Reading Beyond Words:

Contexts for Native History

edited by
Jennifer S.H. Brown & Elizabeth Vibert

broadview press

970.1
R287b
1996

✓ ©1996 The authors

Canadian Cataloguing in Publication Data

Main entry under title:
Reading beyond words: contexts for native history
Includes index.
ISBN 1-55111-070-9

1. Indians of North America — Historiography.
2. Native peoples — Canada — Historiography.*
I. Brown, Jennifer S.H. II. Vibert, Elizabeth .
E76.8.R43 1996 970.00497 C96-930178-2

Broadview Press
Post Office Box 1243, Peterborough, Ontario, Canada K9J 7H5

in the United States of America:
3576 California Road, Orchard Park, NY 14127

in the United Kingdom:
B.R.A.D. Book Representation & Distribution Ltd., 244A, London Road, Hadleigh, Essex SS7 2DE

Broadview Press gratefully acknowledges the support of the Canada Council, the Ontario Arts Council, and the Ministry of Canadian Heritage.

PRINTED IN CANADA

Contents

Acknowledgements

Our first thanks go to the contributors to this volume. They remained cheerful and accommodating through the long process of writing, editing, and re-editing, assisting enormously in shaping a collection which presents diverse perspectives and approaches, yet which exhibits a broad consensus about its overall purpose.

Second, we gratefully acknowledge the initiative and support given to this project by Don LePan and Michael Harrison, president and vice-president of Broadview Press. Their willingness to make an early commitment to us as editors spurred our efforts and enabled us to hold out to contributors the prospect of being part of a real book, not a mirage on the horizon. We also thank the two anonymous reviewers who assisted the final shaping and revisions of the work. The staff of Broadview Press — Barbara Conolly, Linda Steele, and others — have greatly expedited the progress of the book into print. Renée Fossett did double duty as contributor and as preparer of the index.

We express mutual gratitude to each other for making the job of co-editing a rich and pleasurable learning experience and a vehicle for growing collegial friendships. We thank Todd Hatfield and Wilson Brown for endless supplies of moral support, computer expertise, and fine cooking. And we are grateful to our families for timely reminders that there is more to life.

Introduction

Jennifer S.H. Brown and Elizabeth Vibert

THESE ARE EXCITING and challenging times in North American Native history and historiography. The essays in *Reading Beyond Words: Contexts for Native History* convey both the substance and the spirit of current developments, featuring contributors who share a lively interest in the issues and complexities of this field of study. Twenty-one Canadian, American, and Native authors writing from diverse viewpoints — history, anthropology, English, personal life histories, historical and medical geography, Native studies, and linguistics — have composed articles expressly for this collection or in a few instances have recast earlier works to suit its aims. The scholars who joined the project, some of whom are senior and some newly arrived, undertook to write in a way that would reach across to people in other disciplines, to students, and to readers in regions and countries other than their own. They offer innovative and counter-stereotypic perspectives on subjects new and old, familiar and unfamiliar, while making fresh, well-documented contributions to our understanding of the Native past in North America.

Reading Beyond Words

This book emphasizes the importance of "reading beyond" the words and images of the historical documents we consult in the study of Native history, and provides a diversity of tools and ideas for doing so. Intensive case studies highlight major issues surrounding the use of texts ("original" and edited writings, oral documents, images, and artifacts), as sources embedded in ever-changing contexts. Among other topics, the authors engage with such practical matters as comparing and evaluating different versions of archival and oral texts, or deciphering obscure words and categories, relating them to the discursive and conceptual problems posed by the myriad forms of documentation that confront those who venture into this field.

In 1987, Michael Dorris, Modoc Indian author and then head of Native American Studies at Dartmouth College in New Hampshire, offered some sound advice on the pitfalls of doing Native history. In "Indians on the Shelf" Dorris reminds us that whether we are Native or not, whether we hail from New Zealand, the United States, or Germany, we never approach that history with a blank slate. We all carry a host of assumptions and expectations informed by Hollywood westerns and television, by the novels of James Fenimore Cooper, by childhood cowboy-and-Indian games, or by the "council rings" we joined at summer camp. Already in our minds are deep-seated if ill-defined images of "Indians," be they in savage red or dusky, romantic brown. Serious consideration of Native history must therefore begin, Dorris writes, with "an initial, abrupt, and wrenching demythologizing"; we must acknowledge that we begin not from some neutral point, but about ten steps back. Scholars may dream of what Dorris calls "the historian's heaven," a place where "if we have been good little historians" we will finally be told what really, truly happened. However, given the biases, flaws, gaps, and self-serving character of most written sources, "Indian history hardly even offers purgatory."[1]

Illusions of Objectivity

The warning Dorris issues about texts in Native history reverberates widely in the postmodern world of the 1990s. Where once upon a time historical documents seemed to open pathways toward objective truths which could be revealed through the application of proper scholarly methods, many scholars now challenge the very notions of objectivity and ultimate truth. In literary studies, anthropology, sociology, geography, and other fields, it is almost commonplace to characterize meaning, value, and knowledge itself as unstable, uncertain, and subject to multiple understandings. Historians are sometimes thought to be insensitive to this postmodern turn in the humanities and social sciences; the historians who contribute to this book belie that generalization. If there is one conviction that unites the authors in this volume, whatever their disciplines, it is that texts are not transparent. Nor do they simply offer some pre-existent body of "raw facts." The "facts" are socially constructed, moulded by the social and cultural forces in place when the

---

1   In Calvin Martin, ed., *The American Indian and the Problem of History* (New York: Oxford University Press, 1987), 103-104.

JENNIFER S. H. BROWN AND ELIZABETH VIBERT

texts were created, and by the later contexts in which they have been re-read and reinterpreted.[1]

Objectivity, then, like the historian's heaven, is an illusion. Our sources, the texts we study, present us with complex subjectivities, multiple ways of knowing the world. This is part of their fascination. The voices of our documentary texts can be listened for, articulated, balanced with one another; but only through silencing or suppression can they be melded into a single voice or unquestioned truth.[2] Nor can we ever entirely silence our own voices as readers and scholars. None of us is free of the social and cultural contexts in which we are embedded — of the basic human condition which one historian of ideas has called our "predicament of culture." The notion of objectivity is itself a cultural construction, a venerable subjectivity with roots in the optimistic and, as some say, heavily gendered scientific world view which emerged in Europe in the seventeenth and eighteenth centuries.[3]

Language is, of course, one of the main vehicles which conveys cultural meanings in text and context. It is not a neutral medium: the language of any cultural or social group, of any epoch, reflects and helps to constitute that group's view of the world. Accordingly, when we read texts one of our primary tasks is to analyze closely the work of language and the ideological functions which language performs in speech, writing, and action. Those functions are generally referred to as discourse.

---

1 The literature generated by the postmodern turn in the humanities and social sciences is vast. For a useful introduction to concepts, see Terry Eagleton, *Literary Theory: An Introduction* (Minneapolis: University of Minnesota Press, 1983).

2 One recent example of such silencing is the Walt Disney film, *Pocahontas* (1995), which entirely ignores texts documenting early English-Powhatan relations, the true story of the marriage of Pocahontas to John Rolfe, and her journey to England, to invent a spurious love story involving Captain John Smith. Another is the Penguin Books edition of John Tanner's *Narrative of the Captivity and Adventures of John Tanner*, published as *The Falcon* (New York, 1994), which silently omits not only the book's original Introduction, Part II, and appendices, but also all reference to Edwin James, who played the pivotal role of Tanner's editor and amanuensis (see John Fierst's essay, this volume).

3 James Clifford, *The Predicament of Culture: Twentieth-Century Ethnography, Literature, and Art* (Cambridge, MA: Harvard University Press, 1988); Evelyn Fox Keller, *Reflections on Gender and Science* (New Haven: Yale University Press, 1985), especially chapter 4; Ludmilla Jordanova, *Sexual Visions: Images of Gender in Science and Medicine* (Hemel Hempstead: Harvester Wheatsheaf, 1989).

A decade ago, before many students of Native history were even talking about such studies as "discourse analysis," anthropologist Mary Black-Rogers provided an exemplary dissection of a particular form of early colonial discourse. In an essay entitled "Varieties of 'Starving': Semantics and Survival in the Subarctic Fur Trade," she unpacked a term that crops up with startling frequency in European fur traders' writings about Native communities.[1] Looking closely at traders' perceptions of the Algonquian and Athapaskan people with whom they dealt, Black-Rogers showed that "starving" could mean many things besides lack of food. Genuine food scarcity and even famine occurred under that name, but a careful analysis of context and cultural meanings showed that traders applied the term far more widely. Often "starving" had a meaning specific to the fur trade: it was used when Native people were too preoccupied with their own subsistence needs to pay attention to trapping furs (the activity to which traders gave priority). Sometimes writers who used the term were making a cultural value judgment: these European men viewed the things Native people were eating as foods of last resort. In spring, for example, when communities in some regions subsisted on a diet heavy in plant foods but scant in meat, traders called them starving. Finally, Black-Rogers found that Native people frequently declared themselves starving or pitiable when they encountered traders better off than themselves; in fieldwork, she learned that the "pity speech" was a practice with deep cultural roots. Humbling oneself and asking for pity or blessings was the culturally appropriate way of asking anything from a powerful being with whom one hoped to forge an ongoing relationship. Requests for pity, and the "begging tricks" which so annoyed the traders, were metaphorical acts designed to initiate or affirm a social relationship.

Black-Rogers's study underscores the point that culturally defined notions like "starving" need to be carefully interrogated. The unpacking of the diverse meanings of such terms and categories has more than academic interest. As the earliest "ethnographic" records of the indigenous societies of northern North America, fur traders' accounts have been cited extensively, and far too often uncritically. These days, traders' documents are among those routinely mined for information about Native land use patterns by the adversaries in land-settlement cases before

---

1   Published in *Ethnohistory* 33 (1986), 353-83.

provincial, state, and federal courts. In a controversial recent decision, Chief Justice Allan McEachern of the British Columbia Supreme Court drew on selected interpretations of early nineteenth-century fur traders' writings to support his conclusion that life for the aboriginal Gitksan and Wet'suwet'en people was "primitive," indeed "nasty, brutish, and short." McEachern rejected assertions of Native land rights in north-central British Columbia on the basis of a fundamental assumption that fishing-hunting-gathering societies occupied the lowest rung on the ladder of social evolution – a discourse that first came into flower in eighteenth-century Europe.[1] Such a perspective puts Europe at the centre of the world, defining the standards for the rest of humanity and the stages through which all peoples pass to become "civilized." McEachern was echoing Eurocentric, androcentric frameworks which used to be taken as natural (by those in positions of privilege, at least), but which have for some time now been exposed as the cultural creations that they are.

Several authors in this volume pay close attention to the fundamental importance of language in the interpretation of Native history. Maureen Matthews's and Roger Roulette's study of Fair Wind's dream draws on Roulette's linguistic expertise in Ojibwa and the careful record made by anthropologist A. Irving Hallowell to elicit the nuanced philosophical concepts expressed by the medicine man Naamiwan (Fair Wind). At his dream dance in 1933, attended by Hallowell and his interpreter, Chief William Berens, Naamiwan expressed desolation at the loss of his grandson, and declared, in Hallowell's rendition: "I made up my mind to die." With a 1990s awareness of the high rates of suicide in some Native communities, we might interpret this as an intent to commit suicide. But Naamiwan's mental state was clarified by another Ojibwa speaker, his grandson, Charlie George Owen, who explained that Naamiwan wanted to "let himself go," that is, to surrender his life to his spirit helpers as an expression of his grief, powerlessness, and humility. The Ojibwa terminology reveals that he offered himself "in the knowledge that this desperate moment held the potential for a blessing from his spirit helpers and a new direction in life." Context and vocabulary are critical to deciphering these tellings of Naamiwan's dream.

---

1 Allan McEachern, *Reasons for Judgment, Delgamuukw v. B.C.*, Supreme Court of British Columbia, Smithers, B.C. (1991). For scholarly assessments, see *B.C. Studies* 95 (1992), "Theme Issue: Anthropology and History in the Courts."

Similarly, other authors demonstrate that texts are more opaque than they appear. Especially in the early period of Native-European encounters, we gain access to what happened mainly through the words of the newcomers whose discourses "actually do much of the crucially important work of colonialism."[1] As Daniel Clayton argues in his essay, the scientific explorations of such well-known figures as Captain James Cook may be viewed as "handmaiden[s] of European colonialism — as an intellectual strategy for gaining possession of non-European space and symbolic domination over its inhabitants." Captain Cook did not pillage, kill, or colonize, but in the process of recording what he saw (and what he imagined he saw) on the Northwest Coast, Cook contributed to European discourses about indigenous peoples. Subsequent British intervention in the region and in the local people's lives was shaped to a significant degree by the kinds of representations produced by travellers like Cook. It is human nature to view and describe other peoples in relation to ourselves; but in doing so Europeans had the privilege of more power than most. A crucial aspect of that power was "the power to narrate."

Texts of Many Voices

Even though written representations of indigenous peoples are powerful and power-wielding, Native people have not simply been passive victims of representation by foreign traders, missionaries, anthropologists, and others; they have also endlessly and actively represented themselves. The encounter between Native and non-Native peoples has been a long and complex engagement of mutual dialogue, communication, and miscommunication. Given the intensity of the engagement, even the most confidently Eurocentric of texts cannot help but provide glimpses of Native actions, traces of Native voices.

Such traces are clearly present in the writings of French explorer Pierre-Esprit Radisson, whose 1659-60 narrative of his Lake Superior travels is analyzed here by literary scholar Germaine Warkentin. Radisson, who had spent months first as captive and then as adoptive son in a Mohawk community, produced, in English, a discourse truly of the middle ground, crossing boundaries both Native and European.

---

1   Stephen Greenblatt, "Introduction," in Greenblatt, ed., *New World Encounters* (Berkeley: University of California Press, 1993).

JENNIFER S. H. BROWN AND ELIZABETH VIBERT

Warkentin argues that he combined (but never reconciled) the cultural arrogance of the explorer with admiration for the "sagacity" of the Native people he met. The fact that he admitted his debt to his Algonquian guides and associates is noteworthy, given how few European travellers even mentioned the Native guides and companions who made their journeys possible. Describing his presentation of gifts to those attending a Feast of the Dead, Radisson also provided insight into Algonquian social discourse. He recognized gift-giving as a ritual practice for cementing political and social alliances, pipe-smoking as a ritual affirmation of peace.

Jesuit missionary texts from the far western Plateau region in the 1830s and 1840s offer similar gems of insight into the actions and perceptions of indigenous groups. In her study of the Virgin Mary as a multivocal symbol in the conversion of the Salish Flathead, Laura Peers shows how the priests sought to use the Virgin to inculcate not just Christian belief, but the European gender roles and nuclear family structures which accompanied it at this time. Converts obeyed the priests' admonitions to destroy the symbols of their traditional spiritual belief, but the priests' own writings reveal that the Salish bent the new and powerful female figure of Mary to their own purposes. Far from accepting this new model for female piety and submission, Salish women recast her role within their own cultural setting of gender relations and human interactions with the spirit world. In this context, Mary became a powerful, even a warrior woman, capable of crushing a large snake under her heel. While acknowledging that missionary practice became more coercive later in the century, Peers — like so many authors in this volume — forcefully reminds us that Native people were active agents in the making of their own histories, and in shaping the texts of others.

The story of missionary efforts to "civilize" Native children is picked up by J.R. Miller in his account of residential schools in Canada. Miller writes of the difficulty of finding children's voices in the historical record of these institutions. Besides their traces in the written record, the contributions of visual and oral records appear promising. For example, illustrations of Lacombe's Ladder, a visual device used to depict the horrors of Hell, provide startling insight into the impact missionary teachings must have had on impressionable young minds. Photographs of schoolchildren at work convey more starkly than words the strenuous labour regime to which many boys and girls were subjected.

Native roles in shaping texts are of course greatest when they produce those texts themselves. Winona Stevenson thought she had come upon a windfall when she discovered in an archive the mission journals of Church of England catechist Askenootow (Charles Pratt), a Cree-Assiniboine who was also her great-great-grandfather. Yet she soon faced a conundrum: how could the man who animated the pages of the journals differ so greatly from the one she knew through her family oral history? In her essay she places Pratt's texts firmly in the context in which they were produced, probing the influences of the genre of missionary literature, as well as Pratt's personal concerns and motivations. Pratt described his Native charges as "poor heathens," adopting the rhetorical phrases which his superiors in the church expected and used themselves. Yet a number of more subtle subtexts and contradictory narratives in support of his own people emerge in Pratt's writings. They speak to his complex experience as missionary, Cree hunter, and member of a family and community both blessed with a rich history and afflicted by disease and loss of land.

These and other essays in the volume reveal Native writers, speakers, map-makers, and collectors actively asserting the power of their world views, at once resisting and shaping others' perceptions of them. The texts which afford understandings of these processes are not simply open windows on the past. They are at best textured panes of glass, framing outlines of distant shapes, subtle hints of movement. If we approach the texts alert to their refractions as well to our own angles of vision, there is much to learn.

Words and Stories

The words of a document are just that: words on a page. But they survive in a variety of forms, from daily fieldnotes, log-book or journal entries penned by a person on the spot, to posthumously-published narratives complete with illustrative plates and editors' introductions. Form is important, for it has a bearing on content. What did the author of the log-book omit, in the interests of time? How did the journal writer's perception of her audience influence what she recorded, and what she left unsaid? How did a publisher or editor recast a journal to make it suitable for publication as a captivity or adventure narrative?

It is not just well-aged historical documents which pose such intriguing questions. H. David Brumble, writing of the textual complexities underlying Native American "autobiographies," has shown how early anthropologists who recorded Native life stories often wrote without reflecting on the dynamics of the editorial process, as if their own voices were silent. They would highlight a Native speaker as if his or her words were directly quoted and unmediated. Yet naturally enough, these scientific "absent editors" emended and rearranged what their informants told them, asked telling questions to meet their own research agendas, and sometimes compiled composite materials into one "life history" portrait typifying a group or culture as an object for analysis.[1]

The scholars dealing with life histories in this volume take heed of such concerns as Brumble's. Bunny McBride's study of the life of Molly Spotted Elk is a highly personal account of the process by which she came to "know" the Penobscot dancer, actor, and writer through her diaries. McBride is refreshingly honest about the intellectual gulf that initially existed between her subject and herself as author, and about the journey that was needed before she could hear the voices of Molly in the texts. (She was limited to the texts, and other visual and oral accounts, because Molly had passed away some years earlier.) McBride's new book about Molly Spotted Elk does not pose as autobiography. Rather, the work became a "dialogical enterprise," with herself and Molly as "co-authors of a sort," each taking an active role in its production.

The fact that Molly Spotted Elk was no longer alive, and that diaries from key years of her life had been thrown out after her death, left major gaps in her story. This is familiar terrain for those who study the past. For every text that survives for our gaze or ear, countless words and pages have been lost. What serendipity, accident, or purposeful selection led to the preservation of the few? When only one plausible-sounding version of an event or history survives, we tend too often to accept it as adequate, few questions asked. When multiple versions surface, things become murkier, as shown in Frieda Esau Klippenstein's study of the many tellings of a legendary 1828 confrontation between Kwah and James Douglas. Klippenstein shows how two contemporary accounts of the conflict between the Carrier chief and the fur trader, both written by Hudson's Bay Company men and both praising the actions of Douglas,

---

1   Brumble, *American Indian Autobiography* (Berkeley: University of California Press, 1988), especially chapter 3, "Editors, Ghosts, and Amanuenses"; see also Arnold Krupat, *For Those Who Come After: A Study of Native American Autobiography* (Berkeley: University of California Press, 1985), in particular chapter 4 on Paul Radin's constructions of the Winnebago, Crashing Thunder.

became marked as authoritative by the very fact that later writers relied upon them: the texts gained authority by virtue of repetition. Retellings by white authors have shifted in emphasis according to the tenor of their times; what has not changed is the fact that most still rely on two written accounts, to the exclusion of Carrier perspectives on the event. Carrier accounts — oral and written — show some variation, but they share a sense of the brutality of fur traders' actions and the justice of Kwah's response. As Klippenstein points out, the divergences are not surprising. Individuals and communities tell stories which suit their own purposes and reflect their own beliefs. Written accounts produced by those in positions of dominance are as profoundly constructed as the oral accounts of those on the margins.

The subject of story-telling brings to mind the observation of Graham Swift in his novel *Waterland*: humans are defined by their desire to tell stories. In a fascinating analysis of historical writings about the Great Plains droughts of the 1930s, William Cronon has shown how historians use essentially the same rhetorical devices as other story-tellers — and come up with many versions of a story. We configure the events of the past into causal sequences, in the process ordering and simplifying things and giving them new meaning. (That this process and its motivations can be quite different in Native narrative traditions is revealed in the essays by John Fierst and Julie Cruikshank.) We wield what Cronon calls a "rhetorical razor," separating relevant from irrelevant, significant from insignificant, story from non-story. In the very act of making these decisions, in sanctioning some voices and silencing others, we exercise enormous power.[1]

So what are we to do? If the forms and versions of a story each have some claim to validity, if we cannot achieve unitary, unquestionable truth, what hope is there that we can ever understand the past? Julie Cruikshank offers a helpful approach in her contribution to the collection. She finds that the quest for the "correct" version of a story may be less interesting than the rich information that each account reveals about the social processes in which it is embedded. In considering Native oral and Euro-Canadian written accounts of the Klondike gold rush of the 1890s, Cruikshank finds no way to pull together the disparate perspectives into a coherent synthesis; nor is that a desirable aim. Rather, each

---

1   Cronon, "A Place for Stories: Nature, History, and Narrative," *Journal of American History* 78 (1992), 1347-76.

JENNIFER S. H. BROWN AND ELIZABETH VIBERT

account is part of the story, another means by which the past is not only preserved but "constructed and discussed in different contexts, from the perspectives of actors enmeshed in culturally distinct networks of social relationships." Echoing Cronon, Cruikshank stresses that all societies have characteristic narrative structures which help members piece together and maintain knowledge of the world. The exercise, then, is not so much to straighten out the "facts," but to understand how different ways of knowing generate distinct analyses of social processes and distinct interpretations of events, each with its grains of truth and its insights into the actors' various outlooks.

Shifting Contexts

If texts and their mediations by all who touch them need — indeed reward — endless restudy, so too do contexts. Contexts, like rivers, are always in motion, always diverse and differently witnessed, depending on whether their observers are in midstream or on the shore. It is a truism in history that documents ought to be read and placed in context, and their authors located and understood in terms of the period and society that produced them. Yet the apparent simplicity of this recipe creates illusions. Documents and authors exist in multiple contexts, even when they don't cross cultural borders or survive through long periods. Their viewers define and interpret those contexts differently: some widely, some narrowly, some with an emphasis on cultural factors, others on social, political, or economic ones. In doing so, observers cannot help but refract their lines of sight through their own contexts, and through the lens of contemporary concerns and priorities.

This fact complicates our studies, but it also invigorates them. The placing of sources in new contexts opens doors and windows previously closed or not even seen. In the 1960s, for example, university courses on Native and women's history were virtually unheard of. The profession of history offered few contexts in which these subjects appeared as essential, significant or interesting. By the 1980s, the picture had changed dramatically, and today history departments ignore these areas at their peril. One wag has said about one of our own departments that it is visibly divided between those who do maps and chaps, and those who do women and Indians; but most of the chaps who have let us in seem to think the latter categories are needed.

Canadian fur trade studies offer an instance of this kind of sea change in historical consciousness. Before 1980, there were no women in the fur trade, and very few Indians. They were there, of course, in the sources, but most historians were reading right past them, having no context into which to fit them, no questions to ask of them. Today, history students are unlikely to encounter a survey text that discusses the fur trade without these key participants, and they have trouble imagining the contexts in which, thirty to sixty years ago, Harold Innis or E.E. Rich could have written so much about the fur trade and said so little about women and Native people.[1]

Context as Text

Still, the placing of texts into their various historical contexts does not lead to the illusory historian's heaven mentioned earlier. One problem is that text and context are not as distinct as they may seem. Placing a text in context sounds a little like putting a cake into a mould, such that our only task is to watch it rise, shaped and framed by its surroundings. In this vision, context is a given, something as tangible as the metal ring of a cake pan. Yet the shared etymology of these two words — text and context — provides a clue to the contrary. "Text" comes from the Latin *texere*, to weave or knit; the prefix *con-* (with), yields "context," something woven together. Both words are metaphorical extensions of the same root term referring to the weaving of cloth; they allude to the same process of manufacture, construction, or fabrication.

Indeed, Johannes Fabian, in a recent article, "Ethnographic Misunderstanding and the Perils of Context," has observed that "in acts that produce ethnographic knowledge, creations of text and creations of context are of the same kind." Both are constructed, and contexts themselves need to be seen as texts requiring analysis. When the authors in this vol-

---

1 The 1960s and 1970s were marked by far-reaching social change, which had its extension in scholarly fields including fur trade studies. In 1974 A.J. Ray published the path-breaking *Indians in the Fur Trade: Their Role as Hunters, Trappers and Middlemen in the Lands Southwest of Hudson Bay 1660-1870* (Toronto: University of Toronto Press). In 1980 two books, based like Ray's on doctoral dissertations, highlighted the roles of Native women and families in the fur trade: Sylvia Van Kirk's *Many Tender Ties: Women in Fur-Trade Society, 1670-1870* (Winnipeg: Watson and Dwyer), and Jennifer S.H. Brown's *Strangers in Blood: Fur Trade Company Families in Indian Country* (Vancouver: University of British Columbia Press).

JENNIFER S. H. BROWN AND ELIZABETH VIBERT

ume present their discussions, they offer in textual form the contexts that they and their studies and experiences have created. Their writings demonstrate that contexts are not only based on syntheses of research and evidence but are also constructed, taking on dynamic textual lives of their own. They convey what Fabian describes as "a personally situated process of knowing," some of them in a powerfully subjective way. In explicating context, they also generate new contexts which are revealing in their own right. There are, of course, perils along the way, and Fabian highlights some of the non-understandings and misunderstandings through which he has worked in his own ethnographic creations of context. The best safeguard, he argues, is "a communicative view of the pursuit of understanding": a far better approach than "sweeping our failures under the rug of invariably positive accounts of success."[1] The writers in this book vary in their explicitness about their own constructions of texts and contexts, reflecting their diverse styles and approaches to overt expressions of reflexivity. Yet all are sympathetic to a "communicative view" about how historical understandings are arrived at.

Introducing the Editors

An edited collection such as this inevitably involves a complex process of midwifery. In light of all this talk of editorial mediation and textual construction, it is only fair that as editors we place in context the origins of the book and the backgrounds and outlooks we each bring to it. The idea originated in our respective classrooms in Winnipeg and Victoria, where we were frustrated by the lack of sound, comprehensible readings to illustrate our points while teaching about issues of textual and cultural construction in Native history.

The book began to take shape in October 1993, under a brilliant blue sky on Vancouver Island, as the Columbia Fur Trade Conference drew to a close. Sitting on a grassy knoll outside the University of Victoria's Dunsmuir Lodge, we talked about bringing together, for students and others, the best work we could find that would stimulate journeys beyond the straightforward reading of documentary sources in Native history. The issue was to build bridges across a critical middle ground. It is easy to go from glib acceptance of written or published sources to out-

---

1 Johannes Fabian, "Ethnographic Misunderstanding and the Perils of Context," *American Anthropologist* 97 (1995), 41–50.

right rejection and disillusion, once they are found wanting; it is all too easy to privilege one category of text (written or oral; material or linguistic) over others, and to lose sight of the need to consult all available types of sources critically, yet with an open mind. Clearly the book had to be interdisciplinary, presenting in-depth studies which would be fresh and interesting in themselves, yet which would also address broad issues and problems and suggest constructive solutions.

The next task was to identify potential contributors. This was the easy part, given our mutual interests and overlapping collegial networks. As the project developed, we were both struck by how consistently we converged in our interests and goals, favourite writers and works, despite having been educated in different fields of graduate study and even on different continents. It seems appropriate here for each of us to comment briefly on her intellectual upbringing and outlooks, and on some of the baggage that we carried into this project.

Jennifer Brown: I have been crossing national and disciplinary borders for a long time. My Ontario-born parents lived for nearly four decades in the United States. Their maintaining of Canadian citizenship and identity eventually led me home to Canadian fields of research and to a position in history at the University of Winnipeg, Manitoba, in 1983. That move, however, capped twenty years of intellectual peregrinations. During a year in Peru, as my husband did dissertation research in economics, I had the good fortune to work closely with John V. Murra in his studies of indigenous Andean peoples through early Spanish documents. It was he who introduced me to the methodology of ethnohistory. Although I had studied both anthropology and history, never before had the two come together. Their combined application to the documents brought forth knowledge and insights beyond what I could have imagined, not only yielding answers, but raising key questions not previously considered.

Ethnohistory (a methodology, not a discipline in itself) has been variously defined, and sometimes criticized, as a mixture of ethnology and history, or as doing the history of a particular ethnic group. It is both of these and more; it is not simply additive or descriptive. At its best (and the proof is in the doing), the approach possesses a powerful alchemy, enriching and transforming understanding through the combining of data and insights from diverse fields, while always alert to comparative perspectives. Among a wide network of Americanists looking especially at Native peoples after European contact (the field grew out of U.S. Indian claims research in the 1940s), ethnohistory has been a generative force leading anthropologists, colonial historians, and others to treat seriously the histories of peoples who lacked the privileged written sources of the intruders.[1]

John Murra's advice led me to doctoral studies in anthropology at the University of Chicago, where further connections led in turn to the Newberry Library and its D'Arcy McNickle Center for the History of the American Indian, famed not only for its remarkable book collections but as a meeting ground for scholars and tribal historians. For a good many years, my colleagues in the American Society for Ethnohistory have also furnished intellectual stimulation and cordial relationships; they provide an important nexus of communication for scholars of Native North America. Other sources of inspiration include selective reading in interpretive anthropology and on colonial and intercultural encounters, working with Winnipeg graduate students in fur-trade and subarctic Native history, and becoming acquainted with the Ojibwa people of the Berens River who have joined in combining oral and pictorial history with fur-trade, mission, and anthropological documentation, and in sharing their memories of the outsiders who created those documents.[2]

Elizabeth Vibert: My paths have been rather different from Jennifer's. A year of travelling and newspaper-writing in Asia in the middle of my undergraduate degree led me to turn my back on the sciences and begin studies in the politics and history of the "Third World." Back at Dalhousie University in Halifax, the specialty was African studies, and I soon found myself swept up in the political economy of development and underdevelopment (as the jargon had it in the mid-eighties). From there I went to the School of Development Studies at the University of

---

1   On some ways of looking at ethnohistory, see Jennifer S.H. Brown, "Ethnohistorians: Strange Bedfellows, Kindred Spirits," *Ethnohistory* 38 (1991), 113-23; Raymond J. DeMallie, "'These Have No Ears': Narrative and the Ethnohistorical Method," *Ethnohistory* 40 (1993), 515-38, and the references they cite.

2   For some of Brown's Berens River work, see A.I. Hallowell, *The Ojibwa of Berens River, Manitoba: Ethnography into History*, ed. Jennifer S.H. Brown (Fort Worth, TX: Harcourt, Brace, Jovanovich, 1992); Brown with Maureen Matthews, "Fair Wind: Medicine and Consolation on the Berens River," *Journal of the Canadian Historical Association* 4 (1994), 55-74.

East Anglia, England, for a Master's degree. By this time my main intellectual interest was the encounter between indigenous societies and the agents of colonialism.

My shift in focus from Southern Africa to North America came when I started doctoral studies in history at the University of Oxford; actually, it wasn't a shift so much as a stretch to embrace two geographical zones. During a summer visit just before I left for Britain, my grandfather, Harley Hatfield, introduced me to the amazing historical sources generated by fur traders in British North America. A keen historian himself, he shared with me his collection of published trader narratives. With a new interest aroused, not long after my arrival at Oxford I declared my intention to study early British-Aboriginal relations in British North America. In a way it was a surprising decision, since Oxford is hardly a hotbed of Canadian studies. But I quickly found a happy and stimulating home in a familiar place – the African history community. Scholars in this group were beginning to look closely at the ways literary critical approaches to texts can inform historical practice, and I became increasingly intrigued by the process of social construction of written representations. My dissertation supervisor, Terence Ranger, pushed me to draw comparisons between colonial discourses and indigenous cultural contexts in North America, and those in Southern Africa. As a result, my dissertation had an explicitly comparative aspect. My perspectives have been much enriched by the study of multiple historical contexts.

I began teaching history at the University of Victoria in 1993. My encounters with undergraduate and graduate students continue to convince me of the fruitfulness of historically-informed literary approaches, and of the great need for more communication about issues of textual construction and historical methodology. Colonial discourses remain my primary research interest; I am presently exploring the work of gender in fur traders' and other early travellers' writings about Native peoples.[1]

---

1   See, for instance, Elizabeth Vibert, "Real Men Hunt Buffalo: Masculinity, Race and Class in British Fur Traders' Narratives," *Gender & History*, forthcoming. A revised version of the dissertation is to be published as *Traders' Tales: British Fur Traders' Narratives of Cultural Encounters in the Plateau* (Norman: University of Oklahoma Press).

JENNIFER S. H. BROWN AND ELIZABETH VIBERT

Reading the Book

The book is organized into seven sections, following a roughly chronological and topical sequence. Each section has an editors' prologue which introduces its authors and themes.

Part I presents three studies of early encounters, direct and indirect. Its title, "Illusions of Contact," signals questions about how real the contacts actually were. "Contact" (in its Latin etymology) is about touching, and implies the achievement of first-hand or "hands-on" knowledge. Olive Dickason's study, however, vividly depicts how sixteenth-century French cosmographers waged verbal battles over representations of Native peoples, based on slim data and all too ample cultural baggage; amid their contested images lie the roots, and some of the explanations, of stereotypes alive to this day. In the next two essays, Frederic Gleach and Germaine Warkentin take on, respectively, two of the best known figures in early meetings between European explorers and the indigenous people of North America. Their studies challenge popular images of the romantic passion of the Powhatan Indian princess, Pocahontas, and the bravado of the French explorer, Radisson, with more complex, intriguing portraits. They guide us beyond the words of Captain John Smith and of Radisson, toward deeper insights into both Algonquian and European understandings of these meetings.

In Part II, "Trading Texts: Explorers and their Hosts," three authors look critically at some of the documentary sources created as European traders and explorers began to map territory and to seek (and publish) knowledge of lands, trade, and resources in northern North America. As Renée Fossett notes about Inuit maps, texts travelled both ways, as outsiders tried to make sense of Native geographical perceptions and practices, and as Inuit mappers learned the limitations of European cartographical conventions. The essays by Daniel Clayton and Frieda Klippenstein, as noted earlier, juxtapose a variety of British and Native narratives about much-remembered events of contact in British Columbia: the coming of Captain James Cook to the western shores of Vancouver Island in 1778, and the confrontation in the interior between Chief Kwah and fur trader James Douglas in 1828.

Part III concentrates on understanding Native survival, disease, and death through the problematic words and categories of outsiders. Jody Decker demonstrates the difficulties of reading beyond the limited disease vocabularies and medical understandings of European fur traders and medical practitioners when we try to understand epidemics and mortality among Native peoples. Shepard Krech examines the illness and death of a Gwich'in chief on the upper Mackenzie River in the 1820s. Besides the problems of building a narrative from rather thin and biased fur-trade materials, Krech, like Decker, faces the difficulty of translating concepts of illness and curative medicine, not only between Gwich'in and English, but also from British traders' folk concepts into current medical vocabulary.

Native voices in writing are the subject of Part IV. John Fierst vividly conveys the lure and interpretive challenges of the captivity narrative of John Tanner, an American boy drawn deeply and irreversibly into the lives of his Ottawa adoptive family. Theresa Schenck offers a fresh look at a classic of Native history, William Warren's *History of the Ojibway People*, reassessing its approach, aims, and usefulness as historical text. Linguist David Pentland publishes for the first time a rare letter in the Ottawa language and demonstrates what can be learned from such documents. Besides underscoring the fact that Native sources are not exclusively oral, it affords a first-hand look at a small cross-section of Ottawa-Algonquin relationships in the mid-nineteenth century.

Part V, "Religious Encounters in Text and Context," presents three studies of interactions between Native people and Christianity. But these are not stories of simple challenge and conversion. Laura Peers shows how Plateau Salish people recast the Virgin Mary into a figure compatible with their outlooks. Winona Stevenson tells of Charles Pratt, who, for all the mission rhetoric in his notebooks, remained Cree in his values and attachments, and in the memories of his descendants. Maureen Matthews and Roger Roulette explore the fascinating dream texts of Fair Wind and his complex interweavings of Ojibwa and Christian theology.

Texts on Native women's lives are rare in early periods, slightly more common from the mid-1800s onward. In Part VI, Erica Smith analyzes vivid newspaper reports of an attempted-abortion trial in Red River (present-day Winnipeg) to paint a portrait of contemporary British-Canadian thinking about women, and about lower-status Native women in particular. Working with the field notes of a woman graduate student of the 1930s, Alice Kehoe depicts a remarkable Blackfoot woman whose telling of her life counters the "braves and buffalo" stereotypes of classic Plains anthropology and imagery. Bunny McBride recounts the evolving challenges of discovering and telling the life of Penobscot dancer, performer, and actor Molly Spotted Elk.

Finally, in Part VII, Julie Cruikshank examines oral recollections of Skookum Jim, Native "discoverer" of gold in the Klondike Gold Rush; familial memories help to explain why he was really on the scene. J.R. Miller offers fresh perspectives on Indian residential schools through artifacts, photographs, and oral histories. And Trudy Nicks traces the curious life and cultural ambiguities of an Ontario Iroquois collector and world traveller, whose artifacts and souvenirs still present puzzles for analysis.

The authors in this collection draw on a wide range of tools and toolkits to bring a critical understanding to their texts. They list their source materials in either humanities or social science (in-text) referencing style, reflecting their different academic backgrounds. Despite their diversity, however, the extent to which they engage with similar or related conceptual and epistemological problems is striking. We hope that these writings will build some new frameworks for doing Native history, and perhaps undermine a few older ones. In reading the essays ourselves, we were repeatedly reminded that we all share not only some common understandings and premises, but also some major concerns about how best to steer a course among the cross-currents, rocks, and whirlpools that beset travellers on this rapidly flowing river.

Part I. Illusions of Contact

The three authors whose essays introduce this book share a fascination with the dynamics of first encounters between Europeans and indigenous peoples. The phrase "illusions of contact" is ours, not theirs, but it serves to express their shared sense that first contacts between Natives and newcomers had an illusory quality. The people who first met across oceans and cultures thought that to an extent they understood the other side, and each party naturally asserted the validity of its understandings. But both had trouble seeing beyond the blinders of their own prior experiences, cultural values, intellectual traditions, and expectations, and cast their perceptions into their own familiar terms.

Olive Patricia Dickason, professor emeritus at the University of Alberta, Edmonton, is a scholar of many distinguished accomplishments, the author of the widely read *Canada's First Nations: A History of Founding Peoples* (1992), and newly admitted to the Order of Canada. Absorbed by the study of French and Amerindian people who met in early encounters, she has worked extensively in libraries and French archives to trace their respective reactions and responses at first meetings and afterwards, as each side recorded and processed its knowledge and impressions of the other. As a former journalist, Dickason has a special interest in how the cosmographers of sixteenth-century Europe gathered, processed, and promoted their findings and conclusions about the New World as they saw it.

Dickason notes that she is "particularly interested in beginnings, as it is at this stage that basic social patterns are set which can endure for a very long time." Through chronicles and travel narratives, this setting of patterns can be studied from the 1500s even into this century for some regions. Dickason is currently working on a comparative study of first contacts throughout North America.

Frederic Gleach, who earned his Ph.D. at the University of Chicago in 1992, is a visiting scholar in anthropology at Cornell University in Ithaca, New York. He is the author of *Viewing Colonial Virginia: History and the Conflicting World Views of the Powhatans and Europeans*, a volume based on his doctoral thesis which is in preparation for publication. He has a particular interest in Powhatan culture and ritual, and in the conventions of Algonquian warfare.

His essay appeared in an earlier form in the papers of the twenty-fifth annual Algonquian Conference (1994).

Gleach grew up in central Virginia, in and near Powhatan territory. As a child, he sometimes visited Mattaponi and Pamunkey, the oldest Indian reservations in the United States, whose Powhatan residents had state but not federal recognition. He emphasizes "the need to understand the world-views of both the people who made and those who wrote histories, examining both history and its writing as constructive, cultural process." The Pocahontas story, as he observes, is "one of the grand examples of the effects of divergent world-views in the construction of history," and he is working on a commentary on its recent Disneyfication.

Germaine Warkentin is a professor of English at Victoria College, University of Toronto. She works on Renaissance poetry and early Canadian literature. In 1993, she published a highly useful anthology, *Canadian Exploration Literature*, which opens with a vivid passage from Pierre-Esprit Radisson. His writings are a meeting ground for her two scholarly fields, and she is now preparing a new critical, annotated edition of Radisson's works. She has a special fascination with his use of language, English in particular, and his sense of ritual observance and ceremony, both Native and French.

Radisson drew keen comparisons between the social conduct of French and Native life, and he explored ways to bridge the gulf between them through analogy and metaphor. His writings, like those of Dickason's cosmographers and Captain John Smith, highlight many key issues of words, categories, and interpretation that need more attention than they often receive.

1

Europeans and a New World: Cosmography in the 1500s[1]

Olive Patricia Dickason

THE SIXTEENTH CENTURY has been called, with considerable justification, the Age of Cosmographers. As Europeans began to learn about the Americas and other distant regions, the cosmographers' traditional role of describing the universe, the world, and everything in them took on unexpected proportions. The new demands became overwhelming, and classical cosmography collapsed of its own weight. In the process, however, it left a rich heritage for astronomy, geography, history, anthropology, and sociology.

The fashion for cosmography as well as for exploration literature in general was fuelled by the advent of new technologies, which in navigation resulted in expanded geographical knowledge, and in printing resulted in a much increased capacity to disseminate that knowledge.[2] Holland was especially active in publishing. It was in that country that some of the best-known exploration accounts such as *Les Grands Voyages* and *Les Petits Voyages* of Theodore de Bry (1528-1598) and his two sons were published. In France, also a centre for this activity, about 26 cosmographies appeared between 1540 and 1575. Spain, too, had its cosmographers, but an official passion for secrecy did not encourage publication of their work.[3] Nevertheless, Portuguese and Spanish travel accounts were quickly picked up in other countries and translated into a variety of languages.

---

1 The research for this paper was done at The Newberry Library, Chicago. I owe particular gratitude to two members of its staff: John Aubrey for his generous sharing of his encyclopedic knowledge of the library's resources, and Ruth Hamilton for her helpful editorial assistance.

2 A somewhat similar reaction to expanding horizons resulting from technological innovations was seen in sweeping television series such as Kenneth Clark's *Civilization* and Jacob Bronowski's *Ascent of Man*.

3 Ursula Lamb, "Cosmographers of Seville: Nautical Science and Social Experience," 675-86, in *First Images of America: The Impact of the New World on the Old*, ed. Fredi Chiappelli *et al.*, 2 vols. (Berkeley, Los Angeles and London: University of California Press, 1976).

OLIVE PATRICIA DICKASON

This flood of new information challenged accepted beliefs (for example, that Europe, Asia, and Africa comprised the whole world) and even the scriptures (among other things, St. Paul's statement that the Gospel had been heard "unto the end of the World" [Romans 10.18]). To confront these challenges, Europeans turned for reassurance to established authorities, such as the famed Greek geographer Claudius Ptolemy, who wrote in the 2nd century A.D. In 1477, Ptolemy's *Cosmographia* was published in Latin, the *lingua franca* of the day. A spectacular expansion of geographical knowledge during the next 150 years set off a train of more than 40 editions and revisions of this bible of geographers. The most celebrated was Sebastian Münster's version, which first appeared in 1544 and went through numerous editions.[1] An influential contemporary of Münster also drew on classical sources: Johann Boehme's *Omnium Gentium Mores* (Customs of All Peoples) was published in Latin in 1520,[2] and appeared in French in 1539. The French edition was enlarged two years later to include information on contemporary exploration; an English version appeared in 1555,[3] and in 1556 a Spanish edition added a 190-page section on America.

Boehme had a major influence on writers who tackled the new geography in the mid-sixteenth century; Münster, for one, relied heavily on him. Following classical authorities, Boehme presented the world as a centralized evolving hierarchy within which human beings had slowly risen from bestiality. In their most primitive state, early men ate human flesh and mated with whichever women they encountered, without concern about incest. They also indulged in slaughter and robbery, among other vices. This situation improved with the coming of agriculture; human beings then became "more mild, more wise, and better qualified" — in other words, domesticated. Coming down to particulars,

---

1 A helpful survey of the literature of the period is that of Margaret T. Hodgen, *Early Anthropology in the Sixteenth and Seventeenth Centuries* (Philadelphia: University of Pennsylvania Press, 1964).

2 Boehme, *Omnium gentium mores leges et ritus ex multis clarissimis rerum scriptoribus...& libros tris distinctos Aphricam, Asiam, Europam* (Augsburg, 1520).

3 Its complete English title was *The fardle of façions conteining the aunciente maners, customs and Lawes, of the peoples enhabiting the two partes of the earth, called Affrike and Asie* (London: John Kyngston and Henrie Sutton, 1555). It does not include the third part of Boehme's work. A complete translation appeared under the title *The Manners and Customs of all Nations* (London, 1611). The French edition of 1555 was entitled *Recueil de Diverses Histoires*.

Boehme described Tartars, a people living in northeastern Mongolia, as descendants of Japhet (one of Noah's three sons, believed to be the ancestor of Asiatics). He pictured them as not having much hair, loving hunting and fishing, and living on little. Despite their occasional predilection for roasting and eating their enemies, within their own communities they lived peacefully, never arguing. Since this description much resembled early portrayals of New World peoples, many believed that Amerindians were also descended from Japhet. However, when colonists became involved in frontier wars, some would claim it was Japhet's brother, the accursed Ham, who brought ruin to humankind when he "began to divine by Starres, and to sacrifice children by Fire."[1]

Another literature which prefigured descriptions of Amerindians was that of the exotic voyage, of which the *Travels* of Sir John Mandeville (d. 1372) was by far the best known and most influential; for two centuries it was the accepted compendium of world knowledge. This compilation of accounts of medieval journeys to the Holy Land and the East, all ascribed indiscriminately to the knight-adventurer Mandeville, was translated from its original French into an array of languages and widely circulated in countless manuscript versions. With the advent of the printing press, it appeared in nearly 100 editions.[2] Distortions and absurdities accumulated as the different versions had been reverently, if sometimes carelessly, recopied through the years without guides to gauge the accuracy of information. Their influence on perceptions of the Americas is evident. Such passages as that dealing with the inhabitants of the Island of Lamary, who went naked and who had no order in their sexual relationships, who were cannibals and who held everything in common, foreshadowed descriptions later applied to Amerindians by Amerigo Vespucci (1454-1512) and New World chroniclers generally.[3]

Two of the most active cosmographers of the sixteenth century were a French Franciscan monk, André Thevet (c.1517-92), and François de

---

1   Hodgen, *Early Anthropology*, 238.

2   Arthur Layard, ed., *The Marvellous Adventures of Sir John Maundeville Kt.* (Westminster: Constable, 1895), xii-xiii; M.C. Seymour, *Mandeville's Travels* (Oxford: Clarendon Press, 1967), xiii.

3   Vespucci's New World reports are contained in two letters, the first of which, *Mundus Novus*, was published in 1503, and the second, *Lettera delle isole novamente trovate*, in 1505 or 1506. See David Beers Quinn, "New Geographical Horizons: Literature," 2: 635-58 at 639-40 in Chiappelli, ed., *First Images of America*.

Belleforest (1530-83). Thevet, who was also royal cosmographer for four kings of France, was far more fascinated with the stream of information and artifacts coming out of the newly discovered fourth part of the world (the Americas) than he was with his spiritual ministry. He was one of the most widely travelled Frenchmen of his day. The multilingual Belleforest, on the other hand, was more of an historian and literary figure.[1] Historiographer for France for a brief time, his pen was at the service of the occasion. Each man, in his own way, represented the difficulties Christian Europeans faced in reconciling a bewildering array of new information with their orthodox beliefs and classical knowledge. Both authors were read throughout Europe in their lifetimes, and they both reflected and encouraged the climate of opinion that spurred France and other European nations to build their commercial and political empires. This was particularly true of Thevet, who was in a position to influence those policies.

Many charges of inaccuracy were hurled at the two writers, yet they were rarely faulted for their representation of New World peoples as unformed "savages" in their cultural infancy. That was a first impression that Europeans in general saw no reason to alter as one Amerindian society after another went down to defeat before the transatlantic invasion. The fact that it had no relationship to real peoples did not mitigate its fundamental importance to Europe's expansion; by classifying Amerindians as "savages," Europeans justified colonizing them. Thevet and Belleforest, if not leaders in the formation of this perception, were popular representatives of it: the criticisms of their writings came largely from a scholarly elite, rather than from officialdom or the general public.

Thevet's first publication on the Americas was *Les Singularitez de la France Antarctique* (1557), the English version of which was *The New Found Worlde, or Antarctike* (1568). Seven years later, he published his much more developed *La Cosmographie universelle* (1575).[2] As for Belleforest, he considered the works of both Münster and Boehme to be

---

1 Belleforest translated the Danish story that Shakespeare would pick up and develop into the play *Hamlet*.

2 The edition of André Thevet's *Singularitez* used here is the second (1558), ed. Paul Gaffarel (Paris: Maisonneuve, 1878). The *New Found Worlde*, originally published in London, has been reproduced in facsimile in the series Theatrum Orbis Terrarum by Da Capo Press, Amsterdam and New York, 1971. Thevet's two-volume *Cosmographie* was published in Paris in 1575 in two editions. The one used here is that of l'Huillier.

marred by serious lapses; translating both authors into French, he adjusted their texts as he saw fit. He published his version of Boehme in 1570 under the title *L'Histoire universelle*, without crediting the source of most of its material; as Belleforest saw it, in translating Boehme he had so altered and added to the text that "it was no longer he [Boehme] who spoke, but Belleforest."[1] He revised the work two years later, which is the edition used here. When he came to adapting Münster, however, Belleforest acknowledged what he was doing on the title page; this work appeared in 1575 as *La Cosmographie universelle de tout le monde*.[2] Both Belleforest and Thevet accorded more space to the New World and its peoples than did most of their contemporaries, for whom the Orient was a more attractive subject than the Americas (a carry-over from Mandeville's influence).

Thevet wrote that only through direct experience could one hope to understand the world and its peoples, a proposition that was immensely popular during the Age of Discovery. He claimed to be particularly well qualified for such an undertaking, because in his pursuit of knowledge of the rare and the excellent, he had spared no pains. Whereas ancient classical authors had relied largely on their deductive powers and imagination in studying the world because of their limited opportunities for distant travel, Thevet boasted that he could speak from first-hand knowledge because he had travelled everywhere.[3] Not only could he describe the sky and its celestial orders, but he could also depict the world and its peoples in minute detail:

> In dealing with the earth, I have penetrated its depths, and described the locations of the places, the longitudes, latitudes, customs and ways of living of the peoples there; following so completely the cosmographic order that there is not a province, sea, coast, beach, promontory, gulf, harbor, river, mountain, or isle which I have not diligently described, and critically examined in detail, with all the diversity of animals, and strange

---

1   Belleforest, *L'Histoire universelle*, preface.

2   Belleforest, *L'Histoire universelle du monde contenant l'entier description & situation des quatre parties de la terre, la division & estende d'une chacune Region & Province d'icelles* (Paris: Gervais Mallot, 1572); *La Cosmographie universelle de tout le monde... Auteur en partie Münster*, 2 vols. (Paris: Michel Sonnius, 1575).

3   Thevet, *Cosmographie* 2: 975.

OLIVE PATRICIA DICKASON

plants produced in each country: and even lands unknown to both ancients and moderns, which the most learned of whom thought to be un-
inhabited.[1]

Moreover, Thevet claimed that he could supplement his first-hand
knowledge of the New World through his wide acquaintance with others who had made similar journeys: for example, René Goulaine de
Laudonnière for Florida; and for Canada, Jacques Cartier and Jean-
François de La Rocque de Roberval, with both of whom he claimed to
be intimate.[2]

Exaggerating his own qualifications, Thevet downplayed those of
others. Not even Christopher Columbus was spared: Thevet admired
his character ("de fort bon esprit"), but did not think much of his geographical knowledge, ability as a navigator, or capacity to learn languages.[3] Ironically, Thevet in these instances was contradicting his own
dictum that experience counted for more than theoretical knowledge:
Columbus was a natural navigator, which along with his practical experience goes a long way to explain why his voyages were so successful.

Belleforest's pretensions emphasized scholarship rather than travel.
An eclectic man of letters, he frankly admitted that he had not voyaged
to distant lands like "a certain creator of Antarctic singularities."[4] He acknowledged that "the eye is the witness of what the pen put forward,"
but added that things should not be accepted at face value. Rather, he
put his faith in "diligent research" and good judgment, which travel itself did not always ensure. Because he had studied an "infinite number
of books" and manuscripts he could "paint the morals, manners, laws,
customs and religions of nearly all the nations which are on earth." Not
only had he cited 247 authors, including the very best; he had also
delved into different disciplines such as cosmography, geography, and
"corography" (a fashionable word of the sixteenth and seventeenth centuries indicating regional descriptions that were somewhere between
generalized geography and particularized topography). Although these

---

1   Thevet, *Cosmographie* 1: Au treschretien roy.

2   Thevet, *Cosmographie* 2: 1003v; 1019.

3   Thevet, *Cosmographie* 2: 963, 977v.

4   Belleforest, *Cosmographie* 2: 2039.

included first-hand exploration accounts (many the same as those used by Thevet), Belleforest did not claim personal acquaintance with the explorers themselves. He acknowledged that even the best first-hand accounts could be misleading because of language difficulties which impeded communication between Amerindians and Europeans.[1] He believed he could demonstrate, however, that although each region of the earth produced a particular kind of human with special characteristics, all peoples possessed some form of law and political organization:

> Law being natural to man, who is a political animal,... [there] is not, never has been, and never will be, a people so savage ... who does not follow some form of polity, even though the law for him is not written elsewhere than in his own fantasy.[2]

In their professional association the two writers started off on good terms. Belleforest initially sang the praises of Thevet's travels to gather information about extraordinary things that had been hidden from the classical world: peculiar plants with delicious fruits, oddly-formed monsters and, strangest of all, people who went about without any clothes. By the time Belleforest published his own *L'Histoire universelle* thirteen years later, however, the relationship had cooled; he did not list Thevet among the authors he had consulted for his work. By 1575, when both writers published cosmographies, a war of words between them was in full swing. Belleforest now charged that Thevet was an imposter who did not hesitate to appropriate the work of others and was too vain to realize the depth of his own ignorance.[3] Thevet, for his part, missed no opportunity to lambaste "certain historians" who got things mixed up, and who, even worse, passed on false information. However, he added smugly, how could one expect any better from chroniclers who had never visited the New World or any of the other countries they wrote about.

---

1   Belleforest, *L'Histoire universelle*, preface and 293v.

2   Belleforest, *L'Histoire universelle*, épistre. On Belleforest's views on research and first-hand experience, see his *Cosmographie* 2: 2039, 2084, 2115.

3   Belleforest, *L'Histoire universelle*, 2039, 2084.

OLIVE PATRICIA DICKASON

Thevet sometimes forgot his own dictum about speaking only from first-hand experience, as when he defended the existence of New World Amazons[1] on the grounds that they had been reported previously in Asia and Africa. Although he had never met one, he thought that Old World Amazons might have dispersed to the Americas after the Trojan wars of ancient Greece.[2] On this topic, Belleforest gleefully debunked Thevet, pointing out that although Amerindian women accompanied their husbands while hunting and fishing, as well as on the warpath, and were skilled in using bows and arrows, these were not grounds to classify them as the women warriors of legend, the very idea of which he described as folly. Official Spanish historian Gonzalo Fernández de Oviedo y Valdés (1478-1557), upon whom Belleforest depended heavily, denied their existence.[3] Thevet eventually had second thoughts on the subject. Eighteen years later he acknowledged that there were no villages along the Amazon River that were governed by women; however, Thevet now wrote, in the absence of their husbands but also sometimes alongside them, women could and did fight to protect their homes and villages.[4]

What Belleforest and Thevet had in common was their use of accepted techniques for writing travel literature, even as each one considered himself above the general practice. Sixteenth-century writers borrowed freely from each other; uncritical plagiarism was the order of the day, even as it was deplored. The medieval tradition of placing more faith in the written words of accepted authorities – particularly the "ancients" – than in direct observation was still strong. Furthermore, few geographers and cosmographers were able to travel to the distant lands they mapped and described. This was true for scholars in other disciplines as well; for instance, the earliest compilation of New World medicinal plants to be published in Europe was the work of Dr. Nicolás

---

1   In Greek legend, Amazons were women warriors whose domain was on the southern shores of the Black Sea. Fighting the Greeks, they extended their lands to the Caspian Sea.

2   Thevet, *Singularitez*, 331-35.

3   Belleforest, *L'Histoire universelle*, 294; *Cosmographie* 2: 2065.

4   Thevet, *Cosmographie* 2: 957v, 959v-60v.

Monardes (1493-1588), who had never been to the Americas.[1] But this did not prevent it from becoming a best-seller and going through various translations and editions and being considered authoritative. Similarly Jacques-Philippe Cornut's *Canadensium plantarum aliarumque nondum editarum historia* (A history of Canadian plants and other things not yet published), which appeared in Paris in 1635, was based on the study of specimens brought to Europe.

If that was the situation, why did Belleforest (and later critics) make such a fuss in Thevet's case? The answer lies partly in personalities. Thevet, in advocating experience as "the mistress of all things,"[2] downplayed the reliability of established authorities. In the sixteenth century, this was a sensitive point, because the world view of earlier thinkers, so long held to be beyond dispute, was now being proven to be largely in error. A vivid illustration was Mandeville, once the most popular European font of world knowledge, who was becoming regarded as the "father of lies." The irony of Thevet's case lies in the fact that he actually had travelled more than most of his fellow cosmographers (he claimed to have spent seventeen years voyaging).[3] His information, muddled and inaccurate as it sometimes was, contains nuggets of fact that have withstood intense examination and are not found in other contemporary works, such as his descriptions of snowshoes and the making of maple syrup.[4] He is an

---

1 It had the imposing title, *Dos Libros el uno que trata de todas las Cosas que traen de Nuestras Indias Occidentales, que sirven al uso de la Medicina, y el otro que trata de la Piedra Bezaar, y de la Yerva Escuerconcera* (Two books, one of which treats of all the things brought from our West Indies which have medical uses, and the other which deals with the bezoar stone, and the scorzonera grass). It was published in Seville by Herndo Diaz, 1545.

2 Thevet, *Cosmographie* 2: 913 (pagination incorrect; should read 910). For some speculation on the motives of Thevet's detractors, see *André Thevet's North America*, tr. and ed. Roger Schlesinger and Arthur P. Stabler (Kingston and Montreal: McGill-Queen's University Press, 1986), xxxix-xl.

3 Thevet, *Cosmographie* 1: Epistre.

4 Thevet described snowshoes and how they were used in *Singularitez*, 150v, and the making of maple syrup in *Cosmographie*, 1014-14v. According to historian Paul Gaffarel (1843-1920), Thevet preserved "curious details" about the New World that might have been lost otherwise. ("André Thevet," *Bulletin de Géographie Historique et Descriptive* [1888], 166-201.)

OLIVE PATRICIA DICKASON

important early source for Canada.[1] Thevet's problem was that he did not know where to draw the line in making his claims. He assumed, with a naive openness, that "first-hand" reporting left him free to use explorers' accounts, sometimes with acknowledgment, but at other times as if he had been there himself.

On top of this, Thevet never missed an opportunity to point out the errors of others. The irritation he aroused in his associates was expressed by the Calvinist minister Jean de Léry (1534-1613), who had followed Thevet to Brazil. He called the monk a cosmographic liar.[2] The eminent historian Jacques-Auguste de Thou (1553-1617) shared the sentiment:

> In fact, he is ignorant beyond anything one can imagine, having no knowledge of literature or antiquity ... he uses the uncertain for the certain, the false for the true, with an astonishing assurance ... therefore I cannot help but complain about several people who although versed in the sciences, do not perceive the foolishness of this charlatan, but cite him with honor in their writings.[3]

De Thou may have found Thevet's vanity "ridiculous," yet he himself could not escape being a man of his time, as a reading of his history quickly reveals. Renowned as a scholar in his own day, de Thou reported a comet in 1560 as the "most sure announcer of death to a king," and in 1572, a flying dragon.[4] If the weight of classical authority convinced de Thou of the existence of dragons, it did not convince Thevet. The monk asserted that he had never seen one anywhere, any more than he had seen a siren, a griffon, or a unicorn. According to Geoffrey At-

---

1   W.F. Ganong assessed Thevet's works and found value in them in *Crucial Maps* (Toronto: University of Toronto Press, 1964), 386-87 and 427-29. Charles-André-Julien had earlier made a similar assessment concerning Thevet's ethnographic descriptions (*Les Voyages de découverte et le premiers établissements (XVe-XVIe siècles)*, Paris, Presses Universitaires de France, 1948, 381-94). See also B.G. Hoffman, *Cabot to Cartier* (Toronto: University of Toronto Press, 1961), 171-79.

2   Jean de Léry, *Histoire d'un voyage fait en la terre du Brésil, autrement dit Amérique* (La Rochelle: Antoine Chuppin, 1578), preface.

3   De Thou, *Histoire universelle*, 16 vols. (London, 1734). 2: 651-52.

4   Cited by Lynn Thorndike, *A History of Magic and Experimental Science*, 8 vols. (New York: Columbia University Press, c.1923-58). 6: 490-91.

kinson (1892-1960), he was the only cosmographer of his day to deny the existence of the unicorn.[1] Thevet's rival, Belleforest, of course, sided with de Thou, saying that not only were unicorns to be found in India, they had been seen in Arabia. He held that Thevet's denial of the animal had no other basis than his fantasy, "as if nature were incapable of creating this beast."[2] Whatever his claim to first-hand knowledge, Thevet's impressions of Amerindians were remarkably similar to those of stay-at-home Belleforest. Both writers saw New World Natives as "marvellously strange and savage," all living a fundamentally similar way of life, "stirred only by nature's instincts," despite variations in details. Both described these peoples as being much in need of the civilizing hand of Christians, even as they admitted that all men were created essentially the same and that all had developed some degree of civil order.[3] Because of France's close connection with the Tupinambá in the flourishing dyewood trade, both writers relied heavily on Brazil and its peoples for their New World information, which they tended to extrapolate to other regions. Brazilians, particularly the Tupinambá, became the stereotypical Amerindians for the French of the 1500s, and indeed for Europe in general. During the 1600s, the Hurons of Canada would be cast in this role.

The two characteristics of Amerindians that drew the most concern from Renaissance Europeans were nudity and cannibalism.[4] Reading about such humans in pre-Christian classical accounts was one thing; meeting them in actuality was quite another. Both Thevet and Belleforest unquestioningly equated civility with clothing.[5] They also both shared Christian Europe's scandalized reaction to tales of New World

---

1   Geoffrey Atkinson, *Les Nouveaux horizons de la Renaissance française* (Paris: Droz, 1935), 279. Thevet makes his denials in *Cosmographie* 1: 19, 114.

2   Belleforest, *L'Histoire universelle*, 47.

3   Thevet, *Singularitez*, 136-137, and *Singularitez* 1: épistre; Belleforest, *L'Histoire universelle*, 262v, 419, and *Cosmographie* 2: 2081, 2094-95. In the case of Thevet, this sentiment was more evident in his *Cosmographie* than in his *Singularitez*.

4   Atkinson, *Nouveaux horizons*, 67-73.

5   Thevet, *Singularitez*, 135, 141-145. Belleforest remarked of northern Amerindians that they must be called savage because they went naked, even on ice (*L'Histoire universelle*, 268v). Thevet also thought that lack of fixed hours for meals, and eating when hungry, were indications of savagery (*Cosmographie* 2: 930).

OLIVE PATRICIA DICKASON

cannibalism, a custom which Thevet thought explained why Amerindians were without civility, without books, living like "beasts without reason."[1] At the same time, however, neither of the two commented on the French alliance with the man-eating Tupinambá for the purposes of the dyewood trade.

Belleforest turned to classical authority to deal with the problem of such customs as cannibalism and nudity, and cited the widely accepted dictum of Cicero (106-43 B.C.) that there were no people so wild who did not have some idea of God, whether true or false.[2] The fact that cannibals engaged in their butcheries indicated belief in some kind of a god to whom they were making their bloody offerings.[3] The trouble was, of course, that in European eyes, this worship was that of the devil.[4] Thevet, for his part, at first claimed that Amerindians had no religion. Later, perhaps stung by Belleforest's criticism of this assertion, Thevet proceeded in his *Cosmographie* to devote considerable space to the religious beliefs of Amerindians, the most complete we have for this early date. However, he did not retract his previous comment about Amerindians being without religion, as in his eyes the only true faith was Christianity. If the Amerindian way of life included some form of spiritual belief, no matter how strange, then it could not be totally without organization, as Thevet came around to acknowledging. For example, although he reported that Amerindians did not generally practice the virtue of obedience, as most of them had neither princes nor principalities, he admitted that in times of war they selected leaders whom they obeyed.[5] He also found something to praise in their solutions to the problems of living:

> These people desire nothing but what they need to sustain themselves so that they are not curious about foods, nor do they go searching for distant countries; because of the healthfulness of their nourishment they do not

---

1 Thevet, *Singularitez*, 134-36; *Cosmographie* 2: 910.

2 Marcus Tullius Cicero, *De Deorum Natura* 1.16.43.

3 Belleforest, *L'Histoire universelle*, 293v.

4 Belleforest, *Cosmographie* 2: 2054; *L'Histoire universelle*, épistre.

5 Thevet, *Cosmographie* 2, 905.

know what illness is, and so live in continuous health and peace. They have no occasion to become envious of others as they are more or less equal in their possessions, and rich in contentment in their mutual poverty.[1]

Such attitudes meant that they did not need police, because "among themselves they do not do reprehensible things." The only laws they had were those of nature (apparently he was not aware of the highly developed codes of the Mexica and the Maya). That did not prevent Amerindians, in their councils, from comporting themselves as if they were lords consulting the Venetian Senate.[2] This was how the ancient ancestors of Europeans had lived, Thevet said, a remark which pointed to the possibility that Amerindians could also evolve. This hewed to a line of argument that can be traced to the earliest European accounts of the New World.

Belleforest also noted the puzzling fact that even without written laws, Amerindian societies were orderly.[3] However, for every Amerindian who was gentle and accommodating, he wrote, there were many more who, going naked, did not know "what reason is, nor justice, [who] hate being reprimanded and do not accept punishment."[4] Continuing his list of deficiencies, Belleforest added that the older the Amerindian, the more wicked. Children showed a potentiality for good until about the age of twelve, but as they approached adulthood less desirable characteristics became dominant. With such dismal propensities, it was no wonder that God had sent the Spaniards and the Portuguese to subdue Amerindians and bring their villainy under control. Thus, like other Europeans before him, he attributed a divine mission to Christians, who of all peoples of the world, were the most active and talented as discoverers.[5]

Both writers agreed that Mexicans were the most civilized of all Amerindians, including the Peruvians. Mexico's principal city, Themis-

---

1   Thevet, *Singularitez*, 443.

2   Thevet, *Cosmographie* 2: 941v.

3   Belleforest, *Cosmographie* 2: 2095; *L'Histoire universelle*, 268.

4   Belleforest, *L'Histoire universelle*, 322v.

5   Belleforest, *L'Histoire universelle*, preface.

OLIVE PATRICIA DICKASON

titan (Tenochtitlan), was big and rich, with magnificent buildings and streets so straight one could see from one end to the other without hindrance.[1] Belleforest was particularly impressed with reports of the Mexicans' gardens, said to be "the most beautiful that can be imagined." He described in detail their aviaries, zoos, and collections of human oddities.[2] Thevet thought it was little wonder that the Mexica reacted as "badly" as they had toward the invading Spaniards as they had so much to defend.[3] And anyway, had not the Spaniards themselves once reacted similarly toward invading Romans?

Belleforest made more of Peruvian architecture than did Thevet; among other things, he said that Sacsahuaman in Cuzco, a fortified Inca ceremonial centre, was the finest building in the world. The magnificence and richness of Amerindian royal courts, he wrote, surpassed those of the proudest kings in other parts of the earth; these princes gloried in their wealth, were unapproachable, and did not communicate with their people. Peruvian rulers were so autocratic that they forbade their people to use their flocks for sustenance; not even the *caciques* (local leaders) dared to do so without express permission. The Inca ruler Atahuallpa, he said, was the cruellest tyrant on earth. Christian monarchs, by way of contrast, he idealized as popular, gentle, agreeable, and communicative; they were without pomp, without great entourages, and were not surrounded by soldiers, except perhaps in times of emergency. Nor did they make themselves feared. That was the difference, Belleforest ruminated with seemingly unconscious ethnocentricity, between rulers nourished in barbarism and those nourished in gentleness and courtesy.[4]

Fine buildings in the New World were not confined to Peru and Mexico, according to Belleforest. In his *L'Histoire universelle* he praised

---

1 Thevet, *Singularitez*, 382-389; Belleforest, *L'Histoire universelle*, 275v. Estimates for the population of Tenochtitlan range to about 250,000, larger than that of any contemporary European city. See William N. Denevan, ed., *The Native Population of the Americas in 1492* (Madison: University of Wisconsin Press, 1972), 109-111, and David E. Stannard, *American Holocaust* (New York: Oxford University Press, 1992), 42.

2 Belleforest, *L'Histoire universelle*, 316; *Cosmographie* 2: 2054-56, 2081, 2157-58.

3 Thevet, *Cosmographie* 2: 990v.

4 Belleforest, *Cosmographie* 2: 2045, 2050, 2156. See also *L'Histoire universelle*, 279-279v, 311.

the fine houses of "Baccalaos" (Labrador and Newfoundland) which he said may have lacked architecture, but were neat and well built.[1] In his later *Cosmographie*, however, he changed his mind, and presented Labradorians as having no houses other than their canoes, which they pulled ashore, turned upside down, and used for shelter. But he reported the Iroquoian town of Stadacona (on the site of today's Quebec City) as being a seat of royal residence, and Hochelaga (on the site of Montreal) as a city which even Moscow did not surpass in magnificence; it, too, was a royal seat, with fifty palaces made out of wood and bark.[2] Belleforest may have been repeating tales spread about by Cartier's men, who were making the most of their voyages to Canada in 1535-36 and 1541-42, or he simply may have cast their reports into cultural terms that he understood. Thevet's reports were more realistic. Although he, as usual, exaggerated the extent of his first-hand knowledge, there appears to be no reason to doubt his claim that he conversed directly with Cartier, and perhaps with Donnacona,[3] the Iroquoian leader whom Cartier brought home for an involuntary four-year visit to France.

Neither Thevet nor Belleforest allowed their admiration of Amerindian civilization, or even their own reports of the "multitudes" of Amerindian peoples, to interfere with their belief that Europeans' "discovery" of the New World had given them the right to claim suzerainty over those distant regions.[4] Thevet came the closest to recognizing that Amerindians qualified for at least some political rights, if one judges from his repeated comment that they objected strongly to being subjected by Europeans. But he never examined the implications of that observation; in politics as well as in French popular thinking of the day, the point was simply not at issue. Both writers accepted as a "right" France's ambition for colonies. Neither considered that Amerindians had a right to resist, and Thevet was surprised that they did. Neither he

---

1   Belleforest, *L'Histoire universelle*, 261v, 263.

2   Belleforest, *Cosmographie* 2: 2183, 2190-92.

3   Thevet, *Singularitez*, 398-444; *Cosmographie* 2: 1008v-1018v.

4   In Belleforest's words, the New World was "peuplé autant ou plus que autre que j'aye jamais vue." (*L'Histoire universelle*, 323v.) On the right of the French to claim suzerainty over New World lands, see Belleforest, *L'Histoire universelle*, 255, and Thevet, *Cosmographie* 2: 964v-65.

nor Belleforest thought that this was sensible on their part, in view of the benefits France would bring to them.

Of the two writers, Thevet emerges as the more complex, both as a person and in his works. Sincerely dedicated to cosmography, he ranked it next to theology as a discipline because it concentrated the mind on important things, deflecting attention from the minor or the inconsequential.[1] Only by direct observation — in effect, the scientific approach — could man's role in the universe be properly apprehended. Relying on classical authority, in contrast, meant becoming entangled with languages, and their translation and interpretation, increasing the margin for error to the point where white could be presented for black, and green for red.

If Thevet thought of himself as a scientist, although that term was unknown to him, the verdict of posterity is not in accord: he has been referred to as a "bustling journalist." Belleforest, for his part, advocated the methodology of classical scholarship to put new information about the world and its peoples into context, a procedure which he saw as enriching the study of humanity in all its varieties. He stressed the importance of Christianity to history, saying that it raised mankind above the purely human level to realize the overriding influence of God. It was the curiosity of Christians, he wrote, that led the way in learning the secrets of nature and of the Divine.[2] Somewhat less pretentiously than his rival Thevet, he only claimed to present what had been learned about the world and its peoples, whereas Thevet sought to embrace all there was to know about the cosmos. Preposterous as these goals appear today with the advantage of hindsight, they were considered to be realizable at the time.

Thevet and Belleforest present problems to the modern reader. While Belleforest proclaimed a preference for "holy larceny" (which was how he referred to his uncredited borrowings from others) over "stupid arrogance,"[3] Thevet defended his "first-hand knowledge"[4]

---

1 Thevet, *Cosmographie* I: preface.

2 Belleforest, *L'Histoire universelle*, preface.

3 Belleforest, *L'Histoire universelle*, 325v.

4 Thevet, *Cosmographie* I: épistre.

which he claimed to have won at the expense of great danger and much labour. Neither approach saved them from the pitfalls present in the general level of knowledge at their time, not to mention its ethnocentric biases. Their literary duelling only highlights the fact that they were both sixteenth-century Frenchmen for whom Christianity was fundamentally important, and who were both profoundly concerned that their country get its "rightful" share of the newly revealed riches of the New World. Each sought to present "facts" as he saw them; each believed that the "truth" of his cosmographical information would enhance the glory of his country. Astonishingly enough, this attitude was more evident in Belleforest, the historian and unofficial advocate, than it was in Thevet, the official cosmographer.

In their writing styles both were bogged down in detail. Their works are difficult to read, a major reason why the two are not better known today. Thevet's work in particular contains much genuinely new information and could have been more fairly evaluated much sooner if it had been more approachable.[1] Perhaps because of his position, but also because of his approach and personality, he inherited Mandeville's mantle: the absurdities in his work have obscured its real value. Even if his attempts to consider Amerindians in their own terms were not always successful, Thevet prefigured approaches to ethnography that are still in evidence today. This is more evident in his later work than in those considered here; for example, when he compiled biographies of great men of the world, he included six Amerindians, among them one from Brazil's cannibal coast, a gesture that was far ahead of its time.[2]

Thevet, Belleforest, and their colleagues illustrate the importance of examining cosmographers and their works as guides to understanding sixteenth-century Europeans' perceptions of and reactions to the New World and its peoples. Those reactions in turn profoundly affected the course of world history, as well as later European thinking about that history.

---

1 Thevet was the subject of a major study in 1988 by Professor Frank Lestringant, Université de Lille III, for his *doctorat d'état*.

2 Thevet, *Pourtraits et vies des hommes illustres, Grecs, Latin, et payens* (Paris: la veuve Kervert et Guillaume Chaudiere, 1584), 641, 644, 650, 656, 661, 663. All six of the Amerindian portraits and their accompanying texts have been included in Roger Schlesinger, ed., *Portraits from the Age of Exploration*, tr. Edward Benson (Urbana and Chicago: University of Illinois Press, 1993).

OLIVE PATRICIA DICKASON

2

Controlled Speculation:
Interpreting the Saga of Pocahontas and Captain John Smith

Frederic W. Gleach

HISTORICAL DOCUMENTS ARE SHAPED by many factors, including what their authors were able to observe, what they chose to record of those observations, and the biases inherent in their understandings of what they experienced. For a long time now, scholars have worked to recognize biases in the historical documents — and in their own interpretations — in order to construct histories that better reflect "what really happened," and to examine the historical meanings of those things that happened. But what can we do if nobody bothered to write about the particular subject we are interested in, or when there is only passing mention, with no details? These situations are common in the historical record, resulting in the often-heard litany "little is known of ..." in all its variations. This may be accurate in some cases, but it is certainly not very satisfying. As I found in my studies of the Powhatan Confederacy, an alliance of Algonquian nations in seventeenth-century Virginia, we need some way to fill in these gaps.

The most common approach is to look for similar or analogous situations that are better recorded. The question then becomes, how good is the analogy? Or, in the terms I want to work with here, how speculative is the speculation? A related issue arose in anthropology in the 1940s and 1950s, in the form of a debate over the validity of doing cross-cultural comparison. Franz Boas (1940) had argued in the 1890s that detailed study of single cultures was necessary before cross-cultural comparison could be done. Every culture differs in its institutions and understandings, its practices and beliefs, and comparability can be difficult to evaluate (cf. Kluckhohn 1953:509-12). Although Boas and others sometimes used comparative methods, most research emphasized the study of particular cultures viewed in relative isolation. In contrast, Fred Eggan (1954) argued that comparison was not only possible but useful, as long as it was applied with careful control to ensure that the situations were truly comparable — a process he called controlled comparison. I believe the same is true of speculation, and would like to adopt a parallel term first used by Mel Mednick in the 1960s (personal communication): "controlled speculation."

As I use the term here, controlled speculation involves the use of comparative material from other cultural or historical situations to infer crucial information that may be missing or obscured in the historical record of a particular situation; the comparative material is selected from contexts that appear most closely analogous. The speculative inferences are thus controlled by being carefully and explicitly grounded in the ethnographic, historical, and/or archaeological records. My example for this process is an incident that occurred in what is now Virginia in the winter of 1607-1608: the rescue of the English colonist Captain John Smith by the young Powhatan woman Pocahontas.

In plot the story is simple. While exploring the Chickahominy River in December 1607, Smith was taken prisoner by a group of Powhatan Indians, on whose lands the English had recently settled. He was subjected to a series of tests, threats, and rituals, paraded through a series of villages, and was then taken to their paramount chief, Powhatan. While there, he was suddenly seized, his head forced down on a rock, and clubs raised to crush his skull — when Pocahontas, Powhatan's favourite daughter, rushed in and threw her arms around his head to save his life. Powhatan ordered him spared. The next day Powhatan came to Smith with a large company of men, all painted black, who proceeded to sing. Powhatan then told Smith they were friends, and that he would be considered as his son, and could have a village for the English to live in. Smith was then returned to the colony at Jamestown.

The incident from this sequence of events that has captured the imagination of generations is his rescue by Pocahontas. But what did this mean? Did Pocahontas develop a sudden pity, friendship, love, or even lust for Smith, that prompted her to save him? This is perhaps the most common interpretation, particularly in literary treatments of the story, and has been featured in children's books (e.g., Gleiter and Thompson 1985, Graham 1953, Seymour 1961, Wilkie 1969), a romance novel (Donnell 1991), and even a verse of Peggy Lee's hit song, "Fever" (Lee et al. 1958); the 1995 Walt Disney film, *Pocahontas*, was also drawn from this literary tradition. Or was Pocahontas a schemer who saw marriage to a powerful Englishman as a way to escape the drudgery of her life? She was a daughter of Powhatan, but in her matrilineal society she would not inherit from him; might this have motivated her to seek out a better option for her future? Or was Pocahontas acting a part in a ritual,

FREDERIC W. GLEACH

perhaps to adopt Smith? This last interpretation has been the most common among scholars in recent years (cf. Hulme 1992:150, 302n.34), and it is upon this base that I will practice a bit of controlled speculation.

Although this incident has entered the collective consciousness of the United States, being taught in grade schools throughout much of the country, some have questioned whether it even happened. Two recent writers have differed on this point. Lemay (1992) argues from a critical reading of the original texts that the rescue probably happened as described; as he suggests (1992:72-79), the acceptance of the story by Samuel Purchas, who knew both Smith and Pocahontas, argues strongly for its veracity. In contrast, Rountree (1990:38-39) — widely considered the best modern authority on the Powhatans — believes the rescue never happened, following the nineteenth-century argument that Smith invented the story for his own glory (cf. Barbour 1986:lxiii-lxiv). She then asserts:

> The rescue of John Smith by Pocahontas does not bear scrutiny from an anthropological viewpoint, either. We are expected to believe that Powhatan welcomed and feasted a powerful guest whom his astute brother and his most trusted priests had tested and approved, and then suddenly, after "a long consultation," he tried to have that guest's brains clubbed out on an altar stone — a quick death normally meted out to disobedient subjects, not to captured foreigners.... This scenario simply does not ring true. Pocahontas probably did see John Smith for the first time in that January of 1608, but it is highly unlikely that his life needed saving at the time. (1990:39)

Rountree is certainly right in questioning the literal nature of the rescue, but she goes on to dismiss the event as ritual. After describing the successive gathering with Powhatan and his men painted black, she writes:

> This incident, along with the "rescue," has been taken by some historians to be a formal adoption procedure. The incident by itself (conference, decision, announcement) may have been something of the sort, since it approximates descriptions of adoption procedures in other Indian groups (e.g., Iroquois), and Powhatan is known to have placed his real sons in ruling positions and expected them to send him tribute. However, Smith did not write of the "rescue" itself as though it were part of a ritual, and no identical sequence of events is recorded as an adoption procedure for

any other native American group. *We have no information at all about the nature of the Powhatan adoption procedure.* (1990:39, emphasis added)

Rountree does not explain why Smith should be trusted to recognize a ritual from a foreign culture when he cannot be trusted concerning the rescue account. I believe, however, that his interpretations of meanings and reasons are far more likely to be wrong than the simple facts he chose to record. Any outside observer — or even participant — can easily misunderstand or only partly understand the meanings of and reasons for an event. But if Smith, or any other observer from another culture, completely fabricated an incident, we would expect it not to fit with other observations from the culture being described — not to "ring true," as Rountree notes. The question then becomes this: how can one identify the true ring?

Controlled Speculation

Controlled speculation is inherently subjective; it depends upon the scholar's understandings, developed through experience and knowledge of the situations being studied. This lack of objectivity does not make it an inappropriate technique, however. Historical interpretation is inherently a subjective, even imaginative, activity (cf. Collingwood 1956:231-49), despite the "common-sense" theory of history that sees it as derived simply from authoritative statements of historical facts (1956:234-35). The subjectivity of history has been an explicit focus of study in recent years (e.g., Furet 1984), and is as much characteristic of the new, "scientific" histories as it is of "traditional," narrative histories (1984:17-19). The difficulties raised by this subjectivity revolve around the issue of validity of interpretation: what makes one interpretation of a text or an event better, more reliable, more truthful than others?

This is a question that cannot be answered simply. Because interpretations are based on the knowledge and experience of the persons making them, it may be tempting to simply cite "authority." But what constitutes authority? One can know many details of historical documents, and still not understand the meanings of the events they represent. One can have knowledge of theories of social order, and not know which might apply in a particular case. Many kinds of knowledge, some useful and some less so, can be brought to bear upon any given historical ques-

FREDERIC W. GLEACH

tion, but there is no easy way to evaluate them in the abstract. There is no definable One True Way to historical understanding.

But certain methodological approaches can help avoid pitfalls. Like any other historical research, speculation must be grounded wherever possible in documented sources, and those sources must be identified for the reader. When speculating from comparative material, these sources must be evaluated not only for their reliability, but also for their relevance to the context to which they are being extended. This depends on a knowledge of the cultural meanings and relationships involved. One cannot assume, for instance, that a ritual or political institution documented in one society would be the same in a neighbouring society, or in every society sharing the same language. There may be such similarities, but there may not be. Fortunately, there is often information to help determine the likelihood of such parallels or similarities, in the form of passing mentions or partial accounts. The historical record is replete with tantalizing passages that suggest the presence or form of various rituals, beliefs, institutions, or social structures, without fully describing them or even providing certainty of their existence. When partial descriptions from one group seem to match more completely described cultural practices from related or neighbouring groups, and particularly when similarities in other related phenomena can be documented, in the absence of contradictory evidence an assumption of similarity between the two cases is justified. Four criteria can help guide and control this process of speculation:

1. Is there reason to believe the existence of some practice or institution in the context being studied? This might be based on a passing mention or partial description in an historical account, for example.

2. Are there other groups who might provide appropriate comparison? Such might be neighbouring groups, particularly for questions closely tied to a particular environment, or linguistically and/or culturally related groups for questions of cultural meaning. A group that is close in both physical and cultural terms is ideal, but even in such a case there may be marked differences in specific phenomena.

3. Is a similar phenomenon documented in a comparable context? For the controlled speculation to work, there must be at least one case from which comparisons can be drawn. It must be documented in

sufficient detail to evaluate whether it supports or contradicts the original evidence.

4. Is there contradictory evidence? In the strictest sense, any contradiction should refute the comparison, ending the speculation. In practice, such contradictions themselves must be evaluated; they may stem from biased observation in the original documents rather than from inaccuracies in the comparison.

This is merely an outline of the process, and each application will be different. One might use a different starting point, inferring the existence of a practice in a particular group from the observed fact that all or most related groups follow such a practice, and then look for evidence to support or contradict that assumption. Also note that these criteria for controlling speculation are necessary, but not sufficient, criteria. They do not prove an inference, but only demonstrate its plausibility or likelihood.

Controlled speculation is based on certain fundamental assumptions which should be briefly examined. Most importantly, it assumes that there can be meaningful similarities between cultures, and that these similarities may be due to certain kinds of relationships. These may involve direct physical interaction, such as trade or intermarriage, or they may be less immediate, involving historical processes of cultural transmission, such as descent from a common cultural source, with perhaps a shared linguistic base. This assumption encourages comparison, and establishes some ways to proceed. One may need further restrictions on the process in certain cases, using only groups from the same environmental setting, or the same language or language family, or the same time period, to make this assumption valid.

Another set of assumptions involves the nature of historical evidence. The documentary sources are assumed to reflect real phenomena, although they must be interpreted, and biases in observation and transmission must be taken into account. The comparisons made are not between original sources, but between the cultural phenomena represented by the original sources:

The scientific historian does not treat statements as statements but as evidence: not as true or false accounts of the facts of which they profess to be accounts, but as other facts which if he knows the right questions to ask about them, may throw light on those facts. (Collingwood 1956:275)

The sources must be evaluated prior to being used in comparison. This need is particularly obvious when the sources are themselves drawn from different cultural contexts (as, for instance, when comparing observations from the colonial period with those of later ethnographers), but it is always present.

Some situations lend themselves better than others to controlled speculation. Sufficient detail is needed in the original sources to support or refute the attempted speculation, and appropriate comparable cases must be documented in even greater detail. But when used carefully, controlled speculation can be an important tool for interpreting historical events.

Textual and Contextual Considerations of Smith's Accounts

Captain John Smith was a member of the original party of Englishmen who settled at Jamestown, Virginia in 1607. He had gained the status of captain through military service, not from birth as a gentleman (cf. Barbour 1964:3-49). During his time in Virginia he explored widely in the territory surrounding Jamestown. Smith seems to have been determined to justify the status he had achieved, and wrote in detail of his activities. Obviously a literate person, he produced highly readable accounts which form the principal evidence not only for the incidents of his captivity, but for the first years of the colony.

The site chosen for Jamestown was located in the territory of the Powhatan Indians, a confederation of tribes speaking dialects of an Algonquian language, headed by the paramount chief, Powhatan. This territory, called in Powhatan *Tsenacommacah*, was composed of a number of districts, each occupied by the people of a particular tribe, with their own chief; Jamestown was in the district of the Paspeheghs. Powhatan had inherited control over approximately a half-dozen tribes in the late sixteenth century, and had expanded his control to over thirty tribes by 1607. In addition to the chiefs, other marked positions in Powhatan society included priests, war-chiefs, and other councillors; an individual could hold more than one of these positions simultaneously. Opechancanough, who figured prominently in Smith's captivity, was a district chief and Powhatan's war-chief. The war-chief acted not only in actual warfare, but in all relations dealing with non-Powhatan outsiders.[1] Other relevant aspects of the Powhatan world will become clear in the following discussion.

Four published works by Smith included information on the events of his captivity. *A True Relation* (Smith 1986a) was published in 1608, very shortly after these events occurred. It was apparently edited from a letter from Smith, and rushed into print; there are many obvious omissions in the text, and the editor moved several passages, in some cases changing their apparent intended meanings. The Barbour edition cited here notes these editorial changes, but many of them are not recoverable, as the letter is not known to survive. *A Map of Virginia* (Smith 1986b) and the *Proceedings* (Smith 1986c) were published together in 1612. None of these texts mentions the rescue by Pocahontas, although each provides information on other incidents of Smith's captivity. The fact that no account of the rescue was published prior to his *Generall Historie* [1624] (Smith 1986d) is the principal reason some scholars have questioned the truth of the account. As discussed above, however, I agree with Lemay's assessment that the accounts may be taken as essentially truthful, although in some ways they are both naive and biased.

Judging from his accounts, Smith seems to have communicated reasonably well with the Powhatans despite the barrier of language. He apparently studied the Powhatan language, and included word lists and sample sentences in Powhatan in his publications. Communication involves more than words, however, and it is evident in several instances that while he learned enough vocabulary to translate words, he did not understand many of the complexities of Powhatan culture – the ideas, beliefs, and practices being expressed in those words. Rather, he interpreted elements of Powhatan culture within the framework of English ideas. Offerings made to one of the chief Powhatan spirits, for instance, were seen as devil-worship (Smith 1986b:169). As was common at the time, he often referred to the Indians as savages, and oversimplified the meanings both of things that he saw and things he was told. It is the task of the historical researcher to get beyond those simplifications, to better represent a view of the past.

---

1 The existence of war-chiefs for the Powhatans is itself a product of controlled speculation, as it is not specifically described for them. It is a common feature in both Algonquian and southeastern groups, however, and provides the best explanation of the evident relationship between Powhatan and Opechancanough (cf. Gleach 1992:30-31, 136-138).

FREDERIC W. GLEACH

Even more so than in other kinds of historical interpretations, when engaging in speculative reconstruction it is essential to provide the reader with the texts being interpreted. I have kept the original spelling, capitalization, and punctuation in all quotations. Brief editorial insertions have been bracketed, and deletions noted by ellipsis; more extensive clarifications are given in footnotes where necessary.

The Story of Pocahontas and Captain John Smith

In December 1607, the first winter for the English colony in Virginia, Captain John Smith was captured and his companions killed while they were exploring the upper Chickahominy River. When first captured, Smith was brought before the war-chief Opechancanough, whom he impressed with his compass:

> Much they marvailed at the playing of the Fly and Needle, which they could see so plainely, and yet not touch it, because of the glasse that covered them. But when he[1] demonstrated by that Globe-like Jewell, the roundnesse of the earth, and skies, the spheare of the Sunne, Moone, and Starres, and how the Sunne did chase the night round about the world continually; the greatnesse of the Land and Sea, the diversitie of Nations, varietie of complexions, and how we were to them Antipodes, and many other such like matters, they all stood as amazed with admiration. Notwithstanding, within an houre after they tyed him to a tree, and as many as could stand about him prepared to shoot him, but the King holding up the Compass in his hand, they all laid downe their Bowes and Arrowes. (Smith 1986d:147)

This was the first of three threats to his life during his captivity. Smith was then taken to Rasawek, a hunting town between the Chickahominy and Pamunkey rivers (see Figure 1):

> Their order in conducting him was thus; Drawing themselves all in fyle, the King in the middest had all their [Smith's and his men's] Peeces [guns] and Swords borne before him. Captaine Smith was led after him by three great Salvages, holding him fast by each arme: and on each side six went in fyle with their Arrowes nocked. But arriving at the Towne (which was

---

1 Smith, that is; he frequently wrote his accounts in the third person.

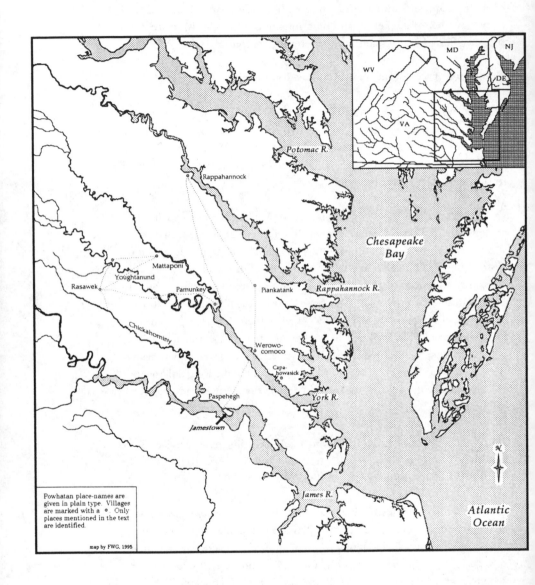

Figure 1: Travels of Captain John Smith in Captivity
Winter 1607-1608

FREDERIC W. GLEACH

but onely thirtie or fortie hunting houses made of Mats, which they remove as they please, as we our tents), all the women and children staring
to behold him, the souldiers first all in fyle performed the forme of a Bis-
sone[1] so well as could be; and on each flanke, officers as Serjeants to see
them keepe their order. A good time they continued this exercise, and
then cast themselves in a ring, dancing in such severall Postures, and singing and yelling out such hellish notes and screeches; being strangely
painted, every one his quiver of Arrowes, and at his backe a club; on his
arme a Fox or an Otters skinne, or some such matter for his vambrace;[2]
their heads and shoulders painted red, with Oyle and *Pocones*[3] mingled together, which Scarlet-like color made an exceeding handsome shew; his
Bow in his hand, and the skinne of a Bird with her wings abroad dryed,
tyed on his head, a peece of copper, a white shell, a long feather, with a
small rattle growing at the tayles of their snakes tyed to it, or some such
like toy. All this while Smith and the King stood in the middest guarded,
as before is said, and after three dances they all departed. Smith they conducted to a long house, where thirtie or fortie tall fellowes did guard him,
and ere long more bread and venison was brought him then would have
served twentie men, I thinke his stomacke at that time was not very good;
what he left they put in baskets and tyed over his head. About midnight
they set the meate againe before him, all this time not one of them would
eate a bit with him, till the next morning they brought him as much
more, and then did they eate all the old, and reserved the new as they had
done the other, which made him thinke they would fat him to eat him.
(Smith 1986d:147–148)

Notice the frequency with which threes appear: Smith was led by three
guards, and the dances performed around Smith and Opechancanough
numbered three. This continued throughout the captivity, and has ritual
significance.

Smith was kept at Rasawek for several days. While he was there an
Indian came threatening to kill him, but was stopped by one of his
guards; Smith was told that this was the father of a man he had killed,

---

1 A simple marching exercise used for new recruits.

2 Armour worn on the arm. Most precisely, the piece worn on the forearm, but commonly extended to the armour of the whole arm.

3 A red dye used by the Powhatans, derived from a root.

seeking revenge (Smith 1986a:49). The Powhatans next marched Smith to a series of villages:

> the King [Opechancanough] presently conducted me to another King-dome, upon the top of the next northerly river, called Youghtanan. Having feasted me, he further led me to another branch of the river, called Mattapanient; to two other hunting townes they led me, and to each of these Countries, a house of the great Emperour of Powhatan.... After this foure or five dayes march, we returned to Rasaweack, the first towne they brought me too, where binding the Mats in bundels, they marched two dayes journey, and crossed the River of Youghtanan, where it was as broad as Thames: so conducting me to a place called Menapacute in Pamaunke, where the king inhabited: the next day another King of that nation called Kekataugh,[1] having received some kindnes of me at the Fort, kindly invited me to feast at his house; the people from all places flocked to see me, each shewing to content me. (Smith 1986a:49-51)

At Pamunkey a ritual was enacted that is crucial to understanding the events of Smith's captivity. The only complete description is given in the *Generall Historie*:

> Early in a morning a great fire was made in a long house, and a mat spread on the one side, as on the other, on the one they caused him to sit, and all the guard went out of the house, and presently came skipping in a great grim fellow, all painted over with coale, mingled with oyle; and many Snakes and Wesels skins stuffed with mosse, and all their tayles tyed together, so as they met on the crowne of his head in a tassell; and round about the tassell was a Coronet of feathers, the skins hanging round about his head, backe, and shoulders, and in a manner covered his face; with a hellish voyce and a rattle in his hand. With most strange gestures and passions he began his invocation, and environed the fire with a circle of meale; which done, three more such like devils came rushing in with the like antique[2] tricks, painted halfe blacke, halfe red: but all their eyes were painted white, and some red stroakes like Mutchato's [mustaches], along

---

1 A younger brother of Powhatan, and, with Opechancanough and Itoyatin, a chief of Pamunkey.

2 In early seventeenth-century English usage this word can be both "antique" and "antic," and here has connotations of both.

FREDERIC W. GLEACH

their cheekes: round about him those fiends daunced a pretty while, and then came in three more as ugly as the rest; with red eyes, and white stroakes over their blacke faces, at last they all sat downe right against him; three of them on the one hand of the chiefe Priest, and three on the other. Then all with their rattles began a song, which ended, the chiefe Priest layd downe five wheat cornes:[1] then strayning his armes and hands with such violence that he sweat, and his veynes swelled, he began a short Oration: at the conclusion they all gave a short groane; and then layd down three graines more. After that, began their song againe, and then another Oration, ever laying downe so many cornes as before, till they had twice incirculed the fire; that done, they tooke a bunch of little stickes prepared for that purpose, continuing still their devotion, and at the end of every song and Oration, they layd downe a sticke betwixt the divisions of Corne. Till night, neither he nor they did either eate or drinke, and then they feasted merrily, with the best provisions they could make. Three dayes they used this Ceremony; the meaning whereof they told him, was to know if he intended them well or no. The circle of meale signified their Country, the circles of corne the bounds of the Sea, and the stickes his Country. They imagined the world to be flat and round, like a trencher, and they in the middest. After this they brought him a bagge of gunpowder, which they carefully preserved till the next spring, to plant as they did their corne; because they would be acquainted with the nature of that seede. Opitchapam [Itoyatin] the Kings brother invited him to his house, where, with as many platters of bread, foule, and wild beasts, as did environ him, he bid him wellcome; but not any of them would eate a bit with him, but put up all the remainder in Baskets. At his returne to Opechancanoughs, all the Kings women, and their children, flocked about him for their parts, as a due by Custome, to be merry with such fragments. (Smith 1986d:149–150)

Smith's statement that this ceremony was to determine his intentions must be questioned. Its complexity seems excessive for such a purpose. The ceremony bears no relation to rites of divination recorded for the Delawares, for instance, all of which were simple mechanical procedures using an object of divinatory power (Newcomb 1956:63). Its repetitions,

---

1   In English usage in the early seventeenth century, "wheat" was the unmarked term for the grain of a cereal, and here refers to maize or Indian corn; "corns" was synonymous with kernels or grains.

sacrifices, and forms seem more like those of ceremonial creations or renewals of cultural relations — the Delaware Big House Ceremony (Speck 1931; cf. 22-24) comes to mind — than like divination. It lasted "eight, ten, or twelve hours without cease" (Smith 1986b:171), and was repeated three times on successive days, with feasting each evening at the conclusion. Rather than being simply the presentation of a static map of the Powhatan world, as understood by Smith, the creation of this diagram was likely part of a much more complex active process.

The nature of that process cannot be known with certainty, but given the context it is possible to speculate with some measure of conviction. At the end of his captivity, when Smith was released, he was made chief of a territory for the English to occupy within Tsenacommacah. When he was first captured, however, he and the rest of the English colony were outsiders to the Powhatan world. Some transformation clearly took place during this time. Given the significance of repetition, sacrifice, and symbolic meanings in the Powhatan culture, this ritual may be best understood as a ritual of redefinition, establishing the forms of the relationship between the colony and the Powhatans, defining the place of the English in the Powhatan world, and transforming them from outsiders to insiders. The sticks thus represented the movement of the English from the margins of the Powhatan world toward its centre, Tsenacommach, represented by the cornmeal.

Given that this all transpired in a language new to Smith, and given his ego- and ethnocentrism, he was unlikely to fully understand such complicated notions. My interpretation of this ceremony as a redefinition rather than a simple presentation of the Powhatan world represents a relatively minor step beyond Smith's understanding, which was necessarily bound by his limited knowledge of the Powhatan language. Taking this step restores meaning to what is otherwise an anomalous account. In the Algonquian world, ceremonial invocations, repetitions, and sacrifices are no more necessary for the explanation of a map than they are for divination — but they are necessary for the kind of creative process I am suggesting here. Repetition, in particular, is a way of making things true, of bringing things into being, although the significant number of repetitions varies. Three seems to have been a ritual number for the Powhatans at this time, and as noted before, the number recurs throughout the events of Smith's captivity. Here the priests entered in three groups, first the head priest, then two groups of three, and three circles were made around the fire. There were also three repetitions of this ritual, in three days.

It is probably significant that the Powhatan world was represented in this ritual by cornmeal – processed, culturally modified corn – and the boundaries of the Powhatan world were represented by "natural" corn. Corn is itself a cultural product, although less processed than cornmeal, and its use to represent the margins, and the fact that clusters were used, further suggest that what was being represented was something more than simply "the bounds of the sea"; the clusters may have stood for surrounding groups of non-Powhatan people, possibly including the varieties of spirit-beings that Hallowell (1976) glossed as "other-than-human persons." The prepared sticks representing the movement of the English are drawn from a different set of symbols entirely.

Let's return now to the narrative of Smith's captivity:

> From hence this kind King [Kekataugh] conducted mee to a place called Topahanocke,[1] a kingdome upon another River northward.... The next night I lodged at a hunting town of Powhatans, and the next day arrived at Werowocomoco upon the river of Pamauncke, where the great king [Powhatan] is resident. (Smith 1986a:51-53)

Note that he was being led at this point by Kekataugh, a Powhatan district chief, instead of by Opechancanough, the war-chief, further suggesting that Smith was no longer an outsider. The meeting at Werowocomoco was the first meeting of Smith and Powhatan, and in this early account he described their conversation concerning the reasons for the English presence in Virginia, and their search for the western sea (1986a:53-55). There is no mention here of the Pocahontas incident, however, and the description of the ritual to which he was subjected while at Pamunkey was moved by his editor to a different place in the book (cf. 1986a:104n.1-41). But it was at Werowocomoco that his rescue by Pocahontas took place:

> Before a fire upon a seat like a bedsted, he [Powhatan] sat covered with a great robe, made of Rarowcun [raccoon] skinnes, and all the tayles hang-

---

1   The Powhatan language included -r- and -t- dialects; this place is commonly called Rappahannock, like the river, although the -t- dialect is preserved in the name of the modern town, Tappahannock.

ing by. On either hand did sit a young wench of 16 or 18 yeares, and along on each side of the house, two rowes of men, and behind them as many women, with all their heads and shoulders painted red; many of their heads bedecked with the white downe of Birds; but every one with something: and a great chayn of white beads about their necks. At his [Smith's] entrance before the King, all the people gave a great shout. The Queene of Appomatuck was appointed to bring him water to wash his hands, and another brought him a bunch of feathers, in stead of a Towell to dry them: having feasted him after their best barbarous manner they could, a long consultation was held, but the conclusion was, two great stones were brought before Powhatan: then as many as could layd hands on him [Smith], dragged him to them, and thereon laid his head, and being ready with their clubs, to beate out his braines, Pocahontas the Kings dearest daughter, when no intreaty could prevaile, got his head in her armes, and laid her owne upon his to save him from death: whereat the Emperour was contented he should live to make him hatchets, and her bells, beads, and copper. (Smith 1986d:150-151)

This is perhaps the most famous incident in the history of Virginia. As noted above, some have doubted that it even happened, and those who have accepted it have generally tried to explain it as an isolated event, whether as a planned adoption or as an unpremeditated rescue by an infatuated young woman. When examined in the context of the other events of Smith's captivity, however, the rescue takes on a great significance. Washing Smith's hands and drying them with feathers is a cleansing act that suggests this was another ritual occasion; the formal organization and attire of the Powhatans supports this contention. Pocahontas was acting here in an important role as mediator (cf. Kidwell 1992:99-101), symbolically saving Smith's life so that he was effectively reborn into the Powhatan world, into the place created through the preceding ritual. It was an adoption, in a sense — not of Smith as an individual, but of Smith as head of the English colony.

The threat of death by clubbing may seem excessive for a ritual of adoption, but it is precisely what one might expect, structurally: a symbolic ending of one existence, and the beginning of a new one. The threat of death was intended to be perceived as real; the end of the prior state had to be marked. Powhatan culture itself provides a good parallel here in the huskanaw, a rite of passage which included the symbolic death of young men[1] and their subsequent rebirth into adult society (Beverley 1947:207-209; Gleach 1992:35-39).

The final episode of Smith's captivity took place two days later:

> Powhatan having disguised himselfe in the most fearefullest manner he could, caused Captaine Smith to be brought forth to a great house in the woods, and there upon a mat by the fire to be left alone. Not long after from behinde a mat that divided the house, was made the most dolefullest noyse he ever heard; then Powhatan more like a devill then a man with some two hundred more as blacke as himselfe, came unto him and told him now they were friends, and presently he should goe to James towne, to send him two great gunnes, and a gryndstone, for which he would give him the Country of Capahowosick, and for ever esteeme him as his sonne Nantaquoud. (Smith 1986d:151)

That this arrangement included not only Smith, but the colony as well, is shown more clearly in the *True Relation*:

> Hee desired mee to forsake Paspahegh, and to live with him upon his River, a Countrie called Capahowasicke: hee promised to give me Corne, Venison, or what I wanted to feede us, Hatchets and Copper wee should make him, and none should disturbe us. (Smith 1986a:57)

The "great house in the woods" in which this took place was most likely a *quioccasin*, "which is their House of Religious Worship" (Beverley 1947:195), rather than a residence. Beverley (1947:195-97) described a *quioccasin* that he entered in the late 1600s that was very similar, and this marginal setting, neither domesticated cultural space, like a village, nor utter wilderness, is typical for such a sacred place. The ritual implications of red, black, and white — colours which recurred in each ceremony in this series — should also be noted, with the Powhatans painted black here. The gifts to be given in return further suggest that this event concluded a protracted ritual.

---

1 Smith originally mistook this, too, for actual death: "In some part of the country they have yearly a sacrifice of children." He was informed otherwise at the time by a Powhatan chief (Smith 1986b:171-172), and more accurate information on the *huskanaw* was available by 1617 (Purchas 1617:952).

Although some have questioned whether either this final ritual or the rescue should be viewed as an adoption ceremony (cf. Rountree 1989:121-22, 1990:39), it seems evident to me that they should be considered together, and together with the other events of Smith's captivity, as a ritual complex "adopting" the English colony. This perspective helps to elucidate the events of Smith's captivity. The ritual sequence apparently began with the act of capturing Captain John Smith. He was captured by a large party, variously reported as 200 to 300 bowmen, led by the Powhatan war-chief Opechancanough. While they may have been on a collective deer hunt, as Barbour (Smith 1986d:147n) suggests, a sense of purposefulness in the actions of the capturing party was apparent even in Smith's accounts of his capture (Smith 1986a:45-47, 1986c:213, 1986d:146-147). This suggests that his capture was more than incidental. He was immediately taken before Opechancanough, whose duties as war-chief would include dealing with outsiders, and his life was threatened — the first of three times this would happen during this captivity. He was then taken to the seasonal village of Rasawek and treated as a captive chief; the three dances that took place there were centred on Smith and Opechancanough, and after the dances he was feasted. He was kept there for close to a week, with his life being threatened again while there.

A few days after this second threat the next phase of his captivity began, a physical transition from the margins of Tsenacommacah to its heart, the village of Powhatan, and a metaphysical transformation from English to Anglo-Powhatan. Smith was first taken to a series of smaller, more peripheral villages, returned to Rasawek, and then taken to Menapacute, one of the main villages of Pamunkey. Pamunkey was one of the most important districts of Tsenacommacah, where Powhatan's brothers Itoyatin and Kekataugh as well as Opechancanough were chiefs. It was while Smith was here that the redefinition ritual took place, creating a place for the English in the Powhatan world. The Powhatans then returned Smith to the periphery of Tsenacommacah, and from this outside position he was brought to Werowocomoco, Powhatan's principal residence at this time. Smith's old life being ended, Pocahontas ceremonially spared him from death, allowing him to begin his new life as a Powhatan. Two days later the ritual was completed, giving both Smith and the colony a specific place in Tsenacommacah. Smith was then returned to Jamestown, early in 1608.

FREDERIC W. GLEACH

In exchange for furnishing Powhatan with the goods he desired, the English would be permitted to remain, with Smith as their chief, safe in their own territory within Tsenacommacah. The colony did not move from Jamestown, however, nor were the "two great guns, and a grindstone" given over. By mid-1609 the Powhatans were attacking the colony with some frequency. Conflict increased after Smith's return to England in October 1609, setting the stage for the later hostility of colonial relations with the Indians of Virginia.

Conclusion

The story of Pocahontas's rescue of Captain John Smith fits with the other events of his captivity to form a cohesive whole. This series of events had meaning within the world-view of the Powhatan Indians, although it was alien to the English colonial world. The likelihood of Smith's being able to create such a construct from his imagination is not great; it is therefore likely that the events happened more or less as Smith described. The meanings of these events either were not recorded by him, or were recorded from an English perspective that must be questioned. Controlled speculation permits some understanding of those meanings, although they must be reconstructed through careful historical and anthropological analysis.

There is no guarantee, of course, that the reconstruction of these events as a ceremonial sequence is precisely correct, but its articulation with the original accounts from Smith, and with known institutions from other groups, suggests that it is a close approximation, at least. This is certainly an improvement over minimalist conclusions that nothing is known concerning Powhatan adoptions, or that these events might or might not have happened based on purely textual criteria such as when and how Smith published the accounts. It also takes us beyond those approaches which define accounts such as Smith's purely as constructs of a European mode of understanding the "Other." We can forget too easily that the Other being observed by Europeans was another group of people who were also engaged in precisely parallel attempts at understanding Others, and that both sides were living, acting co-creators of the events recorded in those accounts. Controlled speculation is one of the tools we can use to re-engage historical documents in the culturally constructed meanings that are an inherent part of the actions they represent. These texts can serve us well as key evidence for the study of human actions and their meanings.

References

Barbour, Philip L.
    1964 *The Three Worlds of Captain John Smith*. Boston: Houghton Mifflin.
    1986 General Introduction. *The Complete Works of Captain John Smith (1580-1631)*, vol. 1. Philip L. Barbour, ed. Chapel Hill: University of North Carolina Press. lxiii-lxxii.

Beverley, Robert
    1947 *The History and Present State of Virginia* [1705]. Louis B. Wright, ed. Chapel Hill: University of North Carolina Press.

Boas, Franz
    1940 The Limitations of the Comparative Method of Anthropology [1896]. *Race, Language, and Culture*. New York: Macmillan. 270-80.

Collingwood, R.G.
    1956 *The Idea of History* [1946]. New York: Oxford University Press.

Donnell, Susan
    1991 *Pocahontas*. New York: Berkley Books.

Eggan, Fred
    1954 Social Anthropology and the Method of Controlled Comparison. *American Anthropologist* 56:743-63.

Furet, François
    1984 *In the Workshop of History*. Jonathan Mandelbaum, trans. Chicago: University of Chicago Press.

Gleach, Frederic W.
    1992 English and Powhatan Approaches to Civilizing Each Other: A History of Indian-White Relations in Early Colonial Virginia. Doctoral dissertation, University of Chicago.

Gleiter, Jan, and Kathleen Thompson
    1985 *Great Tales From Long Ago: Pocahontas*. New York: Torstar Books.

Graham, Shirley
    1953 *The Story of Pocahontas*. New York: Grosset & Dunlap.

Hallowell, A. Irving
    1976 Ojibwa Ontology, Behavior, and World View [1960]. *Contributions to Anthropology: Selected Papers of A. Irving Hallowell*. Chicago: University of Chicago Press. 357-90.

FREDERIC W. GLEACH

Hulme, Peter

1992   *Colonial Encounters: Europe and the Native Caribbean, 1492-1797* [1986].
London: Routledge.

Kidwell, Clara Sue

1992   Indian Women as Cultural Mediators. *Ethnohistory* 39(2):97-107.

Kluckhohn, Clyde

1953   Universal Categories of Culture. *Anthropology Today: An Encyclopedic Inventory*. A.L. Kroeber, ed. Chicago: University of Chicago Press.
507-523.

Lee, Peggy, Eddie Cooley, and John Davenport

1958   *Fever*. Capitol Records 3998.

Lemay, J.A. Leo

1992   *Did Pocahontas Save Captain John Smith?* Athens: University of
Georgia Press.

Newcomb, William W., Jr.

1956   *The Culture and Acculturation of the Delaware Indians*. Ann Arbor:
University of Michigan, Museum of Anthropology, Anthropological
Papers 10.

Purchas, Samuel

1617   *Purchas His Pilgrimage, or Relations of the World and the Religions
·Observed in al Ages and Places Discovered, from the Creation unto this
Present*, 3rd edition. London: Printed by W. Stansby for H.
Fetherstone.

Rountree, Helen C.

1989   *The Powhatan Indians of Virginia: Their Traditional Culture*. Norman:
University of Oklahoma Press.

1990   *Pocahontas's People: The Powhatan Indians of Virginia Through Four
Centuries*. Norman: University of Oklahoma Press.

Seymour, Flora Warren

1961   *Pocahontas: Brave Girl* [1946]. Indianapolis: Bobbs-Merrill.

Smith, John

1986a   A True Relation of Such Occurrences and Accidents of Noate as
Hath Hapned in Virginia [1608]. *The Complete Works of Captain John
Smith (1580-1631)*, vol. 1. Philip L. Barbour, ed. Chapel Hill:
University of North Carolina Press. 3-117.

1986b   A Map of Virginia, With a Description of the Countrey, the
Commodities, People, Government and Religion [1612]. *The
Complete Works of Captain John Smith (1580-1631)*, vol. 1. Philip L.

Barbour, ed., Chapel Hill: University of North Carolina Press. 119-90.

1986c The Proceedings of the English Colonie in Virginia [1612]. *The Complete Works of Captain John Smith (1580-1631)*, vol. 1. Philip L. Barbour, ed. Chapel Hill: University of North Carolina Press. 191-289.

1986d The Generall Historie of Virginia, New-England, and the Summer Isles [1624]. *The Complete Works of Captain John Smith (1580-1631)*, vol. 2. Philip L. Barbour, ed. Chapel Hill: University of North Carolina Press.

Speck, Frank G.

1931 A Study of the Delaware Indian Big House Ceremony. Harrisburg: Pennsylvania Historical Commission.

Wilkie, Katharine E.

1969 *Pocahontas: Indian Princess*. Champaign, Illinois: Garrard.

3

Discovering Radisson: A Renaissance Adventurer Between Two Worlds[1]

Germaine Warkentin

"AFTER THIS WE came to a remarquable place," the explorer tells us. "It's a banke of Rocks that the wild men made a sacrifice to; they calle it Nanitoucksinagoit, which signifies the likenesse of the devill.[2] They fling much tobacco and other things in its veneration. It is a thing most incredible that that lake should be so boisterous, that the waves of it should have the strenght to doe what I have to say by this my discours ... [the rock] is like a great Portall, by reason of the beating of the waves.... I gave it the name of the portall of St. Peter, because my name is so called, and that I was the first Christian that ever saw it."[3] The explorer was Pierre-Esprit Radisson, and his "discours" is the lengthy narrative — the fourth of his six "voyages" — in which with immense verve and unquenchable enthusiasm he described the journey he and his brother-in-law Médard Chouart des Groseilliers made from Quebec to the shores of Lake Superior between August 1659 and August 1660.

---

1   I am grateful to Jennifer S.H. Brown, W.J. Eccles, Allan Greer, David Pentland, Krystyna Sieciechowicz, and John Warkentin, who made valuable suggestions after hearing or reading earlier versions of this paper, or responding to my queries; they are not, of course, responsible for its conclusions. A shorter version of the paper appeared in *Queen's Quarterly* 101 (1994), 305–316.

2   It is not clear how correctly this word was transcribed by the original copyist, who may have confused m/n and h/k. I am grateful to David Pentland, who has suggested the reading *manidoo izhinaagwad*, "it looks like a manitou." The place in question is the "Pictured Rocks" on the south shore of Lake Superior, east of present-day Munising, Michigan, where erosion has carved the sandstone cliffs along the shoreline into fantastic shapes.

3   *The Voyages of Pierre Esprit Radisson*, ed. Gideon Scull (Boston: The Prince Society, 1885; reprinted New York: Burt Franklin, 1967), 190. I am at work on a critical edition of Radisson's writings; though Scull's page numbers are cited here for convenience, his text has been given a preliminary checking against the manuscript and corrected where necessary; punctuation has been lightly modernized, abbreviations expanded, and "ye" normalized to "the."

Most Canadians know who Radisson was; in the seventeenth century he was already cast as the archetype of the explorer as freebooter,[1] and in the twentieth his name still produces fused impressions of valour, bravado, and entrepreneurship to glamorize the mining enterprises, hotels, and venture-capital firms which display it. Yet Radisson always seems to be the centre of someone else's narrative — the historical anecdote, the television series, the children's book — rather than a narrator himself. This is probably because so few of us are aware that he was the first and best teller of his own story. Some time toward the end of his first stay in England (1665-69) he wrote a lengthy account of his travels, which in four separate "voyages," as he termed them, related his adventures up to 1660. Not in his own hand but in that of a scribe, and written — surprisingly — in English, the manuscript reposes in Oxford's Bodleian Library.[2] The diarist Samuel Pepys, who as an increasingly important functionary on Charles II's Navy Board may well have known Radisson,[3] acquired it some time between 1670 and his death in 1703. In the next century it was saved from disposal as waste paper by the collector Richard Rawlinson, who left it and many other manuscripts to the Bodleian. There it sat, ignored, until it was transcribed and published by Gideon Scull in a small edition of 1885. Radisson's narrative, as preserved in this manuscript, provides not only the text in which an important early explorer related his contacts with Native North Americans, but significant information about the context in which that relation took place.

Historians have generally assumed that Radisson wrote down his story as part of the effort he and Groseilliers made to persuade the English to form a company to exploit Canadian furs,[4] and certainly the tri-

---

1   Radisson was accused of being a traitor by both French and English in his own day; see Fr. Silvy (1654-5) and Oldmixon (1708), in J.B. Tyrrell, ed., *Documents Relating to the Early History of Hudson's Bay* (Toronto: Champlain Society, 1931), 78 and 397-79.

2   Oxford, Bodleian Library: Ms. Rawlinson A 329.

3   See Douglas MacKay, *The Honourable Company* (Toronto: Musson Book Company, 1938), 22; and Grace Lee Nute, *Caesars of the Wilderness: Médard Chouart, Sieur des Groseilliers and Pierre Esprit Radisson, 1618-1710* (New York: D. Appleton-Century Company, 1943), 99-100.

4   J.B. Brebner, *The Explorers of North America 1492-1806* (London: A. and C. Black, 1933), 229; Nute, *Caesars of the Wilderness* (in general); Marcel Trudel, *Histoire de la Nouvelle-France*, III: *La seigneurie des Cent-Associés 1627-1663*, vol. 2, *La société* (Montreal: Fides, 1983), 236.

GERMAINE WARKENTIN

umphant but aggrieved conclusion of the fourth or "Lake Superior" voyage (on their return Groseilliers was thrown into jail by Governor Pierre Voyer d'Argenson) gives this some plausibility. Grace Lee Nute further argued that the manuscript was translated from the French.[1] Two late scribal journals of Radisson from the 1680s exist as well,[2] and they are indeed in French. But Radisson was apparently a quick and absorptive student of Native languages;[3] he would have had few problems in learning to speak English, either during the three years (1662–65) when he was much in New England, or in 1665–69 when he spent long periods in Oxford and London. As we shall see, it is by no means impossible that while he was cooling his heels at the court of Charles II in 1668, he used his conversationally fluent though not very correct English to record his early achievements.

Radisson's very skills as a narrator have left him mistrusted by historians and ethnographers, and the linguistic ambiguity of his text has discouraged literary critics.[4] Yet, whatever the purpose to which the written narrative itself was put, it was the information the two explorers gained on the Lake Superior expedition which helped them persuade Charles II to permit the foundation of the Hudson's Bay Company in 1670 and thus, as J.B. Brebner put it, to "change the course of history for

---

1 Nute, *Caesars of the Wilderness*, 30, 99–100, 121.

2 Winnipeg: Provincial Archives of Manitoba, Hudson's Bay Company Archives: Ms. E. 1/1 and E. 1/2 (scribal manuscripts of *Voyage V* and *VI*, in French); London: British Library: a) Additional 11626 (scribal ms. of *Voyage V*, 1682-3, in English translation); b) Sloane 3527 (scribal ms. of *Voyage VI*, 1684, in French).

3 Early in the captivity described in *Voyage I* Radisson observed of his captors, "they untyed mee, and tooke delight to make me speake words of their language and weare earnest that I should pronounce as they" (Scull, 42); these Natives would have spoken an Iroquoian language. It is evident from his general references that Radisson could converse with Algonquian-speakers. However, in *Voyage IV* the "8 ambassadors from the nation of Nadoneseronons" (Scull, 207) spoke a language neither Radisson nor his companions could understand and they required an interpreter; the strangers would have been members of the Siouan language group.

4 Most of the existing work on Radisson was done more than 60 years ago; it was summarized and consolidated by Nute on the basis of her own research, *Caesars of the Wilderness* (1943), the basis for her articles on the two explorers in the *Dictionary of Canadian Biography* (Groseilliers, vol. 1, 1966, Radisson, vol. 2, 1969). Surprisingly, Radisson has not much attracted modern scholars; the four English "voyages" were not translated into French until 1986; see Daniel Vaillancourt, *Des récits de voyages de Pierre-Esprit Radisson* (Master's thesis, Université de Québec à Montréal, 1986).

half the North American continent."[1] Yet to say so is to view that evolving history solely from the Euro-Canadian standpoint, and few of the early explorers of Canada assimilated as fully to Native perspectives as did Radisson. As an adolescent freshly arrived in New France he had twice been captured by Iroquois, and had spent 17 months first as their victim and then as the adopted member of a Mohawk family. From then on, Radisson constantly thought and acted on two separate planes, which for him seem to have been completely consonant with one another. His most famous statement, "We weare Cesars, being no body to contradict us" (Scull, 198), represents one of these planes, that of the self-legitimizing imperial conqueror of "wild men" whom he regarded as living in a state before the establishment of civil order. The other, and more complex, plane is represented by his amiable use of the pronoun "we" in referring to the two explorers and their Saulteaux companions[2] on the journey to Lake Superior.

As his party travelled upriver in August of 1659, they encountered (probably before they left the St. Lawrence for the Ottawa) a group of the hostile Iroquois whose onslaughts had halted the fur trade for over a decade, to the frustration of both French and Natives from the Great Lakes region. A pitched battle, energetically recounted, took place, and Radisson related that his companions "filled their bellyes with the flesh of their ennemyes." He went on,

---

1   J.B. Brebner, *The Explorers of North America 1492-1806*, 229.

2   Radisson does not always name, or name with precision, the Native nations he travels with and meets; in what follows, where he is vague I have specified cautiously which nations he is dealing with, but have sometimes had to leave them unnamed. It is clear however that he travelled from New France with the Saulteaux (people from Sault Ste. Marie, a name early given by the French to the Ojibwe people of that area), and possibly some displaced Hurons, and that they tried to overtake a party of Odawa. The French and Saulteaux at one point engaged in a fray with some Iroquois. Perhaps at the Sault and certainly in modern Minnesota and Wisconsin Radisson encountered more Odawa (possibly the groups today described as "Southwestern Chippewa"). Bruce White has identified some of the "Eighteen severall Nations" (Scull, 209) at the Feast of the Dead with the Dakota (Sioux); see "Encounters with Spirits: Ojibwa and Dakota Theories about the French and Their Merchandise," *Ethnohistory* 41 (1994) 369-405. For information on the indistinct boundaries between the territories and nomenclature of the easternmost of these nations during contact and in the early historic period, see William C. Sturtevant, gen. ed., *Handbook of North American Indians* (Washington, DC: Smithsonian Institution, 1978—), vol. 15, under "Southwestern Chippewa" and "Odawa."

GERMAINE WARKENTIN

we bourned our Comrades, being their coustome to reduce such into ashes being slained in batail. It was an honnour to give them such a buri-all. Att the brake of day we [?]ooked[1] what could accomodate us, and flung the rest away. The greatest marke of our victory was that we had 10 heads & foure prisoners, whom we embarqued in hopes to bring them into our Countrey, and there to burne them att our owne leasures for the more satisfaction of our wives. We left that place of masacre with horrid cryes.... We plagued those infortunates. We plucked out their nails one after an other. (Scull, 183–84)

For a moment — and this was not the only occasion when it happened — Radisson spoke not from his situation as an invading European, but from the position of the Saulteaux, or the Mohawks who named him "Orinha" (lead or stone; Scull, 40) when he lived with them at 12 or 13. He knew what was done with prisoners — he was one himself, endured the "plaguing" as he called it, of the unfortunate, and was saved at the last minute when a Mohawk family adopted him. To judge by his narra-tive, he too joined in the ritual feasting on the flesh of the enemy.

All Radisson's accounts of his voyages have to be read with his adop-tion — and the consequent interaction in his experience of two radically opposed ways of seeing — constantly in view. In one sense, he knew that he could never be the first person to "see" a North American place, as he recognized when he carefully said that he named the portal of St. Peter (Grand Portal, Arched Rock) on Lake Superior after himself be-cause he was the first Christian to have seen that place. In another sense he was likely to present himself as the first even when he did so menda-ciously; interest in the interior was so high in New France that he and Groseilliers could not have been unaware that travellers such as Jean Nicollet (ca. 1633) had already reached out toward Lake Superior (though if any of them wrote of it, their narratives are no longer ex-tant).[2] Groseilliers himself had been as far as Michilimackinac two years before, and later in England when Radisson described that journey, he

---

1 The manuscript says "Looked," which is nonsense; Scull speculates "cooked," but if Radisson's grasp of English was chiefly conversational it could be "tooked." Either "cooked" or "took" would make sense in the context.

2 For the history and motives behind French expansion into the interior at this time, see Marcel Trudel, "L'expansion de l'aire connu," chapter six of his *Histoire de la Nou-velle-France*, III: *La seigneurie des Cent-Associés 1627-1663*, vol. 2, *La société*, 211-50.

did so as if he had been one of the party too, though he had apparently been in New France all the time.[1] As this suggests, his genius as a publicist (it was Groseilliers who was the planner and strategist) stemmed in large part from his ability to believe absolutely in the moment he was living in.

What he tells us about the places to which the pair travelled is always told from this position of absolute belief in the moment. "From this place we went along the Coasts, which are most delightfull and wounderous for it's nature that made it so pleasant to the eye the sperit, and the belly" (Scull, 189), or, "we arrived to a very beautifull point of sand where there are three beautifull Islands, that we called of the Trinity; there be three in triangle" (Scull, 191), or "we went from Isle to Isle all that summer. We pluckt abundance of Ducks, as of all other sort of fowles; we wanted nor fishe nor fresh meate" (Scull, 224). But Radisson was not fundamentally a describer of scenery, which may be one of the reasons he has puzzled readers accustomed to the verbal landscape-painting and more precise itineraries of the "scientific" explorers of the eighteenth and nineteenth centuries. His natural subject-matter was the world of human beings, and particularly the political manoeuvring, the ritual displays, the constant famines and the equally frequent festivals of life in what the American historian Richard White has called "the Middle Ground."[2]

The Middle Ground is White's metaphor for the social space of that broad and shifting border territory between the increasingly European-settled east and the distant and still unknown west, where for a brief period between 1650 and 1815 French and Native Americans established a common cultural language and a shared way of life, typical of neither the settlement nor the "wilderness." White thinks of the Middle Ground in American terms, but Canadians have recognized the same kind of rapprochement in Rupert's Land between 1684 and 1860. In both cases Native people and Europeans built up a set of assumptions about their common interests – the conduct of trade, the control of unpredictable violence, the respective prestige of each group – which slowly assumed the characteristics of a genuine culture. The Middle Ground disappeared

---

1   Radisson witnessed a deed at Quebec in November, 1655; see Nute, *Caesars of the Wilderness*, 43n10.

2   Richard White, *The Middle Ground: Indians, Empires and Republics in the Great Lakes Region 1650-1815* (Cambridge: Cambridge University Press, 1991), esp. Chapter 2.

in the USA by the mid-nineteenth century with the reinvention of Native Americans as an exotic "Other," and in Canada when the Hudson's Bay Company handed over its fiefdom to the new dominion in 1869/70, and government policy decreed that Rupert's Land should become prime agricultural land. Radisson, who had helped to establish that fiefdom three centuries earlier, was one of the early citizens of the Middle Ground, and the peculiar confluence of Native and European in his experience, as well as the two planes of perception which he held in balance with such ease, are symptomatic of its mentality. Radisson's "discours," as he called it, was the discourse of that place. As such, it displayed in equal and never entirely reconcilable parts the ruthlessness of the exploiter and the sagacity of the Native. Only Radisson's confidence in the moment held the two in solution.

He never lost that confidence, no matter how ridiculous the moment, or how serious. Of one attempt to negotiate a bog he related,

> Being come to the height, we must dr[a]gue our boats over a trembling ground for the space of an howre. The ground became trembling by this means: the castor [beaver] drowning great soyles with dead water, herein growes mosse which is two foot thick or there abouts, and when you think to goe safe and dry, if you take not great care you sink downe to your head or to the midle of your body. When you are out of one hole you find yourselfe in another. This I speake by experience, for I meselfe have bin catched often. But the wildmen warned me, which saved me; that is, that when the mosse should breake under I should cast my whole body into the watter on sudaine. I must with my hands hold the mosse, and goe soe like a frogg, then to draw my boat after me there was no danger. (Scull, 192)

The insouciance of this passage is countered by the horror of his evocation of famine in the winter that followed:

> Every one cryes out for hungar; the women become baren, and drie like Wood. You men must eate the cord, being you have no more strenght to make use of the bow, children, you must die. French, you called yourselves Gods of the earth, that you should be feared, for your interest; notwithstanding, you shall tast[e] of the bitternesse, and too happy if you escape. Where is the time past? Where is the plentinesse that yee had in all places and countreys? Here comes a new family of these poore people

dayly to us, halfe dead for they have but the skin and boans. How shall we have strenght to make a hole in the Snow to lay us downe? (Scull, 203–204)

The effect here is enhanced by one of Radisson's most persistent stylistic devices: narration in the present tense. Scholars have stumbled over this fascination with the present, which complicates their attempts to establish a chronology of the explorer's travels. But the point of Radisson's method is not to tell us *when* or *where* something happened, but how it was experienced *as* it happened.

On some occasions the ambiguity of Radisson's mind-set must have been evident even to himself. Toward the end of his fourth or "Lake Superior" voyage he wrote, "before I go further I have a mind to let you know the fabulous beleafes of those poore People, that you may see their ignorance concerning the souls immortality" (Scull, 236). There ensued an extended account of Odawa beliefs about the soul's spirit journey, related not in the contemptuous tone which his opening suggests, but with close and knowledgeable attention to every detail of the soul's progress, from the family's gathering to cover the deceased with "white skins very well tyed" to the moment of feasting and merriment in the spirit world when the soul "who has the choice of very beautifull women" selects a companion for the new life. Yet at the end, he concluded piously, "I have seen right-minded Jesuites weep bitterly hearing me speake of so many Nations that perish for want of Instruction" (Scull, 240). Radisson was only occasionally pious but, well aware of the effect on London merchants of the Jesuits' interest in the potential riches of the fur trade, he was always politic, for he followed this statement with the wily "I have seen also some of the same Company say, 'Alas, what pity tis to loose so many Castors. Is there no way to goe there? The fish and the sauce invite us to it; is there no meanes to catch it?'" (Scull, 240). This instinct for the political infuses every page of Radisson's six narratives. He lived, of course, in an age when the term "political" as we now use it was only being invented.[1] His "politics," consequently, were those of the court, the interest group, and above all the self-validating

---

1 Some of the history of the word "political" is touched on in the essays edited by Anthony Pagden in *The Languages of Political Theory in Early-Modern Europe* (Cambridge: Cambridge University Press, 1987); see especially Nicolai Rubenstein, "The history of the word *politicus* in Early Modern Europe" (41–56), and Judith N. Shklar, "Alexander Hamilton and the language of political science" (339–55).

GERMAINE WARKENTIN

rhetorical "I" of Renaissance disputation. Whatever the nature of his education, he speaks to us from the centre of a set of verbal stratagems designed to maintain the place of that "I" within such competing groups.

Radisson's position between two worlds — both linguistically and historically — thus produces an inevitable clash between the imaginative world of a seventeenth-century man, preoccupied with problems of personal honour and social place, and the tough-minded empiricism of modern Canadian historians, where the problem of the factuality of Radisson's account has frequently taken precedence over an examination of its nature *as* an account.[1] One avenue out of this impasse is a cool-headed examination of Radisson's discursive world, and of the resources of language and narrative method he had available to tell his story. And here again we find ourselves between two worlds.

To take an example: Radisson, as we all know, was a Frenchman; he was expected by many contemporaries to have the loyalties of a Frenchman, and by subsequent scholars to have written like one, which in several cases, if not always, he did. Yet Radisson was not, in any sense known to his time, French in origin. Grace Lee Nute has shown that his father was born at Carpentras in present-day southern France, and suggested that the explorer was born in or near the neighbouring city of Avignon.[2] This would have made him a Provençal, a man of very different culture from the northern French he was to encounter in New France and even from his brother-in-law Groseilliers, who came from the Marne, near Paris. And in the seventeenth century it would have made him the subject of a different state, of the Pope in fact, for Carpentras in the Comtat Venaissin and Avignon in the Comtat d'Avignon

---

1   Sixty years ago A.M. Goodrich objected to the "exasperating" nature of Radisson's writings, which made it so difficult to follow his itinerary; see Albert M. Goodrich and Grace Lee Nute, "The Radisson problem," *Minnesota History* 13 (1932), 245-67, esp. 249. Even J.B. Brebner, who had a keen appreciation of Radisson's imaginative scope, made the same complaint (see Brebner, *The Explorers of North America 1492-1806*, 223-37). More recently Marcel Trudel, in the midst of a careful analysis of the explorers' 1659-60 journey to Lake Superior, described the text as "un document très difficile à interpréter: expliquer les voyages de Chouart et de Radisson, c'est (sauf sur certains rares points) passer son temps à construire des hypothèses"; see Marcel Trudel, *Histoire de la Nouvelle-France*, III: *La seigneurie des cents-associés 1627-1663*, vol. 2, *La société*, 235n76.

2   Nute, *Caesars of the Wilderness*, 40-43.

were both part of a Papal enclave in Provence which remained under the Pope's dominion until the French Revolution. This is why at least two contemporary Hudson's Bay Company documents referred to him as an "Italian," as Nute pointed out in 1943.[1] I doubt that the young Radisson felt much like a subject of the Pope, but his ambiguous status suggests some reasons why he never seems to have behaved with perfect loyalty to the King of France either.

Radisson's unusual origins (fewer than one per cent of those in New France before 1670 came from Provence[2]), his ability to land on his feet, and his expert life-long management of his options, all suggest his implicit awareness of the way language and culture affected those options. His six "voyages" have to be read as the texts of such a man; only then can they be read as historical sources as well. In an important sense, Radisson's literary presentation of himself *is* a historical source, although it has been dismissed, misinterpreted, and trivialized for several centuries. If we are to restore some sort of balance, we need to look closely not only at the extent to which his writing constitutes a merely factual body of information, but at his narrative methods as well, and at the discursive world in which he gave an account of himself.

This cannot be done, however, without examining how his narratives came into being — that is, by looking at the actual linguistic and social context in which they originated. As examples, I want to look first at the language of the four earlier accounts (the two French narratives of the 1680s pose a different set of problems). I will then turn to the way this context illuminates our understanding of Radisson's situation as a late-Renaissance man as we meet it in one of the most remarkable passages of his fourth, or "Lake Superior" narrative. This is his account of the Feast of the Dead as it was celebrated by his Saulteaux and Odawa companions and a group of Dakota Sioux somewhere on the south shore of Lake Superior in the winter of 1659-60.[3]

First, the language of Voyages I-IV. The text of Radisson's first four "Voyages," as the Bodleian manuscript terms them, is in English, and

---

1 Nute, *Caesars of the Wilderness*, 42n8.

2 See R. Cole Harris and Geoffrey J. Matthews, eds., *Historical Atlas of Canada* (Toronto: University of Toronto Press, 1987) I, plate 45.

3 Radisson's identification of the participants in the Feast is very vague; here I follow Bruce White, "Encounters with Spirits" mentioned above, note 13.

GERMAINE WARKENTIN

the question of the relationship of this text with its supposed French original, now lost, has to be faced. That a French original in fact existed has more or less been taken for granted because of an entry of 23 June 1669, in the account book of Sir James Hayes, who as secretary to Prince Rupert and later Deputy Governor of the HBC was the company's early administrative brains. On that date the sum of five pounds was "disbursed for translating a Booke of Radisons."[1] The entry is a useful one, because besides confirming that the founders of the Hudson's Bay Company paid someone to translate something written by Radisson, it ought to provide a latest possible date for the completion of the writing of the text: 1669. But there are difficulties, and they are not easy to surmount.

The first is strictly a matter of interpreting the wording of the account book. The word "book" in seventeenth-century usage did not always mean what it signifies to the twentieth-century reader. It could mean a material book, printed, bound, and offered for sale, but it could also mean a manuscript paper book, a personal account book (the very term Sir James himself used for the document containing the entry[2]), or even the draft of a legal document. Only sometimes did it mean a "title," or a "work" as it does for us today; indeed, there is some probability that Sir James Hayes (or his clerk) would have used "treatise" – or even more likely "travels" or "voyages" – if they had meant what earlier scholars thought they meant. I realize that in casting doubt on the meaning of the account-book entry, we lose the secure dating of these texts, and I realize too that I have only shaken the evidence that Voyages I-IV were translated, not invalidated it. By "book" the clerk could certainly have meant a *manuscript* book written out in French by Radisson. But he could also have meant a legal document or petition of the sort we find Radisson making several times in the 1670s and 1680s. And once the evidence is shaken, it becomes possible to consider alternatives, where the linguistic and literary evidence is both extensive and very suggestive.

A certain amount of contempt has been cast on Radisson's alleged "translator" because of his rough-hewn English. Yet when we approach these texts divested of antiquarian and academic obsessions with genteel

---

1 HBCA, A.14/1, fols. 78v-79, in E.E. Rich, ed., *Minutes of the Hudson's Bay Company, 1671-74* (Hudson's Bay Record Society, 5, Toronto: Champlain Society, 1942), 171.

2 See Rich, ed., *Minutes of the Hudson's Bay Company, 1671-74*, xlviii: £20 paid to Richard Beane "for settling & stateing ye severall accompts in this booke."

or refined language, we discover a vigorous, earthy, and extremely expressive example of seventeenth-century prose, a masterpiece, indeed, of its kind. For example, there is Radisson's comic and forthright account of his party's battle with hunger during the same long, cold winter of 1659-60:

> There came two men from a strange Countrey who had a dogg, the buissinesse was how to catch him cunningly, knowing well those people love their be[a]sts. Neverthelesse wee offred guifts: but they would not, which made me stuborne. That dogge was very l[e]ane, and as hungry as we weare, but the Masters have not suffered so much. I went one night neere that same Cottage to doe what discretion permitts me not to speake. Those men weare Nadoueseronons.[1] They weare much Respected that no body durst not offend them: being that we weare uppon their land with their leave. The dogg comes out, not by any smell, but by good Likes. I take him and bring him a litle way. I stabbed him with my dagger. I brought him to the Cottage, where [he] was broyled like a pigge and cut in peeces gutts and all, soe every one of the family had his share. The snow where he was killed was not lost, for one of our Company, went and gott it to season the kettle. We began to looke better dayly.

If this translator indeed existed, we ought to find out who he was, because he belongs in the same world with that great early realist of English literature, Radisson's younger contemporary Daniel Defoe.

We need not look very far, however, because the linguistic profile of the "translator" shows that he possessed about the same amount of English that Radisson, with his evident verbal gifts, might have learned during his lengthy sojourns in the British colonies in America, and later in England. His prose, for example, is full of French terms that even the most hapless translator would certainly have attempted to translate. To take examples only from the Lake Superior Voyage, we find *castors* for "beavers," and "wildmen" as a literal (and correct) translation for French *sauvages* instead of the more pejorative English "savages" (though in the first or "Captivity" voyage Radisson uses "barbars"). He uses "defends" (Fr.

---

1   That is, Sioux; possibly a hybrid word blending the Algonquian root "Natowewa" (Iroquoian or Siouan) with the Huron "ronnon" (people or nation); for the meaning "people of the snake" (i.e., enemies) in certain Central Algonquian languages see Douglas W. Boyce, "Iroquoian Tribes of the Virginia-North Carolina Coastal Plain" in *Handbook of North American Indians*, v. 15, 289.

défendre) for "forbid" and says "the business was to make a discovery," meaning "now our job was to reveal ourselves," (Fr. *se découvrir*). His "play with an execution," comes from the French *faire jouer*, to set in motion. He uses "cabban" from the French *cabane* to mean Native dwellings; "destinated" from the French *destiner*, to reserve for a particular purpose; and "invented" from French *inventer*, to fabricate or build. The "buttery of Paris" is probably *boucherie*, meaning abbatoir or stockyards. In addition, the grammatical errors (particularly the ones involving verb forms) are those habitually made by someone trying to function in a language he has not quite mastered.

But if Radisson wrote Voyages I–IV in English, why did he then revert to French two decades later to write V and VI? Why indeed are there no other known writings in English from his hand? These are important questions to which, as yet, there is no reply except the one eventually reverted to by everyone interested in Radisson since the seventeenth century: why did Radisson do *anything* he did? But in putting it that way, we should avoid the persistent error of treating Radisson as if he were some kind of semi-literate soldier of fortune, wise in the ways of the wild but an awestruck spectator in London or Paris. Rather, he was skilled, for example, in cultivating over several decades the patronage networks, courtly and mercantile, English and French, which a man needed in this period to keep his head above water in public life. Nor is it necessary to agree with Arthur Adams that Radisson may have dictated his text.[1] This would proliferate speculation unreasonably; indeed the explorer's several references to writing suggest otherwise. The only document of any length which we have in his hand, the long letter to Claude Bernou describing the expedition of Admiral d'Estrées against the Dutch in 1677–78, in which Radisson participated, is both detailed and verbally fluent, and the hand is small, neat, and practised.[2] It is profoundly condescending to continue in the assumption that a figure like Radisson would be only marginally competent in areas that we consider important. And it is counter-productive to assume that what Loren Kall-

---

1   Arthur T. Adams, ed., *The Explorations of Pierre Esprit Radisson*, from the Original Manuscript in the Bodleian Library and the British Museum (modernized by Loren Kallsen), Minneapolis: Ross and Haines, 1961, xvi.

2   The letter is transcribed and translated in an appendix by Nute, *Caesars of the Wilderness*, 303–314. An inspection of the original shows that Radisson's handwriting poses no serious problems, despite Nute's statement to the contrary (308 n.2, n.3).

sen terms his "chaotic narrative,"[1] emanating from a man who had little learning, who may have engaged in ritual cannibalism, who changed loyalties instantly when he thought it served his advantage, and who was not always entirely truthful, is therefore a mangled, semi-literate, and fundamentally untrustworthy document from which the careful historian can draw only guarded conclusions.

In a very limited sense this may be the case. But in Radisson's defence it is worth citing the historian of nineteenth-century culture Steven Marcus. There is a tendency in judging historical works, Marcus writes in his study of Friedrich Engels, to evaluate them "on strictly empirical grounds —did he get every datum, every statistic, every detail right." Literary interpretation can contribute to redressing this imbalance by drawing attention to the way in which the work in question offers "new or augmented *meaning*, insights organized, connected, and developed. Meaning does not imply internal consistency or coherence alone; it does imply a coherent regard which can be assessed by various empirical and critical — though not scientific — means. In short, it remains within the field of our common, complex discourse."[2] If we seek an interpretation of Radisson which gives us this "coherent regard," it will lead us to the resources from which the explorer created meaning, and it is his record as a creator of meanings which may in the long run prove as important a piece of historical evidence as any of the facts he relates, withholds, or reconstructs in the documents themselves.

To suggest why this coherent regard, this creation of meaning, may be important, let us turn to a second example, where the creation of meaning was a central purpose not only of Radisson's text, but of the very event he was describing. The Feast of the Dead was the chief integrative celebration of Huron society. As practised among the Hurons until their dispersal by the Iroquois in 1649, it was described by Champlain, Brébeuf, and Sagard.[3]

---

1 Loren Kallsen, "A Note on Modernization," in Adams, ed., *The Explorations of Pierre Esprit Radisson*, xxix.

2 Steven Marcus, *Engels, Manchester, and the Working Class* (New York: Norton, 1985), 139.

3 For descriptions see H.P. Biggar, ed., *The Works of Samuel de Champlain*, III (1615-18) (Toronto: Champlain Society, 1929), 160-63; *Works*, IV (1608-20) (Toronto: Champlain Society, 1932), 330-33; Jean de Brébeuf's 1636 *Relation* "On the belief, manners, and customs of the Hurons," Reuben G. Thwaites, ed., *The Jesuit Relations and Allied Documents* (New York: Pageant Book Company, 1959), 10, 279-311; Gabriel Sagard, *The Long Journey to the Country of the Hurons*, ed. George M. Wrong, trans. H.H. Langton (Toronto: Champlain Society, 1939), 211-14.

When it was transmitted to their neighbours, the Saulteaux and Odawa, by Hurons fleeing the Huron-Iroquois wars of the mid-seventeenth century, it was also mentioned or described by Lalement, André, and Lafitau.[1] It died out as a ceremony late in the seventeenth century. Every ten or twelve years such a Feast brought together a Huron community and those with whom its members wished to confirm alliances; it may have been held every time a large village changed location.[2] In elaborate ceremonies lasting many days, the participants disinterred the bones of their families buried since the last Feast, and cleansed and reburied them in a common ossuary. Our most detailed account of the funerary aspect of the ceremony is the magnificent, reflective, and melancholy passage in Brébeuf's *Relation* of 1636.[3] As part of the general celebration there were banquets, ceremonial games, and entertainments of all sorts.

In the winter of 1659-60 Radisson and Groseilliers attended the Feast of the Dead which was held among "Eighteen severall nations" (Scull, 209) near the south shore of Lake Superior.[4] According to Harold Hickerson, Radisson's account gives the impression that the two explorers "ran the show."[5] But this reaction illustrates not only Hickerson's susceptibility to the stereotype of the triumphalist explorer, but the neces-

---

1 See Jérome Lalement, in Thwaites, ed., *Jesuit Relations* 23 (209-223); Louis André, in Thwaites, ed., *Jesuit Relations* 55 (137-39); for Nicholas Perrot, see E.H. Blair, trans. and ed., *The Indian Tribes of the Upper Mississippi Valley and Region of the Great Lakes as Described by Nicholas Perrot*, 2 vols. (Cleveland: Arthur H. Clark Co., 1911) I, 86-88; for Lafitau, see Joseph François Lafitau, *Customs of the American Indians Compared with the Customs of Primitive Times*, ed. William N. Fenton and Elizabeth L. Moore (Toronto: Champlain Society, 1977), II, 222-24 and chapter viii in general. See Harold Hickerson, "The Feast of the Dead Among the Seventeenth-Century Algonkians of the Upper Great Lakes," *American Anthropologist* 62 (1960) 81-107, and for recent research, especially Bruce Trigger, *The Huron: Farmers of the North*, 2nd ed. (Fort Worth: Harcourt Brace Jovanovich, 1990), 126-31.

2 Trigger, *The Huron: Farmers of the North*, 126, 131.

3 Jean de Brébeuf, "On the belief, manners, and customs of the Hurons," (1636), in Thwaites, ed., *Jesuit Relations*, 10, 279-311.

4 Many attempts have been made to identify the site of the feast; Arthur Adams tentatively proposed Spring Brook Hill in Kennebec County, eastern Minnesota, but this was on the basis of geographical evidence only; see Adams, ed., *The Explorations of Pierre Esprit Radisson*, lviii-lxi.

5 Hickerson, "The Feast of the Dead Among the Seventeenth-Century Algonkians of the Upper Great Lakes," 103, 16n.

sity of reading a text of this period with an eye to its context in seventeenth-century discourse. This is not to say Radisson was not triumphalist — far from it, as the claim that he and Groseilliers were "Cesars" makes clear. Rather, his model of political discourse was forged in the courts of late Renaissance Europe rather than among the scientists, businessmen, and military officers of the Enlightenment. Radisson was certainly not raised among courtiers, but in the ambiguities of his life between 1662 and 1684 he exhibited an expert's knowledge of their discourse.[1]

The account of the Feast of the Dead is in two parts, separated by the episode of famine mentioned above; the explorers first encountered the Dakota Sioux and arranged to come to the Feast, and later in the winter all gathered to attend it. Radisson's frame of reference was evident in the very first lines, as his party left the Odawa living at Chequamegon, in present-day Wisconsin:

> There came above fowre hundred persons to see us goe away from that place, which admired more our actions [than] the fools of Paris to see enter their King and the Infanta of Spaine, his spouse for they cry out, God save the King and Queene. (Scull, 198)

This is a reference to the royal entry of Louis XIV and his bride, Maria Theresa of Spain, which would take place the next summer (August 26, 1660), and which Radisson would hear about only later, at second hand. But despite his contempt for the "fools of Paris," Radisson was sharply aware not only of the purpose of such pageantry but of the need to engage in precisely the same kind of activity himself when his party reached the Sioux:

> we marched fowre dayes through the woods. The Country is beautifull, with very few mountaines, the woods cleare. Att last we came within a leaugue of the Cabbans where we layed that the next day might be for our entrey. We two poore adventurers for the honnour of our Countrey, or of those that shall deserve it from that day. (Scull, 198)

---

1 Another explorer whose awareness of the necessities of court discourse distinguishes his reports and letters is Pierre Gaultier de Varennes, Sieur de La Vérendrye (1685–1749).

GERMAINE WARKENTIN

Clearly, he and Groseilliers were preparing, for the sake of the honour of their nation, to make the greatest possible impression in their own "entrey":

> The nimblest and stoutest went before to warne before the people that we should make our entry to morow. Every one prepares to see what they never before have seene. We ... arrived att the village by watter, which was composed of a hundred Cabans without pallasados. There is nothing but cryes, the women throw themselves backwards uppon the ground thinking to give us tokens of friendship and of wellcome. We destinated three presents, one for the men one for the women, and the other for the children, to the end that they should remember that journey, that we should be spoaken of a hundred years after, if other Europians should not come in those quarters and be liberal to them, which will hardly come to passe. (Scull, 199)

These are the expected signs of the stereotypical explorer, predatory and culturally self-confident.

But as Radisson's narrative continues, it is clear that the presents the explorers brought were carefully chosen as signifiers within Native systems of social discourse, and that like others from New France the two men were well aware of the role of the exchange of gifts among the First Nations in cementing alliances.[1]

> The first present was a kettle, two hattchetts, and six knives and a blade for a sword, the kettles was to call all nations that weare their friends to the feast which is made for the remembrance of the death. That is, they make it once in seaven years; it's a renewing of friendshippe.... The hattchetts weare to encourage the yong people to strengthen them selves in all places, to preserve their wives and shew themselves men by knocking the heads of their ennemyes with the said hattchetts, the knives weare to shew that the French weare great and mighty and their Confederats and ffriends. The sword was to signifie that we would be masters both of

---

1 See Richard White, *The Middle Ground*, 84-87; also Bruce White, "'Give Us a Little Milk': the Social and Cultural Meanings of Gift Giving in the Lake Superior Fur Trade," *Minnesota History* 48 (1982-3), 60-71 (with useful bibliography), his "A Skilled Game of Exchange: Ojibway Fur Trade Protocol," *Minnesota History* 50 (1986-7), 229-40, esp. 231, and his "Encounters with Spirits" (see note 13).

peace and warrs, being willing to healpe and relieve them, and to destroy our Ennemyes with our armes. (Scull, 199)

After presenting flattering gifts to the women, Radisson continues,

The third guift was of brasse rings, of small bells, and rasades [trade beads] of divers coulours, and given in this maner. We sent a man to make all the children come together. When we weare there we throw these things over their heads. You would admire what a beat was among them, every one striving to have the best. This was done oppon this consideration that they should be always under our protection, giving them wherewithall to make them merry and remember us when they should be men. (Scull, 200)

Initially the most noticeable feature of this passage is its mixture of explication and anecdote: on one hand the solemn gift of the kettle, which the French well knew was a central ceremonial object of peace-time life among Native people (the Hurons called the Feast of the Dead *Yandatsa*, "The Kettle"), on the other the picture of the children competing for the beads. Radisson's mode even when developing an allegory is characteristically amused and practical. But more important is the question, to whom is he telling this story, and why is he telling it *this way*? Radisson's four English voyages constitute a banquet of narrative genres, and he is always the picaresque hero at the centre of the scene. But his presentation of himself and Groseilliers here as "Caesars of the wilderness" has a coherence and purposiveness which go beyond self-congratulation. "We knewed their councels, and made them doe whatsoever we thought best," he says at one point; "this was a great advantage for us, you must think" (Scull, 200).

In due course Radisson related what happened when they reached the rendezvous, where "Eighteen severall nations" (Scull, 209) had arrived to celebrate the Feast of the Dead. A fort was built by the Natives (presumably the Odawa with whom they were travelling, and/or the Saulteaux) and "our Company" exchanged visits with the Sioux, of whom Radisson observes,

The day following they arrived with an incredible pomp. This made me thinke of the Intrance that the Polanders did in Paris: saving that they had

GERMAINE WARKENTIN

not so many Jewells, but instead of them they had so many feathers. (Scull, 211)

Again, Radisson is referring to a well-known European ceremonial occasion. In 1573 Prince Albertus Laski had come to France with a delegation of Polish ambassadors to offer the throne of Poland to Henri III; the richness of their jewels and robes impressed the French deeply, and long remained a standard for exotic magnificence.[1]

A parallel magnificence, improvised in the wilderness, characterized the performance of Radisson and Groseilliers when their turn came to participate. After a brilliant description of the young warriors in their full panoply, passing in their "white robe[s] made of Castors skins painted" down a walkway lined with the members of Radisson's own company, he writes,

The Elders came with great gravetie and modestie covered with buff coats which hung downe to the grounde. Every one had in his hand a pipe of Councell sett with precious Jowells.[2] They had a sack on their shoulders, and that that holds it grows in the middle of their stomacks, and on their shoulders. In this sacke all the world is inclosed.[3] Their face is not painted, but their heads dressed as the foremost. (Scull, 212)

This was not the sober world of the Royal Society to which later figures like Andrew Graham of the Hudson's Bay Company would address their scientific correspondence; this recalls descriptions of court masques by Ben Jonson, or Marc Lescarbot's allegorical "réception," the *Théâtre de Neptune en la Nouvelle-France* (performed at Port Royal, Acadia, in 1606). The warriors' dress was intended to show forth their worth, the long buffalo robes of the elders to attest their position. And Radisson

---

1   I am grateful to W. McAlister Johnson for identifying this reference for me.

2   "Jowells" here is probably used in the general sense of "ornaments"; Radisson elsewhere describes in detail such a pipe, with its feather decorations (Scull, 208).

3   This was probably a medicine bundle. A painting by Charles Bird King, "Okee-Makee-Quid, a Chippewa Chief c. 1825," portrays the Ojibwa chief in full regalia, with his elaborate head-dress, wolf breastplate and calumet; this may be a later version of the kind of ceremonial dress Radisson is describing; see Harold Hickerson, *The Chippewa and their Neighbors*, rev. ed. (Prospect Heights, IL: Waveland Press, 1988), 103.

and Groseilliers must behave in the same way in their turn: "we are called to the councell of New come Cheifes: where we came in great pompe, as you shall heare" (Scull, 213).

But first the Sioux came "to make a sacrifice to the French, being Gods and masters of all things as of peace as warrs," and to present a series of gifts "to Desire our assistance, for being the masters of their lives, and could dispose of them as we would, as well of the peace as of the warrs" (Scull, 213). A present-day ethnographer would be quick to point out that First Nations behaviour here was meant to exhibit ritual courtesy, rather than the political submission the Europeans thought they were receiving.[1] Although it is important to have no illusions about Radisson's motives, we may need to read the explorers' actions with the same insight:

> We made fowre men to carry our guns afore us, that we charged of powder alone, because of their unskillfullnesse that they might have killed their fathers. We each of us had a paire of Pistoletts and sword, a Daggar; we had a role of porkepick[2] about our heads, which was as a Crowne, and two litle boyes that carried the vessells that we had most need of: this was our dishes and our spoons. They made a place higher and most elevate knowing our Customs, in the midle for us to sitt where we had the men lay our armes. (Scull, 214)

It is apparent that the Native people had made as close a study of the Europeans as the Europeans had made of them, something which casts an interesting perspective on colonial relations in New France.

---

1 For a closer reading of these ceremonies from the point of view of Dakota Sioux ritual, see Bruce White, "Encounters with Spirits." For a parallel situation in a later period, with taxonomy and lexicon, see Mary Black-Rogers, "'Starving' and Survival in the Subarctic Fur Trade: A Case for Contextual Semantics," in *"Le Castor Fait Tout": Selected Papers of the North American Fur Trade Conference, 1985*, ed. Bruce G. Trigger, Toby Morantz, and Louise Dechêne (Montreal: Lake St. Louis Historical Society, 1987), 618-49.

2 It is not clear whether Radisson meant porcupine skin or porcupine-quill embroidery; either would have served the purpose. The text quoted suggests that Bruce White ("Encounters with Spirits," 383) is incorrect in stating that the crowns were placed on the explorers' heads by the Sioux, who did, however, make a raised place for the two to sit.

GERMAINE WARKENTIN

The ceremonies which the two explorers then engaged in would as Radisson says of a Native oration, "be too long to writ it," but they centred on the smoking of the calumet or pipe, a political ritual designed to show that conflicts between groups have been resolved. On this occasion a potential source of conflict was represented by the presence of "Cristinos"[1] hovering nearby; would they be incorporated in the activities of the Feast, or would they descend on the celebrants and wipe them out? It was this kind of tension which Radisson and Groseilliers, tempered perhaps by their experience of the Iroquois-Huron wars, were apparently resolved to defuse, and to which they directed their participation in the ritual:

> The day following, we made the principall Persons come together to answer to their guifts. Being come with great solemnity there we made our Interpreter tell them, that we weare come from the other side of the great salted lake, not to kill them but to make ye live, acknowledging you for our brethren and Children whom we will love hence forth as our owne. Then we gave them a kettle. The second guift was to encourage them in all their undertakings, telling them that we liked men that generously defended themselves against all their Ennemyes, and as we weare Masters of peace and warrs we are to dispose the affair. That we would see an universall peace all over the earth and that this time we could not goe and force the Nations that weare yett further to condescend and submitt to our will, but that we would see the neighbouring Countreys in peace and Union. That the Christinos weare our brethren, and have frequented them many winters; that we adopted them for our Children and tooke them under our protection; that we should send them Ambassadors, that I my self should make them come, and conclude a generall peace; that we weare sure of their obedience to us; that the ffirst that should breake the peace, we would be their Ennemy, and would reduce them to powder with our heavenly fire. That we had the word of the Christinos as well as

---

1 At this time "Kristineaux" appears to have been a generalized name for the several nations living north and west of the Odawa, today called "Cree." Radisson had earlier described them thus: "among others they told us of...another wandering nation, living onely uppon what they could come by. Their dwelling was on the side of the salt watter in summer time, and in the land in the winter time, for it's cold in their Countrey. They calle them selves Christinos, and their Confederates from all times by reason of their speech which is the same, and often have joyned together, and have had Company of souldiers to warre against that great nation" (Scull, 149).

theirs, and our thunders should serve us to make warrs against those that would not submitt to our will and desire, which was to see them good ffreinds to goe and make warrs against the upper nations, that doth not know us as yett. (Scull, 216-17)

"The last guift," Radisson genially related, was "for all the women to love us, and give us to eat when we should come to their Cottages" (Scull, 217). As the Feast wound up,

there weare playes mirths, and bataills for sport, goeing and coming with cryes, each plaid his part. In the publick place the women danced with melody. The yong men ... indeavoured to gett a pryse.... The feast was made to eate all up.[1]... Every one brings the most exquisit things to shew what his Country affoards. The renewing of their alliances, the mariages according to their Countrey Coustoms are made; also the visit of the boans of their deceased ffriends ffor they keepe them and bestow them uppon one another. We sang in our language as they in theirs, to which they gave greate attention.... This feast ended, every one returns to his Countrey well satisfied. (Scull, 218)

We will learn more about the discourse and context of Radisson's account of the Feast of the Dead when it can be fully compared with the other contemporary versions mentioned above, in order to see precisely how it differs from what Paul Perron and Gilles Thérien have called the "foundation account" of such an event, the narrative laid down by an early observer which is usually, though not always, the basis for later retellings.[2] But here I want to delve more deeply into the connection between this narrative and what history has always interpreted as Radisson's success in persuading Prince Rupert and the English financiers to

---

1   This may be an early reference to an "eat-all" feast or *festin à tout manger*, see Jennifer S.H. Brown and Robert Brightman, *"The Orders of the Dreamed": George Nelson on Cree and Northern Ojibwa Religion and Myth, 1823* (Winnipeg: University of Manitoba Press, 1988), 143-44.

2   Paul Perron and Gilles Thérien, "Ethnohistorical Discourse: Jean Brébeuf's Jesuit Relation of 1636," *American Journal of Semiotics* 7 (1990), 53-67. Jennifer S.H. Brown has also suggested (private communication) that Radisson's narratives parallel the Native genre of the "coup tale" described by H. David Brumble, *American Indian Autobiography* (Berkeley: University of California Press, 1988).

GERMAINE WARKENTIN

establish the Hudson's Bay Company. It is in this context that Radisson's presentation of his own management of the politics of the Feast becomes important. To understand why, we have to return to Lake Superior.

The Algonquian peoples north of Lake Superior had been active traders with the Huron, but this trade had been disrupted by the Huron-Iroquois wars, which also impaired possibilities of trade with the French.[1] Farther to the north were the "Christinos" or Cree, and the Sioux Radisson's company had been encountering "had a minde to goe against the Christinos, who weare ready for them" (Scull, 211). If the 1660 Feast of the Dead was an attempt by the Sioux to engage in a rapprochement with the Saulteaux and Odawa, and the French with which those peoples were in contact, it also afforded Radisson and Groseilliers an opportunity to bring all these peoples, including the hovering Christinos, to the "dance of Union" (Scull, 217). Radisson in his turn sought to mine the fabulous trove of furs the explorers knew was there; at the end of his journey he was to maintain that the worth of the furs he brought down to Quebec was "very near 600,000 pounds Tournois" (Scull, 241), a fortune at the time.[2] Finally, at precisely the time when he was writing down his "voyages," Radisson was attempting to persuade the English to finance him while he went back for more.

The political discourse in which this complex situation was worked out was not solely, however, that of economic necessity. Rather, its social contexts were those of a series of "honour" societies, social units in which a symbolic display of rank, station, and community and personal repute took precedence over the possession of material wealth and the priorities

---

1 Bruce Trigger, *Natives and Newcomers: Canada's 'Heroic Age' Reconsidered* (Kingston and Montreal: McGill-Queen's University Press, 1985), 159-60.

2 The *Journal des jésuites* (1659-60) reported that the value of the furs was 200,000 *livres* [pounds]; see Thwaites, ed., *Jesuit Relations* 45, 163. Presumably this was the *livre* of Paris; the slightly higher *livre tournois* was a "money of account" by which the various coinages of Europe were given a par value. Although Radisson's 600,000 *livres tournois* seems a colossal brag (John J. McCusker, the chief authority on monetary exchange values in the period, informs me [private communication] that its equivalent in 1994 Canadian dollars would be $7,000,000), it is evident that the furs had an important effect on the economy, as Marie de L'Incarnation indicated in a letter to her son of 17 September 1660; see *Lettre CLXXXV* in Marie de L'Incarnation, *Correspondance*, ed. Dom Guy Oury (Solesmes: Abbaye Saint-Pierre, 1971), 631.

of the individual self.[1] In effect each of these groups, whether Native or European, was communicating with the next in a discourse of power which has to be read symbolically. The initial scene in which this discourse was acted out was the Feast of the Dead, an integrative ceremonial designed to bind alliances. The Feast, however, was conducted with "Christino" neighbours on the fringe, potential enemies from the point of view of the Saulteaux and Odawa, at least as Radisson presented the situation. A political opportunity offered itself to the Saulteaux in the arrival of Radisson and Groseilliers; by involving them in the meeting with the Sioux the French were invited to trade, and they were also in a position to act as ambassadors of peace to the "Christinos" which they were in any case anxious to do. Since Radisson and Groseilliers were acquainted with the conditions of existence in the honour societies which comprised early modern court culture, they enacted their roles in an appropriate fashion as they participated in the interchange, functioning both as peacemakers (a task which later traders like Henry Kelsey and the Sieur de La Vérendrye were also to attempt) and asserting their own symbolic importance. They did so very much in their own terms, as the crowns of porcupine and the little boys carrying their bowls make clear.

Furthermore, not only ritual details like these, but the care with which Radisson related his strategies of self-presentation, were, I suggest, directed specifically and forcefully to an audience at the court of Charles II, and their purpose was equally determined by its assumptions, which were also those of an honour society. At court, too, the two explorers needed to present themselves as men of understanding and authority, familiar with the forms in which power should be displayed. It was Charles's court, as Annabel Patterson has reminded us, which read John Barclay's Latin romance *Argenis* (1621) as political allegory[2] and was

---

1   The prestige-oriented character of the patrilineal and hierarchical society of early modern European society is widely attested; see, for example, Norbert Elias, *The Court Society*, trans. Edmund Jephcott. 2 vols. Oxford: Blackwell, 1983. For the assumptions shared at this time by French and Amerindians (even those in unstratified social groups) see White, *The Middle Ground*, 84; for a specific account of parallel features in a central North American setting see Charles Callender, *Social Organization of the Central Algonkian Indians* (Milwaukee: Milwaukee Public Museum Publications in Anthropology, 1962), esp. 13-26.

2   Annabel Patterson, *Censorship and Interpretation: The Conditions of Writing and Reading in Early Modern England* (Madison WI: University of Wisconsin Press, 1984), 159-202, esp. 180-85.

still preoccupied with issues of royal representation fuelled by the *Eikon Basilike* debate.[1] That Radisson's text was "primitive" by the genteel standards applied to him in the nineteenth century is not important; in reality it was no more primitive than the narratives in Hakluyt and Purchas,[2] which were avidly read by the kind of men who financed such expeditions, or written by Henry Kelsey, who was of course a native speaker of English.

We can see Radisson's narrative from the perspective of Charles's courtiers if we keep in mind the ornate ceremonial of early modern courts, the courtiers' interest in the elaborate devices of heroic romance, and the allegorical readings of their rulers' behaviour in which they so obsessively engaged. At the same time, the behaviour of the Native people appears in a fresh and unexpected light. Although we must filter what Radisson said about their actions through his own devices for "making meaning," it is still possible to recognize in those actions the careful and perhaps even ironic diplomacy of peoples aware that they were operating within a newly threatening political framework, and dealing with a situation which they must at all costs turn to their advantage.

It would be interesting to know to what extent the system of meanings which Radisson and Groseilliers shared with the peoples on whom they reported was truly, in the end, the same system of meanings which Radisson assumed he shared with the men to whom he pressed his case in England. To employ the allegorical-symbolical language of court culture to persuade the king and his cousin Prince Rupert was one thing; to persuade Sir James Hayes, with his ever-present account book, would have been another. It is possible that the two worlds between which Radisson

---

1   *Eikon Basilike: The Pourtraicture of His Sacred Majestie in His Solitudes and Sufferings* began to circulate on the very day on which Charles I was executed, 30 January 1649. The book purported to be by the king himself, and rapidly achieved phenomenal popularity; a debate between Puritans and Royalists raged for some years over its authorship (now attributed with certainty to John Gauden). See *Eikon Basilike*, ed. Philip A. Knachel (Ithaca, NY: Cornell University Press for the Folger Shakespeare Library, 1966), xi-xxxii, and especially Lois Potter, *Secret Rites and Secret Writing: Royalist Literature 1641-1660* (Cambridge: Cambridge University Press, 1989), ch. 5, "The Royal Image: Charles I as Text."

2   Richard Hakluyt, *The Principall Navigations, Voiages and Discoveries of the English Nation*, 3 vols., London: 1599, 1600; and Samuel Purchas, *Hakluytus Posthumus or Purchase his Pilgrimes*, 4 vols., London, 1635; both contain extensive and detailed collections of English travel narratives from the age of discovery.

moved were not those of "civilization" and "wilderness," but between a set of social assumptions of great antiquity where Europeans and Amerindians met almost on common ground, and a world which was being reconceived in terms of the hard factuality of market economics and empirical science. Although he never lost his flair, Radisson two decades later produced a fifth and sixth account which told the story of his actions on Hudson Bay in 1682-83 and 1684 in a different kind of language entirely: more exact and more purely narrative, and more evidently calculated to the needs of merchants and lawyers than to those of the European and Amerindian princes among whom he had begun his career.

References

Manuscripts
London, British Library: Additional 11626; Sloane 3527.
Oxford, Bodleian Library: Ms. Rawlinson A 329.
Winnipeg, Provincial Archives of Manitoba, Hudson's Bay Company Archives: Ms. E. 1/1 and E. 1/2.

Printed Sources
Black-Rogers, Mary. "'Starving' and survival in the subarctic fur trade: a case for contextual semantics." In *"Le Castor Fait Tout": Selected Papers of the North American Fur Trade Conference, 1985*. Eds. Bruce G. Trigger, Toby Morantz, and Louise Dechêne. Montreal: Lake St. Louis Historical Society, 1987.
Brebner, J.B. *The Explorers of North America 1492-1806*. London: A. and C. Black, 1933.
Brown, Jennifer S.H., and Robert Brightman. *"The Orders of the Dreamed": George Nelson on Cree and Northern Ojibwa Religion and Myth, 1823*. Winnipeg: University of Manitoba Press, 1988.
Brumble, H. David. *American Indian Autobiography*. Berkeley: University of California Press, 1988.
Callender, Charles. *Social Organization of the Central Algonkian Indians*. Milwaukee Public Museum Publications in Anthropology. Milwaukee, 1962.
[Champlain, Samuel de] Biggar, H.P., ed. *The Works of Samuel de Champlain*. 6 vols. Toronto: Champlain Society, 1922-36.
Elias, Norbert. *The Court Society*. Trans. Edmund Jephcott. 2 vols. Oxford: Blackwell, 1983.

Goodrich, Albert M., and Grace Lee Nute. "The Radisson problem."
    Minnesota History 13 (1932), 245-67.

Hakluyt, Richard. *The Principall Navigations, Voiages and Discoveries of the
    English Nation.* 3 vols. London: 1599-1600.

Harris, R. Cole, and Geoffrey J. Matthews, eds. *Historical Atlas of Canada.* Vol.
    1. Toronto: University of Toronto Press, 1987.

Hickerson, Harold. *The Chippewa and their Neighbors,* Rev. ed. Prospect
    Heights, IL: Waveland Press, 1988.

——. The Feast of the Dead among the seventeenth-century Algonkians of the
    Upper Great Lakes. *American Anthropologist* 62 (1960) 81-107.

Knachel, Philip A., ed. *Eikon Basilike.* Ithaca: Cornell University Press for the
    Folger Shakespeare Library, 1966.

Lafitau, Joseph François. *Customs of the American Indians Compared with the
    Customs of Primitive Times,* eds. William N. Fenton and Elizabeth L. Moore.
    2 vols. Toronto: Champlain Society, 1977.

MacKay, Douglas. *The Honourable Company.* Toronto: Musson Book
    Company, 1938.

Marcus, Steven. *Engels, Manchester, and the Working Class.* New York: Norton,
    1985.

Marie de L'Incarnation. *Correspondance.* Ed. Dom Guy Oury. Solesmes:
    Abbaye Saint-Pierre, 1971.

Nute, Grace Lee. *Caesars of the Wilderness: Médard Chouart, Sieur des Groseilliers
    and Pierre Esprit Radisson, 1618-1710.* New York: D. Appleton-Century
    Company, 1943.

——. "Groseilliers." *Dictionary of Canadian Biography.* Vol. 1. Toronto:
    University of Toronto Press, 1966.

——. "Radisson." *Dictionary of Canadian Biography.* Vol. 2. Toronto: University
    of Toronto Press, 1969.

Pagden, Anthony, ed. *The Languages of Political Theory in Early-Modern Europe.*
    Cambridge: Cambridge University Press, 1987.

Patterson, Annabel. *Censorship and Interpretation: The Conditions of Writing and
    Reading in Early Modern England.* Madison WI: University of Wisconsin
    Press, 1984.

Perron, Paul, and Gilles Thérien. "Ethnohistorical discourse: Jean Brébeuf's
    Jesuit Relation of 1636." *American Journal of Semiotics* 7 (1990), 53-67.

[Perrot, Nicholas] Blair, E.H., trans. and ed. *The Indian Tribes of the Upper
    Mississippi Valley and Region of the Great Lakes as Described by Nicholas Perrot.*
    2 vols. Cleveland: Arthur H. Clark, 1911.

Potter, Lois. *Secret Rites and Secret Writing: Royalist Literature 1641-1660.* Cambridge: Cambridge University Press, 1989.

Purchas, Samuel. *Hakluytus Posthumus or Purchase his Pilgrimes,* 4 vols. London, 1635.

[Radisson, Pierre-Esprit] Adams, Arthur T., ed. *The Explorations of Pierre Esprit Radisson, from the Original Manuscript in the Bodleian Library and the British Museum.* Modernized by Loren Kallsen. Minneapolis: Ross and Haines, 1961.

——. Scull, Gideon, ed. *The Voyages of Pierre Esprit Radisson.* Boston: The Prince Society, 1885. Reprinted New York: Burt Franklin, 1967.

Rich, E.E., ed. *Minutes of the Hudson's Bay Company, 1671-74.* Hudson's Bay Record Society, 5, Toronto: Champlain Society, 1942.

Sagard, Gabriel. *The Long Journey to the Country of the Hurons.* Ed. George M. Wrong. Trans. H.H. Langton. Toronto: Champlain Society, 1939.

Sturtevant, William C., gen. ed. *Handbook of North American Indians.* Washington, DC: Smithsonian Institution, 1978—.

Thwaites, Reuben G., ed. *The Jesuit Relations and Allied Documents.* 73 vols. in 36. New York: Pageant Book Company, 1959.

Trigger, Bruce. *The Huron: Farmers of the North.* 2nd ed. Fort Worth: Harcourt Brace Jovanovich, 1990.

——. *Natives and Newcomers: Canada's 'Heroic Age' Reconsidered.* Kingston and Montreal: McGill-Queen's University Press, 1985.

Trudel, Marcel. *Histoire de la Nouvelle-France.* III: *La seigneurie des Cent-Associés 1627-1663.* Vol. 2, *La société.* Montreal: Fides, 1983.

Tyrrell, J.B., ed. *Documents Relating to the Early History of Hudson's Bay.* Toronto: Champlain Society, 1931.

Vaillancourt, Daniel. *Des récits de voyages de Pierre-Esprit Radisson.* Thèse de maîtrise. Université du Québec à Montréal, 1986.

White, Bruce M. "'Give us a little milk': the social and cultural meanings of gift giving in the Lake Superior fur trade." *Minnesota History* 48 (1982-83) 60-71.

——. "A skilled game of exchange: Ojibway fur trade protocol." *Minnesota History* 50 (1986-87), 229-40.

——. "Encounters with spirits: Ojibwa and Dakota theories about the French and their merchandise." *Ethnohistory* 41.3 (1994) 369-405.

White, Richard. *The Middle Ground: Indians, Empires and Republics in the Great Lakes Region 1650-1815.* Cambridge: Cambridge University Press, 1991.

GERMAINE WARKENTIN

Part II. Trading Texts: Explorers and their Hosts

The phrase "trading texts" points to a key theme of Part II. In the encounter between European explorers and Native peoples, exchange was not restricted to material goods. World views also travelled into new and sometimes hostile domains. The forms in which those world views were recorded varied: Europeans wrote fieldnotes, journals, and books, while most Native people preserved their accounts orally or through symbols on hides, cloth, wood, or other materials. Until recently, few scholars paid much attention to such non-written texts. The three essays in this section demonstrate both the value of going beyond European writings when trying to understand the histories of indigenous peoples, and the rich promise of turning to the oral texts.

In her essay on "Inuit Maps and the Real World," Renée Fossett illustrates how Inuit maps, whether rendered entirely verbally or as tracings in sand or snow, operated in four dimensions: they incorporated crucial information about distance, difficulty of travel, location of resources, and travel time. European visitors generally failed to grasp the complexity of the maps because they overlooked the centrality of oral descriptions that accompanied the mapping process. Fossett has long been intrigued by the different ways human beings perceive their various worlds. In high school, she once wrote an essay on how North American history might have looked to a teenaged Aboriginal girl four hundred years earlier. She recalls, "the teacher was kind — he gave me an A — but he gently discouraged me from pursuing that line of inquiry, and reported the incident to my parents as a minor act of rebellion."

Fossett became a teacher herself, spending the 1960s in arctic communities where she learned a great deal from Inuit friends and neighbours. She began graduate studies in the 1980s after raising a family, and in 1995 received a Ph.D. in history from the University of Manitoba. In keeping with her passion for the north, her dissertation, *In Order to Live Untroubled*, explores the history of the central arctic Inuit from 1550 to 1940. Fossett is co-author of *Trader, Tripper, Trapper*, a collaborative memoir of Hudson's Bay Company man Sydney A. Keighley (1989), and is working on a biography of Augustine, an Inuk explorer, interpreter, and HBC clerk in the early 1800s.

As a historical geographer, Daniel Clayton focuses on conceptualizations of space and on the dynamics of the extension of colonial power and knowledge over territories and peoples in the British Empire. His essay explores the diverse ways in which both English and Native people represented and recalled the visit of Captain James Cook to Vancouver Island. English intellectual and textual strategies for achieving domination over non-European space and its inhabitants were countered by Native retellings of the same events, which assimilated Cook's visit into a cultural context that gave it quite different meanings.

Clayton's intellectual journeys have taken him along the coast of British Columbia to the Skeena River in the north, and Nuu'chah'nulth territory in the west. He has published numerous articles on maritime exploration and the fur trade in this region. A book growing out of his dissertation (University of British Columbia, 1995) is to be published by Routledge in 1997, under the title *Imperial Visions, Colonial Spaces and Postcolonial Geographies*. He is co-editor with Derek Gregory of a forthcoming volume of essays on colonialism, postcolonialism, and the production of space (Blackwell). Clayton has recently returned to his native Britain to join the faculty of the School of Geography and Geology, University of St. Andrews, Scotland.

Frieda Esau Klippenstein, a public historian based in Calgary, works for Parks Canada on its National Historic Sites projects in Alberta and British Columbia. Her essay on a celebrated clash between the Carrier chief Kwah and Hudson's Bay Company trader James Douglas illustrates the potentialities of marrying traditional historical methodologies with oral history and other means of uncovering the pasts of "peoples without history." Her work at the Fort St. James and Fort Langley fur trade sites in B.C. has confirmed her commitment to the collection and preservation of the oral traditions of Native communities. She works closely with the communities around Fort St. James, where she is helping to devise guidelines for the Nak'azdli (Carrier) Oral History Project.

Klippenstein's essay underscores a message common to all three: accounts of the past, whether written or oral, profoundly reflect the world views of their recorders, and the social settings in which they were produced. Accounts written on paper often receive more legitimacy than they deserve, and the quality of their perspectives on other cultures is variable and always in need of assessment. Klippenstein, Clayton, and Fossett find that the juxtaposition of written sources to the culturally distinct visions of the past carried by spoken words offers rich insights that are otherwise not available.

4

Mapping Inuktut: Inuit Views of the Real World

Renée Fossett

IN INUPIAQ-INUIT LANGUAGES, to describe an activity as *inuktut* is to say that the activity is being done "the way our people do it" or "in our fashion." One can speak *inuktut*, cook *inuktut*, dance, sing, raise children, or practise mapping *inuktut*.

Mapping *inuktut* differs from European cartographic activity in both concept and content. Until about the middle of the present century, most Canadian Inuit societies stored knowledge in memory, and transmitted it verbally. Their mapping activities did not produce permanent artifacts.[1] Archaeological investigations have not discovered any evidence of geographical charts drawn or incised on skin, bone, stone, or ivory; arctic ethnography contains no reports of Inuit making, using, or possessing tangible maps; and there is no oral tradition of mapping on material media.

Inuit did, however, collect vast amounts of geographical information, which they passed on to new generations, and to uninformed strangers without the use of physical maps as navigational aids. Their purpose was to convey information about travel routes, and the medium of transmission was the spoken word. Geographical particulars were given by knowledgeable persons as a list of place-names which a traveller learned by heart before venturing into unknown regions. Maps were sometimes sketched in the snow or sand by the teacher in order to help the pupil visualize the details of routes and relevant terrain, but the graphic repre-

---

1   Examples of Eskimo maps on a material medium are extremely rare and are known to have been used aboriginally only in east Greenland and northern Alaska. The Danish explorer-ethnographer Gustav Holm (1888) reported extensive use of wooden maps as navigational aids in the Ammassalik region of Greenland during his 1882-84 expedition. The four which he collected for Danish museums are the only ones now known to exist. Three are linear pieces of driftwood with carved notches and curves representing coastlines. Relief carving indicates off-shore islands and inland elevations. The fourth is a relief map on a flat piece of wood. In northern Alaska, maps were sometimes carved on ivory or wood, but they were merely decorative, and not used for the purpose of navigation or actual travel (Spencer 1955:47).

RENÉE FOSSETT

sentations were nothing more than incidental by-products of the oral teaching and learning process.

When Captain Thomas Beechey, surveying the Alaskan coast in *Blossom* in 1826, asked local residents for geographical information, they drew a representation of the shoreline with a stick in the sand, then piled pebbles and sand at appropriate places to represent islands, hills, mountains, and river beds. Beechey added comments of his own about the location of certain topographical elements, as did several bystanders, and together they constructed "a complete hydrographical plan" of the Alaskan west coast (Huish 1836:397).[1] Because he had been trained in the European tradition of scientific geography which made representations of actual terrain the goal of cartography, Beechey concentrated on the map as object, and did not realize that the ephemeral representation in the sand was used only in support of the oral instructions.

Other European observers also failed to understand the link between on-the-ground representations and verbal instructions, and the primacy of the oral component. In 1858, on the west coast of Boothia Peninsula, Captain Leopold McClintock of the *Fox* asked local residents for information about a wrecked ship. "One old man, Oonalee, made a rough sketch of the coast-line with his spear upon the snow, and said it was eight journeys [i.e., days' travel] to where the ship sank, pointing in the direction of Cape Felix" (McClintock 1859:234). Like Beechey, McClintock did not recognize the verbal instructions as part of the mapping process or realize the importance his informants attached to them. Unlike Beechey, he also failed to understand the route as drawn in the snow, and could "make nothing out of his rude chart" (McClintock 1859:234).

On Baffin Island in 1884, Franz Boas correctly understood the circumstances of Inuit mapping. "If a man intends to visit a country little known to him," he wrote, "he has a map drawn in the snow by some one well acquainted there" (Boas 1888:235). But like Beechey and McClintock, he thought the graphic representation of terrain was the central element and goal of mapping, as it was in the European cartographic tradition, and missed the point that drawings in the snow were merely devices to help the traveller learn the route.

---

1   For a description of a relief map constructed in similar fashion by a Shoshoni headman, Cameahwait, for Lewis and Clark in 1805, see James P. Ronda (1987:82).

During the nineteenth and twentieth centuries, European visitors to the arctic frequently sought geographical information from local residents, but their manner of doing so reflected their assumption that the purpose of mapping was to create representations of actual terrain, and that the end product of mapping was a hard-copy map. They invited their informants on board their vessels, produced paper and pencil or their own incomplete charts, and requested assistance in filling the empty spaces. Faced with blank sheets of paper in the unfamiliar environment of a ship's cabin, Inuit map-makers attempted to adapt verbal instructions and three-dimensional reconstructions of routes to a two-dimensional visual medium.

Between 150 and 200 of the maps drawn by Inuit on paper for explorers and ethnographers between 1818 and 1924 have been preserved. Except for their translation from sand and snow to paper, the documents retained most of the techniques of mapping *inuktut*, and cannot be understood in terms of European cartographic conventions. Scale, orientation, legend, relief, and completeness in Inuit maps did not conform to the ideals of European scientific cartography.

The drawn maps of Iligliuk, a woman of the Iglulingmiut community of Melville Peninsula in the 1820s, illustrate many of the differences between European and Inuit mapping. Iligliuk's people were spending the winter of 1821–22 at Lyon Inlet on the northwest coast of Hudson Bay when Captain Edward Parry, commander of the British exploration ships, *Fury* and *Hecla*, chose it as his winter station. Iligliuk was a frequent visitor to the ships. She was deeply interested in the activities of the strangers, and in the world beyond her homeland, and constantly sought information about other Inuit. She was especially eager to know about the lives and activities of women in distant places, whether Inuit or European. She examined the illustrated books in the ship's library with intense curiosity, and was always willing to pose for the artists among the crews (Parry 1824:210-11).

In March 1822, therefore, when Captain Parry showed Iligliuk his chart of Repulse Bay, Lyon Inlet, and Winter Island, she was familiar with the uses of pencil and paper, but she had not previously seen a drawn map. Nevertheless, when asked to continue the map to the northward, "Iligliuk was not long in comprehending what we desired, and with a pencil continued the outline, making the land trend as we supposed to the north-eastward and giving the names of the principal places as she proceeded" (Parry 1824:196; see Figures 1 and 3). Her map

RENÉE FOSSETT

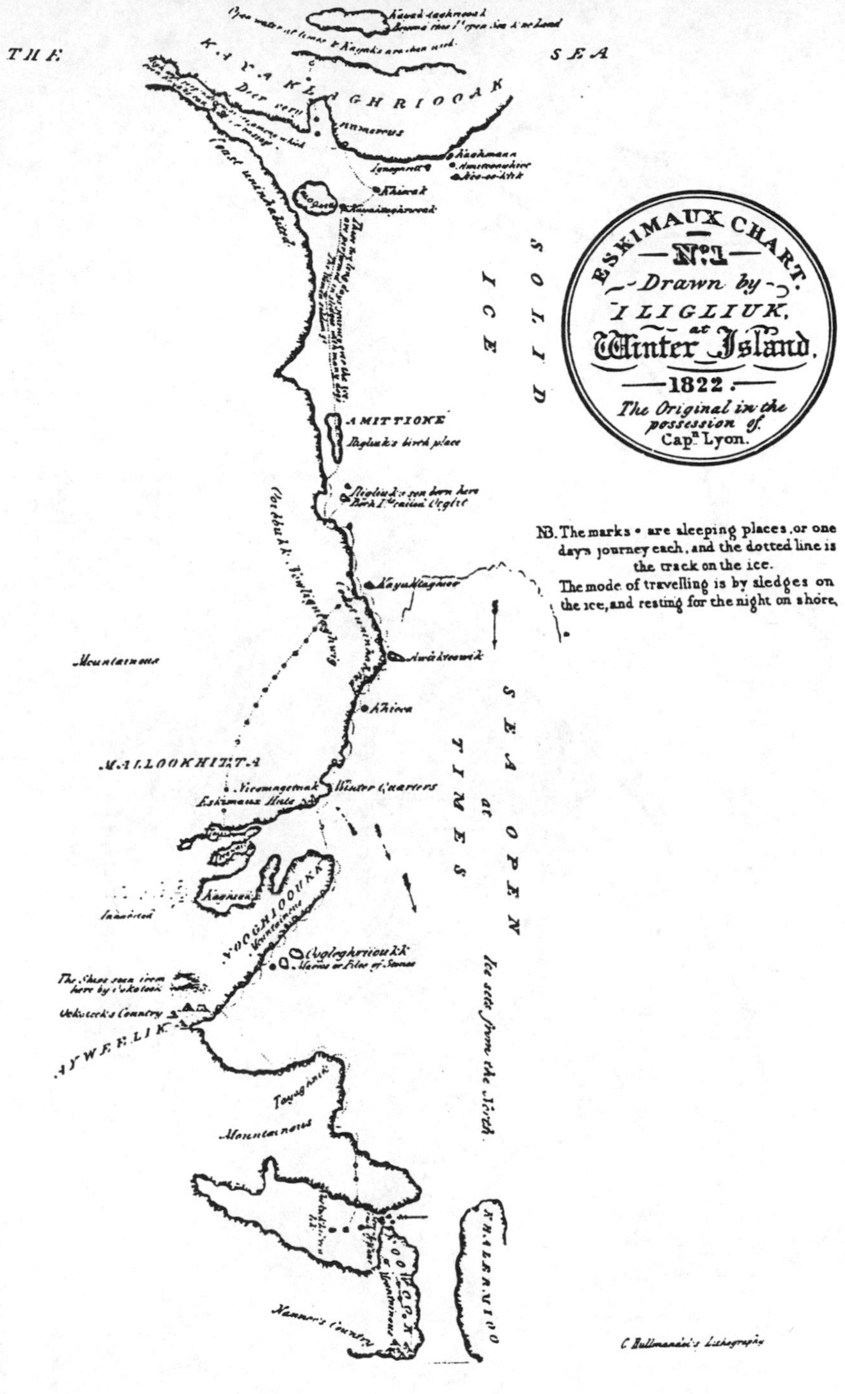

Figure 1. Iligliuk's first map (Parry 1824:facing 197).

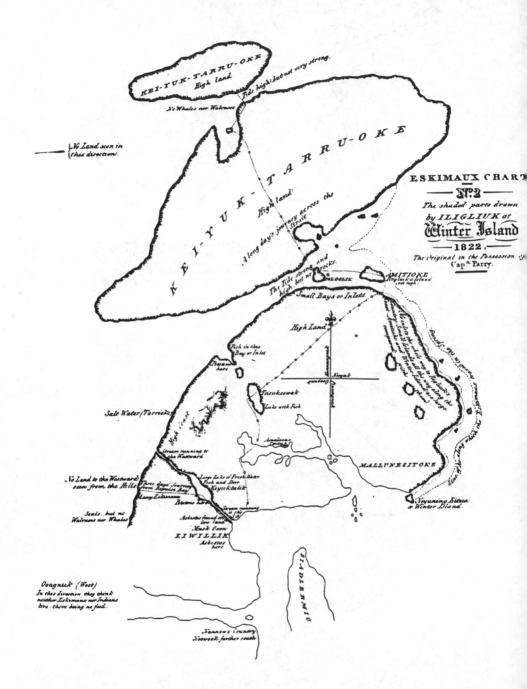

Figure 2. Iligliuk's second map (Parry 1824:facing 198).

RENÉE FOSSETT

included the east coast of Melville Peninsula, Amitioke Island where she had been born, Fury and Hecla Strait, north Baffin Island, and Bylot Island. Although Parry kept her chart for use as a navigational aid, it was, he wrote, some time before he and his officers understood the full extent and accuracy of her geographical knowledge (Parry 1824:185).

Studying the map, Parry and his second in command, George Lyon, realized that while it showed the coast continuing in a more or less straight line northward, the coast actually trended to the east. Parry took Iligliuk ashore, pointed out the four cardinal points, gave her a lesson in "boxing the compass," and then repeated the procedure with his navigational chart. Back on board ship, he gave her a small-scale map of Repulse Bay, Lyon Inlet, and Winter Island, to which she added the Melville Peninsula coast extending first east, then north to Fury and Hecla Strait, and then, to "our surprise and satisfaction ... without taking [the pencil] from the paper, brought the continental coast short round to the westward, and afterwards to the S.S.W., so as to come within three or four days' journey of Repulse Bay" (Parry 1824:198; see Figures 2 and 3).

Because Iligliuk's second map clearly corresponded to the observable landscape, Parry concluded that her earlier drawing, which he called "this curious chart," was simply inaccurate. "With respect to the *relative* geographical position of the lands beyond us," he wrote, " ... it was calculated to give us ideas which our subsequent experience proved to be erroneous" (Parry 1824:197; original emphasis).

Like other European navigators, Parry expected maps to be complete, graphic representations of actual terrain. He and his officers may have formed "erroneous" notions, but Iligliuk's maps did not err. They were intended to convey a different kind of information. Her purpose was to pass on details of routes by "giving the names of the principal places." Parry recorded her comments as she drew, without realizing that it was precisely the list of place-names along the route which was the essence of mapping *inuktut*.

Iligliuk's maps appeared to be deficient in all the elements which the European cartographic tradition valued: completeness, accurate orientation of elements, consistent scale, and correct placement of features on a grid using standard measures of distance. Certainly, Iligliuk did not place much value on topographical completeness. Because the primary purpose of mapping *inuktut* was to inform travellers of routes, topographical features not directly on a route were often omitted. To follow a route, a

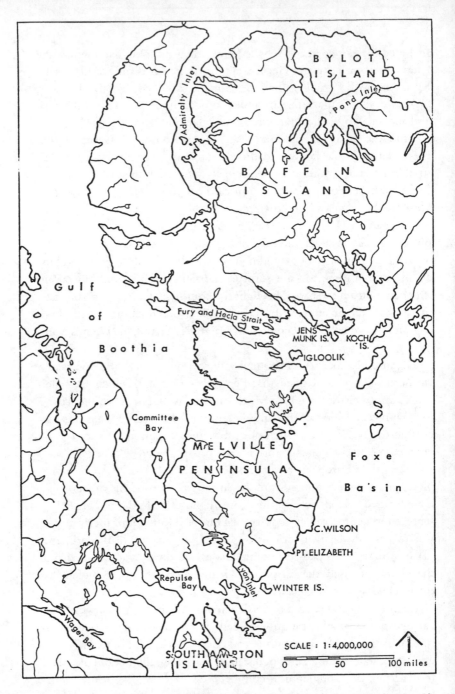

Figure 3. Survey map of Melville Peninsula and Baffin Island. Northwest Territories and Yukon Territory. Ottawa: Department of Mines and Technical Surveys (Spink 1969:59).

RENÉE FOSSETT

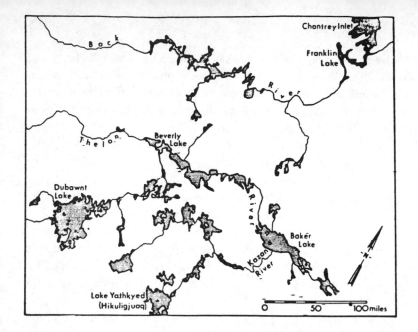

Figure 4. Survey map of Thelon River. Northwest Territories and Yukon Territory. Ottawa: Department of Mines and Technical Surveys (Spink 1969:84).

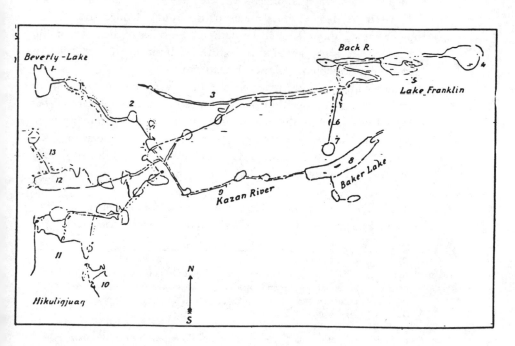

Figure 5. Igjugarjuk's map of his route from Back River to Hikoligjuaq (Rasmussen 1930a: facing 158).

traveller does not need to know what lies off to the side; hills, lakes, and other landforms which do not serve as guide posts are irrelevant. In situations where travellers had to commit route information to memory, elimination of details which had no direct bearing on route identification made the learning process easier.

At the same time, Iligliuk added details which are often missing from European maps. The verbal instructions she gave Parry, and which he pencilled onto her charts, included the location of various resources: a soapstone quarry, a surface asbestos deposit, a peat bog, and a pyrite deposit, as well as caribou crossings, villages, and hunting and fishing sites. She also described the tides, ice conditions, and other obstacles to navigation in Fury and Hecla Strait. More than 150 Inuit maps collected over the next century showed the same concern with resources. The inclusion of sites of life-sustaining resources had obvious survival value for Inuit travellers.[1]

In her first map, Iligliuk paid scant attention to changes in the direction of coasts and rivers, and the actual orientation of topographical features. In giving a spoken list of place-names supported by a sketch intended to help Parry memorize them, she intended to teach him a route. When translated to a visual medium, the routes tended to follow a straight line. Heinrich Klutschak, searching for relics of the lost Franklin expedition in 1878, noted this feature of Inuit maps and called it "straight-line" mapping (Klutschak 1881:76).[2]

Straight-line mapping reflected the Inuit view that identifying, or even knowing, the direction of travel was not always relevant. What mattered was reaching the goal, which one could do by moving from the first named place in the string of instructions to the next, until the end point was reached. During the Fifth Thule Expedition of 1921-24, Knud Rasmussen noted the usefulness of Inuit route instructions.

We worked our way forward by means of the map Pukerluk had drawn for us, and, finding without difficulty both ridges and the special crossing

---

1 In a study of Sami place names in northern Finland, Tuija Rankama noted a similar preoccupation with resources and suggested, "place-names do not exist merely for the sake of aesthetics, but...have a functional role in the lives of the people using them" (Rankama 1993:51).

2 For a discussion of straight-line mapping among other North American aboriginal groups, see G. Malcolm Lewis (1987).

over the river that *he had advised us to make for,* now that the ice was being undermined by the running water, we arrived at the village without any delays whatever. (Rasmussen 1930a:31; emphasis added)

When a map is drawn as a temporary illustration of a route, whether in sand or snow or on paper, straight-line mapping is not a drawback to reaching one's goal.

The distinct approaches of Inuit and their European visitors to the problems of scale and distance in mapping sprang from their different understandings of the purposes of maps, and reflected their different views of the world. While European scientific cartography sought to describe physical reality objectively, Inuit mapping attempted to describe practical reality subjectively. The goal of European scientific cartography was to portray terrain and topography as absolute fact existing outside of human experience. On the other hand, the mapping and the maps of Iligliuk and other Inuit cartographers, with their apparent distortions of scale and distance, reflected a view of the physical environment as a complex of relative conditions important only insofar as they affected human activity. Within the context of arctic physical, social, and cultural environments, mapping *inuktut* was a rational, practical, and appropriate solution to the problems of storing and transmitting geographical information.

Inuit maps on material media tended to show well-known areas in the greatest detail, and smallest scale. In delineating areas farther from the centre of a familiar territory, the map-maker frequently used an increasingly larger scale. Distance was indicated by means that did not accord with European linear measures; travel time was taken into account. A one-day dog team journey across the top of a fifty-mile long esker and a day-long five-mile trek across muskeg bog could be represented by drawn distances of more or less equal length in spite of the fact that actual distance covered was ten times greater on the esker than it was on muskeg. The time required for the two journeys, however, was the same.

When Inuit route instructions were transposed to a material medium, both the creation and interpretation of scale were made more difficult by the fact that the same trip could take varying lengths of time depending on the number and condition of the travellers, the season of the year, and the means of transport. Captain Parry understood the Inuit method of solving problems of scale.

These people give of the distance from one place to another, as expressed in the number of ... days' journey.... No two Esquimaux will give the same account in this respect ... each individual forms his idea of the distance, according to the season of the year, and consequently the mode of travelling in which his own journey has been performed. (Parry 1824:251)

The verbal instructions for an area, even when given by different map-makers, seldom varied, but information about distance did. As Parry indicated, each map-maker made estimates of travel time based on different kinds of information: season of the year, difficulty of particular terrain, method of travelling and condition of travel equipment, number of people in the party, the state of their health, and the degree of their familiarity with the area. Iligliuk's estimates of travel time were for parties of several families travelling together, and she took into account the slower walking speeds of children and the elderly, and the necessity for hunters to spend longer periods hunting. She included all the overnight stops which, given her assumptions about the size and content of the travelling party, would have to be made. She indicated sleeping places at the end of each day's travel, and spaced them evenly on her maps, even when the actual distances between them varied in standard linear measures. Other maps were based on the premise that the travellers were a small party of men or perhaps a single trader moving as quickly as possible, spending a minimum of time hunting, making camp, or resting. They tended to show fewer camp sites farther apart, and an overall reduction in travel time.

The telescoping and expansion of space in drawn Inuit maps were attempts to provide accurate information about time in a material medium which does not express the fourth dimension well. One of the dozens of maps collected by Knud Rasmussen of the Fifth Thule Expedition in the Keewatin District west of Hudson Bay can serve as an example (see Figures 4 and 5). It shows the route of the trader Igjugarjuk from the Back River to Hikoligjuaq (Yathkyed Lake) via the Thelon River, Baker Lake, and the Kazan and Dubawnt rivers. The northern half of the route appears much shorter than the southern leg, although the distances are nearly equal in standard European linear measurements. However, the southern part of the route crosses more difficult terrain, and in terms of time is about twice as long as the northern part. As Rasmussen pointed out, "certain inaccuracies and exaggerations in the proportions have been made deliberately, just for the purpose of emphasizing certain peculiarities of character in the landscape" (Rasmussen 1930b:89). Igjugarjuk chose to distort the linear distances of the two sections in order to convey information about difficulty of terrain and travel time, a means of measurement more relevant to human activity than linear distance would have been.

Igjugarjuk's map also illustrates a point made earlier concerning the omission of irrelevant details. The northern section, showing the route from the Back River to Baker Lake, contains almost no information about terrain or landmarks. The omissions do not indicate an area devoid of topographical features, or ignorance on the cartographer's part. The omissions reflected his opinion that in some places the traveller cannot possibly get lost. One had only to follow the rivers wherever they went. No topographical features were included in the instructions because none was needed to keep the traveller on the right path.

When Inuit cartographers transmitted geographical information orally, details of travel time and difficulty of terrain could be included in a few words. In a very real sense, mapping *inuktut* incorporated information about the fourth dimension — time. When they translated verbal instructions to the visual medium of two-dimensional paper, Inuit took a number of factors into account and produced accurate and informative charts containing reasonable averages of variable information.

The use of symbols on hard-copy maps to indicate particular elements in both the natural and built environments, accompanied by a legend which explains the meanings of the various symbols, is a European cartographic convention. Maps drawn by Inuit seldom included symbols before the twentieth century. Symbols played no part in the oral transmission of travel instructions, and when three-dimensional maps were drawn on the ground, pebbles, sticks, and piles of sand or snow were adequate representations of topographical features. However, when foreign travellers, such as Parry on Melville Peninsula in 1822 and Captain John Ross on Boothia Peninsula in 1830, asked Inuit to produce maps, they translated the verbal instructions of their informants into symbols which accorded with European mapping conventions. The arrows indicating cardinal points on Iligliuk's maps, for instance, were added by Parry; Ross added coastline hachuring to a chart drawn for him by Tiriksiu, a woman at Committee Bay. After Inuit had begun to make maps on paper they tended to use a few symbols which were apparently original to them: Iligliuk used circles to show overnight stops; dotted lines represented routes on a Baffin Island map drawn for Franz Boas; and different people used dots to represent islands, trading posts, and caribou crossings. Yet other symbols appeared for the first time on maps collected by the Fifth Thule Expedition of 1921-24. They included triangles and rayed circles to represent hills, and hatched circles to indicate waterfalls. Their similarity to conventional European map symbolism suggests that the map-makers had learned them from Europeans and had begun to use them consistently as they adapted their mapping techniques to hard-copy maps.

In traditional Inuit mapping, however, the memorized legend *was* the map. People placed more value on the ability to remember place-names in the correct order than they did on drawing skills. Toolemak, a member of the Iglulingmiut community, was judged by Parry to be an indifferent draughtsman.

> His performance in this way, if taken alone, was not a very intelligible delineation of the coast. By dint however of *a great deal of talking on his part*, and some exercise of patience on ours, we at length obtained a copious *verbal illustration* of his sketch, which confirmed all our former accounts. (Parry 1824:303; emphasis added).

Toolemak apparently had the verbal instructions right. The care he took to make sure his European listeners understood them suggests that he also had to "exercise patience." A woman who piloted the *Fox* at Pond Inlet in 1858 made similar efforts to teach McClintock the correct sequence of names. She traced on paper "the shores of the inlet as far as her knowledge extends," and recited *"the name of every point"* (McClintock 1859:150). Toolookah, a map-maker in a south Baffin Island community in the 1860s, made sure that his visitor, the American explorer Charles F. Hall, paid attention to the oral description. In Hall's words,

> Every half minute he would punch me with a pencil I had given him, so that I might pay attention to the Innuit *names of places*. As soon as he had sketched an island, bay or cape, he would stop, and wait until I had correctly *written down the name*. (Hall 1862:355; emphasis added)

In the context of European place-naming customs, a mere list of names would be inadequate as a traveller's guide. In Inuit communities, however, it worked. Names were, and are, highly valued in Inuit society because they "give identity to persons and objects" (Spink 1969:52). Just as names are the essence of each human being, they are also what gives

RENÉE FOSSETT

reality to objects. Reports of visitors to the arctic abound with examples of the Inuit preoccupation with personal names. As McClintock noted,

> The Esquimaux take considerable pains to learn, and remember names.... This woman [at Pond Inlet in 1858] knows the names of several of the whaling captains and the old chief at De Ros Islet remembered Captain Inglefield's name, and tried hard to pronounce mine. (McClintock 1859:154)

Parry made a similar comment, and in particular noticed that although Iligliuk showed no interest in learning to speak English, she asked the names of everyone aboard both *Fury* and *Hecla*, and almost instantly committed them to memory (Parry 1824:204).

Just as every person was identified by a name, so was every nook and cranny of Inuit country. As Captain George Lyon wrote,

> Every streamlet, lake, bay, point, or island, has a name, and even certain piles of stones have also *appellations*, it is easy, in some ensuing year, to find the things which are buried, or even to describe their situation to others. It is remarkable, that in enumerating the various sleeps, or days' journeys along the shore, *every one has a particular name*. (Lyon 1824:343-44; emphasis added)

A few place-names commemorated events which had taken place there, like *alaktok*, "the place where a brown bear was killed." Some were called by the name of a natural resource, like *utkusiksalik*, "the place for pot stone." Most were descriptive of topography: *kujuak*, "the big river," and *kakiati*, "the wind-swept place" (Chipman & Cox 1924:37; Rasmussen 1930b:161-62).[1]

Topographically descriptive names were particularly useful in following route instructions, as Peter Freuchen noted during the Fifth Thule Expedition. "I could always get rather exact topographic descriptions from the Eskimos who had taken the same route. They have a very

---

1   Tuija Rankama's analysis of Sami place names pointed out that toponyms which are obviously descriptive of topography also contain information about resources. Telling a Sami hunter or herdsman to go to *goatnil*, "the counter-current in the river," is the same as telling him where the best fishing is, because he already knows "that the salmon habitually stop to rest in these places and they are therefore good for fishing." Rankama's survey of 333 Sami toponyms found that 15% referred explicitly to resources, and the majority of the 44% which were obviously topographic contained implicit information about resources (Rankama 1993:57).

practical custom of always giving descriptive names to landmarks. *Pingo* everywhere means a round-topped mountain; *Kuksuaq* is the big river; *Tassersuaq* is the big lake, etc" (Freuchen 1961:63). The generic nature of topographically descriptive place-names could, however, create difficulties for travellers in unknown territory, where they could not know with certainty if a particular lake was Big Lake or Windswept Lake.

The practice of cooperative mapping and the presence of one or two long-distance travellers in nearly every community helped to alleviate the problems of repetitive place-names in unfamiliar territory. Thomas Beechey's account of communal mapping on the Alaskan coast was only one of many in which European observers described entire communities involved in recalling geographical information. During the sessions, individuals added details unknown to the others, and corrected or amended one another's information (Huish 1836:397).[1] Members of the community who had travelled widely made significant contributions to geographical knowledge. George Lyon noted that "the importance assumed by a great Eskimaux traveller, is fully equal to that displayed by Europeans who have seen the world. Nothing indeed affords more gratification to a man newly arrived, than to ask him of the places he has recently quitted" (Lyon 1824:342).

Intimate knowledge of home territory was vital to survival, and, in Lyon's words, "even those who have roamed to a short distance only, are acquainted traditionally with their own country" (Lyon 1824:292). It is a truism of social theorists that in hunter-gatherer societies, hunters, usually male, need to know every detail of the natural environments which they exploit. In most Inuit societies, the constant movement of individuals, families, and communities from one resource site to another created conditions in which everyone had an opportunity to acquire a high degree of geographical information (Spink 1969:42, 41–55; Rundstrom 1980:73n2). Women apparently made the most of the opportunities to become expert geographers, cartographers, and navigators. They were frequently recognized, by their own communities and by European travellers alike, not only as equals of the best male cartographers, but in many cases as superior in navigational and cartographic skills.

Among the earliest accounts of Inuit mapping by a named individual are those of Parry and Lyon among the Iglulingmiut in the 1820s. They depended almost entirely on the geographical knowledge and carto-

---

1   Other incidents of communal mapping were witnessed by Charles F. Hall (1879:354–55) and Leopold McClintock (1859:160).

RENÉE FOSSETT

graphic skill of the woman Iligliuk. Captain John Ross, exploring Boothia Peninsula in 1830, was surprised to find himself similarly dependent when the local community answered his requests for a map-maker by producing a woman. However, he conceded, "this personage, woman though she was, did not want a knowledge of geography." He applauded her efforts and understood that her approach to mapping was

> of a different nature from what she might have acquired in an English boarding-school, through the question book and 'the use of the globes.' Tiriksiu, for that was her name, perfectly comprehended the chart; and being furnished with the means, drew one of her own, very much resembling it, but with many more is-lands; adding also the places where we must sleep in our future progress, and those where food was to be obtained. (Ross 1835:261-62).

But while John Ross expressed surprise at the existence of a female cartographer, John Rae had an opposite reaction. During his explorations between Repulse Bay and Boothia Peninsula in 1847, he chanced to meet a married couple, Iillak and his wife Reiluak, at Committee Bay. The geographical information he asked for was given to him in the form of "a chart drawn by the woman, who, as is usual, (at least among the Esquimaux) was much the more intelligent of the two" (Rae 1850:49).

In Inuit communities, women were the recognized geographers at widely separated places and times. At the mouth of the Mackenzie River in 1837, an unidentified woman drew a sketch map of the coast between the Mackenzie River and Point Barrow, Alaska for Thomas Simpson's exploration party (Simpson 1843:148). In 1858 Leopold McClintock not only depended on a woman for geographical information, but he entrusted her with the safety of his vessel and crew as she piloted the *Fox* up Pond Inlet (McClintock 1859:149-150). And at Frobisher Bay in 1861, a woman named Tweeroong made at least one sketch map for Charles Francis Hall, and a second woman, Amergoo, corrected a map drawn by a male compatriot (Hall 1862:355).

Although frequency of travel within a home territory combined with occasional travel into foreign parts offered opportunities for individuals to acquire geographical information, the question of what motivated women to become expert navigators and cartographers remains unanswered. A clue to the prominence of women as geographers among Inuit may have been unwittingly recorded by John Ross. In 1831, he contracted with two local men to act as guides in his exploration of the west coast of Boothia Peninsula. Like many other explorers, Ross quickly discovered that Inuit men seldom travel without at least some members of their families.[1] He described the entourage:

> The mother of the two men led the way in advance, with a staff in her hand; my sledge following, with the dogs, holding one of their children and some of their goods, and guided by a wife with a child at her back.... [A few days later,] the old woman [was] still leading the way. (Ross 1835:530, 532)

A traveller in the arctic in the 1930s, Gontran de Poncins, described similar scenes more vividly:

> [Ohudlerk's] wife had gone on ahead of the sled some fifty yards. There she stopped, turned, called and waved to the dogs, and they broke abruptly out, barking as they ran. Alongside the sled ran Ohudlerk, braking now and then by clinging to a rope tied to the rear of the sled, digging his heels into the snow and dragging with all his strength. (Poncins 1941:50)

> The departure [for seal camp] was a wonderful sight — sleds piled high, dogs barking and choking as they tugged at the heavy loads, the excited cries and calls of the wives gesticulating ahead. (Poncins 1941:344)

The activities witnessed by Ross and de Poncins were typical of Inuit travel. Women broke trail, led the dogs forward, and when necessary harnessed themselves to the sled and pulled, while men stayed beside or behind the sled, keeping it upright, pushing or lifting it over obstacles, untangling the traces, and controlling unruly dogs with voice and whip. The particular division of labour may have arisen from the simple fact of men's greater muscular strength. While men applied muscle power, women concentrated on the details of their territory and accustomed routes, taking on the responsibilities of navigation, and of transmitting their knowledge to new generations.

Reiluak may not have been "more intelligent" than her husband Iillak, as John Rae (1850:49) thought, but she may have been the geographical specialist and navigator in the marital partnership, while Iillak's expertise lay in other areas.

---

1   Among Inuit, men travelled alone or with other men only when short trips of no more than a week or two were planned, and only when the trip had a single, very specific purpose, such as to pick up food from a cache. Athapaskan peoples also preferred to travel in groups which included families. See, for example, the journals of Samuel Hearne, David Thompson, Alexander Mackenzie, John Franklin, and Thomas Simpson.

RENÉE FOSSETT

When comparisons of Inuit and European mapping styles have been made for the sake of illustration, they have often contrasted Inuit customary mapping with European formalized cartography. Such comparisons are useful for initiating discussion, but they can also lead to false conclusions. In comparing aboriginal "popular" custom with European "scientific" form, we may be comparing apples and oranges. The conclusions of many scholars that aboriginal and European societies are radically different in their approach to personal, corporate, and commercial relations are open to criticism. Theories which purport to explain aboriginal social organization have seldom been tested for how they might also apply to European communities of the same size and population density. There are obvious contrasts between the frequent interpersonal relations within any small, face-to-face society and the often more impersonal relations of densely populated state societies. However, obvious differences are also apparent between informal and popular customs and formal and institutionalized conventions within a single society.

As different as Inuit customary mapping activity is from European scientific cartography, the similarities between Inuit charts and the sketch maps which Europeans and Americans without cartographic training make in informal situations are striking. For example, when a gas station attendant tells a tourist how to get to the highway access ramp, or when a hostess gives her guest a hand-drawn chart showing how to get to the party, the purpose of both oral and sketch mapping is to convey instructions on a route, not to create a complete representation of terrain. Traditional Inuit and informal Euroamerican mapping share two obvious features: orality and concentration on route. In both cases, orientation, scale, and distance are likely to be distorted, and information about travel time is likely to be included.[1]

Aboriginally, Inuit mapping was characterized by its orality and concentration on route and travelling conditions. Orality was related to lack of media suitable for graphic mapping. With the exception of the wooden maps used in east Greenland, the only graphic representations of terrain produced in the process of mapping *inuktut* were ephemeral maps drawn in sand or snow in order to help learners visualize, and therefore learn, the topographical details relevant to routes. Travellers reached their goals safely and expeditiously because they had memorized the names of all

---

1   For discussions of the nature and characteristics of mental maps and informal transmission of route information in European and American societies, see Gould and White (1974), and Haynes (1980).

points along the route. Both verbal instructions, that is the list of place-names, and dioramic maps on the ground were four-dimensional, incorporating information about distance, difficulty of travel, travel time, and location of necessary resources. In transposing verbal instructions and dioramic representations to the dimensionally limited medium of paper, Inuit cartographers created or adopted symbols to indicate height, the missing third dimension, and adjusted portrayals of distance and orientation to compensate for the missing fourth dimension, time.

References

Boas, Franz
  1888 *The Central Eskimo.* Bison Book edition. Ed. Henry B. Collins. Lincoln: University of Nebraska Press, 1964.
Chipman, K.G., and J.R. Cox
  1924 *Geographical Notes on the Arctic Coast of Canada. Report of the Canadian Arctic Expedition.* Vol. XI, Part B. Ottawa: King's Printer.
Freuchen, Peter
  1961 *Book of the Eskimos.* Cleveland: World Publishing.
Gould, Peter, and Rodney White
  1974 *Mental Maps.* Harmondsworth: Penguin.
Hall, Charles Francis
  1862 *Life with the Esquimaux: A Narrative of Arctic Experience in Search of Survivors of Sir John Franklin's Expedition.* Reprint. Edmonton: Hurtig, 1970.
  1879 *Narrative of the Second Arctic Expedition Made By Charles F. Hall: His Voyage to Repulse Bay, Sledge Journeys to the Straits of Fury and Hecla and to King William's Land, and Residence Among the Eskimos During the Years 1864-69.* Ed. J.E. Nourse. Washington, DC: US Government Printing Office.
Haynes, Robin M.
  1980 Geographical Images and Mental Maps. London: Macmillan Education.
Holm, Gustav
  1888 Ethnological Sketch of the Angmagsalik Eskimo. Trans. and ed. William Thalbitzer. Meddelelser om Gronland 39(1914). Original title: *Ostgronlandske Expedition. Meddelelser om Gronland.*
Huish, Robert
  1836 *A Narrative of the Voyages and Travels of Captain Beechey...to the Pacific and Behring's Straits; Performed in the Years 1825, 26, 27 and 28.* London.

Klutschak, Heinrich

　1881　Overland to Starvation Cove: With the Inuit in Search of Franklin,
　　　　1878–1880. Trans. and ed. William Barr. Toronto: University of
　　　　Toronto Press.

Lewis, G. Malcolm

　1987　Indian maps: their place in the history of plains cartography. In
　　　　Mapping the North American Plains: Essays in the History of
　　　　Cartography. Eds. F.C. Luebke, Frances W. Kaye, Gary E. Moulton.
　　　　63–80. Norman: University of Oklahoma Press.

Lyon, George

　1824　*The Private Journal of Captain G.F. Lyon of H.M.S. Hecla During the
　　　　Recent Voyage of Discovery Under Captain Parry.* London: John Murray.

McClintock, Leopold

　1859　*The Voyage of the "Fox" in the Arctic Seas: A Narrative of the Discovery
　　　　of the Fate of Sir John Franklin and His Companions.* London: John
　　　　Murray.

Parry, William Edward

　1824　*Journal of a Second Voyage for the Discovery of a North-West Passage
　　　　Performed in the Years 1821-22-23 In His Majesty's Ships Fury and
　　　　Hecla....* London: John Murray.

Poncins, Gontran de

　1941　*Kabloona.* New York: Reynal and Hitchcock.

Rae, John

　1850　*Narrative of an Expedition to the Shores of the Arctic Sea in 1846 and 1847.*
　　　　London: T. and W. Boone.

Rankama, Tuija

　1993　Managing the landscape: a study of Sami place-names in Utsjoki,
　　　　Finnish Lapland. Etudes/Inuit/Studies 17(1):47–695.

Rasmussen, Knud

　1930a　*Iglulik and Caribou Eskimo Texts. Report of the Fifth Thule Expedition,
　　　　1921-24.* Vol. 7:3. Copenhagen: Gyldendal.

　1930b　Observations on the Intellectual Culture of the Caribou Eskimos.
　　　　Report of the Fifth Thule Expedition, 1921-24. Vol. 7:2.
　　　　Copenhagen: Gyldendal.

Ronda, James P.

　1987　"A chart in his way": Indian cartography and the Lewis and Clark
　　　　Expedition. In Mapping the North American Plains: Essays in the
　　　　History of Cartography. Eds. F.C. Luebke, Frances W. Kaye, Gary
　　　　E. Moulton. 81-92. Norman: University of Oklahoma Press.

Ross, John

1835 *Narrative of a Second Voyage in Search of a North-West Passage, and of a Residence in the Arctic Regions During the Years 1829, 1830, 1831, 1832, 1833.* London: A.W. Webster.

Rundstrom, Richard A.

1980 Maps, Man, and Land in the Cultural Cartography of the Eskimo (Inuit). Doctoral thesis, Geography, University of Kansas.

Simpson, Thomas

1843 *Narrative of the Discoveries on the North Coast of America, Effected by the Officers of the Hudson's Bay Company During the Years 1836-39.* London: Richard Bentley.

Spencer, Robert F.

1955 Map making of the North Alaskan Eskimo. Proceedings of The Minnesota Academy of Science. Vol. 23:46-50.

Spink, John

1969 *Eskimo Maps from the Canadian Eastern Arctic.* Master's thesis, Geography, University of Manitoba.

5

Captain Cook and the Spaces of Contact at "Nootka Sound"[1]

Daniel Clayton

BETWEEN 1768 AND HIS DEATH in Hawaii in 1779, the British explorer James Cook commanded three expeditions to the Pacific. He charted the coasts of Australia and New Zealand, and the islands of the Pacific; by 1779 he had completed, in outline, the map of the world.[2] Cook sailed under the patronage of the British Crown and with the backing of Britain's intellectual establishment, the Royal Society and Royal Academy. He had a scientific and humanitarian mandate to "observe the Genius, Temper, Disposition, and Number" of the peoples he met; to "cultivate a friendship with them" through trade; and to show them "every Civility and Regard."[3] The writer Fanny Burney (Madame D'Arblay) spoke for many of Cook's contemporaries when she described him as "the most moderate, humane, and gentle circumnavigator who ever went upon discoveries."[4] His voyages signalled a new scientific curiosity about the world and were meant to be based on an ethic of respect toward other peoples. This popular image was given a scholarly footing in this century by the New Zealand historian J.C. Beaglehole, who viewed Cook as a humble man, a judicious observer, a

---

1   I would like to thank Cole Harris, who made incisive comments on a draft of this essay. The research on which it is based was supported by the Social Sciences and Humanities Research Council of Canada.

2   For an overview of Cook's voyages, see Lynne Withey, *Voyages of Discovery: Captain Cook and the Exploration of the Pacific* (New York: William Morrow, 1987).

3   "Secret instructions for Capt James Cook," 6 July 1776, in J.C. Beaglehole, ed., *The Journals of Captain Cook on His Voyages of Discovery, Vol. III: The Voyage of the* Resolution *and* Discovery, *1776-1780* (Cambridge: Hakluyt Society, extra series xxxvi, 1967), ccxxiii.

4   Charlotte Barrett, ed., *Diary & Letters of Madame D'Arblay, vol.1 (1778 – June 1781)* (London: Macmillan, 1904), 318.

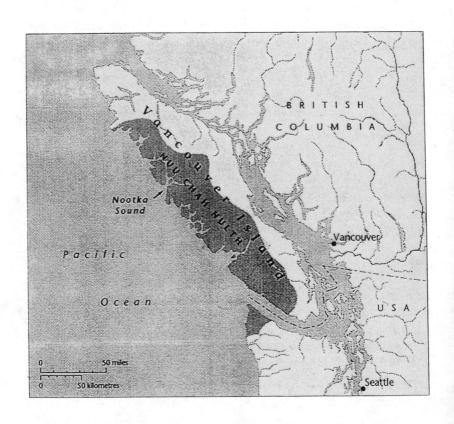

Figure 1: Base map

DANIEL CLAYTON

brilliant navigator, and a journalist who had "a perfectly unassuming and primary wish to tell the truth."[1]

These images of Cook and scientific exploration in the late eighteenth century are beginning to be challenged. Cook did not pillage or colonize, but his voyages can be situated in a longer and more iniquitous imperial history.[2] His discoveries grounded British claims to sovereignty over the Pacific. The scientists and artists who accompanied him contributed to a body of European ideas about non-European lands and peoples that induced, supported, and legitimized imperial expansion. Some scholars now argue that explorers' claims to truth and objectivity cannot be disconnected from questions of power. Did explorers such as Cook simply record what they saw and experienced in an open, objective manner, as Beaglehole suggested, or did they, as some now argue, actively create and order the distinctions between Europe and the wider world that fill their journals?[3] Scientific exploration is increasingly viewed as a handmaiden of European colonialism — as an intellectual strategy for gaining possession of non-European space and symbolic domination over its inhabitants.[4] Europeans, like all human beings, imagined and represented the world in relation to themselves, but with the privilege of more power than most. Many explorers described non-European space as bounteous and ripe for colonization. The Pacific was represented as both an Arcadia of simplicity and innocence that Europeans had lost, and as a region populated by pagans and savages.[5] Europe-

---

1   See J.C. Beaglehole, *The Life of Captain James Cook*, (Stanford: Stanford University Press, 1974). The quotation is from J.C. Beaglehole, *Cook the Writer* (Sydney: Sydney University Press, 1970), 20.

2   For a detailed critique of these celebratory views of Cook, see Gananath Obeyesekere, *The Apotheosis of Captain Cook: European Mythmaking in the Pacific* (Princeton, NJ: Princeton University Press, 1992).

3   See Mary Louise Pratt, *Imperial Eyes: Travel Writing and Transculturation* (London and New York: Routledge, 1992), especially Part I.

4   See Robert Young, *White Mythologies: Writing History and the West* (London: Routledge, 1990).

5   See Bernard Smith, *Imagining the Pacific: In the Wake of Cook's Voyages* (New Haven and London: Yale University Press, 1992), especially Chapters 3 and 4.

ans, as Henri Baudet explained, eyed the wider world with "dissatisfaction and desire," and with "nostalgia and idealism."[1]

Such critical perspectives have flourished in the context of decolonization in the postwar world. Formal colonial power may have been largely dismantled, but colonial ideas and stereotypes about history and Native peoples live on. They are embedded in the nationalisms and self-identities of Europe's former colonies, and some critics claim that they are still part and parcel of European systems of thought.[2] In Australia and New Zealand, Cook is still seen as a founding father and celebrated as a culture-hero. Yet formerly colonized peoples are raising alternative views of history. For many Native groups, Cook stands for a history of colonial violence and dispossession.[3] What the past signifies, and how history is written, are today profoundly contested questions. Scholarship on colonialism has to address these issues of representation, or what Edward Said calls "the power to narrate."[4]

With these issues in mind, this essay explores Cook's encounter with the Nuu-chah-nulth people of "Nootka Sound" on the west coast of "Vancouver Island" in 1778 (see Figure 1).[5] Cook was then on his third

---

1   Henri Baudet, *Paradise on Earth: Some Thoughts on European Images of Non-European Man* (New Haven: Yale University Press, 1965), 55.

2   Much of this debate was provoked by Edward W. Said's *Orientalism* (New York: Random House, 1978).

3   See, for example, Deborah Bird Rose, *Dingo Makes Us Human: Life and Land in an Aboriginal Australian Culture* (Cambridge: Cambridge University Press, 1992), 186–202.

4   Edward W. Said, *Culture and Imperialism* (New York: Alfred A. Knopf, 1993), xiii.

5   I put Nootka Sound and Vancouver Island in scare quotes here and in the title to point out that they are not indigenous place names, and to highlight that processes of naming and mapping were integral to the appropriation of Native land and life by European powers. On this point, see especially J. Brian Harley, "Rereading the Maps of the Columbian Encounter," *Annals of the Association of American Geographers*, 83:2 (1992), 522–42. The Native groups of the west coast of Vancouver Island took Nuu-chah-nulth as their collective name in 1978. Before that Europeans called them "Nootkans." The Native groups of this region did not identify themselves collectively in 1778, nor did they have a single name for the area Cook named Nootka Sound. Cook initially named the inlet "King George's Sound," but changed the name at a later date, thinking that "Nootka" was the indigenous name for the sound. There are many interpretations of Cook's mistake. For instance, the Spanish botanist José Mariano Moziño, who visited the sound in 1792, thought that Cook derived "Nootka" from the Native word "Nut-chi," or mountain. Another Spanish observer

DANIEL CLAYTON

voyage. He had come to the north Pacific in search of the fabled North-west Passage — a water route across northern North America that many at the time thought connected the Pacific and the Atlantic — but stayed at Nootka Sound for a month repairing and resupplying his ships. This was the first encounter of any length between Europeans and Native people in the region. It has been treated by scholars as a historical bench-mark from which British influence on Vancouver Island, and the history of Native-white relations, can be charted. But this encounter, I suspect, does not confer any single or simple history. It represents a fleeting, if re-markable, engagement between Natives and Europeans. Historical and ethnographic records pertaining to initial contact at Nootka Sound al-low us to interrogate issues of representation — philosophies and meth-ods of seeing and recording. I will return briefly to Cook's place in Brit-ish Columbia history at the end of the essay.

★   ★   ★

Cook sighted Nootka Sound on the morning of 29 March 1778. By evening, his ships, the *Resolution* and *Discovery*, had anchored near the south end of the island in the centre of the sound. Figure 2, a map drawn by one of Cook's officers, shows the tracks of Cook's ships into the sound and his anchorage. Following is an excerpt from the official ac-count of Cook's third voyage published in 1784, which was based on Cook's journal of events, reporting his passage into the sound. The ac-count is "official" because it was sanctioned by the British Admiralty; I also refer to it as "Douglas's account" because it was edited by John Douglas, Canon of Windsor and St. Paul's:

> We no sooner drew near the inlet than we found the coast to be inhab-ited; and at the place where we were first becalmed, three canoes came off to the ship. In one of these were two men, in another six, and in the third ten. Having come pretty near us, a person in one of them stood up,

---

claimed that "Cook's men, asking [the Indians] by signs what the port was called, made for them a sign with their hand, forming a circle and then dissolving it, to which the Natives responded Nutka, which means to give away." José Mariano Moz-iño, *Noticias de Nutka: An Account of Nootka Sound in 1792*, Iris H. Wilson Engstrand, trans. and ed. (Seattle: University of Washington Press, 1970), 67.

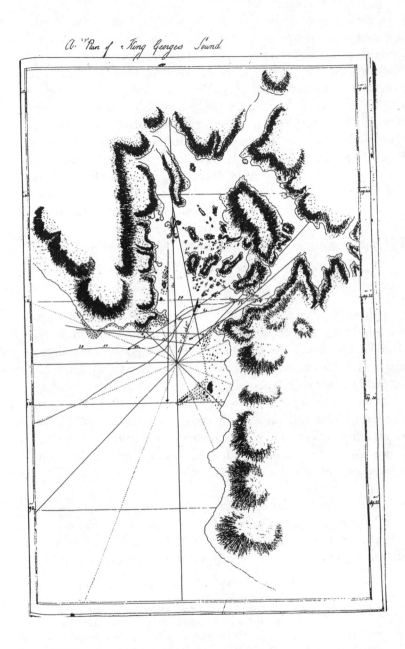

Figure 2: ' A plan of King Georges Sound'
Thomas Edgar, "Log" PRO ADM 55/21, Part I, fol. 150

DANIEL CLAYTON

and made a long harangue, inviting us to land, as we guessed, by his gestures. At the same time he kept strewing handfuls of feathers towards us; and some of his companions threw handfuls of a red dust or powder in the same manner. The person who played the orator, wore the skin of some animal, and held, in each hand, something which rattled as he kept shaking it. After tiring himself with his repeated exhortations, of which we did not understand a word, he was quiet; and then others took it, by turns, to say something.... After the tumultuous noise had ceased, they lay at a little distance from the ship, and conversed with each other in a very easy manner; nor did they seem to shew the least surprize or distrust.[1]

For almost two centuries, it was assumed that these were Cook's words, and this passage was read as a factual account of first contact at Nootka Sound. It established that Cook and his crew had *been there*, looking and recording. During the eighteenth century, exploration became a resolutely empirical science, and European thinkers put a premium on the powers of vision and the category of experience — on firsthand observation. This was the age of En*light*enment. "[T]he two great mythical experiences on which the philosophy of the eighteenth century had wished to base its beginnings," wrote Michel Foucault, were "the foreign spectator in an unknown country, and the man born blind restored to light."[2] The authority and appeal of explorers' narratives rested in good measure on the fact that they had seen new lands and people with their own eyes and compiled their observations on the spot. The fabulous tales of foreign people, and the riches of foreign lands, that an earlier generation of explorers such as Columbus had written were now to be overhauled by careful, systematic studies of people and nature.[3] Scientific exploration revolved around what Barbara Maria Stafford calls "the valorization of the instant": explorers were expected to represent their

---

1   James Cook and James King, *A Voyage to the Pacific Ocean...*, 3 vols. (London: G. Nichol and T. Cadell, 1784), II, 265-66.

2   Michel Foucault, *The Birth of the Clinic: An Archaeology of Medical Perception* (London: Tavistock Publications, 1973), 65.

3   See Bernard McGrane, *Beyond Anthropology: Society and the Other* (New York; Columbia University Press, 1989) for a good discussion of European representations of non-European peoples between the fifteenth and nineteenth centuries.

active, physical engagement with new surroundings.[1] This passage in the official account undertook to mimic the immediacy of first contact. Cook apparently had no preconceptions about these people, and he recorded what happened in clear, factual prose. Communication at first depended on body language — motives and intentions read from gestures. The inhabitants seemingly showed little surprise at the sight of Cook's ships, and invited Cook to land.

Objectivity, and the supposition that an account was therefore reliable and true, were based on a particular textual stance toward the world. The task of the explorer, Stafford suggests, was to find a transparent mode of literary and visual expression that could duplicate the experience of encountering the new.[2] This textual stance constituted the notion of disinterestedness. Scientific explorers, Stafford claims, tried to match words to things without the crutch of memory — to represent people and nature "nakedly without an intervening human screen."[3] Disinterestedness entailed a dedication to observation, a commitment not to let the eye wallow in distant memories and vague connotations. This textual stance also implied detachment. As Stafford continues: "the explorer — committed to the living of actuality, not to recollection; unwedded to the landscape; not endemic to his terrain — is an interloper in a raw world that functions without him."[4] The passage in the official account contains no value judgements about the Natives' behaviour. Rather, it states the facts of contact and implies that the behaviour of the inhabitants was endemic to this particular group of people; that their reaction to Cook's ships was an indication of their "Genius, Temper, and Disposition."

This account of first contact at Nootka Sound may be objective in the sense that I have sketched the term, but how factual is it? In the 1960s the scholar J.C. Beaglehole compared Cook's own journal of his third voyage (housed in the Manuscripts Room of the British Museum

---

1 Barbara Maria Stafford, *Voyage into Substance: Art, Science, and the Illustrated Travel Account, 1760-1840* (London, England, and Cambridge, Massachusetts: MIT Press, 1984), 400.

2 Stafford, *Voyage into Substance*, 28.

3 Stafford, *Voyage into Substance*, 408.

4 Stafford, *Voyage into Substance*, 421.

DANIEL CLAYTON

in London) with what was printed in Douglas's account, and discovered that Douglas had twisted Cook's descriptions and added many lines of his own. Beaglehole published Cook's original journal of his third voyage in 1967, and scholars now rely on it rather than the official account, perhaps in the belief that they are reading a more authentic Cook.

This is how first contact at Nootka Sound is recorded in Beaglehole's edition of Cook:

> We no sooner drew near the inlet than we found the coast to be inhabited and the people came off to the Ships in Canoes without shewing the least mark of fear or distrust. We had at one time thirty two Canoes filled with people about us, and a groupe of ten or a dozen remained along side the Resolution most part of the night. They seemed to be a mild inoffensive people, shewed great readiness to part with anything they had and took whatever was offered them in exchange.[1]

This is a shorter statement than Douglas's, yet it is still matter-of-fact and seemingly objective. But is it a disinterested, on-the-spot account? I.S. MacLaren has studied the four basic stages in the evolution of explorers' narratives — from the log book entry, to the journal, to the book manuscript, and finally to these "official" published accounts — and shows how, from stage to stage in this sequence, the physical scene of writing becomes more distant, the author relies more on memory, and questions of narrative structure become more central. Cook's journal, MacLaren points out, is a second-stage journal, composed after the fact.[2]

MacLaren's argument can be expanded. Explorers' firsthand observations were tempered by the recollection of other lands and peoples. The particular words and details that gave Cook's and Douglas's accounts of first contact at Nootka Sound their own vitality were drawn from a space of comparison that had been opened up during the course of Cook's voyages. Native actions and gestures were fixed as facts beginning a new encounter, and each new meeting was made novel by virtue of a singular collection of statements employed to make it differ from others: here, at Nootka Sound, the Native inhabitants apparently showed little surprise at

---

1 Beaglehole, *Journals*, III, 295.

2 I.S. MacLaren, "Exploration/Travel Literature and the Evolution of the Author," *International Journal of Canadian Studies*, 5 (Spring 1992), 39–68, at 41–58.

the arrival of strangers on their shores; there, in other parts of the Pacific, they appeared to be hostile; here they approached the ships and threw feathers and dust; there they brandished their spears.

Cook's voyages had a textual momentum. Historians may only read the sections in Douglas's account or Cook's journal which relate to their region, but for Cook's eighteenth-century readers, encounters with different peoples made sense as part of a whole. On his third voyage, especially, Cook tried to "*relate* as well as to *execute*" his voyage, as Douglas put it, by weaving his observations into a narrative.[1] Cook highlighted the differences between the peoples he met by pinpointing their different cultural attributes, or "dispositions" as he sometimes called them. Cook distinguished the "Nootkans" from other groups of indigenous people by emphasizing their trading abilities and strong notions of property. Douglas tried to illuminate Cook's space of comparison: he highlighted difference by dividing Cook's various encounters into chapters, by adding information from the journals of some of Cook's officers, and by drawing more acute contrasts than did Cook between Native peoples and Europeans.[2]

More broadly, eighteenth-century Europeans gauged difference, between themselves and non-Europeans, and between the past and the present, through spatial comparison.[3] European thinkers used explorers' findings as evidence of the historical gradation of societies from "savagery" to "civility."[4] Peoples living beyond Europe were thought to exist behind Europe, in "the innocence and simplicity of the first ages ... just as they came from the hand of nature," as John Callender put it in 1768.[5] Cook's voyages contributed to this pattern of thought.

---

1 Cook and King, *Voyage to the Pacific*, I, lxxvii (emphasis in original). Beaglehole also noted that Cook aimed on his third voyage to write a book that would need little editing when he returned home. Beaglehole, *Journals*, III, clxxii.

2 Douglas drew extensively on the journal of William Anderson, surgeon and naturalist on the *Resolution*. Unfortunately, Anderson's journal has since been lost.

3 This comparative conception of identity, difference, and change lay at the heart of what Michel Foucault called the "classical order of knowledge" in eighteenth-century Europe. See his *The Order of Things: An Archaeology of the Human Sciences* [1966] (New York: Random House, 1970), chapters 4-6.

4 See Ronald L. Meek, *Social Science and the Ignoble Savage* (Cambridge: Cambridge University Press, 1976).

5 John Callender, *Terra Australis Cognita...*, 3 vols. (London and Edinburgh: A. Donaldson, 1766-1768), III, book V, 736.

DANIEL CLAYTON

Cook's textual fabrication of difference was also connected to the geographical momentum of his voyages. Cook tried to capture in writing what Paul Carter calls "the zigzag map created by his passage."[1] Carter argues that the place-names Cook bestowed (most famously, "Botany Bay," and others such as "Islands of Direction" and "Repulse Bay") allude to his journey itself, to its dead ends and successes; and to a disagreement between Cook and the scientists on his ships about how to represent the new. Cook did not simply try to capture the new and the strange in a factual, transparent, scientific manner. He also tried to represent the physical and imaginative act of exploring. For instance, as Cook approached Nootka Sound, and glimpsed what appeared to be an inlet, he bestowed the name "Hope Bay," signalling his hope that a good harbour would eventually be found.[2] Cook was not mistaken, of course, but he kept the name because it alluded to the way he had discovered Nootka Sound and his need at that juncture to find an anchorage where he could repair his ships. Cook's European lenses, Carter suggests, became tinted by his experience of travel.

Representation also became more intricate as each new encounter proceeded. Cook went back over his journal, adjusting statements and polishing his observations. While his ships were stationary, his journal was still on the move. Toward the end of his journal of events at Nootka Sound, for example, Cook tried to reassess the Natives' readiness to trade, and their use of iron. Had such facets of Native life been picked up from Europeans, or were they indigenous? Cook knew that the Spanish had sent explorers to the north Pacific in the mid-1770s, though where, precisely, he did not know. He could not resolve the issue, and simply noted that these people "have been so many years in a manner surrounded by Europeans ... and who knows how far these Indian nations may extend their traffick with one another."[3]

Douglas also tried to account for the possibility that these people had been contacted before by Europeans:

---

1 Paul Carter, *The Road to Botany Bay: An Essay in Spatial History* (London: Faber and Faber, 1987), 27.

2 Beaglehole, *Journals*, III, 294-95.

3 Beaglehole, *Journals*, III, 321-22.

They were earnest in their inquiries, by signs, on our arrival, if we meant to settle amongst them; and if we came as friends ...; the inquiry would have been an unnatural one, on a supposition that any ships had been here before; had trafficked ... and had then departed; for, in that case, they might reasonably expect we would do the same.[1]

In this passage from the official account, sixty-five pages beyond the passage chronicling Cook's arrival at Nootka Sound, we are told that Cook did understand the Natives' harangues — that they wanted to know why he had visited them. Yet Douglas still suggested that the Natives had only one culturally endemic or natural way of viewing strangers, that they would have reacted to Cook and the Spanish in the same way. Cook himself seemed to put parameters around the objectivity of his account of first contact, implying that the inhabitants' initial reaction to his ships was influenced by contact with other strangers and may not have stemmed simply from some natural, endemic mode of behaviour.

These processes of revision point to another possible interpretation of these accounts of first contact at Nootka Sound: that Cook, and then Douglas, wrote them as an introduction to and prospect of things to come; that they served a rhetorical purpose. I will return to this line of inquiry shortly. For now, I want to assess first contact from the margins of Cook's field of vision — in terms of what, retrospectively, we can now say he could not have known and did not discover.

A Spanish vessel anchored near Nootka Sound for two days in August 1774.[2] In 1789 an American trader was told by some Natives of the sound that this Spanish ship had terrified them.[3] In 1792 Native people told a Spanish botanist that they thought the Spanish ship was "Quautz"

---

1   Cook and King, *Voyage to the Pacific*, II, 330-31.

2   Another Spanish ship sailed past Nootka Sound in 1775, and scholars have debated whether these Spaniards met any Native people of Nootka Sound. The Spanish naval historian Martin F. Navarrete thought that they did, and made his case in "Viajes en las costa al norte de las Californias, 1774-1790," English translation by George Davidson (Bancroft Library, University of California — Berkeley, P-B 26), 770-83. As far as is known, these were the only two European ships that were in the vicinity of Nootka Sound before Cook arrived.

3   Joseph Ingraham to José Esteban Martínez [1789], Mexico City, Archivo General de la Nación, Ramo: Historia 65, fojas 52-65, at fojas 63-64, in the *Freeman Tovell Collection, BCARS Add.MSS. 2826.*

(a deity), who was coming "to punish the misdeeds of the people."[1] Fear eventually gave way to curiosity, however, and there was some trade between the two groups.

These Native perceptions might usefully be put together with other ethnographic fragments dealing with the arrival of Cook's ships. In the early twentieth century, Chief George of Nootka Sound related a story about how, one day, the tops of three sticks were seen on the horizon. The sticks were soon identified as a watercraft, and people thought that Haitetlik, the lightning snake, was propelling it. Others considered it a salmon changed by magic. Two chiefs thought it was the work of Quautz. As the craft got closer "all the men and women grew very much afraid," and people were advised to hide. "A woman doctor named Hahatsaik, who had power over all kinds of salmon, appeared with a whalebone rattle in each hand; she put on her red cedar bark cape and apron and sang, saying that it must be a salmon turned into a boat." She called out: "'Hello you, you spring salmon, hello you dog salmon, hello you coho salmon.'" A canoe containing another doctor, Wiwai, then went out; then another canoe with chief Nanaimis and ten strong men went to offer the thing two fine beaver skins. Nanaimis stayed in his canoe but got close enough to the thing to see "that Cook was not an enchanted salmon, but only a man." Maquinna, an important Nuu-chah-nulth chief, then went out, saying to Cook, "'I want you to come and stay with me next year.'"[2]

This text is complemented by others recorded in the 1970s and included in a provincial government publication that formed part of the Cook bicentennial celebrations. In a Native account related by Winifred David, the Native people of the Sound "didn't know what on earth" was approaching. Two canoes of warriors were sent out to see, and thought it was "a fish come alive into people." The warriors took a good look at the men on deck. One of them, with a hooked nose, was thought to be a dog salmon. A hunchback sailor was in Native eyes a

---

1 Moziño, *Noticias de Nutka*, 66.

2 F.W. Howay and E.O.S. Scholefield, *British Columbia: From the Earliest Times to the Present*, 4 vols. (Vancouver: S.J. Clarke, 1914), I, 81-83. According to a Native account heard by Augustus Brabant, a Catholic missionary, Cook entered the Sound at night or in fog, and his ships were not discovered until they had reached their anchorage on Bligh Island. Augustus Brabant to John Walbran, July 19, 1905, Roman Catholic Church. Diocese of Victoria. Papers, 1842-1912. *BCARS Add.MSS. 2742.*

humpback salmon. The warriors reported home that this thing contained fish "come here as people." Chief Maquinna sent more canoes out to see what these people wanted. When the Indians were given some thick white pilot biscuits by Cook's crews they thought these men were friendly and should be treated nicely.

In another account related by Gillette Chipps, Cook's ship was viewed as an island and the Indians danced around it: "They say Indian doctors go out there singing a song, find out, try to find out what it was. Rattling their rattles." They saw white faces on both sides of the island. "Maybe it was the same men on the other side when they go around the other side the same person but different places." Cook also visited their village, and his blacksmith, Tom, fell asleep in the big house as the Indians danced and entertained the Captain. During this time the Indians also learned about pilot bread. "They didn't know what the heck to do with it." Some kept it as a good luck charm; others thought it was poisonous and wouldn't eat it. Peter Webster related that Cook's ships got stuck at sea, could not find their way into Nootka Sound, and a whaling canoe went out to guide the ships to shore.[1]

In these Native texts, the new and the strange, remembered from the past, have undergone historical translation. The four Native people who related these accounts all identified Cook by name. British and American traders came to Nootka Sound in increasing numbers in the late 1780s, and it is possible that oral histories of these first dealings with non-Natives in the late eighteenth century may have been adapted and improvised so as to incorporate such a famous figure as Cook. Floating islands, a white man and his blacksmith, now signify Cook and his ships. Strange objects that carry charms or poison have been identified as ship's biscuits. The anthropologists who went to Nootka Sound in the 1970s were probably looking for stories about Cook. Some of the details in these Native accounts can be found in the European record of Cook's stay; others cannot.

Other Native texts, which I am confident refer to Cook's visit rather than that of some other voyager, do not carry as many of these historical traces, though that is not to say they are necessarily any truer or more

---

1   These three accounts are in Barbara S. Efrat and W.J. Langlois, eds., "The Contact Period as Recorded by Indian Oral Tradition," in Efrat and Langlois, eds., *nu.tka: Captain Cook and the Spanish Explorers on the Coast, Sound Heritage*, Vol. VII, no. 1 (1978), 54-62, at 54-58.

authentic than the accounts presented above. When the missionary C.M. Tate was at Nootka Sound around 1880, he recorded some details that had been passed down by Native elders: "we were all down at the ocean beach cutting up a large whale which had been found stranded the previous day when looking across the big water we saw something white that looked like a great seagull." Some thought it was a large bird from the sky that had come to earth to eat the people. "This made us all afraid," the account continues, "and we ran off to the woods to hide ourselves. We peeped out from behind the trees to see what it would do, when we saw it go right past the point and into the bay where our village was." The old people "got very much afraid," but the younger ones "were anxious to know what it was." The wise men of the tribe held a council and one old man said it was a moon from the sky using a sea serpent for its canoe. "As this great thing was now standing still, the old man suggested that two of the young men, who had no wives, should take a canoe, and go off ... to see what it was. If they were swallowed up, they would have no wives or children to grieve for them, and then we would know that it was dangerous." The two men who went out were afraid to go near the moon "for some time," but eventually decided to make "a bold dash" toward it. They found men with a great deal of hair on their faces, and were frightened until one of "the strange men beckoned with his hand for them to go near." They plucked up the courage to paddle alongside the moon's canoe. "Very soon," the account states,

> a rope ladder was dropped down, and one of the moon men beckoned for them to come up. They tied their canoe to the rope ladder, and climbed up the side of the moon's canoe, when they were surprised with everything they saw. One of the men, with bright buttons on his coats, spoke to another man, who went down into the very heart of the moon's canoe, and soon came back with two dishes, one of which was full of round flat bones, and the other full of blood [biscuit and molasses]. The man with the bright buttons pointed to the bones and the blood then pointed to his mouth; but the young man did not understand that they wanted them to eat, until one of the moon men took up a piece of the bone, dipped it in the blood, then put it in his mouth ... at the same time holding out the dishes for them to eat also; but they were afraid to touch the moon's food.

The two Natives soon realized that the moon men wanted the skins they were wearing, and an exchange took place. When the two men returned to shore, people were interested in the beads and strange clothing that they had received but "felt afraid" when they were told that the people of moon's canoe lived on bones and blood. The next day some of the moon men came ashore and one of them had a "crooked stick [flintlock gun] which he made speak with a very loud noise." "After a while," the story concludes, "the moon went away, and everybody felt glad."[1]

The last history I will draw on was told by Muchalat Peter to the ethnographer Philip Drucker in the 1930s. Two people from the community of Tcecis saw an island with people and fire on it that looked like "a spirit thing," a TcExa. When this news reached the village the chief assembled all the people for a meeting. A group of men and a shaman were sent to find out more. As the ship came into sight again the shaman began to sing in order to see the spirit in the thing. "I don't think that's a TcExa," she remarked; "I don't see the spirit of it." When they got alongside they saw men eating fire who asked about "pish." The Indians didn't understand them. When they returned to the village they looked back, expecting the thing to have disappeared, but it had not. The old people of the village thought: "That's our great-great grandchildren coming from the other side of the ocean." Many more canoes returned to the thing and circled it. They did not understand what ladders were for but understood the gesture "come up." Chief u'kwisktcik was the first to go up, and others followed. They exchanged their cedar bark mats and returned to the village to get more blankets. When they returned the whites wanted to trade clothes but the Indians were not interested because they did not know how to wear them. They wanted iron spikes to make hooks. Back at the village, the chief wanted to know if any one had had a bad dream about the ship. When they said they hadn't it was surmised that the ship was not a bad spirit. All the people then went to trade furs. A warrior saw a man with a gun. He "went up to the man, placed [the] muzzle of the gun against [his] own breast, because he had on armour ... that could stop [the gun from] 'blowing.' The white signed that [the] Ind[ian] would fall dead, took the latter's garment, folded it, placed it at the end of the ship, [and] shot [a] hole in [it]. Then they knew that was another Tc'Exa, for no arrows could

---

1   This account is in the Tate Family Papers, *BCARS Add.MSS. 303*, box 1, file 6.

DANIEL CLAYTON

pierce his armor." The people returned to the village and wondered what kind of TcExa this was. A fleet of canoes then came from another village to wed a woman to a TcExa man. As they began their feast, "2 boatloads of whites came ashore and stood looking in the doorway. The white captain gave a hat to the chief of the manuasatxa" (people from another village) but his host "became jealous and said the gift had been meant [for] them," and so it was surrendered.[1]

I have paraphrased these accounts (some of which are long), but have tried to retain their narrative progression and structure. They obviously provide a different set of understandings about Cook's arrival; as such, they help us to probe his way of seeing.[2] Like Cook's journal, these accounts are culturally and geographically situated statements about contact. They also point to aspects of this encounter which are obscured in Cook's journal and the official account, but which shine more brightly in the journals of Cook's officers: a more face-to-face, bodily process of interaction, where touch met sight, words failed to translate the meaning of gestures, and human activity on and around the ships could not be easily summarized.

These stories relate a mixture of wonder, astonishment, curiosity, and fear at the sight of strange objects and people. In the official account, gestures, speeches, and songs are registered matter-of-factly; in these Native accounts such actions are invested with supernatural and spiritual meaning. Cook moved into a space that was inhabited with people and meaning, and had already been represented. Chiefs, shamans, and wise people were called upon to interpret the appearance of this strange phenomenon; they had their own discriminatory categories of knowledge, just as Cook did.

---

1   Philip Drucker, "Nootka Field Notebooks," photocopy from the Smithsonian Institution, National Anthropological Archives, *BCARS Add.MSS. 870*, notebook 2, 19–24. Drucker does not state whether this account refers specifically to Cook. His notebook entry is headed: "First contact with whites."

2   Regarding Tate's narrative, it should be noted that missionaries' enthusiasm for recording events of early contact was tied to a politics of conversion. Such stories about first contact were used to mark the spiritual gulf between (Native) heathenism and (white) civilization which was to be closed by the missionary. Nevertheless, it seems that this account was proffered by a Native person rather than solicited by Tate. See Tate's introduction to this account, and his amended reminiscence of it, in J.S. Matthews, ed., *Early Vancouver: Narratives of Pioneers of Vancouver B.C.*, 2 vols. (Vancouver: J.S. Matthews, 1933), II, 130–31.

Comments about first contact made by some of Cook's officers tally with these Native accounts. Lieutenant David Samwell, for one, observed that the Indians "expressed much astonishment at seeing the Ship."[1] The serenity of Cook's first encounter does not exist in Lieutenant James King's journal, which states:

> The first men that came would not approach the Ship very near & seemed to eye us with Astonishment, till the second boat came that had two men in it; the figure & actions of one of these were truly frightful; he workd himself into the highest frenzy, uttering something between a howl & a song, holding a rattle in each hand, which at intervals he laid down, taking handfulls of red Ocre & birds feather & strewing them in the Sea; this was follow'd by a Violent way of talking, seemingly with vast difficulty in uttering the Harshest & rudest words, at the same time pointing to the Shore, yet we did not attribute this incantation to ... any ill intentions towards us.[2]

Many of the "facts" of first contact included in the official account come from King's journal, then, though Douglas toned down King's animated prose.

Cook and his officers recorded some events that are recounted in the Native accounts, though in a different narrative order. In Chief George's story, Maquinna invites Cook to come and stay next year. Cook and some of his officers state that this invitation was extended as the ships were leaving the Sound.[3] Cook did visit two Native villages, in two boats, with some marines (with "crooked sticks"), and gave out presents. The first village he visited, Yuquot, is that mentioned in the accounts related by David and Tate. (It is depicted on Edgar's map, on the western lip of the Sound.) On the basis of Cook's journal, the second village was Tcesis, as Muchalat Peter's testimony confirms. (On Edgar's map this village is the lower black rectangle depicted to the northeast of the island in the middle of the sound.) The "Surly chief" whom Cook reported meeting there may have been offended because

---

1 Beaglehole, *Journals*, III, 1088-9.

2 Beaglehole, *Journals*, III, 1393-4.

3 Beaglehole, *Journals*, III, 308; John Rickman, "Log," n.d. *PRO ADM 51/4529[46]*, fol.217.

DANIEL CLAYTON

the captain gave a present to a chief from another village and ignored him.[1] Midshipman Edward Riou noted that when Cook visited this second village, on 20 April, he "found more of our Old acquaintances than at the town to the So:ward," confirming that these people had been trading regularly with Cook's ships.[2] Lieutenant John Williamson reported that some Native people asked him how his musket worked, and that they laughed when he told them the ball would pierce their armour. Williamson folded a Native garment about six times, pinned it to a tree, and fired at it, putting a hole through it and embedding the ball in the tree.[3] The only difference between this account and that given by Drucker's informant is that the event occurred on shore. Finally, within two days of Cook's arrival, the Natives of the Sound had boarded the ships and were trading furs and cedar blankets for metal goods. In short, these European and Native texts relate similar details about this encounter, but from different cultural perspectives.[4]

---

1   Beaglehole, *Journals*, III, 304.

2   Edward Riou, "A log of the proceedings of His Majesty's ship Discovery," 20 April 1778, *PRO ADM 51/4529[42]*, fol.78v.

3   Beaglehole, *Journals*, III, 1350. Thomas Edgar also recorded this event in his "Journal," 4 April 1778, *BL Add.MS. 37,528*, fols. 91-91v, a partial copy of which was deposited in the Provincial Library in Victoria, B.C., but not until after Drucker had interviewed Muchalat Peter. Some "facts" from the European record may have been smuggled into Native oral histories over the years. It seems unlikely that this event was, however. Beaglehole was the first scholar that I know of who cited either Williamson's or Edgar's observation.

4   I am fairly certain that these Native accounts relate to Cook rather than to subsequent voyagers, though some of the cultural emphases in them may point to a more composite set of Native understandings of non-Native strangers synthesized from the first ten or so years of contact. After 1778, however, Nootka Sound was not visited again by Europeans until August 1785, when the brig *Sea Otter* under James Hanna arrived to trade sea otter furs. A few days after Hanna arrived a Native group in the sound attacked his vessel and were "repulsed [by Hanna] with considerable slaughter." Surely, the Native accounts that I have presented would have related this slaughter if they were chronicling Hanna's stay; Hanna's actions are recounted in other Native accounts. After 1785, when British and American trading vessels came to Nootka Sound in increasing numbers, the Native people of the sound grew increasingly accustomed to non-Natives and knew some vessel captains by name. The quotation about Hanna's voyage is from an English newspaper: London, *World*, 6 October 1788, in *White Knight Chapbooks: Pacific Northwest Series*, no. 4 (San Francisco: White Knight Press, 1941).

The Native accounts also show that first contact was embedded in a complex human geography. They involve different Native groups, villages, families, and individuals.[1] Native histories were passed down along these lines. Events happened at the intersection of family routines and geopolitical rivalries, human dramas and emotions, material and spiritual life, bonds of kinship and the exploits of individuals. Contact had composite meaning. The bodies of white strangers materialized with hooked noses and beards which were associated with natural and spiritual worlds. The two people in Tate's narrative looked on ship's biscuit and molasses as bones and blood: as signs, perhaps, of cannibalism.

Why were these sentiments of fear and astonishment, picked up by some of Cook's officers, excluded from the official account – especially the observations of King, who helped Douglas edit Cook's journal? To return to my earlier line of inquiry, I suggest that Cook's and Douglas's accounts of first contact did not rest simply on canons of objectivity, or modes of comparison and recollection. They also served a rhetorical purpose. During this era of scientific exploration, and especially in Cook's case, statements about first contact served as parables of Europe's scientific, civilizing mission. Such statements traded on the belief that "successful intercourse" would be had with the Natives.[2] Their lands were discovered, their cultures were recorded, people were treated fairly, and few got hurt, because contact was executed and related in the pacific blink of a scientific eye.

Statements about first contact mesh past, present, and future. When Cook met a new group of people, he assessed the progress of his voyage and shaped its broader message at the site of his discovery. The images of friendship and the prospect of trade that Cook worked into his journal helped to confirm his status as a gentle and humane explorer trading the

---

1   In 1778, over 15 groups of Native people lived at Nootka Sound, each of which hailed from particular villages and owned specific territories. A number of groups on the west side of the sound were at this time allied in a political and economic confederacy. Most of the groups on the east side of the sound were autonomous. See Yvonne Marshall, "A Political History of the Nuu-chah-nulth: A Case Study of the Mowachaht and Muchalaht Tribes," Ph.D. Dissertation, Department of Archaeology, Simon Fraser University, 1993.

2   I borrow this phrase from Tom Dutton's exemplary essay, "'Successful intercourse was had with the natives': aspects of European contact methods in the Pacific," in Donald C. Laycock and Werner Winter, eds., *A World of Language: Papers Presented to Professor S.A. Wurm on his 65th Birthday* (Pacific Linguistics, C-100, 1987), 153-71.

trappings of European civilization. His factual prose confirmed his status as an objective, detached observer.[1] Douglas tried to bolster this image of Cook in his account of first contact at Nootka Sound, by working with some of King's observations to give the event a ceremonial and scientific quality.

When Cook arrived at Nootka Sound he did not jump to conclusions. He narrated the event using the collective pronoun "we" and Douglas followed suit. Cook highlighted the fact that he contacted the inhabitants of Nootka Sound as a representative of his country, and as an ambassador of European civilization. Another officer in the party, Captain Charles Clerke of the *Discovery*, saw himself in a similar light, and wrote at first contact at Nootka Sound: "We could not induce them to come on board, but they had no weapons, & behaved very peaceably & socially, which I hope & flatter myself we shall be able to improve upon."[2]

These ways of visualizing and representing Native peoples relied on a set of disciplinary practices: the control that Cook could wield over his own narrative, the discipline he could exercise over his crews, the confidence he could place in the military superiority of his ships, and the means he had at his disposal for keeping the lid on the unseen and the unthought. But in order to maintain these forms of discipline, Cook had to delegate responsibility. He had to encourage his officers to keep detailed logs so that he might consult them to flesh out his own observations, base his dealings with Native peoples on a division of labour, and plan for the possibility of attack. In short, he had to allow his crews to see and do things out of the scope of his own vision. Cook could not be "the same person but different places," as Gillette Chipps put it in one of the Native accounts.

The principles of consultation and exactitude that Cook forged to maintain his status as the chief author of his voyage disrupted the authority of his representations. Cook's officers paid close attention to their captain's actions, but their journals still drift off in different directions.

---

1   Bernard Smith shows that on his third voyage Cook used his artist, John Webber, to portray images of peace and harmony. This was a "highly selective truth," for Cook allowed tension and violence to breed on his third voyage — much of which he was responsible for, and which ended in disaster when Hawaiian Islanders killed him. Smith, *Imagining the Pacific*, 206.

2   Charles Clerke, "Log and proceedings," 29 March 1778, *PRO ADM 55/22*, fol.151.

These officers recorded many things that are not in Cook's journal, and some of their observations contradict those of their captain. Cook's officers also traded observations and borrowed passages from each other. And what about the "ordinary" sailors who made up the bulk of the ships' companies and were left mostly in the dark about official matters: instructions about what to observe, and how to represent what they saw? "Is it not quite a different path that he travels and can this path ever cross that of the more experienced observer?" wrote one such sailor who sailed on Cook's third voyage; "is it not possible for one traveller to recall what another might forget?"[1]

Cook's crews found the time and space to do things behind his back. At Nootka Sound, truth and objectivity became dispersed and decentred. When, for instance, on 4 April 1778, a large number of canoes full of armed men circled the *Resolution* and *Discovery*, and a Native attack seemed possible, Cook dismissed the event in his journal with a measured, dispassionate prose. He felt sure that his ships had been in no danger. He understood by signs from the Natives that "it was not us they were arming against," was satisfied that this was a quarrel between rival Native groups, and implied in his journal that he simply sat back and observed these rival groups arguing with one another.[2] But Cook's officers wrote different accounts of this event. Cook, evidently, did not just sit back. He sent out King and some armed marines in a boat to assess how dangerous the situation was.[3] Midshipman George Gilbert reported that while Cook did not want to intrude on what seemed to be a Native affair (this being part of his humanitarian mandate), he came very close to firing on some canoes that came alongside the ships.[4] Samwell did not trust the Natives' signs, and judged that "from every appearance" the Natives meant to attack the ships.[5] In sum, while Cook wrote about

---

1   F.W. Howay, ed., *Zimmermann's Captain Cook: An Account of the Third Voyage of Captain Cook Around the World, 1776-1780* [first published in German, 1781] (Toronto: Ryerson Press, 1930), 21-22.

2   Beaglehole, *Journals*, III, 299.

3   Beaglehole, *Journals*, III, 1397.

4   Christine Holmes, ed., *Captain Cook's Final Voyage: The Journal of Midshipman George Gilbert* (Horsham: Caliban Books, 1982), 70.

5   Beaglehole, *Journals*, III, 1092-93.

DANIEL CLAYTON

these proceedings as if he had been in total control of the situation, some of his officers were quite frightened and reported their agitation in their journals.

Cook's officers also produced a great range of opinion about the peoples of the sound. When, for instance, they tried to assess in their journals the meaning of these events of 4 April, they focused on Native speeches and songs (or "harangues" as they called them), and came to different conclusions about what they said about Native manners and customs. Nathaniel Portlock, speaking for some of his fellow officers, stated that the Natives' war songs were "the most warlike and awfull thing they ever heard" and suggested that these people were savage.[1] Samwell thought that these harangues showed that the people of the sound had a "brave" and "resolute" disposition.[2] Lieutenant James Burney, on the other hand, appreciated the harmonies of Native songs, and suggested that while these people were "very apt to take offence at the slightest indignity, ... to do them justice ... any degree of submission immediately pacifies them."[3] Riou noted that Native verbal altercations were passionate, but also emphasized that they were very orderly. One protagonist would not interrupt another's speech, and harangues seldom resulted in fighting.[4] Midshipman James Trevenan put this down to their "fearless independent spirit which apprehended no danger from any other than the person with whom they had particularly quarelled."[5] William Bayly, Cook's astronomer, added that the orderliness of Native harangues showed that these people were "free from malice & design."[6]

---

1 Nathaniel Portlock, "Log," 4 April 1778, *PRO ADM 51/4531[68]*, fol.293v.

2 Beaglehole, *Journals*, III, 1100.

3 James Burney, "Journal of a Voyage in the Discovery," 4 April 1778, *PRO ADM 51/4528/45*, fol.227.

4 Riou, "Log," 4 April 1778, fol.80v.

5 James Trevenan, "Notes Regarding the Death of Captain Cook," 3. *BCARS A/A40/C77T/A2*.

6 William Bayly, "Journals and a log kept on Capt. Cook's second and third voyages around the world," 2nd journal, 12 August 1777-30 June 1778, Alexander Turnbull Library, National Library of New Zealand, Wellington, micro 343.

These officers had different personalities, backgrounds, and literary talents; such differences are reflected in their journal writing.[1] What they recorded also depended in good measure on what they could see from their positions on the ship or on the shore. The kinds of dealings they had with Native people also depended on their rank. It was these issues of location, personality, and rank that were at play in the officers' range of opinion over different events, and in their generalizations about Native people. Bayly complained that he saw very little of the Natives' manners and customs because Cook's ships were tucked away in a cove distant from their villages, and Native people came mostly to trade.[2] Cook's emphasis on the Nootkans' trading abilities, then, was conditioned by the location of his ships. King noted that because of "the narrow confind sphere" of observation at Nootka Sound, it was difficult to distinguish the "invariable & constant springs" of Native life (their natural essence) from fashion and improvisation.[3] And in spite of the seemingly objective nature of his prose, Cook himself confided to an associate in London in 1776 that he and his officers "could not be certain of any information they got" on their travels "except as to objects falling under the observation of sense."[4]

All of this fractures the idea that Cook and his officers captured something original and immediate about the distant and the new in a transparent fashion. These Native accounts signify far more than a different cultural perspective. They point to precisely these micro-geographical aspects of contact, and to these issues of representation: to the variety and physicality of this encounter; to actions and meanings that could not easily be represented or summarized.[5]

Representation, then, was a spatial problematic. It revolved around Cook's movements, his "zigzag" path across the Pacific, the location of

---

1   Their logs and journals, collected by the Admiralty at the end of the voyage, are housed (mainly) in London, in the Public Record Office (Kew), and in the Manuscripts Room of the British Museum.

2   Bayly, "Journals and Log," no.2, n.d., fol.102.

3   Beaglehole, *Journals*, III, 1406.

4   James Boswell, *The Journals of James Boswell, 1760-1795* (London: Heinemann, 1991), 306-307.

5   See Obeyesekere, *Apotheosis of Captain Cook*, who has also made an argument about the dispersion of truth and objectivity.

his ships amid Native peoples, the position of his officers and crew on those ships, and the physical and rhetorical demarcation of distance and difference between Europeans and Natives. In a much broader sense, representation revolved around the traffic of European ideas and agendas in non-European space.[1]

★   ★   ★

In historical discourses on British Columbia, historical truth is most precious at its point of origin, when Native people "entered history" by being contacted by literate Europeans.[2] Cook's discovery of Nootka Sound marked the start of history in British Columbia, so colonial historians argued earlier this century; Cook was invited to land — and, by implication, to take nominal possession of the coast — by friendly Natives who were eager to trade and please.[3] More recently, historians have argued that the images of trade and tranquillity that pervade Cook's journal indicate that the early contact period in British Columbia was beneficial for Native peoples, and that relations of domination did not set in until colonists arrived in the second half of the nineteenth century and Native groups were placed on reserves.[4] In both cases, the historical record of Cook's stay at Nootka Sound has been treated largely at face value. Issues of representation have been sidelined. I suggest that an awareness of such issues should make us more cautious and self-conscious about the ways in which we pattern the past and connect it to the present. Cook's encounter with the Nuu-chah-nulth people of Nootka

---

1 For a stunning account of these spatial dynamics of European contact and representation during this period, see Greg Dening, *Mr Bligh's Bad Language: Passion, Power, and Theatre on the* Bounty (Cambridge: Cambridge University Press, 1992).

2 On the mystique of first contact between Europeans and Native peoples, and how it influences views of history and colonialism, see Carter, *Road to Botany Bay*, introduction.

3 This view was stated most directly and succinctly in 1924, when a cairn commemorating Cook was unveiled at Nootka Sound. See W.N. Sage, "Unveiling of Memorial Tablet at Nootka Sound," *Second Annual Report and Proceedings of the British Columbia Historical Association*, 1924, 17-22.

4 See especially Robin Fisher, *Contact and Conflict: Indian-European Relations in British Columbia, 1774-1890* (Vancouver: University of British Columbia Press, 1977).

Sound does not point in any single direction. The images of peace and trade that pervade Cook's journal are, in part, fabricated truths connected to his own self-estimation as a messenger of European civilization. What followed Cook along the northwest coast of North America was a turbulent and sometimes violent trade in sea otter pelts between Native groups and American, British, and Russian merchants.

None of the texts I have considered defines Cook's stay at Nootka Sound. They each contain partial truths hatched at the intersection of Native and European perceptions of the other in 1778. But taken together, these texts allow us to ask questions about how and why certain representations are taken to be factual and true, while others get buried, ignored, or dismissed.[1] These issues are important in British Columbia because Native peoples pursuing land claims in the courts have encountered judges who think that the observations of white explorers are more factual, objective, and reliable than Native oral traditions.[2] There are strict legal rules about what counts as admissible evidence in court, of course, but in applying such rules to Native land issues judges have also adhered to the ideology of scientific exploration. These judges, and some historians, have assumed that the texts of explorers are reliable because they conform to a European model of what counts as truth — that these texts are truthful because they are first-hand reports that were written on the spot. I have argued that while Cook and his officers may have endeavoured to follow this model, they did not, and perhaps could not, conform to it entirely. When we tackle questions of representation in historical texts (especially texts that represent European-Native encounters), and think about them in relation to these current issues, we begin to see that models of truth are always bound up with cultural relations of power.

---

1 For an assessment of the way these issues are beginning to influence scholarship on Cook, see Paul Carter, "Violent Passages: Pacific Histories," *Journal of Historical Geography*, 20, 1 (1994), 81-86.

2 The most controversial judgement concerning Native land claims in British Columbia is *Delgammuukw et al. v. the Queen*. In his *Reasons for Judgement* (Supreme Court of British Columbia, 8 March 1991), 49, Chief Justice Allan McEachern admitted that he worked with "a different view of what is fact and what is belief" than the Native plaintiffs, who he thought had "a romantic view of their history." This judgement has since passed, largely unchanged, through the British Columbia Court of Appeal. Few land treaties were ever signed between white colonists and Native groups in British Columbia.

DANIEL CLAYTON

References

Barrett, Charlotte, ed. *Diary & Letters of Madame D'Arblay, vol.1 (1778 – June 1781)*. London: Macmillan, 1904.

Baudet, Henri. *Paradise on Earth: Some Thoughts on European Images of Non-European Man*. New Haven, CT: Yale University Press, 1965.

Bayly, William. "Journals and a log kept on Capt. Cook's second and third voyages around the world," 2nd journal, 12 August 1777-30 June 1778, Alexander Turnbull Library, National Library of New Zealand, Wellington, micro 343.

Beaglehole, J.C., ed. *The Journals of Captain Cook on His Voyages of Discovery, Vol. III: The Voyage of the* Resolution *and* Discovery, *1776-1780*. Cambridge: Hakluyt Society, extra series xxxvi, 1967.

——. *Cook the Writer*. Sydney, Australia: Sydney University Press, 1970.

——. *The Life of Captain James Cook*. Stanford, CA: Stanford University Press, 1974.

Boswell, James. *The Journals of James Boswell, 1760-1795*. London: Heinemann, 1991.

Burney, James. Journal of a Voyage in the Discovery. *ADM 51/4528/45*. Public Record Office, London.

Callender, John. *Terra Australis Cognita: Or, Voyages to the Terra Australis, or Southern Hemisphere*. London and Edinburgh: A. Donaldson, 1766-1768.

Carter, Paul. *The Road to Botany Bay: An Essay in Spatial History*. London: Faber and Faber, 1987.

——. Violent passages: Pacific Histories. *Journal of Historical Geography*, 20 (1), 1994, 81-86.

Clerke, Charles. Log and Proceedings, *ADM 55/22*, Public Record Office, London.

Cook, James, and James King. *A Voyage to The Pacific Ocean... Performed Under the Direction of Captains Cook, Clerke, and Gore, In His Majesty's Ships the Resolution and the Discovery. In the Years 1776, 1777, 1778, 1779, and 1780*, 3 vols. and atlas. London: G. Nichol and T. Cadell, 1784.

Delgammuukw et al. v. the Queen. Unreported *Reasons for Judgement* of Chief Justice Allan McEachern, British Columbia Supreme Court, No. 0843 Smithers Registry, 8 March 1991.

Dening, Greg. *Mr Bligh's Bad Language: Passion, Power, and Theatre on the Bounty*. Cambridge: Cambridge University Press, 1992.

Drucker, Philip. Nootka Field Notebooks. *Add.MSS. 870*, British Columbia Archives and Records Service, Victoria.

Dutton, Tom. 'Successful intercourse was had with the natives': aspects of European contact methods in the Pacific. In Donald C. Laycock and Werner Winter, eds., *A World of Language: Papers Presented to Professor S.A. Wurm on his 65th Birthday*. Pacific Linguistics, C-100, 1987.

Edgar, Thomas. Journal. *Add.MS. 37,528*, British Library, London.

——. Log. ADM 55/21, Public Record Office, London.

Efrat, Barbara S., and W.J. Langlois, eds. *nu.tka: Captain Cook and the Spanish Explorers on the Coast, Sound Heritage*, 7 (1), 1978.

Fisher, Robin. *Contact and Conflict: Indian-European Relations in British Columbia, 1774-1890*. Vancouver: University of British Columbia Press, 1977.

Foucault, Michel. *The Order of Things: An Archaeology of the Human Sciences*. New York: Random House, 1970.

——. *The Birth of the Clinic: An Archaeology of Medical Perception*. London: Tavistock Publications, 1973.

Harley, J. Brian. Rereading the Maps of the Columbian Encounter. *Annals of the Association of American Geographers*. 82 (3), 1992, 522-542.

Holmes, Christine, ed. *Captain Cook's Final Voyage: The Journal of Midshipman George Gilbert*. Horsham: Caliban Books, 1982.

Howay, F.W., ed. *Zimmermann's Captain Cook: An Account of the Third Voyage of Captain Cook Around the World, 1776-1780*. Toronto: The Ryerson Press, 1930.

Howay, F.W., and E.O.S. Scholefield. *British Columbia: From the Earliest Times to the Present*, 4 vols. Vancouver: S.J. Clarke, 1914.

Ingraham, Joseph. Letter to José Esteban Martínez [1789], *Freeman Tovell Collection, Add.MSS. 2826*, British Columbia Archives and Records Service, Victoria.

McGrane, Bernard. *Beyond Anthropology: Society and the Other*. New York: Columbia University Press, 1989.

MacLaren, I.S. Exploration/travel literature and the evolution of the author. *International Journal of Canadian Studies*, 5, 1992, 39-68.

Marshall, Yvonne. A Political History of the Nuu-chah-nulth: A Case Study of the Mowachaht and Muchalaht Tribes. Ph.D. Dissertation, Department of Archaeology, Simon Fraser University, Burnaby, BC, 1993.

Matthews, J.S., ed. *Early Vancouver: Narratives of Pioneers of Vancouver, B.C.*, 2 vols. Vancouver: J.S. Matthews, 1933.

Meek, Ronald L. *Social Science and the Ignoble Savage*. Cambridge: Cambridge University Press, 1976.

Moziño, José Mariano. *Noticias de Nutka: An Account of Nootka Sound in 1792*, Iris H. Wilson Engstrand, ed., Seattle: University of Washington Press, 1970.

Navarrete, Martin F. Viajes en las costa al norte de las Californias, 1774-1790. [1802] English translation by George Davidson. Bancroft Library, University of California—Berkeley, P-B 26.

Obeyesekere, Gananath. *The Apotheosis of Captain Cook: European Mythmaking in the Pacific*. Princeton, NJ: Princeton University Press, 1992.

Portlock, Nathaniel. Log. *ADM 51/4531[68]*, Public Record Office, London.

Pratt, Mary Louise. *Imperial Eyes: Travel Writing and Transculturation*. London and New York: Routledge, 1992.

Rickman, John. Log. *ADM 51/4529[46]*, Public Record Office, London.

Riou, Edward. Log. *ADM 51/4529[42]*, Public Record Office, London.

Roman Catholic Church. Diocese of Victoria. Papers, 1842-1912. *Add.MSS. 2742*, British Columbia Archives and Records Service, Victoria.

Rose, Deborah Bird. *Dingo Makes Us Human: Life and Land in an Aboriginal Australian Culture*. Cambridge: Cambridge University Press, 1992.

Sage, W.N. Unveiling of memorial tablet at Nootka Sound. *Second Annual Report and Proceedings of the British Columbia Historical Association*, 1924, 17-22.

Said, Edward W. *Orientalism*. New York: Random House, 1978.

——. *Culture and Imperialism*. New York: Alfred A. Knopf, 1993.

Smith, Bernard. *Imagining the Pacific: In the Wake of Cook's Voyages*. New Haven and London: Yale University Press, 1992.

Stafford, Barbara Maria. *Voyage into Substance: Art, Science, and the Illustrated Travel Account, 1760-1840*. London, England, and Cambridge, MA: MIT Press, 1984.

Tate Family Papers. *Add.MSS. 303*, British Columbia Archives and Records Service, Victoria.

Trevenan, James. Notes Regarding the Death of Captain Cook. *A/A40/C77T/A2*, British Columbia Archives and Records Service, Victoria.

White Knight Chapbooks: Pacific Northwest Series, no. 4. San Francisco: White Knight Press, 1941.

Withey, Lynne. *Voyages of Discovery: Captain Cook and the Exploration of the Pacific*. New York: William Morrow, 1987.

Young, Robert. *White Mythologies: Writing History and the West*. London: Routledge, 1990.

6

The Challenge of James Douglas and Carrier Chief Kwah

Frieda Esau Klippenstein

DOCUMENTING AND INTERPRETING the Native North American past has become a practical as well as theoretical problem for me as a public historian answering both to Parks Canada employers and to members of a Carrier Native community in north-central British Columbia. The Carrier, as these Dene people are known, are central figures in the story communicated at a National Historic Site in the village of Fort St. James. They were the predominant Native group that Montreal-based North West Company fur traders encountered when they began establishing a network of inland posts on the northern Pacific slope in 1805. The task that was given to me — to provide a history of the role of the Carrier in the fur trade "with attention to Native perspectives" — paved a wide path into numerous minefields, as I examined historical and anthropological sources and initiated and supervised an oral history project with Carrier elders. My insistence that an understanding of Carrier perspectives required looking beyond documents to contemporary oral sources was met with some suspicion from academic colleagues, Parks staff, and others. Could I get past the limitations of oral memory and sift through biases to get at "the historical facts"? The attitude articulated by one scholar in his 1958 master's thesis on the Babine Lake Carrier remains predominant: "Incidents that occurred during this [fur trade] period are still remembered by the Babines today even though the facts are often altered" (Hackler 1958:75).

The notion that reliable historical accounts derive only from the written word is challenged by comparing a range of stories about one prominent incident from early fur trade interactions at Fort St. James. The incident involved Kwah (ca. 1755-1850), a Carrier *deneza-cho* of the Stuart Lake area.[1] Kwah's status and leadership qualities were quickly recognized by the first European traders in the region who made him

---

1 The name has various spellings: Kw'eh, K'wah, ?Kwah, Quâs, Qua, Gweh. *Deneza-cho* has most often been translated as "chief." One Carrier elder recently described the position as more akin to "prime minister of the Carrier nation."

"fur trade chief." In this capacity he was expected to channel trade to the post, keep his countrymen from their previous ties to the coastal trade, and generally act as broker between the Carrier and the Stuart Lake post (later known as Fort St. James), which was the district headquarters. Kwah's relationship with the North West Company traders and (after the coalition of companies in 1821) with the Hudson's Bay Company men, was alternately cooperative and stormy. Pivotal confrontations occurred, threatening to change the course of the Carrier-European trade relationship. In 1811, for instance, Nor'Wester Daniel Harmon (1957:143-6) gave Kwah a "drubbing" for his "insolence" in the trade shop, after which Kwah re-established peace by inviting Harmon to a potlatch feast.

The confrontation examined here involved Kwah and Hudson's Bay Company clerk James Douglas in 1828. In both the Carrier communities and in the history books, the conflict between Kwah and Douglas has acquired legendary qualities. Both emerged from it as heroes in their own spheres: Douglas went on to become the governor of the colony of British Columbia, while Kwah's status and reputation were also enhanced. Various renditions of this story survive both in document form and in oral tradition. A comparison of these versions illustrates how historical events and experiences are written from particular perspectives, and suggests that events are interpreted and realities constructed in order to suit specific purposes. The comparison casts doubt on the superiority of written texts and shows how over time — in the written and oral traditions alike — history is shaped and reshaped in the telling.

The story of the confrontation between Kwah and James Douglas is described in historical studies of British Columbia by Bancroft (1886:473-5, 1890:288), Begg (1894:135-7), Morice (1978:139-152), Akrigg and Akrigg (1975:255-6), McKelvie (1949:26-31), Fisher (1977:37), and Barman (1990:44-5). It is told in Bryce's (1904:398-400) history of the Hudson's Bay Company, Van Kirk's (1980:111-13) study of women in fur trade society, and Mulhall's (1986:165) examination of Carrier community dynamics. It appears in biographies of James Douglas (Sage 1930:45-51, 363; Coats & Gosnell 1909:104-10; Pethick 1969:17-22; Gardner 1976:14-17; and Ormsby 1972:239); and in the profiles of Kwah by Bishop (1988:474-5, 1980:199-202). Virtually all of these tellings are based on the same one or two accounts — that of fur trader John McLean, first published in 1849, or that of his fellow trader

John Tod whose story, told to interviewers in 1878, was preserved in manuscript and published forms.[1]

The story-tellers generally agree that the conflict between Kwah and Douglas began in 1823 at Fort George, a trading post at the forks of the Fraser and Bulkley Rivers, in the northern British Columbia region then known as New Caledonia. There, two Hudson's Bay Company men were killed by two Carrier men while the master of the post, James M. Yale, was away. John McLean (1932:166-7) introduced his version as follows:

> Fort George was established a few years ago, and passed through the bloody ordeal ere yet the buildings were completed. The gentleman in charge, Mr Yale, had left his men at work, and gone on a visit to Fort St. James, where he only remained a few days; on his return he found his men had been treacherously murdered by the Indians during his absence. Their mangled bodies were found in one of the houses, with one of their own axes by their side, which evidently had been the instrument of their destruction. The poor men were in the habit of retiring to rest during the heat of the day, and were despatched while they slept.

The Hudson's Bay Company responded with shock and dismay and vowed to avenge the deaths. One of the Carrier was quietly killed under mysterious circumstances,[2] while the other remained at large, repeatedly evading the company's efforts to capture him.

The second chapter in the story followed five years later. In early August 1828 the Carrier fugitive was reported to be in the Nak'azdli Carrier village near Fort St. James, while the district chief factor, William Connolly, was absent. McLean (1932:162-4) did not link the two chap-

---

1 John McLean's 1849 book was edited and republished in 1932. John Tod's memoirs were preserved in the manuscript "History of New Caledonia & The Northwest Coast, Victoria 1878" by an interviewer for historian H.H. Bancroft. Tod's memoirs were also collected by G.H. Wilson-Brown for publication in the Victoria *Daily Times*, in 1905. They were later edited and republished by Madge Wolfenden in 1954.

2 Some versions say he was killed in the mountains "in the Blackfoot country" (Tod 1878, typescript p.20), "by the Blackfeet" (Bancroft 1886:473), by "his own people" (Connolly c.1900:21), or by the Cree (McKelvie 1949:27, HBCA: B 188/a/8, p.83). Others maintain that the Hudson's Bay Company secretly did him in (Morice 1978:142).

ters, but saw the Fort George murders and the Fort St. James episode as two separate stories, even reversing their order in his manuscript:

A native of Frazer's Lake had murdered one of the Company's servants, and, strange to say, no steps were taken to punish him; he concealed himself some time, and finding he had nothing to apprehend, returned to his village. At length he was led by his evil genius to visit Stuart's Lake, then under the command of a Douglas. Douglas heard of his being in the village, and though he had but a weak garrison, determined that the blood of the white man should not be unavenged. The opportunity was favourable, the Indians of the village were out on a hunting excursion, the murderer was nearly alone. He proceeded to the camp accompanied by two of his men, and executed justice on the murderer. On their return in the evening, the Indians learned what had happened, and enraged, determined to retaliate. Aware, however, that Douglas was on his guard, that the gates were shut and could not be forced, they resolved to employ Indian stratagem.

The old chief [Kwah] accordingly proceeded to the Fort alone, and knocking at the gate desired to be admitted, which was granted. He immediately stated the object of his visit, saying that a deed had been done in the village which subjected himself and his people to a heavy responsibility to the relatives of the dead; that he feared the consequences, and hoped that a present would be made to satisfy them; and continuing to converse thus calmly, Mr. Douglas was led to believe that the matter could easily be arranged. Another knock was now heard at the gate: "It is my brother," said the chief, "you may open the gate; he told me he intended to come and hear what you had to say on this business."

The gate was opened, and in rushed the whole Nekasly tribe, the chief's brother at their head; and the men of the Fort were overpowered ere they had time to stand on their defence. Douglas, however, seized a wall-piece that was mounted in the hall, and was about to discharge it on the crowd that was pouring in upon him, when the chief seized him by the arms, and held him fast. For an instant his life was in the utmost peril. Surrounded by thirty or forty Indians, their knives drawn, and brandishing them over his head with frantic gestures, and calling out to the chief, "Shall we strike? shall we strike?"

The chief hesitated; and at this critical moment the interpreter's wife stepped forward, and by her presence of mind saved him and the establishment.

Observing one of the inferior chiefs, who had always professed the greatest friendship for the whites, standing in the crowd, she addressed herself to him, exclaiming, "What? you a friend of the whites, and not say a word in their behalf at such a time as this? Speak? you know the murderer deserved to die; according to your own laws the deed was just; it is blood for blood. The white men are not dogs; they love their kindred as well as you; why should they not avenge their murder?"

The moment the heroine's voice was heard the tumult subsided; her boldness struck the savages with awe; the chief she addressed, acting on her suggestion, interfered; and being seconded by the old chief, who had no serious intention of injuring the whites, was satisfied with showing them that they were fairly in his power. Mr. Douglas and his men were set at liberty; and an amicable conference having taken place, the Indians departed much elated with the issue of their enterprise.

McLean's stories emphasized the savagery of the Fort George killings, the "evil genius" of the "murderer," and the "justice" of Douglas's actions. They dwelt on the treachery of "the old chief's" response and the bravery of the woman who rescued the situation. These images were entrenched by historian Alexander Begg (1894), who cited McLean and followed his text closely; and by George Bryce (1904), who quoted portions of McLean's account and elaborated that the woman who saved Douglas was the "daughter of an old trader, James McDougall."

Building on McLean's version, several variations cited women's involvement in the incident. Credit for saving Douglas's life has been given to "Nancy Boucher, the interpreter's wife," or to "the women of the post" in general. Most often, Douglas was saved by the bravery of his wife, Amelia Connolly, daughter of Susanne Pas-de-nom, a Cree woman, and William Connolly, the district chief factor. These versions described how Amelia pleaded for Douglas, threw goods down from a balcony or second floor, and thus won her husband back (see Akrigg and Akrigg 1975:255-6; Van Kirk 1980:111-13). Admiral Moresby (1909:122), who met Douglas in Victoria in 1852, gave this dramatic rendition:

Douglas ... the centre of a horde of maddened Indians, was at his last struggle, when, like Pocahontas herself, an Indian girl, the daughter of a chief, tore her way to his side, held back the savages, and pleaded his cause with such passion that the red man granted his life to her entreaties.

She lived to share his honours, and to become Lady Douglas, wife of the Governor and Commander-in-chief of British Columbia.

Some thirty years after McLean, John Tod told his version of the story to an interviewer collecting reminiscences for H.H. Bancroft's histories of British Columbia and the North West Coast and, on a separate occasion, to journalists G.M. Sproat and G.H. Wilson-Brown. In Tod's rendition, the details of the Fort George "murders" were different, but the image was the same — that of random savagery: "The Canadians were proceeding on the occasion to Fraser's Lake with 2 Indians in a canoe. A fortnight after leaving, the Indians got up one night, attacked the Canadians and chopped their heads off." The ensuing confrontation between Douglas and Kwah, which Tod set in 1825 instead of 1828, happened when "The Indians were gathered in large numbers for a feast — in charge of an Indian's daughter. Some of the natives came from tribes 400 & 500 miles distant." According to Tod, a woman from the Carrier camp tipped off Douglas that the fugitive was down in the camp. Douglas, with others from the fort, fired at "his would be assassin," but it was "Young Connolly," Chief Factor William Connolly's son (Amelia's brother) who killed the man. Apparently he "rushed in, took the indian by the hair of his head, dragged him outside & finished him with the butt end of his musket." In response, "The Indians finding their friend dead set up an awful howl day & night. Douglas heard it, and all at once hundreds of the savages rushed in through the open gates, with their faces blackened, a sure sign there was going to be mischief."

In contrast to McLean's image of Douglas in "utmost peril," Tod presented Douglas as a rather comical figure, with the Carrier binding him only in order to subdue him and negotiate compensation for the death in the village. It was Kwah's great restraint, rather than the women of the fort, that saved the situation from turning to bloodshed:[1]

Mr. Douglas was first seized, bound & carried away to the mess room of the fort. All this time Douglas kept struggling & swearing, but what could he do. They laid him flat on the table; he kicked & plunged, exhausting himself. The chief looked at him saying, "You are tired now & I can talk

---

1 While in Tod's 1878 manuscript we read only of "the chief," his 1905 memoirs specifically name Kwah.

to you." This only exasperated Mr. D. the more, & he renewed his struggle, damning & swearing, calling them big rascals &c.

The Indians replied by saying, "Oh, you must lie down again", &c. At last the Indians commenced to state that Mr. Douglas killed an Indian; that it was right that he should have been killed, but that it was not right that the Indian should be killed in their camp. Had it occurred anywhere else, outside of their camp they observed, they could do nothing. The chief then stated that what they now wanted was some goods to give the friends of the dead man in return for the body.

Mr. Douglas was again vehement & protested against giving anything in return.

The Chief once more retorted — "then *sit down*".

Mr. Douglas finally asked them what they wanted.

They replied that they wanted clothing, axes, tobacco, guns &c. for the father, mother, brother & sister of the deceased; that they were present & held them responsible for this deed.... Mr. Douglas was set free, & having promised, he gave the goods to quiet the matter. [Tod 1878:29-34 typescript]

In a rather macabre side comment, Tod (1878:23-4, typescript) added that just a few days before the interview an old fur trade colleague had "arrived in town (Victoria) ... bringing with him the scull of this same indian who had been shot by Mr Douglas." Tod offered to the interviewer that he would try "to procure it if possible."

In his *History of the Northwest Coast*, Bancroft (1886:473-5) paraphrased Tod's version, emphasizing the comic elements. Douglas was "a pretty morsel for the gods," totally restrained yet threatening to "cut" the whole Carrier nation "to mince-meat" while the "ruler of the redskins" tried to calm him. Tod was also the key source for McKelvie's (1949) "tale of conflict," and anthropologist Charles Bishop's (1980) profile of Kwah. Akrigg and Akrigg (1975:255-6) followed Tod's version as well, and added in a footnote, "Tod was serving in New Caledonia at the time of the incident and certainly would have been well informed about it."

The manuscripts of John Tod and John McLean have become influential and authoritative versions of the Kwah-Douglas story, partly because they were most readily available. The images they present still pervade modern histories whose authors have access to a broad range of sources, including the Hudson's Bay Company records. What they

FRIEDA ESAU KLIPPENSTEIN

omit, however, is the fact that McLean arrived at his Fort St. James posting in 1833, five years after the Douglas-Kwah incident. Further, he admitted that what he knew about it was related to him by "Waccan, the interpreter." Not only was McLean recording the story second hand, years after the event, but, according to Oblate missionary A.G. Morice, who spent some 18 years (1885-1904) in Carrier country and interviewed Carrier elders for their oral traditions, Waccan (Jean Baptiste Boucher) himself was 140 miles away at the time of the incident. Similarly, our other "authority" John Tod was at Fort McLeod, over 80 miles from Fort St. James, during the confrontation between Kwah and Douglas. His versions, in "History of New Caledonia" and in "Career of a Scotch Boy," were told several decades after the event. Although both Tod's and McLean's accounts are in print and easily accessible, neither is exempt from the vagaries of memory — or the creative reinterpretation of later historians.

Nor can one simply look to the original fur trade records for "the true account." The writer of the Fort St. James journal also received his information second hand. Having returned with the fall brigade, he was not at the post at the time of the incident but heard of it "through Indians" before his arrival. Although he is not identified, he appears to have held a position of authority and could well have been Chief Factor Connolly himself, describing a controversial episode in which Douglas, his son-in-law, and some of his own children were central characters. Perhaps not surprisingly, this version ascribed sinister motivations to the Carrier. The rescue was effected not by women, but by Douglas, who emerged the hero saving himself from peril:

> A short time after my arrival, the old Chief Quâ, with some others, came over on a visit to the Fort, but the old Chief for his misconduct a few days after the murderer had been Killed by Mr Douglas ... was not permitted to enter the House. This circumstance of which, through Indians, I had heard something previous to my arrival is as follows. Some days after that affair had taken place this old Rogue Quâ, with as many other of his Tribe as he could muster, entered the Fort and made their way into the House all armed. Mr Douglas suspecting that they had come with some evil intention immediately ——d(?) his Arms, as also his men, but neither of them were able, from the crowd which surrounded them to use them in turning those intruders out of the Fort. It is true that the Indians in these parts used no other violence than to endeavour to preserve them-

selves from injury, and declared that they had no other view in this than to enter into an explanation with Mr Douglas. But as that could have been done without such a display, the most favourable construction which can be put upon their conduct is that their intentions were by intimidation to extort what they might think proper in compensation for the death of their relation. And nothing but the determination Mr Douglas evinced of defending himself to the last, saved him from being pillaged and perhaps from being Killed. [HBCA: B 188/a/12 p. 94-5, September 1828]

One first hand account of the episode *can* be found. William Connolly's son Henry described the Kwah-Douglas confrontation in his autobiography, an obscure source not referred to in any of the renditions I examined. To call it an "eyewitness" account is problematic, given that Henry Connolly wrote as an elderly man recalling his childhood. Nevertheless, he was on the scene, a seven-year-old boy at the time. In his account, Fort George was "taken by the Indians" while Yale was away. The only two HBC men there were killed, and the fort pillaged and burned to the ground. According to Henry Connolly, Douglas responded to the Carrier fugitive's appearance at Fort St. James by assembling a small garrison, "which consisted of one able man named Peter, my brother Will aged about 18 years, and an old man, Cartier, who was almost helpless." Although Tod claimed it was "Young [William] Connolly" who killed the Carrier man, Henry did not mention his brother's role in the matter. He was clearly aware of other tellings of the story, however, and refuted some points. For instance, he strongly denied that the "murderer" was mangled or mistreated after he was shot: "This is altogether false, for the body was cremated by the Indians." Connolly's (c.1900:22-3) description of the events at the Fort is as follows:

[A]bout a week later the Indians rushed in and in a few minutes the fort was filled. My brother seeing this, ran to shut the gates. One of the Indians aimed at him when another one struck the gun up telling him not to fire yet. He managed to close the gate. The hall in the big house was filled up. On a table lay the blunderbuss, which Mr. Douglas was taking up to put away. The second Chief seeing this rushed up to him and tried to take it from him, thinking he was going to be shot, but Mr. Douglas would not let it go. They were struggling for some time. My Mother was going about looking for Peter. The fellow had hidden himself behind the door

FRIEDA ESAU KLIPPENSTEIN

leading into the hall. She got a big axe and gave it to him saying, "Here, take this and use it." As for Cartier, the poor old fellow had hidden himself in the forge. My brother was the only one going about trying to pacify the Indians. My sister Julia, aged about twelve years, got hold of my father's sword which was in the bedroom. She was going into the big room to slash the Indians right and left. Fortunately my Mother met her and asked what she was going to do. She replied, "Going to Kill some of the Indians," but my Mother told her to put the sword back. If she had used it, we would all have been killed. I think I had a hand in the saving, all through God's mercy. My father had left his fire bag in the bedroom with some tobacco in it, which I took and went through the crowd, I managed to reach the first Chief, Mal de Gorge, and offered him the tobacco which he accepted. He took pity on me as I was crying, and told his brother to leave off. He opened the gate and ordered the Indians to go, and then told his brother to go also, and in a very short time the fort was clear.

Henry Connolly emphasized the vulnerability of his family, the small company complement at the post, and the impressive numbers of threatening Carrier. Although this crisis might have led him to question Douglas's judgement in the incident, he defended Douglas's decision to have the man executed ("he only obeyed the orders of the Company"), and followed up his anecdote with a supportive example of how, as the Governor of British Columbia, Douglas "showed great justice to all." The account is a convincing description of a young boy's intense experience, still a vivid memory at the end of his life. In his version, it was not his sister Amelia's offers of compensation which saved the day, but his own actions which won the chief's sympathy. It is also interesting that he remembered Mal de Gorge rather than Kwah as the central figure.[1] He emphasized that while "some writers mention another Indian who had so much to do in saving our lives ... I am positive it was the Mal de Gorge who saved our lives."

While noting these variations in the written renditions of the story, we should ask whose purposes they served. In several instances, a "moral

---

1 "Mal de Gorge" figured prominently in the Fort St. James journals in the early nineteenth century, as a beaver hunter and leading man. I was not able to confirm his identity or status with contemporary Carrier elders, as they did not recognize the name. Possibly it was a nickname (French for "sore throat") used only by the traders.

of the story" emerged. The message in the Hudson's Bay Company accounts was the inevitability and justice of HBC revenge. To the company the Fort George "murders" represented a savagery and lawlessness which threatened to get out of hand in New Caledonia, where the newcomers in their small, isolated posts were vastly outnumbered by the Carrier and other Native peoples of the area. In the reports the Carrier antagonist was not referred to by name, but rather as "the murderer" or "the criminal," a type rather than an individual, and it was taken for granted that he committed an unjust, savage act. The purpose of the company accounts appears to be to celebrate the idea that "the murderer" was necessarily and finally brought to justice. They also downplayed the volatile aftermath of Douglas's action: while travelling in the district later that fall, Douglas was again threatened by a large group of Carrier. His transfer was arranged shortly after that.

The versions emphasizing Douglas's narrow escape gave him a heroic or legendary quality. His actions were referred to retrospectively as contributing to his later success as governor of the colony. This event was, after all, James Douglas's ticket out of Fort St. James. Derek Pethick (1969:20), in his book on Douglas, says that before the confrontation "there seemed little sign that he was marked for greatness." McKelvie (1949:26,31) described the event as placing Douglas in a position where he could realize his "destiny" and assume his rightful place in the history of British Columbia. In his *Early History of the Province of British Columbia*, McKelvie (1926:21) presented Douglas's transfer from Fort St. James as a promotion. Condensing Douglas's entire New Caledonia experience to a sentence, he asserted: "He so proved his worth [there] that he was called to Fort Vancouver in 1830, where his promotion was rapid." Similarly, Bancroft (1890:288) wrote effusively, "The courage and coolness displayed in this encounter with the savages brought the young man fame and favor not only among his associates, but among the natives themselves."

Several elements of these stories work to exonerate Douglas and keep the responsibility for the unrest squarely on the shoulders of the Carrier. For instance, Tod emphasized that the Carrier *agreed* that the fugitive should be killed, but were offended that it took place in the Carrier camp. Douglas's offence, then, was the violation of an eccentric point of Carrier law — or at least one of which he could plausibly have been unaware. Likewise, Tod's story of an "Indian woman" stealing away to the Fort from her sleeping camp, insisting on speaking with Douglas, and

FRIEDA ESAU KLIPPENSTEIN

informing him that the fugitive could be found in the village added to the idea that the Carrier actually initiated and gave Douglas permission to kill the fugitive. This was brought to an extreme by McKelvie (1949) who embellished Tod's story by spelling out the woman's last, whispered words of encouragement, "You come and get him" — effectively releasing Douglas from responsibility for the unsavoury killing that followed. Also working to exonerate Douglas are the many versions of the story emphasizing Carrier demands for material compensation. These effectively trivialize Carrier motivations, reducing Kwah's anger and actions to a quest for simple compensation in the form of a few store items. Trader Archibald McDonald, for instance, repeating what he had heard of the event, reported simply that the Indians "all assembled, and made a clandestine entry into the Fort, and insisted upon getting a blanket" (1971:27).

Versions emphasizing the women's actions add romance to the story. Certainly the image of the fifteen- or sixteen-year-old Amelia's passionate love and courage triumphing over bloodlust and savagery is memorable. This story has appealed to many writers, appearing in school textbooks[1] and in a feminist account (Van Kirk 1980) illustrating the power and usefulness of the "mixed-blood" wives in counterpoint to the minor roles usually ascribed to them. The historian W.N. Sage (1930:44-5), in contrast, used the story in part to praise "Lady Douglas" for traditional feminine virtues: she was "an excellent helpmeet for her distinguished husband." In Sage's hands the story showed how Amelia Douglas "devoted herself to her husband and her family." Clearly, even the role of one young woman in the event can be interpreted in several different ways.

Personal purposes surely influenced how the story was told. Can it be a coincidence that when Waccan told the story to McLean, Waccan's wife Nancy ("daughter of James McDougall") was the heroine who saved Douglas? When Henry Connolly recalled the events, the action revolved around his apparent ability as a young, distraught boy to capture the sympathy of the chief. When Douglas's acquaintance Admiral Fairfax Moresby recorded the incident, Douglas's wife Amelia emerged as the heroine. The post journal writer, possibly Chief Factor William

---

1   See, for instance, the story of "A Quick-Witted Bride" in D. Dickie (1950:259-60). Dickie's textbook, "authorized for use in the schools of Alberta and Newfoundland," was a part of my own junior high school experience.

Connolly, credited his employee and son-in-law Douglas as bravely saving himself. And Tod, years after watching his peer rise to the highest seat in the land, painted him the young buffoon, with the unnamed "chief" his foil, showing restraint and saving the day. According to James Robert Anderson (1925:236), Douglas himself added a spin to the story some forty-five years after the event (1873). A strong defender of Douglas's reputation, Anderson quoted a letter Douglas apparently wrote to his daughter, responding to some contemporary newspaper accounts of the event: "True, I seized the Indian, a noted murderer, as stated, and secured him after a desperate struggle, but I did not shoot him with my own hands; he was afterwards executed for his crime. It was a desperate adventure, which nothing but a high sense of duty could have induced me to undertake" (Anderson 1925:236).

More notable than the confused details in these various versions is the fact that no written accounts attempted to explain or understand Carrier motivations and behaviour. Why the Carrier killed the two Fort George men in the first place, for instance, has received remarkably little attention. In their biography of James Douglas, Robert H. Coats and R.E. Gosnell (1909:105) commented, "The motive of the deed is unrecorded." A.G. Morice's (1978:141-2) version sheds no more light: "For some reason, the nature of which cannot now be ascertained, two young men had killed two of the Company's servants." While HBC correspondence and journals are also vague on the topic, it is clear that some Hudson's Bay Company officers were aware of some root causes of the conflict. According to John Stuart (HBCA: B 119/e/1 p.8.), district chief factor in 1823 and a founder of the New Caledonia posts, the story can be traced back to a Carrier woman who had been taken as country wife by Mr. Yale, while maintaining a previous connection to one of the Carrier men. A few months after the Fort George killings, Stuart issued a report from McLeod Lake in defence of the Carrier and identified the Fort George people as "the most peaceable and best disposed in the Department." He stated that he believed the killings "proceeded from fear and arose from the impulse of the moment." Apparently "the most creditable of the natives" had told him that

> the evening preceeding the murder one of the men Beaquort had discovered the principal perpetrator in criminal conversation with a woman Mr Yale had in keeping and cautioned both to be more circumspect in future as in the event of his perceiving(?) any thing more of the kind he would

inform Mr Yale. [I]t appears that both got alarmed but in course of the night the young man returned accompanied by another and perpetrated the horrid deed.

Stuart reported that rather than fleeing, those connected with the two Carrier had shown judicious and conciliatory behaviour. They "had themselves buried the deceased and some of them encamped at the Fort to take care of the property until the arrival of Mr George McDougall in the fall." They "obeyed the first summons issued by him on arrival and appeared without arms." Stuart emphasized that "not five pounds worth of property was taken by the whole of the natives including murderers and all, but the Guns and Ammunition they had secreted under the flooring under an apprehension [that they] might be turned against themselves and that a general massacre would be committed on the arrival of our people in the fall." Far from the crazed savages McLean described, the Carrier of Stuart's report had reasonable, logical responses.

In Governor Simpson's official "Report to the Governor and Committee in London 1824-26," he described the Fort George killings as "a very distressing and lamentable occurence arising I fear in a certain degree from the imprudence of Mr Yale." The lower-level company men working in the district were probably not privy to this information — social order in part depended upon their respect for and subservience to the officers in charge. However, Governor Simpson passed on Stuart's report to his superiors in London as follows:

This young man it appears was left in charge of the Post during summer with an Interpreter and two men and had particular instructions from Mr Stuart not to absent himself therefrom on any consideration; he however accompanied by the Interpreter went to visit the neighbouring establishments at Frazers and Stuarts Lakes about 200 miles distant on some frivolous pretext leaving the Post in charge of the two men; while absent two young Indians according to their own report came to the establishment one of whom had formerly been the lover of Mr Yales woman; the servants discovered some familiarities between the woman and this young man and threatened to inform Mr Yale of the circumstance on his return which alarmed them and in order to prevent discovery they formed the horrible resolution of murdering the two men which they effected with a Hatchet while asleep; the murderers afterwards pillaged the Stores of a few articles and accompanied by the woman made their escape. Every means have been used to secure the perpetraters but as yet without success; the well disposed Indians have been called upon for their assistance but they are not inclined to raise hands against their country-men altho' they deprecate their conduct very much, and in the meantime the Establishment has been abandoned. [HBCA: D 4/87, fos. 43-43d]

Simpson's awareness of the apparent logic of the Carriers' actions did not stop him from giving a theatrical twist to the facts as he understood them. Shortly after the confrontation between Kwah and Douglas, Governor Simpson visited Fort St. James and solidified the official HBC interpretation in a way that suited company purposes. The record of Simpson's visit and his interaction with the Carrier survives in the company journals and in the diary of an eyewitness, Archibald McDonald, who was part of Simpson's entourage. McDonald (1971:24-7) recorded that on 17 September 1828 the party made a ceremonial entrance into Fort St. James, adopting "the most imposing manner we could, for the sake of the Indians." The governor rode in on horseback with guns sa-luting, the British flag flying, the bugle sounding, and a piper in full Highland costume playing "Si coma leum cogadh na shea" (Peace: or War, if you will it otherwise). A few days later (September 20) McDon-ald wrote:

> The principal Indians of the place have been sent for, and introduced to the Governor as the Great Chief of the Country. After exhibiting before them our various musical performances, etc, ... an address was made to them through Mr. Connolly and the Linguist [interpreter], in which the Governor laid great stress upon the conduct of the Carriers of late.

In his "harangue," Simpson brought up several events involving grave "misconduct" of the Carrier, including several "murders" of company men, and the recent "rebellion" they displayed when one of these mur-ders was avenged — an oblique reference to the Kwah-Douglas confron-tation.

Apparently, the speech then became a series of threats. According to McDonald (1971:26-8):

> The Governor could not do less than deprecate such proceedings. He represented to them how helpless their condition would be at this mo-ment were he and all his people to enter upon hostilities against them,

FRIEDA ESAU KLIPPENSTEIN

that a partial example had already been made of the guilty parties, but that the next time the Whites should be compelled to imbrue their hands in the blood of Indians, it would be a general sweep; that the innocent would go with the guilty, and that their fate would be deplorable indeed ... and that it was hard to say when we would stop; never, in any case, until the Indians gave the most unqualified proof of their good conduct in future. The chief that headed the party which entered the fort in the summer was pointed at with marked contempt, and it was only Mr. Douglas's intercession and forgiveness that saved him from further indignities.

The speech closed with a glass of rum, a little tobacco, a shake of the hand for the Carrier chief and the *Song of Peace* by the piper.[1] Clearly this was a ritual affirmation of power. No wrongdoing could be admitted by the company, whose officers surely realized how "helpless" they would be if all the Native peoples of the area were to decide to "enter upon hostilities" against *them*. Simpson was attempting to put the Carrier in their place — a place of submission and cooperation. A gradual dissipation of hostilities followed Simpson's visit, but whether it was occasioned by this theatrical display, Douglas's removal, or the conciliatory nature of Kwah cannot be determined.

Not surprisingly, the remarkable story of Kwah and Douglas lives on in the Carrier communities. Carrier versions of the story bring a different sense to it. The first account recorded from Native informants was published in 1904 by A.G. Morice who, in his *History of the Northern Interior of British Columbia*, tried to debunk McLean and Tod and set the record straight. Morice emphasized that his version came from an actual eyewitness "still living near the writer," as well as "many Indians, children or contemporaries of eye-witnesses." Morice's was the earliest account to name "Tzoelhnolle," the Carrier fugitive. Anticipating his critics, Morice insisted that the oral accounts "all agree in the following details." In his version only a "sick woman," lately "delivered of a child," remained in the camp. The "terrified young man," meanwhile, "stupidly" hid under a pile of skins and other "household impedimenta." Far from "meeting justice" or simply being "shot" or "dispatched," the fugitive was subjected to astonishing brutality, being seized and dragged out of Kwah's lodge by Douglas's men, hacked to death with garden hoes until he was "a shapeless jelly," and dragged by a

---

1   See also Simpson (1949:188-221).

rope back to the post to be offered to the dogs. Douglas's actions, far from heroic or dutiful, were shameful.

A similar report of the brutal treatment of the Carrier fugitive was provided by Lizette Hall, a Carrier elder and great-granddaughter of Kwah. In an oral recording in 1966, Hall maintained that the fugitive was pursued at a time when most of the men of the village were absent, and that this gruesome scene took place in the midst of terrorized women and children. The man was torn from his desperate refuge — under the blankets on which a woman (perhaps one of Kwah's wives) had recently given birth:

> And this man came up and, of course, he was hiding. And as soon as they heard about it across the lake there, at the post, a couple of the men, the Hudson's Bay men, came over and started searching for him.... [T]here was a woman who had a baby and she was in bed. Of course that would be in the smokehouse. And he didn't know where to hide so finally they hid him — he crawled in with this woman. He didn't know, at the last moment he didn't know where to go, so he just jumped there and, well, these two men they came searching and of course they threw the blankets off this woman like they did in the old days, like the Hudson's Bay used to do, you know. They bossed these natives and so they threw the blankets off her and there the poor fellow was crouching. And they got him out and they just tore him, literally tore him to pieces. And killed him ... without any fair trial, without even asking any questions.

While Tod emphasized that Douglas's key error was apprehending the fugitive in the village, Carrier accounts specify that it happened in Kwah's own lodge. A statement in Daniel Harmon's "Account of the Indians Living West of the Rocky Mountains," written years before this episode (1811), sheds some light on Kwah's response. As Harmon (1905:254) described:

> An Indian ... who has killed another, or been guilty of some other bad action, finds the house or tent of the chief a safe retreat, so long as he is allowed to remain there ... and if he should [be attacked] the chief would revenge the insult, in the same manner as if it were offered directly to himself.... The revenge ... would be to destroy the life of the offending person, or that of some of his near relations.

FRIEDA ESAU KLIPPENSTEIN

In hiding in Kwah's lodge, then, the fugitive was under Kwah's protection. In Carrier tellings of the story, it was Douglas who was lawless and savage.

Like many of the other accounts, Morice had Kwah accepting gifts as compensation for an affront. Later Carrier sources maintain that Kwah and his countrymen were not motivated by the desire to acquire material goods. Lizette Hall (1966) insisted that the wife of James Douglas did not throw clothes and blankets down, but simply pleaded for her husband's life. Regarding her authority on this point, she added, "I asked my father, you know — it was just between my father and I, and I know my dad wouldn't lie to me." In her published book, *The Carrier My People*, Hall (1992:63) added that her father laughed and replied, "What would he do with women's clothes?"

Nick Prince, a Carrier historian from Fort St. James and a great-great-grandson of Kwah, tells a contemporary version of the story that is also in intriguing contrast to the written accounts. According to Prince, it was neither Kwah nor Amelia Connolly who saved James Douglas's life. In fact, Kwah was so angry that Douglas had "taken the law into his hands" that he entered the house with the clear resolve to kill him. Although Douglas's wife *did* attempt to compensate for the deed by "throwing stuff down," Kwah forbade anyone from accepting the goods. Prince says that it was "two young guys," Kwah's grandsons, who stopped Kwah from killing Douglas. They did this because in Carrier custom it was not for *him* to kill — that was the job of the warrior chief. If Kwah had killed Douglas, he would have been banished by the Carrier communities and he would have lost his hereditary title. It was to protect him from this fate, that his grandsons stopped him — a logical act, as they may well have stood to inherit this title some day. Apparently the sign on Kwah's grave alludes to this intervention; the portion in Carrier syllabics names the two young men who kept Kwah from killing "one man," who remained unnamed.[1]

In the oral tradition, Kwah is heroized for the way he overpowered and humiliated Douglas — and for the way he let him go. A.G. Morice's (1978:139) account described Douglas as a hostage with a knife to his throat, with Kwah's nephew begging the chief for permission to do the deed. "A word from 'old Kwah,'" wrote Morice, "would have cut short [Douglas's] incipient career and sent his ghost to the present abode of his

---

1   Nicholas Prince (personal communication, Fort St. James: 1991, 1994).

ancestors." At Fort St. James, where many people today proudly identify themselves as Kwah's descendants,[1] the English inscription on Kwah's epitaph boldly declares, "Here Lie the Remains of Great Chief Kwah Born About 1755 Died Spring of 1840. He once had in his hands the life of (future Sir) James Douglas, but was great enough to refrain from taking it."[2]

Clearly the significance of this story has evolved along with the status of James Douglas. For instance, in her 1966 oral interview Hall used the Kwah-Douglas story to illustrate the folly and violence of Douglas, while in her more recent book (1992:62-3) she presented it as the source of the benign policies toward Native peoples which Douglas later implemented as governor of British Columbia. Hall declared that after Douglas's wife pleaded for her husband's life, Kwah and Douglas shook hands, and "Douglas promised K'wah his servants would never treat the natives so roughly anymore." She concluded, "James Douglas kept that promise." This interpretation falls in line with several others. Gardner (1976:16), for instance, in her biography of Douglas, asserted that, "In this brief showdown, James had learned something about himself and about the Indian people. He would carry both lessons with him for the rest of his life."

As a public historian, I am interested not only in evaluating the meanings and purposes of written and oral accounts of the past, but also in how events are consciously reinterpreted for commemoration and presentation to wide audiences. It is in such instances that new agendas and contrived meanings are often likely to be imposed. The "Sir George Simpson Centennial Celebration," held in 1928 to mark the centenary of Simpson's visit to New Caledonia, is a poignant example. New meanings were imposed upon the story of Kwah and Douglas, as the significance of Simpson's visit was reconstructed. After hurried renovations to the old fur trade fort, an impressive group of visiting dignitaries met, and Native people from far reaches of New Caledonia gathered. A costumed pageant replayed Simpson's ceremonial entrance into Fort St. James. There were speeches, Native dances, games such as horse racing, and the unveiling of a plaque at Simpson Pass on the high road from Banff to Windermere, British Columbia.

---

1   See Rossetti (1983).

2   For photos of the grave, see Johnston (1943) and Gardner (1976).

Figure 1: "Sir George Simpson" and "James Douglas" enter Fort St. James in the 1928 pageant, a century after the the controversial events of 1828

Figure 2: Aboriginal chiefs greet "Sir George Simpson," at Fort St. James during the Sir George Simpson Centennial Celebration, September 17th 1928.

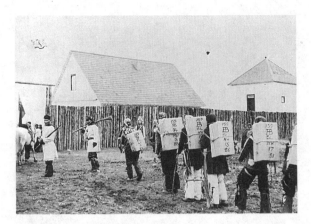

Figure 3: Carrier "packers" enter Fort St. James as part of the procession at the Centennial Celebration, 1928. They are re-enacting transporting HBC packs of trade goods and provisions from Stuart Lake to the Fort.

Figure 4: Native dancing during the pageant celebrations, Fort St. James, 1928.

FRIEDA ESAU KLIPPENSTEIN

Clues to the meanings and purposes of the celebration are revealed in the scripts of the speeches given by visiting dignitaries, later published in a richly illustrated commemorative pamphlet.[1] None of the speeches mentioned Simpson's specific business in Fort St. James, focusing instead on the general goals of his 1828 voyage from York Factory to the Pacific Slope. The speakers celebrated Simpson as a pioneer, a great statesman, and an "empire builder." Charles V. Sale, Governor of the Hudson's Bay Company, and others dwelt on the "courage, endurance and fortitude" of Simpson and the other company men. According to R. Randolph Bruce, Lieutenant-Governor of B.C., these men were "sentinels ... who at great self-sacrifice tenaciously held this great domain." Fort St. James was presented as "the outpost of an empire; the visible sign of British occupation; [and] a centre of government." The essence of the message delivered that day was captured by Lt.-Governor Bruce, who declared, "To-day's pageant gives us courage for the future." Bruce expressed confidence that in the "new era" that was dawning, the Hudson's Bay Company would "lead the van in the march of progress, thus helping to fulfil that great destiny which a benign Providence has provided for this great and glorious country."

None of the speeches mentioned the Fort George murders or the incident between Kwah and Douglas. Several did, however, mention the relationship with "our good friends the Indians." Charles Sale described the relationship between the company and "the Indian and Esquimaux population of Canada" as "for many generations all that both sides could desire." "Between us and them," he said, "is a common interest in the good of the fur trade, the country, and the people. This spirit of good-will and friendship has never been broken.... Since we both desire the same good, we shall never quarrel." Oblate missionary Father Coccola addressed the Native guests directly, calling on them "to carry on, to commemorate the work started so many years ago," and "to follow the spirit displayed by [Sir George Simpson]." Judge F.W. Howay, of the Historic Sites and Monuments Board of Canada, referred most directly to the events of one hundred years earlier, saying,

> Whenever an opportunity offered, Governor Simpson called the Indians together and spoke to them of the trade, congratulating them, if they deserved it, upon their good conduct, or threatening to withdraw the post if they were indolent or criminal. He made them feel that the Company

---

1 Hudson's Bay Company (1928).

was really interested — as indeed it was — in their welfare, and that co-operation would be mutually beneficial.

After the 1928 Centenary, the headlines in the Victoria *Colonist* read, "Great page in story of B.C. related at pageant and historic ceremony." The Victoria *Times* announced, "History lives again in pageant" and "Celebration at Fort St. James great success."[1] Both the pageant and the accounts that followed it expressed and perpetuated myths that did not reflect the reality of the Native peoples at the gathering. Why would they have been interested in celebrating the dawning of a "new era" in which the Hudson's Bay Company "leads in the march of progress"? Why would they "follow the spirit displayed by George Simpson" or celebrate movement toward that "great destiny" of a "Providence" which to them likely did not seem so "benign"? According to Nick Prince, his grandfather, one of the relatively few Carrier in attendance who understood English, responded to the speeches of the 1928 Centenary with the comment, "them white people speak foolish." The commemorative pamphlet claimed that Native people gathered from great distances for the event. In contrast, Prince remembers hearing that, though the Carrier each received fifty cents to take part in "the play," for most of them the primary attraction was not the pageant — they had gathered from Takla, Babine, McLeod Lake, Hazelton, and elsewhere for a potlatch in town, a gathering which had to be kept quiet because the federal anti-potlatch law was in effect.[2] Even the dances and games that were photographed as a feature of the centenary celebration, according to Prince, were seen by the Carrier as part of the potlatch.

At the 1828 gathering at Fort St. James, Simpson made speeches intended to effect a more peaceful relationship between the Carrier and the traders and used threats to achieve acquiescence. A hundred years later, the visit of George Simpson was "rewritten" as a positive event, one worth celebrating. The pageant applauded the conquest of the land, while emphasizing the congenial relationships between traders and Native peoples. The Carrier were asked to commemorate a person who had humiliated them, and to celebrate the anniversary of an event which

---

1 Victoria *Colonist* (19 September 1928), Victoria *Times* (18, 22 September 1928). See also Watson (1928).

2 Nicholas Prince (personal communication, Fort St. James: 1991).

FRIEDA ESAU KLIPPENSTEIN

was not a happy one for them. Besides commemorating what happened in 1828, the centenary celebration also in a way parallelled its purpose – the 1928 event, too, was about fostering peace and eliciting cooperative behaviour from the Carrier. It demonstrated the presumed triumph of British commerce and civilization over a "savage" domain. The message was clear: the British had prevailed.

The story of Kwah and James Douglas, in its several incarnations and in its aftermath, exemplifies the power of historical accounts. It also reminds us that most historical interpretations that have survived in the mainstream were written by those in positions of dominance. This is not to suggest that presenting a "Native perspective" on an event somehow settles the matter. None of us is free of the tendency to invent traditions, or to shape with conscious or unconscious purposes our version of an event. In the telling, events and their meanings can be cast and recast by different parties and by the same party over time. In the Douglas-Kwah story the various written accounts are contradictory on the question of exactly what or who brought an end to the confrontation at Fort St. James. The contradictions do not mean that someone is not telling the truth; rather, they reveal the likely reality that the men, women, and children of the fort were all making desperate attempts to defuse a dangerous situation. When Kwah and the others released Douglas and went home, who really knew what action had effected the desired end? Surely Carrier accounts are more likely than those of HBC participants to contribute to our understanding of Carrier actions and perceptions. European accounts, however faithful to their authors' points of view, are incapable of answering certain questions about the Fort George "murders." For example, in Carrier terms, was Yale lawfully married to the Carrier woman? And as for the Carrier man who apparently had "some previous connection" to this woman, what exactly provoked his extreme reaction?

It is customary for events recorded in written form to be labelled "histories," and those from oral traditions, "myths" or "legends." "Legend," like "folklore" and "myth," connotes a poetic or quaint mix of truth and fantasy and is generally associated with "primitive" people who have a less firm grasp on reality than literate peoples. But what "histories" and "legends" have in common is that in all cases "historical facts" are culturally mediated. They are always interpreted by people with particular perspectives. Perspective is a product of myriad factors, such as cultural background, personal experience, gender, age, social position, as well as the connection of the teller to the event, place, or people involved.

Are all accounts of an event equally valuable — or equally useless — if none is "the truth"? All accounts are not equal. We all make judgements about the value of what we are reading or hearing, although certainly not according to the same criteria. For instance, John Tod's authority came from being a Hudson's Bay Company man in New Caledonia at the time of the incident, from having met Douglas, and from having lived among the Carrier people (not to mention his apparent ability to come up with the actual skull of the man who was killed). As for Morice, his authority came from his direct contact with Carrier eyewitnesses and people connected with eyewitnesses, as well as his fluency in the Carrier language which enabled him to interview them. Among the Carrier themselves, the people recognized by the community as having the authority to tell this particular story ("those who know") are those, like Nick Prince and Lizette Hall, who are direct descendants of Kwah. Their status reflects the traditional methodology of preserving oral histories, whereby stories are "owned" and are "given" to appropriate recipients, generally along family lines.

Accounts of past events are not necessarily more true or more authoritative for having been written on paper. The differentiation between oral and written accounts is ultimately false. Both can preserve unfounded "hearsay" as often as they do the faithful testimony of an eyewitness or an informed participant in an event. Certainly written accounts of the Native North American past are less reliable and less complete if they ignore the meanings and understandings provided by Native oral tradition.

References

Akrigg, G.P.V., and H.B. Akrigg
  1975 *British Columbia Chronicle, 1778-1846*. Vancouver: Discovery Press.
Anderson, J.R.
  1925 Notes and Comments on Early Days and Events in British
        Columbia, Washington and Oregon. Unpublished manuscript.
        Victoria: British Columbia Archives and Record Service, Add Mss
        1912, vol. 9.
Bancroft, Hubert Howe
  1886 The History of the Northwest Coast, 1800-1846. Vol. 2, San
        Francisco: The History Company.
  1890 History of British Columbia. San Francisco: The History Company.

Barman, Jean

1991 The West Beyond the West: A History of British Columbia. Toronto: University of Toronto Press.

Begg, Alexander

1894 *History of British Columbia*. Toronto: William Briggs.

Bishop, Charles A.

1980 "Kwah: A Carrier Chief." In *Old Trails and New Directions: Papers of the Third North American Fur Trade Conference*. C.M. Judd and A.J. Ray, eds. Toronto: University of Toronto Press, 191–204.

1988 "?Kwah (Quâs)." In *Dictionary of Canadian Biography*, vol. 7. Toronto: University of Toronto Press, 474–75.

Bryce, George

1904 *The Remarkable History of the Hudson's Bay Company*. Toronto: W. Briggs.

Coats, Robert H., and R.E. Gosnell

1909 *Sir James Douglas*. Toronto: Morang.

Connolly, Henry

c. 1900 *Reminiscences of One of the Last Descendants of a Bourgeois of the North West Company*. Unpublished typescript in MG 29 B15, vol. 61, file 34 (Robert Bell Papers). Ottawa: National Archives of Canada.

Dickie, Donalda

1950 *The Great Adventure: An Illustrated History of Canada for Young Canadians*. Toronto and Vancouver: J.M. Dent.

Fisher, Robin

1977 *Contact and Conflict: Indian-European Relations in British Columbia, 1774-1890*. Vancouver: University of British Columbia Press.

Gardner, Alison F.

1976 James Douglas. The Canadians Series, Don Mills, ON: Fitzhenry & Whiteside.

Hackler, James

1958 Carrier Indians of Babine Lake: The Effect of the Fur Trade and the Catholic Church on their Social Organization. Master's thesis, Sociology, San Jose State College.

Hall, Lizette

1966 Interview by Imbert Orchard, 14 September 1966, Canadian Broadcasting Corporation, Imbert Orchard Collection, Victoria: BCARS, tape 1044:1, 10–15 in transcript.

1992 *The Carrier, My People*. Cloverdale, BC: Friesen Printers.

Harmon, Daniel W.

1905 *A Journal of Voyages and Travels in the Interior of North America*. Daniel Haskel, ed. New York: Allerton.

1957 *Sixteen Years in the Indian Country: The Journals of Daniel Williams Harmon*. W. Kaye Lamb, ed. Toronto: Macmillan.

Hudson's Bay Company

1928 *Sir George Simpson Centennial Celebration, Fort St. James, 17 September 1928: Unveiling of Tablet, Simpson Pass*. Hudson's Bay Company.

Johnston, W.P.

1943 "Chief Kwah's Revenge." *The Beaver*, September, 22–23.

McDonald, Archibald

1971 [1872] *Peace River. A Canoe Voyage from Hudson's Bay to Pacific by Sir George Simpson in 1828*. Malcolm McLeod, ed. Edmonton: Hurtig.

McKelvie, B.A.

1926 Early History of the Province of British Columbia. Toronto and London: J.M. Dent.

1949 Tales of Conflict. Vancouver: The Vancouver Daily Province.

McLean, John

1849 *Notes of a Twenty-five Year's Service in the Hudson's Bay Territory by John McLean*. vol. 2, London: Richard Bentley. (Reprinted by the Champlain Society, Toronto, 1932, W.S. Wallace, ed.)

Moresby, Fairfax

1909 *Two Admirals*. London: John Murray.

Morice, A.G.

1978 [1904] *History of the Northern Interior of B.C., formerly New Caledonia, 1660-1880*. Smithers, BC: Interior Stationery.

Mulhall, David

1986 Will to Power: The Missionary Career of Father Morice. Vancouver: University of British Columbia Press.

Ormsby, Margaret

1972 "Sir James Douglas." Dictionary of Canadian Biography, vol. 10. Toronto: University of Toronto Press, 238-48.

Pendleton, George

1928 "The Progress of a Governor, A Fur Trade Episode of a Hundred Years Ago." *The Beaver*, September, 54-55.

Pethick, Derek

1969 *James Douglas: Servant of Two Empires*. Vancouver: Mitchell Press.

Rossetti, Bernadette
1983   *Kw'eh Ts'u Haindene, The Descendants of Kwah*. Vanderhoof, BC:
        Yinka Dene Language Institute.

Sage, W.N.
1930   *Sir James Douglas and British Columbia*. Toronto: University of
        Toronto Press.

Simpson, George
1947   "Part of Dispatch from George Simpson...to the Governor and
        Committee of the HBC, London, March 1, 1829." *Simpson's 1828
        Journey to the Columbia*. Hudson's Bay Record Society, vol. 10.

Smedley, J.D.
1948   "Early Days at the Fort, as told by Chief Louis B. Prince, of Fort St.
        James B.C." *Cariboo and Northern B.C. Digest*. Spring.

Tod, John
1878   "History of New Caledonia and the Northwest Coast Victoria
        1878." Original unpublished manuscript. Bancroft Library,
        University of California (Bancroft Collection, Pacific Coast MSS.,
        Series C, No. 27). Photocopy in Victoria: British Columbia Archives
        and Record Service (E/A/T56), and typescript in Ottawa: National
        Archives of Canada (MG29 C15 vol. 3).
1905   "Career of a Scotch Boy Who Became Hon. John Tod," excerpts
        from the victoria *Daily Times*, Sept. 30–Dec. 23, 1905, Gilbert
        Malcolm Sproat, ed., Victoria: British Columbia Archives and
        Record Service (E/E/T565.
1954   "John Tod: Career of a Scotch Boy," Madge Wolfenden, ed., in *The
        British Columbia Historical Quarterly*, XVIII(4): 133–238.

Van Kirk, Sylvia
1980   *"Many Tender Ties": Women in Fur-Trade Society in Western Canada,
        1670-1870*. Winnipeg: Watson & Dwyer.

Watson, Robert
1928   "Fort Saint James, Sir George Simpson Centennial." The Beaver,
        December, 101–103.

Photo Credits

Figure 1: Hudson's Bay Company Archives, Provincial Archives of Manitoba.
Figure 2: Hudson's Bay Company Archives, Provincial Archives of Manitoba.
Figure 3: Hudson's Bay Company Archives, Provincial Archives of Manitoba.
Figure 4: Hudson's Bay Company Archives, Provincial Archives of Manitoba.

Part III. Interpreting Disease, Survival, and Healing

The two essays in Part III confront some major documentary problems in pre-twentieth-century sources concerning Native peoples. We know that Europeans brought new diseases to North America, and that Native death rates were very high when communities were exposed for the first time to such viruses as smallpox. Yet to grasp the particulars of Native medical history, we must rely on texts from one or two centuries ago, written by people whose perceptions of disease and vocabularies for symptoms were variable, idiosyncratic, impressionistic, and often remarkably different from the usages of today.

Jody Decker is a professor of historical and medical geography at Wilfrid Laurier University in Waterloo, Ontario. She has intensively researched the history of infectious diseases among Native people of Rupert's Land (the Hudson's Bay Company territory) before 1870, and is completing a book on the subject. Her essay, "Country Distempers," amply demonstrates the challenges of understanding medical words and categories from past centuries—even those with which we think we are familiar. One complication is that over two hundred years both Native and Hudson's Bay Company traders' concepts and theories of disease and contagion changed and varied according to their experiences and observations, even as the disease patterns themselves were evolving.

Shepard Krech III is a professor and curator of the Haffenreffer Museum of Anthropology at Brown University in Providence, Rhode Island. Like Decker, he has both worked in the Hudson's Bay Company Archives and done fieldwork in northern Canada. He has published widely on Athapaskan peoples and the fur trade and on related museum collections, and is currently completing a book on ecology and the American Indian.

In 1982, Krech published a rather specialized article on "The Death of Barbue, a Kutchin Trading Chief," reading HBC documents for what they revealed about an Athapaskan community's adaptation to the fur trade and about its therapeutic techniques for treating its leader's illness. Reworking it for this volume, he has taken a very different approach. Here he explores the extent to which the textual sources allow him to tell a story about the old chief's illness, and to arrive at an empathetic understanding of Gwich'in (Kutchin) as well as fur-trader perspectives on their interactions and on the efforts at healing in which they both participated. Krech's essay, seeking to follow an individual's last years, his ailments, and the treatments he underwent, through texts that are revealing yet opaque, complements Decker's broader attempt to decipher disease through the documents.

7

Country Distempers: Deciphering Disease and Illness in Rupert's Land before 1870

Jody F. Decker

ALL TEXTS are interpretive. Particularly daunting, however, is the task of analyzing historical texts that refer to matters of health, illness, and disease, and situating them within the context of their original intended meaning. An additional difficulty arises with interpreting historical texts drawn from oral narratives in Native societies. When oral discourse is translated to written text by a non-Native writer, and later reinterpreted by researchers, whose voice has really spoken? Each of these parties may have distinct, ingrained notions of what constitutes health, illness, or disease, notions that have changed and varied over time and across space. For these reasons, words cannot simply be brushed aside. Consider, for example, three diverse associations of the word "jaundice": first, yellow skin and eyes as visible symptoms that allowed identification and labelling of a condition; second, a disease state usually associated with liver disorders, notably hepatitis; and third, a bitter state of mind reflecting envy or pessimism. Medical-historical geographers using the term would query the origin and possible spread of this infectious disease, or analyze the spatial behaviour of its carriers.

But we must go beyond the meaning of words as they were understood through time, to place them into a spatial and social context. Many diseases thrive in certain environments and not in others, and Native groups, since they exploited very different environments, had diverse disease experiences. Distance between places was one of the determining factors in the survival of an infectious disease; for instance, many diseases did not survive the two-month voyage between Europe and North America. To take these points one step further, rival disease theories sometimes aided in the geographic spread of disease. They also affected social relations within a group and the negotiations between patients, families, and physician as to the appropriate way to handle disease and illness. In this paper I expand on these points and highlight some of the documentary and interpretive problems inherent in evidence on disease and illness, and in our efforts to use and understand that evidence. I also examine geographical and historical contexts for the introduction and spread of European diseases into the Western Interior of Canada.

The data presented here come largely from the rich and voluminous archives of the Hudson's Bay Company (HBC) in Winnipeg, Manitoba. The time frame of the discussion is the century from the 1770s, when the HBC moved inland from its posts on Hudson Bay to counteract competition from its Montreal-based competitors, to the 1870s, when Plains Native communities began to be placed on reserves. This was a very dynamic period—one of peopling and de-peopling, major and minor migrations of Native groups and later of white settlers, marked seasonality in the spatial interaction of all population groups, and political upheavals. In deciphering any text on matters of disease and illness during this period, we must include in our explanations both the local and the larger, regional scale.

Context: Diseases, People, and Environment

The Western Interior of Canada is defined here as the region between the Rockies in the west and the Severn River flowing into Hudson Bay in the east, and stretching from the Barren Lands of the Chipewyan and Inuit peoples in the north to those of the agricultural Mandan peoples near the upper Missouri River in the south. Diseases, of course, do not respect political boundaries as they do barriers to passage; therefore, any region is arbitrarily defined when we deal with infectious diseases (unless the political boundary coincides with the natural barrier). Figure 1 shows the Western Interior with the approximate locations of Native groups around 1780. This region formed part of what was known as Rupert's Land, that vast portion of western and northern Canada granted by King Charles II of England in 1670 to Prince Rupert and his fellow investors in the Hudson's Bay Company.

In medical geography, the concepts of disease and illness must be carefully defined and distinguished from each other as we try to explain and predict the incidence, prevalence, and spread or transmission of diseases. Disease organisms enter the human body and survive in the tissues; if they are to spread, they must reproduce and shed their offspring, which in turn must find a new host. The environment plays a major role while these organisms are outside the body, for their very survival depends on conditions such as temperature and humidity, on patterns of settlement and density of population, or on how the landscape has been managed, all of which may encourage or discourage their reproduction.

Infection by an organism does not always result in illness. Humans have the capability to fight off impending infection, but if factors such as poor nutrition, other infections, and undue stress are present, the body may not be able to defend itself, and illness results. Geography plays an important role here too. Nutrients are unevenly distributed in nature, and humans must move or trade between regions to satisfy their nutritional needs. Vitamin D, commonly obtained from oils in fish or iodine contained in seafood, is rarely lacking in populations that exploit a coastal environment, but inland groups are much more prone to rickets or goitre resulting from the absence of those nutrients in their diet. The region around Fort Edmonton and Rocky Mountain House, upstream from Edmonton in present-day Alberta, produced several cases of iodine-deficiency thyroid problems (goitre) according to Dr. John Richardson, the surgeon on the two Arctic expeditions under Franklin in the early nineteenth century (Houston 1984:654-6). Richardson maintained that goitre was more common in mountainous areas, especially among Metis women who drank fresh river water. Natives and traders who drank the less-pure snow water rarely had goitre. This example calls attention not only to variable distributions of disease, but also to the role of cultural practices in their distribution.

With changes in the size and density of populations come changes in their burdens of infection. Small Plains bands (approximately 30-50 people) who frequently moved from one area to another to hunt, gather, or occasionally fish, threatened a parasite's[1] very survival, since their mobility rarely allowed the parasite to repeatedly complete its life cycle. The parasites which did best in these circumstances took a long time to produce a chronic, slow-acting infection in their hosts, or they persisted on plants, and on or in animals. For instance, Natives who exploited fur-

---

1 Parasites are plants or animals that live upon another living organism. Parasites, which are sometimes called pathogens (meaning the origin of suffering), are agents that produce disease. These agents can be micro-organisms such as bacteria and viruses, or they can be multicellular organisms such as worms. Pathogenicity is the ability of a pathogen (commonly called a germ) to produce clinically apparent illness in the body. Pathogens can cause disease in a variety of ways, such as direct invasion of a tissue as in the case of a respiratory infection, or by producing a toxin as in the case of staphylococcal food poisoning. See J.S. Mausner and S. Kramer (1985:268-69) and Mary Wilson et al. (1994:53) for a more thorough discussion.

JODY F. DECKER

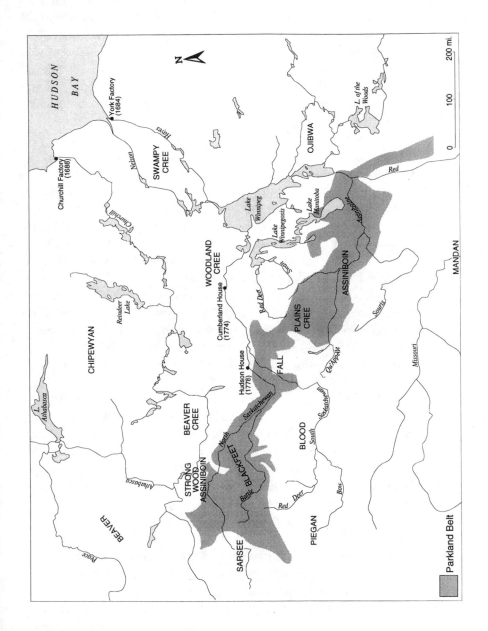

Figure 1: Location of Native Groups and HBC Posts in the Western Interior of Canada, c. 1780.

bearing animals were prone to the animals' parasites. An example is contained in the captivity narrative of John Tanner, a white man living with the Ottawa in western Manitoba in the early 1800s. The community had been harvesting wild rice when Tanner and many others became ill of what appeared to be tularaemia (Martin 1976:58-61), a disease of animals which resembles bubonic plague. The carrier agent *Pasteurella tularenis* lives in water infected by diseased animals. In this case, Native exploitation of a food source in a specific ecological zone was a cultural practice that may have been conducive to disease.

As human populations increased and became more concentrated, parasites became more of a threat because they could easily be transmitted between susceptible human hosts. When Natives and Europeans started to cluster in settlements like Red River (present-day Winnipeg) in the first quarter of the nineteenth century, new diseases such as whooping cough and measles became an increasing threat to all. Native economic and cultural practices of working for and trading with the Europeans contributed to the spread of disease. With some infectious diseases such as syphilis, population density posed a lesser threat than social upheaval, as its transmission depended more on promiscuity than on probability. It is no wonder that groups as small as bands did not have a concept of contagion because, with animal infections or chronic infections, it was not as blatantly evident how disease was spread as it was within larger groups, among whose members transmission occurred quickly and visibly.

In historical studies of disease among Native groups, it is useful to define interaction as the spatial configuration of social contacts within a given territory whose boundaries may be loosely delineated by kinship groups and territorial behavioural patterns. On the Plains, no one Native group owned the land or the resources, but two large overlapping population networks, each with its own alliances, shared this region after 1800: the Plains Cree-Assiniboine and their allies the Saulteaux or Ojibwa; and the Blackfoot tribes and their allies, the Atsina or Fall and the Sarcee (Sharrock 1977:7-21). The structure of contact and activity within and between these two networks set up the potential for the diffusion of infectious diseases. Across the region, population densities remained relatively low among all groups. It is difficult to define the population structure geographically, but generally, we can identify a network of traders and Natives who interacted in summer and tended to be isolated into pockets in winter. The traders did not venture far from

JODY F. DECKER

their respective posts in winter, and Native groups disbanded in order to exploit smaller, dispersed hunting grounds. During the summer, by contrast, the Plains Natives moved throughout the entire region to hunt buffalo, trade, or go to war. Segregation of bands sometimes occurred temporarily, or permanently in cases where some members joined other groups or where entire groups migrated. Such migrations could be due to local, seasonal or annual fluctuations in availability of resources. Native territorial occupation was complex, but in tracing diseases, an understanding of these networks of spatial interaction and social contacts is essential.

The spread of an infectious disease reflects a geographical and temporal pattern of individual contacts. An infectious disease can be propagated through any susceptible population as long as there are enough people within a given time and area. To know where a disease originated and to trace its patterns of spread and decline, we must use whatever geographic scale provides that information. For instance, there were two points of entry of smallpox into the Northern Plains in 1781, one originating from the Dakota Sioux in the southeast and the other from the Shoshone Indians of Wyoming in the southwest. This epidemic, however, had originated in Mexico City in 1779, before branching out to these different regions of the Plains. It did not die out until 1783, when it spread among the more dispersed Chipewyans in the subarctic (Decker 1988). To determine the full demographic consequences of an epidemic, we need to work at this continental scale. For example, to compute the mortality rate, we need to estimate how many people were living in the whole area at this time, to obtain a denominator for this equation.

By what mechanism did smallpox spread through the diverse groups that exploited the different ecological zones of the Western Interior? To answer this question, we need to work at another scale of study—the regional scale. At this more localized scale, spatial interaction is the key to our understanding, and we must address questions such as these: What was the normal pattern of contact of any given Native group with other groups, and with the traders? Was this contact seasonal? What were the population densities of these groups year round? If migration occurred between groups, was it permanent or temporary? Michael Trimble has modelled several spheres of behaviour that could affect the acquisition, introduction, transmission, and maintenance of infectious diseases, reminding us that Native groups were not all alike. Each had its own cultural characteristics, seasonal habits, and range of interethnic contacts. He argues that work or task forces were significant cultural units among the Mandan, Hidatsa, and Arikara who were sedentary horticulturists located along the upper Missouri River. The "farther-ranging area of contact" sphere encompassed warring, hunting, and trading parties. Patterns of movement varied in this sphere. The "extended family and clan" unit coordinated hunting and trading expeditions, managed agricultural endeavours, and attended to the needs of fellow members, but its structure varied among different groups. The post-contact Arikara had no recognizable clan structure, while clans were significant integrating forces in Mandan and Hidatsa societies (Trimble 1989:41-59). Similarly, the flexible social structure of the Teton Sioux allowed them to incorporate other Native peoples into their society, thereby maintaining population growth, whereas the Atsina had no such population buffer against warfare and disease and suffered continual depopulation (Taylor 1989:28).

An analysis of seasonal patterns of contact and movement must heed influences of time as well as of scale. Analyzing one epidemic at one point in time is restrictive: it allows us only to infer that during one episode, some of the exposed population may have benefitted from relatively recent immunity, or to infer whether or not patterns of disease in some of the affected groups were changing over time because of hereditary differences reflective of evolutionary selection. Because diseases such as measles, smallpox, whooping cough, and mumps confer lifelong immunity upon survivors after one exposure, it is necessary to look at the cumulative impact of a series of epidemics upon one region over time. A change in a disease pattern within a region may reflect earlier demographic disturbances. A prior high death rate among children of a group, for example, would lead to lower fertility rates and fewer susceptible children a generation hence.

The human ecology triangle of habitat, population, and behaviour creates patterns of variable exposure to diseases, and their geographical distributions vary accordingly: "Every disease has its cultural ecology, its geographic regionalization, and its patterns of diffusion and change" (Meade et al. 1988:53). Place matters, in matters of disease!

Word Problems: Concepts and Definitions

Disease and illness (or terms such as ailment, malady, and sickness) are not synonymous, but they are often confused with one another in writings. Nor is disease the opposite of health; there is no opposite to disease. As David Jennings explains, we either have a disease or we do not, just as a lung does not have an opposite. Disease is a pathological change in the body that can sometimes be identified through physical signs. Illness (morbidity) is subjective; it is the experience of suffering communicated by complaints. In sum, Jennings says, "diseases cannot have symptoms because they cannot complain or feel, and illnesses cannot have signs because their experiences cannot swell or bleed" (1986:866-7). Patients are concerned with their illnesses while physicians are more concerned with their diseases. AIDS is a disease with which numerous illnesses such as infections are associated. The concomitant pain and suffering are dimensions of the illness, not the disease.

The need to separate the concepts of health, disease and illness is not merely a theoretical or semantic exercise. These concepts are at the very core of any system of thought, and once they are removed from that system, they can lose their meaning and value. They constitute a society's conceptual framework for thinking about health, "a general scheme for explaining, predicting, and controlling dimensions of the human condition" (Englehardt 1981:32).[1] In historical studies, the distinction between disease and illness is an important one. What in one epoch was called a disease may be, in a later period, only a symptom. An example is the word "angina," whose contemporary connotation is chest pain. In the HBC post journals, "angina" was occasionally used, but as a term for what is now known as tonsillitis. It could also have referred to Vincent's Angina (now called trench mouth), with which the patient gets swelling, fever, and mouth ulcers. But this infection was not considered to be any more contagious than is angina in its modern sense.

A second example, more frequently seen in the HBC documents, is the use of the word "asthma." In 1819, Dr. William Todd, writing from a post on the Peace River, said that four Indians had died in the winter of "a kind of asthma which carries them off in the course of two months

---

1 The criterion for membership in the category called disease is important in those societies (predominantly Western) adhering to the biomedical model. Diseases are classified into what is called a nosography, which aids in the understanding of the causes, pathogenesis and nature of disease. The historic English Bills of Mortality and contemporary International Classification of Diseases (ICD) listings are examples of nosographies based on Western concepts of disease. They are the foundation of a physician's salary, one of the determining factors in the allocation of research monies, and the basis of health care insurance payments in the U.S.

after the attack" (HBCA E.10/2/32). He was referring to a respiratory symptom likely caused by whooping cough, which was making its rounds then, but not to the disease we now know as asthma. Same name, different contents, but his asthma was infectious, easily transmitted, and had a much higher morbidity (illness) and mortality (death) rate. Another category of uncertain meaning occurred in a letter by John Black in the Red River Colony in 1853: "Diarrhoea" had been prevalent in the settlement for two weeks and a few people had died, he wrote, "but on the whole it appears that the disease is on the decline" (HBCA A.11/95). Here he named a symptom which may have been infectious, but the identity of the disease (likely dysentery) remains a conundrum.

Whenever we try to identify a particular disease in historical texts, the assumption that a modern disease is an analogue for an old one is problematic (Ramenofsky 1987:137). The host-parasite interaction could have changed through generations, which would alter symptoms and disease patterns. For example, influenza, once known as catarrh, was not given its present name until 1743. This infectious disease was (and is) notorious for changing its strains and causing repeated epidemics in the same population groups. Syphilis appeared in fifteenth-century Europe, also as an epidemic. It initially exhibited fulminating, deadly symptoms, unlike the syphilis of today which is a mild endemic infection (Ampel 1991:659). René Dubos, the esteemed microbiologist and ecologist, noted that the first and second generation of Natives to suffer from a tuberculosis epidemic in a Qu'Appelle Valley reserve initially had meningitis-like symptoms, which by the third generation had changed to pulmonary symptoms (Dubos 1965:175).

Additionally, modern classifications of diseases do not always fit older terminology. Diseases that are sudden and unprecedented (Lyme disease, Legionnaires, toxic shock syndrome, AIDS) start for a variety of reasons. The incidence and prevalence of a disease may change when it is introduced into a virgin population, virulence (the disease-evoking power of a pathogen) may increase or decrease, and ecological systems may be altered (as when a dam is built). It may be that the disease was present all along but not recognized, or identification and reporting skills and procedures may change (Ampel 1991:662-3). I would argue that it often does not matter what we call the disease because we may never be able to identify the infecting agent. We may never know what the fourth-century B.C. Plague of Athens was in modern terminology. In the

JODY F. DECKER

Canadian subarctic, fur traders reported a mysterious disorder that seemed to predominate at York Factory. "The country distemper," as they called it, has eluded attempts at identification by a variety of researchers. We can, however, trace the socio-economic and demographic contexts and consequences of visitations of such pestilences. If we do find congruence between what we understand in modern terms to be a certain disease, and what seemed to be that disease in the historical record, we can usefully analyze how that disease acted in the past in order to predict what it might do in the future.

Ontological and Physiological Concepts of Disease

The causes and the nature of disease for Natives and non-Natives in the eighteenth and nineteenth centuries were interpreted in the framework of one or the other of two theories. According to the *ontological* theory, disease entities had an independent existence from the body; in the *physiological* theory (also called pathological or functional), diseases were said to originate from within the body, even though the precise cause was not known before the age of bacteriology and the rise of scientific medicine in the late nineteenth century. Was a disease due to a new outside invading entity, or was it generated from inside the body? "Catching" or being "struck down" by a disease are ontological explanations of disease still in use today. Was the entity a seed, a micro-organism, or a poison such as a miasma? Spirits, demons, curses, or spells, reified and considered akin to concrete real objects, were also independent entities capable of causing diseases. According to Guenter Risse, ancient societies reified the causes of distress and dysfunction. Such ontologies "were and still are highly functional; they provide the necessary focus for specific therapies ... and were bound to lessen fear and anxiety in both the affected individual and his circle of family and friends" (Risse 1980:580). If the entity was not an enemy to be expunged, then was the sickness due to the body's own attempts to heal itself by displaying a fever? On the other hand, the physiological disease theory holds that disease cannot exist as an entity without the patient. Each patient is unique and real in this view; definitions and classifications of diseases are arbitrary. Patients vary, but the disease does not (Englehardt 1981; Risse 1980).

Europeans vacillated between these two theories. The etiology or cause of disease was highly disputed and remained for most people a mystery. The basic framework which supplemented or replaced magical and religious explanations was humoral medicine, according to which bodily humours played essential roles in functional integrity and thus in maintaining health. This concept, laid down in antiquity, led to the establishment of the physiological disease concept. Rather than reifying disease, ancient Greek, Indian and Chinese civilizations stressed the body's individual "psychophysical" characteristics (the constitution) as the cause of a disease (Risse 1980:581). Concepts of humoral medicine varied among cultures, but the basic premise was that the elements (fire, water, earth, air) and bodily humours (air, bile, phlegm, blood) existed naturally in a state of opposition. Disease resulted from imbalance and the individual was held responsible. However, environmental explanations for disease, such as miasmas or swampy exhalations (as in malaria, meaning literally "bad air"), were also thought to account for some diseases until bacteriology ascribed specific micro-organisms to specific diseases. Epidemics of typhoid, diphtheria, and cholera fuelled the ontologists' fires. But as micro-organisms were reified, environmental and social factors were relegated to the background.

The nineteenth century was the age of heroic medicine: administer violent cathartics and extract at least six pints of blood, because as the medical journals demonstrated and, as respected physicians such as Benjamin Rush admonished, "desperate diseases require desperate remedies" (quoted in Duffy 1982:5). As John Duffy notes, "the medical world was still debating whether diseases were distinct entities, or symptomatic of basic constitutional disturbances" (1982:5). It is true that from the time of the French Revolution and the rise of hospital medicine in the 1790s, through to the emergence of bacteriology in the late nineteenth century, significant advances were made in medical knowledge. The practice of medicine changed very slowly, however, especially in Rupert's Land where physicians were few and far between.

We get glimpses of how European disease concepts functioned in the region from the York Factory medical journals, the only surviving medical journals in the 200-year history of the Hudson's Bay Company (HBCA B.239/a/166-180). They were written from 1846 to 1852 by what were called "regular doctors," as opposed, for example, to barber-surgeons or apothecaries. These doctors came from well-established and respected medical schools such as Edinburgh. One graduate of this school who wrote four years of these journals was Dr. William Smellie, M.D., L.R.C.S.E. (Licentiate of the Royal College of Surgeons of Edinburgh). The training that Dr. Smellie received in Edinburgh formed

JODY F. DECKER

the basis of his medical practice in Canada. He was typical of the physicians of his day, operating within two disease theories: a confused, frustrated doctor bleeding, purging, inducing vomiting, blistering, and correcting bodily imbalances. These imbalances were due to external, remote causes often referred to in the journals as effluvia. Purging kept the entire system open; bleeding relieved tension; and blistering relieved compression. So Dr. Smellie "cupped" (application of a glass vessel with no air in it to the skin to draw blood to the surface) the loins of one patient six ounces for haemorrhoids, did a fiat venisection (another method of bloodletting that removed larger quantities of blood than did cupping) of four ounces for chicken pox, and applied croton oil to make a blister rise as treatment for a stroke. His diagnosis for an ulcer on the side of a labourer's neck was that it was "not the result of a blow but a constitutional affection" (Decker 1994).

The Indians also bled, purged, and cupped. George Keith asserted that the Athapaskan-speaking Beaver Indians did not know how to use herbs, but they practised blood-letting. Assiniboine healers did cupping with a buffalo horn to alleviate pains or extract objects such as worms from the body (Corlett 1935:108). The Indians sometimes had the traders bleed them. During the measles epidemic in 1819, an Indian arrived at an unidentified post with a "distemper" and the trader bled him in the arm and described the blood "as black nearly as Ink." The Indian died the next day. After another measles epidemic in 1846, a Native woman complaining of pain in her right ear, with an offensive discharge from it and swelling, came in to see Dr. Smellie. She had never recovered her hearing after an attack of measles the summer before (HBCA B.239/a/166, 5 September 1846).

For the vast majority of the company's employees, self-medication was the traditional first resort. Neither trader nor Indian relied on HBC "regular doctors." One HBC officer, John McLean, wrote in 1849:

> I have now passed 24 years of my life in this country; I have served in every quarter of it; and I own that I have never yet known a single instance of an Indian being retained at any inland post for medical treatment. I may mention however, by way of exception to the general rule, that the depots along the coast are well supplied with medicines, and that there are medical men there who administer them to the natives when they apply for them. In the interior we are allowed to doctor ourselves as we best can. What with the salubrity of the climate, and our abstemious

fare, we are enabled, with the aid of a little Turlington Balsam, and a dose of salts, perhaps, to overcome all our ailments. Most of us use the lancet, and can even 'spread a plaster or give a blister', when necessary, but the Indians seldom trouble us. (Wallace 1932:315)

Such excerpts from the primary documents give us a sense of a practice of pluralistic medicine. A perusal of the HBC medical journals and daily post journals indicates that Natives suffering from acute infectious diseases such as measles and smallpox tended to ask for European assistance. Did they think that it took a European treatment to cure a European disease? The journals record that the Natives also sought help for respiratory-related disorders, especially consumption, which was a chronic disease, perhaps not considered to be infectious by them. Yet there is no mention in the journals of Natives seeking treatment for chronic venereal diseases.

The basic tenet of the biomedical or Western health model is that diseases derive from a single pathology at the cellular level, and manifest themselves in symptoms (complaints or feelings expressed by an individual), in syndromes (a constellation of signs and symptoms) or in culturally-recognized diseases that follow a predictable course. The biomedical model is reductionist in assuming that disease is accounted for by measurable biological variables; it is also dualistic in that it separates the mind from the body. Neither of these factors operates in a traditional Native spiritual model. However, in the biomedical model, diseases and illnesses are classified into a highly developed taxonomy. The person playing the sick role is then labelled, which can be an advantage, as it is a comfort to the sufferer whose legitimate disease, once recognized, elicits an accepted treatment regime. In other words, labelling is a part of the "business" of health. In traditional Native philosophy, labelling of diseases as such is not as important because it is individuals and the society in which they live, not specific pathogens, that are responsible for disease. However, Subarctic Algonquian peoples (Cree, Ojibwa) believed some individuals could become a "windigo," which was a fearsome prospect to these people as it was a symbol of cannibalism and elicited a variety of treatments (Asikinack 1987:3-12).[1]

---

1   Windigo stories are told to young people as a lesson about selfishness. When you hoard something in a sharing society, you indirectly feed off the "flesh" of another human, as Asikinack explains.

JODY F. DECKER

Native traditional cosmologies or world views are governed by a sense of interrelatedness with the environment and the forces of nature. Nature is to be lived in accordance with, not controlled. The Woods Cree believed that living creatures supplied food and medicine for humans and that the only expectation was that an offering be given (Young *et al.* 1990:25). Writing from somewhere around the North Saskatchewan River on his 1772 inland journey, Matthew Cocking revealed to us not only his own cultural baggage, but also indicated the congruence of Native medical practices with the environment:

> these [gifts] were to be given to the ground to induce it to favour them with plenty of furs & provisions: They [Natives] have a notion that these gifts have a great effect; & when anything happens contrary to their desires they commonly use this method to appease the ill Domon [demon]. When sick they are very foolish, for they throw away many necessaries, also present to others as payment for singing their god-songs that they may recover. (quoted in Warkentin 1993:146-7)

Disease could be induced by the breaking of a taboo imposed by the spirits, by the capture of the essence of a person by evil spirits, or by the intrusion of objects (Kemnitzer 1980:275). Among the Blackfoot, the cure for the disease was elimination of evil spirits represented in the body by disease objects (Corlett 1935:104). In a letter to Roderic MacKenzie in 1810, George Keith wrote that the Beaver Indians of the Mackenzie River district also cured diseases by performing "absurd gestures" and pretended "to extract hair, toads and small pike fish" from their affected parts (Masson 1960:89, Vol.2). The shaman did very little to treat the affected part, but he did try to appease or defeat the powers that had sent the disease. Such a seer of visions could be a community leader and one who received special honours. Indeed, among the Plains societies, the most highly valued power coming to a successful vision seeker was the art of healing. Medicine men or shamans received through dreams special marks of favour from a spirit to engage in healing, and, among other abilities, their success in vision quests "brought the capacity to control diseases" (Dugan 1985:161). In Western societies, in contrast, the seeing of visions is often thought symptomatic of a diseased state.

While shamanistic curing did have its successes, the Native panacea for many diseases and illnesses, the sweat bath, was often a double-edged sword. The lodge was usually constructed of willow bark, which contains salicin, the active ingredient in aspirin, and/or conifer branches, whose oils are a decongestant. Inside the lodge, other herbs and roots were added to the heated rocks to produce medicinal vapours (Taylor 1977:58). After sweating for some time, however, it was customary to plunge into the cold snow or a nearby body of water. High temperatures accompanying many infectious diseases such as smallpox could be lowered so dramatically by such actions that shock and often death ensued. David Thompson, recalling the smallpox epidemic on the Plains in 1781, stated that more men than women and children died "from the fever, rushing into Rivers and Lakes" (Tyrrell 1916:236). In these instances, death resulted from a secondary problem rather than the apparent primary cause, the smallpox virus. This fact complicates efforts to estimate the mortality rates caused by the virus itself.

Mortality rates ascribed to the infecting disease are termed "case fatality rates." During the smallpox epidemic from December of 1781 to the spring of 1782, William Tomison at Cumberland House reported in numerous entries that many Native tents in his district contained no live bodies, and those who survived the epidemic told him they had no friends or relatives alive (HBCA B.49/a/11). In such grim circumstances, was there a major case-to-case transmission of smallpox which resulted in high case fatality rates, or was the high mortality more a matter of environmental and cultural factors? Absence of medical attention or of able bodies to acquire food, cultural practices such as smoking from the same pipe and using the same blankets to scare away the "eyed monster," and utilization of the sweat bath followed by cold shocks all contributed to mortality. The virus itself may not have been as lethal as is sometimes assumed, and overestimations of its fatality rate may easily occur. Similarly, other factors such as non-infectious diseases, alcohol, warfare, suicide, and starvation contributed to mortality, but determining their relative importance is highly problematic. Underestimations of mortality rates can also occur. In epidemics of measles and whooping cough, weakened victims often died later from secondary respiratory infections. Such infections, however, could also have been due to the reactivation of latent tubercular infection, which may have been triggered by coughing, induced in diseases such as measles, whooping cough, and smallpox (Mercer 1990:101). In short, interpreting the causes and rates of mortality and morbidity in the historic record requires careful analysis of challenging evidence.

Explaining Contagion

There are two ways that people construct notions of disease and illness. One way is from our own memories—our personal knowledge of having had measles or the "flu." The second source is secondhand information. Donald Ross, HBC chief factor at Norway House (Manitoba), wrote in 1833, "that awful calamity the cholera is it seems raging with deadly violence in Canada and the States—it will reach us of course next summer if not sooner." (Glazebrook 1938:102). Cholera never did diffuse into the Western Interior, but Donald Ross had learned an attitude, and any reader of his statement learns only his opinion, not a fact.

Ways of explaining illness and disease vary across cultures, as do behaviours associated with illness, and reactions to the ill by members of the group. As societies change and evolve, theories of what constitutes and explains a disease or an illness also change. Groups also have folk understandings of illness which are embedded in names of illnesses, and beliefs about causation and cures. In many societies, diseases are not the only explanations for illness; demons and spiritual intrusions, curses, or disharmony with nature are among the explanatory factors. Such culturally derived belief systems reflect world views and group experiences, but Western-style scientific investigation aims and claims to go beyond these parameters.

One of the most important early Western explanations of disease centred on the idea of contagion. The Italian physician Girolamo Fracastoro proposed the first consistent scientific theory of contagion in his famous treatise *De Contagione* in 1546. He proposed that the entity causing an infection was a "seed of contagion" and that each infectious disease had a different seed (Ackerknecht 1982:99-101).[1] His ideas, however, had little impact until they were confirmed through discoveries in bacteriology by Pasteur, Koch, and others late in the nineteenth century. But if the concept of contagion was not recognized or understood earlier, how did ordinary people, European or Native, account for the spread of disease? Their theories of causation ranged from foulness of the air (mal-

---

1 Amazingly, Fracastoro described and analyzed several contagious diseases such as smallpox, measles, leprosy; named and described syphilis; and was the first to describe typhus. Dubos (1965:166-7) also points out that this remarkable man gave us this timely warning: "syphilis too will pass away and die out, but later it will be born again and be seen again by our descendants, just as in bygone ages we must believe it was observed by our ancestors."

aria), artificially poisoned water, and swampy exhalations in the form of a miasma, to the magical powers of some chiefs or the ire of the Great Spirit (Veith 1981:227).

A disease can be present without illness, as in the case of infections with latent periods such as smallpox or measles. Even though the organism is in the body, the patient may not feel ill. If the disease does manifest itself, it may first appear as a mixture of signs and symptoms, known in epidemiology as the prodromal stage of illness. The prodrome, typical of infectious diseases, often defies a definitive diagnosis until the characteristic rash of the disease appears. In many cases, despite such clues, the identity of an illness remained an enigma to the traders and medical men in Rupert's Land. Terms such as "the distemper," "a sickness," the "prevailing complaint," and the "prevailing disorder" were therefore common in their writings. The whole concept of contagion and of a silent or latent period where the disease is inside the body but not evident on the outside, was puzzling to both Natives and European fur traders; and their responses to the appearance of disease changed and varied through time, as the following examples demonstrate.

A Blackfoot who survived the 1781-82 smallpox epidemic told David Thompson: "We had no belief that one Man could give it to another, any more than a wounded Man could give his wound to another" (Tyrrell 1916:337). Another Plains group, the Assiniboine, thought that smallpox had eyes and could see who was afraid of it, so they gathered around the ill rather than isolate themselves, smoked from the same pipe, ate from the same dish and used each other's blankets (Lowie 1901:43). The usual remedies of the Indians failed and the cold plunge that often followed what the traders described as their "grand remedy," the sweat bath, led to more deaths.

Several Plains Natives, especially the Cree, came to some of the posts for what the traders referred to as "the grand medicine" or vaccination during the 1837 smallpox epidemic. It was their firsthand knowledge of the ravages of this disease during the 1781-82 epidemic that led them to flee from it when smallpox next struck the Plains in 1837. By the time of this latter epidemic, both Natives and Europeans understood the idea of quarantine, but neither understood latency. Dr. William Todd, who played a pivotal role in this epidemic by vaccinating and inoculating as many Indians as he could, wrote the following about an Indian who had come to him from Carlton House on the North Saskatchewan River:

another point which may be considered extra-ordinary the time the contagion must have remained in the System without any visible effects, the man was twelve days on the March and five days here before the Eruption broke out it can only be imputed to climate which ultimately proved injurious. (HBCA B.159/a/17)

Dr. Todd was guided by the tenets of ontological theory in ascribing the eruption of the disease to an external climatic factor. He thought that the disease would not have spread if it was not visible on the body, and that quarantine would suffice as a preventative measure when the disease was manifested.

Finally, during the last great smallpox epidemic on the Plains in 1869, an incident described by Captain William Butler suggested that the Crees' understanding of contagion had clearly changed and grown to include the concept of spreading an infectious disease through its victims and its discharges:

In the immediate neighbourhood of Fort Pitt two camps of Crees established themselves, at first in hope of obtaining medical assistance, and failing in that ... they appear to have endeavoured to convey the infection into the fort, in the belief that by doing so they would cease to suffer from it themselves. The dead bodies were left unburied close to the stockades, and frequently Indians in the worst stage of the disease might be seen trying to force an entrance into the houses, or rubbing portions of the infectious matter from their persons against the door-handles and window-frames of the dwellings. (Butler 1872:368)

This apparent recognition of smallpox as contagious came just as Cree lands were being sold to Britain to become part of Canada in 1870. Through most of the 200-year history of Rupert's Land, however, neither Native peoples nor Europeans clearly grasped the concept of contagion, and the consequences were indeed appalling. A disease such as measles or smallpox with an average latency period of twelve days could be carried a considerable distance on horseback by an unsuspecting traveller. Some epidemics, especially those of measles and smallpox, were spread far and wide by fleeing, mounted victims who had no idea of the concept of contagion (Decker 1991:392).

Contextualizing Illness and Disease

The term environment has been used in this essay to mean the totality of factors, both physical and cultural, that affect an organism. The dynamic interaction between humans and the environment necessitates contextualizing every illness and disease. Major contextual factors affecting the course of a disease include ecosystems, levels of immunity, nutrition, public health and quarantine measures, the carriers' theory of disease, and cultural practices.

Illness has always existed. The signs and symptoms were always there, although they may not have been recognized culturally, for illness is cultural while disease is pathological. Indeed, there are those who argue that disease does not exist, and that only cultural practices exist (Delaporte 1986). This is not a denial that bacilli, viruses, and tumours that cause disease do exist. Some viruses change through time and alter their manifestations of illness; new diseases then appear (Ampel 1991).[1] The tubercle bacillus causes tuberculosis, but housing conditions (crowding, cleanliness, and ventilation), nutritional status, and treatment help determine the course of the disease. To move beyond an analysis of diseases *per se* and to address other questions such as cultural change and adjustment, Michael Trimble argues that variables such as individual social behaviour, village organization, and clan obligations must also be included in a contextualized analysis (Trimble 1989). Our concepts of disease are closely related to our behaviours and values, and these are culturally determined and transmitted.

Ways of coping with illness manifest themselves within the bounds of certain underlying expectations or conformities in a given society. Illness can elicit a variety of responses. First, the action can be predictable, for instance, going to a physician or shaman. However, a person may be ill but unable to obtain the needed care due to geographic isolation. Or the people close to the patient may also be sick and unable to help, as was the case in Native communities in many epidemics. Second, victims may decide to take no action if it is their belief that fate will take its course. The fur-trade doctor often behaved on that premise. Finally, a person may have a disease which will bring on illness, but may be still unaware of it. The latency period in infectious diseases is an example. In

---

1   Ampel gives a good review of where "new" diseases could come from and the diverse ways epidemics start.

such cases, one is capable of spreading the disease in a ghostly state, but such a carrier is a nightmare in more than the ghostly sense to researchers who trace diffusion patterns of diseases.

Such actions and their interpretations are important, for they are the basis of explanation in most historical texts. Historical data are typically fragmentary, imprecise, and scattered, yet they are no less valuable than those data which deal with probability. Terms such as "the prevailing disorder" or "severe sickness" used in the HBC journals provide important clues even if they are problematic. We cannot always be sure whether an outbreak with "severe sickness" is a portion of a larger epidemic, but HBC records often provide some data on the geographical extent of the outbreak. Converting such a term as "severe sickness," suggestive of illness and not death, into a standard unit of measurement for demographic or cartographic purposes, however, presents challenges.

The risks we take if we make sweeping generalizations from fragmentary documentation are enormous. We cannot assume, for instance, that all Plains Natives or all fur trade physicians changed their understanding of contagion at the same rate, regardless of the efficacy of communication. Adoption of new disease theories by different cultural groups was (and still is, for the most part) a very slow process. The fact that the Crees' concept of contagion changed over time, for example, does not mean that their allies, the Assiniboine followed suit. Nor does it mean that all individuals were aware of or adhered to this concept; Butler's description pertained only to Fort Pitt. This was also the case with vaccinations for smallpox. Some members of the same Native group did not agree to vaccination, while others thought it was the best medicine.

Epidemics of infectious diseases played a major role in altering Native societies in the eighteenth and nineteenth centuries (Decker 1991, Krech 1983, Ray 1974, Taylor 1977). To understand the full significance or impact of regional details about such disease episodes, many researchers have situated their studies within a wider comparative or international framework. John Moore, for example, argued that regional studies on disease and depopulation can inform general studies of social evolutionary theory, which account for cultural continuity and discontinuity (Moore 1989:127). Susan Vehik has explored the use of ethnographic data on disease and depopulation for understanding pre-contact and early contact Plains societies' population sizes and settlement organization (Vehik 1989:115-125). And in her book *Vectors of Death*, the archaeologist Ann Ramenofsky valiantly attempted to infer population estimates from archaeological evidence and ethnographic data. As more regional analyses of disease and depopulation have become available, western hemispheric aboriginal population figures have been reassessed, most notably by William Denevan (1992) and Douglas Ubelaker (1992). Denevan now estimates the pre-contact North American aboriginal population to have been 3,790,000, a drop of over 600,000 from his 1976 estimate (Denevan 1992:xxix). Approximately five per cent of that total population resided north of the present-day Canadian border (Heidenreich 1990).

Changes in standard of living, advances in medical therapy, efforts at disease prevention and control, and the changing periodicity of different epidemics have contributed, through time, to a global mortality transition from largely infectious to non-infectious causes of death. Alex Mercer recently examined the relative importance of these factors in the epidemiological-demographic transition for England since the eighteenth century. His discussion of the ways human beings react to diseases as social and biological beings has laid the groundwork for comparative studies with other countries. He argued, as I did in a study of the impact of infectious diseases on the Plains Natives, that a long-term perspective on mortality decline, and a sense of the cumulative impact of diseases and disease control, is necessary to fully understand the reasons for depopulation and the underestimation of various disease-control measures (Mercer 1990:9; Decker 1991).

On a final note, one pragmatic reason for analyzing records of historic epidemics is the potential for applying our knowledge of the best-documented episodes to other less well understood episodes at different times and places. Ann Herring's examination of the 1918-19 influenza pandemic at Norway House, at the north end of Lake Winnipeg in Manitoba, provides, for example, "a possible simulation of conditions that might have existed from time to time in some historic and prehistoric North American Aboriginal communities" (Herring 1994:75).

Epidemics are cyclical; diseases arise and peak, but later their effects on a population wane. Just as this cyclical propensity means that we are always on the defensive against micro-organisms, so, too, should we be on the defensive about interpreting historical texts. Careful reading and interpretation of all the available historical evidence helps us to better understand their patterns and their human consequences.

JODY F. DECKER

References

Ackerknecht, Erwin
    1982 *A Short History of Medicine.* Baltimore: Johns Hopkins University
        Press.

Ampel, Neil
    1991 Plagues—What's Past is Present: Thoughts on the Origin and
        History of New Infectious Diseases. *Reviews of Infectious Diseases*
        13:658-65.

Asikinack, William
    1987 Legends through Anishinabe Eyes. *Contemporary Native American*
        Cultural Issues: Proceedings from the Native American Studies Conference.
        Lake Superior State University, 3-12.

Butler, William F.
    1872 *The Great Lone Land.* London: Gilbert and Rivington.

Cocking, Matthew
    1993 An Adventurer from Hudson Bay: Journal of Matthew Cocking,
        from York Factory to the Blackfeet Country, 1772-73. Germaine
        Warkentin, ed. *Canadian Exploration Literature.* Toronto: Oxford
        University Press, 142-53.

Corlett, William Thomas
    1935 *The Medicine-Man of the American Indian and his cultural background.*
        Baltimore: Charles C. Thomas, 97-122.

Decker, Jody
    1988 Tracing historical diffusion patterns: the case of the 1780-2 smallpox
        epidemic among the Indians of Western Canada. *Native Studies*
        Review 4(1-2):1-24.

    1991 Depopulation of the Northern Plains Natives. *Social Science and*
        Medicine 33(4):381-9355.

    1994 The York Factory medical journals, 1846-52. Paper presented to the
        History of Medicine lectures, Department of Medicine, McMaster
        University.

Delaporte, François
    1986 *Disease and Civilization: the Cholera in Paris, 1832.* Cambridge, MA:
        MIT Press.

Denevan, William
    1992 The Native Population of the Americas in 1492. 2nd ed. Madison:
        University of Wisconsin Press.

Dubos, René
  1965 Man Adapting. New Haven, CT: Yale University Press.
Duffy, John
  1982 Medicine in the West: an Historical Overview. *Journal of the West*
       21(3):6-14.
Dugan, K.M.
  1985 *The Vision Quest of the Plains Indians. Its Spiritual Significance.*
       Lewiston, NY: Edwin Mellen Press, Studies in American Religion,
       13.
Englehardt, H. Tristram, Jr.
  1981 Changing Concepts of Health and Disease. In Arthur L. Caplan, H.
       Tristram Englehardt, Jr., and James J. McCartney, eds. *Concepts of
       Health and Disease. Interdisciplinary Perspectives.* London:
       Addison-Wesley. 221-45.
Glazebrook, G.P. de T., ed.
  1938 *The Hargrave Correspondence.* Toronto: Champlain Society.
Heidenreich, Conrad
  1990 Native Peoples circa 1740. *The National Atlas of Canada*, 5th ed.
       Ottawa: Energy, Mines and Resources Canada.
Herring, Ann
  1994 "There were young people and old people and babies dying every
       week": The 1918-19 Influenza Pandemic at Norway House.
       Ethnohistory 41(1):73-10555.
Houston, Stuart
  1984 New light on Dr. John Richardson. *Canadian Medical Association
       Journal* 131:653-60.
       Hudson's Bay Company Archives, Provincial Archives of Manitoba,
       Winnipeg.
  1781 Cumberland House Post Journal by William Tomison, B.49/a/11.
  1838 Fort Pelly Post Journal, B.159/a/17.
  1853 London Inward Correspondence, A.11/95.
  1819 Private Papers, E.10/a/32.
1846-52 York Factory Medical Journals, B.239/a/166-80.
Jennings, David
  1986 The Confusion Between Disease and Illness in Clinical Medicine.
       Canadian Medical Association Journal 135:865-70.

JODY F. DECKER

Kemnitzer, Luis S.

1980 Research in Health and Healing in the Plains. In W. Raymond Wood and Margot Liberty, eds. *Anthropology on the Great Plains.* Lincoln: University of Nebraska Press, 272-83.

Krech, Shepard III

1983 The Influence of Disease and the Fur Trade on Arctic Drainage Lowlands Dene, 1800-1850. *Journal of Anthropological Research* 39(1):123-4655.

Lowie, Robert

1901 *The Assiniboine.* New York: Anthropology Papers of the American Museum of Natural History (4), part 1.

Martin, Calvin

1976 Wildlife Diseases as a Factor in the Depopulation of the North American Indian. *Western Historical Quarterly*, 7:47-62.

Masson, L.R., ed.

1960 Les bourgeois de la compagnie du Nord-ouest: récits de voyages, lettres, et rapports inédits relatifs au Nord-ouest canadien. 1889-90. 2 vols. New York: Antiquarian Press.

Mausner, Judith, and Shira Kramer

1985 *Epidemiology. An Introductory Text.* Toronto: W.B. Saunders.

Meade, Melinda, John Florin, and Wil Gesler

1988 *Medical Geography.* New York: Guilford Press.

Mercer, Alex

1990 *Disease, Mortality and Population in Transition.* Leicester: Leicester University Press.

Moore, John

1989 Quantitative and Qualitative Variables in Human Evolution. In Gregory R. Campbell, ed., Plains Indian Historical Demography and Health. Perspectives, Interpretations, and Critiques. *Plains Anthropologist* (34) 124:127-32.

Ramenofsky, Anne

1987 *Vectors of Death. The Archaeology of European Contact.* Albuquerque: University of New Mexico Press.

Ray, Arthur, J.

1974 *Indians in the Fur Trade.* Toronto: University of Toronto Press.

Risse, Guenter B.

1980 Health and Disease. History of the Concepts. In Warren T. Reich, ed., *Encyclopedia of Bioethics.* New York: Free Press, 579-85.

Sharrock, Susan

 1977 Cross-tribal, Ecological Categorization of Far Northern Plains Cree
 and Assiniboine by late Eighteenth and Early Nineteenth Century
 Fur Traders. *Western Canadian Journal of Anthropology* 7(4):7-21.

Taylor, John F.

 1977 Sociocultural effects of epidemics on the Northern Plains:
 1734-1850. *Western Canadian Journal of Anthropology* 8(4):55-81.

 1989 Counting: The Utility of Historic Population Estimates in the
 Northwestern Plains 1800-1880. In Gregory R. Campbell, ed.,
 Plains Indian Historical Demography and Health. Perspectives,
 Interpretations, and Critiques. *Plains Anthropologist* (34) 124:17-30.

Trimble, Michael K.

 1989 Infectious Disease and the Northern Plains Horticulturists: A Human
 Behavior Model. In Gregory R. Campbell, ed., Plains Indian
 Historical Demography and Health. Perspectives, Interpretations,
 and Critiques. *Plains Anthropologist* (34) 124:41-59.

Tyrrell, J.B., ed.

 1916 *David Thompson's Narrative of his Explorations in Western America,
 1784-1812*. Toronto: Champlain Society.

Ubelaker, Douglas

 1992 North American Indian Population Size: Changing Perspectives. In
 John W. Verano and D.K. Ubelaker, eds., Disease and Demography
 in the Americas. Washington, DC: Smithsonian Institution Press.

Vehik, Susan C.

 1989 Problems and Potential in Plains Indian Demography. In Gregory R.
 Campbell, ed., Plains Indian Historical Demography and Health.
 Perspectives, Interpretations, and Critiques. *Plains Anthropologist* (34)
 124:115-25.

Veith, Ilza

 1981 Historical Reflections on the Changing Concepts of Disease. In
 Arthur L. Caplan, H. Tristram Englehardt, Jr., and James J.
 McCartney, eds., *Concepts of Health and Disease. Interdisciplinary
 Perspectives*. London: Addison-Wesley, 221-45.

Wallace, William S.

 1932 *John McLean's Notes of a Twenty-five Years Service in the Hudson's Bay
 Territory*. Toronto: Champlain Society.

Wilson, Mary E., Richard Levins, and Andrew Spielman, eds.

 1994 *Disease in Evolution: Global Changes and Emergence of Infectious Diseases*.
 New York: New York Academy of Sciences.

JODY F. DECKER

Young, David, Grant Ingram, and Lise Swartz

1990 *Cry of the Eagle. Encounters with a Cree Healer.* Toronto: University of Toronto Press.

8

Retelling the Death of Barbue, A Gwich'in Leader

Shepard Krech III

OVER THE PAST quarter century, anthropology and history have converged greatly, as anthropologists have increasingly embraced historical modes of analysis and writing, and historians anthropological ways. Their mutual boundary increasingly permeable, the two disciplines have drawn on each other as well as on other fields. What each has borrowed from the other varies considerably because theoretical inspiration is so broadly based. But in recent years, the convergence has had one notable outcome: some historians whose work was formerly most firmly based in statistics and the social sciences have returned to narrative approaches, finding common ground with some anthropologists headed toward similar goals. Both now try more often to write stories which have beginnings, middles, and ends, stories with plots and sub-plots, stories cast chronologically, stories elegantly told. Scholars in both disciplines continue to draw from each other as well as from literary theory, in the process emphasizing, to put it more crudely than one might, art over science. The results have been salutary. At the same time that historians have embraced culture – and contemporary culture theory – anthropologists have acknowledged the importance of their "voice" in ethnography and placed a greater emphasis on style. Increasingly, both anthropologists and historians wish to tell stories, not because they share antiquarian interests of many "old" narrative histories, but because they are aware of the expressive limitations of their craft and yearn to analyze in a more compelling way culture or the actions of indigenous and non-indigenous people across cultural and social boundaries.[1]

---

1 For the turn to history in anthropology, see Shepard Krech III, The State of Ethnohistory, *Annual Review of Anthropology* 20, 1991, 345–75, and Sherry Ortner, Theory in Anthropology Since the Sixties, *Comparative Studies in Society and History* 26(1), 1984, 126–67. For the return to narrative, see Lawrence Stone, The Revival of Narrative: Reflections on a New Old History, *Past & Present* 85, 1979, 3–24; Eric Hobsbawm, The Revival of Narrative: Some Comments, *Past & Present* 86, 1980, 2–8. One recent example for North America, among many, is John Demos, *The Unredeemed Captive: A Family Story from Early America* (New York: Knopf, 1994).

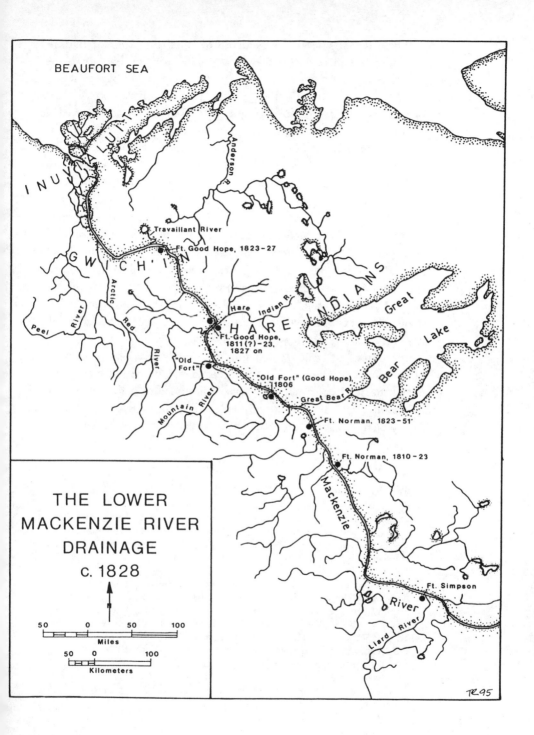

THE LOWER
MACKENZIE RIVER
DRAINAGE
c. 1828

BEAUFORT SEA

I N U V I A L U I T

G W I C H ' I N

H A R E   I N D I A N S

Peel
River

Arctic Red
River

Anderson R.

Travaillant River

Ft. Good Hope, 1823-27

Hare Indian R.

Ft.-Good Hope,
1811(?)-23,
1827 on

"Old
Fort"

"Old Fort" (Good Hope),
1806

Great Bear R.

Great
Bear
Lake

Mountain River

Ft. Norman, 1823-51

Ft. Norman, 1810-23

Mackenzie

Ft. Simpson

River

Liard River

n

50   0   50   100
Miles

50   0   100
Kilometers

TR95

These developments have led me to retell the story of Barbue, a Gwich'in Indian leader in the 1820s.[1] The story enables us to see — dimly, 170 years later — how individuals participated in historical events as well as in the making of history. Unfortunately, little is known about Barbue. I am unaware, for example, of oral historical accounts, which are of great potential, concerning him, and what we do know comes largely from journals and correspondence kept by Hudson's Bay Company (HBC) traders who managed the fur-trading post where Barbue traded. This story relies especially on the analysis of information in daily post journals, which are one of the most common document types in the voluminous HBC Archives in Winnipeg, Canada. Often, they represent the major if not sole direct source of written information on indigenous people and on everyday events that affected the residents of posts. The clerks who kept the journals were careful to mention their own comings and goings. They also often mentioned the seasonal motions of Native people. They sometimes named the groups and their individual leaders, who visited them for the purpose of exchange. The trade, after all, was the reason the clerks were there.[2]

In contrast to trade, which gripped both Native and non-Native, other aspects of Natives' lives were either not witnessed or, if experienced, deemed irrelevant for journals intended as a formal record of mercantilist endeavour. For post managers, the segments of Natives' lives which lay beyond what the clerks considered of immediate or "his-

---

1   This essay revisits an analysis of Barbue in The Death of Barbue, a Kutchin Trading Chief, Arctic 35, 1982, 429–37, which has been extensively reworked for this volume. I would like to thank Jennifer Brown for urging me to rethink the analysis for this collection; the Arctic Institute of North America for the necessary permission; Jennifer Brown and Elizabeth Vibert for their thoughtful comments on an earlier version; and Tuija Rankama for the map.

2   The Hudson's Bay Company Archives are quoted extensively in this essay. Abbreviations are used for specific records in the notes that follow. The full citations are: HBCA B. 39/b/2, Fort Chipewyan Journals, 1822–25; HBCA B. 80/a/2–14, Fort Good Hope Journals, 1823–38; HBCA B. 181/a/2–12, Fort Resolution Journals, 1819–37; HBCA B. 200/a/6, 10–11, Fort Simpson Journals, 1825–26, 1828–31; HBCA B. 200/b/3, Fort Simpson Correspondence, 1826–27; HBCA B. 200/d/4,6,1155,17,44, Fort Simpson Accounts, 1824, 1826–28, 1834; HBCA B. 200/e/3,7, Fort Simpson Reports, 1823–24, 1826–27; HBCA D. 4/92, Governor George Simpson Correspondence Outward, 1828; HBCA D. 5/3, Governor George Simpson Correspondence Inward, 1823–30.

torical" importance constituted non-events.[1] Thus, scholars who have depended on post journals for their analyses of indigenous culture and history have not only had to determine the meanings that Native people assigned to certain events, but have faced the awkward problem of seeking in the journals the traces of what Native people considered to be significant events. Moreover, traders rarely said enough about a single individual in post journals to allow insight into one person's life. Fortunately, post journals can often be supplemented — as they are here — with reports, correspondence, and the recorded observations of explorers. Still, this fuller record is ordinarily woefully inadequate for more than a skeletal biography.[2]

The story of Barbue is that of a man whose last six years concluded what had evidently been a full life lived in the area of Fort Good Hope, a Hudson's Bay Company post positioned strategically in the northwestern subarctic to capture the fur trade over a vast region. The HBC employees who met him and whose words about Barbue and other Gwich'in we must interpret, were mainly of Scottish and Canadian origin. John Bell, who kept the post journal in 1825-28 when the events concerning Barbue unfolded, was born on the island of Mull off the west coast of Scotland. He had earlier served at North West Company (NWC) posts in the Mackenzie River region. After the NWC/HBC amalgamation in 1821, the HBC kept him on. He was posted at Fort Good Hope during the 1820s and 1830s. Later, in 1832, HBC governor George Simpson, whose caustic and judgmental remarks about many of his colleagues startle readers even today, said of Bell:

---

1   Raymond D. Fogelson, The Ethnohistory of Events and Non-Events, *Ethnohistory* 36, 1989, 133–47.

2   Native accounts, where they exist, can also of course be critical in the reconstruction of biography. Scholars who have explored the use of biography in history of northern indigenous people include Carol Judd, Sakie, Esquawenoe, and the Foundation of a Dual-Native Tradition at Moose Factory, in *The Subarctic Fur Trade: Native Social and Economic Adaptations*, ed. Shepard Krech III (Vancouver: University of British Columbia Press, 1984), 81–98; Charles A. Bishop, Kwah: a Carrier Chief, in *Old Trails and New Directions: Papers of the Third North American Fur Trade Conference*, eds. Carol Judd and Arthur J. Ray (Toronto: University of Toronto Press, 1980), 191–204; and Jennifer Brown, "A place in your mind for them all": Chief William Berens, in *Being and Becoming Indian: Biographical Studies of North American Frontiers*, ed. James A. Clifton (Chicago: Dorsey Press, 1989), 204–225. See also James H. Merrell, "Minding the Business of the Nation": Hagler as Catawba Leader, *Ethnohistory* 33, 1986, 55–70.

A Scotchman, about 35 Years of Age, has been 13 Years in the Service. Writes a good hand, but his Education has been very limited. A quiet, steady well behaved Man, but wanting in the Manner address necessary to acquire influence over Indians or Servants, and does not possess any qualification likely to bring him into particular notice: equal however to the management of a smaller Trading Post. Not likely to come rapidly forward to an interest in the business. Stationed at McKenzies River.[1]

But Bell surpassed Simpson's prediction. He later explored and opened up the trade in the Peel River region and became chief trader in charge of the Athabaska District. But in Barbue's time, he was a mere clerk in charge of a small post. In the hierarchy of the new HBC, the difference between clerk and chief trader had to do with power and financial stake: a clerk held no shares in the company, while each chief trader had one. At the highest ranks were the chief factors, each holding two shares and playing major roles in decision making.

Two other HBC officers at Fort Good Hope in Barbue's time were brothers: Peter Warren Dease and Charles Dease, Canadians whose father, Dr. John Dease, was Irish-born and an administrator in the Indian Department, and whose mother perhaps came from Kahnawake. -Charles Dease was roughly Bell's age and, like him, had previously served as a clerk with the North West Company. He was a minor figure in this story: he kept the post journal only during the summer of 1825. For the tale of Barbue, it is fortunate that Charles did not loom larger as a recorder of events, for far less is known about him than about Peter Warren Dease, who was nine years older and who had responsibility for the post journal in 1828-29, the year Barbue died.

Formerly a NWC clerk who had joined the trade in 1801, Peter Warren Dease had over twenty years of experience in the Mackenzie River region. Simpson delegated both Deases to assist John Franklin's Second Land Expedition in 1825-27, strongly recommending Peter Warren at the time. He was promoted to chief factor in 1828, and later undertook significant exploration of the Arctic coast. In 1832 he came under Simpson's scrutiny in his Character Book:

1   Glyndwr Williams, ed., The 'Character Book' of George Simpson, 1832, in *Hudson's Bay Miscellany 1670–1870* (Winnipeg: Hudson's Bay Record Society, 1975), 151–236, 201–202; R. Harvey Fleming, ed., *Minutes of Council Northern Department of Rupert Land, 1821–31* (London: Champlain Society for the Hudson's Bay Record Society, 1940), 427–28.

About 45 Years of Age. Very steady in business, an excellent Indian Trader, speaks several of the Languages well and is a man of very correct conduct and Character. Strong, vigorous and capable of going through a good deal of Severe Service but rather indolent, wanting in ambition to distinguish himself by any measure out of the usual course, inactive until roused to exertion and over easy and indulgent to his people which frequently occasions a laxity of discipline, but when his temper gets ruffled he becomes furiously violent. His judgement is sound, his manners are more pleasing and easy than those of his Colleagues, and altho' not calculated to make a shining figure may be considered a very respectable Member of the Concern.

The traits that so irritated Simpson pleased others, however, who found Dease an amiable, sociable, unpretentious man with talents for music as well as leadership. Bell may have been one of these people; in 1830, he married Peter Warren Dease's daughter.[1]

Bell, the two Deases, and others did not say a great deal about Barbue, and because so little is known about him, his life must be fleshed out with what we can learn of the lives of other Gwich'in who lived at his time yet remained nameless in the fur-trade record. Enhanced in this way, Barbue's story offers us a way to talk about Gwich'in culture and behaviour during the period when they and Europeans first encountered each other, and to embed analysis in narrative in order to tell a more compelling story of the past.

There is much we do not know about Barbue —for example, when he was born. But in January 1827, Barbue was, in Bell's words, an "old Chief" or "old man," which indicates an eighteenth-century birth. If he was in his late fifties or older in 1827 then he was born prior to the 1780s. We do know far more about Barbue's final years and death, however. Barbue was ill in January of 1827, so ill that Bell thought he was dying. Barbue did not die that winter, which may have surprised Bell, but he did

---

1   Williams, ed., The 'Character Book' of George Simpson, 1832, 184; Fleming, ed., *Minutes of Council Northern Department of Rupert Land*, 433–36; Jennifer Brown, *Strangers in Blood: Fur Trade Company Families in Indian Country* (Vancouver: University of British Columbia Press, 1980), 37–38, 113. On Peter Warren Dease's mother, see I.S. MacLaren, The HBC's Arctic Expedition 1836–39: Dease's Field Notes as Compared to Simpson's *Narrative*, in *The Fur Trade Revisited*, eds. Jennifer S.H. Brown, W.J. Eccles, and Donald P. Heldman (East Lansing: Michigan State University Press, 1994), 465–79. On Bell's marriage, see Sylvia Van Kirk, *"Many Tender Ties": Women in Fur-Trade Society, 1670–1870* (Winnipeg: Watson and Dwyer, 1980), 281.

not live much longer. He succumbed at last, in the summer of 1828, to some debilitating disease.

Barbue's death was one of many at the time. The Gwich'in who traded at Fort Good Hope were suffering from diseases of some kind, as were their neighbours who traded there and elsewhere along the Mackenzie River. Many diseases came from outside the region, were epidemic, and on occasion caused frightful symptoms and fatalities. Barbue's death, from some chronic ailment, was the recorded exception to the many deaths from epidemics during this period. If he had not been a "chief," which is what traders called the men designated as representatives of the groups with whom they exchanged goods for furs and skins, he might not have caught their attention and thereby entered their historical record. Their interest was also drawn by the indigenous medicine men, or shamans, whom they called "jugglers" and whose therapeutic techniques were so unusual that they could not be ignored.

Although brief, Bell's and the Deases' remarks open a window through which one can gain access to Gwich'in history. They both offer fresh historical data on therapeutic techniques and adaptations of the Gwich'in shortly after they had been drawn into the fur trade, and capture, in a very personal way, a traumatic era in Gwich'in history.

★   ★   ★

Barbue was a member of one of the easternmost bands of Gwich'in; the traders called his band the Upper Loucheux. The Gwich'in lived in a vast portion of the western subarctic, in what today is the northwestern corner of the Northwest Territories and the northern Yukon Territory in Canada, and in eastern interior Alaska. Gwich'in, meaning people or dwellers, was the term appended to the geographical names of the major bands by which these people knew themselves: people of the flat-land, people of the head of the waters, people among the lakes, and so on. There were nine or ten regional bands in all, which inhabited territory extending from the middle Yukon River on the west to the Anderson River, which parallels the lower Mackenzie River, on the east. The Gwich'in spoke related dialects of a language distinct from those of their neighbours on all sides. The linguistic and cultural gulf was greatest with the Inuvialuit who lived to the north and east, and least with other Athapaskan-speaking people to the south and west.

The Gwich'in were boreal forest people, even though their hunting often took them above the tree line into alpine tundra of the northern cordillera, as well as north of the tree line. Their country was drained by rivers which flowed into either the Arctic Ocean or Bering Sea. The Gwich'in fished for whitefish and trout in lakes and rivers throughout their territory and for salmon in Pacific-drainage rivers. They hunted moose and caribou as well as beaver and many smaller animals wherever these were found. Their patterns of movement throughout their territory were cyclical and largely predictable, with smaller bands fusing into larger ones as seasons, weather conditions, and distribution of resources permitted, and as planned activities and unforeseen circumstances demanded.[1]

We don't know when the first encounters between white men and the Gwich'in took place, but we can guess. For the first half of the eighteenth century, these Gwich'in almost surely did not possess any direct information concerning people of European extraction whose trading parties came closer to their territory every year. Whether they became aware of them over the next several decades is not known, and may never be unless future archaeological investigations prove revealing. Even if they were aware of Europeans — and if they were it may be that information about Russian traders came first, via Inupiat or Athapaskans to the west — no assumption about the meaning of that knowledge to the Gwich'in should be made. The assumption that the mere presence of the West, or its first coming, was somehow of earth-shattering significance is just that: a premise embedding cultural (and historical) assumptions, badly in need of "unpacking," demanding testing. Even the very terms we use get in the way. It does not help to state that the arrival of Russians or Europeans spelled the end of "prehistory" and the beginning of "protohistory" or "history" itself. Such labels are problematic. Knowledge of these outsiders, or the arrival of the outsiders themselves, may indeed in some way have been significant; but it did not have to be, nor was it in all instances.[2]

---

1   See Richard Slobodin, Kutchin, *Handbook of North American Indians, vol. 6: Subarctic,* ed. June Helm (Washington, DC: Smithsonian Institution, 1981), 514–32.

2   On this point — the meaning of the encounter of the west and non-west — see, e.g., Marshall Sahlins, *Islands of History* (Chicago: University of Chicago Press, 1985), Inga Clendinnen, *Ambivalent Conquests: Maya and Spaniard in Yucatan 1517–1570* (New York: Cambridge University Press, 1987). Events recorded here unfolded in the early fur trade era, a period initiated by fairly regular, direct trade with traders of European extraction at a post in or near a particular group's territory, or by travel to a more distant post. For discussion, see Shepard Krech III, Introduction, in *The Subarctic Fur Trade: Native Social and Economic Adaptations,* Shepard Krech III, ed. (Vancouver: University of British Columbia Press, 1984), ix–xix.

Whatever the nature of earliest contact, Gwich'in and white men definitely encountered each other in 1789. That year, Alexander Mackenzie swept relentlessly to the Beaufort Sea down what he called River Disappointment (because it did not produce a Northwest Passage). In recognition of this feat of exploration, white men who followed called this the Mackenzie River. Along its lower reaches, Mackenzie met Indians he called "Quarrellers," because they spoke in guttural, staccato fashion, vociferously and determinedly defending the positions they took. They were Gwich'in — a name Mackenzie seemed not to know. Other traders called these people Squinters, Squinteyes, or, in French, Loucheux.[1]

Over the next fifteen years, traders and Gwich'in surely gained increasing knowledge of each other, but the trade in furs coveted by the mercantilist companies represented by Mackenzie and others did not greatly affect the Gwich'in. Few traders ventured as far north as the lower reaches of the Mackenzie River, and the Gwich'in probably carried on as they had before.

But they could not do so after 1806, when Barbue was a young adult and fully in his prime. That year, the North West Company established a fort on the Mackenzie at the mouth of Blue Fish River, some sixty miles north of Great Bear River. In English, the post was called Good Hope; in French it was known as Bonne Espérance. Although well upstream of Gwich'in territory, Good Hope was within reach of their canoes or overland treks, and it quickly became clear that the Gwich'in were eager to trade — indeed, several had come to a post at the junction of the Liard and Mackenzie Rivers the year before. As a result, by 1811 Fort Good Hope had been moved downstream to a site opposite the confluence of the Hare Indian and Mackenzie Rivers. The Gwich'in also knew that white men were eager to exchange. Trading companies competed briefly with each other in this region several times during the first two decades of the nineteenth century. Although the competition was less intense and disruptive on the lower Mackenzie than elsewhere, and ended in 1821 with amalgamation, nevertheless the die was cast. Most Native people who were enticed by the trade had their lives changed by it in some way, no matter how minor.

The Hare Indian River was still distant for many Gwich'in wishing to trade. One October, for example, two Gwich'in spent nine days en route to

---

1 By the close of the nineteenth century, the easternmost Gwich'in had adopted the term Loucheux when they referred to themselves in English.

SHEPARD KRECH III

the post from Arctic Red River, and the next month others walked for six days from Trading (Travaillant) River. With only the Indian trade to contemplate, the newly merged company therefore decided to move Fort Good Hope even farther downstream to make it more accessible, and in 1823, New Good Hope, as it was called, was built on the border of Hare Indian — Gwich'in territory. It was nearer two favoured trading rendezvous for the Gwich'in: the mouth of Arctic Red River and Trading River, which was closer yet. But in 1827, New Good Hope was closed because it was too difficult to find adequate food, and Fort Good Hope moved back to its former upstream location. There is no question that the upstream location was awkward for many of the Gwich'in, and after a decade the HBC laid plans to establish another post deep in Gwich'in territory, accomplished in 1840 with the establishment of Peel River Post.[1]

In moving toward monopoly control of the fur trade, the HBC underwent stringent geographical reorganization, instituted routine record keeping and communications, and placed a strict emphasis on post self-sufficiency and "economy." The region from Hudson Bay to the Rocky Mountains became the Northern Department, within which were two districts, the more northerly (north of Great Slave Lake) of which was called the Mackenzie River District. Until 1840, Fort Good Hope was the northernmost post in the Hudson Bay territory and the only option for eastern Gwich'in wishing to participate directly in the exchange for European goods.[2] Until the 1850s, the only white men in this region — the

---

1   There is some question exactly when Fort Good Hope was first established, and where it was located. On its locations, see Alexander McKenzie, *Journal of Great Bear Lake, 1805–06*, Manuscript collections, British Columbia Archives and Records Service, Victoria, BC; Willard F. Wentzel, Notice Regarding the Map of Mackenzie's River by Mr. W.F. Wen[t]zel, of the North-West Fur Company, *Wernerian Natural History Society Memoirs, 1821–22* (4), 1822, 562–63, Plate XVII; Willard F. Wentzel, Letters to the Hon. Roderic McKenzie, 1807–1824, in *Les Bourgeois de la Compagnie du Nord-Quest*, vol. 1, L.R. Masson, ed. (New York: Antiquarian Press, 1960), 75–153, 110; Wentzel, Account of MacKenzie River, 1821, Unpublished manuscript MG19, A20, Ottawa: Public Archives of Canada; George Keith, Letters to Mr. Roderic McKenzie, 1807–1817, in *Les Bourgeois de la Compagnie du Nord-Quest*, vol. 2, L.R. Masson, ed. (New York: Antiquarian Press, 1960), 65–132, 104–105; E.E. Rich, ed., *Journal of Occurrences in the Athabaska Department by George Simpson, 1820 and 1821, and Report* (London: Champlain Society for Hudson's Bay Record Society, 1938), 393–95.

2   On changes in record keeping and organization, see, e.g., Harold A. Innis, *The Fur Trade in Canada*, rev. ed. (Toronto: University of Toronto Press, 1962), 283–338.

only Europeans to keep records in which Barbue's name might appear — were traders and explorers; missionaries, preoccupied elsewhere, had not yet reached the Mackenzie.

★   ★   ★

Barbue's name first turned up in post records in 1823. His name is ambiguous, although the word is certainly of French origin. In French, *barbue* is the brill, a species of flatfish in the same family as turbot and common in European saltwaters, and the related term *barbeau* is the barbel, a whiskered freshwater fish. According to John Franklin, French-speaking traders used barbue for the freshwater catfish they encountered in the waters through which they canoed. But barbu (fem. barbue) also means bearded (the connection with fish with whiskers or barbels being an obvious one). Perhaps French-speaking employees of the North West Company gave Barbue his name because he had whiskers or a beard, neither of which was common among his people. The feminine ending —it should have been Barbu —was conceivably an orthographical aberration. Yet another possibility is that Barbue's eyes somehow reminded traders of the brill, whose most conspicuous feature is having both eyes on the top side of the body — but this seems more far fetched than the suggestion that Barbue had whiskers.

The connection between the name Barbue and indigenous naming patterns is equally speculative. At birth a Gwich'in was often given a name connected in some way with a parent; the parent was then named after the child, a practice known as teknonymy. Thus, Barbue's name in Gwich'in might have been catfish, after the name of his eldest son. Alternatively, Barbue's name might have derived from some sociological or supernatural connection he held with catfish — perhaps he was born into the matrilineal clan with which "fish" was associated; or perhaps he had a special supernatural relationship with catfish that he advertised with an emblem on his clothing.[1]

---

1   On these various possibilities, see Cornelius Osgood, *Contributions to the Ethnography of the Kutchin*, Yale University Publications in Anthropology No. 14 (New Haven: Yale University Press, 1936), 140; Robert A. McKennan, *The Chandalar Kutchin*, Technical Paper No. 17. (Montreal: Arctic Institute of North America, 1965), 58; Slobodin, Kutchin, 523, 527. On catfish as barbue, see John Franklin, *Narrative of a Journey to the Shores of the Polar Sea, in the years 1819, 20, 21, and 22* (London: John Murray, 1823), 93. I wish to thank Sheila ffolliott and Jennifer Brown for helping me rethink the derivation of Barbue's name.

In 1823, Barbue was identified as a Hudson's Bay Company "chief" or trading leader. He was clearly no stranger at Fort Good Hope, but other than his status as a leader we know little about his relationship to traders prior to this year. In recognition of that status, the traders gave him goods and clothing as they did other men they identified as band leaders. Exactly what they gave Barbue that year other than clothing is not known; four years later his present consisted of "1 coat Shirt 1 pr Leggins & 1 lb beads." Barbue came not merely for a present, however, but to trade. He could not manage the trip annually – he did not come in 1824, for example – but when he missed a year it was a "long stay from the Fort." Barbue was clearly more than a procurer of furs, or trading chief, for in 1825 he promised his services for John Franklin's second polar expedition and the next year met Franklin at the mouth of Arctic Red River.[1]

The HBC was interested in the Gwich'in for the furs they brought to exchange, for provisions, and for various services including guiding and translating (as in Barbue's case). For their part, the Gwich'in were eager to trade with the newcomers from the moment they arrived near Gwich'in territory. The earliest image of them is as people with well-established commercial tendencies who immediately embraced the trade at Fort Good Hope. In 1806, some Gwich'in travelled a considerable distance in order to exchange beaver and marten pelts for blue and white beads and various iron works. They craved beads, as well as dentalium shells, from the start. At no time were they represented as passive in the exchange. In 1814, for example, Gwich'in were "near creating an uproar" because there were too few beads at Fort Good Hope. For the "want" of beads, "their favorite article," they "preferred taking back to their tents the peltries they had brought to trade."[2]

In 1825, Barbue arrived at Fort Good Hope with 1500 muskrats and some beavers. In the 1820s, the Gwich'in brought mainly muskrats, martens and provisions to the post, and with Hare Indians were responsible for a large percentage of muskrats and martens traded in the Mackenzie River District — each year, they exchanged roughly 20,000

---

1   HBCA B.80/a/2, 6; B.80/a/4/fo. 2; John Franklin, *Narrative of a Second Expedition to the Shores of the Polar Sea, in the Years 1825, 1826, and 1827* (London: John Murray, 1828), 183.

2   McKenzie, Journal of Great Bear Lake; the quotation is from Wentzel, Letters to the Hon. Roderic McKenzie, 1807–1824, 110.

muskrats and 2,000 martens, which amounted to three-quarters and one-third of district totals respectively. The HBC encouraged the marten trade, because marten pelts were worth a great deal and were easy to transport. But muskrats were worth far less and were a greater nuisance to ship because of the weight and bulk of thousands of pelts. In the late 1820s, the most valuable furs traded in the Mackenzie River District in both volume and price were beaver, marten, lynx, muskrat, and bear. The company tried to promote the trade in beaver and lynx everywhere, but was less successful at Fort Good Hope than at posts farther south in the district.

The trade in provisions, or meat and fish, was also important at Fort Good Hope, which was regarded as a "meat post" where supplies might be obtained for wider use. In 1826 alone, the Gwich'in and Hare Indians brought in approximately 10,000 pounds of fresh meat, 3,500 pounds of dry meat, 1,000 caribou tongues, and 3,000 fish. These provisions were destined for consumption at the post and, if needed, elsewhere in the Mackenzie River District.[1]

Already traders themselves when Europeans arrived, the Gwich'in were attracted by a range of novel goods brought by HBC traders, especially what were known as "iron works" and "dry goods": kettles, knives, daggers, files, flints, fire steels, ice trenches, bonnets, belts, capotes, gartering, blankets, and leggings. They also exchanged their furs for combs, powder horns, and tobacco boxes. But most important by far were guns, powder, ball, shot, tobacco, and beads. As mentioned, the Gwich'in coveted beads especially, threatening not to trade at all unless they could obtain large white beads. In the 1830s, some western Gwich'in drawn to Fort Good Hope boycotted the exchange when they discovered that few or no beads were on hand. And the fact that they carried Russian knives, kettles, and other metal items was a warning for the HBC that there existed an alternative market for western Gwich'in furs: Russian traders to the west, to whom the Gwich'in had access through middlemen.[2]

The trade in beads was of enormous potential profit to the Hudson's Bay Company. In Barbue's day, beads were traded whenever possible,

---

1   HBCA B.200/d/4, 11, 17.

2   HBCA B.200/d/4, 17; HBCA B.80/a/7–14 passim. See Shepard Krech III, The Eastern Kutchin and the Fur Trade, 1800–1860, Ethnohistory 23, 1976, 213–35.

and for decades they remained "necessaries," not baubles, to the Gwich'in, who used them not simply for decoration, but increasingly as a general-purpose money.[1] George Simpson was in favour of weaning the Gwich'in from their dependence on "beads and baubles," which is of interest since Simpson never let his mind wander far from profits, and the profit in beads was astronomical. But Simpson worried. Although beads "affords us the largest immediate profits," he wrote, they could "easily be dispensed with, and when no longer fashionable the attraction to our establishments will be at an end." Accordingly he promoted an exchange in dry goods and iron works. These, he was confident, "will soon become necessaries to them and tender them dependent on us."[2] He was only partly successful, because the potential profit on beads and dentalium shells, as well as on guns, was substantial. Profit was the difference between expenditures for goods, transportation and transaction, on the one hand, and revenues received for furs obtained in exchange for those goods, on the other. The potential can be seen in differences between cost of goods and value of furs in exchange: the marten exchanged at Peel River Post at mid-century, for example, were worth approximately twelve times the cost of a gun, more than 60 times the cost of dentalium shells, and roughly 150 times the cost of beads. On specific items, the mark-up was as high as 15,000 per cent. But overall net profits were far lower, ranging perhaps from 80 to 200 per cent above costs.[3]

The Gwich'in also valued guns highly, both as items of prestige and for use in hunting and warfare. During the 1820s and 1830s, they took large quantities of ammunition for defence against the Inuvialuit.[4] The

---

1   Krech, The Eastern Kutchin and the Fur Trade; Krech, The Early Fur Trade in the Northwestern Subarctic: The Kutchin and the Trade in Beads, in *Le Castor Fait Tout: Selected Papers of the Fifth North American Fur Trade Conference, 1985* (Montreal: Lake St. Louis Historical Society, 1987), 236–77.

2   HBCA D.4/22 fos. 41d–42.

3   Krech, The Eastern Kutchin and the Fur Trade, 221. One figure in that essay on page 221 is a typographical error: an 83% profit appears incorrectly as 8%. In rethinking this analysis, I acknowledge my debt to Elizabeth Mancke's excellent discussion of the difficulty of calculating profits in *A Company of Businessmen: The Hudson's Bay Company and Long-Distance Trade, 1670–1730* (Winnipeg: Rupert's Land Research Centre, University of Winnipeg, 1988), 70–82 especially.

4   Shepard Krech III, Interethnic Relations in the Lower Mackenzie River Region, *Arctic Anthropology* 16, no. 2, 1979, 102–122.

policy of the HBC to exchange powder, ball and shot for provisions, in order to encourage the provision trade, reinforced the trade in guns and ammunition. Guns remained popular, in spite of the fact that some were "very subject to freezing" and others broke easily; one brand, Wilson's guns, was particularly prone to defective workmanship: "many is the criple his Guns have made among the Indians."[1]

In this region, "poverty" was a recurrent problem more for the Hudson's Bay Company than for Native people. This is counter to the myth that mercantilist enterprises quickly thrust indigenous people into indebtedness and dependency. The HBC sought to guarantee that Native people would return with their furs by advancing them goods prior to the beginning of a trapping season, hoping that they would work all winter to pay off the season's advances. That strategy did not always work, especially when Native people traded competing companies off against one another. In the Mackenzie River District it sometimes failed because the HBC could not provide enough men to transport sufficient trade goods to pay for furs, once those men were in the Mackenzie River District. During Barbue's time, the company was in debt to Natives in the Mackenzie River District, as it would again be in succeeding decades. In 1829 came "again the same complaint" from Fort Good Hope: "Stores full and Shops empty of Goods." No white beads were left for the Gwich'in trade but dry goods were exchanged despite their being "not to [their] liking." The following year, the HBC was 1500 Made Beaver (MB) in debt in the district.[2]

★ ★ ★

Three years after he entered the historical record in 1823, Barbue was in conflict with his Gwich'in neighbours because his youngest son, in what John Bell and others called a "frantic fit" or "jealous fit," shot his wife. The incident happened in the winter of 1826. The woman who was shot and presumably killed, Barbue's daughter-in-law, was from another Gwich'in band that the traders called the Lower Loucheux. So when

---

1   HBCA B.80/a/4/fo. 6; HBCA B.200/a/11/fo. 29.

2   HBCA B.200/d/27/fo. 3d; D.5/3/fos. 419d–420; for quotation, see HBCA
B.200/a/10/fo. 25. The Made Beaver was the standard against which both furs and
trade items might be measured — e.g., one beaver pelt or twelve muskrats per MB; or
one gun for every 20 MB.

SHEPARD KRECH III

Barbue announced, in late August 1826, that he and his son were going to the territory of the Lower Loucheux "to settle an affair," John Bell feared greatly that it "will not terminate to his satisfaction." Bell explained the source of his anxiety: the father of the woman who had been killed "threatened to revenge his Daughter's Death." What happened in the short term is not clear, other than that the Lower Loucheux did not bring their furs to Fort Good Hope "as customary" that summer because they were said to be "in dread of the Upper Indians." This "unfortunate affair" was unsettling not merely to the social relations and amity between Gwich'in bands but to the trade, on which the traders always had an eye.[1]

However, any worry that fractured relations might upset fur returns in the long term came to naught, as relations were smoothed over between the bands. The next year, Bell was relieved to report the result of a "long conversation" with the "Lower Chief," in which Barbue, who functioned also as a post interpreter, was translator. Bell attempted to "prevail upon" the chief of the Lower Loucheux "to come with his relations next season & bring their furrs." Bell may have offered him some inducement above the tariff, for he told the Lower Chief that "if he came & brought good hunts I would recompense him." The chief promised to come. His relationship with the HBC was becoming more complicated, just as his authority as a trading chief was becoming more dependent on the sanction of the company. Like trading chiefs elsewhere, he tried to influence succession – in this instance, to ensure that the position of trading chief descended to his son. As Bell put it, "He styles himself the Principle Chief of the Lower Tribe & says he has a Son who is also looked upon as Chief & as he is getting an old man he would wish his son to succeed him as Chief." He was clearly asking Bell to sanction that move. Bell promised nothing, "but told him that if his Son's conduct was satisfactory he would be rewarded accordingly." Subsequently, Bell "Made the Old Man a present of a Bonnet of Strouds. 1 knife. 1 steel & a few Beads with which he was pleased."[2]

As these accounts indicate, Barbue was more than a trading leader and an interpreter. He seemed to function as leader in indigenous con-

---

1   HBCA B.80/a/4/fo. 14; B.80/a/5/fo. 6; see Franklin, *Narrative of a Second Expedition*, 184.

2   HBCA B.80/a/6/fos. 6d–7. The position of trading chief was not linked to the matrilineal clan system, clans functioning largely in marital and ceremonial contexts.

texts which involved interband political relations — and relationships between different Gwich'in bands were not always smooth. As the leader of one Gwich'in band, the "Upper Loucheux," he was linked — through the marriage of his son, and through trade and other interactions — to the "Lower Loucheux," a band living to the north. Such interband marriages probably served to offset the dangers of long-term feuds.[1]

Leadership among the Gwich'in was more sharply defined than in other Athapaskan groups living along the Mackenzie River. In Barbue's time, the approximately 120 Gwich'in known to HBC traders were said to "have two Chiefs" with "nearly an absolute authority among them." In the bands called Upper and Lower Loucheux, descent of leadership was patrilineal. After Barbue died, Peter Warren Dease polled the members of Barbue's band who happened to be at the post "regarding a successor to the deceased Old Chief," and the people declared themselves "unanimously in favor of his eldest Son present who will in future be their leader." As with the "Lower Tribe," the evidence for HBC influence on succession is difficult to read definitively.[2]

Friction between Gwich'in bands, which was played out both in specific events like the "frantic fit" and shooting incident, and in sorcery and deaths attributed to sorcery, may have been caused in part by middleman profits and trading enmities. Barbue was a middleman to other Gwich'in living farther from Fort Good Hope and to Mackenzie Inuvialuit, and he appears to have acted no differently than many other Gwich'in who, in the first half of the nineteenth century, were quick to seize mercantilist opportunities and charge high prices for the goods they traded to more distant groups.[3]

★　　★　　★

In 1826, Barbue was troubled not only by relations with the Lower Loucheux but by the Inuvialuit, who lived along the northern edge of the Mackenzie Delta in coastal villages. In spring, a large group of Inuvi-

---

1　See Shepard Krech III, The Nakotcho Kutchin: A Tenth Aboriginal Kutchin Band?, *Journal of Anthropological Research* 35, 1979, 109–121.

2　On "absolute authority," HBCA B.200/e/3/fo. 3d; for succession of Barbue, HBCA B.80/a/7/fo. 11d.

3　Krech, The Eastern Kutchin.

aluit left the coast in umiaks and kayaks and headed south up the Mackenzie River. Their destination was Arctic Red River, where they intended to trade with Gwich'in. Even allowing for exaggeration of numbers, John Bell's report that "60 boats manned with from eight to nine men each" accompanied by "a great number of small Canoes" arrived at Arctic Red River indicated a major trading force. They met "a small Party" of thirty Gwich'in and proceeded to exchange goods. Not entirely unexpectedly, some "Misunderstanding took place about the Trading of Furs," and the Inuvialuit stole "some triffling articles" from the Gwich'in "with impunity."[1]

This was a typical incident marking the complex relations between Inuvialuit and Gwich'in in Barbue's day. The Inuvialuit tended to be coastal and the Gwich'in to remain inland, but they both exploited resources in the Mackenzie Delta. Moreover, the Inuvialuit needed flint for projectile and spear points and knives, and several excellent and favoured sources were located well within Gwich'in territory. Gwich'in and Inuvialuit met annually, and all their meetings were potentially volatile. The Inuvialuit were contemptuous of all their Northern Athapaskan neighbours, including the Gwich'in. Hostilities erupted with regularity and people on both sides were killed – on four occasions in the 1820s alone. But the Gwich'in and Inuvialuit also traded and hunted with each other, and the Gwich'in used their geographical location and possession of guns to control the terms of the trade, possibly exacerbating hostilities. In Barbue's day – and for decades afterward – a fundamental difference between Gwich'in and Inuvialuit was that the former possessed guns and the latter did not. Armed, the Gwich'in answered Inuvialuit contempt with firepower and prevented Inuvialuit from having access to HBC posts – first Fort Good Hope, later Peel River Post. Without guns, it is unlikely that they could have maintained their balance of power and their middleman trading position in the face of Inuvialuit assertiveness.[2]

One potential problem the Gwich'in faced was maintaining a reliable supply of guns and ammunition. Their demand for guns was constant and high, but because of transportation and provisioning problems, the HBC was not always able to meet it. Not all Gwich'in who wanted guns pos-

---

1   HBCA B.80/a/5/fo. 2d.

2   Krech, Interethnic Relations.

sessed them, and not all who owned them were able to keep them in prime condition or to obtain ammunition. When supplies lagged there were repercussions on Gwich'in-Inuvialuit relations. In the late 1820s, Barbue's "very evident disappointment" at the lack of goods at Fort Good Hope may have been compounded by fear. In 1828, Inuvialuit ascended the Mackenzie all the way to the Narrows to trade. They were more hostile than they had been in recent meetings, while the Gwich'in "were destitute of ammunition & could not use such firearms as they had of which," Peter Warren Dease reported, the Inuvialuit "are in great dread." The Gwich'in made a "great demand for Powder & Balls," but there were none to trade.[1]

The Gwich'in put great stock in their middleman position. They maintained it in Barbue's day but not after mid-century. By then many had died from disease and the demographic balance of power had shifted. Those who survived valued peace and direct access to muskrats, whose optimum habitat was the upper Mackenzie Delta, a dangerous no-man's land separating Gwich'in and Inuvialuit, more highly than feuding and middleman profits. HBC traders also changed their attitude toward the Inuvialuit. Formerly suspicious and antagonistic toward them, they groomed Gwich'in interpreters to translate and open trade and became bold enough themselves to overcome their traditional attitude.[2]

★   ★   ★

Feuding with other Gwich'in and quarrelling with the Inuvialuit in 1826-27, Barbue was also forced to contend with hunger. Caribou failed to appear in the winter of 1827 and the Gwich'in "consequently ... suffered privations all winter." In the spring of 1828, caribou left Gwich'in territory early for coastal calving grounds and many Gwich'in starved. Struggling to hold his own, Barbue seemed not the least bit inclined to visit Fort Good Hope. Hungry, having only recently repaired his relations with the Lower Loucheux and perhaps apprehensive about the Inuvialuit, he had his hands full.[3]

---

1   HBCA B.80/a/7/fos. 3–3d.

2   Krech, Interethnic Relations.

3   On "suffered privations," HBCA B.80/a/5/fo. 20.

So did the traders, for reasons both within and outside their control. When they had moved Fort Good Hope downstream, they had evidently been assured that the Gwich'in would supply provisions. After all, it had been for the convenience of the Gwich'in that they had moved. But the Gwich'in did not bring them food, probably because game was scarce. In June 1825, Chief Factor Edward Smith spoke to them "on their indifference about the supplying the Post with provisions." The Gwich'in complained "of Starvation, sickness, and the early Spring," which adversely affected the caribou hunt. The next year, illness kept the Gwich'in from Fort Good Hope. Compounding the problem was the fact that the traders could not manage to feed themselves. At Fort Good Hope and elsewhere, they understood poorly the distribution and habits of animals and fish, and were consequently at risk when their principal producers failed to supply them.[1]

The traders were also anxious at New Good Hope, the downstream location of Fort Good Hope, because it was so close to Inuvialuit territory. After relocation upstream, George Simpson wrote that they abandoned the downstream site because "the Indians of the Interior were averse to going so near the Camps of the Esquimaux, with whom they are continually at war." This explanation is simplistic, however.[2] More relevant is the fact that the traders constructed the Inuvialuit as unrelentingly hostile to all white men. When John Franklin received an "unwelcome reception" from these "ferocious savages" on his second expedition, their suspicions were confirmed. Chief Factor Edward Smith, who was closer to the action than was Simpson, remarked in June 1827 that Fort Good Hope "is the worst situated and the most exposed" of all posts in the region, and that "what renders it more so is its proximity to the lands of the Esquimaux – who have too often proved themselves to be turbulent and hostile to Whites." He thought that if the Gwich'in would agree to come the extra distance upriver, then the "danger would be removed and the situation better in every respect and as good for returns."[3]

---

1 On "indifference," HBCA B.200/a/6/fo. 29; also HBCA B.200/e/3/fo. 3d. See also Krech, The Eastern Kutchin and the Fur Trade.

2 The opinions are George Simpson's in HBCA D.4/92/fo. 29.

3 On "unwelcome reception," see HBCA B.80/a/5/fo. 7; Edward Smith is quoted from HBCA B.200/e/7/fos. 2d–3.

But that was only part of the story. To explain the relocation upriver to the Gwich'in, the traders needed more palatable reasons than their own fear of the Inuvialuit. In June 1827, Chief Factor Edward Smith informed the Gwich'in and Hare Indians of the move and emphasized the "difficulties" the HBC had coming so far downriver twice a year, the "risk of their supplies being stopped by the Ice," and the "General Scarcity of Provisions" which almost guaranteed that winter would be a marginal season. John Bell was somewhat relieved to discover that the Gwich'in "consented more readily" to the move than he thought they would.[1]

Neither Barbue nor other Gwich'in nor other Athapaskans were exempt from the hunger and starvation that were such problems for the Hudson's Bay Company traders. Simpson remarked, "there is more danger to be apprehended of starvation" in the Mackenzie River region "than in any part of North America."[2] Several winters stood out in their extreme difficulty for Natives and whites alike: in 1810-11, several traders died at The Forks (later called Fort Simpson, and located at the conjunction of the Mackenzie and Liard Rivers), and the early 1830s, just after Barbue's death, were also extremely difficult. At these times many suffered; often local hardships were severe. Starvation was caused in part by ecological cycles, faunal movements, and harsh climatic conditions. Most critical were the population cycle of the hare, whose numbers plunged with regularity every decade, and extreme fluctuations in precipitation and temperature, which affected where caribou foraged and hence where they were available. These factors had always affected Native people. But there were also "new" influences accompanying European traders like epidemic diseases and faunal depletions that resulted from the demand for furs. Another problem arose when Native people thought they could depend on traders for provisioning in times of extreme hardship and moved near posts, only to discover that traders were often unable to provide for themselves, much less others, and that posts located conveniently for transportation were poorly situated for animals and fish.[3]

---

1   HBCA B.80/a/6/fo. 1

2   E.E. Rich, ed., *Journal of Occurrences in the Athabasca Department by George Simpson, 1820 and 1821, and Report* (Toronto: Champlain Society for Hudson's Bay Record Society, 1938), 393.

3   See Shepard Krech III, Disease, Starvation, and Northern Athapaskan Social Organization, *American Ethnologist* 5, 1978, 710–32.

Thus the traders suffered equally. Given the difficulties they experienced, it is no surprise that they listened closely when Hare Indians and Indians living near Great Bear Lake urged them to move Fort Good Hope back upriver. For the "Outer Half-Breed Loucheux," a Hare Indian band wanting the post near "its former site at the Rapid," it was an "old subject." Other Hare Indians preferred that the post be not so far upriver, but "a convenient distance between the Rapid and the site of New Good Hope." Their reason: "they now dread to approach the vicinity of the Rapid" because it was "the receptacle of so many of their deceased relations."[1]

★   ★   ★

In the spring of 1826, sickness struck Barbue's people with fury just as they were resolving tensions with Barbue's daughter-in-law's relatives that resulted from her death, and engaged in hostilities with the Inuvialuit. Barbue himself escaped death — how is not known — but only for the moment. The drama that engulfed his people was repeated often in the nineteenth century along the Mackenzie, and especially near Fort Good Hope during the mid-1820s, when "mortality" was said to be "so prevalent" among the Gwich'in and Hare Indians.[2] The decade before, a variety of diseases affected Northern Athapaskans on the Mackenzie River and in the region immediately to the south. Infections entered the region mainly through the annual summer transport of trading goods, which had to reach posts at all costs. From 1819 to 1823, for example, measles, dysentery and influenza ravaged the Chipewyan and Beaver who lived in the region drained by the Slave, Hay, and Peace rivers. Colds, influenza, and other contagious diseases afflicted Europeans and Indians alike, but Indians suffered far more because most lacked immunity to those diseases.[3]

---

1   On "former site at the Rapid," HBCA B.80/a/5/fo. 14; for "dread to approach," HBCA B.200/b/3/fos. 6d–7d.

2   HBCA B.80/a/5/fo. 2d.

3   For specific examples, see Rich, 1938, 81; Franklin, *Narrative of a Journey*, 137, 158; HBCA B.39/b/2, B.181/a/2, 4. For comprehensive analysis, see Krech, Disease, Starvation and Northern Athapaskan Social Organization, and Krech, The Influence of Disease and the Fur Trade on Arctic Drainage Lowlands Dene, 1800-1850, *Journal of Anthropological Research* 39, 1983, 123–46.

Diseases seared Fort Good Hope in the mid-1820s. One was a "contagious distemper," some unidentified affliction. It was horrifying at this post, where by 1826 it had killed "a great number of men, women and children indiscriminately," among them "some of the principal hunters." By January 1827, Chief Factor Edward Smith, after hearing from John Bell, wrote his superiors that "Many of the Loucheux and Hare Indians have droped into the Grave." Fortuitously for those who remained, by the end of the next month, this particular disease had run its course.[1]

Barbue's band was affected along with others. In June 1826, Barbue and thirty followers arrived at Fort Good Hope with fewer furs than John Bell had anticipated. Bell thought that their failure "is doubtless to be attributed to the mortality so prevalent among the Natives of the Lower part of the River." Included among the deceased was Barbue's son-in-law, "a man of Consequence." This man was "an Indian much respected & beloved by his relations, and his death is much lamented by the Loucheuxs." Bell witnessed the ritual mourning in which mourners occasionally put their own lives at risk. He reported: "I have never witnessed among savages such an affecting Scene of sorrow. Two of the Deceased's Brothers were at the fᵗ at the time, one of which made a rash attempt to Drown himself, by running head foremost into the middle of the River but was fortunately extricated from his perilous situation by his relatives."[2]

The next year, Barbue himself complained of sickness apparently unrelated to the epidemics that raged. Twice during the winter and spring of 1827, reports reached Fort Good Hope that he was dying. Moreover, Bell was implicated in Barbue's illness: "The Chief is dying and but slender hopes entertained of his recovery, and according to Indian superstition did not hesitate to say that I was the cause of his sickness by throwing bad Medicine upon him! in Consequence of his Sons having destroyed the Boat left by Captⁿ Franklin & Party last fall below Red River." Bell concluded, "so much for Savage Superstition!"[3]

---

1   HBCA B.80/a/4/fo. 10d, B.80/a/5/fo. 5d, B.200/b/3/fo. 16.

2   HBCA B.80/a/5/fo. 2d.

3   HBCA B.80/a/5/fo. 20.

Gwich'in disease theory was far more complex than Bell allowed, and made sense to them in ways he could not fathom. When they became ill, the Gwich'in sought explanations in taboo infraction, spirit loss, and sorcery. They blamed sorcerers for epidemics, and sorcerers were not just other Gwich'in; they could also be Hare Indians, other Athapaskans, Inuvialuit, or Europeans. Thus it made perfect sense to the Gwich'in to accuse Bell himself of "throwing bad Medicine" on Barbue. In later decades, they would blame other traders for diseases.[1]

Bell sent Barbue some European medicine, unspecified. Barbue later appeared, improved and denying the earlier report that Bell was considered to be the cause of his sickness. But the next year Barbue was sick again. On 2 July 1828, he arrived at Fort Good Hope, complaining "much of a difficulty of breathing & violent palpitation of the Heart." Four days later, he was "much troubled by spasms which almost cause suffocation when he sleeps." That day, Peter Warren Dease gave Barbue "a dose salts" and four days later "a dose of Physic." The salts had "a good Effect" and the Physic provided "some relief."[2] That Barbue was willing to try HBC remedies is not surprising: many Indians were. John Richardson, the doctor who accompanied John Franklin on his expeditions, made up small packets of medicines for Indians to use, and Franklin noted that other Indians "set a great value upon medicine."[3]

Bell and Dease may have involved themselves in Barbue's cure out of genuine concern for his welfare, or because they did not wish to be blamed again for his illness. Because Barbue was the trading chief, they were definitely concerned about the effect of his death on relationships among Gwich'in themselves as well as between the Gwich'in and the Inuvialuit. Of course, they were concerned above all about the impact of his death on the trade in furs.

The salts and physic sent to Barbue may have taxed but did not exhaust the supply of medicine at Fort Good Hope. Although this isolated post had a far smaller medicine chest than Fort Simpson, district head-

---

1 See Shepard Krech III, 'Throwing bad medicine': Sorcery, Disease, and the Fur Trade among the Kutchin and other Northern Athapaskans, in Krech, ed., *Indians, Animals and the Fur Trade: A Critique of Keepers of the Game* (Athens: University of Georgia Press, 1981), 73-108.

2 HBCA D.80/a/7/fos. 4–5.

3 Franklin, *Narrative of a Journey*, 312.

quarters, by 1831 it was supplied with a variety of purgatives, carminatives, and emetics – purges, vomits, Epsom and Glauber salts, cream of tartar, cinnamon bark, lavender, rhubarb, castor oil, camphor, blue vitriol, and essence of peppermint; expectorants like Spanish liquorice, flour of brimstone, and Turlington's Balsam (also useful in the treatment of wounds); tonics like hartshorn; Peruvian bark, a febrifuge; blistering plaster, which was a solid covering used to irritate and raise blisters on the flesh; and tincture of opium, a sedative.[1]

The traders gave some medicine to Native people, but they reserved much for themselves in these pre-antiseptic and pre-anesthetic days: a draining toe received "lint & salves"; a man constipated for eleven days was given a purge, with grease held in reserve; another man suffering "indisposition" was given a physic (usually a purgative) "which operated copiously and afforded him relief"; and an inflamed hand was treated with a poultice. Some cases were regarded as incurable: one Indian "dreadfully eat up with the venerial Disease" elicited the following comment from Robert McVicar, the clerk: "I regret to observe that there is no Medicine in the Fort calculated to effect a cure of that nature." And to cure an outbreak of influenza in 1835, "nature must effect a change."[2]

★   ★   ★

On 6 July, after the salts and physic, Barbue, "in order to get more relief ... got himself bled by making Deep incisions with a Knife in the Legs & Breast."[3] There was no further word for a week. Then Barbue was again bled, and Dease recorded the circumstances, as well as his own reaction, in some detail the day after:

> Contrary to my advice the Old Chief allowed himself to bleed all night from about 6 P.M. yesterday to 11 A.M. today profusely and then accord-

---

1   HBCA B.200/d/4, 44. Approximately one-half of the items listed were present in 1823.

2   These cases are from Fort Resolution: HBCA B.181/a/4/fo. 21; B.181/a/8/fo. 9; B.181/a/9/fos. 4, 12, 32; B.181/a/11/fo. 18; B.181/a/12/fo. 25. For general comments, see E.E. Rich, The Fur Traders: Their Diet and Drugs, *The Beaver* 307(1), 1976, 43–53.

3   HBCA B.80/a/7/fos. 4–5.

ing to his intentions, prepared his Canoe etc. to leave this with his family & join his relations below. when he was down near the Water Side I heard an alarming Cry & immediately was told the Old Chief was Expiring. on going to the spot found him in a very pitiful State. he had fallen in a kind of Fit from Extreme weakness. complaining much administered such restoratives as we have which recovered him from that State which I attribute chiefly to the quantity of blood he lost since yesterday.[1]

The Gwich'in were said to practise phlebotomy "*ad libitum*, and for every complaint, from a headache to a pain in the big toe."[2] But Dease objected to the bleeding of Barbue only because it went on too long. He shared with Barbue a belief in the efficacy of phlebotomy; indeed, throughout North America, leeches, when they could be had, were used in this era to treat colic, fevers, and whooping cough, and dry and wet cupping were widespread therapeutic techniques. Fevers attributed to violent passions or "atmospheric vicissitudes" were treated by blood letting. A proper diet and leeches placed, or blisters raised, on the stomach were prescribed for gastritis thought to be caused by too much alcohol or exposure to cold and damp.[3] Bleeding was common at Mackenzie River posts. When Alexander McKenzie was "very unwell and delerous" in 1806, he bled himself and later "recovered a little." At Fort Resolution, one man who "over stressed by carrying a large log of wood" became sick and was bled, which "immediately ... gave him some ease." Another, ill for some time, had two pounds of blood removed from his arm.[4]

Dease was worried about the political and economic consequences of Barbue's death but, unlike Bell, he demonstrated a more sophisticated knowledge of Gwich'in disease theory. As he wrote: "In this precarious

---

1   HBCA B.80/a/7/fo. 5d.

2   Strachan Jones, The Kutchin Tribes, *Annual Report of the Smithsonian Institution for 1866* (Washington, DC, 1872), 320–27, 325.

3   W. Brockbank, *Ancient Therapeutic Arts* (London: William Heinemann, 1954); J. Eberle, *Notes of Lectures on the Theory and Practice of Medicine, delivered in the Jefferson Medical College, at Philadelphia*, 2nd ed., corrected (Cincinnati: Covey and Fairbank, 1834). According to Elizabeth Vibert (personal communication), John Buchan's *New Domestic Medicine* was a popular nineteenth-century reference.

4   Alexander McKenzie (Ms.:13); HBCA B.181/a/5/fo. 5; B.181/a/12/fo. 31.

situation of the old man I feel much anxiety as his death may be the cause of warfare among his Relatives & the Lower Loucheux or Rat hunters, as it is said the latter said they would throw bad medicines on him on account of some family feuds & the old man's Sons threaten to make war if he Dies." The "family feud" must refer to Barbue's son's killing of his wife, mentioned earlier. Barbue's sons dispatched someone to convince "some of the Jugglers above to attend" Barbue and counter the sorcery; to induce them to come they sent "a hatchet & Tin Dish ... as a Fee." Three arrived "with their wares etc." Despite acknowledging that the Gwich'in had their own theory of sickness (and accordingly, health), Dease remained the sceptic to the end, thinking that the medicine men came "as much as I think for the sake of Getting something to eat from us, as an attempt to cure the Old Chief as all their Art consists of puffing & blowing upon the Patient & using some mysterious words."[1]

The "jugglers," as the traders called them (medicine men or shamans), who attempted to cure Barbue, were either Gwich'in or Hare Indians. Shamans of both groups were renowned during this period.[2] In cases like Barbue's, the job of a Gwich'in shaman was usually to divine or otherwise identify the cause of sickness; to extract disease, if magically intruded, by sucking, blowing, or biting out its symptoms; to prescribe additional or other therapeutic courses of action; and, in some instances, to undertake revenge.[3]

In common with other Northern Athapaskans, the Gwich'in were firm believers in the powers of their shamans during this period. A Gwich'in medicine man (very few were women) began to acquire his power during adolescence, when an animal such as a weasel, wolf, marten, or mink came to him in dreams and forged an alliance. With the aid of animal spirit-helpers and various songs and fetishes, a shaman undertook magical flight, wounded himself without leaving scars, performed miracles, forecast hunting success, death, or other events, changed the weather to be more auspicious for hunting, killed his own enemies or those of others, and cured the sick. By the mid-nineteenth century, Gwich'in shamans were wealthy, prestigious, and powerful. Given the

---

1 HBCA B.80/a/7/fo. 5d.

2 Franklin, *Narrative of a Journey*, 291.

3 W.L. Hardisty, The Loucheux Indians, *Annual Report of the Smithsonian Institution for 1866* (Washington, DC, 1872), 311–20.

frequency of epidemic disease, the attribution of disease to sorcery, the need for shamanistic therapy, and payment for the services of shamans, one can readily understand why.[1]

★ ★ ★

Two days later, Barbue ate "a few Hartle berries" gathered by Gwich'in women. The medicine men left since he appeared improved. Yet ominous signs remained: "He complains that the palpitation will not allow him any Sleep, as soon as he slumbers he almost Suffocates." Dease said, "I dread giving him any opiates."[2]

By "hartle berries," Dease may have meant whortleberries, but whatever he meant or whatever they were exactly, they were probably brought to Barbue either for nourishment or for their perceived medicinal qualities.[3] The Gwich'in have long been aware of the healing properties of many plants, including yarrow (*Achillea*), alder (*Alnus*), anemone (*Anemone*), mossberry or crowberry (*Empetrum*), juniper (*Juniperus*), Labrador tea (*Ledum*), puffballs (*Lycoperdon*), and spruce (*Picea*). Each had its use for the symptoms they wished to ease. They boiled yarrow roots for headaches and alder bark for colds and tuberculosis. Alder buds were useful for venereal disease. They placed poultices of boiled anemone leaves on wounds, administered roots as tonic, used mossberries for stomach ache, and prescribed juniper berries for chest pains, Labrador tea to increase urine flow, and puffballs for sores. They used spruce gum, cones, and twigs widely for a variety of ailments.[4] There is no doubt that

---

1 Hardisty, The Loucheux Indians; Jones, The Kutchin Tribes; Osgood, *Contributions to the Ethnography of the Kutchin*, 161–62; McKennan, *The Chandalar Kutchin*.

2 HBCA B.80/a/7/fo. 6.

3 I am grateful to Jennifer Brown for guidance on identifying "hartle berries."

4 On the Gwich'in, see Douglas Leechman, The Vanta Kutchin, *Bulletin No. 130, Anthropological Series No. 33, Department of Northern Affairs and National Resources*, (Ottawa: National Museums of Canada, 1954); Osgood, *Contributions to the Ethnography of the Kutchin*; McKennan, *The Chandalar Kutchin*. For comparative data on other Northern Athapaskans, see Catharine McClellan, My Old People Say: An Ethnographic Survey of Southern Yukon Territory, Parts 1–2, National Museum of Man Publications in Ethnology No. 6 (1–2), (Ottawa: National Museums of Canada, 1975); A.G. Morice, Déné Surgery, *Transactions of the Canadian Institute* 7 (1904), 15–27.

yarrow, alder, anemone, juniper, and other plants were biochemically efficacious.[1]

The day after eating the hartle berries, Barbue remained sleepless. He or his sons again sent for a medicine man, who arrived the following day. In the meantime, Barbue asked Dease to "[apply] a Blistering Plaister to his Breast." Dease warned Barbue about its effects, but Barbue decided to go ahead despite the pain. The next day, Dease reported that "after the Plaster had been Distributed and the blister broken," he cut it open and "found it had drawn a great deal."[2] However, Barbue still did not get the relief he wished. What followed was perhaps therapy of last resort. Dease had not witnessed it before. Fascinated, he reported what he saw at great length:

> This evening we were witnesses to a remedy of their own of a rather Singular Nature & one they say resorted to only in Extreme cases, which I may say is nothing more or less than burying the Patient alive, the manner thus — a hole is dug out or rather a kind of Grave about 1½ ft. deep & sufficiently long & broad to contain the body. it is then partly filled with moss the Patient then laid in & covered with moss every part except the face then Earth or Sand laid over that. on the middle of the body a fire was kindled & allowed to burn untill the Patient can not endure the Heat of it underneath. it was then taken away & 4 other fires kindled one on each side & one at the feet, also at the head. after the old man had complained some time while the first fire was burning it was removed & in the space of 20 minutes time when Mr. Bell & I saw him again with the 4 other fires around him, he appeared to be & in fact was in a profound sleep & breathing very freely. It is such an uncommon manner of treating a weak Patient that the novelty induced me to insert it in my Journal. I sincerely wish the effects may be beneficial in restoring the old man so that he may rejoin his relatives again.[3]

---

1   Each of the plants named forms a base for botanical drugs listed in the United States Pharmacopoeia or National Formulary. See Virgil J. Vogel, *American Indian Medicine* (New York: Ballantine, 1973).

2   HBCA B.80/a/7/fo. 6.

3   HBCA B.80/a/7/fos. 6–6d.

Although bizarre to Dease, the fires lit on and around Barbue clearly brought him immediate relief. That four and not some other number of fires were lit may have been significant, four having special meaning not only for other Northern Athapaskans but for many North American aboriginal people.[1]

Phlebotomy and the application of heat were the only two physical therapeutic techniques tried on Barbue. Both persisted among the twentieth-century Gwich'in, who applied steam-heat by lying on moss-covered hot rocks.[2] Although no surgical techniques are mentioned in treatment of Barbue's illness, Gwich'in medicine men and women were certainly knowledgeable in them. In the late 1890s, for example, a Klondiker named George Mitchell went toward the Yukon gold fields via the Mackenzie and Peel rivers and wintered in Gwich'in territory. On a trip with Gwich'in, Mitchell broke his kneecap and later described in detail the immediate effort to immobilize the leg, and the later diagnosis and surgery — each by a different woman. One surgeon made three cuts around the knee with a flint blade to release blood, pinned and joined together the split cap halves with caribou bone and sinew, and placed a poultice made from the inner bark of willow and herbs on the wound, which healed without infection. Other patients were also treated successfully. Mitchell described the skilful repair of a badly slit stomach and of an upper chest bullet wound, and noted that scurvy was treated with a spruce decoction, and that when an enema was needed, a caribou bladder and revolver barrel served nicely.[3]

★　　★　　★

That night after Barbue was — to use Dease's imagery — buried alive, he slept. But he improved no further. On 20 July, "a Different remedy was tried which consists of the skin of a Muskrat. they singe it & the Patient then eats the skin & drinks the liquor." But Barbue defecated often, "pass[ing] a very bad & unsightly bilious kind of matter." An Indian

---

1　Osgood, *Contributions to the Ethnography of the Kutchin.*

2　McKennan, *The Chandalar Kutchin.*

3　Angus Graham, Surgery with Flint, *Antiquity* 4, 1930, 233–37; Angus Graham, *The Golden Grindstone: The Adventures of George Mitchell* (Toronto: Oxford University Press, 1935).

brought "fresh bustard," which was goose, that Barbue ate. But this was his last meal and he declined rapidly. On 21 July, at two o'clock in the morning, Dease and Bell "were awakened by the cries of one of the Loucheux who came to tell us that the old chief had Expired. On going to the Spot, we found but too true. he breathed his last without a struggle while in the act of taking a drink of water and retained his speech & recollection all along."[1] His widow was "incessant in her lamentations & frequently joined by the other women & men." She later "threw herself into the Water." Barbue, it seems, was subsequently buried, for Dease wrote that pickets were placed "round the Grave."[2]

The mourning practices that Dease observed were typical among Gwich'in and other Northern Athapaskans, who, upon the death of a relative, destroyed their food and property, singed their hair, cut and otherwise mutilated their bodies, and threw themselves into the water.[3] But the burial of Barbue is puzzling. Although Dease remarked that it was "according to their own custom," it was typical of neither the Gwich'in nor Hare Indians.[4] The Gwich'in preferred placing the dead on stages or scaffolds, or enclosing them in hollow wood then hanging them from trees. A year or so following death they burned the body, ostensibly to keep maggots from eating the corpse.[5] For the Gwich'in, "the idea of their bodies being destroyed by worms is horrible." Perhaps Barbue was buried because he was a trading chief and died where Hudson's Bay Company traders held sway or perhaps his burial marked the beginning of changes in burial customs.[6]

---

1   HBCA B.80/a/7/fos. 6d–7.

2   HBCA B.80/a/7/fo. 7.

3   See, e.g., Franklin, *Narrative of a Second Expedition*; Hardisty, The Loucheux Indians; George Keith, Letters to Mr. Roderick McKenzie, in L.R. Masson, ed., *Les Bourgeois de la Compagnie du Nord-Quest*, Vol. 2 (New York: Antiquarian Press, 1960), 65–127.

4   HBCA B.80/a/7/fo. 7.

5   Hardisty, The Loucheux Indians; Jones, The Kutchin Tribes; W.W. Kir[k]by, A Journey to the Youcan, Russian America, *Annual Report of the Smithsonian Institution for 1866* (Washington, DC, 1872), 416–20.

6   Hardisty, The Loucheux Indians, 319. On burial, compare treatment of Sakie, the Cree leader, at Moose Fort following his death; see Judd, Sakie, Esquawenoe, and the Foundation of a Dual-Native Tradition at Moose Factory.

There is no evidence that the Gwich'in blamed Barbue's death on sorcery, but they did regard the actions of the medicine men as failure. Two days after Barbue died, Dease reported that an Indian named Travaillant "went to pay a visit to some Indians above in order to the restitution of some articles that were given to them for Juggling. as the Old Chief Died they now wish them to be restored & put in his Grave." Dease added wryly, "If the same custom was observed in all countries, the Medical profession would require to be cautious in receiving patients so as to Effect a Cure."[1]

★   ★   ★

Barbue's death did not cause significant change in the lives of the Gwich'in. His eldest son succeeded him as trading chief, and the Gwich'in carried on very much as they had before. In important ways, they had been caught up in a history in which consequential events were initiated by outsiders, but in equally significant ways, Europeans did not so much present exclusively novel circumstances to which the Gwich'in were forced to adapt as they intensified patterns and relations already in place. For example, the processes of exchange were familiar to the Gwich'in. They were zealous traders at the dawn of their contact with Europeans. They valued dentalium shells before Europeans arrived to trade these commodities. Their animosities with Inuvialuit were well established. And they had always either adapted to periodic scarcities of rabbits, caribou, and fish or faced hunger and perhaps starvation. In other words, although Europeans themselves and many of their trade goods were novel, some Gwich'in probably made only slight adjustments in their lives to accommodate the newcomers.

But many of the circumstances described here are clearly attributable to the European and Canadian presence. Traders brought epidemic diseases into the Mackenzie River region, and Gwich'in subsequently died in large numbers from those diseases. Traders introduced firearms, and relations between Gwich'in bands became tense as a result of mortality caused by those guns. Traders established posts that attracted all Native people who learned of them, but the Gwich'in, armed with guns, successfully prevented the Inuvialuit from having direct access to European traders, which heightened tension among all three ethnic groups.

---

1   HBCA B.80/a/7/fo. 7d.

It is overly simplistic to take a position that the Gwich'in either actively made their own history or were passive bystanders in a history whose important events were effected by other people. The answer is rather that they did both: like indigenous people everywhere, the Gwich'in actively determined the course of events even as they were caught up in expanding European-based mercantilist economies and, later, European-initiated evangelical advances. The Gwich'in influenced the direction of events as they assigned their own meaning to them. One cannot argue that the Gwich'in did not fundamentally affect European and Canadian traders who moved to their territory when the consequence of their not bringing expected food was the marginalization and subsequent abandonment of a post, as happened at New Good Hope.

It is currently fashionable to argue that Native people were active agents throughout their lives, and that they determined the course and outcome of events far more than the people of European descent with whom their relations became increasingly intertwined. What weakens this position, if it is taken to the extreme, is epidemic disease, the wild card in the meeting between European and Native American. No matter that in the case scrutinized here, Barbue himself died not in an epidemic but — so it seems — from a chronic disease of old age. Many other Gwich'in who lived at his time did succumb from epidemic diseases, which killed them or left them weakened and exposed to starvation. And if we can trust the anecdotal evidence in post journals, the epidemics that arrived in the mid-1820s were devastating.

In fusing analytical and narrative goals, and in its focus on biographical fragments, this retelling of the story of Barbue brings an especially personal dimension to the history of earliest encounters between Gwich'in and people of European background. It reminds us that the history of the Gwich'in is not just about them, nameless, and named whites, despite the obstacles that our sources place in the way of successfully recovering Native names, identities, and personalities. Here one Gwich'in at least has retained an identity. In the absence of Native testimony it nevertheless remains difficult to provide Gwich'in perspectives on the particular events recorded here. There is no doubt they had their own perspectives on all that unfolded, and that they gave intense meaning to happenings like the demise and death of Barbue; it is simply the inaccessibility of those perspectives that is at issue.

Barbue's death may not in itself have been widely significant, but the moment in Gwich'in history measured in epidemiological and demographic terms was. The Gwich'in who survived the epidemics kept on living, for the most part, traditional ways of life in the bush. But they also continued to visit Fort Good Hope periodically in order to exchange furs, provisions, and services for trade goods. While traditional cultural sentiments and values surely persisted, the Gwich'in were increasingly affected by the trade. More than a decade would pass after Barbue's death before a trading post, initially known as Peel River Post and later Fort McPherson, was established squarely in Gwich'in territory. But by that year, 1840, which was almost two decades before missionaries penetrated this far north with their proselytizing agendas, the trade for pelts and provisions, the new desire for tobacco and guns and enhanced desire for beads and dentalium shells, the temptation on the part of some Gwich'in to seek provisions at posts when hungry, and especially, the epidemics that ravaged entire populations — all had left their impact on Barbue and other Gwich'in, on Gwich'in demography, Gwich'in adaptations, and Gwich'in culture. The records of Barbue's demise, placed as fully as possible into their cultural and historical contexts, afford insights into these processes.

Part IV. Native Voices in Writing

The three chapters in Part IV look at nineteenth-century writings in which Native authors and communities hold centre stage. The first two essays examine works which have been widely read and reprinted since their appearance more than a century ago: *A Narrative of the Captivity and Adventures of John Tanner during Thirty Years Residence among the Indians in the Interior of North America* (1830), and William W. Warren's *History of the Ojibway People* (1885). The third translates and analyzes a previously unpublished letter sent in 1845 by several Ottawa chiefs on Manitoulin Island (Ontario) to the Algonquin chiefs at Oka (Quebec); written in the Ottawa language, it is a document of special historical and linguistic interest.

The fact that these writings all relate to Ojibwa and Ottawa history reflects the active role long played by these peoples in Native interactions with Europeans. Many of the descendants of the Algonquian groups who met Radisson in 1659-60 (see chapter 3) came to appreciate the power of the written word and to cultivate it for themselves. They counter stereotypes of Native people as solely oral or as lacking their own authors who would cultivate literacy—like any other useful tool—when they could.

John Fierst has spent several years researching the *Narrative* of John Tanner, a Kentucky boy taken captive by Ojibwa Indians in 1790. With support from the National Endowment for the Humanities and others, he and an interdisciplinary editorial team are preparing a new edition of the book, thoroughly documented and annotated. Fierst explores the many levels and the remarkable accuracy of the text, and the complex ways in which it expresses Tanner's voice, his participation and assimilation into Native worlds, and the voice of its equally interesting editor and amanuensis, Dr. Edwin James.

Theresa M. Schenck is both a member of the Blackfeet Tribe in Montana and a descendant of Cree, Ojibwa, and Metis on both the U.S. and Canadian sides of the border. In her doctoral thesis (Rutgers University, 1995) and publications, she has examined Ojibwa social history and clan structures and their relations with the fur trade, notably through one of her ancestral lines, the Cadotte family of Madeline Island, Lake Superior. Long interested in the Ojibwa history penned by their relative, William Warren, she looks at the origins and background of Warren and his book and assesses both the value and limitations of his perspectives and contributions.

David H. Pentland is a professor in the departments of linguistics and anthropology at the University of Manitoba. Some years ago, he discovered in Montreal the 1845 Ottawa-language "Letter to the Chiefs of the Alqonquin, Lake of Two Mountains" which he presents here; his essay is the first study to focus on this text. Pentland's contribution offers a model for how such documents can be treated to productive analyses of language, style, authorship, and context, to reveal the elusive Native writers and worlds behind them.

We need far more complete and careful studies of all such texts. Whether written in Native or European languages, in the roman alphabet or in the Cree syllabic system widely adopted across the North, these letters and narratives record Native outlooks and authors. They speak volumes if they are read attentively.

Readers may note that various authors use three different spellings of the name most often applied to the people known among themselves as Anishinaabeg: Ojibwa, Ojibway, and Ojibwe. The first two varients reflect the fact that English-speakers tend to pronounce the final syllable with either a long or short "a." Properly, the sound falls in between, which is why Ojibwe linguists prefer the third spelling, "Ojibwe."

9

Strange Eloquence: Another Look at *The Captivity and Adventures of John Tanner*

John T. Fierst

I FIRST LEARNED OF John Tanner in the fall of 1979, while living in St. Paul, Minnesota. I had a casual interest in the Boundary Waters Canoe Area at the time and was reading Grace Lee Nute's *The Voyageur's Highway: Minnesota's Border Lake Land.*[1] In it Nute included a vignette of Tanner, entitled "An Indian Captive." Describing him sentimentally as a "blue-eyed lad," she told how he had been kidnapped from his father's cabin "near the mouth of the Miami River." The Great Miami River, which flows through southwestern Ohio, enters the Ohio River a mile below Cincinnati.[2] Having grown up in Cincinnati, I have many memories of this part of the world. Nute's description of Tanner reminded me of how, on an occasional Sunday afternoon, my father, to give my mother some relief from her six children, would herd us into the car and drive down to the Anderson Ferry, a car ferry that still operates on the Ohio River. In this splendid fashion, by ferryboat, we would cross the Ohio between Cincinnati and Kentucky, not far from the mouth of the Great Miami. These childhood memories, more than anything else, first stirred my interest in John Tanner, foreshadowing the appeal his story would have for me.

The next day I borrowed a copy of *A Narrative of the Captivity and Adventures of John Tanner*[3] from the St. Paul Public Library, and over the weekend read it at the kitchen table in my apartment. I was greatly impressed but could not then have explained why. I have discovered since,

---

1 Grace Lee Nute, *The Voyageur's Highway: Minnesota's Border Lake Land* (St. Paul: Minnesota Historical Society, 1941), 68-70.

2 Tanner was taken near the mouth of the Great or Big Miami River (as opposed to the Little Miami, which flows into the Ohio above Cincinnati).

3 John Tanner, *A Narrative of the Captivity and Adventures of John Tanner During Thirty Years' Residence Among the Indians in the Interior of North America*, Edwin James, ed. (New York: G. & C. & H. Carvill, 1830).

in the course of editing the *Narrative*,[1] that such a personal response to his story is not unusual. Because of the pathos of Tanner's life and because he crossed several cultural boundaries, his story appeals powerfully to readers of very different backgrounds.

In the spring of 1790, Manito-o-geezhik and his son Kish-kau-ko, warriors from an Ojibwe village on the Saginaw River,[2] captured John Tanner, a nine-year-old American, during a raid against the Virginia settlements in Kentucky. They and five others came down the Great Miami River, crossed the Ohio, and waited in the woods at the edge of Tanner's father's farm, or station,[3] located a mile below the mouth of the Great Miami. After abducting Tanner, they paddled back across the Ohio, abandoned their canoe, and, with a party of whites in pursuit, led him north along the Great Miami. A difficult race through the Ohio wilderness brought them finally to a Shawnee town on the Maumee River in northwestern Ohio. From there they descended the Maumee, which drains into Lake Erie.

Tanner's capture was not without precedent. The uncertain boundary between white settlement and Native homeland in North America had a long history of captivities. Hundreds of captives had been taken before Tanner, both by Natives and whites.[4] They were the embodi-

---

1 The John Tanner Project is funded through grants provided by The National Endowment for the Humanities and The National Historical Publications and Records Commission (both of the United States). The other editors on the project are D. Wayne Moodie, Lacey Sanders, John D. Nichols, Roger Roulette, Bruce M. White, and Paul Hackett.

2 The Saginaw River flows into Saginaw Bay on the west side of Lake Huron. The region was occupied at the time by Ojibwe-speakers often referred to as Chippewa in American usage. See Helen Hornbeck Tanner, *Atlas of Great Lakes Indian History* (Norman: University of Oklahoma Press, 1986), 133-134; and Virgil J. Vogel, *Indian Names in Michigan* (Ann Arbor: University of Michigan Press, 1986), 30.

3 Americans used this term to refer to the early fortified settlements they established in Kentucky. Tanner's Station is now the site of Petersburg, Kentucky, in Boone County.

4 Many whites taken captive, particularly at a young age, chose to remain on the Native side of the boundary. To some whites this seemed a contradiction and made them question what they assumed was true about the superiority of their own societies. In the social bonds of Native societies, speculated the essayist J. Hector St. John de Crevecoeur in the late eighteenth century, there must be "something singularly captivating, and far superior to anything to be boasted of among us; for thousands of

ments of cultural conflict, as one writer expressed it.[1] Whites were taken captive for ransom, or in retaliation for white depredations, yet often, as well, their Native captors took them to replace deceased relatives. It was the custom in many Native groups to allow a family member – a child who had died from disease or a son who had been killed in war – to be replaced by a captive. In most cases the captive would eventually gain full status within the adoptive society; the race of the captive, it seems, did not stand in the way of cultural acceptance.

Accounts of returned captives were widely read when published. The earliest of them mark the beginning of a distinctively North American form of literary expression, the captivity narrative. Captivity narratives in their three-hundred-year history have served a variety of purposes: Puritan divines used them to illustrate God's providence and to provide religious instruction; British authorities, to stir up fear of the French during the French and Indian War; Americans, to stir up fear of the British during the Revolution, and later to justify territorial expansion; reformers, to argue for social change; popular fiction writers, to create sentiment and sensation for their readers.[2]

The reasons for Tanner's abduction were probably mixed. Political tensions gathering along the Ohio River, having to do with the construction of American settlements north of the river, accounted in part for Manito-o-geezhik's raiding party. Yet the primary reason for Tanner's kidnapping was made clear in the *Narrative* – he was to replace the deceased son of Manito-o-

---

Europeans are Indians, and we have no examples of even one of those Aborigines having from choice become Europeans!" Crevecoeur, *Letters from an American Farmer* (New York: E.P. Dutton, 1957), 209.

1 Paula A. Treckel, review of "The White Indians of Colonial America," by James Axtell, *William and Mary Quarterly* 33 (1976): 143-48. Axtell is cited below. Treckel's essay was printed under "Letters to the Editor," along with Axtell's response.

2 Interest in captivity narratives continues today, with the captivity genre receiving long overdue attention from scholars. Two articles provide a good introduction to captivity literature: Annette Kolodny, "Among the Indians: The Uses of Captivity," *New York Times Book Review*, 31 January 1993, 1, 26-29; and James Axtell, "The White Indians of Colonial America," in *The European and the Indian: Essays in the Ethnohistory of Colonial North America* (Oxford: Oxford University Press, 1981), 168-206. Axtell offers some answers to St. John de Crevecoeur's question about the drawing power of Native societies (see note 4 on page 221). Other treatments of captivity literature include Richard Vanderbeets, *The Indian Captivity Narrative: An American Genre* (Lanham, MD: University Press of America, 1983); and June Namias, *White Captives: Gender and Ethnicity on the American Frontier* (Chapel Hill: University of North Carolina Press, 1993).

JOHN T. FIERST

geezhik. On the Maumee River British traders tried to ransom Tanner, but Manito-o-geezhik refused to give him up. The traders, who treated Tanner kindly and gave him plenty to eat, told him that for now he must be content to become Manito-o-geezhik's son, "in place of the one he had lost."[1] Tanner related that when he learned he had to remain a prisoner, he cried for the first time since he had been captured.

Manito-o-geezhik's party descended the lower Maumee to Lake Erie and continued on to Detroit. From Detroit Tanner was taken on horseback to Saginaw, where he was adopted into Manito-o-geezhik's family, with whom he spent the next two years. Up to this point his story, as he later told it to Edwin James, his editor, resembled other accounts of captivity. It emphasized the ordeal of capture, the captive's initial journey, and the harsh trials of adaptation to a new life.

But then in 1792, something happened that moved Tanner's experience beyond the stereotype of "captivity." That summer Manito-o-geezhik sold him to Netnokwa, an influential Ottawa or Odawa[2] woman from the village of L'Arbre Croche, located on the northern edge of Michigan's southern peninsula. An exchange of "whiskey, blankets, tobacco, and other articles of great value"[3] for this eleven-year-old boy started Tanner on a different road. He began his life with the Ottawa, with whom he would live closely for a period of approximately twenty-six years (1792-1818), most of which he spent west of Lake Superior.

I still associate the Narrative with Quetico Provincial Park in Ontario and the adjacent Boundary Waters Canoe Area Wilderness in Minnesota. But its principal settings are in fact Lake of the Woods (northwestern Ontario), the Red River Valley, and the prairies and parklands west and northwest of Winnipeg (Manitoba). In the spring of 1794 Netnokwa and Tawgaweninne, her Ojibwe husband, left L'Arbre Croche, setting out for Red River to join Tawgaweninne's relations. Their

---

1   Tanner, Narrative, 29.

2   The Ottawa speak a southeastern dialect of Ojibwe. When they first encountered Europeans the Ottawa were living on Manitoulin Island, in Lake Huron. By the time of the Narrative most of the Ottawa were living along the coasts and rivers of Michigan's lower peninsula, and in contiguous areas that are now part of Ontario, Ohio, Indiana, Illinois, and Wisconsin. See Johanna E. Feest and Christian F. Feest, "Ottawa," in Handbook of North American Indians, vol. 15 (Washington: Smithsonian Institution, 1978), 772-86.

3   Tanner, Narrative, 36.

move was part of a western migration of Ottawa and Ojibwe to the region then known as Rupert's Land in the latter decades of the eighteenth century. Their journey proved difficult. Tawgaweninne died en route. Not until a year later, in the fall of 1795, did Netnokwa, Tanner and other members of her small family arrive at Lake Winnipeg. It would be twenty-three years before Tanner would leave this part of the world on a first return journey to the United States in the spring of 1818.[1]

Many Ottawa and Ojibwe moved to the Red River country because of the depletion of game and the spread of disease in their homelands, and also to take advantage of "westward moving trade opportunities," according to Laura Peers.[2] The period 1780 to 1804 for these westernmost Ottawa and Ojibwe was a period of expansion and adaptation, as they spread out along the rivers and lakes in the region. Following this movement came years of crisis for them (1805 to 1821). Violent competition in the fur trade disrupted their lives and ended only when the Hudson's Bay Company and the North West Company merged in 1821. Most of the events Tanner described in his *Narrative* took place during this rivalry. The *Narrative* gives us an intimate view of the changes and tensions of the times.

Tanner's book is an early ethnohistorical text of major importance. In it Tanner reveals his Ottawa associates to us in a personal way, not as distant hunter-gatherers, not in the anthropologist's timeless present, not as the enigmatic figures in Ernest Hemingway's story "Indian Camp,"[3] but as real persons in a distinctive landscape, passing through a specific period in their history. Well-known historical figures like William Clark, Lewis Cass, and Lord Selkirk[4] appear in the *Narrative*, but they were not

---

1 Tanner, *Narrative*, 40-49, 239.

2 Laura Peers, *The Ojibwa of Western Canada, 1780 to 1870* (Winnipeg: University of Manitoba Press, 1994), 27-97.

3 Ernest Hemingway, "Indian Camp" *In Our Time* (New York: Charles Scribner's Sons, 1925), 15-19.

4 William Clark, U.S. army officer, explorer, Indian agent, Governor of Missouri Territory, is famous for the transcontinental expedition he and Captain Meriwether Lewis led to the Pacific Coast between the years 1803 and 1806. Lewis Cass, Governor of Michigan Territory, Secretary of War under Andrew Jackson, Democratic nominee for the presidency in 1848, and Secretary of State under James Buchanan, befriended Tanner and his family. Thomas Douglas, fifth Earl of Selkirk, was the Scot-

the main actors. In Tanner's perspective, the important figures were Native: Peshauba, She-gwaw-koo-sink, Blackbird, Wasso, the Black Duck, the Little Clam, Netnokwa. The landscape had Native place names: Keneshewayboant, Hill of the Buffalo Chase, Me-nau-ko-nos-keeg, War-gun-uk-ke-zee, the Dry Carrying Place, the Lake of the Sand Hills, names that require the context of oral tradition to decipher.

Because the language and outlooks of the Ottawa so deeply shaped his point of view, Tanner saw the major events in this time of adaptation and crisis as a Native participant. His description of the epidemic that early in the winter of 1802-1803 devastated beaver populations throughout the region is far more telling than the account books of the fur traders. Deeply struck by the silent spread of death among the beavers, he remembered the details vividly: "I found them dead and dying in the water, on the ice, and on the land; sometimes I found one that, having cut a tree half down, had died at its roots; sometimes one who had drawn a stick of timber half way to his lodge, was lying dead by his burthen. Many of them, which I opened, were red and bloody about the heart."[1] Although we cannot know exactly how Tanner interpreted the meaning of the epidemic, we can assume, because he profoundly internalized the cognitive reality of the Ottawa with whom he lived, that he attributed it to the influence of other-than-human powers, and we can sense how disturbing the contagion must have been to the Ottawa and Ojibwe trappers who relied on the beaver for their livelihood.

Tanner's concerns about sacred power and keeping the patronage of the manitos, powerful beings who guided the course of a person's existence, run throughout the *Narrative*, or better, inform it. Tanner, more often than not, expressed these concerns indirectly, through his actions. His struggle with Aiskabawis, for example, which begins in chapter eleven, and is central to the *Narrative*, can be understood as a contest of power between Tanner, a practitioner of the Midewiwin, or Grand

---

tish nobleman whose concern for the plight of the dispossessed of the Highlands led him to attempt to establish colonies for them in North America, Selkirk's boldest adventure being the establishment of the Red River Colony in the heart of the fur trade country. This exacerbated the conflict between the North West Company and the Hudson's Bay Company. The Northwesters viewed Selkirk (a major stockholder in the Hudson's Bay Company) and his colonization plan as a threat to their interests. Tanner assisted Selkirk's mercenaries in their defence of the Red River colony.

1 Tanner, *Narrative*, 104.

Medicine Society, and a local shaman who gained influence in Tanner's village in the wake of the Shawnee Prophet enthusiasm, a revitalization movement which centred on the figure of Tenskwatawa, the half-brother of the Shawnee leader Tecumseh.[1]

Tanner's *Narrative* demonstrates how far to the northwest the influence of the Shawnee Prophet spread after 1806, but Tanner revealed more about this nativist revitalization movement than simply its physical range. He graphically recalled how echoes of the Prophet's ideas affected his Ottawa companions and himself in the Red River Valley. The level of detail recorded in the *Narrative*, as shown in the descriptions of Tanner's metaphysical struggles with Aiskabawis, is striking.[2] Unfortunately for Tanner, Aiskabawis managed to persuade Tanner's in-laws that Tanner had shot bad medicine at several of their children and caused their death. Tanner's loss of power in this contest with Aiskabawis is a turning point in the *Narrative*, and stands at the beginning of events leading to his return to the United States.

Tanner actually returned to the United States three times, in 1818, in 1820, and finally in 1824. His *Narrative* ends with this last return, describing his attempt in the summer of 1823 to bring his children down to the Catholic mission on Mackinac Island, a venture to which his former wife and her relatives were opposed. As a consequence, Tanner was shot and nearly killed on the Malign River east of Rainy Lake. He spent the winter of 1823-1824 recuperating at Rainy Lake in the Hudson's Bay Company trading house, under the care of Chief Factor John McLoughlin, and returned to Mackinac Island the next spring.

---

1 Tenskwatawa, the Prophet, promised that, if his teachings were adhered to, relations with the Master of Life would be restored and Native people would be freed from dependence on the whites. Emissaries of the Shawnee Prophet carried his message to the Ottawa and Ojibwe. See R. David Edmunds, *The Shawnee Prophet* (Lincoln: University of Nebraska Press, 1983). For an overview of traditional Ojibwe beliefs, see Christopher Vecsey, *Traditional Ojibwa Religion and Its Historical Changes* (Philadelphia: American Philosophical Society, 1983). Vecsey discusses the Midewiwin on pages 174-90 and the Shawnee Prophet enthusiasm on page 193.

2 Other examples of Tanner's uniquely detailed observations include his descriptions of the warfare between the Ojibwe and the Dakota, and his account of Lord Selkirk's mercenaries who employed Tanner in the winter of 1816-1817 as their guide when they seized Fort Daer and Fort Douglas on the Red River, two posts held by the North West Company at the height of its rivalry with the Hudson's Bay Company.

JOHN T. FIERST

While serving as Ojibwe interpreter at the U.S. Indian agency on Mackinac Island in the 1820s, Tanner told the story of his life to Dr. Edwin James, the post surgeon at the American fort on the island. Their conversations were probably a mixture of English and Ojibwe. James spoke a broken Ojibwe, and Tanner, since he had a poor command of English, may well have spoken in Ottawa. The account was edited by James and published in April 1830 by G. & C. & H. Carvill, a New York bookseller.

The *Narrative* runs to 426 pages (fifteen chapters) and includes a long introduction by Edwin James and a set of appendices with vocabularies. The appendices (four chapters) also present an early study of Algonquian cultures in central North America. Edwin James based them on what he had learned from Tanner and on his own ethnographic studies and observations made during his assignments in the West.

The manuscript has never been recovered. It is even difficult to find references to Tanner's publisher, to whose office at 108 Broadway Tanner delivered the manuscript in the summer of 1828. There was no mention of Tanner in the New York newspapers that summer, although they often reported the arrival of unusual travellers. We can only wonder about Tanner in New York — this Ottawa hunter from far beyond the Great Lakes, hardly able to make himself understood in English.

In New York Tanner sat for his portrait in Henry Inman's studio on Vescy Street. Inman, one of the most accomplished American portraitists in his day, painted Tanner in a style and pose accepted as the standard for male portraiture in Jacksonian America. Tanner faces nearly frontward. The red colour of his hair and the blue of his eyes stand out. He is wearing a dark green great-coat with gold buttons, a white stock and high white collar, a white tie, and tie pin. He looks uncomfortable in the tailored clothes of a bourgeois gentleman — a long way from Lake of the Woods. His expression is one of armed neutrality. The publisher probably commissioned the painting, intending to have an engraving made from it. Cephas G. Childs, later a partner of Inman's,[1] produced a mezzotint from the portrait, and it is this image of Tanner, the only like-

---

1   Information about Inman and Childs was supplied by Thomas O'Sullivan, Curator of Art at the Minnesota Historical Society, in a personal letter to Robert M. Frame, now in possession of the John Tanner Project. The original painting is owned by the Essex Institute in Salem, Massachusetts.

ness known, that the reader encounters upon opening the *Narrative* to the title page.

On its surface, the *Narrative* seems somewhat nomadic. A lack of calendar dates offers an impression of Tanner wandering from one hunting story to the next. Yet his account is far from being a series of disconnected episodes. Few other fur trade sources possess its vitality and imaginative coherence. I remember sensing this strange eloquence even as I read the *Narrative* for the first time. I gradually came to appreciate that there is a structure to John Tanner's *Narrative*, though it is not a structure typical of story telling in the European tradition. What struck me above all else were its many instances of foreshadowing. In a dream, one time, spirits gave Tanner a horse for his next day's journey. Through songs and prayers, Netnokwa located game for her sons to kill. On the way to war, Peshauba divined correctly that the Ojibwe would return home unharmed but also unsuccessful.[1]

Both Tanner's capture and his return were foreshadowed. A passage in the opening chapter of the *Narrative* hinted at the future:

> When my father returned at night, and found that I had been at home all day, he sent me for a parcel of small canes, and flogged me much more severely than I could suppose the offence merited. I was displeased with my sisters for attributing all the blame to me, when they had neglected even to tell me to go to school in the forenoon. From that time, my father's house was less like home to me, and I often thought and said, "I wish I could go and live among the Indians."[2]

Three paragraphs later John Tanner got his wish; he was carried off. In chapter fourteen Tanner recalled a dream his sister Lucy had, foreshadowing his return to Kentucky in 1818: "My sister Lucy had, the night before my arrival, dreamed that she saw me coming through the cornfield that surrounded her house."[3]

Tanner, like his Ojibwe and Ottawa adopted relatives, accepted the reality of dreams, as he accepted other-than-human involvement in his

---

1 Tanner, *Narrative*, 52, 108, 140.

2 Tanner, *Narrative*, 24.

3 Tanner, *Narrative*, 252.

JOHN T. FIERST

life. To dismiss the significance to Tanner of such phenomena is to close oneself off from his world. A special instance of foreshadowing occurs in chapter ten. Peshauba, approaching the time of his death, told of his existence before coming to live in this world. To be able to speak of one's existence before birth was a special gift and a sign of great spiritual power.[1]

I remember before I came to live in this world, I was with the Great Spirit above. And I often looked down, and saw men upon the earth. I saw many good and desirable things, and among others, a beautiful woman, and as I looked day after day at the woman, he said to me, "Pe-shau-ba, do you love the woman you are so often looking at?" I told him I did: then he said to me, "Go down and spend a few winters on the earth. You cannot stay long, and you must remember to be always kind and good to my children whom you see below." So I came down, but I have never forgotten what was said to me. I have always stood in the smoke between the two bands, when my people have fought with their enemies. I have not struck my friends in their lodges. I have disregarded the foolishness of young men who would have offended me, but have always gone into battle painted black, as I now am, and I now hear the same voice that talked to me before I came to this world: it tells me I can remain here no longer.[2]

The foreshadowing in the *Narrative* is expressive of the extent to which Tanner absorbed the complex of divinatory beliefs and practices of the Ottawa. Edwin James, Tanner's editor, did not, in any large degree, have access to this reality, this web of meaning behind Tanner's words. But he did try faithfully to record Tanner's thoughts in English. James was a compassionate man of high ideals, and devoted to his work.

---

1   "Other-than-human" is the anthropologist A. Irving Hallowell's term. Hallowell referred to the phenomenon of having knowledge of one's existence before birth as "precognition." See Hallowell, *The Ojibwa of Berens River, Manitoba: Ethnography into History*, edited with preface and afterword by Jennifer S.H. Brown (Fort Worth, TX: Harcourt Brace Jovanovich College Publishers, 1992), 63-64; also, Hallowell, "Spirits of the Dead in Saulteaux Life and Thought," in *Culture and Experience* (Philadelphia: University of Pennsylvania Press, 1955), 170.

2   Tanner, *Narrative*, 176.

Considered a radical for his times, he advocated temperance, fought against the U.S. Indian Removal Bill in 1830,[1] and later, as an abolitionist, helped slaves to escape from the American south. James's character is sewn into the fabric of the *Narrative*. His part in its composition presents challenges for analysis, yet Tanner's account is no less authentic because it was mediated through James's voice. While it would have been impossible for James to leave himself out of the *Narrative* completely, neither did he take possession of it. It remained Tanner's account. However, what is really at question is not the fact of mediation but the degree of trust we can place in James. In the course of my research I have found no evidence to believe that he was dishonest. We should be grateful that it was James who took down Tanner's story, not because he gave us the whole story but because, from within the limits of his own perspective, which blended Christianity and Jeffersonian idealism, he painstakingly gave us an accurate one. There were barriers to what James could have known. But, from our perspective, more important than what he and Tanner were unable to tell us is what they did tell us — what we can learn about Tanner and his world through a study of this imperfect document.

The circumstances that brought these two together and created this book seem almost providential. Some knowledge of Tanner — of an American boy taken captive during the warfare in the Ohio Valley — must have circulated generally among the fur traders. Surveyor and map maker David Thompson, employed by the North West Company in 1797, noted in his journal on 23 August of that year that they came across Tanner on Rainy River: we "came up with 2 canoes ... 3 men, 3 women and an American Slave of 10 years — he is adopted."[2] One would guess that over time others like Thompson brought down from the upper country stories of this American living among the Ottawa. Tanner himself learned from a trader that his brother had been as far as Mackinac Island in search of him.[3]

---

1   The Indian Removal Bill was passed by the U.S. Congress in the same month that Tanner's *Narrative* was published, April 1830. With the passage of the Removal Bill, many Native Americans who had been living east of the Mississippi River were forced to surrender their lands and their freedom and were exiled to reserves in Oklahoma.

2   Sean Peake, in a personal communication, brought my attention to this reference to Tanner. For the original journal, see David Thompson Papers, microfilm reel 25, Archives of Ontario, Toronto.

3   Tanner, *Narrative*, 162.

JOHN T. FIERST

It is likely that Tanner and James first crossed paths in Cape Girardeau, Missouri, in 1820, when Tanner made his second return journey to the United States: "At Cape Guirardeau, where I left my canoe, and where I remained but a very short time, I saw some of the gentlemen of Major Long's party, then on their return from the Rocky Mountains."[1] Tanner was referring to Major Stephen Long's 1819-1820 expedition across the Great Plains, which broke up in Cape Girardeau the fall Tanner was there. The purpose of the expedition, on which Edwin James served as botanist, had been to survey the high plains and to determine the source of the Red River.[2] It was James who eventually wrote and prepared for publication the official account of the expedition.

A student of natural history, James was eager to make his contribution to the scientific description of the North American continent. Typical of young American scientists in the early nationalist period, most of whom were amateurs, he had little support or leisure to follow his interests, which makes his accomplishments all the more noteworthy. The concerns of his medical profession constantly distracted him from his scientific pursuits. Given their circumstances on Mackinac Island, one would guess that James recorded Tanner at a daunting pace. Yet he was the perfect observer. His experiences and his training as a botanist served him well in this case, for he preserved in the *Narrative* a level of detail, a degree of specificity, that can only be admired.

When all is said about James's participation, however, the integrity of the *Narrative* and the world that informs it have impressed me the most. The reader enters that world through the senses, as the following passage beautifully demonstrates.

> The weather was very cold, and the ground hard frozen, but no snow fell; so that it was difficult to follow the tracks of the moose, and the noise of our walking on hard ground and dry leaves, gave the animals timely warning of our approach. This state of things continuing for some time, we were all reduced nearly to starvation, and had recourse, as a last resort, to medicine hunting. Half the night I [sung] and prayed, and then lay down to sleep. I saw, in my dream, a beautiful young man come down

---

1   Tanner, *Narrative*, 260.

2   This is not the Red River of the *Narrative*, which flows north between Minnesota and North Dakota into Manitoba and eventually into Lake Winnipeg, but the Red River of the south-central United States, which rises in the Texas Panhandle.

through the hole in the top of my lodge, and he stood directly before me. "What," said he, "is this noise and crying that I hear? Do I not know when you are hungry and in distress? I look down upon you at all times, and it is not necessary you should call me with such loud cries." Then pointing directly towards the sun's setting, he said, "do you see those tracks?" "Yes," I answered, "they are the tracks of two moose." "I give you those two moose to eat." Then pointing in an opposite direction, towards the place of the sun's rising, he showed me a bear's track, and said, "that also I give you." He then went out at the door of my lodge, and as he raised the blanket, I saw that snow was falling rapidly.

I very soon awoke, and feeling too much excited to sleep, I called old Sha-gwaw-ko-sink to smoke with me, and then prepared my Muz-zin-ne-neen-suk ... to represent the animals whose tracks had been shown me in my dream. At the earliest dawn, I started from the lodge in a heavy fall of snow, and taking the course pointed out to me, long before noon I fell on the track of two moose, and killed them both, a male and a female, very fat.[1]

Having read the *Narrative*, I wanted to learn more about John Tanner, but the secondary literature proved disappointing. Most interpretations of Tanner have been superficial, stressing the miseries of "savage" life, the unreliability of Tanner's account, or the mysteriousness of Tanner himself.

The earliest descriptions of Tanner often took their lead from comments Henry Rowe Schoolcraft made about him in his *Memoirs*, published in 1851.[2] Schoolcraft served in the 1820s under Lewis Cass as Indian agent at Sault Ste. Marie. After Tanner returned from New York in 1828, Schoolcraft hired him to work at the agency as an interpreter. His later statements about Tanner were very unflattering and stood in vivid contrast to the John Tanner depicted by James in the *Narrative*:

Tanner was a singular being – out of humor with the world, speaking ill of everybody, suspicious of every human action, a very savage in his feelings, reasonings, and philosophy of life, and yet exciting commiseration by the very isolation of his position.... He came out to Mackinac with the traders about 1825, and went to find his relatives in Kentucky, with

---

1 Tanner, *Narrative*, 189.

2 Henry Rowe Schoolcraft, *Personal Memoirs of a Residence of Thirty Years with the Indian Tribes on the American Frontiers: with Brief Notices of Passing Events, Facts, and Opinions, A.D. 1812 to A.D. 1842* (Philadelphia: Lippincott, 1851).

JOHN T. FIERST

whom, however, he could not long live. His habits were now so inveterately savage that he could not tolerate civilization. He came back to the frontiers and obtained an interpretership at the U.S. Agency at Mackinac. The elements of his mind were, however, morose, sour, suspicious, antisocial, revengeful, and bad. In a short time he was out with everybody. He caused to be written to me a piteous letter.... I felt interested in his history, received him in a friendly manner, and gave him the place of interpreter. He entered on the duties faithfully, but with the dignity and reserve of an Indian chief. He had so long looked on the dark side of human nature that he seldom or never smiled. He considered everybody an enemy. His view of the state of Indian society in the wilderness made it a perfect hell. They were thieves and murderers.[1]

It is difficult to imagine Tanner gaining the favour of someone as devoted to the victory of "civilization" as Schoolcraft, whose guiding conviction was that "Man was created, not a savage, a hunter, or warrior, but a horticulturist and a raiser of grain, and a keeper of cattle."[2] Schoolcraft's agrarian idealism, his low opinion of the world of the Ojibwe hunter, and his association of truth with civilization were manifest in his attacks upon Tanner, his underlying criticism being that Tanner chose to remain "savage." My impulse, on reading Schoolcraft, was to defend Tanner. The view of Native society presented in the *Narrative* was anything but "a perfect hell." In writing the introduction to the *Narrative*, James himself had felt a need to defend Tanner from Schoolcraft:

He returns to the pale of civilization, too late in life to acquire the mental habits which befit his new situation. It is to be regretted, that he should ever meet among us with those so destitute of generosity, as to be willing to take advantage of his unavoidable ignorance of the usages of civilized society. He has ever been found just and generous, until injuries or insults have aroused the spirit of hatred and revenge; his gratitude has always been as ardent and persevering as his resentment....

The preceding remarks would not, perhaps, have been hazarded, had not some harsh imputations been made to rest on the character of our

---

1   Schoolcraft, *Memoirs*, 315-16.

2   Henry Rowe Schoolcraft, "The Indian Viewed as a Man Out of Society," *Historical and Statistical Information Respecting the History, Condition and Prospects of the Indian Tribes of the United States*, vol. 6 (Philadelphia, 1851-57), 27.

narrator, in the district where he has for some time past resided, in consequence of differences growing, as appears to us, entirely out of the circumstance of the Indian character, with many of its prominent peculiarities, being indelibly impressed upon him.[1]

If Tanner needed defending, his defence lay in the *Narrative* itself. The
Narrative, however, is not a transparent text. It is deceptively complex.
Because of its ethnographic content and the layers of mediation involved
in its composition, its meanings do not lie on the surface. The reader
needs to be drawn in. And for an editor to do so requires more than simply
reprinting the *Narrative* and attaching a new introduction to it, as was
done in 1956 and in 1994.[2] Annette Kolodny, in a review of the series of
captivity narratives reprinted in facsimile editions by the Garland Publishing Company in the late 1970s, criticized the series for its "total lack of editing or editorial apparatus ... hampering its potential usefulness to sea-
soned scholars and rendering it all but inaccessible to the novice."[3] Her
criticism is especially justified in the case of Tanner's *Narrative* (volume 46
in the series), since much can be learned about Tanner from sources outside the *Narrative*. I first realized this when I came across a letter that he
had written to U.S. President Van Buren in 1837, complaining about
Schoolcraft's treatment of him.[4] The documentary record was adequate
to piece together a sense of the tensions in Sault Ste. Marie in the late
1820s and early 1830s that fostered both Schoolcraft's and James's state-

---

1 Tanner, *Narrative*, 4.

2 Tanner, *Narrative*, with an introduction by Noel Loomis (Minneapolis: Ross and
   Haines, 1956). In 1994 Penguin Books reprinted the Ross and Haines edition of the
   Narrative under a different title: *The Falcon: A Narrative of the Captivity and Adventures of
   John Tanner*, with an introduction by Louise Erdrich (New York: Penguin Books,
   1994). The Penguin edition makes no reference to Edwin James anywhere in the
   book, not even on the title page, and it omits both James's original introduction and
   his appendices. While the attention to Tanner is welcome, the effacement of James is
   misleading and regrettable.

3 Annette Kolodny, review of *Narratives of North American Indian Captivities*, selected
   and arranged by Wilcomb E. Washburn, *Early American Literature* 14 (1979): 228–35.

4 John Tanner to Martin Van Buren, 11 November 1837, Office of Indian Affairs
   (OIA), letters received, 1831–80, Michigan Superintendency, National Archives Record Group (NARG) 75, microfilm copy.

JOHN T. FIERST

ments and the letter Tanner sent Van Buren.[1] This convinced me that the *Narrative* itself could be treated with the same documentary care.

It seemed to me that readers would benefit tremendously from a text edited in the manner of some of the better examples of documentary editing, such as the two-volume correspondence of American Revolutionist Benjamin Rush, where the editor, Lyman Butterfield, succeeded in capturing "the people, the issues, the tensions, and spirit of an age."[2] The *Narrative* is ideal for this kind of treatment. As history, the text can be verified by documents in the Hudson's Bay Company Archives in Winnipeg, in the National Archives of both Canada and the United States, in county, state, and provincial records, and in the journals and letters of missionaries, explorers, and travellers, who encountered Tanner or passed through his world. Moreover, the themes and content of the *Narrative* are consistent with Ojibwe oral traditions and with information recorded over years of ethnographic study among related peoples in the region.

A documentary approach to the *Narrative* is by necessity interdisciplinary. It encompasses a study of Native languages; an historical sense of traditional Ojibwe and Ottawa cultures; insight from participants in the culture itself, and from oral traditions that surround the *Narrative*;[3] a familiarity with relevant ethnographic research; a reconstruction of the landscape, both physical and cultural; a grounding in the broader history of the period; and a knowledge of the documentary sources that exist to corroborate the *Narrative*.[4]

---

1   John T. Fierst, "Return to 'Civilization': John Tanner's Troubled Years at Sault Ste. Marie," *Minnesota History* (Spring 1986), 23-36.

2   J.H. Powell, review of the *Letters of Benjamin Rush*, edited by L.H. Butterfield, *Mississippi Valley Historical Review* (September 1952), 325-27. For a description of documentary editing, with suggested readings, see Mary-Jo Kline, *A Guide to Documentary Editing* (Baltimore: Johns Hopkins University Press, 1987), 1-29. For Kline, one goal of the documentary editor is to preserve "the nuances of a source that has survived the ravages of time."

3   Roger Roulette is responsible for the interviews of Ojibwe elders undertaken in conjunction with the Tanner project. Roulette, whose first language is Ojibwe, has devoted himself to the study of Ojibwe religion and culture. He works as a consultant and instructor of Ojibwe at the Manitoba Association for Native Languages.

4   For a discussion of the interdisciplinary nature of documentary editing see, Barbara Oberg, "Documentary Editing as a Collaborative Enterprise: Theirs, Mine, or Ours?" *Documentary Editing* 17 (March 1995): 3. According to Oberg, "the editorial project crosses the lines of established disciplines and traditional academic departments...calling upon the skills of numerous specialists." She argues that the goal of

To edit the *Narrative* requires looking at Tanner's world, to the degree possible, from the inside out. It requires the editors to think critically about issues of mediation and representation and to try to understand Tanner on his own terms. His memory was remarkably accurate; the depth of his transculturation is abundantly clear. A study of how he remembered may yield as important an insight into his world as anything else, for the text preserves not only what Tanner recollected but also the habits of mind he unconsciously displayed, even mediated through James's English. Tanner's world is embedded in the details of the *Narrative*, and it is on the details that editorial attention needs to be focused. By clarifying the details — identifying persons and places, fleshing out patterns barely visible, explaining meanings, and providing broader contexts — a good edition will knit together a sense of the life and setting Tanner knew. The reader can then judge whether or not Schoolcraft was right when he claimed that James had made "a mere packhorse of Indian opinions" of Tanner.[1]

The antipathy Schoolcraft expressed toward Tanner grew out of his racial beliefs and out of the controversy referred to above, but it had a further source, made clear in a footnote appended to his attack on Tanner.[2] In brief, Tanner was accused of murdering Schoolcraft's brother, James L. Schoolcraft, who was shot through the heart at close range on 6 July 1846. Tanner disappeared from Sault Ste. Marie that same day. Although the evidence suggesting Tanner had committed the murder was very strong, there was wide room for speculation, since Tanner was never apprehended and since there is no record of his life afterwards. Speculation has continued ever since. A.H. Clark's article, "The Tanner Case," which appeared in the *Sault Ste. Marie Evening News* two days before the 100th anniversary of the murder, was typical. Clark resurrected an old theory, that a third person, Lt. Bryant Tilden, had killed both Schoolcraft and Tanner that July morning.[3]

---

editing is "broadly humanistic" and suggests that editorial projects "can be a counterforce to the modern universities' segregated departments, compartmentalized epistemology, and fragmented learning."

1 Schoolcraft, *Memoirs*, 601.

2 Schoolcraft, *Memoirs*, 316-17.

3 A.H. Clark. "The Tanner Case," *Sault Ste. Marie Evening News*, 4 July 1946. Clark concluded what really became of Tanner was "as much of a mystery as it always has been."

July 6, 1846 was also an unfortunate day for John Tanner's *Narrative* because its significance became overshadowed by interest in the murder. Ever since, Tanner and his book have been subsumed under the word "mystery": "A man without a country, he lived in a shadowy half-world, fully accepted by neither the whites nor the Indians, until he mysteriously disappeared after the murder of James Schoolcraft in 1846," as Maxine Benson put it.[1] At the heart of darkness lived a man half white and half red, graphically symbolized on the dust jacket of Walter O'Meara's biography of him, *The Last Portage*,[2] with the muddied face of Tanner divided into red and white halves, as though he had fallen asleep under a sun lamp. Such romance serves only to marginalize and exoticize.

Tanner's *Narrative* has commonly been a voice in the margin,[3] although there have always been a few who have sensed its importance. The anthropologist Paul Radin, for example, who introduced the 1940 edition of the *Narrative*, wrote:

> Tanner was an unusual man in many respects and clearly possessed great powers of observation as his account of his life among the Indians amply attests. For the customs of the Ottawa and Ojibwa Indians of the Old Northwest between the years 1790 and 1825 few better sources of information exist. Yet his work is only inadequately known. In part this is due to its extreme rarity, in part to prejudice against accounts written by white captives.[4]

In past years, the *Narrative* did not fit easily into progressivist lines of thought, other than to represent a way of life sadly eclipsed. Today it invites readings that look for an appreciation of the past in other voices, in memories of traditions quite distinctive from Western traditions. To understand the *Narrative* challenges us to go beyond nineteenth-century ra-

---

1 Maxine Benson, "Schoolcraft, James, and the White Indian," *Michigan History* 54 (Winter, 1970), 318.

2 Walter O'Meara, *The Last Portage* (Boston: Houghton Mifflin, 1962).

3 The phrase is taken from Arnold Krupat, *The Voice in the Margin: Native American Literature and the Canon* (Berkeley: University of California Press, 1989).

4 *An Indian Captivity (1789-1822). John Tanner's Narrative*, with an introductory comment by Paul Radin (San Francisco: Works Projects Administration, 1940).

cialist theories as well as New Age romanticisms, to the wonder waiting restlessly behind James's prose. Tanner's book —far more than a captivity narrative — is a mnemonic landscape, a bundling of clues or markers, pointing back toward his world. It is the richness of detail in Tanner that makes his story so attractive, that persuades us of his credibility, and that makes possible a compelling dialectic between his past and our present.

In Marcel Proust's *Remembrance of Things Past*, it is a morsel of cake dipped in lime-flavoured tea that stirs the narrator's memory and through memory allows him access to the world of his childhood. Similarly in Tanner, each passage of text, so freighted with meaning, offers access to a small part of the world Tanner knew. That world was the traditional world of the Ottawa and Ojibwe on the eve of their being dispossessed by the tide of white settlers who would lay claim to their homelands. Tanner's *Narrative* provides us a living sense of the world these people had known before that came to pass. No other text does this in such a profound way, for any Native group. The *Narrative* is wonderful to read, as well as instructive; it shares these features with other great literary works. But it is the humanity of his story that makes us identify with Tanner. What is truly mysterious is that so little attention has been paid to him. In our age of cultural pluralism, this is a voice in the margin that speaks to us all.

JOHN T. FIERST

References

Axtell, James
1981   The White Indians of Colonial America. In *The European and the
        Indian: Essays in the Ethnohistory of Colonial North America*. Oxford:
        Oxford University Press.
Benson, Maxine
1990   Schoolcraft, James, and the 'White Indian'. *Michigan History* 54
        (Winter): 316-18.
Butterfield, Lyman, ed.
1951   *Letters of Benjamin Rush*. 2 vols. Memoirs of the American
        Philosophical Society, vol. 30, pts. 1-2. Princeton: Princeton
        University Press.
A.H. Clark
1946   "The Tanner Case," *Sault Ste. Marie Evening News*, 4 July.
Crevecoeur, J. Hector St. John de
    1957 *Letters from an American Farmer*. New York: E.P. Dutton.
Edmunds, R. David
    1983 *The Shawnee Prophet*. Lincoln: University of Nebraska Press.
Feest, Johanna E., and Christian F. Feest.
    1978 Ottawa. In *Handbook of North American Indians* Vol. 2. 772-86.
        Washington: Smithsonian Institution.
Fierst, John T.
    1986 Return to 'Civilization': John Tanner's Troubled Years at Sault Ste.
        Marie. *Minnesota History* (Spring): 23-36.
Hallowell, A. Irving
    1955 *Culture and Experience*. Philadelphia: University of Pennsylvania Press.
    1992 *The Ojibwa of Berens River, Manitoba: Ethnography into History*, edited
        with preface and afterword by Jennifer S.H. Brown. Fort Worth,
        TX: Harcourt Brace Jovanovich College Publishers.
Hemingway, Ernest
    1925 "Indian Camp" *In Our Time*. New York: Charles Scribner's Sons.
Kline, Mary-Jo.
    1987 *A Guide to Documentary Editing*. Baltimore: Johns Hopkins
        University Press.
Kolodny, Annette
    1979 Review of *Narratives of North American Indian Captivities*, selected and
        arranged by Wilcomb E. Washburn, *Early American Literature* 14,
        228-35.

1993 Among the Indians: The Uses of Captivity. *New York Times Book Review.* 31 January, 1, 26-29.

Namias, June.

1993 *White Captives: Gender and Ethnicity on the American Frontier.* Chapel Hill: University of North Carolina Press.

Nute, Grace Lee.

1941 *The Voyageur's Highway: Minnesota's Border Lake Land.* St. Paul: Minnesota Historical Society.

Oberg, Barbara.

1995 Documentary Editing as a Collaborative Enterprise: Theirs, Mine, or Ours? *Documentary Editing* 17, no. 1: 1-5,15.

O'Meara, Walter.

1962 *The Last Portage.* Boston: Houghton Mifflin.

Peers, Laura.

1994 *The Ojibwa of Western Canada, 1780 to 1870.* Winnipeg: University of Manitoba Press.

Powell, J.H.

1952 Review of the Letters of Benjamin Rush, ed., L.H. Butterfield, Mississippi Valley Historical Review (September): 325-27.

Radin, Paul

1940 *An Indian Captivity (1789-1822). John Tanner's Narrative.* San Francisco: Work Projects Administration.

Schoolcraft, Henry Rowe

1847 *Historical and Statistical Information Respecting the History, Condition and Prospects of the Indian Tribes of the United States.* Collected and prepared under the direction of the Bureau of Indian Affairs, per Act of Congress of March 3.Vol. 6. Philadelphia, 1851-57.

1851 *Personal Memoirs of a Residence of Thirty Years with the Indian Tribes on the American Frontiers: with Brief Notices of Passing Events, Facts, and Opinions, A.D. 1812 to A.D. 1842.* Philadelphia: Lippincott.

Tanner, Helen Hornbeck

1986 Atlas of Great Lakes Indian History. Norman: University of Oklahoma Press.

Tanner, John

1930 *A Narrative of the Captivity and Adventures of John Tanner During Thirty Years' Residence Among the Indians in the Interior of North America.* Edwin James, Ed. New York: G. & C. & H. Carvill.

Tanner, John

> Letter to Martin Van Buren, 11 November 1837, Office of Indian
> Affairs, letters received, 1831-80, Michigan Superintendency,
> National Archives Record Group 75, microfilm copy.

Vanderbeets, Richard

> 1983   *The Indian Captivity Narrative: An American Genre*. Lanham, MD:
> University Press of America.

Vecsey, Christopher

> 1983   *Traditional Ojibwa Religion and Its Historical Changes*. Philadelphia:
> American Philosophical Society.

Vogel, Virgil J.

> 1986   *Indian Names in Michigan*. Ann Arbor: University of Michigan Press.

IO

William W. Warren's *History of the Ojibway People*: Tradition, History, and Context

Theresa Schenck

FOR MORE THAN one hundred years, William W. Warren's *History of the Ojibway People* has been considered by many to be the most authoritative work ever written on the Anishinabeg, as the Ojibwa call themselves. Although it was written between 1849 and 1852, it was not published until 1885 by the Minnesota Historical Society, more than 30 years after the author's death in 1853. Reprinted in 1957 and 1984, it continues to be an important and widely used source for almost every study of the Ojibwa people.

Scholars who have used Warren's book have found it especially valuable not only for the information it presents on Ojibwa migration, totems, ceremonies, and warfare, but also because it is considered to have been written from the Ojibwa viewpoint, since the author was himself part Ojibwa. In his classic study of the Midewiwin or Grand Medicine Society, for example, W.J. Hoffman included whole sections of Warren's text (1891:160-162). Ruth Landes referred to it in her discussion of the social organization of the Ojibwa of the Rainy River district in northwestern Ontario (1937:31-52). A. Irving Hallowell used it as background for his study of acculturation among the Lac du Flambeau Ojibwa (1955:337). Selwyn Dewdney found it an important tool for interpreting the birchbark origin and migration scrolls of the Minnesota Ojibwa (1975). And Harold Hickerson used it to support several of his main ideas, notably that the Ojibwa were an amalgam of clans or totems (1970:46); that the Midewiwin unified these various groups into a single tribe (1963:77-78); that Chequamegon on the south shore of Lake Superior had been their religious and political centre since the early historic period (1962:67; 1970:56); and that Ojibwa-Dakota warfare was the result of competition for furs (1962:35-38).

More recently, many Ojibwa themselves have come to regard Warren's *History* as sacred tradition. Native authors Gerald Vizenor (1984) and Edward Benton-Benai (1988) have based whole portions of their works on it. And in 1993, when the Chippewa Valley Museum in Wis-

THERESA SCHENCK

consin prepared its exhibit, *The Paths of the People*, in cooperation with the Ojibwa of Lac Courte Oreilles and Lac du Flambeau, Warren's narrative was used as the basis for the account of the Ojibwa migration into the area and for their earliest history (Pfaff:1993).

Although the influence and importance of Warren's work cannot be denied, it is essential that we look at it critically. In his preface Warren expressed concern that he was unable to reconcile discrepancies of time or date with "the more authentic records of whites" (1984:26). Later, in a brief, hand-written biography of her brother, Mary Warren English (n.d.) stated that "frequently it [the book] was hurriedly written and many times during great physical weakness." She added that Warren himself recognized that the manuscript was in need of careful revision, but that due to his untimely death he was never able to review it. In view of the author's own realization of certain inadequacies in the text, it is somewhat surprising that this history has come to be regarded with such veneration among both scholars and Ojibwa themselves.

The complete title of the original work was *History of the Ojibways based upon Traditions and Oral Statements*. It was not to be a history founded on the writings of missionaries and travellers, who, according to Warren, could collect only superficial information through temporary observation or imperfect interpreters. Rather it would be an "account of the principal events which have occurred to the Ojibway within the past five centuries, as obtained from the lips of their old men and chiefs who are the repositories of the traditions of the tribe." It would therefore be "the first work written from purely Indian sources" (1984:26). This, then, is how Warren viewed his *History*: a collection of lodge stories and legends which would present the Indians' own account of their past.

Warren considered himself eminently suited for the task of recording tradition. In his preface he wrote:

> The writer of the following pages was born, and has passed his lifetime, among the Ojibways of Lake Superior and the Upper Mississippi. His ancestors on the maternal side, have been in close connection with this tribe for the past one hundred and fifty years. Speaking their language perfectly, and connected with them through the strong ties of blood, he has ever felt a deep interest in their welfare and fate, and has deemed it a duty to save their traditions from oblivion, and to collect every fact concerning

them, which the advantages he possesses have enabled him to procure.
(1984:25)

The advantages he possessed were his direct, personal knowledge of his subjects and their language, and his extraordinary (for the nineteenth century) education. Born in 1825 to the trader Lyman Warren and his part-Ojibwa wife, Marie Cadotte, William spent his early years on Michael's Island (now Madeline Island) across from Chequamegon Bay on Lake Superior. There he listened to the stories told by the Ojibwa elders, among them his grandmother's brother, Tug-waug-aun-e, leader of the Crane clan, and Pezhike, leader of the Loon clan. There he also heard the fur-trade tales of his half-Ojibwa grandfather, Michel Cadotte, and of the countless other traders and voyageurs who passed through the offices of the American Fur Company. Likewise, during these impressionable years he witnessed his own father's religious conversion and intense involvement in the founding of the Presbyterian mission at La Pointe on Madeline Island in 1830-31. The Warren home, where the missionaries were lodged, became the site of numerous prayer meetings and discussions (ABCFM Papers:18.3.7[1]: Hall to Greene, 17 Sept. 1831; Hall Journal, 1831-1833).

However, not all of Warren's youth was spent among his Ojibwa relatives on Madeline Island. When he was only six years old he was sent to be educated at the Rev. William Ferry's mission school on Mackinac Island in Michigan, where most of the students were, like himself, of mixed parentage. He returned home once a school was firmly established at La Pointe in 1832, and then in 1836, at the age of twelve, he was sent with his brother and his older cousins to Clarkson, New York in the care of his paternal grandfather. There he attended Clarkson Academy, and later the Oneida Institute in Whitesboro, New York, a seminary established to prepare poor young men, including Negroes and Indians, for the ministry. He returned to Madeline Island in 1841, strengthened in his religious convictions, educated far beyond the average resident of the Lake Superior region, but having somewhat forgotten the Ojibwa language.

Back among his Ojibwa relatives the young Warren quickly recovered his use of his native tongue, according to his sister (English:n.d.), and he was soon employed as interpreter by various Indian agents of Lake Superior. Married in 1843 to Matilda Aitken, the part-Ojibwa daughter of the trader William Aitken, he moved his family to Crow

THERESA SCHENCK

Wing, Minnesota, in 1845. There he established friendships with several of the leading chiefs, notably Esh-ke-bug-e-coshe, or Flat Mouth, and thus was able to record many of the traditions of the Ojibwa of the upper Mississippi River.

In a newspaper column written in 1851, Warren described the technique he used to gather information:

> In order to arrive at the truth of a fact obtained of an Indian, respecting their past history, a person must go from one old man to another of different villages or sections of the tribe, and obtain the version of each; if they all agree in the main fact, even if they disagree in the details, you can then be certain that the circumstances had happened and that the tale has a substantial origin. (*Minnesota Democrat*, 11 February 1851)

It was this method, he believed, which gave his work great accuracy (1984:25).

One problem encountered early in Warren's *History* is the issue of voice. Although he claimed to have written the work purely from Native sources, it was often Warren who spoke, and not his Ojibwa informants. This is clear from his use of the third person plural in referring to the Indians. Warren never felt himself to be one with his mother's people. *They* are the fast-disappearing "red race of North America." The bones of *their* ancestors are sprinkled through soil on which *our* homesteads are now erected. *We* owe *them* sympathy and attention now, before *their* traditions fall into total oblivion (1984:23-25, emphasis added). The five years he had spent among his father's family had separated him, to a certain extent, from his Native roots.

Warren nevertheless acknowledged himself to be "in language, thoughts, beliefs, and blood, partly an Indian" (1984:55). He believed that his Christianity, however, gave him superior understanding in certain matters.

> Respecting their own origin the Ojibways are even more totally ignorant than their white brethren, for they have no Bible to tell them that God originally made Adam, from whom the whole human race is sprung. They have their beliefs and oral traditions, but so obscure and unnatural, that nothing approximating to certainty can be drawn from them. (1984:55)

Warren, educated for ten years in religious schools, could find no acceptable Native explanation of creation. In fact, he believed that the name they gave themselves, *An-ish-in-aub-ag*, meant "spontaneous people," rather than simply "the people," and that they possessed no reliable account of their origins; it was a subject "buried in darkness and mystery." Without the Bible, all was "a perfect chaos of confusion and ignorance." Like his missionary teachers he adhered to the then-common belief that all aboriginal inhabitants of North America were descended from the ten lost tribes of Israel and attempted to find similarities between ancient Hebrew customs and those of the Ojibwa (1984:57-75).

It was in the tradition of the Midewiwin or Grand Medicine Society, however, that Warren found the earliest history of the Ojibwa, the story of their migration from the East, from the shores of the great salt water, to Sault Ste. Marie, and thence to Chequamegon. Indeed the paths of the Anishinabeg described to Warren are identical with those found more than a century later by Selwyn Dewdney in his study of the birch-bark scrolls of the Ojibway of Minnesota and southwestern Ontario (1975:57-80). Henry Rowe Schoolcraft, whose mother-in-law was Ojibwa, also recorded a tradition of migration from the East (Mason 1962:1), which is supported by both archaeology and linguistics (Siebert 1967:39-40; Seeber 1982:135-143). In fact, in the nineteenth century only Warren's contemporary George Copway, a Mississauga Ojibwa from southern Ontario, mentioned a tradition of migration from the West, "from Red and Sandy Lakes, the home of their forefathers" (1851:29).

Other important events of Ojibwa history which the Ojibwa elders related to Warren concerned totemic origins, migration into Minnesota, and narratives of warfare with the Dakota and the Fox. For information on these subjects Warren relied solely on Native people, and thus these accounts accurately represent the Ojibwa viewpoint, or rather, the viewpoint of the Ojibwa of Chequamegon and the upper Mississippi. Seen in this light, Warren's *History* becomes not the "History of the Ojibwa People," but more accurately, the "History of the Southwestern Ojibwa," the Ojibwa of Wisconsin and Minnesota, as they themselves saw it in the middle of the nineteenth century. It is therefore *their* voice; this is the context in which it should be understood.

One of Warren's greatest contributions, especially in the eyes of the Ojibwa people, was his thorough treatment of totemic traditions. Ever since they were first contacted by the French, the Algonquian-speaking village groups on the northern shore of Lake Huron had been known by their totemic designations: the Ouasouarini (sturgeon), the Outchougai (osprey), the Atchiligouan (another kind of sturgeon), the Amikouai (beaver), the Noquai (bear); almost every group was known by an animal name (André 1688:11-13; Thwaites 1959[18]:229-231). Those who were not, such as the Oumisagai and the Pauoitigoueieuhak, were named from the location of their summer villages, although records indicate that even these place-named groups had a totem: in the document ratifying peace with the Iroquois in 1701, the Sauteurs (as the Ojibwa were known throughout the French records) signed with a Crane, and the Mississauga with an Eagle (NAC C11A[F-19]:43).

The totem, then, was originally the family or clan name of the people who lived in a given village, and was the most important feature of identification of the group. Later, as clans mixed in larger villages, the totemic name and sign were retained, serving in much the same way as a person's family name. Schoolcraft called it "the most striking trait in their moral history" (Mason 1958:94) and "a link in the genealogical chain by which bands are held together" (Williams 1956:190). The French cartographer Joseph N. Nicollet, who visited the upper Mississippi River in 1836, explained it thus:

> Their totem name is the only one they disclose without hesitation or reserve. It is not a sacred name, neither is it connected with any favors of the spirits. There is no mystery attached to it. The totem being an institution of purely civic nature, they are inclined to quote with pride the name of the great family to which they belong. It is simply a collective name. (Bray 1970:187)

By the time Warren heard the stories of the origin of the totems, significant changes had taken place since the totems were first listed in the *Jesuit Relations* in the mid-seventeenth century (Thwaites 1959[18]:229-231;[44]:245-251). Many groups had migrated around the north shore of Lake Superior in their flight from the Iroquois invasion (Blair 1911:173), while others had gone south toward Detroit, often joining with the Ottawa, the Potawatomi, and the Menominee.

The oral tradition of the Lake Superior Ojibwa of the nineteenth century identified five great totems: the Crane, the original totem of the Sauteurs or Outchibouec; the Bear, Moose, and Catfish, also original totems in the seventeenth century; and the Loon, which had not been mentioned previously, but which had grown to importance in the latter part of the eighteenth century. Totems which had not migrated to the south shore of Lake Superior, but which were also quite ancient, such as the Otter, the Beaver and the Sturgeon, did not figure in the mythology of the region, and so they were simply not listed among the principal families (Warren 1984:44-45).

So important were the totems to the Ojibwa people that Warren, recounting the stories of Ojibwa migration throughout the Lake Superior area, almost always identified the totems of the chiefs, the leaders and founders of each village. It is thus easy to follow the migrations of totemic bands and trace the movements of the Ojibwa across the south shore of Lake Superior and into the headwaters of the Mississippi River. Furthermore, even today the same totems often predominate in the villages where the people first settled: the Marten at Lac Courte Oreilles in northern Wisconsin and the Catfish at Leech Lake in northern Minnesota.

The German ethnographer Johann Georg Kohl, who spent the summer of 1855 at La Pointe, supported Warren and Schoolcraft in their emphasis on the importance of the totem. He remarked on "how proudly the Indians always talk of the totem to which they or their wives belong," and "how deeply this aristocratic element is rooted in them" (1985:148). Two of his informants were Mongosid, grandson of Bi-aus-wah, the first chief of Sandy Lake, who belonged to the Loon totem, and Warren's uncle Michel Cadotte, Jr., whose wife and mother were both of the Crane totem. "La marque des Grues est la plus noble et la plus grande marque parmi les Ojibbeways," Cadotte explained to Kohl (1985:149).

Like his uncle, Warren emphasized the pre-eminence of the Crane totem. In doing so he was both reflecting his own genealogy (his maternal grandmother was the daughter of White Crane, leader of the Crane totem at La Pointe), and representing the traditional viewpoint of the Ojibwa of this region. The Sauteurs who ratified the Peace of 1701 signed with the mark of the Crane (NAC C11A [F-19]:43); in 1750 the first chief of Sault Ste. Marie was Taco8agané, a Crane (NAC C11A [F-97]:107v); in 1825, at the Treaty of Prairie du Chien, and in 1826 at the Treaty of Fond du Lac, the Crane chief of Sault Ste. Marie, Shingaba Wossin, was recognized as the "principal chief." George Copway acknowledged that, with few exceptions, the chiefs of the Ojibwa were of the Crane totem (1847:16). Numerous other examples support Warren

248   THERESA SCHENCK

and the Ojibwa elders in upholding this tradition (Schenck 1994: 398–401).

Schoolcraft, on the other hand, emphasized the importance of the Reindeer or Caribou (Addik) totem, the totem of his mother-in-law. He claimed that this was the family which had ruled at Chequamegon "since earliest times" (Mason 1962:40). The Caribou totem, however, had migrated to Chequamegon only in the mid-eighteenth century, as even Schoolcraft realized (1851a:135) and as Warren had also acknowledged (1984:52).

Warren's account of how the leader of the Crane totem had relinquished leadership to the Loon clan (1984:87-88) can be substantiated in the historical record. In 1826, at the Council of Fond du Lac just southwest of Lake Superior, the fourth speaker, Tahgwawane (Tug-waug-aun-e, son of White Crane and chief of the Cranes of La Pointe) did not want to speak, became embarrassed, and called on another speaker to "explain better what I mean" (McKenney 1972:379). That other speaker was Pezhike, or Buffalo, a leader of the Loon clan of La Pointe, and descendant through his mother of the Caribou chief Waubojeeg. "The name of a speaker has come down to me from my fathers ... I am no chief. I am put here as a speaker," he said (McKenney 1972:379-380). Henceforth, however, he was recognized as chief of La Pointe, and Tahgwawane was considered second chief.

While the totem was recognized as the outstanding feature of Ojibwa social organization, warfare with the Dakota and the Fox was central to Ojibwa history as Warren recorded it. The Ojibwa believed that there had been a time five generations earlier when they had been at peace with the Dakota. It appears from historical documents that this peace, first recorded as established by Radisson and Groseilliers in 1661 (Adams 1961:135-142), was maintained almost unbroken, often with great difficulty, until 1736. Until then the Ojibwa generally hunted without reprisal on Dakota land, and married with them, thereby creating a new totem, that of the Wolf. This totem is found only near the Dakota borders, and still predominates today among the Ojibwa of the Upper St. Croix River in Wisconsin.

According to Warren, the first incursions into Dakota lands were made by Bi-aus-wah, a chief of the Loon totem, who led his people from the southwest shore of Lake Superior to the rich hunting grounds of the Upper Mississippi. Warren dated Bi-aus-wah's settlement at Sandy Lake in Minnesota, located about 60 miles west of Fond du Lac (near present-day Duluth) by difficult portages, at about 1730. This date may be too early since at this time the historical record only begins to mention the Sauteurs at Fond du Lac (Margry 1888:[6]578). Certainly, however, the Ojibwa were at Sandy Lake by the mid-eighteenth century, for Joseph Marin mentioned in his journal of 1753-1754 that three years earlier the Sauteurs had asked to hunt on the Crow Wing River, located about fifty miles southwest of Sandy Lake (Bailey 1975:96).

Warren's method of determining dates has led to numerous errors of chronology. Recognizing the "somewhat uncertain manner in which the Indians count time by reference to generation" (1984:26), he tried to reduce an Indian generation to a given number of years in order to determine dates. Considering that the Indian generation comprised about half an average lifespan, and believing that Indians used to live longer than whites, he somehow arrived at forty years as the length of an Indian generation. A plate of copper on which the Crane family kept its record indicated that, in 1842, eight generations had passed since the Ojibwa had first come to Chequamegon, and five generations since the white race had come among them. Warren then estimated in 1852 that, since one more generation had passed since that copper plate was shown to him, the Ojibwa had arrived at La Pointe 360 years earlier, or about 1492, and that the first whites had arrived there 240 years earlier, in about 1612 (1984:89-90). Both dates are far earlier than either the historical or the archaeological records indicate.

Warren failed to realize that a generation is more correctly analyzed according to the age of parents when children are born, and that it consists of a single cohort born generally over a period of 25 to 30 years. Frederick Baraga, a nineteenth-century missionary to the Ojibwa of Lake Superior, recorded in 1847 that "men ordinarily marry when 18 or 20 years old" (1976:49). Thus Ojibwa generations were probably about the same as those of whites. Warren's generous estimate of the length of Indian generations has led many to believe that the Ojibwa had been at Chequamegon far longer than can be shown in the archaeological record (Birmingham 1992:179-180).

Warren's account of first contact may be compared with one related by Schoolcraft. In 1827 Ke-wa-kons, a chief at Sault Ste. Marie, told Schoolcraft that seven generations had passed away since the French had first appeared there (Schoolcraft 1851b:250). If a generation is taken to be 25 or 30 years, that would put the French at the Sault about 200 years earlier, approximately the period when Jean Nicollet was living with the

Nipissing, one of the groups allied to the Ojibwa. But figuring a generation at 40 years would have the French at the Sault in the mid-sixteenth century, which is clearly absurd.

In interpreting the role of the Ojibwa in the fur trade, Warren was largely influenced by his familial connections to the trade. Although he recognized that it was competition for hunting grounds that led to the Ojibwa-Dakota warfare, Warren concluded that it was competition in the fur trade that led the Ojibwa into Dakota hunting grounds (1984:127). However, while the Ojibwa were not averse to acquiring items which made their life easier, and they most certainly did participate in the fur trade, there was a limit to how many axes, guns, knives, kettles, and clothes they could take with them as they moved on their seasonal rounds. It is more likely that they engaged in the fur trade because it fitted into their way of life, and that their first concern was to feed and clothe their families. Thus competition for food more than for furs led the Ojibwa westward. A comparison of population estimates of the eighteenth and nineteenth centuries with fur trade records of the same period (Henry 1966:198; Tyrrell 1968:282-298; Jackson 1966:222; Mason 1958:158-160), suggests that one pack generally represented the number of furs acquired in a season by one family. Furthermore, each pack, estimated at sixty to seventy skins by the explorer David Thompson (Tyrrell 1968:298), probably corresponded to that family's consumption of food (including a favourite item, beaver tail) during one winter, and indeed was not excessive. Warren, himself a product of the fur trade, misinterpreted the principal motivation of Ojibwa expansion, like so many historians after him.

Not all warfare between the Ojibwa and the Dakota was related to competition for land and animals. Warren explained that an Ojibwa mourned the death of a relative for one year, but that there were two ways in which he could "wipe the paint of mourning from his face" before the period expired. One was through the rite of the Midewiwin, an expensive procedure, and the other was "to go to war, and either kill or scalp an enemy, or besmear a relic of the deceased in an enemy's blood" (1984:264). So Warren gave three reasons for spring and summer warfare: a desire for blood and renown, revenge for old injuries, or "to wipe away the paint of mourning for the death of some near relative" (1984: 304). This important insight into another aspect of Ojibwa-Dakota warfare has been largely overlooked by historians.

Another motive for warfare was glory, "the sake of being mentioned in the lodge tales of their people as brave men" (Warren 1984:355). The warrior ethic was an important cause of prolonged warfare, as men on both sides sought status and recognition among their people (Pfaff 1993:27-28). Alexander Henry the Elder recounted one such incident unrelated to competition for land or furs. After a successful winter hunt in the interior, the Ojibwa of the Chequamegon region did not immediately return to Henry with their furs. Instead, 400 strong, they set out in search of the enemy; on the fourth day they found and attacked the Sioux (Dakota). The battle raged all day; as the enemy fell back, the Ojibwa pursued them, losing only 35 men. Later they expressed to Henry their disappointment that the Sioux did not even "do the honours of war" to the slain, that is, scalp them. It was an affront, a disgrace, "because we consider it an honor, to have the scalps of our countrymen exhibited in the villages of our enemies, in testimony of our valour" (Henry 1966:203-204).

Warren recounted numerous incidents of battles waged for the glory of victory, which, like that related by Henry, can be understood only in the light of the warrior ethic. Any study of Ojibwa-Dakota warfare needs to take into account all these motives; competition for furs was not the sole cause.

It has been suggested that Warren's account of Ojibwa-Dakota warfare "is not supported by French documents, has many inaccuracies, and runs counter to Sioux oral tradition" (Anderson 1984:47). Warren, however, was presenting the Ojibwa viewpoint, Ojibwa memories of events, often exaggerated or glorified, but most assuredly as he had heard them. Certainly the ferocity, if not the frequency of conflict, is substantiated in many French documents (NAC C11A [F-43]:32-40; [F:65]:168-171; [F-67]:105; [F-75]:174-12181; [F-77]:109; C11E [16]:204v-205). Furthermore, the French records, too, are biased, and do not always tell the whole truth. The French witnesses to this warfare had their own agenda, and did not always want the truth to be known. The commandant at La Pointe, Denis de La Ronde, for example, had hopes of exploiting the rich mineral deposits on the south shore of Lake Superior in the 1730s, and his contemporary, the Chevalier de La Vérendrye, was mainly interested in attaining the glory of his discoveries.

In recording Ojibwa traditions Warren was greatly influenced by common beliefs of his times. The Ojibwa of La Pointe believed that

THERESA SCHENCK

their Chequamegon village was the oldest and most important after Sault Ste. Marie. They had forgotten an earlier village on Michigan's Keweenaw Peninsula which preceded the settlement on Chequamegon (Blair 1911:173; Margry 1888[6]:40-41). Nor did they know that their ancestors had been found at Lac Courte Oreilles by Radisson and des Groseilliers as early as 1660, when other unnamed peoples were inhabiting Chequamegon Bay (Adams 1961:124-128).

Schoolcraft did much to popularize the idea that the Ojibwa once had an extensive village at La Pointe on Lake Superior with a powerful chief who had authority over all other chiefs (Mason 1958:11). Warren, too, was under the impression that the Ojibwa formerly had "principal chiefs" who ruled the whole tribe (1984:316), that Chequamegon was once a vast settlement (1984:97), and that bands were formerly much larger and more concentrated (1984:319). In 1855 Kohl was told that "the chiefs who resided here have always laid claim, even to the present day, to the rank of princes of the Ojibbeways" (1985:2) None of these accounts is borne out in the historical or the archaeological record; they were rather beliefs which grew firm in the telling, exaggerations which resulted from a natural desire (perhaps on the part of both narrator and recorder) to glorify the past.

Both Schoolcraft and Warren erred in thinking Chequamegon the ancient seat of Ojibwa power. To the Ojibwa who were the sources of these tales, Chequamegon was indeed the most important location, the place to which they resorted in the summer for ceremonies and trade, and probably the first place to which their ancestors had come after leaving the Keweenaw peninsula. There were indeed fifteen lodges at Chequamegon as early as 1683 (Margry 1888:[6]38), but Radisson and Groseilliers had found none when they came through in 1660 (Adams 1961:124-126). There is no archaeological evidence of any large settlement until after 1720 when the French established a post on Madeline Island (Birmingham 1992:186). All earlier remarks about a large settlement appear to refer to Jesuit descriptions of a temporary village of Ottawa and Huron refugees located on the bay between about 1660 and 1672 (Thwaites 1959[50]:273.297[51]:259-265;[3381254] 165-173).

Warren also described a system of "civil polity"(1984:99), a level of clan organization that was simply not in keeping with Ojibwa band society in which each family or village group was relatively equal and independent, and no one chief was seen as having power over any other (Smith 1973:16). The Jesuits had long lamented the seeming lack of authority among chiefs (Thwaites 1959[38]:265;[66]:221). In 1693 the Ojibwa leader Chingouabé had told Frontenac that, among his people, he could speak only for those "immediately allied or related" to him (NAC C11A[F-12]: 232). Indeed, throughout the historic period no great chief ever ruled over all the Ojibwa, except in the imagination of his descendants. Both Warren and Schoolcraft seem to have been influenced in this respect by Euro-American ideals of leadership.

Schoolcraft and Warren generally agreed on most aspects of Ojibwa tradition, and it is likely that they influenced each other. Certainly Warren read Schoolcraft's published works, and even borrowed his material on Waubojeeg (Schoolcraft 1851a:134-144; Warren 1984:248-255). When he disagreed with Schoolcraft, as he did with regard to the meanings of Anishinabeg (1984:56) and Ojibwa (1984:37), he did so with great respect, for Schoolcraft, though a contemporary of Warren, was of an older generation. Schoolcraft likewise acknowledged his use of Warren's work (1851-1857[2]:135-167), an early version of which was published in 1849 in the *Minnesota Pioneer*. By and large, except for the emphasis on different totems, they reinforced each other's work.

Warren set out consciously to record and preserve Ojibwa tradition, fearing the eventual demise of the Indian people as well as the possibility that he himself would not survive to complete his work (1984:27). His success in preserving Ojibwa tradition has been his greatest contribution, and for this alone his work stands unequalled. The question is whether the traditions he recorded are truly the history of the Ojibwa people.

In the late twentieth century tradition has become for many something sacred, infallible, and immutable. To the Ojibwa, as to other aboriginal peoples, however, oral tradition was and is a dynamic process, continuously being gathered and dissected (Cohen 1989:10-11). Although traditional stories were handed down from generation to generation, they most certainly varied with the teller and were often revised and embellished. As Schoolcraft's Ojibwa mother-in-law told him in 1826:

> Now, the stories I have heard related by old persons in my nation cannot be so true, because they sometimes forget certain parts, and then thinking themselves obliged to fill up the vacancy by their own sensible remarks and experience ... their fertile flights of imagination. (Mason 1962:6)

Again, as Schoolcraft noted in 1834:

THERESA SCHENCK

Tradition does not reach far, where there is neither pen nor pencil to perpetuate the memory of events. Oral history is very uncertain at best. Every repetition varies the language at least.... And fiction would often be called on, to supply the lapses. (Mason 1958:59)

Warren himself realized that certain of the tales told to whites were "made up for the occasion" (1984:58).

But Warren believed that the traditions he was relating went beyond the superficial information obtained by outsiders, and that the stories he told were unattainable by anyone who did not live with and know the Ojibwa as he did. In his mind, they were truly Ojibwa history, all that could be known of a time beyond the written record. Warren's work, while not an historical document, is nevertheless an important source for history. It must, however, be used cautiously and critically, and be complemented by both documentary evidence and recent archaeological findings.

Oral tradition expresses a people's perception of their past, enlarged and renewed by each successive generation. It can give as many clues to this past as can ethnographic studies of the present (Vansina 1985:199). Once it is written, however, it often ceases to grow, and risks being canonized as an infallible compendium of a people's past. It is precisely this which has occurred with regard to Warren's *History of the Ojibway People*. The context in which it was written, the viewpoint it portrayed, have often been forgotten; scholars and Native people alike are reluctant to criticize it. Yet in this important work history and tradition must both receive careful study. They may not always agree, and neither is without error, but one can certainly be used to understand and to illuminate the other.

References

Adams, Arthur T., ed.
> 1961 *The Explorations of Pierre Esprit Radisson.* Minneapolis, MN: Ross and Haines.

American Board of Commissioners of Foreign Missions
> 1825-55 Papers. Houghton Library, Cambridge, MA.

Anderson, Gary C.
> 1984 *Kinsmen of Another Kind: Dakota-White Relations in the Upper Mississippi Valley, 1650-1862.* Lincoln: University of Nebraska Press.

André, Louis
> 1688 Préceptes, Phrases et Mots de la Langue Algonquine, Outaouaise pour un Missionaire nouveau. Manuscript in the Archives of St. Mary's College, Montreal. Photocopy in Smithsonian Institution, Washington, DC.

Bailey, Kenneth P., ed.
> 1975 Journal of Joseph Marin, August 7, 1753-June 20, 1754. Huntington Library: San Marino, CA.

Baraga, Frederick
> 1976 Chippewa Indians as recorded by Rev. Frederick Baraga in 1847. New York: Studia Slovenica.

Benton-Benai, Edward
> 1988 The Mishomis Book: The Voice of the Ojibway. St. Paul, MN: Red School House.

Birmingham, Robert A.
> 1992 Historic Period Indian Archaeology at La Pointe in Lake Superior: An Overview. Wisconsin Archaeologist 73(3-4):1775-98.

Blair, Emma Helen, ed.
> 1911 *The Indian Tribes of the Upper Mississippi Valley and Region of the Great Lakes.* Cleveland, OH: Arthur H. Clark.

Bray, Martha Coleman, ed.

 1970 *The Journals of Joseph N. Nicollet*. St. Paul: Minnesota Historical Society.

Cohen, David William

 1989 The Undefining of Oral Tradition. *Ethnohistory* 36(1):9-18.

Copway, George

 1847 *The Life, History and Travels of Kah-ge-ga-gah-bowh*. Philadelphia: James Harmstead.

 1851 *The Traditional History and Characteristic Sketches of the Ojibway Nation*. Boston: Benjamin B. Mussey.

Dewdney, Selwyn

 1975 *The Sacred Scrolls of the Southern Ojibway*. Toronto: University of Toronto Press.

English, Mary Warren.

 n.d. Biography of William Warren. Manuscript in Warren Family Papers. Madison: State Historical Society of Wisconsin.

Hallowell, A. Irving

 1955 *Culture and Experience*. Philadelphia: University of Pennsylvania Press.

Henry, Alexander [the Elder]

 1966 *Travels and Adventures in Canada and the Indian Territories between the years 1760 and 1776*. Ann Arbor, MI: University Microfilms [1809].

Hickerson, Harold

 1962 The Southwestern Chippewa: An Ethnohistorical Study. American Anthropological Association Memoir 92.

 1963 The Sociohistorical Significance of Two Chippewa Ceremonials. American Anthropologist 65:67-85.

 1970 *The Chippewa and Their Neighbors: A Study in Ethnohistory*. New York: Holt, Rinehart and Winston.

Hoffman, W.J.

 1891 The Mide'wiwin or "Grand Medicine Society" of the Ojibwa. Bureau of American Ethnology, 7th Annual Report, 143-300. [1885-1886.]

Jackson, Donald, ed.

  1966 *The Journals of Zebulon Montgomery Pike with Letters and Related Documents.* 2 vols. Norman: University of Oklahoma Press.

Kohl, Johann Georg

  1985 *Kitchi-Gami: Life among the Lake Superior Ojibway.* St. Paul: Minnesota Historical Society Press. [1860.]

Landes, Ruth

  1937 *Ojibwa Sociology.* New York: Columbia University Press.

Margry, Pierre, ed.

1879-88 *Découvertes et Établissements des Français dans l'ouest et dans le sud de l'Amérique septentrionale.* 6 vols. Paris: Maisonneuve.

Mason, Philip P., ed.

  1958 *Schoolcraft's Expedition to Lake Itasca: The Discovery of the Source of the Mississippi.* East Lansing: Michigan State University Press. [1834]

  1962 *The Literary Voyager or Muzzeniegan.* Lansing: Michigan State University Press.

McKenney, Thomas L.

  1972 *Sketches of a Tour to the Lakes, of the Character and Customs of the Chippeway Indians, and of Incidents Connected with the Treaty of Fond du Lac.* Barre: Imprint Society. [1827.]

National Archives of Canada

         MGI: Archives des Colonies. Séries C11A, C11E.

Pfaff, Tim

  1993 *Paths of the People: The Ojibwe in the Chippewa Valley.* Eau Claire, WI: Chippewa Valley Museum Press.

Schenck, Theresa

  1994 Identifying the Ojibwa. In William Cowan, ed., *Papers of the 25th Algonquian Conference,* 395-405. Ottawa: Carleton University.

Schoolcraft, Henry Rowe

  1851a *The American Indians, Their History, Condition and Prospects, from Original Notes and Manuscripts.* Buffalo, NY: George H. Derby.

  1851b *Personal Memoirs of a Residence of Thirty Years with the Indian Tribes on the American Frontier.* Philadelphia: Lippincott, Grambo.

1851-57   *Information Respecting the History, Condition and Prospects of the Indian Tribes of the United States, Collected and Prepared under the Direction of the Bureau of Indian Affairs*, 6 vols. Philadelphia: J.B. Lippincott.

Seeber, Pauleen McDougall
    1982   Eastern Algonquian Prehistory: Correlating Linguistics and Archaeology. In Margaret G. Hanna and Brian Kooyman, eds., *Approaches to Algonquian Archaeology*, 135-145. Calgary: Archaeological Association of the University of Calgary.

Siebert, Frank T., Jr.
    1967   The Original Home of the Proto-Algonquian people. In Contributions to Anthropology: Linguistics I, 13-47. *National Museum of Canada Bulletin 214*. Ottawa.

Smith, James G.E.
    1973   Leadership among the Southwestern Ojibwa. Publications in Ethnology, No. 7. Ottawa: National Museums of Canada.

Thwaites, Reuben Gold, ed.
    1959   The Jesuit Relations and Allied Documents, 73 vols. New York: Pageant Book Co. [1896-1901.]

Tyrrell, J.B., ed.
    1968   *David Thompson's Narrative of his Explorations in Western America 1784-1812*. Toronto: Champlain Society.

Vansina, Jan
    1985   Oral Tradition as History. Madison: University of Wisconsin Press.

Vizenor, Gerald
    1984   The People Named the Chippewa: Narrative Histories. Minneapolis: University of Minnesota Press.

Warren, William W.
    1849   Answers to Inquiries respecting the History, Present Conditions and Future Prospect of the Ojibwas of Mississippi and Lake Superior. In *Minnesota Pioneer*, St. Paul, 5-26 December 1849.
    1851   A Brief History of the Ojibwas. In *Minnesota Democrat*, 11 February 1851.
    1984   *History of the Ojibway People*. St. Paul: Minnesota Historical Society Press. [1885.]

Williams, Mentor L.

1956 *Schoolcraft's Indian Legends*. East Lansing: Michigan State University
Press.

11

An Ottawa Letter to the Algonquin Chiefs at Oka

David H. Pentland

ON 13 FEBRUARY 1845, eleven Ottawa chiefs from Manitoulin Island (in northern Lake Huron, Ontario) addressed a letter to the Algonquin chiefs of Lac-des-Deux-Montagnes or Oka (on the lower Ottawa River near Montreal, Quebec).[1] Although the letter refers only indirectly to historical events, it is of great importance in that it preserves a specimen of the Ottawa dialect of the Ojibwa language of that era, and of Ojibwa rhetoric. It also tells us something of the chiefs' concerns and perspectives at that moment, in their own words, without the intervention of government officials or missionaries.

Many thousands of pages have been written or published in or about Algonquian languages, including complete translations of the Bible and full-length grammars and dictionaries from as early as the seventeenth century. Almost all their writers, however, were people whose first language was English or French.[2] Even today there are few works by authors whose primary (or only) language is an Algonquian language such as Ojibwa; 150 years ago hardly any documents were composed and written down by one Ojibwa for the benefit of another.[3] Almost all

---

1 The literature on the culture and history of the Ojibwa-speaking peoples, including the Ottawa and Algonquin (also spelled Algonkin), is vast. A useful summary is vol. 15 of the Smithsonian Institution's encyclopedic *Handbook of North American Indians* (*HNAI*, Washington, 1978), especially the chapters on the Southeastern Ojibwa (by E.S. Rogers), the Ottawa (by Johanna E. and Christian F. Feest), the Nipissing (by Gordon M. Day), and the Algonquin (one chapter, by Day and Trigger). Each article outlines the group's culture and history, with maps and an authoritative guide to the literature up to the early 1970s.

2 Virtually every published work and manuscript in existence before 1890 is listed in James C. Pilling's monumental *Bibliography of the Algonquian Languages* (Washington, 1891).

3 John Nichols, in his introduction to "*Statement Made by the Indians*" (London, ON, 1988), p. 1, mentions that there are a few nineteenth-century letters, indigenous sacred texts, and diplomatic communications written by native speakers of Ojibwa in various archives.

of the nineteenth-century literature in Ojibwa is religious — hymns, prayers, and parts of the Bible — and most is translated from English, French, or Latin. The content of these texts is often foreign to North America, and the style is usually heavily influenced by the European original. Even the relatively few original Ojibwa-language works, such as sermons, were usually composed by missionaries who had learned the language in their adult years. Although many missionaries were said (by their compatriots, at least) to have mastered various North American languages, it is reasonable to suspect that they actually spoke with a noticeable accent, sometimes uttered ungrammatical sentences, and had a style more European than Native. The chiefs' letter is virtually indistinguishable from missionary writings in its spelling, choice of words, and grammar, but its structure is quite different, much more like a formal Ojibwa speech than a European letter.

Since their first contacts with Europeans, at least, the Ojibwa-speaking peoples have not formed a single political unit. The Ottawa, Algonquin, and their kin are usually treated as separate "tribes" (or *nations*, as the French called them), because although they all speak the same language, they are politically — and to some extent culturally — distinct from each other, much like the Canadians, Americans, Australians, and other English-speaking "tribes." Although historians and anthropologists tend to treat them as distinct entities, this letter shows that the Ottawa of the Lake Huron area recognized their kinship with the Algonquin who lived near Montreal, and sought to establish closer relations with them at a time when both groups were being pushed about by forces beyond their control.

The Text

The original letter is item 2 in file 1 of Manuscript 317, the N.O. Greene Papers, in the Department of Rare Books and Special Collections, McGill University Libraries, Montreal. N.O. Greene was a Montrealer about whom little is known, but who acted as an agent for the Mohawk chiefs of Oka in the 1880s, and collected material concerning Oka. The letter consists of a single sheet of laid paper watermarked "Morbey & Saunders 1844," folded to make two pages, each 32.5 x 20.2 cm (about 12 3/4 x 8 in.); the text of the letter covers both sides of the first page and the back of the second page contains the address. The sheet has been folded to form an envelope and sealed with a red wax

DAVID H. PENTLAND

seal. A green silk ribbon has been interlaced through the first page parallel to the signatures and sealed with another red wax seal.[1]

In the upper right-hand corner of the envelope the address "Aux
chefs des Algonkins, Lac des deux Montagnes" ('To the chiefs of the Algonquin, Lake of Two Mountains') is written in French, apparently in
the same handwriting as the letter itself. Below this is the "real" address
in three lines:

Ganachatageng daji Ogimâg	The chiefs at Kanesatage
Omizinaiganiwâ (Odichkwâgamig)	(the Nipissing) their letter
Nissadjiwon.	below the rapids

The last line was written by another person; it seems like an unnecessary
addition, since the letter carrier must surely have known that
Ganachatage (Kanesatage, or Oka) was on Lac-des-Deux-Montagnes
(Lake of Two Mountains), downstream from the Long Sault, the rapids
on the Ottawa River.

The letter was doubtless delivered by hand, not by the Post Office.
There are no postal markings on the cover, and in any case in 1845 there
was no post office anywhere near Manitoulin Island.[2] Moreover, it is
unlikely that the writers of the letter would have considered using the
postal service even if it had been readily available. As a formal message
from the chiefs of one community to the chiefs of another, it would
have been only proper for it to be carried by a trusted envoy, who
would have to travel — presumably on snowshoes — at least 700 kilometres along the traditional trade route up the French River from Lake
Huron to Lake Nipissing, then down the Mattawa and Ottawa rivers to

---

1   I would like to thank Dr. Richard Virr, Curator of Manuscripts in the Department
    of Rare Books and Special Collections at McGill, for granting permission to publish
    this letter, and for supplying the detailed description of it. I have worked mainly from
    a photocopy received nearly twenty years ago from his predecessor, Gerald French,
    when I enquired whether the library had any manuscripts written in Algonquian lan-
    guages, but some details were cleared up only when I checked the original document
    in March 1995.

2   The post office at Manitowaning, the site of the Indian Agency office on Manitoulin,
    did not open until 1846, according to Frank W. Campbell, *Canada Post Offices 1755-
    1895* (Boston, 1972), p. 101.

Oka. Probably the messenger was expected to deliver the message orally, as a formal speech to the Algonquin chiefs of Oka; the written version would have been only a back-up to the speech, or in imitation of the Europeans' way of doing things. In any case, the envoy was presumably aware of the message he carried, and could have clarified phrases in the letter and supplied details that are now obscure.

Wikwemikong. 13 ᵐᵉ Fevrier 1845.

Wikwemikong, 13th February 1845.

Ganachatageng daji Ogimâg –

The chiefs at Kanesatage:

Enawemina, kin a niss[we]wanagizien, enigokodeeia kit anamikon, gaie go ki Mekade okwanaiemeg, gaie ki kitchi Ji-maganichimag, gaie kit ikwemag, gaie kit abinodjiimag nin danamikawag.

My relative, you who are of three groups, with all my heart I greet you, and also your priests, and your great warriors, and your women, and your children I greet them.

Kit inenimigona sa Kije Manido Mi-sode gego Debendang djiwi inawendi-ang, nongo- memindange ga ako odes-sigoiang Jesos odijitwawin, gaie echkam djiwi sagitoieng iwi ki kitchi inawendi-winina, ondjita gaie kit inenimigona gego bwaianawitossig djiwi anamietadi-eng. Ki bagossenimin sa djiwi anamietawien.

God, the Master of All Things, thinks that you and I should be relatives, now especially since we (here) have been reached by the religion of Jesus, and that you and I should more and more love this, our great relationship, and there is a reason why he thinks it is not impossible that we should pray for each other. So I ask you to pray for me.

Enawemina, ningi iji nondage, anomaia endogwe djiwi debwewinagak, ki wi bi Andakim giwe, Nibissing idik wa bi danakieg, gichpin dach iwi debwewina-gak; ki bagossenimin djiwi win-damawien gichpin inendaman, wi bid-jibiamawien: mi gaie ga iji nondageia,

My relative, I have heard recently – I wonder whether it is true – that you intend moving toward here, that Lake Nipissing is where you are supposed to be going to live, if this is true. I ask you to tell me if you are thinking thus, that you will write me. And also

wi bi ijad ajonda bejik kit ogimam,
manda ge ani nibing: gichpin dach ba
ijagwe, apidji ninda kitchi minwendam
gichpin wi bi gagizid iwi getchi
agawadaman wi wabandama **Kidona-**
ganina *getchi apitendagwak, mi sa eji*
bagossenimina.

I have heard that one of your chiefs is
going to come here next summer. If
he comes, I would be greatly pleased
if he would bring with him that
which you greatly desire me to see,
our Dish which is highly valued;
that's what I ask of you.

Enawemina – Gichpin bidjibiamawien
eji bagossenimina, windamawichin eji ai-
iaien, gaie eji bimadizien. Nin win ki
wonenim nandach ejiwebizia, ni mino
aia ajonda Saganach Aking a danakiia,
anodj gego menezia, nindodinamâg
genawe[ni]mid Saganach. Awi dach ga
bi naganag begik Nikanis Kitchi Mok-
oman Aking ka machi ningikendazin ge
ijiwebizid.

My relative, if you write me as I ask
you to, tell me how you are doing,
and how you live. As for myself, you
are probably unaware of how I live. I
am doing fine here in the land of the
English where I live; the various
things I need I am supplied by the
Englishman who takes care of me. As
for that one friend of mine whom I
left behind in the United States, not
yet do I know how he will fare.

Nind achkwa ojibiige sa Enawemina.
Enigokodeeia ni bagossenima Deben-
dang ki bimadiziwinina, djiwi mini-
nang, ojawendjigewin, djiwi weweni na-
gadoiang omikan getchi gwaiakomok,
djiwi dach bindiganinang mamawi odogi-
mawiwining, a pegich ijiwebag.

I am finished writing, my relative.
With all my heart I ask the Ruler of
our lives to give us his blessing, that
we may properly follow his path that
is truly straight, that he may take us in
together into his kingdom; hopefully
it may be so.

Nin daw Enawemina getchi sagiina, nin
a nisswabewizia &c.

I am, my relative, he who greatly
loves you, one of the triumvirate(?),
etc.

Ogimâg –

The chiefs:

Bemassige, Adawich, Bebamidabi, Makonse, Assiginak, Ozaweie, Tekamassimo,
Bemanikinang, Johnis, Ginochameg, Schkakoyan.

The handwriting is very clear and easy to read, but some of the Ojibwa expressions are difficult to translate or explain.[1] At two places in the second paragraph of the manuscript words are underlined, apparently for emphasis: the name "Jesos" (Jesus) and the phrase meaning "it is not impossible." One word, "**Kidonaganina**" (our dish), is written in larger, more carefully shaped letters (here boldfaced), also to draw attention to it. Despite the care that must have gone into the preparation of the letter, there are two words which seem to be miscopied from an earlier draft; I have supplied the missing parts (in each case, one syllable) in square brackets. Other minor copying errors —misplaced dots, etc. —have been silently corrected.

The three groups referred to in the letter's opening sentence are probably the Algonquin, Nipissing, and Mohawk, the largest components of the population at Oka. Although the letter was sent by one group of chiefs to another, the writer refers to himself and the recipient in the singular: "my relative" (not "our relatives"), "I greet you (sing.)" (not "we greet you all"), and so on. This is a common rhetorical device in Ojibwa; English does the opposite, when a single writer employs the editorial *we*.

The most obscure point is "Kidonaganina" (with the inclusive *we* — "yours and mine"). The chiefs at Wikwemikong were surely not interested in some ordinary tableware from Oka, nor claiming joint ownership in it, but *onaagan* is just the ordinary word for a dish or plate. I surmise that it was a dish of religious significance — a piece of Communion silver, for instance — and perhaps one of special historical importance to the Ojibwa nation as a whole. Another unknown is the friend left behind in *Gichi-mookomaan-akiing*, the Land of the Big Knives, but the Ottawa of Canada had close ties to other Ottawa in the United States; many residents of Manitoulin Island had in fact been born in Michigan.

Two of the chiefs whose names are appended to the letter had their portraits painted by Paul Kane a few months later — Sigennok (Assiginak) or The Blackbird, and Makonse (Muck-koze) or Young Bear.[2] A

---

1   I have consulted a number of Ojibwa speakers, as well as various Algonquian linguists and all of the available dictionaries, but a few words seem to have gone out of use (in the dialects spoken by my consultants, at least), and some expressions which are easy enough to translate in isolation do not make much sense in context. I would particularly like to thank Roger Roulette for his suggestions about the most difficult words and phrases.

2   J. Russell Harper, ed., *Paul Kane's Frontier* (Toronto, 1971), 274-5, pictures III-42 and III-52.

DAVID H. PENTLAND

few others may have signed the Manitoulin Island treaties in 1836 or 1862.[1] For 1836, Paimausegai can be equated with Bemassige, the first name in the letter, and possibly Pesciatawick with Adawich, and Nainawmuttebe with Bebamidabi. The letter's Tekamassimo may be Francis Tehkummeh, who signed the 1862 treaty. However, it is dangerous to base any identifications on vague similarities between names: except for Bemassige, the differences in spelling may indicate different people. A chief named A-towish-cosh (or A-to-nish-cosh) also signed in 1862, but he cannot be the same as the letter's Adawich, who was a spokesman for those who opposed the surrender of most of the lands that had been granted in 1836.[2] It should be noted that only Assiginak (Jean-Baptiste Assiginack), who signed both treaties, his son Benjamin Assiginack, who signed in 1862, and possibly one or two other chiefs were literate: all the others signed the treaties with a drawing of their totem. In the letter all eleven names are in the same handwriting, with no added drawings.

The writer of the letter was obviously a Catholic, educated by French missionaries. The handwriting is a fine example of French – not English – copy-book style, the address and date are in good French, and the Ojibwa words are spelled according to the French system, adhering closely to the orthography adopted toward the end of the eighteenth century by the Sulpician missionaries at Oka, Quebec.

However, the letter is written not in the Algonquin dialect of Ojibwa spoken at Oka[3] but in the Ottawa dialect. The most obvious dialect difference is in the demonstrative pronouns and related words: Ottawa has *maanda* "this" and *azhonda* "here" (spelled "manda" and "ajonda" in the third paragraph of the letter) where other dialects have *ow* and *omaa* and Algonquin has *(o)'o* and *(o)'ondii* or *(o)'ondazhi* respec-

---

1   Canada, *Indian Treaties and Surrenders* (Ottawa, 1891), vol. 1, pp.113, 235-7. Names were often badly misspelled by government officials, and were further distorted by the printer's inability to decipher the handwritten documents.

2   Douglas Leighton, "Jean-Baptiste Assiginack," *Dictionary of Canadian Biography* 9 (1976), p. 10. Adawich was one of J.B. Assiginack's sons.

3   According to Ives Goddard, "Central Algonquian languages," *HNAI* 15 (1978), p. 583, the dialect spoken at Oka "is taken to reflect the speech of the Nipissing segment of the mission population"; I have retained the traditional name Algonquin, which is what speakers of the dialect call it.

tively.[1] Another important difference is that Ottawa drops final *n* from some words;[2] this is extensively attested in the letter, for example in "Enawemina" *enaweminaa* "you (sing.) who are related to me" (Algonquin *enaweminaan*) and "enigokodeeia" *enigokode'eyaa* "with all my heart" (Algonquin *enigokode'eyaan*) in the first sentence. While the Ottawa dialect is somewhat different from the Algonquin dialect of the intended readers, the recipients would have followed it well enough to understand the message; the difference is only about as great as between standard spoken British and American English.

The writer of the letter was probably Jean-Baptiste Assiginack, whom Paul Kane described as "an acute and intelligent Indian," the principal chief on Manitoulin Island.[3] Born around 1768, perhaps at Arbre Croche (Harbor Springs, Michigan),[4] he was educated by the Sulpician missionaries at Oka, where he would have learned the French handwriting, orthography, and French phrases included in the letter. He did not, however, speak either French or English well, as Kane observed:

> He receives a salary from the British Government as interpreter. This is paid him from policy, for although useless as an interpreter, from not speaking the English language, his natural eloquence is such that he possesses great influence over his tribe; indeed, it is to the untiring volubility of his tongue that he owes his name, which signifies "The Blackbird."[5]

Converted to the Roman Catholic religion while at Oka, Assiginack had returned to Arbre Croche in 1827 to assist with the establishment of a mission there; since no priest had been provided he himself catechized

---

1 Richard Rhodes, "A preliminary report on the dialects of Eastern Ojibwa-Odawa," *Papers of the Seventh Algonquian Conference* (Ottawa, 1976), pp. 131-2; Rhodes notes that *azhonda* is characteristically Ottawa. The Algonquin forms are from an unpublished grammatical sketch by David Jones.

2 Rhodes, "A preliminary report" (1976), p. 139, calls this "perhaps the single best diagnostic" of the Ottawa dialect.

3 Harper, ed., *Paul Kane's Frontier* (Toronto, 1971), p. 54.

4 Leighton, "Jean-Baptiste Assiginack," *DCB* 9 (1976), pp. 9-10.

5 Harper, ed., *Paul Kane's Frontier* (Toronto, 1971), p. 54.

DAVID H. PENTLAND

and preached.[1] Not far away was the British military base on Drummond Island, east of Sault Ste. Marie, but in 1828 the island was ceded to the United States. Assiginack, a steadfast ally of the British and leader of a contingent of Ottawa warriors during the War of 1812, therefore brought his band to the new British base at Penetanguishene in Upper Canada (Ontario). In 1832 he and his followers moved to Coldwater, and a few years later to Manitouwaning on Manitoulin Island, where a new reserve had been established under the direction of Thomas Gummersall Anderson, the Indian Superintendent (and no doubt "the Englishman [zaaganaash] who takes care of me" mentioned in the letter).

Although the settlements at Coldwater and (later) Manitouwaning were established under the auspices of the Church of England, and despite his long association with Anderson, a staunch Anglican,[2] Assiginack continued preaching, converting many Ottawa and other Ojibwa to Catholicism.[3] His dedication to the Catholic Church is also evident in the letter, which devotes two paragraphs – about one third of the whole – to religious sentiments, sending greetings to gimekadewigonayemag "your priests" (literally "the ones who wear black robes") and asking for prayers in the name of Gizhe-manidoo, "God" (a literal translation of the French le bon Dieu) and mizoode gegoo Debendang "the one who rules all things together," an expression probably created by missionaries to express "the Lord."

However, the letter also includes two long paragraphs about purely temporal matters. Assiginack was writing mainly to seek confirmation of a rumoured move of the Algonquin from Oka, and to ask that a certain dish be sent. Had there been no rumours and no impending visit, it is unlikely that he would have bothered to send a messenger bearing a letter to ask for the others' prayers or to tell them he was well provided for. This mix of religious, business, and personal subjects in a single document is apparently unique in the published Ojibwa literature, but there may well be other unpublished letters of similar content in one archive or another.

---

1 Leighton, "Jean-Baptiste Assiginack," DCB 9 (1976), p. 9.

2 W.R. Wightman, Forever on the Fringe (Toronto, 1982), p. 11.

3 Leighton, "Jean-Baptiste Assiginack," DCB 9 (1976), p. 9.

The style of the letter is very different from most other Ojibwa documents, such as the list of grievances submitted to the United States government by the Lake Superior Chippewa in 1864.[1] Although the dialect is almost the same, the 1864 petition is basically a straightforward recital of events, organized by topic and chronology, with no striking rhetorical devices. There is, however, a very close stylistic parallel in a testimonial letter given to James Evans, the Methodist missionary, by six chiefs at Rice Lake (near Peterborough, Ontario), around 1837.[2] The Rice Lake letter is in English, but is obviously translated rather literally from Ojibwa. If the opening paragraph, "Brothers, We the Chiefs of this Tribe our young men, wives, & Children shake hands with you the Chiefs your young men women & children, in our hearts," were translated back into Ojibwa it might use exactly the same words as our letter: "My relative ... with all my heart I greet you, and also your priests, and your great warriors, and your women, and your children I greet them." The closing of Evans's letter is also similar to Assiginack's conclusion:

Evans:
Brothers — May the Gt Spirit bless you the Chiefs young men women & children & help you to listen to his good words — & may we after death meet you in heaven. We have no more to say — but put our totems to this paper.

Assiginack:
I am finished writing, my relative. With all my heart I pray that the Ruler of our lives will give us his blessing ... that he may take us in together in his kingdom.

Every one of the nine paragraphs in the Rice Lake letter begins "Brothers," possibly a loose translation of the word here given as "my relative" and used in a similar way.

---

1 John Nichols, ed., *"Statement Made by the Indians": A Bilingual Petition of the Chippewas of Lake Superior, 1864* (London, ON, 1988). Nichols points out (p. 6) that at least part of the petition was first drafted in English and then translated into Ojibwa: "fur trader" was miscopied as "fat trader" and translated into Ojibwa as "a trader who is very fat."

2 Margaret Ray, "Brief of the Rice Lake Indians," *The Bulletin* 7 (1954), pp. 38-40.

The similarities between the two letters reflect not a special style used in written communications of this kind (which are very rare in any case), but rather the style of formal speeches in Ojibwa. The Rice Lake testimonial, with its shorter phrases and more poetic language, appears to be a little closer to the traditional spoken style; Assiginack's style may reflect some influence (such as longer sentences, and a more direct approach) from English speeches and letters, as he had long served as an official interpreter for the British government.

The Context

In 1835 a reserve was established at Manitouwaning, near the east end of Manitoulin Island, where the Indians of the region could be gathered under the benevolent guidance of the colonial government and the Church of England, supervised by Assiginack's friend Captain Anderson.[1] From 1841 on the Anglican mission was supervised by the Rev. Frederick A. O'Meara, assisted by a doctor and a schoolmaster. By 1845 about 380 Indians in the district were Anglicans, but only 180 actually lived at the mission. In competition with this government-supported establishment with its single missionary, O'Meara complained, were three or four Methodist missionaries, and a Roman Catholic mission run by two Frenchmen.[2] The Methodists probably spent most of their time travelling around the Ojibwa villages north and east of the island, but the Catholics were well entrenched at Wikwemikong, only 15 kilometres to the northeast, with about 700 converts.[3] Since he was employed as an interpreter by the government, Assiginack had to live at Manitouwaning, but most of his co-religionists had settled near Wikwemikong.

---

1   Frederick O'Meara, *Report of a Mission to the Ottahwahs and Ojibwas, on Lake Huron* (London, [England] 1846), pp. 3-4, credits Captain Anderson with the whole idea, but in *Forever on the Fringe* (Toronto, 1982), pp. 13-15, W.R. Wightman suggests that while Anderson may have picked the specific location, "the conceptual frame in which his ideas were placed" belonged to Sir John Colborne, lieutenant governor of Upper Canada (Ontario), and the Rev. John Strachan.

2   O'Meara, *Report of a Mission* (London, [England], 1846), pp. 6, 21-22.

3   "Nous comptons à peu près sept cents néophytes dans cette peuplade," Father Hanipaux reported in *Annales de la propagation de la foi* 18 (1846), p. 465. In his *Report of a Mission* (London, [England], 1846), p. 22, O'Meara estimated the number of Catholics at 750, of whom 508 were actual residents in the village.

The Holy Cross Mission had been established in 1838 to draw to-gether Catholic Indians scattered around the shores of Lake Huron; by 1845 the settlement had developed to an extent which pleasantly sur-prised the newly arrived Father Joseph Hanipaux, a Jesuit, who thought it resembled a French hamlet.[1] His fellow missionary, Father Jean-Pierre Choné, who had already been there for a year, painted a less rosy pic-ture: he complained that most of the Indians around Lake Huron had abandoned Christianity and that the trade in alcohol was causing many problems.[2] However, the mission thrived under the Jesuits, who estab-lished boys' and girls' schools and a program of agricultural instruction on the mission farm.[3]

For their subsistence the residents of Manitoulin Island depended on crops of corn and potatoes, and the fish they could catch in Lake Huron. There were some wildfowl on the island, but few deer or other game animals.[4] The traditional Ojibwa balance between hunting, fishing, and horticulture was obviously impossible since there were so few animals to hunt. Furthermore, the soil of Manitoulin Island was generally thin, in-terspersed with sandy, rocky, and swampy areas. Only about one-fifth of the land could support agriculture, and none of it was of the highest quality.[5] Even in the early days of the settlement questions had been raised about the climate and fertility of the soil.[6] A decade later the Rev. Peter Jones wrote,

---

1 *Annales de la propagation de la foi* 18 (1846), p. 462: "J'ai trouvé-là [à Wikwemikong] mieux que je n'attendais; des maisons en bois, même assez grandes, des cabanes à peu près semblables à celles des charbonniers de vos forêts, forment une espèce de village comme les pauvres hameaux de France."

2 *Annales de la propagation de la foi* 20 (1848), p. 140.

3 Wightman, *Forever on the Fringe* (Toronto, 1982), pp. 28-9.

4 Hanipaux, *Annales de la propagation de la foi* 18 (1846), p. 463: "La pomme de terre et le blé de Turquie sont la nourriture commune. Ils ont souvent du poisson, qu'ils pêchent dans le grand lac; quelques oiseaux, c'est tout ce que la chasse leur fournit, car il y a peu d'animaux dans les bois."

5 On the differing assessments of the island's agriculture potential, cf. Wightman, *Forever on the Fringe* (Toronto, 1982), especially pp. 67-72.

6 William H. Smith's *Canadian Gazetteer* (Toronto, 1846), p. 107.

DAVID H. PENTLAND

The Colonial Government have made an attempt to locate the scattering tribes of Indians in Upper Canada on the great Manitoulin Island; but, on account of many disadvantages, the Indians in general have refused to settle on it. Some of the Ottawa Indians have made attempts at improvements on this island, and have grown a few potatoes and some Indian corn.[1]

But, as Assiginack told Jones in 1852, "the weather is so cold here, that nothing grows to perfection."[2]

By the mid-1850s it was clear that the Manitoulin experiment had been a failure. Some groups had never moved to the island, and others left for more congenial locations over the years. The scheme had considerable merit and was stoutly defended to the end by both Anderson and Assiginack (despite his reservations about the weather), but the island provided few resources other than fish, and could not have supported the numbers it was proposed to settle there.[3]

While the population of Manitoulin Island was increasing in the early 1840s as various groups (not all of them Ojibwa-speaking) were attracted there from the United States or from other communities in Canada, the number of Ojibwa speakers at Oka, Quebec, was declining. Only three years after Assiginack's letter was dispatched, the Hudson's Bay Company finally closed the trading post at Lake of Two Mountains which had been in operation since the early eighteenth century; for at least two decades individuals and groups of Algonquin trappers had been moving away, reducing its business to the point of unprofitability.[4]

The mission at Oka had been established in 1721, bringing together Ojibwa speakers (mainly Algonquin and Nipissing), and Iroquoians (mainly Mohawk), from an earlier mission at Ile-aux-Tourtes and else-

---

1   Peter Jones (Kahkewaquonaby), *History of the Ojebway Indians* (London [England], 1861), p. 43; the book, probably written soon after Jones retired from mission work in 1850, was published posthumously.

2   Donald B. Smith, *Sacred Feathers* (Toronto, 1987), pp. 221-2.

3   For the complex causes of the project's failure, cf. Ruth Bleasdale, "Manitouwaning: an experiment in Indian settlement," *Ontario History* 66 (1974), pp. 147-157, and Peter S. Schmalz, *The Ojibwa of Southern Ontario* (Toronto, 1991), pp. 162-4.

4   C.C.J. Bond, "The Hudson's Bay Company in the Ottawa Valley," *The Beaver*, spring 1966, pp. 15-16.

where. The land for the mission was granted by the French Crown to the Seminary of St. Sulpice of Montreal for the purpose of "maintaining and instructing" the Indians gathered there.[1] The Iroquois at Oka took up farming and in the summer months also worked as river pilots and raftsmen, but the Algonquin retained their traditional dependence on hunting, trapping, and fishing, residing at the mission only for short periods each year.[2] However, the anthropologist Frank G. Speck noted that in the 1920s the Algonquin still considered Oka "their capital" and referred to it simply as *oodenaang*, "the village."[3]

The nineteenth-century mission records show that the Ojibwa-speaking part of the community included individuals from many ethnic groups, including the Ottawa, Mississauga, Tête-de-Boule and Saulteaux, in addition to the Algonquin and Nipissing;[4] as they often intermarried or married people from the Iroquois part of the community, ethnic distinctions became blurred. Assiginack's letter shows that even other Ojibwa speakers found it difficult to apply the traditional labels accurately in the Oka context: in French he addressed the chiefs of the Algonquin, but in Ojibwa called them *odishkwaagamiig* "people from the last stretch of water," or Nipissing.

In addition to the Indians actually living at Oka, the Sulpicians had also ministered to other Ojibwa-speaking groups living further north in the Ottawa River valley. However, in 1845 the task of visiting the various trading posts was handed over to the Oblate order of missionaries. In the early 1840s the Sulpicians built a small chapel at Maniwaki, at the junction of the Gatineau and Desert rivers, and in 1851 the Oblates established a mission there. In 1854 the Canadian government allocated about 180 square kilometres for the Maniwaki Indian Reserve, and a

---

1 Peter Hessel, *The Algonkin Tribe* (Arnprior, ON, 1987), p. 91. Brian Young's *In its Corporate Capacity: The Seminary of Montreal as a Business Institution, 1816-1876* (Kingston and Montreal, 1986) gives a detailed picture of the activities of the Sulpicians in the nineteenth century.

2 M. Jean Black, *Algonquin Ethnobotany* (1973), pp. 30-1.

3 Frank G. Speck, "Boundaries and hunting groups of the River Desert Algonquin," *Indian Notes* 6(2) (1929), p. 107.

4 M. Jean Black, "Nineteenth-century Algonquin culture change," *Actes du vingtième Congrès des Algonquinistes* (1989), pp. 64-5; Black also notes that fur traders and government officials seem to have been less sensitive to ethnic differences than were the missionaries at Oka.

DAVID H. PENTLAND

large part of the Algonquin left Oka to occupy it.[1] In 1870 another group obtained a reserve at Golden Lake, Ontario, where some had resided since 1807.[2] Others settled further south in Ontario: George Copway reported that around 1842 a band of 81 Indians from Oka joined some stragglers from his own community of Rice Lake, to form a settlement 40 kilometres north of Kingston, Ontario.[3]

Although a majority of the Ojibwa speakers from Oka eventually settled at Maniwaki, the rumour Assiginack had heard was correct – some did in fact move to the Lake Nipissing district in the 1840s. In September 1848 four families from Oka arrived at Mattawa House, on the Quebec-Ontario border, and two groups of "Montagnais" (here meaning "people from Lake of Two Mountains," not the well-known Montagnais of eastern Quebec and Labrador) later settled north and south of the Mattawa River, just east of Lake Nipissing.[4] The date of the move is difficult to pin down, since the Algonquin based at Oka had always hunted in the area east of the lake, where, John McLean reported in 1823, "they pass the greater part of their lives without visiting the Lake [of Two Mountains]."[5]

Conclusion

The letter is invaluable as an example of nineteenth-century Ojibwa prose actually written by a native speaker without any direct influence

---

1 Peter Hessel, *The Algonkin Tribe* (Arnprior, ON, 1987), pp. 92-3, and Frank G. Speck, "Boundaries and hunting groups of the River Desert Algonquin," *Indian Notes* 6(2) (1929), p. 115, present an uncomplicated account of the founding of Maniwaki; in her article "Nineteenth-century Algonquin culture change," M. Jean Black shows that the full story is much more complex.

2 Gordon M. Day, "Nipissing," *HNAI* 15 (1978), p. 790; Day and Trigger, "Algonquin," *HNAI* 15 (1978), p. 795; Hessel, *The Algonkin Tribe* (Arnprior, ON, 1987), pp. 72, 85.

3 *The Traditional History and Characteristic Sketches of the Ojibway Nation* (London [England], 1850), pp. 194-5.

4 Diary of the Hudson's Bay Company trader Colin Rankin, and unpublished notes by Father J.E. Gravelle, parish priest of Chiswick, ON, quoted by Murray Leatherdale, *Nipissing from Brulé to Booth* (North Bay, ON, 1975), pp. 96-8.

5 *John McLean's Notes of a Twenty-five Year's Service in the Hudson's Bay Territory*, ed. W.S. Wallace (Toronto, 1932), p. 40.

or participation by speakers of a European language. It is as close as we are ever likely to get to the real spoken language of the time, and particularly to the special style appropriate for formal speeches also reflected in the testimonial letter from Rice Lake. As a historical document, however, its importance is less clear. The many records written by missionaries and government officials tell far more about the Manitoulin Island situation than does the letter. Most of the documents concerning Oka have also been preserved in the Sulpicians' extensive archives. Yet they are unlikely to contain much further information about the move to Lake Nipissing, or about the projected visit to Manitoulin; apparently only a few families moved up the Ottawa River in the 1840s, and a trip by a single Algonquin — even if he was a chief — would probably have passed unnoticed by the missionaries, unless the dish he was to bring was the property of the church.

Jean-Baptiste Assiginack would have welcomed a visit by a fellow Catholic chief from Oka, especially one bringing a sacred relic, if that is what "our Dish which is highly valued" actually was. Having come from Michigan, Assiginack no doubt still had friends and relatives in the United States; as the American government had threatened to dispossess all the tribes who had sided with the British during the War of 1812, his concern was not misplaced, but the reference to the particular friend "whom I left behind" is obscure. During a period when many Ojibwa were abandoning their traditional homes in Michigan and southern Ontario to live on Manitoulin Island, and a number of people from Oka were moving back to their hunting territories up the Ottawa River toward Lake Nipissing, perhaps Assiginack hoped to persuade some of the Algonquin to join their kinsmen at Manitouwaning and Wikwemikong. As one of the strongest supporters of the Manitoulin project, as well as an active promoter of the Catholic church, the opportunity to attract more Ojibwa-speaking Catholics to the island might have greatly appealed to him. His more immediate object, however, was to strengthen the ties between the Ottawa and their Algonquin relatives at a time when increasing white settlement, conflicting government policies, and even competition between different religious sects was making cohesion among his people increasingly difficult.

Perhaps the greatest historical value of the letter is that it provides direct (and probably unique) information about the specific concerns of Assiginack and his fellow chiefs in 1845. Hitherto we have known only what interested the missionaries and officials, and what *they* claimed the

DAVID H. PENTLAND

Indians were saying: now the concerns of some aboriginal leaders on Manitoulin Island are available for comparison.

References

Black, M. Jean. *Algonquin Ethnobotany: An Interpretation of Aboriginal Adaptation in Southwestern Quebec.* Doctoral dissertation, Ann Arbor: University of Michigan, 1973.

——. Nineteenth-century Algonquin culture change. *Actes du vingtième Congrès des Algonquinistes.* Ed. William Cowan. Ottawa: Carleton University, 1989, pp. 62-69.

Bleasdale, Ruth. Manitouwaning: an experiment in Indian settlement. *Ontario History* 66, 1974, pp. 147-157.

Bond, C.C.J. The Hudson's Bay Company in the Ottawa Valley. *The Beaver,* Spring 1966, pp. 4-21.

Campbell, Frank W. *Canada Post Offices 1755-1895.* Boston: Quarterman Publications, 1972.

Canada. *Indian Treaties and Surrenders from 1680 to 1890.* 2 vols. Ottawa: Brown Chamberlin (Queen's Printer), 1891. Facsimile reprint Toronto: Coles, 1971.

Choné, Jean-Pierre. Lettre du R.P. Choné, missionnaire de la Compagnie de Jésus dans le Haut-Canada, à son Supérieur. *Annales de la propagation de la foi* 20, 1848, pp. 140-152.

Copway, George (Kahgegagahbowh). *The Traditional History and Characteristic Sketches of the Ojibway Nation.* London (England): Charles Gilpin, 1850. Facsimile reprint Toronto: Coles, 1972.

Day, Gordon M. Nipissing. *Handbook of North American Indians.* v. 15, *Northeast.* Ed. Bruce G. Trigger. Washington: Smithsonian Institution, 1978, pp. 787-791.

Day, Gordon M., and Bruce G. Trigger. Algonquin. *Handbook of North American Indians.* v. 15, *Northeast.* Ed. Bruce G. Trigger, Washington: Smithsonian Institution, 1978, pp. 792-797.

Feest, Johanna E., and Christian F. Feest. Ottawa. *Handbook of North American Indians.* v. 15, *Northeast.* Ed. Bruce G. Trigger, Washington: Smithsonian Institution, 1978, pp. 772-786.

Goddard, Ives. Central Algonquian languages. *Handbook of North American Indians.* v. 15, *Northeast.* Ed. Bruce G. Trigger, Washington: Smithsonian Institution, 1978, pp. 583-587.

Hanipaux, Joseph. Lettre du R.P. Hanipaux, missionnaire apostolique de la Société de Jésus, à son Frère. *Annales de la propagation de la foi* 18, 1846, pp. 461-465.

Harper, J. Russell, ed. *Paul Kane's Frontier, including Wanderings of an Artist among the Indians of North America, by Paul Kane.* Toronto: University of Toronto Press, 1971.

Hessel, Peter. *The Algonkin Tribe: The Algonkins of the Ottawa Valley, an Historical Outline.* Arnprior, ON: Kichesippi Books, 1987.

Jones, Peter (Kahkewaquonaby). *History of the Ojebway Indians, with Especial Reference to their Conversion to Christianity.* London (England), A.W. Bennett; Houlston & Wright, 1861. Facsimile reprint Toronto: Canadiana House, 1973.

Leatherdale, Murray. *Nipissing from Brulé to Booth.* North Bay, ON: North Bay and District Chamber of Commerce, 1975.

Leighton, Douglas. Jean-Baptiste Assiginack. *Dictionary of Canadian Biography* 9. Toronto: University of Toronto Press, 1976, pp. 9-10.

Nichols, John D., ed. *"Statement Made by the Indians": A Bilingual Petition of the Chippewas of Lake Superior, 1864.* London, England: Centre for Research and Teaching of Canadian Native Languages, University of Western Ontario, 1988.

O'Meara, Frederick A. *Report of a Mission to the Ottahwahs and Ojibwas, on Lake Huron.* (Missions to the Heathen, no. VI.) London (England): Society for the Propagation of the Gospel, 1846.

Pilling, James Constantine. *Bibliography of the Algonquian Languages.* Washington: Bureau of [American] Ethnology, 1891.

Ray, Margaret. Brief of the Rice Lake Indians. *The Bulletin* (Records and Proceedings of the Committee on Archives of the United Church of Canada) 7, 1954, pp. 38-40.

Rhodes, Richard. A preliminary report on the dialects of Eastern Ojibwa-Odawa. *Papers of the Seventh Algonquian Conference.* Ed. William Cowan. Ottawa: Carleton University, 1976, pp. 129-156.

Rogers, E. S. Southeastern Ojibwa. *Handbook of North American Indians.* v. 15, *Northeast.* Ed. Bruce G. Trigger. Washington: Smithsonian Institution, 1978, pp. 760-771.

Schmalz, Peter S. *The Ojibwa of Southern Ontario.* Toronto: University of Toronto Press, 1991.

Smith, Donald B. *Sacred Feathers: The Reverend Peter Jones (Kahkewaquonaby) and the Mississauga Indians.* Toronto: University of Toronto Press, 1987.

Smith, William H. *Smith's Canadian Gazetteer; comprising Statistical and General Information Respecting all Parts of the Upper Province, or Canada West...* Toronto: H. & W. Rowsell, 1846. Facsimile reprint Toronto: Coles, 1970.

Speck, Frank G. Boundaries and hunting groups of the River Desert Algonquin. *Indian Notes* 6(2), 1929, pp. 97-120.

Wallace, W.S., ed. *John McLean's Notes of a Twenty-five Year's Service in the Hudson's Bay Territory.* Toronto: Champlain Society, 1932.

Wightman, W.R. *Forever on the Fringe: Six Studies in the Development of the Manitoulin Island.* Toronto: University of Toronto Press, 1982.

Young, Brian. *In its Corporate Capacity: The Seminary of Montreal as a Business Institution, 1816-1876.* Kingston and Montreal: McGill-Queen's University Press, 1986.

Part V. Religious Encounters in Text and Context

Discussions of meetings between mission Christians and Native communities have often tended either to worship the missionaries as heroes or martyrs, or to brand the churches as agents of deculturation, dislocation, and worse. The essays in Part V explore three contexts in which religious interactions initiated complex human intellectual and social responses and innovations that the churches would not have expected, did not fully understand, or perhaps did not even notice.

Beginning in 1839, Jesuit priests founded a number of missions among the Salish people of the Plateau region of western North America. Laura Peers, while working with Jacqueline Peterson on *Sacred Encounters*, a major travelling exhibition and catalogue centred upon these events and their aftermaths, worked through the mission records and also met Salish people who reflected deeply on their Native and Roman Catholic religious roots. Most striking to her was the way in which the Salish made the Virgin Mary their own. Rather than accepting the priests' image of Mary as a loving and submissive wife and mother, they saw her as a woman of strength and as a powerful guardian in their increasingly troubled lives. In this article, as in her recent book, *The Ojibwa of Western Canada, 1780 to 1870* (1994), Peers sensitively articulates the different faces that Native people gave to outsiders' concepts and divinities, even as they followed the clergy and appeared to be adopting their doctrines.

Winona Stevenson is a professor of Native Studies at the University of Saskatchewan, Saskatoon, and a member of the Fisher River First Nation, Koostatak, Manitoba. While doing a master's thesis in history at the University of British Columbia, she decided to work on her Church of England Native missionary ancestor, Askenootow (Charles Pratt), of whom her family preserved many stories and recollections. His mission journals and writings showed an image of him startlingly different, however, from the one she knew through oral histories. Stevenson's essay tackles thoughtfully and creatively the challenge of reconciling the different faces of a nehiyopwat (Cree-Assiniboine) who struggled to serve and remain faithful to both his people and his church. Writing of the ordeal that she went through as she tried to make sense of a great-grandfather's seemingly double life, she calls upon approaches that literary criticism has lately provided for the analysis of Native texts, integrating them with her own deeply felt perspectives and reflections.

In 1933, the small Ojibwa community of Pauingassi on the upper Berens River, Manitoba, was visited by an American anthropologist, A. Irving Hallowell and his travelling companion and translator, William Berens, chief of the reserve at the mouth of the river. They met with Fair Wind (Naamiwan), a widely known and respected medicine man, and attended a drum ceremony that Fair Wind had been given in a dream after the death of a favourite grandson some twenty years before. Hallowell recorded Fair Wind's telling of this vision in an English translation furnished by Chief Berens.

Fair Wind's grandson, Charlie George Owen, still tells the story of Fair Wind's dream, and has shared it on several occasions with Roger Roulette and Maureen Matthews. Roulette is an Ojibwa teacher and linguist with the Manitoba Association for Native Languages in Winnipeg, and Matthews is a documentary journalist with the Canadian Broadcasting Corporation who has won national acclaim for her CBC Radio *Ideas* programs on Aboriginal topics (including a 1993 program on Fair Wind's Drum).

Matthews and Roulette compare in depth Hallowell's English and Owen's Ojibwa versions, examining key categories and expressions that convey the essentials of these texts. Of particular interest are the Christian elements that Fair Wind borrowed into his ceremony from visiting missionaries who hoped they might convert him; also, Chief Berens' English translation preserves phraseology suggestive of Berens' own Methodist experience. Most importantly, however, Charlie George Owen's texts offer a sophisticated and classically Ojibwa account of a formative religious and cultural event and its sequels, and of a powerful leader who through words and texts has touched the lives of many.

12

"The Guardian of All": Jesuit Missionary and Salish Perceptions of the Virgin Mary[1]

Laura Peers

In December [1841], the Indians departed for the winter hunt ... from the first evening the chiefs assembled for prayer asked that the expedition be dedicated to Mary. It was accordingly agreed that twice a day all would assemble for prayers. After prayers, they would hear an instruction, preceded and followed by hymns. Every morning, at sunrise, before leaving for the hunt, and every evening, before retiring, they would recite the Angelic Salutation three times, together with their families.[2]

On Christmas Eve 1841, a young Interior Salish (Flathead) child in the Bitterroot valley in what we now call western Montana, entered a friend's lodge and saw "a very beautiful person" who wore "garments such as I had never seen before. Beneath the feet of this person there was a snake, and, beside the snake, a kind of fruit I had not seen before. Around this person, there was a very bright light. The person looked at me in a kindly manner ... [and] told me that she was happy that our village had chosen to be called the name St. Mary's."[3] It was the second time in a decade that the Virgin Mary had appeared to a Salish child. In late December, as they left for the bison hunt (dangerous because it took

---

1   This paper was drafted while I was Research and Curatorial Associate on the De Smet Project, Washington State University. An earlier version was presented at the 1990 meeting of the American Society for Ethnohistory, Toronto, and at the Washington State University Anthropology Colloquium, 18 April 1991. I would like to acknowledge the contributions of Dr. Jacqueline Peterson, Salish elder Frances Vanderberg, Dr. Allan Smith, Gerald McKevitt, S.J., and Dr. Lillian Ackerman, who have, in conversation and in their writings, given me many ideas.

2   Nicolas Point, S.J., *Wilderness Kingdom. Indian Life in the Rocky Mountains: 1840-1847; The Journal and Paintings of Nicolas Point, S.J.*, trans. Joseph P. Donnelley (New York: Holt, Rinehart and Winston, 1967), 43.

3   Point, *Wilderness Kingdom*, 41.

them into the territory of their Blackfoot enemies), the Salish requested that the hunt be dedicated to Mary, and agreed to follow the intense worship described above despite the bitter cold, the rigorous exertions, and the dangers of the hunt. Jesuit missionaries had been working among the Salish for only three years.

The Jesuits' accounts of this worship, first made as reports to superiors, slightly later as letters of exhortation to potential financial patrons of the western missions, and decades afterward as personal reminiscences, are complex texts which can be read in several ways. The background of the history of Marian devotions in Europe, of Salish culture and religion, and of the Jesuit missions to the Salish, serves as the multifaceted context in which to interpret them, a kaleidoscopic lens with which to view Salish and Jesuit actions and perceptions. What do these texts really mean? What did the Virgin mean to the Salish in that first sustained contact with missionaries? For that matter, what did she mean to the Jesuits? How was this new and very powerful Christian being, who had no parallel in traditional Plateau religious beliefs, reconciled with or added to those beliefs? Furthermore, how has she been perceived? What have missionaries hoped to communicate to Native converts by introducing devotions to her? And what have Native peoples "read into" her image?

There is yet another lens through which I have read and interpreted these intriguing texts — a more personal one, no less positioned than that of Native convert or Jesuit missionary. In the course of the research for this paper, both Salish and Jesuit advisors pointed out to me that my interpretations are very much ethnohistorical ones, in both the ethnographic and the historical senses of that word: they do not reflect the personal and often painful sense of connection to this history that many Salish and Jesuit people still feel today, or the shifting meanings of Mary in changing times and living cultures. I am neither Salish nor Catholic; hence my reconstruction of the meaning of Mary to the Salish and their Jesuit missionaries in the nineteenth century is very much a distanced, academic one, though I have tried to use this academic lens to see what it would have been like to be a Salish or Jesuit person relating to the Virgin in the mid-nineteenth century. If we speak of contextual lenses through which to look at documents and events, though, we must acknowledge that we look through those lenses with our twentieth-century eyes. We must take a close look indeed to understand how a person from another era and another culture would have viewed the same events and texts.

Jesuit Missions to the Salish

Jesuit missionary Pierre-Jean De Smet established a network of missions among the tribes of the eastern Plateau between 1839 and the 1850s.[1] Unlike the situation in which many other missions to Native people were founded, the Jesuits arrived on the Plateau at the request of the Interior Salish, Nez Perce, and Coeur d'Alene, who had received extensive preconditioning in Christianity from fur traders, Christianized Native fur trade employees, missionaries (early Protestant missionaries on the Plateau itself, and both Catholic and Protestant missions on the northwest coast, at Red River, and in California), and Salish and Coeur d'Alene prophecies. The Jesuits arrived during a turbulent period in Plateau history during which the Salish and Coeur d'Alene were being devastated by epidemic disease and intensified warfare with their more powerful Blackfoot and Bannock enemies. At the same time came the stimulus of increasing contact with foreign peoples, ideas, and objects. On the Plateau, the early fur trade era was one of both cultural florescence and, all too often, mourning.

The rapid influx of new ideas, objects, and diseases, as well as the increasing warfare which preceded De Smet's initial visit in 1839, caused large numbers of Plateau peoples to be receptive to Christian — and, in particular, Catholic — sources of spiritual power to revitalize traditional sources and meet the new needs of a new age. The Salish and their neighbours were thus amazingly enthusiastic about the Jesuit missions, and for the first few years of the missions many of them eagerly participated in an intensive program of worship involving prayers and instruction several times a day. Many of the peoples of the northeastern Plateau enthusiastically adopted Catholic forms of worship, learned their catechism, prayers, and hymns, were baptized and confirmed, and provided a heady atmosphere for the Jesuits. One of De Smet's colleagues, Father Gregory Mengarini, summarized this period:

---

1   On the Plateau missions and their historic context, see Jacqueline Peterson and Laura Peers, *Sacred Encounters: Father De Smet and the Indians of the Rocky Mountain West* (Norman: University of Oklahoma Press, 1993).

LAURA PEERS

the Flatheads are fervently devoted to religion, they place great emphasis upon all related to it. On all occasions they perform the rituals in an excellent manner. The rosary, medals, and the scapular ... constantly hang on their breasts. Such importance is placed upon them that when they are lost, even grown men cry in sorrow. Reciting prayers and singing [hymns] is their life.[1]

Fur traders, early miners and settlers, and, later, government officials also noted the Salish and Coeur d'Alene attachment to Catholicism, even after disputes which emerged between the converts and their missionaries resulted in the temporary closure of missions. It is important to note, however, that Christianity did not entirely replace traditional beliefs for Native converts, but was integrated into them: although they were persuaded by the priests to destroy traditional medicine bundles and sacred objects, they replaced these, as Mengarini's statement implies, with holy medals, rosaries, and scapulars. Even Mengarini admitted that "the prayers of our Indians consisted in asking to live a long time, to kill plenty of animals and enemies, and to steal the greatest number of horses possible."[2] As many scholars have noted, this process of addition and integration is typical in Indian mission situations.[3] Indeed, one of the Jesuits at the Plateau missions believed that, "with the Indians particularly, it is better to graft than to fell": an unusual admission by the clergy that syncretism might play a functional role as a step in the process of conversion and assimilation.[4] But how did these peoples deal with the concept and powers of the Virgin Mary, and why was she so popular among them?

---

1 Gregory Mengarini, S.J., *Recollections of the Flathead Mission*, trans. Gloria Lothrop (Glendale, CA: Arthur H. Clark, 1977), 221.

2 Mengarini, *Recollections*, fn. p. 159.

3 See, for instance, John Webster Grant, *Moon of Wintertime* (Toronto: University of Toronto Press, 1984); and James Axtell, *The Invasion Within: The Contest of Cultures in Colonial North America* (New York: Oxford University Press, 1985).

4 Cornelius M. Buckley, *Nicolas Point, S.J.: His Life and Northwest Indian Chronicles* (Chicago: Loyola University Press, 1989), 290.

The Jesuits brought to the Plateau centuries of experience in imparting Christianity to Native peoples in Asia, South America, and eastern North America. They also brought a conventional, European view of Christianity in which the Holy Family were commonly represented as white Europeans, and were viewed as models of European gender roles. The Virgin Mary was seen by lay people as well as priests as the epitome of a European woman, embodying the values, virtues, and behaviour expected of Catholic women: she was frequently described as humble, reserved, and modest, implying a retiring personality concerned with the woman's place allotted within the home rather than the European man's role of leadership and public participation outside the home. She was also described as a nurturing mother, loving, healing, forgiving, a symbol of purity and fertility, and as suffering and sorrowing for her Son. Again, this is strongly evocative of the generative, nurturing, patient, and enduring qualities to which European women were urged to aspire. When described or appealed to as Queen of Heaven (and she was often depicted and thought of as powerful, a symbol of divine majesty) the Church insisted that Mary was ultimately subordinate to the higher male authority of her Son and of God the Father.[1] Mary was thus seen as both human and superhuman, powerful, and bound by conventional European gender roles. Based on this model, pious and good Catholic women were expected to be supportive and obedient wives and nurturing mothers whose authority within the home, although considerable, was sharply limited by and subject to the authority of their husbands.

This was the image of Mary which the Jesuits brought to the Plateau and attempted to inculcate in their converts using pedagogical techniques perfected at missions around the world. Hymns and simple prayers, pictures, stories, and the drama of processions were used to teach all of the basic Catholic precepts, but from the very beginning the Virgin Mary, and devotions to her, played an especially important role at the Plateau missions. "Marian devotions" introduced to the Salish, Coeur d'Alene, and other Plateau tribes in the 1840s included the saying of the rosary; prayers and hymns addressed to Mary, such as the *Ave Ma-*

---

1   See Ann Taves, *The Household of Faith* (Notre Dame, IN: University of Notre Dame, 1986), 39, 82. On European images of Mary, see Marina Warner, *Alone of All Her Sex* (New York: Knopf, 1976).

LAURA PEERS

ria or Hail Mary; miraculous medals (the standard prayer inscribed on which read, "Mary conceived without sin pray for those who have recourse to thee"); the wearing of scapulars (small cloth badges printed or embroidered with the image of Mary, worn as a devotion to her and thought of as protective by many Catholics); and the holding of special days of worship and rituals celebrating her life and divine assistance. One of the Jesuits' first activities after erecting rough bark-roofed chapels was to carve and paint pictures and statues of the Virgin and to celebrate the Feast of the Immaculate Conception of Mary:

> a small wooden statue of Our Lady ... was carried in triumph by the tribe to the very place where their patron had appeared.... After the erection of the little monument, there was established a kind of pilgrimage in the name of Our Lady of Peace. Thereafter, no one passed that way without saying an Ave Maria. And every evening, everyone knelt to recite three Ave Marias.[1]

Sodalities (associations of converts), such as the Congregation of the Immaculate Heart of Mary, devoted to the conversion of sinners, were also established among the Salish and Coeur d'Alene at the Jesuit missions.[2]

The Jesuits hoped that by introducing the Virgin Mary, with her conventionalized behaviour and piety, and these means of worshipping her, they would be able to inculcate Christian values, gender roles, and patterns of family relationships on the Plateau and eradicate what they saw as a "pagan" lifestyle.[3] Thus, the sodalities in honour of the Virgin which they established were ostensibly to promote the conversion of sinners, but also reinforced European concepts of "good" behaviour versus sin: "Individuals were often invited to membership [in sodalities]

---

1   Point, *Wilderness Kingdom*, 46; see also Mengarini, *Recollections*, 224.

2   Sodalities: Mengarini, *Recollections*, 222. For accounts of Marian devotions at the missions, see Point, *Wilderness Kingdom*, 38, 41-46, 147; Mengarini, *Recollections*, 221-24; Buckley, *Nicolas Point, S.J.*, 208; Hiram Martin Chittenden and Alfred Talbot Richardson, eds., *Life, Letters and Travels of Father Pierre-Jean De Smet, S.J., 1801-1873* (New York: Francis P. Harper, 1905), vol. 1, 334, 367; and Thomas Connolly, S.J., ed., *Quay-Lem U En-Chow-Men: A Collection of Hymns and Prayers in the Flathead-Kalispel-Spokane Indian Language* (Pablo, MT: Salish-Kootenai College, 1983; rev. ed., orig. pub. 1958).

3   For other Jesuit efforts to alter Plateau women's roles, see Lillian Ackerman, "The Effect of Missionary Ideals on Family Structure and Women's Roles in Plateau Indian Culture," *Idaho Yesterdays* 31:1-2 (1987), 64-74.

because of their exemplary behaviour. Members of the sodality served to set an example of Christian living and piety for the rest of the community."[1] The Jesuits picked the leaders of the sodalities from among their converts, choosing those whom they felt to display the most Christian (and European) behaviour. The use of images of Mary and of the Holy Family at the missions provided a visual model of the European gender roles and nuclear family structure which the Jesuits expected their converts to adopt.[2] The celebration of Marian festivals at the missions was also meant to reinforce European, Christian models of social structure. Typically, in Euro-American public devotions to Mary, especially processions and the more elaborate festivals, the power of Mary and her images is celebrated; at the same time, the typically male control of such events and the behaviours and supporting roles expected of women during the event act as a powerful reinforcement of culturally assigned gender roles.[3]

Jesuit texts mention their attitudes toward Plateau women, whom they judged by the European standards they brought with them; they also mention their use of the image of Mary to effect change in Plateau society. Father Joset, for instance, praised the women of one group of Plateau tribes who were, he said, "submissive and affectionate," and judged these "the best disposed to profit by instruction."[4] Similarly, De Smet noted with approval a Salish convert who received punishment from her father "with the most humble and praiseworthy submission."[5] And even five decades after the founding of the missions, the Virgin was

---

1   Personal communication from Gerald McKevitt, S.J., Santa Clara University, 19 February 1992.

2   See the images of Mary and the Holy Family in Nicolas Point's sketches and paintings of the Plateau mission in Point, *Wilderness Kingdom*, and Peterson and Peers, *Sacred Encounters*.

3   Robert Orsi, *The Madonna of 115th Street* (New Haven, CT: Yale University Press, 1985), 211.

4   Joset papers, box 1351, folder 13, "Ethnography of the Rocky Mountain Indians," Oregon Province Archives of the Society of Jesus, Crosby Library, Gonzaga University, Spokane, Washington. I am grateful to the Society of Jesus for permission to research in and quote from the Oregon Province Archives.

5   Chittenden and Richardson, eds., *Life, Letters and Travels of Father Pierre-Jean De Smet, S.J.*, vol. 1, 324.

still being overtly used as a symbol of proper womanhood to Salish girls at the mission boarding school: "The ideal set before these girls ... was Mary, the ever Blessed Mother of Jesus Christ, and her place in her home with St. Joseph and the Child Jesus was the model of the Christian wife and mother."[1]

Salish Perceptions of the Virgin Mary

Native people in mission situations have often identified many aspects of Catholicism with existing aspects of their cultures. Catholic saints and guardian angels were perceived to function in essentially the same way as traditional guardian spirits, and Christian sacred objects were seen as tokens of and means of communication with the sacred, just as were personal and tribal sacred objects. Sweetgrass, cedar, sage, and tobacco were identified with the incense used in Catholic rituals; holy medals were equated with medicine objects; Jesus has been identified with traditional beings, particularly male culture heroes, tricksters, and creator figures. Mary, however, fits less easily into traditional belief systems, particularly in Native cultures which do not have important female supernatural beings.

This was the case with the introduction of the Virgin to Plateau converts: she was, in concept, a completely new deity. There are only two female supernatural figures in the traditional cosmology of the Salish. One of these is known as *Em'tep*; the other is known as the mother of the Creator, *Amotkan*. According to an account collected by Mengarini in the 1840s, the mother of *Amotkan* prevented him from destroying humans a fourth and final time.[2] *Em'tep* is portrayed in later ethnographic accounts as essentially the opposite of *Amotkan*, as living at the bottom of the world, and as being evil. The word *Em'tep* has been used to signify both Hell and Queen Victoria.[3] These beings and their actions do have

---

1   William L. Davis, S.J., *A History of St. Ignatius Mission* (Spokane, WA: C.W. Hill Printing, 1954), 52.

2   Mengarini, *Recollections*, 152.

3   Mengarini, *Recollections*, 149-52; Harry H. Turney-High, *The Flathead Indians of Montana* (Memoirs of the American Anthropological Association no. 48, 1937) 22; James Teit, *The Salishan Tribes of the Western Plateaus* (facsimile reproduction: Seattle: Shorey Bookstore, 1973; orig. pub. in 45th Bureau of American Ethnology Report, 1927-28) 184-85; Teit, however, implies *Em'tep* is male and also confuses the two beings at one point in his account.

elements similar to Mary (one is a powerful intercessor and mother; the other is a queen); however, they were minor figures in the traditional cosmology, and have not been equated with Mary by the Salish or other Plateau people. Even the name by which Salishan-speaking peoples know this new being is still essentially an English one. She is "Malee," the Salishan gloss of Mary, and has not been given an "Indian" name.

Thus, Plateau converts did not turn to Mary so enthusiastically because they already knew her in an older guise; their perception of her and their devotion to her is more complex than that. I believe that Plateau people linked Mary with their own view of women and of "proper" women's roles — which were entirely different from European perceptions — and with the special powers and images of the Virgin which the Jesuits emphasized in their teachings. The combination of these qualities made her, in Plateau eyes, a special and powerful figure who could aid them in a way no other traditional or Catholic being could. It is at this point that I begin to "read into" the Jesuit texts about their Plateau converts' worship of Mary, and about Plateau cultures; I am training my own academic lens on the worship of Mary to contrast Jesuit and Plateau perceptions, and the image we get becomes truly kaleidoscopic.

Plateau peoples did not have the same expectations or gender roles for women as Europeans, and their perception of Mary seems, accordingly, to have been quite different. If a loving but submissive Mary was the model for young European Catholic women to emulate, little wonder that the Jesuits were dismayed by the roles and attitudes of Plateau women, whose economic and social power and autonomy contrasted sharply with the European Catholic model. Eastern Plateau women had control over all household possessions and food, even game once it was killed; they harvested the camas lily roots and bitterroots, which constituted a crucial part of their diets; and "not only the clothes they wear but almost everything else, including the tent, the saddles, the sacks, cords, etc., belong[ed] to the women" as well.[1] These women enjoyed a considerable degree of autonomy and influence; they often refused to feed their husbands if displeased with them; they could be warriors; and they frequently stood up in council to make their own points and harangue male leaders. This did not accord with European ideas about virtuous female behaviour. Thus, Mengarini complained strongly about "the an-

---

1   Point, *Wilderness Kingdom*, 94.

LAURA PEERS

cient custom of female despotism," stating that women were not only "masters over their men," but that they absolutely refused to concede any of this power to their husbands.[1] Joseph Joset, another early Jesuit missionary, similarly complained that many Plateau women were "independent and hawty."[2]

These very different cultural expectations of women led Plateau Indians to see Mary as a different kind of role model for women than that which the Jesuits had envisioned. In early accounts of the missions, converts were quoted as describing Mary as a very strong woman, emphasizing, for instance, the fact that she was commonly portrayed as crushing a large snake beneath her heels.[3] This image of Mary continues to clash with Church-sanctioned ones among older Plateau Catholics a century and a half later. I have heard Salish women say, "The Church is all wrong about Mary; she's much stronger than that," and describe Mary as a warrior woman. From the very beginning, converts perceived Mary as a Plateau woman and related to her in a Plateau manner involving traditional norms for relating to supernatural beings and traditional expectations of guardian spirits. Plateau converts were not interested in Mary as an example of submissive womanhood; they were interested in her powers, her strength, and her ability to protect.

That Plateau converts related to Mary as they would to a traditional guardian spirit is suggested by a body of hymns which were introduced by the Jesuits in the 1840s and were later indigenized both in content and in musical form by the Salish and Coeur d'Alene. The hymns were re-collected in their altered forms in the 1870s and published for use at the missions. One of them is a hymn to Mary whose words are:

> You beloved mother, so good;
> You're the guardian of all;
> Virgin good, all pure
> Our guardian, we pray to you.

---

1 Mengarini, *Recollections*, 215-16. See also Joset's description of the roles of women in various Plateau tribes (Footnote 22), and Ackerman, "The Effect of Missionary Ideals on Family Structure and Women's Roles in Plateau Indian Culture."

2 Joset papers, box 1351, folder 13, "Ethnography of the Rocky Mountain Indians," Oregon Province Archives of the Society of Jesus, Crosby Library, Gonzaga University, Spokane, Washington.

3 E.g., Point, *Wilderness Kingdom*, 41.

Mother Mary, good guardian;
Mother Mary, I pray to you;
About all of my sadness,
My guardian, I pray to you.
To the hungry you are pitying;
Pray for the dying;
Hopefully in our awakening, we'll all be happy.[1]

Another hymn, apparently created by the Salish early in the history of the missions, says:

My soul is pitiful because of the dangers of the world.
But Mary, you love me
You, who are the mother of God, are also my mother.[2]

The most important word in these two hymns, a word which serves as a key to understanding Plateau attitudes and perceptions, is "pity." The notion of "pity" has been explored more thoroughly for Great Lakes and Plains peoples than for Plateau tribes, but was also part of Plateau spirituality. Traditionally, Plateau people, like their neighbours to the east, begged powerful spirits to "have pity" on them and bestow powers and gifts to sustain life. As Mary Black-Rogers has discussed for the Ojibwa, to "pity" someone was the same thing as "to bestow a blessing":

To be pitiable, then, seems the correct state for a person who wishes to receive a gift of power — a promise of help in getting through life. However, the word does not refer to a state, but to an action (or transaction). To "give the blessing" and to "pity" is all one act. To "be pitied" and to "receive a gift" of this kind is all the same thing. Such gifts consisted of specific powers, abilities to perform life's jobs both great and small.[3]

1　Connolly, ed., *Quay-Lem U En-Chow-Men: A Collection of Hymns and Prayers...*, 59.

2　Hymn text from Mary Michael, a Coeur d'Alene, whose ancestors learned it from Salish elders in Arlee, Montana; information courtesy Dr. Loran Olsen, Department of Music, Washington State University, who served as ethnomusicologist to the De Smet Project and Sacred Encounters exhibition.

3　Mary Black-Rogers, "Varieties of 'Starving': Semantics and Survival in the Subarctic Fur Trade, 1750-1850," *Ethnohistory* 33:4 (1986), 367. On the concept of "pity," see also Bruce White, "Encounters with Spirits: Ojibwa and Dakota Theories about the

The use of "pity" and "guardian" in the Marian hymns of the Plateau is thus a direct continuation of traditional Native perceptions and expectations of powerful beings. Mengarini reported that before one Salish man he knew became a Christian, he used to pray to a large tree in this manner:

... one of the oldest Flathead leaders recalled, when he was young, orphaned and poor, he gave way to his sorrow one day. With tears in his eyes he allowed his arms to encircle a large tree, all the while murmuring, "My tree, have pity on me so that I may become a chief, have many horses, ... and that I may overcome my poverty."[1]

This spiritual relationship paralleled the Native ideal of proper social relations, in which powerful and wealthier beings and humans were expected to bestow gifts and assistance on those less fortunate. In praying for "pity," supplicants emphasized their poverty, their weakness, their danger, and their dependence for life upon more powerful supernatural beings. In fact, this paralleled typical appeals to saints by European Catholics, for whom, as Ann Taves has written, "In return for obedience and devotion, supernatural patrons provided the graces and favors believed necessary for salvation or well-being in this world."[2] At the Plateau missions, then, converts emphasized their "pitiable" state in prayers and hymns to Mary, and asked her aid and intercession for the sick, the hungry, and dying sinners. Little wonder, then, that the Salish and Coeur d'Alene addressed Mary as "the guardian of all." In this hymn we find the answer to the riddle of why the winter hunt of 1841-2 was dedicated to Mary: "To the hungry you are pitying," it says, just as Na-

---

French and their Merchandise," *Ethnohistory* 41:3 (1994), 380-81, 386; Bruce White, "Give Us a Little Milk: The Social and Cultural Meanings of Gift Giving in the Lake Superior Fur Trade," *Minnesota History* 48 (2), 1982, 62. While these consider Ojibwa and Dakota uses of "pity" and more comparative work needs to be done to link them specifically to the uses of "pity" by Plateau converts, consider the similarity between the uses of "pity" in the Marian hymns and the Ojibwa notion that "to 'pity' another is to adopt him and care for him as a parent...cares for a child" (cited in White, "Give Us a Little Milk," 62).

1   Mengarini, *Recollections*, 158.

2   Taves, *Household of Faith*, 86.

tive people would have pleaded with their traditional guardians and with the spirits of the animals they hunted to "pity" the hungry.

To these traditional powers of guardian beings was added a Catholic twist. Much of Mary's power and appeal was based on her maternal role and the superhumanly strong power of a mother's love. It was as a mother that Mary particularly appealed to nineteenth century Catholics, Native and non-Native. Not only was it said that Jesus could refuse his Mother nothing, but Mary embodied the tender, nurturing, forgiving qualities of motherhood; she was (and remains) an easy figure to have recourse to. In Mary, the traditional Native concept of pity was fused with the ideal of Christian love and charity and the universal bond between a mother and her children.

These kind, forgiving qualities constituted a great difference between Mary and traditional Plateau guardians, who were apt to take revenge if the rules for using their power were disobeyed. Some ethnographic accounts state that traditional guardians could kill or injure people if displeased.[1] While it is true that Christian supernatural patrons offered their earthly and spiritual favours "in return for obedience and devotion," as did traditional Plateau guardians, Mary and other saints were not likely to make you ill or kill you if you asked for something inappropriate (or inappropriately).[2] Furthermore, Mary and devotions to her represent what John Long has termed a "democratization of power" inherent in Christianity: Mary is a powerful figure to whom all converts, women as well as men, marginal as well as respected members of the community, have access, and to whom access was easier than the fasting and life-long observance of taboos, sacrifices, and rituals which was involved with obtaining a traditional guardian spirit. She was, indeed, "the guardian of all." As Long writes, Christianity "was associated in the Indians' minds with power — over sickness, other-than-human danger, conjurors, danger while travelling, and starvation. This power was obtainable through prayer (appeals to God or Jesus [or, in this case, Mary]), and observance of the Sabbath."[3]

---

1   E.g., Turney-High, *The Flathead Indians of Montana*, 32–33.

2   Taves, *The Household of Faith*, 86.

3   John Long, "Manitu, Power, Books, and *Wihtikow*," *Native Studies Review* 3:1 (1987), 15–16.

LAURA PEERS

Mary's role as mother seems also to have been crucial in introducing a family metaphor into human-supernatural relationships on the northeastern Plateau, where traditional guardians and supernatural beings were addressed by terms of respect but not of kinship.[1] The Salish and Coeur d'Alene were undoubtedly aware of this practice among other Native groups and also learned it from other elements of Christianity (particularly the concept of "God the Father"). As Ann Taves has written, "Prayers to Mary and the saints in heaven ... presupposed the existence of social relationships between faithful Catholics and supernatural beings, and provided a means of interacting with them."[2] The concept of "social relationships" between humans and supernatural beings was a familiar one to the Salish, though the patterning of these relationships in terms of the human family may have been new to them.

It was in their emotional relationship with this new mother-figure that Plateau peoples most deeply related to this concept of social relations based on ideals of human kinship. Just as she was strong and powerful, as they were, Mary, like many Plateau women in an age of disease and warfare, had lost a much-loved son; she was someone they could understand and appeal to. Certainly many of the Indianized hymns dwell on this relationship, and events such as the first apparition of Mary on the Plateau – to a dying girl, who cried: "Oh, how beautiful! I see Mary, my Mother" – also underscore it.[3] This affective mother-child relationship may also have been linked to the importance placed on holy medals at the early Plateau missions: think of Mengarini's statement, cited earlier, that, when such medals were lost, "even grown men cry in sorrow." In one early incident, a dying child was cured when a medal of the Blessed Virgin was placed around her neck and the parents prayed to the Virgin to save the child. In essence, placing the medal around the child's neck symbolically made her a child of the Virgin. The Virgin's love for her infant Child was known to be supernaturally strong; and

---

1 E.g., Turney-High, *The Flathead Indians of Montana*, 27-28; Mengarini, *Recollections*, 158-59; Teit, *The Salishan Tribes of the Western Plateau*, 185, 193-94, 384; and personal communication with Dr. Allan Smith, Department of Anthropology, Washington State University.

2 Taves, *Household of Faith*, 47.

3 Point, *Wilderness Kingdom*, 38. For hymns, see Connolly, ed., *Quay-Lem U En-Chow-Men: A Collection of Hymns and Prayers*....

what mother would not do anything in her power to heal her sick child?[1]

Mary's strength and maternal qualities come together in her most powerful attribute, one which was deeply meaningful to Plateau converts: her ability to intercede on behalf of the dead, in purgatory and even in Hell. The scapular to which Plateau peoples were so attached was worn on the basis of Mary's promise that "whosoever dies clothed in this shall never suffer eternal fire,"[2] and in the most common Catholic prayers and hymns Mary is asked to "pray for the dead" and to "pray for us now and at the hour of our death." The idea of Hell was a Christian import to the Plateau, and was resisted by some converts because it was so foreign to their traditional cosmology. The threat of the torments of Hell, and the vivid imagery associated with it, was used by both Protestant and Catholic missionaries to persuade Native people to convert and to exhort backsliders to reform. The concept that Mary could preserve the worst of sinners from the torments of Hell was clearly important to Salish and Coeur d'Alene converts, particularly in light of their continuing high mortality rates throughout the nineteenth century. Mary's intervention was also meaningful in its relation to belief in the "communion of saints," a central tenet of nineteenth-century Catholicism which held that for those

> who believe in life eternal and the communion of saints ... the holy ones in heaven [are] living and present with us.... Death has not removed them from us.... They are present to our hearts, and we can speak to them, pour into their open and sympathizing hearts our joys and griefs, and ask and receive their aid, as readily and as effectively as when they were present to our bodily senses.[3]

To a people ravaged by waves of epidemics, and for whom the death of elderly tradition-bearers became even more devastating in the face of pressure to assimilate, such beliefs filled a need for contact with the dead and for reassurance about their own cultural continuity.

---

1 "Even grown men cry": Mengarini, *Recollections*, 221; child healed by Marian medal: Point, *Wilderness Kingdom*, 94.

2 Warner, *Alone of All Her Sex*, 328.

3 Warner, *Alone of All Her Sex*, 328.

LAURA PEERS

The reality of death and mourning as a link between Plateau peoples and their appeals to Mary is not unique to this mission situation. Robert Orsi has observed of a European immigrant community in New York City which faced great hardship and change, "Their own suffering was used to create a deep bond of sympathy with the redemptive suffering at the heart of Christianity," and these deep emotions created ties to Catholicism on the Plateau as well.[1] Plateau hymns make much of Mary's suffering at the Cross in an emotive style suggesting great empathy and experience with pain and death, and contemporary Salish Catholic women have assured me that Mary must have been (or become) an extraordinarily (superhumanly?) strong woman to have seen and withstood her Son's suffering. She was, the women tell me, "a Warrior woman." Her strength, her survival, her love, and her ability to transcend death were, and remain, deeply meaningful to Plateau converts. On both personal and community levels, then, relationships with and devotions to Mary involved what has been called "a *psychodrame* of disintegration and reintegration": a movement, through appeals to Mary, from despair to hope, sickness to health, the finality of death to the possibility of contact with the dead, suffering to survival.[2] As a new and powerful figure who could be seen in Plateau terms, the figure of the Virgin provided a powerful catalyst for both cultural adaptation and continuity during the continued turbulence of the nineteenth century.

Conclusion

In 1855, Father Hoecken wrote from one of the Plateau missions to Father De Smet:

> There is among our converts a universal and very tender devotion to the Blessed Virgin, a most evident mark that the Faith has taken deep root in their souls. Every day, morning and evening, the families assemble in their lodges to recite the rosary in common, and daily they beg of Mary to

---

1   Orsi, *Madonna of 115th Street*, 221.

2   Orsi, *Madonna of 115th Street*, 177.

thank God for them for having called them from the wild life of the forest
... to the blessings of the true religion and its immortal hopes.[1]

This last text is more than simple missionary rhetoric. It incorporates the different Native and Jesuit perceptions of the Virgin Mary and of the effects of Catholicism on Plateau peoples; in addition, it shows how easily any single lens or perspective can blur our understanding of the complex reality at the missions. True, Plateau converts did take up Marian devotions most enthusiastically; it is hard for us, in this secular age, to imagine the hours of prayer and song and worship they engaged in every day, even during the bison hunts and other seasonal movements. And while Father Hoecken's claim that "daily they beg of Mary to thank God for them for having called them from the wild life of the forest ... to the blessings of the true religion" is most likely an overstatement by a gratified missionary, it is probable that given the desire of northeastern Plateau peoples for new sources of power to revitalize traditional belief systems, they may well have expressed satisfaction with new religious practices and even denigrated the waning power of their traditional ones.

We need, then, to read between the lines of this text, to train other lenses on it. What a superficial reading of Father Hoecken's statement misses, of course, is the meaning of the Virgin to Plateau converts, the manner in which Plateau peoples "translated" the Virgin into a recognizably Plateau holy woman who could, using both Catholic powers and Plateau expectations, protect and sustain them. This was more complex than a simple replacement of traditional beliefs and religious practices. It involved new as well as traditional spiritual and physical needs, new ideas about sacred beings as well as traditional relationships with them, new powers and holy objects, some of which were used like old ones and some of which were used in new ways to accomplish traditional goals. All of these things motivated Plateau peoples to pray daily to Mary in their mat lodges.

Sparked by these intricate recombinations, however, the behaviour upon which Father Hoecken remarked did not involve an abandonment of traditional perceptions of women or expectations of guardian beings.

---

1 Hoecken to De Smet, in De Smet, *Western Missions and Missionaries* (New York, 1863), 296; also quoted (same letter) in Chittenden and Richardson, *Life, Letters and Travels of De Smet*, vol. 4, 1229.

The figure of the Virgin Mary continued to be perceived in very different as well as very similar ways by Plateau peoples and the Jesuits who converted them. While Plateau peoples accepted what they were told about Mary's powers and maternal qualities, they saw her as a woman much like their own — which was a very different figure than what the Jesuits saw. It seems probable that Marian devotions at the Plateau missions initially functioned to reinforce conventional Plateau ideas about women and their proper roles and that, where the Jesuits saw a celebration of the virtues of "sweetness and humility," their Native converts were "identifying their wives and sisters [and other female relatives] ... with a very powerful woman."[1] One can see in the mind's eye the processions which were held on certain Marian feast days, with the Jesuit priests leading a line of Native converts to a statue of the Virgin — and with Native and European each seeing a different face on the same statue.

Finally, I am aware that Marian devotions were not always as beneficent or functional as I have portrayed them here. The attitude of the Church in its dealings with Native peoples hardened over the course of the nineteenth century, so that the Jesuits on the Plateau went from believing that "'tis better to graft than to fell," to applying policies designed to force assimilation. By the late nineteenth century, the rules for one mission school stated that every new pupil must "remain silent until he can speak English," and the image of the Virgin was used in those schools as a model for teaching the Euro-American gender roles which the Jesuits had originally intended, just as the Holy Family became the model for a Euro-Americanized nuclear family.[2] Men and women chosen by priests to lead certain devotions, particularly the sodalities, were termed "puppets" by more than one Native dissenter, and such Church-sanctioned leadership roles acted to alter traditional leadership and political patterns, creating factions among Plateau tribes when they most needed (during the influx of settlers, miners, and government agents) to act together.[3] In these ways, devotions to Mary became intimate and powerful tools of assimilation. The analysis of Plateau attitudes toward

1   Orsi, *Madonna of 115th Street*, 207.

2   Mission rules: illustrated in Peterson and Peers, *Sacred Encounters*, 144–45. Virgin as role model in schools: Davis, *A History of St. Ignatius Mission*, 52. See also Ackerman, "The Effect of Missionary Ideals..."

3   Robert Burns, "Roman Catholic Missions in the Northwest," *Handbook of North American Indians*, vol. 4: *Native-White Relations*, ed. Wilcomb E. Washburn (Washington, DC: Smithsonian Institution, 1988), 500.

Catholic religious figures such as Mary needs to be placed in the ethno-historical context of the upheaval experienced by northeastern Plateau peoples throughout the nineteenth century.

Despite attempts to impose this Euro-American face on Plateau perceptions of Mary, however, many Plateau Catholics still see her as a Plateau woman, and still appeal to her in traditional ways. These are the women who tell me that "The Church is all wrong about Mary; she's much stronger than that." Such strength and tenacity in their perceptions and worship of the Virgin Mary mark them as "active participants ... in their own history instead of victims of an imposed and alien one."[1] In the end, these people have retained central aspects of their identity and culture while finding a new and powerful guardian figure: "The Guardian of All."

References

Ackerman, Lillian. "The Effect of Missionary Ideals on Family Structure and Women's Roles in Plateau Indian Culture." *Idaho Yesterdays* 31 (1-2), 1987, 64-74.

Axtell, James. *The Invasion Within: The Contest of Cultures in Colonial North America*. New York: Oxford University Press, 1985.

Black-Rogers, Mary. "Varieties of 'Starving': Semantics and Survival in the Subarctic Fur Trade, 1750-1850." *Ethnohistory* 33:4 (1986), 353-83.

Buckley, Cornelius M. *Nicolas Point, S.J.: His Life and Northwest Indian Chronicles*. Chicago: Loyola University Press, 1989.

Burns, Robert, S.J. "Roman Catholic Missions in the Northwest." In *Handbook of North American Indians*, vol. 4: *Native-White Relations*, ed. Wilcomb E. Washburn. Washington, DC: Smithsonian Institution, 1988.

Chittenden, Hiram Martin, and Alfred Talbot Richardson, eds. *Life, Letters and Travels of Father Pierre-Jean De Smet, S.J., 1801-1873*. 3 vols. New York: Francis P. Harper, 1905.

Connolly, Thomas, S.J., ed. Quay-Lem U En-Chow-Men: A Collection of Hymns and Prayers in the Flathead-Kalispel-Spokane Indian Language. Pablo, MT: Salish-Kootenai College, 1983(1958).

Davis, William L., S.J. *A History of St. Ignatius Mission*. Spokane, WA: C.W. Hill Printing, 1954.

De Smet, Pierre-Jean. *Western Missions and Missionaries*. New York, 1863.

---

1 Long, "Manitu, Power, Books, and Wihtikow," 2.

Grant, John Webster. *Moon of Wintertime: Missionaries and the Indians of Canada in Encounter Since 1534*. Toronto: University of Toronto Press, 1984.

Joset, Joseph, S.J. "Ethnography of the Rocky Mountain Indians." Joset papers, box 1351, folder 13, Oregon Province Archives of the Society of Jesus, Crosby Library, Gonzaga University, Spokane, WA.

Long, John. "Manitu, Power, Books, and Wihtikow." *Native Studies Review* 3:1 (1987), 1–30.

Mengarini, Gregory, S.J. *Recollections of the Flathead Mission*. Gloria Lothrop, trans. Glendale, CA: Arthur H. Clark, 1977.

Peterson, Jacqueline, and Laura Peers. *Sacred Encounters: Father De Smet and the Indians of the Rocky Mountain West*. Norman: University of Oklahoma Press, 1993.

Point, Nicolas, S.J. *Wilderness Kingdom. Indian Life in the Rocky Mountains: 1840-1847; The Journal and Paintings of Nicolas Point, S.J.*. Joseph P. Donnelley, trans.; introduction by John C. Ewers. New York: Holt, Rinehart and Winston, 1967.

Orsi, Robert. *The Madonna of 115th Street*. New Haven, CT: Yale University Press, 1985.

Taves, Ann. *The Household of Faith*. Notre Dame, IN: University of Notre Dame, 1986.

Teit, James. *The Salishan Tribes of the Western Plateaus*. Facsimile reproduction: Seattle: Shorey Bookstore, 1973; orig. pub. 45th Bureau of American Ethnology Report, 1927-28.

Turney-High, Harry H. *The Flathead Indians of Montana*. Memoirs of the American Anthropological Association no. 48, 1937.

Warner, Marina. *Alone of All Her Sex*. New York: Knopf, 1976.

White, Bruce. "Give Us a Little Milk: The Social and Cultural Meanings of Gift Giving in the Lake Superior Fur Trade." *Minnesota History* 48 (2), 1982, 60-71.

——. "Encounters with Spirits: Ojibwa and Dakota Theories about the French and their Merchandise." *Ethnohistory* 41:3 (1994), 369-405.

Charles Pratt or Askenootow (1818-1888), Assiniboine/Cree CMS Catechist, George Gordon's First Nation, Saskatchewan, c. 1850.
(photo credit: Colin R. Pratt [1905-1983] in possession of author)

13

The Journals and Voices of a Church of England Native Catechist: Askenootow (Charles Pratt), 1851-1884[1]

Winona Stevenson

ASKENOOTOW, OR CHARLES PRATT, was a nehiyopwat (Cree-Assiniboine) who spent thirty-three years as a Church Missionary Society catechist on the plains and parkland fringe of present-day Saskatchewan. The primary interpretive problem that I encountered at the outset of this study arose from the discovery of two contradictory historical representations of Pratt's personal character and self-identity. One view came from family oral history, the other from his own hand – his mission journals written between 1851 and 1884.

At first glance, representations of him from the collective memory of his descendants seemed diametrically opposed to how he represented himself to his Church Missionary Society superiors. These contradictions in Charles Pratt's journals not only engaged me with all the interpretative problems that face any scholar; they reached into the very core of my being. I am nêhiyaw, a Cree person, and Askenootow is nimosôm, my grandfather.[2] Against the backdrop of a lifetime of stories I heard about nimosôm, the picture he gave me of himself in writing caused tremendous emotional turmoil – shock, confusion, pain, and at some points, even shame. Although schooled in the norms and conventions of the Western academic enterprise, I have always found it almost

---

1   I come from the second youngest line of Charles Pratt genealogy (granddaughter of Colin Richard, first son from Josiah's fourth marriage [to Harriet Favel], Josiah being the eldest son of Charles Pratt) and wish to acknowledge my elder relations – although the views taken in this paper are purely my own. Sincere thanks to Frank Tough for his careful reading and comments on the first draft and the unconditional support and encouragement he has offered as friend and colleague for the past ten years. Thanks also to the editors, Jennifer Brown and Elizabeth Vibert, and to the word warrior, Gerald Vizenor, for his postmodern androgogy and "ruins of representation." *kinanâskomatinâwâw nimosôm* Colin Richard Pratt *mina nohkom* Clara Pratt (Anderson) for keeping our family history alive.

2   Charles Pratt's son Josiah was the father of Colin Richard, who was the father of Bernelda Winona, my mother.

impossible to separate myself from my work – I am subject as much as I am observer. What I study has affected my real life in ways most academic historians studying the "Other" can never fathom. Thus, this study was also a personal journey. The path was not easy: it was much like a wagon trail, two parallel ruts heading in the same direction. In the beginning the road was bumpy, full of potholes and unsuspected turns. As the journey progressed the ruts smoothed out, the path became manageable, and the end came into view. The journey is not over yet, but many of the contradictions and confusions have been reconciled. More significantly, the process allowed this student/granddaughter the opportunity to gain a deeper understanding of Charles Pratt's motives, actions, and perspectives.

The study required more than the conventional tools of historical analysis. Oral history directed the path of inquiry which led me to locate new tools for textual analysis, especially those offered by psychology, anthropology, and literary criticism. This study, then, will trace a portion of my journey through oral history, archival data, and a variety of theoretical approaches in my attempt to reconcile the journals of Charles Pratt with the oral history passed on by his descendants.

Askenootow was born in 1816 at the fish barrier between Mission and Echo Lakes, Qu'Appelle Valley, in present-day southern Saskatchewan.[1] His people were nehiyopwatak, or Assiniboine-Crees, sometimes referred to in the historical literature as the Young Dogs. His Assiniboine-speaking mother named him Askenootow, Worker of the Earth. His father, Zacharria Floremond, was of Cree and French ancestry.[2] At the tender age of six years his people sent him to the Red River Settlement to learn how to read and write under the care of the Anglican Missionary John West at the Church Missionary Society (CMS) establishment.

---

1 Except where otherwise stated, the material on the life and times of Charles Pratt comes from Winona L. Stevenson, "The Church Missionary Society Red River Mission and the Emergence of a Native Ministry 1820-1860, with a Case Study of Charles Pratt of Touchwood Hills" (Master's thesis, University of British Columbia, Vancouver, 1988).

2 Saskatchewan Archives Board, University of Regina, Collection R, Vital Statistics Register 106, Gordon's Indian Reserve, "Gordon's Indian Reserve Register of Marriages, 1874-1931," no. 18, 1 October 1874 (hereinafter SAB, Vital Statistics, Gordon Reserve Marriages); National Archives of Canada, Church Missionary Society Archives Microfilm (hereinafter CMS), reel no. A.88, George Harbidge to Josiah Pratt, 1 July 1824.

During his six years at the Red River Indian Mission School, Askenoo-tow was baptized Charles Pratt and he acquired a well-rounded education for his time. Like his classmates, Pratt was trained for Indian mission work so his education consisted of academic and liturgical training, animal husbandry, agriculture, carpentry, masonry, and gun repair. At school he was tutored in Cree and learned to hunt, gather, and fish under the careful guidance of the mission hunter Asau. When Pratt left the mission school he joined the servant ranks of the Hudson's Bay Company as a boatman in the Swan River District. Eighteen years later, he joined the CMS as an itinerant missionary catechist.

Throughout his lengthy CMS career, Charles Pratt established five missions, served as an interpreter for Treaty No. Four in 1874 and adhesions, and with his lifelong friend George Gordon (Kaneonuskatew or One Who Walks on Four Claws), founded the Gordon's Indian Reserve located near present-day Punichy, Saskatchewan. At the age of 66, Askenootow suffered a paralytic stroke and was bedridden in his home on the Gordon's Reserve until his death in 1888. He was survived by eight children.

Discovering the journals of Charles Pratt came after years of hearing family stories, or oral histories, about his life and the "old days." My generation grew up hearing about how he and George Gordon, the namesake of our reserve and mosôm Charles's good friend, ran the buffalo before they founded the reserve. We heard about our grandfather's role as interpreter in the Treaty Four negotiations and how he spent his entire adult life as a catechist for the Anglican church. As children, we heard that he wanted ordination but was refused, that he worked hard for the church but was ill treated, and that he was a pipe-carrier and partook in ceremonies beyond the watchful eyes of his Anglican superiors and Indian Agents. We also heard that his children suffered much for his labours, that they often went without adequate shelter and comforts, and worked hard to help their father run the mission. This was especially true for mosôm Josiah, the eldest son, our grandfather's father. "I think it made him kind of mean when he grew up," my grandmother would say.

Our grandparents were wonderful storytellers. The way they interacted with their listeners, us children, as well as their body language, tones, and inflections, combined to bring the stories of mosôm Charles to life. When grandma Clara Pratt told stories, her eyes danced and glistened. The eyes of Old People, especially grandparents, are windows to the past through which we are honoured by visions of our deceased relatives. Oral history, in both its content and its form, conveys the humanity, character and environment of our ancestors in ways the written word simply cannot duplicate.

Mosôm Charles Pratt was represented to us as a man who loved his people and worked hard to help them adjust to changing conditions. He was a generous man who willingly gave his last morsel to others in need. He was a man of prayer, a humble man yet full of fiery pride – a trait handed down through the generations, I might add. He also instilled a strong sense of cultural pride in his children and grandchildren who, in their turn, spoke fluent Cree and passed cultural traditions down the generational line. This was the Charles Pratt I knew when, as a graduate student in history, I began researching his life in the archives at the University of British Columbia in 1986.

Discovering that nimosôm left hundreds of pages of unpublished journal entries and correspondence between the years 1851 and 1884 was like finding a pot of gold at the end of the rainbow.[1] However, I soon found out that finding his journals was not an end in itself – it was the beginning of a long and difficult personal journey.

The words I encountered in Charles Pratt's journals caused such confusion and pain that they inhibited my scholarly abilities. Much to my shock, I realized that he wrote like every other missionary I had ever read. This was my grandfather, but his language and his message differed little from those of tenacious evangelicals I've gone to great lengths to avoid all my life. His constant sermons and biblical paraphrasing were a violent affront to my nurtured image of who he was. For example, in his first journal, written in 1851 at Fort Pelly, Pratt described a series of encounters with the Saulteaux Medicine Man, Cha-wa-cis, of Fort Pelly (see appendix). The aggressive, evangelical proselytism and self-righteous arrogance that permeated those pages left me cringing, with mixed feelings of shame, confusion, and sadness. The intensity of my first reaction slowly faded as I read on; eventually Pratt's zeal toned down, but it never entirely ceased. In early January 1859 he wrote,

---

1   Charles Pratt's original journals and correspondence are in the Church Missionary Society Archives at the University of Birmingham, England. Microfilm copies of this collection are at the National Archives of Canada and many university libraries.

WINONA STEVENSON

very little fruit of my labors, I pray God to look down, with an eye for pity up us, & to bless his own word, to the souls of the poor heathen for Jesus Christ sake, his well beloved son, Amen. myself & family are Invited to the Companies fort. with all the cree Indian around me none of them were wanting all came to the invitation of a feast for the new year.[1]

And on 20 December 1859 in the Qu'Appelle Valley:

I have much reason to be thankful, that we are all still in good health, because his compassion fail not, hundreds of our fellow brethren are dying with the scarlet fever, as some suppose it to be, it is now within twenty miles distance from us, poor indians scattered all over as sheep without a shepperd. O may the time be drawing near, when they shall be gathered to the Redeemers fold. Blessed Jesus, hasten their own time, for this sheep which thou hast. which are not of the Jesus fold, for them also bring, that they may hear the voice, & that we may be in one fold & one shepperd even thou, O thou sheperd of Isreal.[2]

Pratt's journals were rife with condescending judgments and representations of the "poor heathen," the "Indians," his "fellow brethren." His broken English also caught me off guard, not because it demonstrated his relatively weak command of the English language, but because it highlighted his self-abasing and subservient representations of himself. Where was the man who had such pride and love for his people? Where was that Pratt tenacity? Where was my grandfather in this text?

Thus far, hath the Lord helped us, who am unworthy of the least of all his mercies. & my garden has come on well.[3]

---

1 CMS, A.95, Pratt Journal, 1 January 1859. The excerpts taken from Charles Pratt's journals and correspondence have not been edited except in cases where misspelled words are difficult to deduce. The reason why I decided not to edit Pratt was to avoid misrepresenting him and his identity. Pratt received a rudimentary English education and his primary language was Cree, and it is quite possible that during the long months he spent on the Plains his only use of English was in his journals. Because language was a large part of who he was, I decided to keep true to his own words and spelling.

2 CMS, A.95, Pratt Journal, 20 December 1856.

3 CMS, A.95, Pratt Journal, 20 August 1858.

my son Josiah teaching the cree boys who come in for teaching. It is his to be hoped, that a grain ... may chance to fall in the earth will spring up. I pray that God may not have oversight of my feeble work.[1]

In his written words, Askenootow did not present himself as my grandparents represented him — I barely recognized this man. The only wisps of familiarity traceable from oral accounts were his references to life around him: the Christmas feast at the local HBC post, his anxiety over the raging scarlet fever epidemic, concern for his garden, and the glint of pride that showed through for his eldest son's ability and support.

My initial examination of Charles Pratt's journals led me to accept that they fell into the genre of missionary literature, which has come under considerable analysis and criticism by historians in the last two decades. Its inherent biases and ethnocentrism have led numerous writers to point out that any discussion of Aboriginal-missionary relations must include the realization that missionaries, and their respective churches, were instrumental colonial agents. Frantz Fanon, for example, states that the Christian missions, "by condemning the customs and religions of the natives as heathen and unhuman ... bolster and uphold colonial racism [sic] ideology. At the same time they weaken the power of resistance of the indigenous population."[2] Missionaries set out with the intention of radically transforming Indigenous societies, and knowingly or not, provided the religious and ideological rationale for the larger colonial enterprise.

In light of the missionary agenda, the form and content of missionary literature confront historians with a range of interpretative problems. Sarah Carter and others have demonstrated that missionary writings are rife with racism, notions of cultural superiority, and zealous evangelicalism such that careful critical analyses are required to separate useful information (facts) from rhetoric and attitude (interpretation).[3] This recent interpretative trend has opened up a new field of research known in the

---

1   CMS, A.95, Pratt Journal, 9 January 1859.

2   Renate Zahar, *Frantz Fanon: Colonialism and Alienation* (New York: Monthly Review Press, 1974), 22.

3   Sarah Carter, "The Missionaries' Indian: The Publications of John McDougall, John McLean and Egerton Ryerson Young," *Prairie Forum* 9, 1 (1984): 27-44.

vernacular as "Indian–missionary relations." These studies attempt to explain missionary attitudes, perspectives, and behaviours in their relations with Aboriginal peoples.

Aboriginal missionary literature, however, poses even more complex interpretive problems. For example, the term "Aboriginal missionary" is not easy to digest because most often "Native" and "missionary" are conflicting terms. Not only is "Aboriginal" perceived as something distinctly Other than (opposite to) a "missionary," but there is also an inherent inequity in Aboriginal-missionary relations which manifests itself in the subjugation of the former to the domination of the latter.

In Canada a number of biographies have been written about individual Aboriginal missionaries but none has attempted a critical analysis of its subject's writings. Katherine Pettipas, in *The Diary of Henry Budd*, never broached the topic except to say that Budd's journals and correspondence "differ little in style and attitude from those of his European counterparts."[1] Penny Petrone, in *Native Literature in Canada*, delved somewhat deeper. She claimed that the handful of Native converts who left written records in the mid-nineteenth century all wrote the same way because their parochial school education trained them in a prevalent literary genre of that era, the sermon. According to Petrone, Native converts were instructed in sermon composition, "a typical blend of straightforward exposition and practical admonition, a mixture of spirituality and practicality expressed in balanced prose."[2] Noting that they were profoundly influenced by the Bible, she found that their writing "reflects a derivative and imitative style." Accordingly, Native missionaries, like their European counterparts, "produced passionate sermons and lectures, as well as prose narratives that advocated the assimilation into the blessings and benefits of Christianity and progress."[3]

No doubt prevailing literary genres had a tremendous impact on students, especially when imposed as they were on Native mission school children. However, this is not an adequate explanation, especially in cases where representations of a subject in the oral record contrast so

---

1   Katherine Pettipas, *The Diary of the Reverend Henry Budd, 1870-1875* vol. 4, Manitoba Record Society (Winnipeg, 1974), xix.

2   Penny Petrone, *Native Literature in Canada: From the Oral Tradition to the Present* (Toronto: University of Toronto Press, 1990), 40.

3   Petrone, *Native Literature in Canada*, 69.

vividly with his self-representations in the written records, as I found in comparing the different voices of Charles Pratt. A closer reading of Aboriginal missionary literature indicates that reasons far more complex than just training and mimicry compelled Aboriginal missionaries to engage in the sermon discourse.

The attempt to reconcile the contradictions between the oral and written representations of Charles Pratt began with basic, conventional historical questioning: for whom was Pratt writing and why? Like all missionaries in the field, Pratt was writing for an exclusive audience — his CMS superiors. He was expected to keep a weekly journal on the progress of his mission work, his activities and relations with the HBC and other fur traders, and to provide some useful information about his real and potential congregations.[1] The CMS wanted to hear that the missions were expanding, that congregations were growing, that Native people were settling down to farm, and that its Native workers were conducting themselves appropriately — as European missionaries would.

Most European missionaries were cautious and critical of their Native counterparts. They had little faith that Native missionaries could do their job as instructed. The Reverend John Smithurst believed that "the day for a native ministry will I doubt not arrive, but I look upon it as rather distant."[2] In Pratt's day, Native church workers lived under a looking glass — a stern eye — because their teachers and superiors had little faith in their abilities. As Smithurst wrote in 1850,

> entrusting a congregation to a native minister must be done with great caution. The native character is generally unstable. A native does well enough under the guidance of a European but when left to himself sinks into indolent listlessness and does next to nothing ... they would appear to me far better suited to break up new ground than to be left in charge of an

---

1 While a letter of instruction to Pratt has not been located, one was been found for James Settee, a Swampy Cree catechist who attended the Red River Mission School with Charles Pratt, when he was sent to establish a new mission at Beaver Creek in 1843. Settee was instructed to keep three books, one each on student enrolment, student progress and a record of the mission hunter's activities. He was also told to keep a weekly journal but was not instructed specifically on what he should be recording. I have deduced what the journal was to contain by comparing Native catechist journals with the instructions Settee received on the operations of the mission. CMS, A.96, Reverend Smithurst to James Settee, 1 October 1843.

2 CMS, A.96, Smithurst to the Secretaries of the CMS, 1 August 1845.

old station.... At a future time it may be different when the native character has been steadied by a longer and better Missionary.[1]

Not all European missionaries harboured such doubts. In fact, the Bishop of Rupert's land, David Anderson, ventured to say in 1870, "I believe some of the most effective of your staff or Missionaries are several of the Native clergy."[2] Even with that vote of confidence, however, Native church workers laboured under strenuous conditions. They were paid far less than their European counterparts, they were delegated the hardest tasks, and they were forced to deal with condescending attitudes, distrust, scepticism, and racism.[3] The negative opinions that CMS missionary teachers held of Native people were no doubt internalized in varying degrees by Native clergy at deep psychological and emotional levels.

Paulo Freire tells us that the internalization of colonialist ideas results in self-deprecation, fatalism, feelings of subservience, inferiority, and low self-esteem.[4] And Frantz Fanon, well known for his work on colonial relations and the impact of colonialism, describes how the mind of the colonized is affected often to the point of self-hatred:

> The racial stereotype of the colonized designed by the colonizer is eventually adopted by the former. In social psychology this process, which in many cases leads to self-hatred on the part of the victims of prejudice, is seen as one of the of many possible reactions of an out-group (the colonized people) to the prejudices of an in-group (their colonial overlords).[5]

As Fanon concludes, "the oppressed learn to perceive the cause of their oppression in their own inferiority."[6] In the case of Charles Pratt, I

---

1 CMS, A.96, Smithurst to Henry Venn, 6 August 1850.

2 CMS, A.99, Bishop of Rupert's Land to Mr. William Fenn, 17 December 1870.

3 See Winona L. Stevenson, "'Our Man in the Field' The Status and Role of a CMS Native Catechist in Rupert's Land," *Journal of the Canadian Church Historical Society* 33, 1 (1991): 65-78.

4 Paulo Freire, *Pedagogy of the Oppressed* (New York: Continuum Publishing reprint, 1988).

5 Zahar, *Frantz Fanon*, 22.

6 Zahar, *Frantz Fanon*, 19.

would venture that he not only internalized, in varying degrees, the views of his CMS superiors; he was also in the unenviable, even ironic, position of having to constantly demonstrate his abilities and evangelical orthodoxy — to disprove entrenched prejudices, a no-win task. He also, no doubt, realized that his superiors expected him to acknowledge and act out his "inferiority."

To a large degree this helps explain why Charles Pratt's journals convey the same Eurocentric, patronizing attitudes and self-righteous zeal as those of his European counterparts; in his writing he attempted to mollify or pacify the fears and doubts his superiors held about him. This is especially evident in Pratt's case because he always had a rather tenuous hold on his job and his missions. In many ways he did not measure up to the standards and expectations of the local CMS authorities. He was not well educated (clearly evident in his grammar and syntax), he continued to live more like a nehiyopwat than a missionary (he was a migratory buffalo hunter who also trapped furs, spoke his language, wore leather clothing and long hair), and he was unable to amass a strong sedentary congregation. As a result his superintendent, Abraham Cowley, often questioned his value as a CMS worker. For example, on 18 December 1873, Cowley wrote, "[I] urge only an additional European for Touchwood Hills. The work there I feel is suffering from the incompetency of Mr. Pratt to sustain & extend it. Under a European he would work I have little doubt."[1]

Pratt was constantly subjected to the condescending paternalism of his European superiors. For example, in October 1856 the Reverend Chapman, then CMS Secretary in London, chided Pratt for his apparent lack of evangelical enthusiasm. Chapman's letter illustrates that from the perspective of his superiors, Pratt's problems were due to his own lack of faith and study:

A mighty charge is committed to you; one for which in your own strengths you are quite unfitted — But you can do all things through Christ strengthening you. The whole secret of success lies in feeling close to him. In meditation upon his Holy Work you have access to him ... read slowly; verse by verse, sentence by sentence, word by word. Reflect

---

1   CMS, A.100, Abraham Cowley to Mr. Wright, 18 December 1873.

deeply on each syllable, apply it to your work, apply it to your own heart — turn it into prayer — turn it into praise — turn it into humiliation.[1]

A year after Pratt's wife Catherine died in 1868, the Reverend Abraham Cowley even tried to arrange a second marriage for him, "to a woman in whom I felt I cd. [could] repose confidence, assisting in the work of the Society, but failed, & am sorry of it."[2] Cowley was confirmed in his low opinion of Pratt in 1874 when Pratt, then 53 years old, chose to marry a much younger woman, Elizabeth, the sixteen-year-old daughter of an unbaptized hunter named Kashepuyas.[3] In 1883 Cowley wrote, "Mr. Pratt is a sincere Christian, but weak in simplicity, & unequally yoked in marriage."[4]

The CMS was most frustrated by Pratt's apparent lack of frugality and foresight. Charles Pratt was constantly chastised for sharing his supplies which always left him and his family destitute most of the year. Clearly Pratt's generosity was more in line with Cree notions of hospitality and generosity than with Christian notions. On 6 August 1884 Cowley wrote, "Year after year have I had to remonstrate with him [Pratt], being so careless of himself, allowing Indians to sponge upon him, till he is reduced to great extremities; often to almost starvation."[5]

Pratt was also always under the threat of being fired or relocated, or having his missions closed at the whim of the Corresponding Committee. Cowley noted of him on 28 December 1853, "Charles Pratt is to leave Fort Pelly & for the present to be suspended."[6] On 21 October 1855 at Fort Pelly, Pratt wrote, "I have everything prepared for the winter. Mr. Hillyer think is advisable to go & winter at the Capel [Qu'Ap-

---

1 Church Missionary Society Archives, University of Birmingham, Bundle C C1 I1 Individual Letter-books, J. Chapman to Charles Pratt, 8 October 1856 (hereinafter CMSA. Bundle C C1 I1).

2 CMS, A.100, Cowley Journal, 9 September 1871.

3 SAB, Vital Statistics, Gordon Reserve, Register of Marriages, no. 18, 1 October 1874.

4 CMSA Bundle G1 Ci/P1, "North West America Index, Precis Book vol. I, 1881–1889," no. 107, Archdeacon Cowley to CMS, 9 June 1883.

5 CMS, A.122, Abraham Cowley to Christopher C. Fenn, 6 August 1884.

6 CMS, A.86, Cowley Journal, 28 December 1853.

pelle] River ... I hope to return to Fort Pelly Indians."[1] On 2 September 1858, he mentioned yet another move: "The Bishop of Rupert's advised me to leave the Q'Appelle Mission & leave it Mr. J. Settee, & go to, Little Touchwood hills, which is, about seventy miles."[2] Even when he was well into his old age, the CMS required Charles Pratt to operate as an itinerant missionary. In 1875 Joseph Reader, Pratt's supervisor at Touchwood Hills, noted, "Charles Pratt is growing old and if he spends his strength as he has hitherto done he will soon be unfit for travelling."[3]

Given the strenuous conditions Pratt laboured under, it is no wonder he used a language which he believed would best mollify his superiors. In order to retain his position and keep his missions open, Pratt had to convince them he was doing things their way and that his people were receptive and responding to the Christian call.[4] His strategy was to employ a technique, aptly named by Gerald Berreman "impression management," to attempt to control the impression his readers developed about him and his work.[5] Charles Pratt wrote the way he did because he was under constant pressure to prove himself and gain approval.[6] Clearly, nimosôm Charles Pratt adopted a discourse that he believed would best satisfy superiors; but his journals contain more than sermons. A closer read indicates the presence of a number of subtexts or narratives, and a variety of literary strategies.

Recent postmodern historians like Hayden White have promoted taking a rhetorical approach to history, to consider the active role of language, texts, and narrative structures in the creation and description of historical reality.[7] White suggests that treating historical documents as

---

1   CMS, A.95, Pratt Journal, 21 October 1855.

2   CMS, A.95, Pratt Journal, 2 September 1858.

3   CMS, A.81, Reader to H. Wright, 22 January 1875.

4   Stevenson, "'Our Man in the Field,'" 74.

5   Gerald D. Berreman, *Behind Many Masks: Ethnography and Impression Management in a Himalayan Village* (New York: Society for Applied Anthropology, 1962), 1-5.

6   Berreman, *Behind Many Masks*, 1-5.

7   Hayden White, *The Content of the Form: Narrative Discourse and Historical Representation* (Baltimore, MD: Johns Hopkins University Press, 1987).

WINONA STEVENSON

literature and subjecting them to the same sort of literary analysis as fiction offers a new mode of analysis and insight.

This approach has been applied in a relatively new field of scholarly inquiry: literary studies of Native American autobiographies. Since the first Native writers were Christian converts, educated at mission schools, studies of these texts serve as useful models for the historical analysis of Pratt's writings. One of the leading scholars in this field is Arnold Krupat. Krupat expands on Penny Petrone's sermon genre in his discussion of the "salvationist discourse" which, he claims, pervaded missionary literature during the Great Awakening, from the mid-eighteenth to the early twentieth century. The salvationist discourse was noted for its "dialect of aggressive Protestantism." This salvationism, "illustrating God's plan and power," explained all human actions "in relation to God's will" and all events as mere "variants of Biblical origins."[1] According to Krupat, Native Christian converts, "defining themselves exclusively in relation to salvationist discourse," drew their sense of self "entirely from Christian culture"; in other words they traced their lineage through Biblical genealogies.[2] There is no doubt Charles Pratt traced his people's lineage back to Noah and the Biblical "lost tribes." HBC trader Isaac Cowie noted this fact in the 1870s and it is also evident in Pratt's 1851 conversion sermon to the Saulteaux Medicine Man Chawa-cis (see appendix).[3] Clearly, Pratt's journals are vivid examples of salvationist discourse which demonstrate that he did derive a certain "sense of self" from Christian culture. However, Pratt's voice is not monoglossic; although the salvationist discourse is the most pervasive in his journals, a closer reading unearths other less apparent voices.

Mikhail Bakhtin asserts that the language of any speaker is never exclusively his or her own but is "heteroglossic and polyvocal." Likewise, the speech of every individual is enabled by and infused with the speech

---

1 Arnold Krupat, *The Voice in the Margin: Native American Literature and the Canon* (Berkeley: University of California Press, 1989), 142, 144.

2 Krupat, *The Voice in the Margin*, 147, 145.

3 Isaac Cowie, *Company of Adventurers, A Narrative of Seven Years in the Service of the Hudson's Bay Company During 1867-1874* (Toronto: William Briggs, 1913), 235; Stevenson, "'Our Man in the Field,'" 71.

of others — it is a plural construct.[1] Arnold Krupat adds, "Speech is social and meaning is open and in flux, inevitably a dialogue among speakers, not the property or in the power of any single speaker."[2] According to Krupat, this is especially true of American Indian autobiographies, which, he claims, are "dialogic models of the self" because the autobiographer "generates a textual self that is in greater or lesser degree inevitably dialogic."[3] This "textual self," Krupat explains, "derives from a prior actual or biographical self" which "in its historical formation, is collectively rather than individualistically constituted."[4] Thus, Native American autobiographies are the "textual result of specific dialogues (between persons, between cultures, between persons and cultures)." The Indian subject, then, "is the human result of specific dialogical or collective sociocultural practices."[5] When Pratt's journals are viewed in this framework it is evident that his "textual selves" are the historical products of the many dialogues surrounding him as well as his own bi-cultural experiences[6] as a nehiyopwat and CMS catechist.

Charles Pratt's texts were heteroglossic because they consciously or unconsciously included the voices of missionaries, Cree hunters, HBC traders, starving widows, scarlet fever survivors, and his family, as well as giving voice to his own various roles — the catechist, the hunter, the family man, the nehiyopwat. Because his intended readers were CMS missionaries, the sermon (the missionary voice) pervaded. However, all these voices, and probably more, influenced him and found their way into his journals.

Although Pratt's other voices are difficult to discern — blanketed as they are by his salvationist discourse — they can be found. David Murray, another critic of Native literature, claims that the way in which Native

---

1 Mikhail Bakhtin, cited in Krupat, *The Voice in the Margin*, 135, and Arnold Krupat, *Ethnocriticism: Ethnography, History, Literature* (Berkeley: University of California Press, 1992), 18.

2 Krupat, *The Voice in the Margin*, 136.

3 Krupat, *The Voice in the Margin*, 133, 133–34.

4 Krupat, *The Voice in the Margin*, 134.

5 Krupat, *The Voice in the Margin*, 134.

6 Krupat, *The Voice in the Margin*, 133, 141.

WINONA STEVENSON

writers "represented themselves to *whites*" can help us to understand how Christian Indians thought of themselves and their actions.[1] According to Murray, Native missionaries employed a variety of genres or literary strategies which articulated the historically determined "perceptions of their own inferiority and the injustices done to them."[2] The two genres most prevalent in Pratt's writing were the complaint and the theme of the "poor Indian."

The "poor Indian" was a central motif in Native literature while Pratt was writing.[3] His journals are rife with accounts of his people as heathens, backward, starving, and dying and he painted a grim picture of their spiritual and material condition: "I trust through the mercy of our God, for his son sake he will visit the poor heathen with the message of salvation to my poor parishing countrymen."[4] In most instances, however, Pratt identified with the "poor Indian," a clear instance where his heteroglossia was operative. His personal identification served as a strategy that not only described his actual condition but also had the effect of "mounting a criticism"[5] against his CMS superiors for that condition. Murray suggests that by identifying with the subjects — "the poor Indian" — Native missionaries such as Samson Occum of the Mohegan tribe in New England turned the phrase "poor Indian" "from a term of self-derogation almost into an expression of solidarity."[6] Despite his relatively weak command over the English language, Pratt also made strategic use of irony and metaphor to add an extra punch. For example, on 21 September 1856 Pratt wrote:

21st The Lords day, Thank be to I am enjoying another sabbath day ... *while our bodies are falling away, for want of food, I trust he is feeding our souls*

---

1 David Murray, *Forked Tongues: Speech, Writing and Representation in North American Indian Texts* (Bloomington: Indiana University Press, 1992), 53.

2 Murray, *Forked Tongues*, 52.

3 Petrone, *Native Literature*, 69.

4 CMS, A.95, Pratt Journal, 1 January 1857.

5 Murray, *Forked Tongues*, 54.

6 Murray, *Forked Tongues*, 54.

with that bread of life which if a man eat thereof he shall live for ever, O may he ever more give us that bread (emphasis added).[1]

On 7 March 1869 at Mission Lake: "Indeed I may say, with sorrow that after I ommit family prayers at night after a hard days toile, *for want of a candle or lamp.* O may the Lord Jesus have pity on my weakness that *the true light may shine more & more into the perfect day*" (emphasis added).[2] And, a few weeks later he wrote,

> I was almost unable to proceed with my usual ... work, *for in want of shoes for my feet.* I am so reduced for want of better, praised to be to our heavenly father.... I believe his, his the kingdom, the power & the glory, until *he shall put all his enemies under his feet* (emphasis added).[3]

The above excerpts also demonstrate Pratt's use of a genre, which Murray describes as "part aggressive, part conciliatory and submissive,... [a] mixture of complaint and accusation" against his CMS superiors; he invoked "God to criticize those acting in his name."[4] To paraphrase Murray's analysis of the Pequot missionary William Apes, Pratt used "Christianity as his club" to beat his European overlords.[5] I would conjecture that Charles Pratt employed this strategy, in part, to protest his subordinate treatment by the CMS — the fact that he received one-third to one-half the salary of his European counterparts would be enough in itself to cause bitterness and resentment.[6] The personal humiliation of his poverty — no candles, shoes, or food — and the condescending attitudes of his superiors also must have been very difficult to endure. By strategically couching his humiliation in metaphor he covertly chastised the CMS. But sometimes he took a more direct approach, as in July 1877:

---

1   CMS, A.95 Pratt Journal, 21 September 1856.

2   CMS, A.81, Pratt Journal, 7 March 1869.

3   CMS, A.81, Pratt Journal, 21 March 1869.

4   Murray, *Forked Tongues*, 57, 63.

5   Murray, *Forked Tongues*, 63.

6   CMS, A.86 Abraham Cowley Report, 30 September 1874; and CMS, A.99, Bishop of Rupert's Land to Christopher C. Fenn, 17 December 1870.

Many thoughts arose in my breast today. I thank & praise the Lord, I can say, I am not ashamed of the gospel of Christ, but I really feel half ashamed to be amongst people for I & my little boys are naked nothing our have naked bodies I have never felt so in all my journies through life.[1]

Two narratives that are prevalent in other Native missionary texts never appeared in Pratt's journals – the "confessional" and the cultural critique. According to Murray, the "confessional" is the personal account of conversion, lapses and tribulations, and finally, being "rescued from rum and degradation by Christianity."[2] At no point in his journals did Pratt describe such personal experiences nor did he discuss any lapses or personal weaknesses. The only conversion stories he told were those of his converts. Why he never recorded any deeply personal religious experiences is difficult to determine. Perhaps he never had a lapse or personal tribulation of a religious character; or if he did, perhaps he refused to give his CMS superiors the satisfaction they would have derived from his admission, given the stereotypical attitudes of the time.

Descriptions and explanations of traditional religious beliefs are also missing from Pratt's journals. In fact, Pratt never attempted to explain any local Saulteaux or Cree traditions. Rather, he wrote of events, alluding to them as if he assumed that his readers had some understanding or prior knowledge of their meanings. For example, when Pratt described his encounter with Cha-wa-cis in 1851, he simply wrote, "I paid a visit to the old man, with a piece of tobacco, & had a long discourse with them."[3] The significance of the tobacco would only be known by people familiar with the customs of Cha-wa-cis's people. Later, in January 1872, he mentioned that the Blackfoot or Piegan people "sent seven white bladder of tabacoe of peace" to the tribes of the Saskatchewan with the message that "whoever would do evil & break the peace" faced penalty of death.[4] Again, he appeared to assume his readers would be aware of the significance of this action. Perhaps his readers did know, or

---

1   CMS, A.104, Pratt Journal, 7 July 1877.

2   Murray, Forked Tongues, 57.

3   CMS, A.95, Pratt Journal, 13 August 1851.

4   CMS, A.99, Pratt Journal, 15 January 1872.

perhaps Pratt was so entrenched in Cree thought that the probable ignorance of his readers simply slipped his mind.

Also unlike his contemporaries, Charles Pratt seldom condemned his people's religious practices. Although he freely referred to them as "heathen" and "pagan" he gave few details of their religious practices and only recorded one zealous outburst against paganism, or more precisely, against a stone image.[1]

One could conjecture that Pratt's non-fulfilment of some of the stereotypes held by his European superiors and peers was a subtle act of resistance. Clearly, his refusal to conduct himself and his mission according to standards prescribed by his superiors was as much an act of resistance as it was personal inclination. The same can also be said about his covert criticisms of the CMS for his poverty and lack of support. What emerges in Pratt's journals is what James C. Scott describes as a "hidden transcript" consisting of "a bewildering array of resistance and compliance."[2] The "subtle mixture of outward compliance and tentative resistance" in Pratt's writings stems from a much more complex discourse inherent in the colonial conditions of his life. Although Pratt could be charged with collaborating with colonial agencies in his role as a catechist, the "tentative resistance" of his writings and his often non-compliant actions indicate that he did not entirely buy into the colonialist ideology. He used his position in the colonial institution because it offered him the best opportunity to help his people adjust to changing conditions.[3] And since he was a part of the Anglican Church, the forms his resistance could take were naturally set by its parameters. According to

---

1 "[T]raveling through lofty hills, I spied an Image of stone on an high hills to this I ascended on horse back to see the Image. My heart mourned within me to think of the Kingdom of darkness reigning over this vast empire. I prayed that the Lord Jesus may be exalted upon this hills I call'd to mind of the stones which the deceiver of mankind used to tempt our Lord, I then lifted the head of the Image which was painted red, threw down the hill. with the expression, [']Art thou, who hast reduced my countrymen.['] such were my thoughts this days travel." CMS, A.95, Pratt Journal, 11 September 1858.

2 James C. Scott, *Weapons of the Weak: Everyday Forms of Peasant Resistance* (New Haven, CT: Yale University Press, 1985), 289.

3 Stevenson, "'Our Man in the Field,'" 73–75.

James C. Scott, "symbolic compliance is maximized precisely in order to minimize compliance at the level of actual behavior."[1]

To what degree did Pratt actually *intend* his writings to be more than records of his activities? Pratt himself is silent on this point. The only clue he gives about the content and form he selected for his journals comes from a passage dated 31 January 1860:

> I am still very busy preparing my letters & journal. I have copied this journal, sent it to the Bishop of Rupertsland, in Red River. I hope to be excused, making so many mistakes, in my writing. I am writing in haste, because starvation is approaching near us, & I must endeavour to — make a journey to the plains amongst the cree Indian camps, for provisions. I would write but a [...] more, there is but little in this imperfect journal, to seed what is down here in this journal, is sketches of my work & troubles. I write least as possible not to deceive God or man, & yet my judgment is with the Lord and my word with my God.[2]

James C. Scott claims that such relative silence as Pratt's is not uncommon. Many forms of resistance require the actors to remain mute about their intentions because the kind of resistance they engage in may depend for its effectiveness on the appearance of conformity.[3] As already demonstrated, Pratt's focus on his "work & troubles" constituted literary techniques that criticized the attitudes and policies of the CMS. Of tantamount concern to Pratt was his inability to meet the daily needs of his family and the lack of support he could offer his people. According to Scott, intentions are nearly always founded and manifested in survival and persistence, and are inscribed in the acts themselves. A CMS Native catechist who shared his provisions with the people around him, directly against his superior's dictates, was "saying" by his actions that his and his people's need for food, and his need to follow Cree protocol, took precedence over CMS policy. Likewise, a CMS Native catechist who lived by hunting buffalo, fishing, and trapping rather than establishing

---

1 Scott, *Weapons*, 26.

2 CMS, A.95, Pratt Journal, 31 January 1860.

3 Scott, *Weapons*, 301.

sedentary farming missions was "saying" that his and his people's survival took precedence over the ideals and policies of the CMS.

The foregoing analysis of Charles Pratt's journals is not one that conventional historical methods alone could produce. Oral history opened the way to a new line of rigorous questioning that challenged the written word in ways most historians are unfamiliar with. As Julie Cruikshank observes in chapter 18 of this volume, an awareness of the spoken word leads "to more cautious handling of written sources." Based on her work among Yukon Aboriginal Elders over the past two decades, Cruikshank has found that using both kinds of sources, written and oral, does not necessarily offer a synthesis or the "real story." Rather, she claims, both serve to open windows on the past as constructed "in different contexts, from the perspectives of actors enmeshed in culturally distinct networks of social relationships." In contrasting Native and Euro-Canadian memories and narratives of Skookum Jim and the Klondike gold rush, she points out that the issue is less one of straightening out facts than of identifying how much distinct cognitive models may generate different kinds of social analysis, leading to different interpretations of a given event, one of which is included in official history, while the other is relegated to collective memory.[1]

That Charles Pratt left two sets of historical records, one to his CMS superiors in the form of his mission journals, and one to descendants in the form of oral history, allows far more insight into the parallel worlds in which he lived and died. The intent of Askenootow's journals was to convince his superiors that the mission field was ripe and that he was conducting his work according to their standards and desires. In so doing he represented himself as approaching as closely as possible to the ideal missionary. His journals were filled with salvationist discourses, denigrations of his own people, and subservient, even servile, self-abasement. However, careful analysis reveals wisps of another, less evident personality, one which is closer in substance to the man represented in the collective memory of his descendants. The grandfather I grew up hearing stories about inscribed himself in his texts through a variety of narratives and literary strategies. My task, as a granddaughter and a student, was to take direction from preceding generations and to take full advantage of the scholarly tools available to locate him in his text. In

---

1   Julie Cruikshank, "Discovery of Gold on the Klondike: Perspectives from Oral Tradition" (ch. 18, this volume).

many ways this has been a cyclical journey — I ended up about where I began. Charles Pratt was a generous, selfless, feisty, and proud man who used his position in the CMS to help his people adjust to dramatically changing conditions in their world. But I knew that already, because nimosôm Colin Pratt told me.

Appendix

Charles Pratt, CMS catechist meets Cha-wa-cis, Saulteaux Medicine Man, Fort Pelly, July 1851[1]

12th Tuesday morning. Getting home our house wood. At even[ing] Indians from the plain arrived here — a principal man, by named Cha-wa-cis, with a few Indians with him, but no sermon they came, they received rum from the master of the fort & made them all drunk all night both men and women. The said old man came to my tent at night encompanied by his young man with his great conjuring articles in his hand, quite displeased with me forbided me to build home. He told me the following words — "Who told you to come here. I never told you to come & build on my lands, go back go back, from whence you came, & do not pressure further to build, & if you still build you shall find the dread of me so long as I here. you shall not be safe go back & build on you own land." I told him, "there was but little wood on my land to build but if you wish me to build on my own country I shall build in the middle of your territories." he sat studying a while & them asked me "do you pray." I replied "yes my friend I do pray to the almighty God our heavenly father who made heaven & earth & all things that are there." He answered with a high tone "I dont pray. God tells me all the praying go to the devil & as for me & my children we will not pray." I told him "let me speak my turn, my friend. The God that told you to hate prayer, is the devil, who even how means to destroy mens souls to everlasting fire. & now I will tell you god tells me, who is the God of gods & a Lord of Lords — who created the heaven & the earth by his words & in whose hands our life & breath depends. God tells me that you & me & every body must pray to him through his son Jesus Christ with all our hearts" I told him further. "The Great God said that the wicked shall be turned to

---

1   CMS, A.95, Pratt Journal, 12–14 July 1851. The quotation marks around direct quotations in the following passages have been added.

hell with all the nations that forget God! Think around my friend, how much all our country-men are passing their lives living without God & without hope in the world." He still ... threatened me closely, when an indian came in & siezed him by the right arm & led him out. I scarce had my sleep this night for he came a second time & began to me again, but some other indian came in & led him out, so he did not come again.

13th Wednesday morning. I paid a visit to the old man, with a piece of tobacco, & had a long discourse with them, he seemed very sorry for what he had said to me last night, not knowing that I was one of his country-men, at even[ing] he came with another indian to my tent, after supper ended I took the Great Bible, the Old & New Testaments, the present I received from Mr. Coleman, holding the two volumes in my hand I told them to look at these great books of wisdom & knowledge in thence their lies the unreachable riches of Christ the Everlasting father offered to all man-kind of every tribe through the whole world around. they made deep sighs. I told them "I suppose you wonder to see such books you have seen the outside of them & now I will tell you some-thing of the inside." I began to read the 1st Chap of Gen[esis] Telling them In the beginning God created all things in heaven & earth. by the wand of his almighty power in six days & all very good. & on the sev-enth day to be keept holy unto God through-out all generations telling them how God has formed man out of the dust of the ground & breath-ing into his nostrils the breath of life & man became a living soul. I told them repeating the prophets & good men of old spoke as they moved by the holy ghost fore telling of things to come, & for all this people still went on sinning the sting of death prevailing amongst mankind till they filled the measure of the unequity. God could not bear longer with their sort a great flood of waters up on the face of the earth to destroy them. save one good man [h]is wife & three sons & daughter in law these that were righteous & obeyed God commands were saved & of clean beast by seven, of unclean beasts by two kept alive in the ark remained their, till God removed the waters from the face of the earth, & so these came forth of the ark with all their creatures. from these three sons of Noah. Shem. Ham. & Japheth, was the ... of the nation to their present time. I showed them of the distinguishing characteristics of the three sons of Noah, The one of them was a man & his descendents after him, the sec-ond did not think so much of God or his souls as much as making instru-ments of music. *The third son thought less of God & of his soul wandered from*

God land & was left to himself & was lost to the present time & we are his
offspring I here we are still lost. Thanks be to God for his unspeakable gift. Who
has found out away to redeem us back into himself, though the offering up of his
son to die for us that he might deliver us from the curse of the law [emphasis
added]. The wrath of God that was upon us, Jesus Christ hath taken
away upon himself by his dying for us. but he did not die long death
could not confine him in his grave nolonger than a part of three days &
three nights, he burst the tomb layed his grave-clothes aside & rose from
the dead like a triumphant conquerer. He was of a great people after his
resurrection, Instruction to his people telling them "Go ye therefore &
teach all nations baptizing them in the name of the father & of the son &
of the holy ghost, teaching them to observe all things whatever I have
command you, & lo I am with you always even unto the end of the
world. Amen." Then he ascended up into heaven where he was before,
be now this present moment he siteth on the righ hand of God – making
continuall intercession for us. He is ever holding out his hands unto us
telling us to come unto him that we might have life. O let us not delay
or neglect his offers of mercy we are the people for whom he came to
seek & to save, we cannot get to God without him, for his word says
NO man can come to the father but by me. Even if we come to God it
must be through his son no other way. For there is no other name under
heaven given amongst men whereby we can be saved but through Jesus
Christ, he is the way the truth & the life. We must served God in spirit
& truth for such he seeketh to be worshipped, O let us then with one
heart & voice cry mightly [sic] unto God that [we] may obtain mercy &
find grace to help in time of need. I proceeded further that all that are in
the graves shall rise again at the last day to appear before this Great God,
that we have so long neglected & will every one according as is work
have has ... those that have obeyed God laws to the ressurection of life.
& those that have done evil & disobeyed the commands of the most high
shall be thrust out from the presence of God & from his holy angels. To
dwell with the devil & all bad spirits. Were the soul dieth not & the fore
shall never be quenched. My dear friends do not let these words sound
in your ears as an idle tale, they are the words of the everlasting God,
who continually watches over people what heed they to his word you
must understand that God have his word to us as well as to the white-
man. otherwise we should have never it. Thanks be to God we now
hear it. we indeed ought to be truly thankful seeing & hearing the things
that Kings prophets, & wise men of old have denied to see the things

that we see & have not seen them & hearing things, that we hear & have not heard Them. We then see that God has mercy upon us. O let us not cast his word behind our back to trample under foot what the good men of old have wished for. They saw it but afar off & counted themselves pilgrims & strangers in the earth. If we do not take heed to the word of the living God, it will ... unto us Instead of a blessing.

14th Thursday. At our usual occupation. the plains Indians their returning back to the plains the old man went off quite pleased. he told me to build on & try to get the house up. Do not be afraid there will be no danger.

References

Berreman, Gerald. *Behind Many Masks: Ethnography and Impression Management in a Himalayan Village.* New York: Society for Applied Anthropology, 1962.

Carter, Sarah. 'The Missionaries' Indian': The Publications of John McDougall, John McLean and Egerton Ryerson Young. *Prairie Forum* 9, 1, 1984, 27-44.

Church Missionary Society Archives, University of Birmingham, Bundles Numbered C C1 I1 (Individual Letter-books) and G1 Ci/P1 (North West American Index, Precis Book 1).

Freire, Paulo. *Pedagogy of the Oppressed.* New York: Continuum Publishing reprint, 1988.

Krupat, Arnold. *The Voice in the Margin: Native American Literature and the Canon.* Berkeley: University of California Press, 1989.

——. *Ethnocriticism: Ethnography, History, Literature.* Berkeley: University of California Press, 1992.

Murray, David. *Forked Tongues: Speech, Writing & Representation in North American Indian Texts.* Bloomington: Indiana University Press, 1992.

National Archives of Canada, Church Missionary Society Microfilm, reel nos. A.81, A.86, A.89, A.95, A.96, A.99, A.100, A.112.

Petrone, Penny. *Native Literature in Canada: From the Oral Tradition to the Present.* Toronto: University of Toronto Press, 1990.

Pettipas, Katherine. *The Diaries of the Reverend Henry Budd, 1870-1875.* vol. 4. Manitoba Record Society. Winnipeg. 1974.

Saskatchewan Archives Board, University of Regina, Collection R, Vital Statistics Register 106, Gordon's Indian Reserve.

Scott, James C. *Weapons of the Weak: Everyday Forms of Peasant Resistance*. New Haven, CT: Yale University Press, 1985.

Stevenson, Winona L. "Our Man in the Field": The Status and Role of a CMS Native Catechist in Rupert's Land. *Journal of the Canadian Church Historical Society* 33, 1, 1991, 65-78.

White, Hayden. *The Content of the Form: Narrative Discourse and Historical Representation*. Baltimore, MD: Johns Hopkins University Press, 1987.

Zahar, Renate. *Frantz Fanon: Colonialism and Alienation*. New York: Monthly Review Press, 1974.

14

Fair Wind's Dream: Naamiwan Obawaajigewin

Maureen Matthews and Roger Roulette

IN THE SUMMER of 1933, A. Irving Hallowell, an American anthropologist, made his first visit to the Ojibwe[1] community of Pauingassi, Manitoba. At the time Pauingassi was a small summer fishing settlement on the upper Berens River. Most importantly it was the home of Naamiwan (Fair Wind), a famous medicine man, and his family. Hallowell was drawn to this community by the reputation of its residents. His friend and collaborator, Chief William Berens, told Hallowell that the people who lived up the Berens River were more traditional – "the real Indians," as Berens's son Percy put it, less influenced by Christianity and, from Hallowell's anthropological point of view, less acculturated than the Cree he had met in northern Manitoba.[2]

Naamiwan's Pauingassi was a kind of Ojibwe Mayo Clinic. On a high grassy hill overlooking a strategic narrows in Fishing Lake just north of Little Grand Rapids, he built two large pavilions and a sweat lodge. Here he conducted a variety of ceremonies including the *Waabanowin*.[3] People

---

1   We have chosen the word Ojibwe to identify these people because this is how they speak of themselves to other people. Many contemporary Ojibwe think this name originated with their distinctive moccasins which had a small vamp and tightly gathered sole (*ojibwaawan makizinan* "puckered moccasins"). In their language the Ojibwe people refer to themselves as *Anishinaabe(g)*. Hallowell often used the term Saulteaux, a common Manitoba usage recalling the first French encounters with Ojibwe people around the rapids of Sault Ste. Marie, Ontario in the 1600s. Hallowell (d. 1974) was a professor of anthropology at the University of Pennsylvania for many years.

2   A.I. Hallowell, *The Ojibwa of Berens River, Manitoba: Ethnography into History*, ed. Jennifer S.H. Brown (Fort Worth, TX: Harcourt Brace Jovanovich, 1992) and Percy Berens in "The Search for Fair Wind's Drum" (CBC Radio, *Ideas*, Toronto, 1993) transcript, 2.

3   *Waabano* means "what is represented by the east" and the word is sometimes used to refer to dawn. This dance was performed throughout the night and lasted until dawn. It was held in the spring and summer to celebrate rebirth and revitalization or healing. The Ojibwe of 60 years ago celebrated either the Sun Dance or the *Waabano* and the dividing line is roughly between plains and forest. The Ojibwe word for Sun Dance is *Niibaagweshimowin* (during the night dance) and the main difference

came to him from miles away because of his reputation as a healer. About 1914, Naamiwan's power was augmented by a vision which gave him the right to create an innovative dream drum ceremony. The ceremony introduced to Pauingassi by Naamiwan had a Minnesota history.[1] The dream drum dance originated in the 1870s with the vision of Tail Feather Woman, a Sioux who dreamed about a drum which would bring peace between the Sioux and the Ojibwe and protect them both from white soldiers. The original "Squaw Drum" was given to an Ojibwe group in Minnesota and it was supposed to travel. A new drum was to be built every four years and the songs and the dance were to be passed on to others. In less than 35 years the dream dance *(Boodaade)*[2] had become a part of Naamiwan's powerful practice.[3] By the time Hallowell and Chief Berens visited him, Naamiwan's reputation had been cemented by miraculous cures he was able to accomplish with his dream drum, including his apparent success in stopping the deadly progress of the 1918 influenza epidemic.[4] By 1933, Naamiwan was in his eighties. He was blind, but still an imposing figure, very much in charge of the ceremonies he had been given the right to conduct.

---

between the ceremonies seems to be that the *Waabano* incorporates a giveaway element and the *Niibaagweshimowin* doesn't. On the occasion when Hallowell recorded the dream dance, it followed a three-day *Waabano* ceremony.

1 Thomas Vennum, Jr., *The Ojibwa Dream Dance Drum: Its History and Construction* (Washington: Smithsonian Institution, 1982) 44, 70.

2 *Boodaade* means "something is blown" and refers to the gift of or the breath of life. *Boodaajigan* is a small flute which was used in the ceremony to indicate when a giveaway was to take place and whose turn it was. *Boodaade (potáte* in Hallowell) was the local word for the dream dance.

3 The first dream dance drum was sold to someone in Little Grand Rapids in 1910. Hallowell mentioned in his field notes that the people paid $100, and named the man who sold it. Four years later Naamiwan had his dream. Sometime later Naamiwan sold the first drum to his nephews in Poplar Hill, Ontario and constructed a second. There were at least four dream dance drums in Little Grand Rapids and one, named *"Niinimoshe"* or Sweetheart, in Pikangikum.

4 Jacob Owen, in "The Search for Fair Wind's Drum" (CBC Radio, *Ideas*, 1993) transcript, 19; Ann D. Herring, "There Were Young People and Old People and Babies Dying Every Week: The 1918-1919 Influenza Pandemic at Norway House," *Ethnohistory*, 41 (1) (1994), 73.

Figure 1: Naamiwan (Fair Wind) and his wife Koowin in front of his large Waabano pavilion at Pauingassi, Manitoba. This photograph was taken by A. Irving Hallowell in the mid-1930s. Zaagajiwe (Charlie Moose Owen) stands behind Naamiwan; and his younger brother Joseph Owen sits with them. In the pavilion are Omishoosh (Charlie George Owen), a grandson, Naamiwan's eldest son, Aangish (Angus Owen), and Naamiwan's youngest son Wejaanimaash.

MAUREEN MATTHEWS AND ROGER ROULETTE

While Hallowell and Berens were in Pauingassi that summer, Naami-wan conducted a drum dance which Hallowell considered unique. When Hallowell wrote about this ceremony in 1940, he focused on the feature of Naamiwan's dance which impressed him most, the fact that Naamiwan's drum became an active medium between the living and the *(d)jiibayag,*[1] or spirits of the dead.[2]

Hallowell's description of the ceremony became important when we made a radio program about another drum, very beautifully decorated, which Hallowell had photographed in the community of Poplar Hill (*Azaadiikaang*), farther up the river in northwestern Ontario.[3] The story of these drums emerged as we put together the memories of people on the river and Hallowell's careful yet tantalizingly brief description of the ceremony. Hallowell never described either drum or connected them to the Minnesota dream dance, but his detailed account in "Spirits of the Dead" opened a window on Fair Wind and a rich religious tradition. His photographs, most of them maddeningly unlabelled, eventually gave us an entrée into the communities where Naamiwan, Hallowell, and Chief William Berens are all vividly remembered.[4] When we showed the pictures of the elaborately decorated drum to current residents of Poplar Hill, they recalled the story of the vision by which Naamiwan received his drum. These people still revere the dreamer, Naamiwan.

---

1   A. Irving Hallowell, "Spirits of the Dead in Saulteaux Life and Thought," *Journal of the Royal Anthropological Institute* 70 (1940), 29–51. Reprinted in *Culture and Experience* (Philadelphia: University of Pennsylvania Press, 1955), 151–71. Hallowell rendered this term *djibaiyak*. Contemporary linguists tend to use *j* to indicate a collapsed *dj* sound but the elders we spoke to in Pauingassi separate these two consonants, so we've used a *dj*, as Hallowell did, to more accurately render their way of speaking.

2   When Hallowell saw a dream dance conducted in a nearby community by Kiwitc, he mentioned Naamiwan's drum and its role as a medium. Kiwitc said, "I have not gone *that* far" (Hallowell, "Spirits of the Dead," 165).

3   "The Search for Fair Wind's Drum" aired in May 1993 on the CBC Radio program *Ideas*. An Ojibwe version of the show, "*Naamiwan Odewe'iganan,*" aired on CBQ Thunder Bay in November 1993. The shows were made by Maureen Matthews, assisted by Jennifer Brown and Roger Roulette.

4   In Poplar Hill, Hallowell is still called *Aadizookewinini* (Story man); in Pauingassi he is called *Midewigimaa* (Mide chief) because of his interest in learning about the Midewiwin.

When they say his name, they linger over the long vowels, fondly recalling the old man and his gifts.[1]

It was in the summer of 1933 that Hallowell and Chief William Berens created their invaluable firsthand record of Naamiwan's dream. Hallowell incorporated the account in a 1940 article on the spirits of the dead. The *Boodaade* ceremony was presented as an unusual instance of Ojibwe conversations with the *(d)jiibayag*, but because of Hallowell's careful attention to ethnographic details, the text, which he wrote as anthropology, now has great historic value. It helped us initiate and understand the significance of our conversation with Charlie George Owen, the grandson and religious heir of Naamiwan, who ultimately told us five versions of the same dream. More than 60 years later, we have been able to piece together a fascinating story that Hallowell and Chief Berens only partly understood.[2]

Looking at Hallowell's text critically, in the rich context provided by the memories of the people of Pauingassi and Poplar Hill, we are able to do several things. We can assess the accuracy of Berens's and Hallowell's ethnographic observations and their representation of Ojibwe philosophy by comparing them with contemporary explanations provided by Naamiwan's descendants, most of whom are unilingual Ojibwe speakers. We can also compare the persistence and accuracy of Ojibwe memories with a text which is more than 60 years old. Finally, we can add contexts provided by other sources – linguistic, historical, and anthropological – to help complete a picture which neither Hallowell, Chief Berens, nor the people on the river would have been able to draw.

Hallowell began to draw his picture of the dream dance by describing the structure *(boodaadewigamig)* in which the ceremony took place: "a circular structure made of poles, which has four doors, facing north,

---

1   In Ojibwe one usually attaches the suffix *-ban* to the name of a deceased person; when we die, we will be Maureeniban and Rogeriban. However, some people were so powerful in life that linguistically they are treated as if they are still alive. Naamiwan is one such person; no one we spoke to used the term *Naamiwaniban* although he has been dead since 1944. This suffix has turned out to be a useful marker in tracing others with powers like Naamiwan's and in identifying men from other communities who conducted dream dances of their own. These powerful men are not lurking about to be feared; rather their accomplishments in life were such that they live on through the "life" *(bimaadiziwin)* they gave to others.

2   Jennifer Brown with Maureen Matthews, "Fair Wind: Medicine and Consolation on the Berens River," *Journal of the Canadian Historical Association* 4 (1994), 55–74.

south, east, and west. The northern door is used as entrance."[1] The photographs he took in 1932 of a dream dance pavilion in Poplar Hill show a circular structure like an inverted open-work basket, nearly 20 feet high and 30 feet around, with a spotless brushed sand floor and a round hole at the peak. This gap in the top of the pavilion was the opening for spirit beings (*aadizookaanag*[2]), who were either the dream helpers (*bawaaganag*) of the leaders of the ceremony or those specially summoned to participate in the event.[3]

It was a cloudy, windy afternoon when Naamiwan conducted his dream dance. Hallowell must have been sitting, taking notes near the perimeter wall of the pavilion with William Berens at his side, translating as they watched. It is crucial to remember that these events took place in Ojibwe. Hallowell depended utterly on William Berens for his understanding of everything he heard. In this productive collaboration, Chief Berens was bringing to bear his considerable linguistic talents, his

---

1   Hallowell, "Spirits of the Dead," 165. Hallowell's observation about the doors is interesting. Contemporary Ojibwe *Midewiwin* pavilions have only two doors — east and west — and strict rules about entering only from the east and departing only through the western door. The eastern door is apparently symbolic of renewal and the western door represents endings — of days, lives. One is thought to go in a western direction when one dies. On the Berens River in the 1930s the people spoke of the land of the dead (*oniboog gaa-ayaawaad*) being in the south so there may be some difference in directional symbolism.

2   *Aadizookaanag* (*ätsokának* in Hallowell) is the general term for divine beings or those who have qualities of divinity, including the animal spirits, and for the mythic characters of the winter legends. It is possible for a person, given a remarkable life and the passage of time, to become one of the *aadizookaanag*, or "Our Grandfathers," as Hallowell glossed the term. *Bawaaganag* (*pawáganak* in Hallowell) are divine beings who identified themselves as a guide in a person's life.

3   A *bawaagan* visited a person during a fast or dream to give particular gifts. All people have a *bawaagan* but only those who sacrifice and fast are likely to be given gifts by their helpers. These are mostly men, willing to give up something important in order to hunt successfully or heal people. Most men feel they have to acquire a guide if they want to assure the health and safety of their families. Women are not as likely to fast in order to receive a gift partly because one has to pay dearly for gifts and one is sometimes expected to sacrifice the health of children one might have. Jacob Owen, Naamiwan's grand-nephew, learned that he would be very powerful but that this power would come at a high cost; he would never have any children. This was one of the factors in his becoming a Christian. It enabled him to escape the obligations of his vision and have a family. Naamiwan's son Angus and his wife had no children and the people in Pauingassi would have understood this to be the price he paid for his great powers.

knowledge of Ojibwe philosophy, and his prestige as a visiting chief. This is how Berens and Hallowell related the beginning of the ceremony:

> The dance was opened by old Fair Wind, who with lighted pipe in hand (the stem pointing toward the drum) and his hat off, made some opening remarks. Then he circled the pavilion, took his place and smoked for a while.[1] Before the actual drumming started he made a speech, in a voice which expressed deep feeling, and was punctuated by many gestures. The gist of it was an explanation of how he had obtained the dance.[2]

It may seem surprising that Naamiwan would reveal the details of his dream publicly and, in particular, reveal them to a visiting anthropologist. Ojibwe dreams involving *bawaaganag* or dream helpers are usually secret; the gifts are personal and to reveal them would rob the recipient of acquired powers. But Naamiwan's gift was different in that it involved the entire community; the dream was meant to be shared with those who would benefit. Interested community members participated in the construction of the drum, the pavilion, and in the dance. They built the drum, made the women's dance capes and other regalia that Naamiwan envisioned, and they learned the songs associated with the ceremony. Ultimately his power and prestige were enhanced by sharing the vision, the drum, and the ceremony with many others including Hallowell.[3] And just as Naamiwan evidently had no inhibitions about revealing his dream, his descendants were equally willing to tell us. It was the only way they could explain their reverence for the drum in which we were so interested. Nevertheless, certain details were guarded in Naamiwan's and other tellings of the dream. He never named the giver of the gift, for instance. The identity of the giver was not meant to be a complete secret, however, and oblique references could be found by an attentive listener.

---

1   The smudge (*wiingashkosige[win]*) which is typically done before a ceremony is meant to keep out the negative spirit beings — the ones who could create havoc in the ceremony, while welcoming the positive spirit beings.

2   Hallowell, "Spirits of the Dead," 165-66.

3   St. John Owen, told to Roger Roulette, September 1994.

MAUREEN MATTHEWS AND ROGER ROULETTE

Naamiwan's preliminary smoke was typical of ceremonial performances. It marked out the space into which the spirit beings were invited.[1] To an Ojibwe speaker like Naamiwan, the tobacco (*asemaa*) and the pipe (*opwaagan*) would be categorically alive. They actively play a ceremonial role and are linguistically animate, while the smoke (*bate[wan]*) is a decidedly separate entity and is not animate. Ojibwe grammar has two genders, animate and inanimate. Animacy has to do with free will and the autonomy to initiate action, and while tobacco is thought to have this capacity, smoke is just a messenger. Animacy is a floating category, partly related to the nature of the object or being, and partly related to the context of the action being described. For instance, a person, who is almost invariably animate, may be jokingly spoken of by others as grammatically inanimate when his actions are beyond his own control and he is not apparently accountable. In any case, when the smoke drifts up and disappears it is thought to have crossed the barrier between planes of existence, whereupon the spirits receive it as a formal invitation to attend the ceremony.[2] Naamiwan was very bold to have invited the spirits at the outset of the ceremony and then to tell his dream to the people when the spirits were already in attendance. Most would do it the other way around, waiting until the crowd was prepared before making an invitation to the spirits.

After describing the preamble, Hallowell quoted William Berens's translation of Naamiwan's dream. Naamiwan started by remembering emotions of grief and desperation, a state of being which, while deeply felt and very unwelcome, offered the possibility of intervention by spirit helpers who might take pity on their protégé:

He spoke about one of his grandsons, who grew to be a good-sized boy and then fell sick. He said:

"I tried to cure him, but I found I was unable to help him. Others tried, too, but they also failed. Finally he was so weak he had to be fed

---

1   One would say *zagaswe'aa* (this being [whom we don't know] is offered a smoke). Naamiwan would have gone around the pavilion in a clockwise direction. During Naamiwan's dance, there was a moment when the dancers went counter-clockwise and this was remarked on by nearly everybody because it was such an unusual occurrence. Hallowell, "Spirits of the Dead," 168.

2   Those things which disappear or are imperceptible to the eye, for instance, the smell of crumbled sage in the air, seems to be able to cross this barrier.

with a spoon. Then one day he slept away.[1] After that, even in the day-time it was dark to me. I was full of grief.

"One day I was away in the bush by myself. The tears were running down my cheeks all the time, thinking about this boy. I put down my gun and my mittens. I made up my mind to die. I lay down on the point of a rock, where I could be found. When I closed my eyes, towards the sky I saw something like a nest. When I looked toward the east, I heard something saying: 'This is something that will stop you from crying. You'll not die. For this is one of the finest things to play with.'"[2]

One of the telling things about this description is how authentic it sounds to an Ojibwe speaker in its style, in its sequence of thoughts, and in the concise details and simple declarative nature of its sentences. "I put down my gun and my mittens" is easily said in Ojibwe: *Ningii-asaag niminjikaawanag zhigwa nimbaashkizigan*. Even more than the phrasing, the ideas ring true. Hallowell wrote, for example, that the boy "slept away." This is not a typical English-language representation of death, but in Ojibwe it is the way one would refer to the peaceful death of a loved one (*gii-nibaa*).[3] To Ojibwe ears the expression *gii-nibaa* reveals a tender personal relationship to the deceased.[4]

However, some of the ideas, expressed as concisely as they are here, convey in English to us *now* something quite different than they meant *then* in Ojibwe to Naamiwan. This is particularly true of Naamiwan's declaration, "I made up my mind to die." We cannot help but read these

---

1 Charlie George Owen confirmed the child's grave illness in the same way. "*Zhigwa mii owe, zhigwa ani-aazha gakina gegoon e-gii-gashkitoopan e-odaapinang. Emikwaanensan gaye gii-odaapinaadj. Eyezhi-dakomaadj ini emikwaanensan, e-gii-gashkitoodjash.*" (This is an indication of his ability to take something [food]. When he also took a small spoon [in his mouth], he then bit on the small spoon in his feeble way.) Charlie George Owen to Margaret Simmons, 17 March 1995.

2 Hallowell, "Spirits of the Dead," 166.

3 This would not be confused by an Ojibwe listener with ordinary sleep. There are many specialized terms for sleep. To take a nap is *zhiibaangoshi*; *nibaase* is to dose off accidentally. Hallowell renders sleep *nipá*.

4 Hallowell mentioned, at the close of the ceremony, that Naamiwan spoke to all the participants as they left. "To some he said 'Good Night' in English; to others, the women in particular, he said, *nipá* (sleep well)." *Mino-nibaan* is to tell someone to sleep well. Hallowell, "Spirits of the Dead," 168.

Figure 2: The dream dance drum and drummers at Poplar Hill, Ontario in 1932. Photo by A. Irving Hallowell. Omishoosh (James Owen, centre), was a cousin of Naamiwan. He and his brothers, Gezhiiyaash (John Owen) on the left, and Joozhii (Joseph Owen Moose), bought Naamiwan's first drum and introduced the ceremony to Poplar Hill, probably in the early 1920s.

words within our own contemporary context, the graphic news stories of suicide epidemics in "remote" Ojibwe communities.[1] It is easy, given these recent tragic events, to interpret Naamiwan's declaration as the articulation of a death wish. But Naamiwan was not talking about suicide. He was talking about surrendering the course of his life to his spirit helpers (*bawaaganag*). Charlie George Owen, Naamiwan's grandson, used his eloquent Ojibwe to clarify Naamiwan's state of being:

*Gii-ikido iinzan e-wii-**bagidinidizod** egaa-omaa ji-ayaasig.*	Apparently he said that he was going to **let himself go** so that he wouldn't exist here any more.
Daabishkoo ji-nibod e-gii-inendang. Endasa gagwaadagitood.	It was as if he was giving up on life. The reason was all his pain/hardships.
*Mii gaa-izhi-**bagidinidizod**.*	So he **gave himself up**.
Mii-sh iinzan imaa e-bimishing gegoon gaagii-noondang.	And so, apparently, while he was lying there he heard something.
Mii gaa-ikidod. Gaawiin da-izhisesinoon, gidinendamowin iinzan ogii-initaan gegoon.	That's what he said. "It [your death] will not happen," he apparently thought he heard.
*Meshkoj iga-miinigoo wegonen ge-onji-**nanayendaman** maanoo **zanagiziwin** gaye ge-onji-**nanayendaman** iga-miinigoo.*	"In return we will give you that which will **ease your mind** and also **ease your hardship**."

Because of his grief, Naamiwan had no further purpose for his life: his *bawaaganag* could do with it what they would. He offered his life as an expression of his deep unhappiness, his powerlessness, and his humility, but it is crucial to remember that he did so in the knowledge that this desperate moment held the potential for a blessing from his spirit helpers

---

1 Randy Turner, "Death stalks desperate reserve, suicide problem out of control" (*Winnipeg Free Press*, 25 February 1994, A1); Bill Redekop, "Second suicide rocks reserve" (*WFP*, 1 March 1994, B1), "Suicide epidemic endless" (*WFP*, 4 March 1994, A1); and "The Hard Way Out," CBC Television, *The Fifth Estate* (3 January 1995).

and a new direction in life. Naamiwan was not proposing to take his own life, since in Ojibwe philosophy there is a powerful sanction against suicide. Naamiwan would have understood that if he took his own life, his spirit would be unable to find its way to the land of the dead (*oniboog gaa-ayaawaad*) and the desired reunion with his ancestors.[1]

Naamiwan knew a lot about the land of the dead and about the road one travelled to get there. His drum acted as a guide along this path for the recently deceased, and through the drum, Naamiwan was able to speak to those who resided there. Toward the end of his life, he boasted that he could go there and bring back a blossom from the flowers which lined the path. The two old men who told us this mused about his claim: "I wonder if he ever did?"[2]

The dream and the drum not only gave Naamiwan unusual access to the land of the dead; they also gave him access to new healing powers and the right to conduct a new ceremony. As Robert Brightman has pointed out, the dream legitimated Naamiwan's theological innovation in the eyes of the community. Since they understood the drum and Naamiwan's ability to hear it speak as gifts from which they would all benefit, they were willing to participate in his new ceremony. His relatives explained his increased powers as a consequence of the dream.[3] However, one of Hallowell's great insights was that, within their own world view, the Ojibwe are rigorous empiricists. A dream alone is not sufficient to give a person the credibility Naamiwan clearly had. One had to be good at curing people. When we met Charlie George Owen, the first thing he told us was how his grandfather, Naamiwan, brought him back from the dead. Charlie George had been dreadfully ill and, while unconscious, he had walked quite a distance along the flower-lined path to the land of the dead. On hearing his grandfather's voice call

---

1 This literally means "where the dead exist." Hallowell referred to the land of the dead as *djibaiyàking*, which means "where the dead are." *(D)jiibayakiing* is a less specific term and can also refer to a graveyard or morgue. There is a second instance in which *Anishinaabeg* cannot reach the land of the dead; if one has too many possessions which one wants to hang on to when one dies, the burdens will bear the soul down. Anyone can go there but in these two instances the difficulty is in making the journey.

2 Stanley Quill and Whitehead Moose in conversation at the school in Pikangikum, March 1994.

3 "The Search for Fair Wind's Drum," transcript, 18.

to him, he returned to his family. "I'm proud to be 73 years old," he told us. "I should have been dead."[1]

As further confirmation of Naamiwan's gifts, Charlie George then told us his grandfather's dream:[2]

Ngikendaan o'owe.

I know about this.

*Mii **awe ndede** nitam ikwewan e-gii-ayaawaad...Niizhing aaniish gii-bi-wi-iwi.*

My father [*Waanajens*] the first woman he had...he had had two wives.

Zhigwa dash nitam e-gii-ayaawaad gwii-wizensan, mii awe gaagii-nibod.

And, the first[child] that he [and his first wife] had was a boy. That is the one who died.

*Zhigwa dash **gii-gichi-minjinawezi** nimishoomis ono oozisan.*

And he **was very regretful**, my grandfather, about his grandson.

Zhigwa dash, gii-maajaa o'owedi, e-gii-babaami'eyaadj mii onoweni' onji.

And so, he left [Pauingassi] going that way [pointing east toward Turtle River] for his [grandson's] sake.

Zhigwa, gigikendaamin o'omaa, gi-noondam maawiin. O'owe gaa-ani-izhi-gamaag o'owe, owe gaa-izhigamaag o'owe zaaga'igan omaa, zhigwa omaa bi-ziibiwan na.

Further, we know that place, both where it is and what sort of place it is, here [in Pauingassi]...you see, it [Turtle River] flows toward us here.

***Miskwaadesiwiziibi*[3]** *gididaamin. Zhigwa omaa **bikodinaa** aapiji. Omaa **bikodinaa.**[4]*

We all call it **Turtle River**. And at that place there is **a very steep hill with a rounded off top** [sort of **bul-**

---

1 Charlie George Owen to Maureen Matthews, October 1992. For a version of this healing dream, see "The Search for Fair Wind's Drum," transcript, 19.

2 16 October 1992.

3 This is the name of a small reddish turtle, not the big snapping turtle called *Mikinaak*.

4 Precise Ojibwe geographical terminology in Charlie George's version of the dream made it possible for us to visit the mouth of the Turtle River and find the rock upon

MAUREEN MATTHEWS AND ROGER ROULETTE

	bous —like a very lofty bun]. That steep hill is right here [in this area].
Mii iwe izhi-wiindamaw.	Tell her that because **I'm certain** about it.
Mii-sh omaa, mii zhigwa omaa gii-ikido, mii imaa e-gii-izhi…e-gii-izhi mawigwen, biinish e-gii-nibaad.	This place which exists as he [Naamiwan] said, this is where he would have cried until he had fallen asleep.
*Mii dash omaa gaagii…gaagii-onji miin-indiban onoweniwan, **ono dewe'iganan**.*	This is where he was given these [gifts], **this drum**.
***Ishpiming** ogii-izhi-bawaadaan maawiin.*	As I understand, he saw him [the drum, animate] through a dream which came **from the direction of the sky**.
Gaawiin wiin oshkiinzhigong ngii-onji-inaabisii ikido.	However, it wasn't through his eyes that he saw, [Naamiwan] said.
"Wedi nake ngii-onji-inaab," ikido.	"I looked from here," he said [gestures to back of head].
"Ngii-waabandaan dash e-bagone'aag ishpiming," o'owe.	"I saw a hole in the sky, this way," here [gestures to back of head again].

---

which Naamiwan experienced his vision. Our boat driver knew exactly where the Turtle River was but he was unsure which of the many outcrops might have been the one on which Naamiwan "laid down his mittens and his gun." We wandered along the shore for a while and then saw a likely looking spot a short distance from the mouth of the little river. It was indeed *bikodinaa*, as Charlie George put it, a bulbous rock. *Bikodinaa* is one of many highly specific Ojibwe words which characterize land forms. The word left us in no doubt that we had come upon the right place. In another version of the dream Charlie George said, "*Mii-sh omaa gaagii-izhi-ogidajiwegobanen wedi*," "the rock leans back from the shore," and so it does, climbing up about twenty feet in height. A forest fire has drastically altered the landscape since Naamiwan's day, but even with the effects of the fire, it is still a remarkably secret yet open spot. Its lack of ostentation and the many signs of human occupation confirmed our feeling that we had found the right place.

"Mii owe gaa-miinigooyin," mii e-gii-igooyaan.

"This, which is alive, is who we give you," This is what I was told.

"Mii a'awedi gaagii-miinigooyaan," gii-ikido....

"He, over there, [the drum] is who was given to me," he said....

Mii iwe e-gii-igod awegwenan.

This is certainly what was told to him, but by whom, I do not know.

*"Mii a'a menigooyan meshkoj **ji-bi-maadiziyan**, aaniin minik waa-bi-maadiziyan," e-gii-igoogwen aweg-wenan.*

"This is what we give you **so that you may live**, but only for as long and as well as you are predestined to live," is what he was told by whom I don't know.

*Mii owan dash onoweniwan niibiwa gaa-onji-gashkitood omaa **bimaadiziwin**.*

These, here [the drum and gifts]...these many things, are the ones through which he [Naamiwan] acquired **life**.

O'owe gaagii-aabaji'aad ono'.

This one whom he was able to have...this [drum].

*"Mii dash izhinikaanig wa'awe,' gii-ikido, '**Gibaabaanaan**,[1] Gaa-gizhe-waadizidj.'"*

"For this," he said, "you call him [the drum], '**Our Father, the Gracious One.**'"

Mii owe na omiinigoowin wa'awedi gaagii-onji odewe'iganid....

And, you see, this gift, is the reason why he had a drum....

---

1   Gibaabaanaan is definitely a name and indicates the Southern Ojibwe roots of the dream dance complex. It is not the word people in Pauingassi use to refer to one's father. There, they use an older form for father (*dede*) as Charlie George does in the second sentence of this story. However gibaabaanaan is now commonly used to refer to a father among Southern Ojibwe. It was initially adopted for addressing missionaries and incorporates the English/French root *papa* but is now used to refer to biological or categorical fathers in everyday conversation. The drum's name probably still had these Christian implications in Pauingassi at the time of Naamiwan's dream.

Iwe ḍash gii-izhise o' gaagii-izhi-naagozid o'owe omaa gegoo gaagii-ateg.	This is what occurred, his appearance [the drum], the thing [design] that was here[indicating the pattern drawn on the drum face].[1]
*Gegii-gaagiigidod, e-gii-gaganoonaad ono **dewe'iganan**, ogii-nisidotawaan gaa-izhi-gaganoonigod.*	When he spoke, when he spoke to the **drum**, [Naamiwan] understood his speech [that of the drum].

It is remarkable how closely this version follows Hallowell's account. The basic details are the same, evidence of the skill of William Berens as translator and explainer. One has to admire both the accuracy of Hallowell's understanding and the precision of Ojibwe memory.[2] Some ambiguous elements of Hallowell's version are clarified by placing the two versions side by side and some new information is revealed by a more leisurely translation of the Ojibwe words. Charlie George's versions each offered some new insights. His accounts were not identical but some of the phrasing was echoed in each rendition.

Like Hallowell, Charlie George started his account with the death of Naamiwan's grandson. He was able to be very specific about this child, because the language lends itself to situating people in familial terms. This boy was Charlie George's elder brother. Their mother died when Charlie George was a small baby. Like Charlie George, who was the next eldest grandson, this boy was probably raised by his uncle Angus, the childless eldest brother of his father, Waanajens, and by Angus's wife, Mishko'o (One who dresses red), who was the sister of Charlie

---

1   The pattern on the drum is seen in a photograph from the 1950s. It's a four-sided cross very much like a Maltese cross, carefully inscribed and painted blue and purple, encircled by two thin lines of blue and purple. We were told it was called *Gaagige anang* – "the forever star."

2   The Ojibwe have a very specific understanding about how one remembers. It involves ideas having a place within the mind, a place where they can be located when they need to be retrieved. A person is judged as having remembered well when verifiable quotes are accurate and the story line and details are consistent. They are not expecting word-for-word versions of the story. Charlie George Owen would be judged a very good rememberer, one who, because of his fondness for his grandfather and his obligations to the memory of Naamiwan, purposely holds on to the memory (*minjimenjige[win]*) of the dream.

George's mother. Like Charlie George, this first grandson would have been seen as the heir to Naamiwan's gifts through Angus.

The Ojibwe phrase used to describe Naamiwan's reaction to the death of his grandson was the phrase "very regretful," *gichi-minjinawezi*, which implies more than simple grief. It means that Naamiwan felt himself to blame for the death, either because of some wrong done in the past which was ultimately visited on his grandson, or because he was insufficiently powerful to heal the boy. He may have thought it was punishment he deserved for some arrogance or impropriety.

The operative Ojibwe idea here is *onjinewin*. It means, roughly, that what comes around, goes around. It is the condition in which one finds oneself when one has offended some powerful being, human or non-human, and is, or should be, anticipating the consequences. Several terms deal specifically with the repercussions of *onjinewin*. *Baataa'idizowin*[1] is when the insult or deed rebounds directly on the perpetrator, *obaataa'aan* is when it is visited on a loved one, a child for instance, and *baataa'aa* is when it comes back to a member of the extended family or community.[2]

When the memory of great Ojibwe religious leaders like Naamiwan is celebrated, it is for the life (*bimaadiziwin*) they have given to others. They have saved many people from illness caused by *onjinewin*. Naamiwan gave Charlie George life when he needed it. Naamiwan's failure to give life to his elder grandson initiated the dream, and the gift of life through the gift of the drum concluded it. This concept of life, as Hallowell thought, was crucial to understanding the dream. In one of the other versions of the dream, Charlie George expressed Naamiwan's grief specifically in terms of lost life. *"Aah, e-niwii-banis ge-waabamag noozis," iinzan gii-ayinendam e-bi-maajaadj e-mamawidj.* ("Oh, I will miss out in life, [it will be shorter] because of not seeing my grandson," he thought, apparently, as he left crying.) The gift of new life Naamiwan was given

---

1   *Baataa* is the root used in all these words. It implies that the deed has been done and the consequences are inevitable. This sanction, rather than the forces exerted by public institutions such as courts, generally governed Ojibwe behaviour. This is exemplified in the word *maanoo* which means "let it be." Why nag or punish someone who will inevitably suffer in the end?

2   For instance, William Berens experienced an illness caused by something his father did. He was healed only after his father returned from the land of the dead through the medium of a shaking tent to explain the offence, and after appropriate medicines were given to him by a spirit being. Hallowell, "Spirits," 164.

in the dream was limited by his fate. That is, the quality and length of his life were controlled both by preordination and by his deeds with respect to other people and to his spirit helpers. However, through the dream he was still getting a bonus which he was able to direct toward others as well.

A gift from one's *bawaagan* had to be paid for with deliberate personal suffering such as prolonged fasting and isolation or by foregoing certain things in life, but it could also be earned at times of real grief and desperation as was the case with Naamiwan. *Bagosendam* is the Ojibwe term Naamiwan would have used to describe this unhappy state which nonetheless had such possibilities. *Bagosendam* is the act of hoping for divine intervention in one's favour during difficult times in one's life.[1] The gift of the drum was an example of such an intervention by a *bawaagan*.

William Berens and Hallowell were obviously interested in the question of how one earned such a gift. They recorded Naamiwan's explanation, offered during the ceremony. Naamiwan framed the gift in terms of familial obligations. The *bawaaganag*, who are never overtly identified, are often referred to in conversation or prayer as "Our Grandfathers" (*Gimishoomisinaanig*).[2] Naamiwan's expectation that they would help him was based on his sense of their familial obligations to him. A powerful grandfather would necessarily share extra gifts, extra life, with a grandchild in need. As Naamiwan explained to his visitors at the drum dance: "If any of you heard one of your children crying, you would run to the child at once to find out what had made him cry. He might have hurt himself, and you would try to give him something to amuse him, so he would stop crying."[3]

The *bawaagan* gave the drum to amuse Naamiwan; it was something to "play with." But it was no ordinary toy. In the Ojibwe version of the

---

1   Mary Black-Rogers explores the concept of pity and sharing in a fur trade context. "'Starving,' and Survival in the Subarctic Fur Trade: a Case for Contextual Semantics," *Selected Papers of the Fifth North American Fur Trade Conference, 1985*, eds. Bruce G. Trigger, Toby Morantz, and Louise Dechène (Montreal: Lake St. Louis Historical Society, 1987), 618-49.

2   When simply referring to "my grandfather" one would say *nimishoomis*. *Gimishoomisinaanig* is the inclusive first person plural form (we, including you) and is a formal way of referring to our grandfathers.

3   Hallowell, "Spirits of the Dead," 166.

dream it is clear that the drum was alive.[1] Charlie George said, "*e-gii-ga-ganoonaad ono* **dewe'iganan**, *ogii-nisidotawaan gaa-izhi-gaganoonigod*" (when he spoke to the **drum**, he [Naamiwan] understood *his* speech [that of the drum].) In both of his other versions of the dream, Charlie George even implied that the drum had life before it was made, and that this life suffused the object once Naamiwan's son (Waanajens) built it. The drum was given a very beautiful name, *Gibaabaanaan, Gaa-gizhe-waadizidj*, which means "Our Father, the Gracious One."[2]

The drum, which is now in a museum in Red Lake, Ontario, is still called *Gibaabaanaan, Gaa-gizhewaadizidj* by those who know the name. Although they regret the absence of the drum, older members of the community are not distressed by the drum's residence in a museum. In the museum, the drum lives in a relatively dignified state of retirement and does not have to hear harsh words spoken about himself by fervent Christians in the community.[3] These sharp critics of "pagan" belief would be surprised by the syncretic nature of Naamiwan's thinking. When Hallowell visited Pauingassi, the Christian elements of the ceremony were perceived to be a very important part of the gift of the drum.

Naamiwan was not the only one to receive this gift. At the ceremony Hallowell witnessed, his son Angus was also able to understand the voice of the drum and, through it, to speak to the dead and to other spirit beings. Angus's gift was legitimated by a dream which was crucial for his acceptance as Naamiwan's heir. Fortunately, Hallowell and William Berens recorded Angus's dream as well, a dream which includes some intriguing references to Christianity:

---

1   The animate verbs used in conjunction with the drum are the same as those used to describe the actions of a person. The drum is a categorical person. If the drum were inanimate, the drum would have "made a sound" (*noondaagozi),* but, the drum not only spoke (*ganoonigod*), he carried on a conversation (**gaganoonigod**), which is the same verb reduplicated.

2   "*Gizhewaadizidj*" translates roughly as "gracious one," but it is hard to translate simply because it incorporates many ideas including notions of generosity, thoughtfulness and sensitivity. The contemporary pronunciation is without the final *j (gizhe-waadizid)* but Charlie George and others used an older form with a definite *d* followed by a *j* (*ch* sound) at the end of the word.

2   James Strang to Roger Roulette, Pikangikum, March 1994.

MAUREEN MATTHEWS AND ROGER ROULETTE

My beloved friends, when I was a boy, I never expected to be sitting here beating this drum. Even when I was a young man, I never thought of it. Later when I was a full grown man, I worked hard on the York boats, just like my father had done. Yet I knew nothing. Even when I got married, I was still ignorant. Recently one of my brother's sons slept away.[1] He is sleeping over there [pointing in the direction of the grave]. I did not like to see his grave like that of an animal covered with snow. I went there and put my tent over the grave.

A few months later, I went up north to hunt. I was crying, even while I was hunting. Finally, I made up my mind that I would rather sleep than live. Then I heard a voice saying to me: "I'll give you something to ease your mind and that of others. But you must take care and carry things through as you are told."

Even a minister's name was mentioned. But the minister did not tell me half of what he should have told me. He did not even know what *pinésï* [Thunderbird] was. He is one of those that tries to make us believe that stones striking together makes the noise we hear (thunder). I do not believe this. I mentioned it today only because I know something different on account of what I have dreamed.

There are many parallels here with Naamiwan's dream, some interesting details, and a few remarkable differences. The similarities include the sadness and desperation which attended the death of the boy and the description of the gift as something to gladden the heart. It is interesting how unexpected the gift was for Angus, who described a workaday world of York boats and travelling before being given his gift. But Angus's dream was also different in that he only heard about the drum; he did not see it. And his vision contained a confusing element – the mention of a minister who didn't tell what he should have and didn't know what Thunderbird was.

---

1   Charlie George Owen was raised by Angus, his father Waanajens's eldest brother. Angus's wife, Mishko'o, was Charlie George's mother's sister. Charlie George's mother had only two children, the boy whose death provoked the dream and Charlie George.

Charlie George does not remember this dream of Angus's and so we cannot be certain whether this is the death of the same boy or that of another nephew of Angus. We are presuming it is the same boy.

Angus's dream hints at the identity of the giver of the gift again. Hallowell was confused by what he heard and he specifically asked whether the drum was the gift of a *bawaagan* or the *(d)jiibayag* (spirits of the dead):

> When I later inquired whether the dance was a gift of the *djibaiyak* or some *pawágan*, I was answered in the negative. It came directly from God. In this it contradicts, of course, one of the fundamental principles of even contemporary Saulteaux dream revelation. But the mixed character of the elements of the ceremony is obvious even in a superficial description.[1]

This is an instance where the memories of Naamiwan's descendants are useful in piecing together Christian overlay and Ojibwe world view. It's easy to forget that these Ojibwe people were familiar with missionaries; Methodists in particular, had been visiting the area since the 1870s.[2] Hallowell was told that Naamiwan had been a professing Christian before he experienced the drum vision.[3] Even after his Ojibwe epiphany, Naamiwan conducted a kind of church service on Sundays. "It wasn't church exactly. They just followed him. It was part of the gift of the drum."[4] There was a bell on a wooden tower next to the dream dance lodge,[5] and Adam Owen, a grandnephew of the old man, remembered Naamiwan ringing it and praying from a Cree syllabic Bible.

In a few of the stories about Naamiwan there are undercurrents of glee whenever he experienced any come-uppance. St. John Owen is lay minister of the Mennonite congregation in Pauingassi now, and another grandnephew of Naamiwan. He told us one story about Naamiwan's bell which still provokes mirth. One Sunday morning Naamiwan pulled the rope to ring his bell and instead brought it crashing to the ground, barely missing his head. Ojibwe listeners would also perceive such an event as a bad omen, and a symptom of his lack of complete mastery over the Christian lexicon. Particularly for those who look back now,

---

1   Hallowell, "Spirits of the Dead," 168.

2   Brown and Matthews, "Fair Wind," 61.

3   Hallowell, "Spirits of the Dead," 402, n. 40.

4   Adam Owen in transcript of "The Search for Fair Wind's Drum," 17.

5   A photograph of the *boodaadewigamig* with the bell tower beside it appears in Gerald Malaher, *The North I Love* (Winnipeg: Hyperion, 1984), 56.

this is an easy judgment to make. The reality is that Naamiwan was neither the Christian the missionaries hoped for, nor the pure, unacculturated Ojibwe Hallowell would have favoured, but rather an intelligent old man interested in new ideas, seeking to adapt them within his Ojibwe world.[1]

The Christian references in the description of the dream also remind us of the role of William Berens in the creation of this account. One passage in particular raises a few questions. Naamiwan is quoted as saying:

> I'm going to explain to the great visiting Chief [Berens][2] the meaning of those dishes that have just been brought in here, and are lying there with a little food in them. When a person has lost a brother, a child, or some other relative, we call upon them to look down upon us. They have been on this earth once, and before that they were sent from above to come on this earth. Jesus, too, came from above to be the boss of the earth.[3]

Just as Naamiwan's dream passed the test of expressing Ojibwe ideas in the right style and phrasing, this section fails. A statement like "look down upon" is not an idea easily conveyed in Ojibwe; one looks at things in particular and their relative position is revealed by context. A person might look about (*ayinaabi*), look skyward (*ishpiming inaabi*) or look at his feet (*oganawaabandaanan ozidan*). The phrase which would express the kind of "looking" a departed spirit might do is *ganawaabamigooying* ("to observe" or maybe "to watch over" in the caring sense), and in any case interactions with spirit beings usually take place on a level plane. "Sent from above to live on earth" is another phrase that evokes missionary patter rather than Ojibwe thinking. Ojibwe speakers would talk about the souls of the dead being out be-

---

1 Brown and Matthews, "Fair Wind," 69.

2 Charlie George Owen says that this explanation was addressed to Chief William Berens, a Christian and *Ogimaakaan*. (Hallowell was called Mide Chief, *Midewigimaa*.) *Ogimaakaan* means "like a chief" and is the commonly used expression for the elected leader of the community. *Ogimaa* is chief and -*kaan* indicates not the actual entity but a substitute. *Manidookaan* is "like a god," or "a substitute for god" (*manidoo*, god, plus -*kaan*).

3 Hallowell, "Spirits of the Dead," 167.

yond what we know – in that irretrievable other world (*oniboog gaa-ayaawaad*), not coming "from above."[1]

Given the divergence here from Ojibwe linguistic possibilities, we must conclude either that William Berens introduced these expressions because of his familiarity with Christian phraseology, or that Naamiwan was speaking in English. Since Naamiwan's grandson Charlie George Owen says he knew virtually no English, Berens is the likely source. His choice of these ready phrases probably reflected his missionary schooling and his Christian, English-speaking mother's influence.[2] His contribution to Hallowell's perception of what was going on here is crucial. Hallowell would not have interjected such a phrase; indeed, he was not particularly interested in the Christian aspects of these Ojibwe lives although he recorded instances of Christianity where he found them. William Berens, however, was a practising Christian who kept Sunday even on the trapline.[3]

There is another possibility. Some of the Christian elements of the ceremony may have come with the dream drum. Thomas Vennum Jr., who has written extensively on the dream drum tradition in Minnesota and Wisconsin, has observed that, although the dream drum was initially very aboriginal in iconography and ceremony, it quickly picked up Christian references.[4] Michael Reinschmidt, writing about the dream dance among the Sauk in Oklahoma, observed the same thing.[5] We know that the first dream drum in the area came from Jackhead (on the west side of Lake Winnipeg) to Little Grand Rapids (about ten miles south of Pauingassi), a community often visited by Methodist missionaries. A better understanding of the drum ceremo-

---

1   It is possible for a soul to come back but it's a more immediate thing. In some dreams about the trip to the land of the dead, a river must be crossed. Only very few come back after crossing the river, and they come back more or less immediately. In other instances, people actually visit the land of the dead and see their ancestors but are brought back by someone with the power to do so, or for some other reason are not meant to stay.

2   Jennifer S.H. Brown, "'A Place in your Mind for Them All': Chief William Berens," *Being and Becoming Indian: Biographical Studies of North American Frontiers*, ed. James A. Clifton (Chicago: Dorsey Press, 1989), 204-225.

3   Percy Berens, conversation, October 1992.

4   Thomas Vennum, Jr., personal communication, February 1995.

5   Michael Reinschmidt, "The Drum Dance Religion: Historical and Contemporary Reflections," *European Review of Native American Studies* 8 (1) (1994), 27.

nies in Little Grand Rapids and Jackhead could help to answer some of the questions we still have about Hallowell's account of the dream dance.

These confusing sections of Hallowell's text remind us of the limitations of ethnographic categories, the impossibility of ethnographic purity, and the mental baggage we all bring to the problem of trying to conveying accurate ethnographic information across linguistic and perceptual barriers.[1] To complicate things further, Naamiwan may have offered these religious comparisons out of deference to both his guests, in effect tailoring his remarks to accommodate what he perceived to be their interests and religious convictions. In any case, Naamiwan's dream dance, as witnessed by Hallowell, was a fundamentally Ojibwe observance incorporating several Christian flourishes. In attempting to explain this composite Ojibwe ceremony, Hallowell concluded:

> [It] also illustrates extremely well how diverse strands of belief and practice can be welded together under the influence of a strong personality, and yet still kept within the framework of the Saulteaux interpretation of the universe. To my mind, the dance indicates the dynamic character of the syncretic processes, and the fact that it is of fairly recent origin shows that there is still some religious vitality left in the non-Christian beliefs of the Indian population along the river. The unique features it embodies stamp it as a creative, rather than a decadent, product.[2]

Sixty years later, this syncretic process is still going on. The oldest residents of the community, men and women who once participated in Naamiwan's dream dance and in the *Waabano*, are now the leaders in the local Mennonite church and they continue to think of the world in very Ojibwe terms. Jacob Owen, the oldest man in Pauingassi and predecessor of St. John Owen as Mennonite lay preacher, carries on an active medical practice specializing in the sorts of ailments caused by breaking Ojibwe sexual taboos.[3] He told us that this ability to cure is a

---

1   Compare the points made by Joel Scherzer, "The Kuna and Columbus: Encounters and Confrontations of Discourse," *American Anthropologist* 96 (4) (1994), 902-924.

2   Hallowell, "Spirits of the Dead," 168-69.

3   Taboos, for instance, against having intercourse with a woman during menstruation, and against bestiality or incest. Such healing powers are thought to be a gift of Thunderbirds. Charlie George Owen identifies Jacob Owen as so gifted, in "Thunderbirds"(CBC Radio, *Ideas*, Toronto 1995) transcript 5.

gift from Jesus, yet he gave us indications of a very traditional *bawaagan* at work as well.

It is common for professed Christian men and women of this generation to believe profoundly in the existence of Thunderbirds who confer such healing gifts on their protégés. In spite of missionization and other pressures, it seems that much of this Ojibwe philosophical framework will last as long as people think and speak in Ojibwe. As long as people speak the language, some aspects of the weather, for example, can only be referred to in terms of the presence or absence of Thunderbirds. The phrase *bimisewag* ("they [Thunderbirds] are sweeping by") indicates racing storm clouds in a fast-moving front.

At the same time, the Ojibwe language has adapted to accommodate Christian personalities and concepts. Some of the most useful old Ojibwe categories have expanded to include new Christian meanings, a process well under way when Hallowell was in Pauingassi. In 1994 we visited Pikangikum, up the Berens River in northwestern Ontario. This Ojibwe reserve has a very high rate of language retention. We made a presentation about the Ojibwe vocabulary of Naamiwan's dream to a high school Native language class and were surprised by the reaction when we spoke about Naamiwan's apprentices, or *oshkaabewisag*. It turned out that, among Christian Ojibwe speakers in Pikangikum, *oshkaabewis* is the word for Jesus. The idea of apprenticeship has been borrowed to explain the relationship of Jesus to God, the Father. Yet it is a crucial word for understanding what the old people say about Naamiwan and his beliefs. Our tapes are peppered with it. The transmutation of *oshkaabewis* into a powerful Christian term is an illustration of one source of the breakdown of communication between generations in these communities. If communication is to be re-established, such word changes need to be acknowledged and the historical meanings of words taught to young people.

The question still remains: who gave the gift of the drum to Naamiwan? Was it the same *bawaagan* who instructed Angus in his dream? Are we to believe Hallowell and Chief Berens and accept that it was God, a Christian God? If we look closely at Hallowell's own evidence, there are many reasons to think he was mistaken.

It may be a translation problem. There are two ways to say God in Ojibwe. One is *Gaa-dibenjiged* or *Gaa-dibendang*, which means something like "the all-encompassing power of life." This word is almost never spoken but may have been the response to a seriously asked question about the source of metaphysical gifts. In the discussion surrounding Angus's conversations with the spirits of the dead, some of the questions in fact originate with "the master (*kadabéndang*)."[1] The other word that Naamiwan might have used for a god is *manidoo*, which can mean any spirit being including a Thunderbird, in which case the answer was diplomatic, once again demurring from identifying the giver. *Manidoo* had also, by this time, become the way of expressing the notion of a Christian God in Ojibwe and therefore had a new Christian meaning attached. However, we know Hallowell understood these points by 1940, when he published the description of Fair Wind's dance; he had written about them in an article on the empirical aspects of Ojibwe thought.[2]

At the same time, there is strong evidence that it was a Thunderbird who gave the gift. The first clue to the identity of Naamiwan's *bawaagan* is in Hallowell's version of the dream, in a reference to a nest in the sky. Hallowell inserted a footnote after the mention of the nest, expressing his belief that this was "an allusion to the drum," from which we can only guess that he meant its shape.[3] Our reading is that the nest was a sign that the giver of the drum was a Thunderbird. In fact, in Angus's dream, it becomes clearer yet that the Thunderbird (*binesi*) was the *bawaagan* who gave the gift. *Binesiwag* are very particular that things be done exactly right and carried through to the end, no matter what the task – even murder.[4] Angus was told "to carry things through as you are told." This is typical of the kind of instruction a Thunderbird would give. And Angus's dismay that the minister in his vision did not know what *binesi* was, is another indication that *binesiwag* must be playing a role. He refuted the minister, saying, "I know something different [about Thunderbirds] on account of what I have dreamed." It is in dreams that one comes to know Thunderbirds.

---

1 Hallowell, "Spirits of the Dead," 168.

2 A. Irving Hallowell, "Some Empirical Aspects of Northern Saulteaux Religion," *American Anthropologist* 36 (1934), 389-404.

3 Hallowell, "Spirits of the Dead," 402, n. 37.

4 We were told a story of a battle during which Naamiwan and Angus were sent bad medicine by rivals in a nearby community. At the end of the battle the two challengers were dead. "They carried it through to the end," we were told, and this was evidence that their power came from Thunderbirds. St. John Owen to Roger Roulette, September 1994.

Figure 3: A. I. Hallowell's photograph of the *oshkaabewisag* and *oshkaabewisikwe-wag*, the young men and women who were the religious apprentices in Pauingassi, taken in the mid-1930s. They are wearing ceremonial regalia kept for them by Naami-wan. In the front row, left to right, are Zaagajiwe (Charlie Moose Owen), Asemaa, Omooday, and Wewaanj. Middle row: Anang (Mary Anne Keeper), Animigiizhigong, A'aasii, Odaab, Waagidiniigan and Wawezhi'o. In the back row are Mados, Omishoosh (Charlie George Owen), Moonzogimaa, Boozijii, Gisayenaan, Jiibay, and Es (Jacob Owen). Jacob Owen wears a feather indicative of his familiarity with Thunderbirds. We would like to thank Henry Neufeldt for his assistance in identifying the individuals in Hallowell's photographs.

MAUREEN MATTHEWS AND ROGER ROULETTE

One of Hallowell's photographs shows Naamiwan in front of his Waabano pavilion. A carved wooden bird is mounted on a pole near the entrance. This is a remarkably overt representation of a Thunderbird. Only a supremely confident medicine man would be so daring. Hallowell himself recorded a story of Naamiwan understanding the voices of Thunder, which, he pointed out, was by no means usual among the Ojibwe.[1] There is ample evidence that Thunderbirds conferred the right to conduct the dream drum dance,[2] the practice of which was brought to the Pauingassi area by a man named *Niiskaadwewidang*. Hallowell translated his name as "when pinesi [Thunderbird] calls there is always rain,"[3] and his Thunderbird credentials are clear from his name alone. Similarly, anthropologist Ruth Landes recorded the dream of a woman who received the gift of a dream dance during World War I in the Emo area of northwestern Ontario. Maggie Wilson learned eighty songs from a chorus of Thunderbirds who tormented her in her sleep.[4] But the most telling evidence of all on this subject comes from Charlie George Owen, Naamiwan's grandson:

*Binesi debwe ayaa ishpiming. Gaa-noondaagozid miziwe giizhigong. Mii-wan dash onoweniwan dinoowikaanan gaagi-ganoonigod ji-boodaadang. Binesi aanish, **miigwan** badakijige awiya, na.*	**Thunderbird** truly does exist up there. He [Thunderbird] is heard everywhere throughout the heavens. This is who told him [Naamiwan] to do the *Boodaade* [dream drum] ceremony. It is the Thunderbird, as one should know, for whom one wears the **feather** which you see [worn by Jacob Owen in one of Hallowell's photographs].

---

1 Brown and Matthews, "Fair Wind," 59.

2 Thomas Vennum, personal communication. February 1995. He has looked at many recorded dream dance visions. By far the most common dream helper is the Thunderbird.

3 Hallowell wrote this name "Niskatwewitang," which could mean "one who disturbs by his loudness," but in any case it is definitely about Thunderbirds.

4 Ruth Landes, *Ojibwa Religion and the Midewiwin* (Madison: University of Wisconsin Press, 1968), 207-212.

*Giishin awiya wii-ayaan ogichidaawi-win bigo miigwanan ji-badakijiged. Mii iwe ayaad odinoowikaan daabishkoo owe dinoowikaan ji-niimi'iwed awiya ji-**boodaadang**.*

If someone wants to be powerful they must wear the feather. Only if someone has something like that, would they be able to perform the **Boodaade** ceremony.

Mii we[1] dinoowikaan mii endinoowang odinoowikaan. Mii niin gaa-izhi-nisido-tamaan o'owe.

This is what this type of thing is [the *Boodaade*]. This is how I understand it to be [the process of receiving gifts and power and the symbolism of the feather].

Gaawin wiin igo omichi- inendamowini-waang aaniish o'owe gaagii-gaagi-igidowaad....

These were just not their own thoughts, they used to speak....

gii-miinaawag aaniish, mii dash gashki'ewiziwin ogii-ayaanaawaa. Ogii-bimaaji'aawaan awiya. Giishpin awiya michi-inendang gegoon izhichiged gaawn gegoon oga-inaabajitoosiin. Aabiinj igo gaawn gegoo. Apooshke biinish da-ani-onji-aakozi.

because it was given, then they [Naamiwan and others] had the power. They healed many. If someone does something on his own for the sake of doing it, he won't be able to benefit anyone. Absolutely nothing will come of it. He will eventually make himself sick.

Margaret Simmons:
*Mii na iwe **baataa'idizowin** gaa-iji-gaadeg?*

Margaret Simmons:
Is that what they call (*"baataa'idizowin"*) **accountability for a wrong which one must pay**?

---

1 This text is peppered with the word *mii* which indicates that Charlie George is certain about the story he is relating. In the first version of the dream, Charlie George says, "**Mii iwe** *izhi-wiindamaw.*" ("Tell her that because **I'm certain** about it.") Some people end a story with "*Mii iwe,*" ("I have spoken") to indicate the story's veracity and their certainty. Older people who are fluent Ojibwe speakers frequently embed in their sentences phrases and suffixes indicating degrees of certainty. There is a subtle declension of certainty from personal experience to hearsay which can be expressed by such words as *gondasha* (of course) and *maawiin,* which means simply "I think so." For instance, Charlie George often uses the suffix "*-banen*" (e.g., *bimosego-banen, ogidajiwegobanen*) to indicate that he was told about something but did not see for himself. This suffix, which he uses with such ease, has disappeared among con-

Omishoosh:	Charlie George Owen:
Mii iwe Baataa'idizowin. **Onjinewin**.	That **certainly** is it — ("Baataa'idizowin"). ("*Onjinewin*") **the payment for a moral wrong.**[1]
Mii iwe.	I have spoken.

temporary Minnesota speakers. It's only used by older people in Manitoba, but if one leaves it out one loses the sense that the things being told are hearsay, not firsthand experience. In contemporary conversation, "*-banen*" is often replaced by the less-subtle word, which means "apparently," the word "*iinzan*."

1 Charlie George Owen to Margaret Simmons, March 1993.

Part VI. Women's Lives through Words and Images

Students of women's lives constantly confront the reality that most historical documents were written by and about men. Those who study women of colour find their subjects doubly silenced by gender and race. The authors of the following essays recover and interpret the image constructions and experiences undergone by three Native women previously almost invisible. They employ a range of research strategies — from the analysis of images of women in popular discourse and in ethnology, to the literary techniques of biography.

Erica Smith's experiences in women's history have parallelled the development of her field. An undergraduate in Manitoba in the early 1970s, she recalls how at that time historians of women were still demonstrating that their subject was a proper one for historical inquiry, and that women despite their subordination were active agents in history. After raising a family, Smith returned to graduate studies in the late 1980s and again found a discipline in transformation. Now with the rise of postmodernism, many feminist scholars were dissecting their own terms of reference and discovering that the project of recovering women's lives was enmeshed in language.

Smith is currently exploring the experiences of British and Native women at Red River Colony (present-day Manitoba) in the nineteenth century. Her analyses of old texts about and occasionally by women reveal strands of discourse that seem to operate "like independent spirits in history," structuring understandings of woman, race, civilization, and other foundational categories in ways that differ markedly from our late twentieth-century views. As her essay on the journalistic coverage of the Corbett abortion trial of 1863 reveals, Smith finds the potent and historically-specific discourses of the day to be a primary apparatus for defining women's experiences.

In her portrait of Insima, an elderly Blackfoot woman, and the young woman student ethnographer with whom she shared her stories in the 1930s, anthropologist Alice Beck Kehoe analyzes dominant ethnological discourses — specifically, tales of brave hunting Plains tribes — and reveals their contrasts with women's experiences long neglected in the standard ethnographic narratives. Kehoe knows this territory intimately. An internationally renowned professor of anthropology at Marquette University (Milwaukee), she has studied Plains peoples and Native American ethnohistory for over thirty years.

Her interests in the history of anthropological practice and the sociology of scholarly knowledge find expression in this close study of an ethnographic experience going back six decades. Her essay on Insima evokes, too, her memories of graduate student days at Harvard University where women among the anthropologists might be seen but were seldom heard.

Bunny McBride's essay reveals the issues she encountered and the insights she gained while researching and writing about the life of a remarkable Penobscot woman, Molly Nelson. Raised on an Indian reservation in Maine, Nelson spent much of her life from the 1920s to the 1950s as an actor, dancer, and writer in New York and Paris. McBride's textual engagement with this fascinating figure resulted in a biography, *Molly Spotted Elk: A Penobscot in Paris* (1995). Here, McBride reflects on her book as "a dialogical enterprise" in which both the researcher and the subject were active creators. Her essay, "The Spider and the Wasp," describes in intimate detail the process by which she came to know Molly Spotted Elk (her stage name) through Molly's daughter, through her diaries, and through a range of other sources gathered in the United States and France. A decade of research and community development work in Micmac and other communities in northern Maine provided McBride with further context, and led also to a travelling museum exhibit and book-length study (*Our Lives in Our Hands*, 1990) chronicling the work of contemporary Micmac basketmakers. That research in turn contributed to a Micmac victory in a long-standing claim against the U.S. government for federal recognition and the right to re-establish a tribal land base.

"The Spider and the Wasp" recounts McBride's personal journey of discovery, reflecting on issues of responsible representation of other cultures; on the search for an authorial voice that would speak meaningfully across ethnic and gender divides to Native, scholarly, and broader readerships; and on the challenges facing a non-Native biographer seeking to "understand and internalize" her subject. All three authors in this section have worked with texts which sometimes contain only rumours of women's voices, traces of women's actions. They demonstrate the rich rewards awaiting diligent attempts to uncover the historical experiences of those previously silenced.

15

"Gentlemen, This is no Ordinary Trial": Sexual Narratives in the Trial of the Reverend Corbett, Red River, 1863[1]

Erica Smith

FOR NINE DAYS in February of 1863, often late into the night, a melodrama of chaste and fallen womanhood unfolded in the modest courthouse in Red River Settlement (present-day Winnipeg). The Reverend Griffith Owen Corbett, an Anglican minister in the parish of Headingley, stood accused by Simon and Catherine Thomas of having seduced their daughter Maria, a sixteen-year-old girl of mixed descent and a servant in the Corbett household.[2] According to Maria Thomas's testimony, her employer had repeatedly forced himself upon her. When she became pregnant, Corbett, who had some medical knowledge acquired by attending lectures at King's Hospital in London, subjected her to several attempted abortions. He failed to interrupt the pregnancy and she gave birth to a child shortly before the trial. Corbett was arrested and, on the basis of Thomas's testimony and that of about 100 witnesses, found guilty of the crime of attempting to procure an abortion. The court sentenced him to six months' imprisonment, in spite of the eloquent rhetoric of his counsel, James Ross, who had hoped to acquit his client by persuading the jury that Maria Thomas was a "common prostitute" in the parish.

Among the attentive spectators sat Ross's colleague, William Coldwell, a journalist from Canada and now resident in the colony.

---

1   Thanks are due to Leona Crabb and Kerry Abel, who read and commented on an earlier draft of this paper.

2   The daughter of Simon Thomas and Catherine Linklater, and a pupil in Rev. James Hunter's Sunday school, Maria's family connections were British, Anglican, and Cree. A brother, born in 1844, was named Thomas, a fact suggesting a link with Governor Thomas Thomas, although it may merely reflect the tendency in Red River to name children after influential persons. Of note is the fact that only Maria Thomas's Cree connections were stressed in the trial. James Hunter Journal, NAC mfm. A91; Anglican Parish Registers, Provincial Archives of Manitoba (PAM), MG-7.

Coldwell took shorthand notes (unfortunately lost) which he and Ross later reworked into a journalistic tour de force in their newspaper, *The Nor'Wester*. Grandly entitled "The Trial of the Century," the story was serialized as a front-page, three-month sensation.

Taking advantage of the inherent theatricality of nineteenth-century court proceedings, *The Nor'Wester*'s opening editorial on the subject dramatized the trial as a "tragedy" headed for an inexorable "*dénouement*," a "deplorable finale," and a "final curtain,"[1] with the participants in the proceedings as *dramatis personae*. James Ross, the son of an Okanagan woman and a prominent retired Scottish fur trader, stage-managed the courtroom drama[2] as well as its literary reconstruction, and cast himself simultaneously as author, director, and lead. Several Headingley residents, witnesses called to testify about the plaintiff's character, appeared briefly in minor roles. The Reverend Corbett's appearance was exceedingly brief; Ross was likely reluctant to highlight an English man of the cloth as the villain of the piece.

The two major female actors, Maria Thomas and the English wife of the accused, Abigail Corbett, played opposing roles. They were cast as one of the nineteenth century's most powerful and pervasive dualities of womanhood: the fallen woman and the chaste wife, or "angel in the house."[3] As paired metaphors, the women had a symbolic import that far outweighed their actual roles in the legal proceedings. Abigail Corbett was never called to the witness box and remained a shadowy presence, but as an Englishwoman and wife, she enacted the pivotal role of Thomas's counterpart by opposition.

---

1   *The Nor'Wester*, 3 March 1863.

2   Joseph James Hargrave, *Red River* (Montreal: John Lovell, 1871), p. 271.

3   Coventry Patmore, *The Angel in the House* (London: George Bell and Son, 1896). *The Angel in the House* was a poetic construct which captured the imaginations of several generations of writers and social commentators. Patmore wrote the poem, he said, as a celebration of married love. But modern historians, analyzing its gender politics, found that his Angel operated as an influential prescription for flesh-and-blood women. Edmund Gosse, *Coventry Patmore* (London: Hodder and Stoughton, 1905); Carol Christ, "Victorian Masculinity and the Angel in the House," in Martha Vicinus, ed., *A Widening Sphere: Changing Roles of Victorian Women* (Bloomington: Indiana University Press, 1977).

The Nor' Wester's staging of this event is a prime example of how the construction of a narrative gave new meaning to real persons and events. In a deconstructive vein, this paper mines James Ross's journalistic elaboration of key social and literary themes for answers to the questions: Why did this particular discourse of sexuality emerge in Red River in 1863? Where did Ross acquire it and why did he give it so much attention? What practical impact did the polarization of women have on Red River?

The Corbett trial has been interpreted as reflecting a social and political conflict which was indigenous, and in some senses unique, to Red River.[1] But a closer examination of *The Nor' Wester*'s consciously literary techniques and strategies reveals that its writers saw Red River's identity and destiny as tied to a larger story whose plot was dominated by British social structures, institutions, and modes of thought. The leading gentlemen of the trial proceedings were primarily British-born or British-oriented middle-class Victorians whose ideas, attitudes, dreams, and fantasies informed Red River's official sexual code. This is not to imply that their attitudes were uniform or fixed within a stable and homogeneous "Victorian frame of mind." They did, however, share the collective sexual anxieties of their day, as well as its common-sense thinking about women, which naturalized the perceived gulf between respectable women and prostitutes.

Labelled the "great social evil,"[2] the "problem" of prostitution permeated every sector of British society, and generated masses of printed material penned by purity campaigners, politicians, philanthropists, novelists, and journalists. By the 1860s, "the prostitute" was imprinted on middle-class consciousness as a cultural archetype of moral depravity and physical contagion.[3] James Ross was aware of and attuned to this mode

---

1   Frits Pannekoek, "The Rev. Griffith Owen Corbett and the Red River Civil War of 1869-70," *Canadian Historical Review* 57 (1976), pp. 133-50.

2   Barbara Kanner, *Women in English Social History 1800-1914*, vol. 2 (New York: Garland, 1988), p. 483. E.M. Sigsworth and T.J. Wyke, "A Study of Victorian Prostitution and Venereal Disease," in Martha Vicinus, ed., *Suffer and Be Still: Women in the Victorian Age* (Bloomington: Indian University Press, 1973), p. 80. Leonore Davidoff and Catherine Hall, *Family Fortunes: Men and Women of the English Middle Class*, 1789-1950 (Chicago: University of Chicago Press, 1987), p. 89.

3   A major study of Victorian prostitution is Judith R. Walkowitz, *Prostitution and Victorian Society: Women, Class and the State* (New York: Cambridge University Press, 1980).

ERICA SMITH

of thinking, as his speeches and cross-examinations indicate. It is worth-while to examine how the son of an old fur trader acquired and applied that discourse.

With the encouragement of his teacher and mentor David Anderson, the Bishop of Rupert's Land, Ross had won a scholarship to the University of Toronto's Knox College in 1853, graduating with distinction five years later. As a student, he inhabited a landscape of knowledge marked by the intellectual currents and gender assumptions of the educated classes of Britain. Thus it was to Britain that he turned for his iconography when he constructed, for the benefit of the court, a portrait of Maria Thomas which transformed a mixed-blood daughter of Red River into a typical Victorian prostitute who traded sexual favours for money and dress, articulated inappropriate sexual knowledge, and gadded about in public, destroying the domestic happiness of respectable families and the reputations of respectable neighbourhoods.

Ross proceeded first to discredit Thomas's credibility by questioning her virtue:

> Maria says ... that she had now for the first time known a man. From the evidence you will hear — I think you will easily draw the inference that she must have had sexual intercourse before this time ... her high principle succumbed before a bribe and ... she willingly bartered her character and her chastity for gain.[1]

Ross's further "evidence" revealed that Thomas had accepted money and a dress from Corbett. The significance of the monetary gift paled momentarily, however, as the dress aroused a flurry of interest in the courtroom. The women of the parish who testified about Maria's character perceived the dress as a social marker with which she inappropriately adorned her body. To them, its stylishness ("black French merino" with a "fine black silk fringe") indicated its expensive quality and, implicitly, Maria Thomas's social pretensions. Ross, however, also perceived the dress to have been a temptation to this suggestible and corrupted young woman and invested it with moral significance.

The tendency to judge character from dress, the inner state from the outer, flourished in nineteenth-century discourse and was, in the 1860s,

---

1   *The Nor'Wester*, 30 March 1863.

particularized in the image of the prostitute. Searching for the origins of the great social evil, the influential English surgeon and social reformer William Acton, for example, wrote that woman's vanity and love of dress sounded the first alarm bell of a predilection for a life of prostitution. Acton's concern reverberated widely, as when a New England doctor opined: "As a medical man, I will give my opinion as to what encourages prostitution; idleness and the love of finery."[1] In Rupert's Land, the theme echoed in the frequent refrain of fur traders who made pejorative associations between Indians' love of fine clothing and their low moral development.[2]

Thomas's apparently difficult confinement left marks on her body which were interpreted as further evidence of moral failure in addition to physical decline. As she stood in the witness box "with her babe in her arms,"[3] the presiding judicial officer, recorder John Black, noted the pathos of her "wistful, withered, haggard" countenance. Although Black sympathized with Thomas's plight, he was also convinced of the inevitability of the standard denouement of illicit sexual encounters: lost virtue, banishment from respectable society, broken health, a sad death.

> To the unfortunate woman herself, the consequences of this prosecution cannot alas! ... affect her very much. By some one or other, she has already been deprived of all that makes female character valuable — her virtue; and probably there is now nothing on earth that concerns her but preparation for death.[4]

---

1 Sigsworth and Wyke, 82. For the connection between finery and prostitutes, see Mariana Valverde, "The Love of Finery: Fashion and the Fallen Woman in Nineteenth-Century Social Discourse," *Victorian Studies* vol. 32 (Winter 1989) 169-188. Valverde uncovered a veritable "debate on finery" in the official documents on prostitution.

2 Erica Smith, "Something More Than Mere Ornament: Cloth and Indian-European Relationships in the Eighteenth Century," master's thesis, University of Winnipeg, 1991.

3 NAC, James Hunter Journal, mfm. A91. James Hunter to Henry Venn, 7 January 1863.

4 *The Nor'Wester*, 12 May 1863.

No doubt the clergymen in the courtroom, shaken by the disclosures and anxiously awaiting the verdict, were reminded of Genesis and Eve's punishment for her ill-conceived curiosity, as Ross went on to draw a connection between Maria Thomas's prurience and her persual of Corbett's medical books:

> Maria ... was a girl of lewd tendencies, and of a reckless, licentious disposition, who seized every opportunity to revel in those improper delights which an inspection and perusal of medical works would offer her! ... who more likely than she to pry into these books, examine the woodcuts, and read eagerly the details and explanations given?[1]

Thomas's exposure to "obscene pictures" swept away whatever remnant of innocence she might still have possessed. Illustrations of sexual matters were in themselves indecent, and potent stimuli to misbehaviour. As a later Canadian clergyman warned: "No man can look upon obscene pictures without the danger of photographing upon his mind that which he might subsequently be willing to give thousands of dollars to obliterate."[2] Ross reflected this widespread perception when he declared that the medical illustrations would "leave a vivid and lasting impression" on a susceptible mind.[3]

Turning to the prostitute's celebrated opposite, the chaste wife, Ross introduced the absent Abigail Corbett in a domestic vocabulary which drew attention to her exemplary relationship to her husband. As a faithful wife, "the dear partner of his bosom," she was "in continual tears — plunged in hopeless grief" over her husband's tribulations.[4] Notions of the stability of the respectable monogamous family as a domestic sanctum permeated his opening address to the jury:

---

1   *The Nor'Wester*, 30 March 1863.

2   Rev. Sylvanus Stall, *What a Man Ought to Know* (Philadelphia, 1901), p. 241. Cited in Michael Bliss, "'Pure Books on Avoided Subjects': Pre-Freudian Sexual Ideas in Canada," J. Atherton, J.P. Heisler and Fernand Ouellet, eds., Canadian Historical Association. *Historical Papers* (1968-70), p. 95.

3   *The Nor'Wester*, 30 March 1863.

4   *The Nor'Wester*, 13 March 1863.

I implore you [to find Corbett innocent] by all that is valuable in life, by all that is precious in domestic happiness, by all that is dear in an unsullied name.[1]

In contrast to his detailed portrait of Maria Thomas, Ross sketched Abigail Corbett in brief, broad strokes, confident that the audience to which he spoke would fill in the details themselves. The judge, the medical men, his fellow journalists and legal colleagues had British cultural ties; they knew and shared his terms of reference:

I need not speak of Mrs Corbett's character, or paint her noble, pure feelings. We see it in her very face, we notice it in her conversations, in her manner, her every movement: she is a refined, honest, pure-hearted noble Englishwoman.[2]

As Ross constructed her, Abigail Corbett epitomized that quintessential symbol of respectable Victorian womanhood, universally admired in the 1860s and beyond: the angel in the house. Ross moulded her to fit the particulars most frequently applied to this paragon: sterling character, noble sentiments, refined emotion, genteel deportment, and most importantly, sexual purity.

Victorian discourse about woman's sexual purity turned frequently on discussions of her natural passivity. Countless pamphlets, treatises, sermons, and books were devoted to the invention of a passive, asexual feminine ideal. In 1850, the writer of one influential article in the *Westminster Review* noted approvingly, if impressionistically: "Women whose position and education have protected them from exciting causes, constantly pass through life without ever being cognizant of the promptings of the senses."[3] The reformer William Acton was more direct, although

---

1   *The Nor'Wester*, 13 March 1863. A number of Ross's private letters also upheld the sanctity of the woman-home-family triad. "Ah yes! – It has been well remarked that 'mother' 'home' and 'heaven' seem to sound the sweetest words in our language, and when, papa, the last two become synonimous [sic] terms, they become a hundredfold sweeter," he wrote to his father. PAM, Alexander Ross Collection, James Ross to Alexander Ross, 13 July 1854.

2   *The Nor'Wester*, 30 March 1863.

3   William Greg's article, "Prostitution," published in the *Westminster Review* in 1850, is reprinted in *Prostitution in the Victorian Age: Debates on the Issue from 19th Century Critical Journals* (Westmead, England: Gregg International, 1973).

no less impressionistic: "Many of the best mothers, wives and managers of households, know little of or are careless about sexual indulgence. Love of home, children, and of domestic duties are the only passions they feel."[1]

By the 1860s, women's sexual passivity was a matter for debate.[2] When Maria Thomas claimed that she had been drugged and was therefore unable to resist Corbett's advances, she provoked an outburst from Ross in which he revealed his own assumptions. Women were by nature passive, he argued, but for a pure woman, apathy and supineness posed no danger, as he put it, to "her most sacred parts." As a protection against predatory males, nature had provided woman with an innate involuntary response that sprang immediately to her defence the instant her chastity was threatened.[3] She was thus rendered "sacred from the rude touch of impure hands."[4] As he believed that no sleeping draught had the potency to overcome nature, Ross's subsequent question was rhetorical:

What kind of medicine could put her into such a profound sleep as to make her unconscious while a man lay with her! ... the thing is preposterous. In such circumstances the girl would involuntarily shrink from the ravisher, even in her profoundest sleep. She would become cognisant of

---

1   By 1860, the passionless wife had her masculine counterpart in the domesticated, sexually restrained, middle-class husband. Sexual control, or the mastery of passion, was one of the great moral imperatives aimed at men during this time. Too complex to flesh out here, the masculine gendering of sexuality awaits fuller treatment, but it may be briefly noted that the consequences of his sexual transgression were far-reaching and disastrous for Corbett. Disgraced and labelled "an awful blackguard" by his clerical colleagues in Red River, he returned to England shortly after the trial. When he begged the Archbishop of London, A.C. Tait, for a position, he did so on the basis of his "blameless life for some twenty years...prior to the storm which burst out abroad." Tait had been alerted to the scandal by David Anderson, Bishop of Rupert's Land, and delayed giving Corbett his answer until, he said, he was "satisfied respecting the past." PAM, M627, Lambeth Palace Library, Tait Papers.

2   Acton's passionless stereotype was being vigorously challenged by the 1860s, mostly by medical men who argued that women as well as men were capable of sexual arousal. See Carl Degler, *At Odds: Women and the Family in America from the Revolution to the Present* (New York: Oxford University Press, 1980), especially chapter 11.

3   See Peter T. Cominos, "Innocent Femina Sensualis in Unconscious Conflict," in Martha Vicinus, ed., *Suffer and Be Still: Women in the Victorian Age* (Bloomington: Indiana University Press, 1973), p. 157.

4   *The Nor'Wester*, 30 March 1863.

her impending shame and dishonor — innocent nature would recoil and revolt and she *must* awake.[1]

The angel in the house, by definition physically weak and vulnerable to the storms and stresses of life, spent most of her life confined to the home. Thomas's robustness and "romping" behaviour, in contrast, proved that she did not belong to that frail sisterhood, for in spite of her ordeal, Ross said,

> she was vigorous and healthy walked briskly, foolishly gossiped, as usual, and jested with great glee on impure topics.... Instead of finding this sick girl in bed or passively reclining on some couch or sofa — she was from home romping about the neighborhood doubtless pursuing her vocation of impure gossip and wretched scandal.[2]

Ross's words call to mind William Acton's report of the general medical opinion that "as a rule" prostitutes were endowed with "iron bodies" and resilient constitutions.[3] The passage also highlights the extent of the inconsistencies and confusions in Victorian conceptualizations of female sexuality: Maria Thomas was at once "withered" (according to Black) and "vigorous," a contradiction that both counsel and judge overlooked.

In summing up his case, Ross drew conclusions from his own construct of Maria Thomas as a fallen woman. It was for the most part a decontextualized abstraction, largely uninfluenced by the evidence at hand. What accounted for Ross's exaggerated construction of Maria Thomas as a prostitute?

On one level, given Ross's financial interest in the fledgling newspaper, a trial involving illicit sex was simply good copy: *The Nor'Wester* was pandering to the public's fascination with scandalous exposés. It was also a form of self-advertisement for the editors, who proudly proclaimed that their reportage of the "trial of the century ... no doubt rivals some of the *causes les plus célèbres* of other lands."[4]

---

1 *The Nor'Wester*, 30 March 1863.

2 *The Nor'Wester*, 30 April 1863.

3 Marcus, *The Other Victorians*, p. 5.

4 *The Nor'Wester*, 3 March 1863.

ERICA SMITH

But *The Nor'Wester*'s higher purpose was to be a conveyor of moral truths, and Ross's dichotomizing of womanhood sprang from wider concerns. By 1863 Red River was a substantial community of considerable interest to outsiders observing its moral condition. *The Nor'Wester*'s coverage attracted critical comment in the *Montreal Witness*;[2] but Red River was also drawing positive attention from a variety of easterners who were converging on Red River in the 1860s.[3] Acutely aware of an opportunity to advance the reputation of his mixed race, Ross was determined to demonstrate his and Red River's devotion to and defence of British values.

In this project, he drew support from the racial ideas of Daniel Wilson, the Scottish-born professor who held the chair in history at the University of Toronto when Ross was a student there, and whose best-known work, *Prehistoric Man*, was published in 1863. Addressing the question of intermarriage between Indians and whites, Wilson wrote that the offspring of such unions constituted an important "ethnical element" which could only benefit the development of the Canadian nation.[4] Worried about the role of people of biracial ancestry in the new order, Ross seized on the professor's appealing thesis, optimistically predicting in *The Nor'Wester* that Red River's "fusion of races ... would do no discredit to any community," and that mixed-bloods "can claim equality with pure whites in all those qualities which go to constitute merit."[5]

---

1   They condemned the two editors for printing such "disagreeable records" in a "family magazine," a judgment perhaps not unmixed with professional envy. Hargrave, p. 271.

2   William Coldwell, the journalist who took shorthand notes of the trial, had professional as well as attitudinal ties to Canada. Like Ross, he was concerned to present Red River in the best possible light to reassure Canadian expansionists, whose ambitions they shared. Doug Owram, *Promise of Eden: The Canadian Expansionist Movement and the Idea of the West 1856-1900* (Toronto: University of Toronto Press, 1980), p. 82.

3   Suzanne Zeller, *Inventing Canada: Early Victorian Science and the Idea of a Transcontinental Nation* (Toronto, University of Toronto Press, 1987), p. 261.

4   *The Nor'Wester*, 14 October 1863. See also Red River Bishop David Anderson's exegesis of Hebrews 1, 1-12, a synthesis of Christianity, ethnology, and history, in which the sons (the Native and mixed-blood catechists of the youthful and vigorous colonial church) surpass the stately father (the Church of England). Anderson, *Children instead of fathers: a Christmas ordination sermon, preached at St. John's Church, Red River, on Sunday, December 25, 1854* (London, 1854).

In fact, most visitors to Red River appeared impressed by its moral progress. Travellers frequently praised the colony as an oasis in a desert, an example of the triumph of civilization over brute nature. Sir John Henry Lefroy's sigh of relief on reaching Red River after his western subarctic travels ("Here again one encounters civilization")[1] was a typical refrain among such gentleman adventurers returning from the wilderness and encounters with "primitive" Indians. The colony's schoolchildren were commended in these accounts for their "decorum," and high-achieving men such as James Ross were singled out as "improved" and a "credit" to their race.[2] Such improvement narratives by influential outsiders helped to foster pride in the emergence of a civilized society at Red River. By mid-century the leading families of the settlement were also fashioning their own image of a community devoted to British definitions and requirements of respectability.[3]

At first glance, then, Ross's public construction of his countrywoman as a prostitute – condemning Maria Thomas in order to achieve the elevation of the mixed-blood community to which they both belonged – would appear to be a major paradox. It is important to recall, however, that being defined as "prostitute", placed Maria Thomas beyond the pale of respectable society and its discourses. Moreover, the prostitute metaphor was remarkably flexible and could be expanded to draw attention to all kinds of social problems. Ross found it a useful vehicle to highlight his most pressing concerns: community respectability and the purification of Red River's sexual mores.

The first requisite of respectability was to exorcise the ghost of a fur-trade past haunted by images of illicit sexual congress. In the censorious Christian discourse of the clergymen of Red River, Native women living with men in unions not sanctioned by the church were little better

---

1   NAC, MG 24 H25, Sir John Henry Lefroy Journal, 1843-44.

2   Robert Coutts, "Anglican Missionaries as Agents of Acculturation: The Church Missionary Society at St. Andrews, Red River, 1830-1870," in Barry Ferguson, *The Anglican Church and World of Western Canada 1820-1970* (Regina: Canadian Plains Research Center, 1991), p. 56. Adam Thom, a former resident, reporting on the progress of the mission to an Aberdeen audience, held James Ross up as an "example of the progress of Red River" in particular and of "civilization in general." PAM, Alexander Ross Collection, Adam Thom to Alexander Ross, 27 March 1855.

3   The 1860s saw the establishment of a cricket club, a public library, a reading club, a temperance society, and a scientific institute in Red River.

than prostitutes, regardless of the stability and longevity of their marriages "according to the custom of the country." Seizing on the rhetoric of shame as a way out of burdensome relationships, and the notorious example of Hudson's Bay Company Governor George Simpson, several fur trade officers abandoned their country wives. They frequently spoke of their past relationships in a vocabulary of sexual disgust.[1]

As mid-century Red River distanced itself from old fur-trade ways, the polarization of women as either promiscuous or pure was made absolute. Within the prevailing racial discourse, Indian women were agents of men's ruin and white women agents of men's salvation. On this theme, the views of the Red River elite were in tune with those of the Aborigines Protection Society, a humanitarian organization founded in London, England, in 1837. The report of its rescue mission, published in 1856, represented a wave of protest, a kind of backlash against the sexual licence of the British colonial social order in western North America and elsewhere. Viewing the social landscape of Rupert's Land through a filter of popular ethnological and gender assumptions, the society concluded that Native women's promiscuity was responsible for the "low morals" of Hudson's Bay Company men. Like Britain's social reformers exhorting middle-class women to reclaim prostitutes, they also expressed a deep commitment to the notion that British women should effect "the mental and moral improvement" of the Company's servants. Marriage to respectable white women was the fur traders' best hope of reclamation and deliverance from their deplorable liaisons.[2] However, commentators for the Society admitted that their solutions were more idealistic than practical since white wives were in short supply in Ru-

---

1 Sylvia Van Kirk, *"Many Tender Ties": Women in Fur-Trade Society, 1670-1870* (Winnipeg: Watson and Dwyer, 1980), especially chapter 7. The language of George Simpson is the most obvious example of a fur trade officer's distaste for Indian women's sexuality and his own sexual past. See also the letters of his friend and colleague, James Hargrave, discussed in Jennifer S.H. Brown, "Changing Views of Fur Trade Marriage and Domesticity: James Hargrave, His Colleagues, and 'The Sex,'" *Western Canadian Journal of Anthropology*, vol. 6 (1976), p. 3. Hargrave's comments echo the obsession with "the woman question" that plagued British male discourses at the time; in them the term "the Sex" (signifying women) was a common phrase.

2 Aborigines Protection Society, *Canada West and the Hudson's Bay Company* (London: William Tweedie, 1856), pp. 6, 16. William Acton expressed precisely the same sentiments in *Functions and Disorders of the Reproductive System* (1857). See Stephen Marcus, *The Other Victorians: A Study of Sexuality and Pornography in Mid-Nineteenth-Century England* (Toronto: Bantam Books, 1967), p. 32.

pert's Land. They were also silent about the question of whether the majority of HBC servants found such preachings to have any real meaning in their lives. Indeed, many of these men had neither the means nor the inclination to adorn their lives with the graces of a white angel, a "lovely, tender exotic."[1]

Yet traders, too, were men of their time. Ambitious and conscientious veterans of the fur trade were, like Alexander Ross, father of James, concerned about their families' standing within the shifting social patterns of their ever-widening world. Instead of acquiring white wives, however, most officers with families in Red River focussed intense attention upon elevating their daughters. They were to serve as bridges from a cloudy past to a respectable present and bright future. The fathers' concern to train the girls for British-style middle-class domesticity and marriage to white men has been well documented.[2] But the paternal anxiety to cultivate and protect their sexual purity went beyond a wish to see them advantageously established. In her study of nineteenth-century girlhood, Deborah Gorham has noted the pervasiveness of the "daughter-as-redeemer" theme in the novels of the time. In these books, daughters as agents of salvation rescue fathers from the consequences of past moral transgressions.[3] This insight is worth exploring with reference to Red River's racially mixed families. The purity of half-British daughters, if carefully cultivated, could in effect wipe famil-

---

1   The word "exotic" applied by Chief Factor James Douglas to white women in the Northwest and vaguely assumed to be a term of admiration, could mean quite the reverse. Douglas, married to a woman of mixed descent, was possibly using the term ironically to undercut the prevailing discourse. To William Acton, for example, it meant an unusual freakish person (Marcus, 16). Similarly, it is difficult to ignore the satirical implications of such descriptions of the ideal (white) wife immortalized by Chief Factor Donald McKenzie in his epigram: "[N]othing can give greater comfort to a husband than the satisfaction of having a wife who is nearly mute," or the parodic elements in John Stuart's impression of Frances Simpson disembarking at Red River: "Grace was in all her steps – heaven in her Eye – In all her gestures Dignity & love." Quoted in Brown, "James Hargrave," p. 103, and G.P. de T. Glazebrook, *The Hargrave Correspondence* (Toronto: Champlain Society, 1938), p. 57, respectively.

2   Van Kirk, "Many Tender Ties," especially chapter 7; Thomas F. Bredin, "The Red River Academy," *The Beaver*, (Winter 1974), p. 14.

3   Deborah Gorham, *The Victorian Girl and the Feminine Ideal* (Bloomington: Indiana University Press, 1982), pp. 42-43.

ERICA SMITH

ial slates clean of the immoral past and elevate the respectability of the paterfamilias, his country wife, and the community in the process.

Red River fathers such as Alexander Ross spared neither effort nor expense to nurture their daughters' moral development and safeguard their chastity.[1] Their project was both reanimated and legitimized after 1860 by Darwin's buoyant discoveries about the developmental potential of the human race as it progressed towards perfection. One of their tenets was that if mixed-blood daughters were to mature properly, it was necessary to minimize maternal influences. Thus Red River reversed the British trend of mothers inculcating moral values in young children, as well-intentioned fathers with Native wives involved themselves in the early religious education of their daughters.[2] British-style schools took over where the fathers left off.

Significantly, calls for such schools came both from the gentlemen of the HBC's Northern Council as well as the governor of Assiniboia, Eden Colvile, for whom the education of "the young women of this Country" was "a matter of great importance."[3] The schools aimed to provide the enabling conditions and fertile ground for the flourishing of sexual purity[4] and were thus usually under the charge of governesses from Britain. One of these "excellent importations" was Harriet Mills, who arrived in Red River in 1851, "on the invitation of the Bishop of Rupert's Land, to establish a school for young ladies."[5] The school flourished and was tellingly described by the young Peter Jacobs, a student at the boys' school, as "swarming with angelic beings."[6]

But the most powerful moulding force in the elevation of girls in Red River was Matilda Davis, herself a daughter of the country. Like James Ross, she arose as a shining example of what exposure to a civi-

---

1 Van Kirk, *"Many Tender Ties,"* p. 148.

2 W.J. Healy, *Women of Red River* (Winnipeg: Russell, Lang & Co., Ltd, 1923), pp. 80-81.

3 E.E. Rich and A.M. Johnson, eds., *London Correspondence Inward from Eden Colvile, 1849-1852* (London: Hudson's Bay Record Society, 1956), p. 156.

4 Two examples are the St. Cross school and Miss Davis's Academy.

5 Rich and Johnson, pp. 156, 260.

6 PAM, MG 2C14, Alexander Ross Collection, Peter Jacobs to James Ross, 19 December 1853.

lized British milieu could accomplish. Her HBC officer father, John Davis, sent her to England to be educated. When she returned to establish a school in the Red River parish of St. Andrew's in about 1840, she brought with her solid British middle-class values and a trunk full of books and pamphlets with such titles as "Home Life," "The Excellent Woman," and "A Mother's Mission."[1] According to the celebratory written and oral testimony of several Red River descendants, Davis not only taught a solidly academic curriculum, but also stressed "all the feminine accomplishments of the day" and the graceful deportment she had learned during a stint as governess in the homes of some of Britain's "prominent families."[2] One former pupil later told her daughter of being taught by Miss Davis "how to sit, how to walk," during her stay at what she referred to as "finishing school."[3]

Davis also imported the high-minded doctrine of duty upheld by educated British women of her generation. Intent on raising the level of her countrywomen,[4] she joined the crusade popularized by the influential English philanthropist and social reformer Hannah More, who exhorted her middle-class female readers to elevate the moral tone of society by educating their less fortunate sisters. More's writings, an enduring staple of British girls' school literature, also guided the education of Red River's young women.[5]

School records, James Ross's newspaper, and reports of church sermons all help to document Red River's pursuit of middle-class British ideals in this period. The columns of *The Nor'Wester* provided guidance to families aspiring to gentility through prescriptive homilies with such titles as "The Happy Woman," "Comfort at Home," and "The Gentlemen at Home." Similarly, Red River's Presbyterian minister, John Black, a brother-in-law of James Ross, preached domestic propriety in texts such as that which one parishioner glossed simply as "husbands love

---

1 PAM, MG 2 C24, Matilda Davis School Collection.

2 Mrs. George Bryce, *Early Red River Culture*, Historical and Scientific Society of Manitoba, Transaction no. 57 (Winnipeg: Manitoba Free Press), p. 15.

3 Winnipeg, Museum of Man and Nature Library. Flora Smith Oral History Tape 106.

4 Bryce, *Early Red River Culture*, p. 15.

5 Healy, *Women of Red River*, p. 260.

your wives [and] wives love your homes."[1] Other preachers warned about the dangers of female vanity and emphasized standard proper comportment of the body, modest dress, and sedate behaviour.[2]

The new sexual code was reflected in the shift from the HBC's earlier stress on the teaching of basic literacy and Christian morality to a more explicit directive in 1851. Its educational goal was now "to weaken the mischievous and destructive energy of those violent and untamed qualities of human nature which so frequently manifest themselves in society in a half-civilized state."[3] The discreetly worded reference to unregulated sexuality was not lost on Red River's teachers, who applied themselves assiduously to their mission. In the memoirs of former pupils, the governesses emerge as strict guardians of reputations, ever vigilant "for signs of promiscuous behaviour."[4]

Maria Thomas probably escaped such surveillance, for the project of bringing daughters up to a suitable standard was anchored in class values, and reserved for those who could afford the costs. Elite colony residents showed little interest in educating the "abandoned" daughters of country marriages, who were assumed to lack the budding virtues of chastity and piety which, with careful cultivation, could be brought to flower.[5] An education based on "the social etiquette of the day" would be a wasted effort on them.[6] Maria Thomas, described as a "poor girl," and the daughter of "poor folk," was raised by a Cree-speaking mother who testified in the Cree language at the trial. Thus the Thomas family inhabited the lower rungs of Red River's social ladder, and their circumstances prohibited Maria from receiving an education in refinement.

Maria Thomas was no passive victim, however. Her responses to Ross's cross-examinations countered his claims with certainties of her own. Unlike Ross's theatrical narrative, Thomas's formulation of her

---

1 PAM, Alexander Ross Collection, Jemima Ross to James Ross, 28 June 1854.

2 Healy, *Women of Red River*, p. 34.

3 E.H. Oliver, *The Canadian North-West: Its Early Development and Legislative Development*, vol. 1 (Ottawa: Government Printing Bureau, 1914), p. 365.

4 Healy, *Women of Red River*, p. 82.

5 Bredin, "The Red River Academy," p. 11.

6 Bredin, "The Red River Academy," p. 11; Bryce, *Early Red River Culture*, p. 14.

story appeared as straight chronicle, stripped of imaginative glosses.[1] Its coherence was diffused, however, because it was printed in several scattered fragments, comprising her "answers" to questions which *The Nor'Wester* did not specify. In contrast, the speeches of Ross and Judge Black were given dozens of uninterrupted column inches. Thomas's story was thus framed within their narrative and meaning system, or so it would seem at first glance.

A closer scrutiny reveals, however, that the papers on which Ross and *The Nor'Wester* inscribed their drama were not blank pages. They were palimpsests, scored and criss-crossed with traces of older stories — both Native and European — that proved difficult to erase even as late as 1863. These stubborn scripts of sexuality and sex-related practices (enduring country marriages and Cree courtship patterns, for example) interrogate *The Nor'Wester*'s dichotomous metaphors. As layered texts, heavily written over in the Corbett trial, they also offer counter-readings for understanding how Red River responded to new ideas and made sense of a changing and tension-ridden social order. But that is, indeed, another script and another story. What is of note here is that the scaffolding for the staging of the trial, its forms of dramatic and textual representation — the metaphors, allusions, and vocabulary — are themselves sources of historical knowledge.

---

1   The content of Thomas's version was, I suspect, left more or less intact because it was not considered worthy of notice, let alone editorial reworking. The known facts about her life are scanty. She died in 1867 and the child, Anne Elizabeth, was raised by the Thomas family. Hargrave, *Red River*, p. 287.

ERICA SMITH

16

Transcribing Insima, a Blackfoot "Old Lady"[1]

Alice Beck Kehoe

SUE SOMMERS[2] had completed only one year of graduate work in anthropology at New York's Columbia University when she arrived in Browning, Montana, on the Blackfeet Indian Reservation early in the summer of 1939. Ruth Benedict, her professor and organizer of the Columbia University Laboratory for ethnography, was already there, living in a tent. Sommers recalled that Professor Benedict had her sleeping bag on the ground, and was grateful when the young woman lent her an air mattress. Several other graduate students enrolled in the Laboratory project later became well-known anthropologists, including Oscar and Ruth Lewis, Esther Goldfrank, and Lucien Hanks and Jane Richardson,

---

1   David Reed Miller and Susan Miller introduced me to Sue Sommers Dietrich. After procrastinating for a couple of years I telephoned her home in south-suburban Chicago in August 1993 and made an appointment to interview her about the 1939 Blackfoot project. Sue was a delightful interviewee and a gracious hostess. She lent me three folders of her typed interviews with Insima so that the fragile sheets could be copied and archived by Mark Thiel, Marquette University archivist, and she invited me to return. Less that two months later, Sue Dietrich was killed by a car near her home.

   The estate of Susan Dietrich has consented to the use of these interviews for this volume.

2   Sylvia Sue Roma Sommers, named after the women's rights activists Sylvia Pankhurst and Susan B. Anthony, was born in 1914 in Trenton, New Jersey, where her parents had immigrated from Russia. She earned a Bachelor of Arts in sociology from Hunter College in 1936, worked as a social worker in Harlem, and in 1938 enrolled in Columbia University's graduate program in anthropology. The following summer, at Ruth Benedict's invitation, she joined the Laboratory project on the Blackfeet Reservation.

   Sommers served in World War II and afterward married Donald Dietrich, a psychoanalyst who, in 1948 and 1949, accompanied by Sue, did comparative psychology field research on three Plains reservations (one of them the Blackfeet). Sue Dietrich devoted herself to activities related to Quaker missions to promote peace, particularly a series of trips to Viet Nam and China. She visited the Blackfeet Reservation several times after the 1949 fieldwork with her husband, remaining in contact with the Yellow Kidney family.

who later married (Goldfrank 1978:128). Benedict planned that they would divide and cover the four Blackfoot reserves, the North Blackfoot, Blood, and North Piegan in Alberta, Canada, and the Blackfeet (South Piegan[1]) in Montana, comparing the four societies and investigating their histories. Sue Sommers joined fellow student Gitel Steed and her painter husband, Bob, at Two Medicine River on the Montana reservation. Benedict gave the inexperienced students the simplest of instructions: "See if you can establish contact with a family and live with them."

Sommers arrived on the reservation during the South Piegans' annual reunion, the North American Indian Days powwow. She dressed in jeans and commercial moccasins, twisted her long, thick hair into two braids, and went into the campground. A group of women, noticing her, exclaimed over her braids. A middle-aged man, Jim Little Plume, came over and escorted Sommers to the tipi of Yellow Kidney, then about 70 years old, where she was invited to sit beside the fire hospitably burning in the tipi. A tourist from Connecticut came in with his two sons, saying that he wanted his boys adopted into the tribe and given Indian names. The tourist took out a notebook and asked each person's name, writing down the replies. When he came to Sommers, Jim Little Plume spoke up, "She is Long Braids, she is my wife." As soon as the man departed, everyone in the tipi laughed heartily at the joke. Little Plume showed up daily to escort Sommers around the reservation, and every morning he placed a bouquet of wildflowers at her tent.

Yellow Kidney and his wife Insima (*I'nssimaa*, "Gardener, Planter") agreed to set up a large tipi next to their house for the Steeds and Sommers. Tipis are often erected in the summer to shelter a family's guests, and this tipi was so comfortable that Benedict preferred it to the accommodations of the other students on the Canadian reserves. In the evenings, the Steeds and Sommers often joined the Yellow Kidney family in their home. Officially, Yellow Kidney spoke only Blackfoot and required anthropologists to hire interpreters at 25 cents an hour, but after hours, his English proved adequate if not fluent, and he would comment on the day's interpreter. Yellow Kidney's neighbour and long-time comrade (*itakkaa*, "buddy," "partner") was Jappy Takes Gun On Top, who had been stepfather to D.C. Duvall, the half-Piegan collaborator

---

1 Piegan and Peigan are variants of Pikuni, the closest English spelling for the Blackfoot term *Piikani*. The South Piegan in Montana are the *Aamsskaapipiikani*.

Figure 1: Insima with her pet raven (undated)
Credit: Patricia Dietrich, photographer unknown

with Clark Wissler on the American Museum series of ethnographies of the Blackfoot (Wissler and Duvall 1908). Yellow Kidney was half-brother to Jim's deceased father, the original Little Plume, and their families had been neighbours on Two Medicine River early in the century. Cuts Different, widow of that Little Plume, remained close to her brother-in-law.

Sommers wanted to interview the three women in the family: Insima, her daughter Agnes Chief All Over, and Cuts Different. Although she obediently recorded extended interviews with Yellow Kidney, Philip Wells, and other respected older men throughout July, in mid-August she began interviewing Agnes Chief All Over and her fascinating mother. Jim Little Plume had interpreted at first, but he was killed on 9 July when Bob Steed's roadster, in which he was a passenger, overturned rounding a dangerous curve. Agnes took over the task of interpreting, and gave Sommers pages of her own life history as well.

Insima was 72, the same age as her husband Yellow Kidney, and had the Christian name Cecile. She had formerly been married to Yellow Wolf, more than 20 years her senior, who died at 82 about ten years before the Laboratory project. Insima was listed as "Cecile" in the 1907-08 Allotment Census, where her father is given as Isadore Sanderville, son of a non-Indian supposedly of the same name and a Piegan woman called Catch For Nothing. He had married Margaret, daughter of the Piegans Red Bird Tail and Twice Success. Cecile had two older brothers, Oliver and Richard (Dick), and a sister Louise (Mrs. John Croff in 1908). Dick Sanderville served on the Blackfeet Tribal Council as early as 1909.

Sue Sommers found Insima captivating. "Five by five feet," energetic and funny, and "really controlling, of the men, of everybody," Sommers recalled her. (One day, Insima picked up Sommers and threw her down, just in fun.) Insima much enjoyed imitating men, putting a pillow under her skirt to appear as a man's big paunch belly (see Appendix for one story of her joking). Her serious side was as a midwife and herb doctor. Sommers remembered her "running up and down the hills" picking medicinal herbs on one occasion while Sommers laboured to get a car out of a stream crossing. Told of his wife's energy, Yellow Kidney remarked, "That's how she keeps in shape for when she wants to chase after men."

Ruth Benedict expected Sommers to take down Indians' life histories. Yellow Kidney's was an obvious choice, since he was a prominent elder in the community. Sue learned that as a young man Yellow Kidney had been in a circus, doing stunts on a horse, but the thick folder of typescript from days of interviews with him mentions nothing of this; instead, the practised informant retold a list of Piegan bands, details of the All-comrades' societies, of the Sun Dance, of bison hunting. Trying to take a life history, Sommers found that Yellow Kidney veered off into what she called "folktales," well-known stories of battles and the foundation myths for medicine bundles and their rituals (Wissler 1912). Yellow Kidney had become familiar with what anthropologists wanted, from George Bird Grinnell (e.g., 1892, 1901)in the late 1880s through Walter McClintock, Clark Wissler and Duvall (1908), and James Willard Schultz, who married into Yellow Kidney's community. Salvage ethnography was the task, recording from the last generation to have lived as independent nations, experiencing the bison hunting, ceremonies, and warfare they lost when they settled upon the reservation in 1884. Personal histories were considered idiosyncratic, unscientific in the effort to obtain *the* culture of *the* tribe, and Yellow Kidney's circus exploits were definitely not subjects for a respected elder's recorded life history (cf. DeMallie 1984).

In accordance with the classic ethnographers' expectations that each "primitive" society had "a culture," whose tribal members hewed unthinking to a tradition passed on by their forebears over thousands of years,[1] Yellow Kidney told how it was supposed to have been. For example, "In buffalo days [there was] never a woman who vowed [the Sun Dance] and wasn't pure. Have that just lately. Only being very bad to family" (8-4-39:33). The technical word for Yellow Kidney's accounts is "normative." Wissler (1971 [1938]:206) understood that Indians collaborated, for their own reasons, with their ethnographers in this skewed model: "The old people I knew came to adult life before reservation days and so saw the breakdown of tribal life and independence. Some of them were discouraged as to the future, but by living in the past and capitalizing their ancestral pride, they carried on."

---

1   One might term this the Holiday Fruitcake paradigm: firmly moulded, dark, studded with traits, infused with spirits, ritually bestowed and hardly nibbled at until, at last, Civilization came and, by the hand of Acculturation, discarded it.

Men's and Women's Business

Yellow Kidney and Insima were each requested to dictate life histories to young "Long Braids." Sommers collected her interview material into one thick folder labelled "Yellow Kidney," another labelled "Insema," and thinner transcripts from other Piegans. With one small exception, the July interviews were all with men. On 1 August 1939, Sommers got five pages of typescript from Short Chief (Good Leader Woman?), identified only as a woman over 80 whose first husband had been Heavy Gun. After another week with Yellow Kidney, on 11 August Sommers interviewed Agnes Chief All Over. At last, from 16 to 18 August, she could work with Insima, Agnes Chief All Over interpreting.

In contrast to her husband's didactic presentations of "Plains Indian culture," Insima said nothing of battles and myths. Her reminiscences focused on who married whom, and how good, or bad, the husbands were. Both she and her daughter Agnes recalled their childhoods and especially their relationships to women and girls. Notably absent from Insima's interviews are data on midwifery or herb doctoring, the specialties for which she was well known in her community, or on how she managed her professional and familial commitments. Insima seems to have offered "women's business," that is, marital concerns and childrearing (Goldfrank 1978:140), in complement to the "men's business" of warfare and ritual performance presented by her husband.

"Insema Interviews" is the heading on the folder of typescripts. Immediately we are engrossed in a woman's account of coping with the actuality of reservation life. Men recited the glories of the "buffalo days"; for Insima, the real battles lay in surviving her nation's economic and political collapse. Sommers, if she had followed other mid-century anthropologists, might have labelled her recording of Insima's history a study of "acculturation," or how the Indian adopted a more Western style of life. Perhaps one factor in Sommers's neglect of publishing these field data was her inchoate understanding that the popular term was a biased, ethnocentric distortion of the indigenous nations' protracted contests with the invaders. From a First Nations' perspective, the Blackfoot adopted substitutes for their principal economic resource, the bison, and accepted opportunities to learn English, reading, and other means of dealing with the conquerors. To call these strategies "acculturation" — that is, moving *toward* Western culture — misses the essential point that

ALICE BECK KEHOE

indigenous people were struggling to *retain* as much of their heritage as possible under the much altered circumstances of the reservation.

Sommers's informants were members of a community formed out of the Grease Melters (translated "Fries" by Agnes Chief All Over; McClintock [1910:57] gives it as *Ich-poch-semo*), a band that dispersed onto farms around 1896, in Yellow Kidney's recollection (7/7/39:1). Sets of brothers formed its core: Yellow Kidney's father was a brother of the Three Suns (Big Nose), respected chief of the Grease Melters at the formation of the reservation in 1884. Yellow Kidney's half-brother was Little Plume, and Yellow Kidney had brought up his brother's son, Jim Little Plume, who became "Long Braids's" friend and guide. A young boy Sommers met, Buster Yellow Kidney, said to be *minipoka*, favourite child, to his maternal grandfather Yellow Kidney, today occupies the place of knowledgeable elder once held by that grandfather.

Insima's notion of a life history was a history of lives. She began the first lengthy interview with stories about her neighbour Running Owl (born 1859). Running Owl's daughter Susie and Insima's Agnes were close friends and they got married at the same time:

> When Agnes was 15 she wanted to get married and she did [to Sam Middle Calf]. Gave her a house. Had a bed on the floor. At same time Susie married [John] Calf Tail. Running Owl didn't like to see this. Running Owl would follow both girls. First night they went to bed he went in and sat and smoked and smoked. Had lamp lit and watched them all night for several nights. Johnny [Calf Tail] told Susie, "Since your Father doesn't want you to marry me, I'm going to leave you," and he did. Not long after that Susie was killed by Jim Little Plume. Agnes' husband left her also.

This is both personal and social history, documenting the early age and instability of marriage among the Blackfoot of the early reservation period. Sommers' experience as a social worker in Harlem had prepared her to listen to accounts of lives quite different from those of most Columbia University Students. Her kind, gentle and attentive friend, Jim Little Plume, had, she was told at his funeral that July, "got up drunk one morning and shot his wife, child, and seven other people. He had been in prison for twenty years [but] he had gotten out before [Sommers] arrived and no one spoke of it to her; [she] was impressed at how accepting Indians are" (interview, 8/29/93). Sommers recalled, in 1993, that she and the Steeds attended Jim Little Plume's funeral, conducted by a priest. Two hundred people were there, she estimated, and Insima and Yellow Kidney "went over and gave prayers" in addition to the priest's service. Sommers went with a man named Yellow Owl to dig Jim's grave along the Two Medicine river (interview, 8/29/93). Half a century later, Sommers remembered Jim Little Plume fondly, and like the Indians, in our interview preferred not to dwell on the tragedies of his life. She had said to Insima at his wake, "Why hadn't you told me about his past?" Insima answered, "Would it have made a difference?" That was one of the most important lessons I had ever learned," Sommers believed, "of great importance to my life."

Insima's Reminiscences

Sommers's typescript for 16 August 1939 launched into "Indian's [Insima's] life." (Apparently Sommers initially misheard *I'nssimaa* as "Indian.") The young woman's transcription style of writing as rapidly as she could in English has the virtue of recording the stream of tale-telling. Sommers did not realize the importance of including her own queries in the text, so we can only guess where she asked for clarification or more information. Minor problems arise from Sommers's unfamiliarity with the dramatis personae of the Reservation, and from Agnes's occasional tendency to give a literal but inappropriate translation: for example, saying "daughter" for what Insima likely termed *itan*. As Sommers's fellow students Hanks and Richardson [1945:31] noted for the North Blackfoot, the term *itan* also includes "(female speaker) daughter of sister; daughter of comrade ... first generation female descendant of husband's senior," and extends to *otanimm*, "emotionally attached as to a daughter, adopted as a daughter." Her linguistic naivétè led Sommers to write (8/16/39, p. 28) that Fine Shield Woman, Pikuni first wife of James Willard Schultz, was Agnes's "daughter," although elsewhere Insima noted that Agnes was a year younger than Fine Shield Woman's son Hart; in English terminology, Fine Shield Woman was Agnes's first cousin. Occasionally, Agnes was careless using "he" versus "she," a common slip stemming from the fact that gender in the Blackfoot language distinguishes animate from inanimate, but not masculine from feminine.

ALICE BECK KEHOE

Here is part of Insima's response — translated as she spoke by Agnes Chief all Over — to the ethnographer's request for her life history:

Yellow Wolf [Insima's first husband] told father that he was going to Browning's Willow Creek to see if it was a good place to build a home. Moved with another family.

Moved. Camped right where Browning is now.[1] Rode and looked Willow Creek over and decided on a place on which they can settle down, and soon to get cattle and cut hay.[2]

Next day, moved to mountains to cut house logs ... and poles for corrals. When through, hauled them down as far as Browning on wagons. Build houses there. Finished. From there used to go to Old Agency for rations. Yellow Wolf got mowing machine, rake, and grindstone from government. Bear Paw joined them and asked, Why they didn't let them know they were going to move. Yellow Wolf thought, I wouldn't want to move. After [he] bought machinery a white man came — Mr. Stuart, he married an Indian woman. Told Yellow Wolf, "I heard about this place and you're going to have a lot of hay. Come to put it up for you so you can give me some." Agreed. First time [that] they learned how to cut hay and put it up. When through, put up corral and barn. Then heard some cattle was to be issued to them.

Black Bear said, they should winter cattle at Cut Bank because here, there isn't much shelter. "We'll take hay down there."

Yellow Wolf went to Old Agency. Each family got four cows and four calves regardless of size of families. They told him about milk and he knew how to milk and so did it right away, but didn't know how to make butter.

North of Browning, they found a place [to winter cattle] — thick trees for good shelter. All three — yet — Black Bear and Bear Paw had hayracks and in no time had half the hay there. Sometimes made 3 trips a day. When enough hay there, they moved there. Made house there of cotton[wood] trees.

---

1 The Blackfeet Agency was transferred to Willow Creek, near Joe Kipp's trading post, in 1895, and the town of Browning grew up around Kipp's by 1900 (Farr 1984:40-42).

2 Cattle were issued to the Piegans beginning in 1890, as part of the 1886 treaty negotiations (Ewers 1958:307; Farr 1984:98).

[Insima] left Agnes because grandmother took Agnes and would[n't] let her go. Father agreed to let her stay and they go ahead. Will build house for them and then send for them.

Yellow Wolf went to agency and when he returned told wife to tell Mother [mother-in-law and son-in-law traditionally did not speak directly to one another] he wanted Agnes to go to school. Grandmother had Agnes — same story as for daughter. Didn't even know when she was brought to school. Policemen come around and collect children. Finally caught. Crying but taken to the school. Told that all children under six had to go to school, even if they were five or three — if older, whites claimed they were younger than they were.

When it occurred to Insima that Sommers would be unfamiliar with Blackfoot custom, she interjected explanations. For example, after mentioning how closely her second pregnancy followed Agnes's birth, she described methods of avoiding too-frequent pregnancies:

Usually don't have intercourse with husband a month or six weeks after that [childbirth]. Afraid of husband then — don't want to have another child right away but they usually do have a child every two years. After tenth day [after childbirth], going to get out of bed, they put entirely new clothes on. Mother gets any old lady [telling her] that her girl is getting out of bed and to go help her put them on. When old lady gets there, takes all the clothes off. Makes sweet smoke — blankets, moccasins, stocking, etc., and hold them over smoke and then puts the clothes on her. Paints girl's face. Not paid for this. This lady must be old enough to no longer have children. Take all the girl's old clothes that she wore in bed, blanket, and she keeps these. This is to keep the girl from being caught [pregnant] right away.

Agnes' "daughter" [that is, her *nitan.'a*, Fine Shield Woman] was married to Mr. Schultz [James Willard Schultz]. Almost died when she gave birth to Hart Schultz. Potato [Fine Shield Woman's mother] went to Mother and asked her to help her daughter so she wouldn't have any more children. We almost lost her. Father agreed that something should be done. There was a round copper bracelet with a hole — put a buckskin string through it and put it on the woman's neck. Told her, if a dog has puppies don't pick up or take one (it's all right if they're older and running around) or you'll be caught then. Never did have another child.

[Insima's] Mother also fixed up Louis Champagne's wife for birth control. Mother didn't like to do it anymore — only helped — felt it was killing. Doesn't know where she learned how. She only had one child.

Later in the interviews, Insima indulged in reminiscences of her childhood:

Insema went hunting when she was very small. In winter went with Boy Chief and Louis Champagne [Yellow Wolf's nephews] and her far away husband [the term for sister's husband (Hanks and Richardson 1945:31)], Morning Plume. A far away husband never says anything out of the way before girl marries and girl does not know how to treat a far away husband.

It was a cold but a nice day. Before she knew how to ride, her Mother used to tie her on the horse. Boy Chief and Morning Plume and Yellow Wolf chased a buffalo. The sky was clear —not a cloud. After each killed a buffalo, they started to cut them up. Then the clouds started to come up like a smoke. Hurried because it looked bad. Insema had an extra horse with her and Morning Plume had four extra horses and so did Yellow Wolf. She had just followed Morning Plume to the hunt. As fast as they cut meat and packed on horses, the cloud was traveling fast. We started back. Blizzard came and it sure was cold. Many had gone buffalo hunting but in all different directions.

While going, her moccasin ripped on heel — all at once felt a sting — didn't know but her heel had frozen. Got lost and way above the camps and stood around and heard dogs barking down below. When they came home — they — Mother and Father — were sure mad at her. When I got off horse I just fell backwards. They had told me not to go but I wanted to go and pick out my own meat. When I go inside tipi, my heel started to thaw and burn badly but I was ashamed to say anything. Went to another old lady and told her, my heel froze. She took a dried gut, cooked it in a fire until brown. Chewed it and put it on the frozen heel. Didn't sting anymore. Next morning, my heel blistered. Put more gut on. Blisters broke — put more gut on.

Next day, heard one boy missing, never returned and many men went on hunt. Blizzard was over. It was the equinox and storm. Boy had frozen to death. His blanket coat was raggy and leggings torn. Horse was right by him.

[Insima] got a lot of meat from men, hind legs, ribs, heart, liver, kidney, and some guts and ribs. Men didn't mind that she had come. Many times she went in the summer — followed the men. Never went with Father. He would never get chance to go because he had two fast buffalo horses and some one would ask to borrow them and they would bring him meat.

Remembering hunting brought to mind the early reservation period when the bison herds disappeared:

People claimed they were being starved.... That was when they first learned to make a garden. Potatoes, rutabagas and carrots — about 57 years ago [1882]. Men plowed and women put in seeds. When first issued rations — flour, meat, bacon, rice, crackers, coffee, tobacco — big long plug, salt, tapioca — called it fish eggs. In fall when garden ready, issued it to them like rations. Have a great big slab of bacon. Scared of the flour because they found bones in it. Claim it was ghost bones — bones from human skeleton.[1] Had to use it but would pick bones out. When we started to eat it, two or three died every morning complaining of their stomachs. White man there [at Old Agency] with Indian wife who talked English and acted as interpreter [probably Malenda Wren (Farr 1984:29)].

Woman would tell them what husband dreamt last night, that he made two or three coffins and sure enough next morning he have to make that many coffins. Then buffalo all gone — no other way to live — not permitted to roam — had to stay right there. Think flour poisoned them. Didn't like smell of cows and so didn't like to eat them and didn't like so many different coloured animals.

At Old Agency, women did all the work. Agent, Grey Beard, put out two saws and two axes and when he'd open up tool house all the women rush over. Hand out saw and tallest would grab, and same with rest. Pick out best friend to help her with the saw. Be 4 women with 2 axes. Usual to pay them paper money and white paper. The white paper was for

---

1 Rodent bones may have occurred in the flour. The necessity of shipping food long distances without refrigeration, the government practice of accepting the lowest bids, and chicanery from suppliers all contributed to the likelihood of contamination in flour and other rations.

ALICE BECK KEHOE

sugar. Saw and axes would put up a cordwood and get $4 for one cord-wood. Green paper — a dollar. Each get $4, and $1 for sugar.

Men would go up to mountains and haul timber for the agency. One with big load — get $7 — way up to mountains. In those days wagons very scarce. Build little log houses. Wouldn't stand long and roofs broke in. Took men a long time to [learn how to] guide a team and how to put harness on. Put harness on up side down. An old man when first learning how to cut hay — didn't know he had to oil it [the machine]. Started to get hot and smoke. Had wife follow with a bucket of water to pour on it. Stand awhile till wife returned with water.

Horses and cattle increased fast. Had over 510 heads of cattle. Father have over 480 horses; he had no cattle. Agency didn't issue cattle to old people. Insema had 22 head of horses.

Insema's fourth daughter was Molly. Molly was born one year after Yellow Wolf's fourth wife had left the family. Katie was the fifth child. She was born three years later. A third daughter had died when she was nine years. (Couldn't remember her name — she had no Indian name.) She had died of pneumonia. Her clothes and toys were buried with her. Molly died when Fannie [Molly's daughter] was very small and Insema raised her. Fannie went to school, staying in dormitory, [and got pregnant by] the principal. Blamed it on young Indian man because she didn't want to get the principal in trouble. He sent Fannie to Minot, N.D. and he paid all expenses and hospital fees there.

Husband [Yellow Wolf] got a salary as a policeman, but the amount was forgotten. He was paid every month. He never actually quit, nor was he fired, but he just didn't return to work. He wasn't paid after he failed to return to work. The salary was stopped after they had moved to Wil-low Creek. They were living at Willow Creek when Yellow Wolf died. At the time of Yellow Wolf's death, they had both a house and a tent. Yellow Wolf and Insema lived in the tent. Emma and her husband John Little Plume [not related to Yellow Wolf's brother] lived in the house, with Emma's husband's father and mother. Katie and her husband ([Paul] Home Gun), Agnes, her second husband James Big Top and her daughter Mary, lived in Yellow Wolf's tent.

Everyone was there because Yellow Wolf was very rich, and he knew he was going to die. Those who lived there all the time were Insema, Yellow Wolf and Mary, with Emma and her husband in their own house. (No one lived in Yellow Wolf's house throughout the summer.) Yellow Wolf died at 82 [c. 1927]. He did not die of any illness. He had been shot in war, a little below the shoulder, and the bullet had never been removed. It had swelled and finally burst inside. He [Insima?] cut her hair.[1]

She kept everything. All Yellow Wolf's clothes were put in a sack and buried with him, together with all his little things, pipe, tobacco, matches. He had given his saddle away while he was still alive, and had refused to ride again. Insema gave it to her father. Mrs. Powell — a white woman married to a fullblood — took her to Browning. She stayed with the woman less than a year. She did nothing at all. The woman's daughter-in-law did all the cooking and called them when food was ready. Her other two daughters came after them to eat. Insema did not pay anything for her keep during the time she was there. When father was living, Insema did a lot of work for her, beading and making repairs for her. This woman asked to take Insema home with her because she was older and felt Insema would be happier with her than with her children, who were young and often went out. Insema took only [her granddaughter] Mary with her.

When Agnes had her baby, Insema was nearby but not present. Every time Agnes suffered, she had to run out and cry. Thus she was constantly running in and out. However, she was present at the second birth. (It is always like this — mothers hate to be present at the first birth their daughter has. Mother might stay if she felt others are not helping enough and she can do more for her daughter, everyone thinks she is brave in such a case.) There was no medicine smoke at that time. it had been stopped by the [blank: agent or priest?] If the girl suffers for two or three days, they make a [blank] to bring child right away. Medicine man and wife called on Agnes to change clothes and make medicine so that she does not have another child soon. His wife took care of changing her clothes, and he painted her face yellow. Gave her no medicine or anything to wear. Told her that if she let no one wear her shawl she would not have another baby right away. He lied, for she had one three years later, and she so informed him. He was paid with a work horse.

Insema adopted Mary after Agnes left her husband. She left in the summer and remarried in the fall. Agnes' new husband told Agnes to let Mother and Father keep Mary since they already had her. "Sometimes we'll take her home with us." Mary got used to her grandparents. Agnes

---

1 It was Blackfoot custom that close family members, particularly widows, cut off their hair as a sign of grief and mourning. (Note Agnes's slip in choosing the English pronoun, since Blackfoot uses one animate form for both masculine and feminine.)

ALICE BECK KEHOE

got her clothes and shoes. Insema cared very little when Agnes left her first husband, because she knew he drank and gambled away the cattle and horses; he would never gather wood or go to work. Glad to be rid of him.

If grandparents love their grandchildren and feel that they can take better care of them than their parents, the mother cannot object. Nowadays, it is not necessary to go to court in order to adopt grandchildren. However, to adopt an unrelated orphan, it is necessary to go to court and pay $25.00. The child is then registered in your name and when you die, your property goes to adopted children.

Glad she picked out second husband because he was known as a good man. Agnes knew the second husband [James Big Top] when he was married to Minnie. They would come and stay several nights. Minnie's mother came down for a week. Minnie used to say he was good to her, but his mother was mean to her. Agnes didn't speak much to him. Heard later that Minnie had quit him.

Agnes met him in town, Browning, one day and he asked if she was going back to her husband. When she told him she was not, he asked her to marry him. She said nothing. He asked her again every time he met her. Told mother first time he asked. She finally said yes but said she had heard his mother was mean. He said she acted that way to Minnie because Minnie was running around with his brothers.

When Agnes married her second husband, Insema stopped the taboo [against mother- and son-in-law speaking]. Agnes and husband would visit her, but son-in-law and mother-in-law never spoke to each other. Agnes told her, "You should stop avoiding your son-in-law, it's unusual, you should think of your son-in-law as your son." She was glad not to have to avoid her son-in-law because now he could visit her. She thought of how she had had to avoid her first son-in-law and she would have to go out — only one place in tipi and both couldn't be present. Liked the new arrangement.

Mary [Middle Calf, Agnes' daughter, born 1902] got married that year. Agnes' first husband picked the man for her. Agnes knew nothing about it. She lived quite a distance from Mary. Nobody told Insema about it — she found out about it from others. When Yellow Wolf died, Mary's father came and took her home, and it was during that time that she was married.

Jack, Mary's husband, had given no gifts when he married. (That is not done anymore, Mary got nothing from anyone until later on. Insema started getting bedding, furnishing and tent for her.) Mary did not know Jack before they were married. They were both young.

Six years after Yellow Wolf died, Yellow Kidney's wife died. Insema had not known Yellow Kidney before she married him. His wife was the same age as Insema. Insema went to Browning and while there went to visit an old lady, Mrs. Bird. While she was visiting, Walter McGee and John Mountain Chief, policemen, came in and told her she was wanted at the Indian Agency. She wondered whether she had done something wrong and was under arrest. Decided to go and find out what it was about. Mrs. Bird told her that she would go there with her when Mrs. Bird had finished her cooking. They both went. They found a place, a small room, and Yellow Kidney waiting there. Yellow Kidney didn't know either what they wanted with him. They had just brought them together there.[1] "Wonder if they came after me over that man." They gave me a chair and told me to sit down. They placed her on one side of the desk and Yellow Kidney on the other.

Another policeman, Mr. Tevenus, started to talk to her. He said, "We sent for you because you are going to marry that man." She didn't wish to marry him — she had never know him before (she was very young at the time of her first marriage, and hadn't known any better). They said she wouldn't have to be rustling for herself, and she'd have someone to help her and do things for her. She didn't answer. Walter McGee started to talk kindly to her. Asked her if she had made up her mind. She told them, "The reason I am saying nothing is that I have children and grandchildren and Yellow Kidney might not like them." They said, "The reason we brought you together was that we thought you two would get along together. You are both good workers and will have a nice home soon." They wouldn't let her go until she said yes. Yellow Kidney had been listening to all this. His wife had died only two weeks before.

She said, "It's up to him to say whether he wants to marry me." They started to talk to him. Yellow Kidney said he'd marry her.

I went home but not with him. After I went out they told him to go where I was staying. He came there in a rig. He brought lots of grub, dress goods, a blanket and a shawl. When she got home she explained to Mary and Jack. They told her to marry him.

---

1   This passage show the paternalism of the reservation Agent, treating mature widowed men and women as if they were too feckless to make suitable living arrangements.

"I'd like to marry him but he's stranger and I feel ashamed."

Yellow Kidney: "I have some things for you and you can take all that's in the rig." When Yellow Kidney's wife had died they had taken everything that belonged to his wife. Mary Little Plume took all the cooking utensils. Stayed with Mary and Jack quite a while, when finally Yellow Kidney suggested they fix up his place for their own. They came here and cleaned up the place.

We can leave Insima here. She went on to tell of the marriage of her youngest daughter Katie to Paul Home Gun, "a good worker" who "never drinks or gambles," and Agnes's marriage to George Chief All Over after Agnes's second husband died. She also told stories of jealous husbands, and of the adventure of a mistreated Blackfoot youth and his orphaned comrade, who went over the mountains to the Flathead Valley and returned with two Salish Flathead women escaping from cruel husbands. This story resembles men's standard tales of war exploits, except that Insima emphasized the Salish women's active participation in the escape.

Insima's reminiscences are firsthand accounts of the early reservation period that in recent years has increasingly drawn historians' interest. Because scholars during that time were engaged in salvage ethnography, there was little contemporary description outside official documents and newspapers, and particularly little directly and candidly from Indians. The memoir Sommers transcribed is doubly rare because it is from a woman speaking freely and at length.

How valid is this document? Discourse analysis, formerly confined to linguistics, has entered general anthropology and made us more sensitive to the parameters of ethnographic work, to "issues of power and perspective, questions of how authoritative knowledge is legitimated, of self-awareness and authenticity of voice in the presentation of data, and of the constraints of the historical and cultural contexts within which knowledge develops" (Rubinstein 1991:12-13). In 1939, these issues were stuff for the researcher to grapple with before reaching the final draft of a monograph: it was unseemly to expose one's struggles. The persona one presented in print, to the public, was the aloof observer before whose magisterial gaze the events of the field fell into orderly categories. Sommers, who had been a social worker before entering graduate school, could not maintain such an objective analytical stance. World War II pre-empted her personal crisis over a career decision, and after the war she engaged herself in international social activism. Her 1939 typescripts remained raw data.

Rubinstein identifies a "folktale" (as Sommers would have called it) told within the profession of American anthropology, about naive graduate students supposedly cast into the field with only a blank notebook, to flounder about, shiver and shake, until a kind Native adopted them and taught them what they ought to know. Fifty years later, Sommers remembered herself as such a stereotypical innocent. But as Rubinstein points out (1991:14), all those graduate students who *felt*, as they arrived in a strange land, like babes cast adrift, had in fact been prepared by years of academic study of scientific observation and social analysis. They had all read the classics of ethnography *and* heard their professors informally tell their own field experiences. Benedict's instruction, as Sommers recalled it, seemed maddeningly simplistic, yet Sommers knew, from the seminars she took, what an ethnographer was expected to do once he or she "establishes contact with a family and lives with them." Her professor was on the reservation, ready to listen to her students' experiences and suggest how they might proceed. Sommers's fellow student Jane Richardson recalled that they

> sought out the tribal elders to obtain their recollections of Blackfoot life in more free-spirited times. The old ones liked to talk for hours about war deeds, or the sadly vanishing religion of the medicine bundles (Hoffman 1988:118).

This was, Richardson explained, "the formal method of anthropological research [she] had learned ... at Columbia" (Hoffman 1988:118).

In Sommers's typescripts we have admired a Blackfoot's matron's *story*, in every sense of that word, told to a young woman who showed herself respectful, empathetic, and fascinated by the lively "Old Lady." Insima, who had listened for too many years to men's stories of war and prescriptions of correct ritual, wanted young Long Braids to hear and record the affairs of real life, how Blackfoot people *lived. I'nssimaa*, the Gardener, would plant, would cultivate, a text on women's business — the business of maintaining life. Sommers had paid her dues for more than a month, dutifully recording the standard accounts of men; now, the feminist consciousness nourished in her childhood could resonate with her hostess's Blackfoot pride in womanly accomplishments. Sommers's transcript is perhaps naive in that she made no effort to learn the

ALICE BECK KEHOE

Blackfoot language (which is difficult for English speakers), she put on paper only the translated formal interviews with no minutiae of context, and she left out her own presence, her queries, her reactions.

As a straightforward narrative, however, Sommers's "Insema" folder documents both Blackfoot history and women's history. Its particulars reverberate against dry official archives and sweeping summaries. It is only a text, one woman's selected memories, but we owe gratitude to Ruth Benedict who let her student work in a much less-travelled way; to Sue Sommers who persisted; and especially to Insima and her daughter Agnes who wanted their stories to be history.

Conclusion

Insima's narratives convey the spirit with which the Piegans adapted to the new economy, carefully selecting ranch land and moving into cabins once they could no longer obtain sturdy bison skins for tipis. Insima partnered her husband in hauling wood and ranching while her mother, according to Blackfoot custom, cared for Insima's young child. It was hard for Insima's mother to see the granddaughter constrained by dresses, shoes, school buildings, kept from the outdoor exercise and work that make women strong. The older woman's fears of sickness were well founded, for mortality rates, especially among children, were appalling in the early reservation period. Yet, in spite of the terrible toll taken by malnutrition and diseases after the collapse of their indigenous economy, the Piegans maintained their communities throughout the radical step of becoming ranchers in widely separated hamlets along the prairie streams.

Clark Wissler (1971[1938]:239) remarked, "so far as I could see, the morale of the women was far less shattered [by reservation life] and it was they who saved tribal life from complete collapse." Wissler may very well have met Insima; his collaborator Duvall commissioned her in 1904 to make a cradleboard for the American Museum collections.[1] His evaluation of women's business on the reservation seems well borne out by Sommers's transcript of her interviews with Insima.

---

1   Duvall wrote Wissler, "Mrs. Yellow Wolf is making the Baby Board and her mother is making the dog travois" (letter of 12 October 1904), then on 10 November "Mrs. Yellow Wolf, and Boy, also failed to make some of the things" (Wissler papers, American Museum of Natural History).

Appendix: Insima Plays the Dirty White Man

[Interview of 8-17-39 or 8-18-39, Insima speaking, Agnes Chief All Over interpreting]

"She [Insima] was picking [choke]cherries. There was an old lady 'Steals Good' heard that another old lady had almost been raped. She got mad and said 'I wish I had been there with my butcher knife.' She was grinding cherries as she spoke. As she spoke she shook her big butcher knife. Insima thought 'I'll see what you can do.' Mary and Jack were camping there too. Told Mary 'I'm going to play a trick on her. When you see me go to her out of the brush you tell her you're going to the house to put the baby to sleep.' Insima went in the tent and put Yellow Kidney's pants on. Cut the fur off a pair of old chaps. Rubbed syrup all over her chin and pasted the fur all over chin and cheeks. Put coat on and dish towel around her head. Put her hair up under an old hat.

"Went way around and from east walked up to camp. When Mary saw her she said her piece. She [Steals Good] was facing the grinding. Insima said 'Hello.' She looked up and said 'Hello.' Made signs 'Eat some of these cherries, they're good.' Took some and spit them out and said 'No good.'

"'They're good.' Stopped grinding and started backing away. She moved near her and drew her near and said 'Lot of fat, lot of fat.' 'No, no, I haven't any meat.' Insima grabbed her any place — kept yelling, 'No good, no good.' She kept hollering for Insima to come — half crying. She kept calling for Mary. Insima had her around the waist and reached under her dress and she cried out. She hollered and hollered. Insima held her tight and pushed her. She cried. Mary finally came running. Insima had an old axe over her shoulder and had dropped it. Insima was holding her under one leg to lift her. Mary was pushing them apart, talking English.

"She grabbed the axe and said to Mary 'Here's his axe — that dirty white man. I'm going to give it to Jack so he'll know.'

"Insima circled around to her tent and washed and changed. 'What's wrong? I was picking cherries across the river and heard you screaming.' Steals Good bawled her out. Asked her which way did white man go? Mary said 'Down that way?'"

ALICE BECK KEHOE

"Insima; 'Why didn't you grab your knife?' 'Well, right from the start he grabbed me and threw me down, and I never thought of my knife. There's his axe, I'm going to give it to my son.'

"'It was me. I wanted to see if you'd use your knife.'

"Old lady took after her and did grab her."

References

Benedict, Ruth
    1939 Letter to Oscar and Ruth Lewis. Unpublished, in possession of Ruth M. Lewis, Urbana, IL.

DeMallie, Raymond J., ed.
    1984 *The Sixth Grandfather: Black Elk's Teachings Given to John G. Neihardt.* Lincoln: University of Nebraska Press.

Dietrich, Sue Sommers
    1939 Field Notes, Blackfeet Indian Reservation, Montana. Typescript in author's possession.
    1993 Interview with Alice B. Kehoe, 29 August 1993, in Dietrich's home in Olympia Fields, IL.

Ewers, John C.
    1958 *The Blackfeet: Raiders on the Northwestern Plains.* Norman: University of Oklahoma Press.

Farr, William E.
    1984 *The Reservation Blackfeet, 1882-1945.* Seattle: University of Washington Press.

Goldfrank, Esther S.
    1978 *Notes on an Undirected Life.* Flushing, NY: Queens College Publications in Anthropology, no. 3.

Grinnell, George Bird
    1892 *Blackfoot Lodge Tales.* New York: Charles Scribner's Sons. See *American Anthropologist* o.s., 1896, 9:286-87; n.s. 1899, 1:194-96; 1901, 3:650-68 ("The Lodges of the Blackfoot").

Hanks, Lucien M., Jr., and Jane Richardson
    1945 *Observations on Northern Blackfoot Kinship.* Monograph 9, American Ethnological Society. Seattle: University of Washington Press.

Hoffman, Edward
    1988 *The Right to be Human: A Biography of Abraham Maslow.* Los Angeles: Jeremy P. Tarcher.

McClintock, Walter

    1910 *The Old North Trail*. Lincoln: University of Nebraska Press (1968
            Bison Book facsimile reprint).

Rubinstein, Robert A.

    1991 Introduction. In *Fieldwork: The Correspondence of Robert Redfield & Sol
            Tax*. Boulder, CO: Westview Press.

Schultz, James Willard (Apikuni)

    1907 *My Life as an Indian*. New York: Forest and Stream.

    1962 *Blackfeet and Buffalo*. Keith C. Seele, ed. Norman: University of
            Oklahoma Press.

    1974 *Why Gone Those Times? Blackfoot Tales*. Eugene Lee Silliman, ed.
            Norman: University of Oklahoma Press.

Wissler, Clark

    1911 *The Social Life of the Blackfoot Indians*.s Anthropological Papers, vol. 7,
            pt. 1, 1-64. New York: American Museum of Natural History.

    1912 *Ceremonial Bundles of the Blackfoot Indians*, Anthropological Papers,
            vol. 7, pt. 2, 65-289. New York: American Museum of Natural
            History.

    1971 [1938] *Red Man Reservations*. New York: Collier. (Originally
            published 1938 as *Indian Cavalcade or Life on the Old-Time Indian
            Reservations* by Sheridan House.)

Wissler, Clark, and D.C. Duvall

    1908 *Mythology of the Blackfoot Indians*. Anthropological Papers, vol. 2, pt.
            1, 1-163. New York: American Museum of Natural History.

17

The Spider and the WASP: Chronicling the Life of Molly Spotted Elk

Bunny McBride

To fail to understand another person's life story is, in general, to reject one's own humanity. (Langness, 136)

Strands in the Web

MOLLY NELSON, a Penobscot Indian[1] of the Spider Clan[2], was born on Indian Island, the 315-acre reservation across the river from Old Town, Maine. The oldest of eight children, she arrived on 17 November 1903 in the middle of what Penobscots called "winter fish moon."[3] Soon after her maternal grandmother pulled her from the womb, her parents had her baptized by the reservation's priest and gave her a Christian name — Mary Alice. But they and everyone else on the island pronounced it the Indian way: *Molliedellis*. For short, they called her Molly. Her mother, a Penobscot-Maliseet named Philomene, was a basket

---

1   The Penobscot are one of many Algonquian-speaking groups. Along with the closely-related St. Francis Abenaki, Maliseet, Passamaquoddy, and Micmac, they belong to a cluster of Eastern Algonquians known as the Wabanaki ("Dawnland") Indians. For more information, see Speck's 1940 ethnography on the Penobscot. Cf. Prins 1994b; Snow 1978.

2   The existence of "clans" among Penobscots has long been debated (Morgan 1877, Speck 1915, 1917, 1940:205-213). Siebert reviewed and challenged the ethnographic and historical evidence of clans in his 1982 paper, "Frank G. Speck, Personal Reminiscences." He argued that Penobscots were organized in patrilineal descent groups identified by animal totem or tutelary emblem. Each group included individuals related through blood, marriage, or adoption. Siebert identifies at least sixteen totemic groups, including Bear, Otter, Raccoon, Bobcat, Whale, and Insect. The latter emblem represents the Nelson and Newell families. Molly's daughter, Jean Archambaud Moore, and Molly's sister, Dr. Eunice Nelson-Bauman (as well as other family members) specify the Insect and identify themselves as members of the Spider Clan.

3   So-named because throngs of tomcod used to swim the waters around Indian Island at that time of year. See Speck 1940:263-64.

maker and traditional healer. Her father Horace, who was Penobscot-Passamaquoddy, had attended Dartmouth College in Hanover, New Hampshire for a year, then quit the assimilation track to return home. Back on the reservation, he pursued work that responded to the seasons – hunting, fishing, gardening, canoe-building, rowing the ferry between Indian Island and Old Town, and hawking baskets to summer tourists. He also served terms as tribal chief, and as the Penobscot representative to the Maine state legislature in Augusta, the state capital.

Molly entered the world four centuries after Europeans first came to northeastern America's shores to fish, and three centuries after the French, followed by the English, began to colonize the land of her ancestors. The culture surrounding her on that tiny island reservation carried the mark of generations of change and adaptation to the economic, social, and religious demands of the dominant white newcomers. Yet, remarkably, remnant Penobscot traditions still hung in the air like the scent of pine. Molly breathed in deeply. She learned the Algonquian languages of her parents (Penobscot and Maliseet) and sat in rapt attention at the feet of wizened elders who told her tales of the culture hero Gluskap and other mythical characters in traditional Penobscot lore. And, roaming the island's extensive woodlands for hours on end, she discovered the rhythms and solace of nature. From the time she was young she somehow recognized the preciousness of such knowledge, and throughout her life it provided a cultural-historical rootedness that steadied her when winds of racism blew in her direction.[1]

Intensely curious, Molly also felt drawn to the world beyond Indian Island, especially to cosmopolitan centres of academics and artists. Performing for primarily white audiences who applauded cliché over authenticity, Molly wrestled with the discrepancy between internal and external definitions of who she was.[2] The knotted thread that ran through her life was an identity search – a struggle to figure out what of her past she wished to carry into her future, and a relentless effort to fit together the two worlds that tugged at her.[3] In dozens of diaries penned

---

1   See Fischer, in particular his comments on "authentic anchorages," 1986:200.

2   For a discussion of Indian princess and squaw stereotypes, see Green 1975. Cf. Green 1980 and 1989; Friar and Friar, 229-46.

3   In the words of Fischer, 196, she sought "a voice or style that [did] not violate [her] several components of identity."

from girlhood through late middle age, she articulated how she grappled with this issue in her personal and professional life. For several years, through the channels of art and love, she achieved the bicultural equilibrium she yearned for. At those blessed moments she epitomized the culturally enlarged person referred to by Malcolm McFee as "the 150% [Wo]man" (in Clifton, 29.)[1]

Thinking About Webs

This essay explores challenges and insights experienced while writing Molly's biography. Although her diaries are rare and invaluable resources, they have presented distinct challenges: finding verification; identifying scores of individuals; deciphering thousands of pages of minute scribbles; shedding cultural assumptions and developing the sensitivity needed to interpret obscure passages and read between the lines; and figuring out how to weave Molly's own words into a contextual narrative composed with material from a wide variety of other sources gathered in America and France.

Beyond the virtues and problems of diaries, this essay ventures into questions of perspective, reflecting on a non-Indian biographer's gradual understanding and internalizing of her subject. It also explores the issue of responsible representation and the search for a voice that translates across the ethnic divide to speak meaningfully to Native, scholarly, and general communities.

Entering the Web: WASP Meets Spider[2]

Our meeting was not face to face. Molly died in 1977 — four years before I moved to Maine and began working with my husband on a federal recognition and community development project with the Aroostook Band of Micmacs. By 1987 this work had brought us into contact not only with Micmacs, but with members of the state's three other tribes

---

1   In his 1989 book, *Being and Becoming Indian: Biographical Studies of Native American Frontiers*, Clifton, ed., presented profiles of fourteen "marginal men and women, people whose lives were spent on the borders between ethnic groups" (29). Cf. Bataille and Sands, 19-24, who discuss this issue relative to Colson's *Three Pomo Women*.

2   Several paragraphs of the text in this section and the next one appear in slightly different forms in my biography about Molly (McBride 1995).

Molly Spotted Elk, 1930

406 BUNNY MCBRIDE

(the Penobscot, Passamaquoddy, and Maliseet). That year an article appeared in a regional newspaper announcing that Molly and two other Penobscots had been selected as inductees for a new Indian Hall of Fame in Page, Arizona.[1] Although I had heard of Molly and had been prodded more than once by my husband to write about her, I was not drawn to her until seeing that article. It included a close-up photograph that seized my attention. Her elegant, fine-featured face was warm, inviting. Her blackberry eyes summoned me closer. To my surprise, at second gaze the alluring eyes were wary, impenetrable. This ambiguous image haunted me for days, so much so that I telephoned Molly's youngest sister, Dr. Eunice Bauman-Nelson, whom I had met through my work with the Micmacs. I talked with her about the possibility of writing an article, perhaps a book, about Molly. Soon thereafter, Eunice spent a long weekend with us at our home in Hallowell.

For me, time stopped as I sat on our deck overlooking the Kennebec River, listening to her reminisce about her sister. Molly's life, marked by tradition mixed with independence, professional determination, and artistic and intellectual cosmopolitanism, defied stereotypes of women born in the early years of this century – particularly American Indian women. By the time Eunice left, I knew I wanted to find out more about Molly, and share my findings in a book.

Eunice suggested I contact Molly's daughter, Jean Archambaud Moore, who had in her keeping Molly's diaries, photos, letters, and other memorabilia. I phoned Jean, then living in Tennessee, and told her of my wish to write about her mother. My desire grew as I listened to this keen-witted woman talk about her mother in a deep, earthy voice. Her recollections were vivid and brilliantly told. She had been approached by others interested in writing Molly's life story, so I offered to send her samples of my work to help her decide if she felt I was the right one for the task.

A dozen days later, Jean telephoned to invite me to Tennessee. We worked together intensely for a week, from early morning until deep into the night, recording her recollections of Molly and sorting through boxes of memorabilia. Jean, indefatigable, sat hour after hour, day after day, on a wooden chair at her desk. As afternoons gave way to evenings, she would lean more heavily on her bureau, propping herself up with her elbows. That desk held the tools of her fortune-telling trade, includ-

---

1   As of this writing, plans for this museum have not come to fruition.

ing a crystal ball and cards. On our last evening together, I learned that she practised her trade personally as well as professionally:

"Would you like to know why I chose you to tell my mother's story? she asked.

"Indeed, I would."

"You see this painting?" she queried, pointing above her desk to a picture of the Mohawk Indian "Saint" Kateri Tekakwitha[1] – one of several paintings of this young heroine of the Jesuits for which her mother had posed.

"Yes, I've been looking at it all week."

"Well, two weeks before you first phoned me, I noticed it was crooked, and straightened it out. The next day, I found it had shifted again, and once more levelled it. This happened again and again. When I straightened it on the day you telephoned, I asked out loud, '*Mother, what are you trying to tell me?!*' After your call, the painting remained evenly hung. Apparently, my mother felt comfortable about entrusting you with her story."

Until hearing this, I had given little thought to the idea that I might be entering a family whose world view differed dramatically from my own. I had assumed Jean chose me because she liked the writing samples I sent her, or because Eunice had recommended me, or perhaps because I sounded pleasant on the phone. Although these things may have had some bearing on her decision, it was clear that a psychic factor foreign to me had played a major role. Somewhat belatedly it dawned on me that in many ways Molly was my quintessential "Other." We hailed from dramatically different times and societal niches. Our personalities were strikingly different. Molly's friends and family say she was highly suspicious and sometimes paranoid, while mine say I am overly trusting. The choices Molly made rarely matched my own. Even the dreams she noted in her diary were a world apart from mine in content and interpretation. I dreamed at night (most often about missing a plane or train)

---

1 Born in 1656, Kateri Tekakwitha converted to Christianity. At age twenty-one she joined the French Catholic Indian mission village at Kahnawake, Quebec, where she lived a pious life of prayer and service until her untimely death in 1680. Beloved, and reputed to have performed miracles, she has long been considered a saint by the Catholic Iroquois and other Indians. For decades a committee of prominent Indian laypersons and Canadian priests have pressed the Vatican to proclaim her sainthood. In 1980 the Pope took a step in this direction by beatifying her in an official ceremony in Rome.

and dismissed those dreams in the morning. But Molly had prescient sleeping and waking dreams of cathedral forests, whispering moons, green snakes, and white-robed death. To her, these visions were highly symbolic. Moreover, unlike me, she read palms and tea leaves for insights, and believed communication between the dead and the living was possible.

How could a WASP raised in middle-class suburbia presume to glean and reconstruct the truth of Molly's life? I remember vividly the first time I saw a pair of her size-five dance moccasins. Glancing from them to my own size nine-and-one-half feet I thought, "I'll never be able to step into her shoes and tell her story." Curiously, rather than incapacitating me, this humbling thought alerted me to what should have been obvious from the beginning: this was Molly's story, not mine, and telling it credibly required listening, responsiveness, and, in measure, a surrendering of ego. This brings to mind a comment Rayna Rapp made in an interview concerning the problem of subjectivity in ethnographic research: "What you have to do is use yourself in the fullest sense as the widest instrument, [recognizing] that there are parts of the research that you have not been prepared for or did not know how to pre-think, or were not ready to hypothesize when you entered the library, the village, or the stage of action. [You need to] be open to them, to allow them in and hear them" (in McBride 1980:176).

Accepting this, and taking my cue from Molly's undaunted spirit, I opened myself up for surprises and I continued my journey to the far-off land of her life. One by one, I shed the assumptions that hindered my travel, increasing the space I had for her in my mental suitcase. At first she was a phantom on the horizon, but as I strolled the paths and sidewalks that she frequented on Indian Island and in New York and Paris, she gradually came into focus and became my guide. I pored over her diaries and examined countless photographs of her. I interviewed her surviving friends, associates and family members, and unearthed dozens of articles chronicling her performances. I devoured the impassioned love letters she received from Jean Archambaud. I stood at the foot of the stairs where she died. Bit by bit I came to know her, until finally, as I wrote my way toward the end of her life, our souls touched. It happened like this:

Molly was a hiker. When I started her biography, I swam regularly. By the time I finished it, I had surrendered swimming for daily hikes through the Flint Hills of northeastern Kansas where I now live. The switch was not conscious, but looking back, I believe I traded water for soil because putting foot to ground made me feel closer to Molly. Always, when I walked, I imagined her with me, challenging me up the slopes with her strong graceful stride. Hiking in her mental company, I began to have visions — graphic images of her and events in her life. Just before I began the last chapter of her biography, I had a startling vision of Molly's death. Ironically, she was never more alive to me than at that moment. It was then that our alien souls finally met. In this meeting, a holy happening in the mind's eye, I swear, Molly gave me the conclusion to the book. Or, perhaps, the conclusion gave me Molly.

Paradoxically, I had much in common with the Molly I came to know. But treating her as my quintessential other — anticipating and struggling to see and comprehend the unfamiliar aspects of her character and life — had been a vital step toward seeing her whole and beholding her distinct gestalt. The fact that Molly's life contrasted with my own brought great meaning to the task of writing her biography, for it forced me to look at life anew through the eyes of another. For me, our differences made this a story worth telling — and our commonalities made it possible.

Ruth Underhill once commented that after her intensive 1930s collaboration with Maria Chona for *Papago Woman*, Chona had transformed from informant to biographer, and she and Underhill had become "two of a kind" (in Bataille and Sands, 64) — distinct, yet kindred, united in the purpose of telling a story well. I recognize this feeling even though my collaboration was with a woman I never saw face to face. This WASP entered a spider's web — and got stuck long enough to glimpse its intricate design.

Maps for the Web: Molly's Diaries

Jean's level of trust proved to be as extraordinary as the crooked painting message from her deceased mother. When I left her home after our first visit, I carried with me a box of precious goods: Molly's diaries — a dozen of them, covering 19 non-consecutive years from 1920 to 1959. As a writer and would-be anthropologist, Molly articulated in these diaries how she grappled with the question of identity in her personal and professional life. Because she was supremely private and often felt alone and out of place, her diaries were vital confidants. She relied on them as Anais Nin relied on her journal: as "the only steadfast friend I have, the

Molly as she appeared in Texas Guinan's clubs, 1928

Molly in street clothes, c. 1930

only one which makes my life bearable; because my happiness with human beings is so precarious, my confiding moods rare, and the least sign of non-interest is enough to silence me. In the journal I am at ease.... I [have found] one place of truth, one dialogue without falsity" (in Moffat and Painter, 14). Moreover, Molly's daybooks provided private platforms for asserting that she was a subject in her own right, and not just the object of others.[1] While diaries penned by women in general are not unusual, Native records of reflection on self and society are exceptional. Molly's journals, as much as her artistic achievements, make her life noteworthy.

Although the diaries were rare and invaluable resources, they presented distinct challenges — problems (and opportunities) quite different from those I experienced during the 1980s when helping Micmac elders record their oral histories. Beyond the tedium of deciphering thousands of pages of Molly's minuscule scribbles and identifying scores of people alternately noted by their real names, initials, and nicknames, I had to corroborate the historical accounts in the diaries. Bit by bit, with considerable effort, I managed to do this. If Molly noted that an article appeared about her in a magazine or newspaper, I was able to track it down. If she mentioned giving a particular performance, I could find evidence of it in reviews and promotional material. Friendships, love relationships, and work associations referred to in her daybooks were repeatedly confirmed through interviews with those who knew her. In short, Molly's journals withstood an intensive veracity test when held against oral histories and personal correspondence, as well as written and photographic records unearthed in national, local, and university archives and libraries in France and the United States.

When working on the Micmac oral histories, I met frequently with the individuals who told their life stories, which allowed for follow-up questions to elicit explanations and expansions of their recollections. I did not have this luxury with Molly. Diaries chronicling key years of her life had been thrown out after her death, leaving major gaps in her story. And information in the surviving pages was not always clear or complete. When facts or feelings in the diaries were foggy or fragmented, I had to flesh them out with other sources (interviews, newspapers, letters, archival records, etc.) — many of which were tough to come by. Even identified resources could be elusive. For instance, some of the

---

1   See Blodgett.

elderly people who knew Molly wavered in their recollections; others were too ill to talk for long periods of time; and one of Molly's old associates died two weeks after our first (and therefore last) interview. Another, who eagerly agreed to send me photographs of artwork by his aunt, for whom Molly had often posed, passed on before he was able to do so. After his death, his aunt's possessions became contested property in the settlement of his estate, making it impossible to obtain the promised photos.

Molly's diaries offered a candour that was sometimes lacking in the Micmac oral histories. I had considerable trust among Micmacs who told their stories, for these recollections were part of the ethnographic research needed to substantiate their federal recognition case. Still, I knew full well that I was receiving filtered information — only what they were willing to share publicly. Although Molly's sense of privacy sometimes carried over into her diaries, she wrote them for herself so they were relatively uncensored. She protected their confidentiality with penmanship so minute that I had to make enlarged photocopies of her pages in order to read them at all.

Effective use of the diaries required developing a sensitivity that made it possible to interpret obscure passages and read between the lines. While self-reflection, soul searching, and personal struggle are present in the diaries, Molly usually used journal writing as a means of wrestling out of, rather than immersing herself in, the sorrows that plagued her. Her determination to be cheerful and to carry on in the face of great difficulty inspired me. But at times it left me confused about her true feelings. When I interviewed dancer Lisan Kay, one of Molly's old friends from both New York and Paris, she told me Molly was always upbeat and never depressed. Molly fooled her — and she almost fooled me. Only after reading all (and transcribing much) of her surviving journals did I learn how to read between the lines. There I discovered the ambiguity that haunted Molly through much of her life — ambiguity toward and from dominant white society concerning her place in it. I came to understand that the aim of Molly's journals, at least in part, was to affirm her Native self in the coercive arena of acculturation.[1]

While distinct in some ways from the diaries of mainstream women, Molly's daybooks also reflect a theme common in the journals of

---

1   See Bataille and Sands, 8, 11.

women cross-culturally. Moffat and Painter, in their book *Revelations: Diaries of Women* (4-5), identify this theme as

> an unconscious call ... for a redefinition of [the] concepts [of Love, Work, and Power] into a less divisive, more organic pattern for existence, one where their capacities for both love and work blend, allowing them to be fully human and balanced, true to the power of their individual natures.

Also, as in other Native women's autobiographies, Molly's diaries focus on personal growth, private relationships, and domestic details.[1] In addition, they provide social commentary on a range of topics, from politics and racism to the emptiness of high society life. Molly had an anthropologist's eye, and in her travels frequently recorded culturally-based values, customs, and tastes that differed from her own – from the profound to the prosaic. During her first months in France she devoted a half dozen pages to descriptions of French cheeses and eating habits.

Of course, beyond deciphering, interpreting, and fleshing out the diaries, it was essential to gather information needed to place Molly in a contextual narrative. In addition to ethnohistorical research pertaining to the Penobscot, this included exploration on a range of relevant topics – from vaudeville to film, from world's fairs to World War II.

More Strands in the Web

Molly's two-pronged identity began in childhood. As a girl, she attended the reservation's Catholic mission primary school on weekdays and zealously collected tribal legends from Penobscot elders on weekends. One day she would learn a traditional tribal dance, and the next day she would scrub floors in exchange for classical ballet lessons. As a teenager, she spent summers (and frequent school terms) away from the reservation performing in vaudeville with an Indian troupe to help support her seven younger siblings. This sense of responsibility toward family lasted throughout her lifetime, and diary notes such as this are common: "Giving my heart and soul to my dancing and my career to help my [family] is my task."

In vaudeville – as in Old Town's secondary schools, where some Penobscot children ventured after reaching the limits of the reservation

---

1   See Bataille and Sands, 8.

Molly and the U.S. Indian Band of the 1931 Colonial Exposition in Paris. They are standing in front of the U.S. exhibit: a replica of George Washington's Mount Vernon home.

BUNNY MCBRIDE

school – Molly often encountered racist heckling. Referring to an incident at school, she told her diary, "The white boys [of Old Town] shun the ... Indian girl like poison." On another occasion, after one of her Indian vaudeville shows, she noted, "Cried after performance. Why? Heard a cutting remark." Sometimes she fought back: "A front row couple made fun of us. I flirted with the fellow and the girl became silent." In another instance, she challenged an audience's insults by writing a "criticism on ... racial feeling to the Boston Telegram."

In her early twenties Molly studied journalism and anthropology at the University of Pennsylvania, thanks, in part, to anthropologist Frank Speck, whose extensive Maine Indian research included long visits to Indian Island. Short of funds, she left Philadelphia after a year for a season with the Miller Brothers' 101 Ranch Wild West Show, where she found a circus atmosphere that starved her artistic soul.[1] During the second half of her twenties, she assumed the name Molly Spotted Elk, and moved to New York City. There she modelled for a host of artists, danced in Broadway productions, delighted the high society crowd in Texas Guinan's famous speakeasies, and performed in a much touted production with the Provincetown Players, an esteemed theatrical company. In 1928 she won a starring role in *The Silent Enemy* (a docudrama about Ojibwa Indians), and ventured off to the wilds of northern Ontario for a rugged year of on-location shooting at Lake Temagami. There, art and nature came together, which gave Molly enormous pleasure. The much-publicized film gained critical acclaim from every corner – but failed at the box office because it was a silent picture released amid a flurry of new "talkies."

Back in New York, Molly grew sick of the milieu, repertoire, and hours of nightclub work. Feeling straitjacketed by her audiences' stereotypic views of "Indian maidens,"[2] she made this prescient diary entry:

> How I wish I could always have the proper atmosphere to do my work as it should be.... The more I dance, the more I want to interpret my emotions without limitation, to create a freedom of primitiveness and aban-

---

1   For a detailed look at Indian participation in the 101 Ranch, see Collings and Miller.

1   Molly was unhappy heir to what Hinsley, 53, calls "the transformation of the aborigine from historical actor to aesthetic object." Cf. Green, 1975, 1980, 1989.

don. If only one could dance solely for art! Maybe someday I will have that chance. If not in America, then in Europe.

Two years later she travelled to Paris and performed the opening dance for the extravagant 1931 International Colonial Exposition. Lured by French audiences who appreciated her desire to perform authentic Indian dances rather than the cliché "jumping and whooping" that thrilled American crowds, she decided to remain in Paris after the Exposition. In the years that followed, she danced and lectured professionally, worked on an "Indian novel," and mingled with well-known American literati and French anthropologists.

Molly's most frequent and intimate French companion was Jean Archambaud, a journalist with *Paris Soir*, the city's leading daily newspaper. As special correspondent, Jean spent considerable time outside the office, gathering up material for a wide variety of feature stories. His interests, gravitating toward natural history, philosophy, and the arts, were decidedly pan-cultural. So it is not surprising that within days of Molly's arrival in Paris, he approached her for an interview. He was smitten from the start. Over the next few weeks, during timeless talks in cafes and long strolls through Parisian parks, he discovered that she, like him, relished art, literature, and history, and felt uneasy if she spent too much time away from nature. She spoke with a captivating blend of passion and knowledge about an American Indian culture that intrigued him profoundly. He pursued her as a reflection of something deep within himself, and several weeks after their first meeting, he proposed marriage.

The feeling was mutual, yet Molly resisted marrying Jean for years, certain that a formal union would kill her career. She had always given priority to her profession: "The fire of ambition must be first," she had told her diary when writing about work and love at age twenty-three. A few years later she had noted, "In the joy of one's work there lies the secret of all happiness." Now, confronted with a love as strong as her ambition, she wrote, "Sooner or later, I, as a woman, will have to make a choice between two things.... I will be happy in my work and lonely ... or happy with someone and discontented with myself and my work." Yet the fact that Jean, unlike a string of previous white suitors, loved her not as a "novelty" or "sexy savage," but as a true soul mate (his "missing half," as he put it), eventually won her over. His interest in her heritage seemed to rise from the centre of his being, prompting Molly to note in her diary, "At times, I would swear Jean had injun feeling – for he understands so well. As it is, the arms of the forest enveloped him in his childhood, and its warmth and mysteries saturated his white skin and soul."

Molly's fears about the limitations of marriage were gradually eclipsed by what she described as the "companionship, honesty, honor, understanding, and confidence" that she found with Jean. A remarkable partnership emerged. Jean welcomed Molly's input in his work, and they frequently co-authored newspaper and magazine articles on American Indian topics. He supported her career enthusiastically, sometimes painting costumes for her, playing the drum while she danced, and translating her public lectures and the Penobscot legends she had written down. They finally wed in 1939 – eight years after their first meeting (and four years after the birth of their daughter, whom they named Jean, after her father).

In France Molly experienced the wonder of bridging the cultural gap through art and love. But that bridge began to crumble when the Germans occupied the country in 1940. Her husband, unable to obtain a United States visa and in a dangerous position because of his political writings, escaped on the eve of occupation. Neither he nor Molly knew for certain where he would shelter himself. Molly, determined to get their child out of harm's way, made a harrowing journey with the little girl, trekking on foot over the Pyrenees Mountains into Spain, taking a train to Lisbon, and finally boarding a refugee steamer that carried them home.

Back in the States, Molly's life took a tragic turn – beginning with the death of her husband in a French refugee camp, followed by her demise as a performer and a gradual retreat into reclusiveness on her home reservation.

Respinning the Web: Responsible Representation

The diaries provided an opportunity both to glean from and to include Molly's voice in her biography. Because many daily entries are fragmented or obscure, the journals are not suited to stand on their own as a cohesive narrative accessible to a general readership. But a selection of *telling* passages, woven together with a narrative informed by all of the diaries plus a wide variety of other sources, made it possible for us to be co-authors of a sort. This helped curb what George Stocking (103) calls the "inherent ambiguity and asymmetry of almost all ethnographic relations." James Clifford (1983:147-48) has explored the difference between ethnographic texts constructed by researchers who believe extensive experiences within a community empower them "to speak as an insider on behalf of the community's truth or reality," and those born of a "dialogical enterprise in which both researchers and natives are active creators." Surely such dialogue is more difficult to achieve with a deceased subject, but keeping the principle foremost reminded me to guard against letting my voice eclipse Molly's.[1] Aiming to avoid the ownerial ethnographic view epitomized by Bronislaw Malinowski's comment about his Trobriand subjects ("It is I who will describe them or create them"[2]), I used her words as much as possible. Further, I repeatedly backtracked to examine my own words in the light of a growing understanding of her — and revised them as needed. This was essential as a "check against assimilating the other to the self" (Fischer, 201). In retrospect, I believe the most telling passages in the book were written at moments when I felt like an "editor-recorder" working in partnership with Molly to create her autobiography.[3]

There is, of course, a danger in becoming so close to one's subject, particularly in this time of postcolonial political correctness. In the wake of worldwide decolonization efforts of the 1960s and 1970s, including the Red Power movement in North America, Indian cultures began to revitalize rather than disappear through assimilation as expected. Depictions of Native Americans, in turn, shifted. According to James Clifton's sometimes hyperbolic essay, "Alternate Identities and Cultural Frontiers" (3-4), now the "task for scholars was to document how Indians had been exploited, to show how they had overcome injustice, to stress how they had perpetuated old ways and their identities, and to forecast a more beneficent, independent future." This, Clifton complains, led to "glamorized" accounts — "moralizing stories about the contributions of larger-than-life heroic figures to serve, in the phrasing of modern pop-sociology, as role models." I confess I was tempted to present Molly in exaggerated dimensions — to bolster her fame and pain to drive home

---

1 Cf. Clifford 1986:15.

2 In Stocking, 103.

3 Bataille and Sands, 11, use the term "editor-recorder" in their discussion of assisted autobiographies.

the points of cultural genocide and its collateral damage of identity confusion and diminished self-worth. For one brief moment, I even toyed with the idea of dramatizing her story in a novel. But, beyond thwarting my personal desire to get to the "truth" (or at least *a* truth), I realized this would have been disrespectful. It would have robbed Molly's story of its subtleties, and obscured the fact that her life was emblematic of the lives of many American Indian women.

Barbara Meyerhoff (90), writing about her research among elderly Jews, touched on this question of responsible representation, and offered an eloquent description of the mental turmoil ethnographers experience when (and if) they reach the point of genuine empathy with their subjects — particularly if those subjects have been victimized by dominant society:

> I wanted my people to be loved and admired as a result of my study, for in addition to being survivors, they were presently poor and maltreated. I wanted to protect them, even from my responses. But finally I accepted the necessity for sacrificing that desire. A reverential, protective attitude would allow the reader to distance him- or herself from them. The elders' accomplishments were important precisely because they were not heroes or saints.... My work would have to be a full-length portrait, light and darkness with more shading than sharp lines. Since neutrality was impossible and idealization undesirable, I settled on striving for balance. If these people emerged as real in their entire human range and variety, arousing admiration and disappointment, laughter and tears, hope and despair, I would be satisfied.

I, too, settled on striving for the balance of a full-length portrait. But there is more to the challenge of responsible representation than this. What if the painting of Kateri Tekakwitha had straightened out for someone other than me? No doubt Molly's biography would have been different from the one I wrote. My effort to be true to her voice greatly influenced but surely did not silence my own. Inevitably, the book became a "negotiated reality" (Clifford, 14). It is about my encounter with Molly, even though I never appeared in her diaries or on my pages, and never used the word "I" in telling her story. As Gerald Berreman (339) has noted, "All observation is selective, all recording of observation is selective again, and the published account is selective of the recorded observations." Certainly, the selections of another author, informed by a distinct vantage point, values, and purpose, would not match mine.

While gleaning the whole truth is surely impossible,[1] it is nonetheless the task of the biographer and ethnographer to reach toward it. This I did, aiming for a truthful biography that not only chronicled facts about and surrounding Molly, but also echoed her attitude toward and feelings about life. I was aided in my endeavour by Molly's sister Eunice and daughter Jean. Not only did both of these women welcome frequent interviews, but they reviewed each chapter as it was completed. They corrected facts as needed and occasionally helped me rethink interpretations — but not once did they request censorship of anything. While sharing my commitment to getting at the truth of Molly's life story, their vantage points were distinct from mine. Their input (and to a lesser degree interviews with many others) helped me in my effort to do what Eric Wolf (95) calls "circumnavigating man" — exploring multiple facets of a life from multiple angles or mindsets.

I think it is important to note that when I got stuck in my wrestlings to understand Molly's life and translate it into a book, I had the benefit of an in-house sounding board to help bounce me out of such predicaments. I am married to an anthropologist who specializes in American Indian studies. His willingness to brainstorm with me on the issues I confronted and to give critical feedback on each chapter brought many insights — and welcome escape from the hermitage of my study.

Drawing Others into the Web: Purpose and Audience

Although my view of Molly and her cultural context was informed and bent by the perspectives of her family, friends, and associates, I came to the task of writing her biography with a particular purpose that held firm and played a significant role in shaping the book's tone and some of my choices about its content. First of all, *I* wanted to understand Molly and the forces that shaped her. Second, I wanted to write a book that prodded readers to reach across the cultural divide as Molly did. Molly's life offered insights for a society struggling with its own multicultural identity. It seemed to me that if I could introduce readers to Molly in a way that encouraged them to take her arm and walk through her life with open minds, they might be witnesses to unexpected strengths and strug-

---

1   Cf. Crapanzano in Clifford and Marcus, 6.

gles that would shatter well-harboured stereotypes and open channels of communication. The readers in my imagination had many faces: Penobscots, American Indians in general, humanities scholars, and a broad general public including women from all walks of life. To bring this huge varied audience into focus, I kept specific individuals from each group in mind as I wrote. Then I sought a non-esoteric voice that wedded fact and feeling, aiming to speak to them all with at least a measure of meaning.

Although I cast my net wide in terms of readership, perhaps most important to me was the construction of a text that would be useful as a cultural root in the Penobscot community today and in years to come. In part, this feeling grew out of my previous work with the Aroostook Band of Micmacs. Most of the ethnographic research and writing that my husband and I did about them was produced to educate legislators (and the public) concerning the validity of the band's federal recognition effort. Alongside this legal endeavour grew a social one – a struggle for self-recognition and cultural reclamation – that also called for research and writing. The Micmac community was often the primary (and sometimes only) audience for this work.[1]

Not coincidentally, the coming together of distinct cultures was both the process and the purpose of writing Molly's biography. And clearly, Molly held this as a central purpose in her life. She endeavoured to build a bridge between Penobscot culture and the larger world in which she moved. From the time she was a girl, she tried to preserve and foster respect for traditional culture by defining it to the public through dance, song, lecture, and writing. The first stage name she chose for herself was *Neeburban*, the Penobscot word for Northern Lights. In many ways this name symbolizes the light or insight Molly sought for herself and shared with others through her art. Although she never used the words pluralism or cultural emancipation, that is what she strove for. She once told her diary, "With patience, hard work will be the means of reaching that hilltop I want to reach so badly – not fame but realization."

---

1   For example, the Micmac oral histories were compiled in an unpublished manuscript, entitled *In Our Own Words*. Like other internal documents produced for the band, copies are on file at the Aroostook Band of Micmac headquarters (as well as in the hands of those who shared their stories). For a twentieth-century overview of the Micmacs, see Prins 1994a. For a deeper historical account covering the last five hundred years, see Prins 1996.

The Web is Spun

The resurrection of Molly's life in a biography was something made possible, perhaps even anticipated, by Molly herself. The diaries and other life remnants she left behind are testimonies of her efforts to escape and eradicate social domination through self-identification, cultural definition, and cross-cultural communication. It is as if she recognized that her life was emblematic of these fundamental issues of the human condition — and that it "might serve to renew the self and ethnic group as well as contribute to a richer, powerful dynamic pluralist society" (Fischer, 197).

At its best, a retrospection on such a life can help us gain a vision for the future — not only for the society in which we wish to live, but for the methods and missions we bring to our disciplines. As Clifton (xi) avers: "Using biography as a magnifying glass, peering closely at the experiences of particular individuals, we aim at revealing more texture and intricacy than what emerges from other types of anthropological and historical studies, and at generating some new insights."

Among the insights I gained in writing Molly's biography is the realization that only through an intimate encounter with another can we perceive and begin to actualize our shared humanity. And inevitably, the striving that is necessary to truly understand another person (and another culture) leads to self reflection and a new perspective on one's own beliefs and values.

Some years ago I interviewed several anthropologists about the purpose each brought to research and writing. Clifford Geertz's simple response summed up all the others. He said that he practised anthropology "to make it possible for people to comprehend one another" (in McBride 1980:90). Indeed, we explore and write about the lives of others with our eyes focused on possibilities. And, in the words of Scott Momaday, "The possibilities of storytelling are precisely those of understanding the human experience" (in Fischer, 225).

References

Bataille, Gretchen M. and Kathleen Mullen Sands

    1984 *American Indian Women Telling Their Lives*. Lincoln: University of Nebraska Press.

Berreman, Gerald D.

    1968 "Ethnography: Method and Product," In *Introduction to Cultural Anthropology*. Ed. James Clifton. Boston: Houghton Mifflin, 337-73.

Blodgett, Harriet

    1991 "Dear Diary: How do I need you? Let me Count the Ways," *New York Times Book Review*. 22 September, 24-25.

Chona, Maria

    1979 *Papago Woman*. Ed. Ruth M. Underhill. New York: Holt, Rinehart and Winston.

Clifford, James

    1983 "Power and Dialogue in Ethnography: Marcel Griaule's Initiation," in *Observers Observed: Essays on Ethnographic Fieldwork*. Ed. George W. Stocking. Madison: University of Wisconsin Press. 121-56.

Clifford, James, and George E. Marcus, eds.

    1986 "Introduction: Partial Truths," in *Writing Culture: The Poetics and Politics of Ethnography*. Berkeley: University of California Press. 1-26.

Clifton, James A., ed.

    1989a "Alternative identities and Cultural Frontiers," in *Being and Becoming Indian*. Ed. James A. Clifton. Chicago: Dorsey Press. 1-37.

    1989b *Being and Becoming Indian: Biographical Studies of North American Frontiers*. Chicago: Dorsey Press.

Collings, Ellsworth, with Alma Miller

    1971 *The 101 Ranch*. Norman: University of Oklahoma Press.

Fischer, Michael M.J.

    1986 "Ethnicity and the Post-Modern Arts of Memory," in *Writing Culture: The Poetics and Politics of Ethnography*. Eds. James Clifford and George E. Marcus. Berkeley: University of California Press. 194-233.

Friar, Ralph, and Natasha Friar

    1972 *The Only Good Indian: The Hollywood Gospel*. New York: Drama Book Specialists.

Green, Rayna

    1975 "The Pocahontas Perplex: The Image of Indian Women in Popular Culture." *Massachusetts Review* 16 (Autumn): 698-714.

1980 "Native American Woman: Review Essay." *Signs* 6 (Winter): 248–67.

1989 "The Indian in Popular American Culture," in *History of Indian-White Relations*, Handbook of North American Indians, vol. 4. Washington, DC: Smithsonian Institution. 587–606.

Hinsley, Curtis

1983 "Ethnographic Charisma and Scientific Routine: Cushing and Fewkes in the American Southwest, 1879–1893," in *Observers Observed: Essays on Ethnographic Fieldwork*. Ed. George W. Stocking. Madison: University of Wisconsin Press. 53–69.

Langness, L.L., and Gelya Frank

1981 *Lives: An Anthropological Approach to Biography*. Novato, CA: Chandler and Sharp.

McBride, Bunny

1980 *A Sense of Proportion: Balancing Subjectivity and Objectivity in Anthropology*. Master's thesis, Columbia University.

1995 *Molly Spotted Elk: A Penobscot in Paris*. Norman: University of Oklahoma Press.

Meyerhoff, Barbara

1989 "So What do You Want from Us here?" in *In the Field: Readings on the Field Research Experience*. Eds. Carolyn D. Smith and William Kornblum. New York: Praeger. 83–90.

Miller, Jay

1989 "Mourning Dove: The Author as Cultural Mediator," in *Being and Becoming Indian: Biographical Studies of North American Frontiers*. Ed. James A. Clifton. Chicago: Dorsey Press. 160–82.

Moffat, Mary Jane, and Charlotte Painter, eds.

1975 *Revelations: Diaries of Women*. New York: Vintage Books.

Prins, Harald E.L.

1994a "Micmac," in *Native America in the Twentieth Century, An Encyclopedia*. Ed. Mary B. Davis. New York: Garland Publishing.

1994b "Penobscot," in *Native America in the Twentieth Century, An Encyclopedia*. Ed. Mary B. Davis. New York: Garland Publishing.

1996 *The Mi'kmaq: Resistance, Accommodation, and Cultural Survival*. NY: Harcourt Brace College Publishers.

Siebert, Frank T.

1982 "Frank G. Speck, Personal Reminiscences," in *Papers of the Thirteenth Algonquian Conference*. Ed. William Cowan. Ottawa: Carleton University. 91–126.

Snow, Dean R.

    1978 "Eastern Abenaki," in *Northeast*. Ed. Bruce G. Trigger. Handbook of North American Indians, vol. 15. Washington, DC: Smithsonian Institution. 137-47.

Speck, Frank G.

    1915 "Basis of American Indian Ownership of the Land," in *University Lectures Delivered by Members of the Faculty in the Free Public lecture Course 1914-1915*. Philadelphia: University of Pennsylvania. 181-96.

    1917 "Game Totems Among the Northeastern Algonkians." *American Anthropologist* 19:9-18.

    1940 *Penobscot Man: The Life History of a Forest Tribe in Maine*. Philadelphia: University of Pennsylvania Press.

Stocking, George W., ed.

    1983 "The Ethnographer's Magic: Fieldwork in British Anthropology from Tylor to Malinowski," in *Observers Observed: Essays on Ethnographic Fieldwork*. Ed. George W. Stocking. Madison: University of Wisconsin Press. 70-120.

Wolf, Eric

    1964 *Anthropology*. Englewood Cliffs, NJ: Prentice Hall.

Part VII. Words and Things, Documents
        and Collectors

New texts (in their broadest sense) are constantly being discovered and produced for the endlessly diverse fields of Native history that draw our attention now and for the future. In this final section, three authors explore a range of "texts" produced from the 1890s to the present. They include written and oral accounts, old and new, of key events and actors in the Klondike gold rush; pictorial and oral depictions of the experiences of Native children in white-run boarding schools; and an eclectic collection of artifacts which were assembled by a fascinating and worldly late Victorian Mohawk doctor and whose messages and meanings have been read and reread ever since.

Julie Cruikshank's study of contrasting written and oral accounts of Skookum Jim (Keish to his Tagish relations) and his role in the Yukon gold rush provides intriguing insights into the way texts are embedded in the social milieus that produce them. Written accounts of the gold rush by Pierre Berton and others provide readings of Skookum Jim strikingly different from those of the oral narratives told by Tagish people, refracting the divergent social contexts and concerns of the tellers. Cruikshank does not blend or marry these disparate narratives, or winnow them down to some shared grain of truth. Rather, she illustrates how differing kinds of narrative, through their very difference, enhance our understanding of the past. In her words, the narrative forms of a community "help members construct, maintain and pass on an understanding of how the world works or should work." Taken together, they all provide rich insights into how people understand their own past and present, even as they tell about others.

Before becoming a professor of anthropology at the University of British Columbia, Cruikshank lived in the Yukon for many years; she returns regularly to work with Athapaskan and Tlingit elders, recording their oral traditions and life stories. This work has fed her interest in how history is constructed differently in differing cultural contexts. Internationally known for her studies of the social meanings of oral narrative, the social construction of anthropology, and the social commentary contained in museum collections, she is the author, with Angela Sidney, Kitty Smith, and Annie Ned, of the award-winning *Life Lived Like a Story: Life Stories of Three Athapaskan Elders* (1990) and the oral history-based book *Reading Voices* (1991).

Historian J.R. Miller, a professor at the University of Saskatchewan, also combines distinct kinds of texts for glimpses into the lives of Native children in Canadian residential schools from the 1880s to the 1960s. He explores the nature and impact of residential schools through every available medium: archival sources, extensive interviews with former students, attendance at their school reunions, and detailed study of visual images for clues to the experiences of children whose voices seldom penetrated the historical record.

Miller's interest in schooling grew out of his time teaching Canadian Studies in Japan in the early 1980s. Efforts to understand Japanese education led him to the scholarly literature on schools as laboratories for social engineering. His interest piqued, he returned to the Canadian prairies to begin a major project on the dozens of Native residential schools that dotted the Canadian West for eight decades. Since the mid-1980s his research and publications have centred on Native-White relations in Canada. His widely read works include *Skyscrapers Hide the Heavens: A History of Indian-White Relations in Canada* (1991) and an edited volume, *Sweet Promises: A Reader on Indian-White Relations in Canada* (1991). He is currently completing a book on the history of residential schooling for Native children.

Trudy Nicks is a curator of ethnology at the Royal Ontario Museum in Toronto. Her essay brings to light the diverse interpretive angles from which museum collections can be read: in this instance, the cultural artifacts, tourist curios, and natural history specimens amassed by a nineteenth-century Mohawk medical doctor and insurance executive. Approached as an entity and studied as a text, the Oronhyatekha collection constitutes a valuable record of cross-cultural exchange and interaction. It documents the collector's ambivalent cultural position in his era: Dr. Oronhyatekha was at once deeply engaged in Victorian society (a society smitten with the habit of collecting), and made use of that engagement to advance distinctly Iroquoian political aims.

Nicks's fascination with the Oronhyatekha collection grew out of her ethnological work at the Royal Ontario Museum where she is engaged in a major research project in oral history and preparing an exhibition of contemporary traditions in Iroquois beadwork with several communities in Ontario, Quebec, and New York State. Much of her research has focused on the artwork of Iroquois, Mi'kmaq, and Ojibwa peoples in the nineteenth and twentieth centuries and the artistic, social, and economic significance of the items they produced specifically for tourists or for exhibition. She has also written widely on the forging of partnerships between museums and Native communities, and co-chaired the 1992 Task Force on Museums and First Peoples sponsored by the Assembly of First Nations and the Canadian Museums Association.

18

Discovery of Gold on the Klondike: Perspectives from Oral Tradition[1]

Julie Cruikshank

THE GOLD RUSHES in northwestern North America during the mid- and late-nineteenth century have a special fascination for Western audiences. Stories from these times persist partly because they appeal to popular imagination and partly because they dramatize aspects of social life that seem problematic. This is particularly true of the Klondike gold rush, perhaps because its circumstances draw together so many elements central to European and American folklore. In northern Canada, it is still possible to hear contrasting accounts about incidents from these times, some from written records and others in the daily conversation of elderly Native men and women.[2] The question of which versions are "correct" may be less interesting than what each story reveals about the cultural values of its narrator.

The problem of whether or to what extent oral narrations about the past can be equated with Western notions of history has long been discussed in anthropology.[3] As ethnohistorians look more closely at oral testimonies, they are paying increasing attention to ideological, sym-

---

1   This is a revised version of "Images of Society in Klondike Gold Rush Narratives: Skookum Jim and the Discovery of Gold" which appeared in *Ethnohistory* 39(1):20-41.

2   For historical accounts based primarily on written records, see, for example, Zaslow 1971, Wright 1976, Coates and Morrison 1988. Discussions of gold rush accounts narrated by aboriginal men and women appear in Slobodin 1963, McClellan 1963, 1970a, McClellan *et al.* 198, and Cruikshank 1991.

3   Very early, Lowie (1917:165, 166-67) denied that oral tradition had any value as historical evidence. Malinowski (1926) and Radcliffe-Brown (1952) each proposed that narrative accounts served primarily as charters to justify the present social order. More recently, structuralists argued that oral traditions are statements about the human mind rather than commentaries on the past (Levi-Strauss 1966:66, 232-37). Rosaldo (1980) and Cohen (1989) have each demonstrated that historical insights are most likely to come when we analyze oral tradition on its own terms rather than treating it as an example of some other process.

bolic, and metaphorical meanings in them. Sensitivity to ethnocentric bias in Western writings has increased awareness of the value of the spoken word and has also led to a more cautious handling of written sources and to recognition that *both* oral and written traditions are part of larger social processes.[1] Even so, Edward Steinhart's (1989) recent comparison of trends in African and American oral history concludes that conventional archaeological, documentary, and ethnographic sources continue to be privileged as the standards against which oral accounts are judged to establish the "factual truth" of cultural history.

My attempts to combine oral and written accounts from the Yukon Territory suggest that both kinds of narratives share common problems not always addressed in ethnohistory. This paper examines one particular incident from the Klondike gold rush in order to demonstrate possibilities that exist for combining written and oral accounts. Comparing such accounts shows, for example, how culturally distinct ideas about family and community organization may influence *interpretations* of events. Such an approach directs us back to the social processes in which all accounts are embedded and raises questions about the authority we accord to documentary evidence.

The circumstances surrounding the discovery of gold that triggered the Klondike gold rush in the Yukon in 1896 come to us both in the written record and in stories from indigenous peoples passed on by word of mouth. The term "discovery" is somewhat problematic in this context, because it implies a discrete, bounded incident. Yet knowledge that gold existed in this area was far from new in 1896. Robert Campbell, a trader with the Hudson's Bay Company, recognized gold in the gravel near his trading post at the junction of the Yukon and Pelly Rivers in the early 1850s. Robert McDonald, a Church of England missionary, reported traces of gold in Birch Creek near the Yukon-Alaska border in the 1870s (Ogilvie 1913:84-87). Prospectors had worked their way north from the California goldfields, following strikes on the Fraser River and in the Cariboo district, confident that the Cordilleran would

---

1 Some of the most impressive ventures in this direction come from analyses of colonial encounters in Surinam (Price 1983), in the South Pacific (Sahlins 1985, Obeyesekere 1992), in Africa (Netting 1987), and in South America (Hill 1988). Certainly, some historians working exclusively with written documents pay close attention to symbolic aspects of documents; for example, see Robert Darnton's (1984) account of cat trials in pre-revolutionary France, and Carlo Ginsberg's (1980) and Natalie Davis's (1983) writings about life experiences in sixteenth-century Europe.

yield more. In 1887, geologist George Dawson (1898:133) named several prospectors who were making a reasonable living panning gold on the Pelly River. Yet the term "discovery" always refers back to the same event — the almost accidental finding of a creek where placer gold lay in amounts sufficient to signal a major rush. The event is still celebrated annually on 17 August, which is a Territory-wide holiday, Discovery Day, with numerous organized festivities in Dawson City.

Narratives from Native elders, by contrast, focus less on an event than on a process. The oral accounts considered here come from three Native women with whom I recorded life histories over a number of years: Mrs. Kitty Smith and Mrs. Annie Ned, each born in approximately 1890, and Mrs. Angela Sidney, born in 1902. Each incorporated references to the gold rush into her life story (Cruikshank et al. 1990).[1] Parallel accounts have been recorded with other Native elders (see Skookum Jim Friendship Centre)[2] but I refer here specifically to Mrs. Sidney's, Mrs. Smith's, and Mrs. Ned's accounts because we discussed them together so fully. The written accounts come from books and from archival documents — private and published journals, lawyers' records, newspapers — located while I was trying to put the oral narratives into some broader historical context.

What becomes clear in working with these accounts is that neither oral nor written versions can be treated simply as historical evidence to be sifted for "facts"; furthermore, combining the two kinds of accounts does not really give us a synthesis, the "real story." Instead, both of them have to be understood as windows on the way the past is constructed and discussed in different contexts, from the perspectives of actors enmeshed in culturally distinct networks of social relationships. All societies have characteristic narrative structures that help members construct and maintain knowledge of the world. The exercise here is less one of straightening out facts than of identifying how distinct cognitive models

---

1   I began working with Mrs. Sidney and Mrs. Smith in the early 1970s, and with Mrs. Ned a few years later. We collaborated for more than a decade on projects documenting life history, oral narrative, place names, and songs. Several booklets from this work have been published by the Yukon Native Language Centre (e.g., Sidney 1982, 1983; Sidney et al. 1977, Smith 1982, Ned 1984).

2   In 1975, the Skookum Jim Friendship Centre, based in Whitehorse, conducted a series of taped interviews with several elderly Native men and women who talked about their memories of Skookum Jim. Tape recordings from that project are stored in the Yukon Archives, Whitehorse.

generate different kinds of social analysis, leading to different interpretations of events, one of which gets included in official history, the others relegated to collective memory.

Tagish Society in the 1890s

To approach the oral accounts intelligently, we have to understand some basic principles about the way social behaviour was organized in the southern Yukon at the turn of the century. The individuals who appear in the following accounts were all Tagish men and women. Tagish people were hunters and fishers whose territories encompassed much of the lake system at the head of the Yukon River (see Figure 1).[1] They travelled widely in the course of the year, dispersing and regrouping as seasons and resources required. This apparent fluidity in group composition has led some anthropologists to characterize social organization of subarctic hunters as "flexible." However, in the southern Yukon, day-to-day activities were profoundly influenced by two kinship groups, Wolf and Crow. Anthropologists call these two divisions *moieties*, which means "halves." Membership in these two groups is determined by birth, and in the Yukon each person belongs to the same group as his or her mother; in other words, descent is *matrilineal*. By customary law, a person from one moiety can only marry someone from the opposite "side." Because this rule was strictly enforced in the past, every family grouping was composed of members of both moieties: alliances between moieties were repeatedly forged through marriages, partnerships, and trade, linking people from widely separated areas in networks of clearly understood responsibilities.

Some anthropologists believe that moieties in the southern Yukon are very old and that matriliny originated in the interior and spread to coastal Tlingit tribes at some point in the distant past (Dyen and Aberle 1974:388–89). During the last two centuries, however, long-standing

---

1   Anthropologists follow linguistic boundaries in designating territorial groups, while recognizing that such boundaries were never firm because of physical mobility and widespread intermarriage (see Helm 1981, and especially McClellan 1981). At the turn of the century, at least eight distinct languages were spoken in the Yukon. Seven of these were members of the Athapaskan language family (Gwich'in, Han, Tutchone, Southern Tutchone, Upper Tanana, Kaska, and Tagish). Inland Tlingit, an unrelated language, was spoken in the southern Yukon, at Teslin Lake. By then most Tagish speakers were bilingual, speaking Tagish and Tlingit.

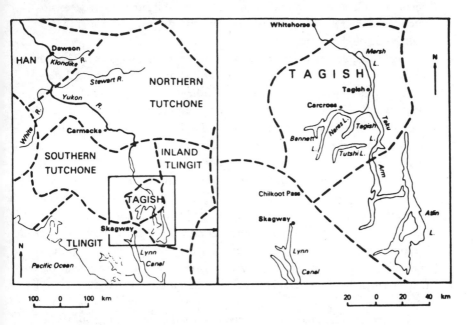

Figure 1: The Southern Lakes, Yukon Territory

trade alliances with coastal people also brought considerable Tlingit cultural influence to the interior. Some time after the arrival of Russian fur traders on the Pacific coast in the late eighteenth century, Tagish people became involved in trade networks with coastal Tlingit traders. After the intense demand for Pacific sea otters depleted this species, European traders redirected their efforts to obtaining land furs from across the mountains. Coastal Tlingits established themselves as middlemen in this trade by the nineteenth century, asserting control over the trading activities of interior groups like the Tagish, whom they visited on a regular basis (see McClellan 1981). Tlingits began by importing marine products and later added trade goods from Russian, British, and American traders. They jealously guarded their monopoly, effectively barring white traders from going to the interior, and interior Natives from going to the coast until the 1880s. Inevitably, the coastal Tlingits held the balance of power in these arrangements, and they regularly established trading partnerships with interior men, who were then obligated to trade exclusively with their Tlingit partner. These partnerships were frequently formalized through marriage.

Tagish people gradually began to adopt the Tlingit language as well as a number of Tlingit customs.[1] Each Tagish moiety incorporated clans with Tlingit names, for example Deisheetaan (a Crow clan) and Dakl'aweidí (a Wolf clan). Moiety and clan arrangements were expected to guide behaviour at birth, at the onset of puberty, at marriage, at death, and on other less formal occasions. Within any family, adult siblings were careful to observe rules of avoidance; however, the eldest brother had a definite commitment to see to the welfare of his sisters. He was recognized as the "boss," that is, responsible for younger brothers and sisters throughout his lifetime (McClellan 1970a:6). Sisters, in turn, prepared special clothes for an older brother and later prepared special food for him (McClellan 1961; 1975, 2:414-15; 432-33). The expectations and obligations attached to moiety and clan membership provide a context essential to understanding oral interpretations of events discussed below.

Written sources make little reference to the devastating impact of epidemics on Tagish demography during this period. There are not even rudimentary census figures for the southern Yukon before the twentieth century. By contrast, census figures for the coastal Chilkat, one of the Tlingit communities trading regularly to the Yukon interior, show that between 1861 and 1890 the Chilkat population declined by half, from 1,616 to 812 (De Laguna 1990:205). Boyd (1990:144) notes that the population of the community of Hutsnuwu (Angoon), to which members of the Tagish Deisheetaan clan trace their origin, declined by nearly two thirds between 1842 and 1890, largely as a result of a measles epidemic in 1848, followed by a smallpox epidemic in 1863. Inevitably, these epidemics must have affected Tagish people, and their oral accounts give some indication of how diseases were still decimating Tagish families by the end of the 1890s.

By the 1880s, Tlingits were losing their ability to maintain the blockade against a growing number of white prospectors, and Tagish people

---

1 Angela Sidney, one of the narrators of accounts about Skookum Jim, was one of the last living speakers of the Tagish language. She learned it as a child but said that by the time she was five or six years old, most people were using Tlingit as their principal language.

were making regular trips down to the coast by 1883 (Schwatka 1885:59). In 1887, geologist George Dawson (1888:203b) noted that the Tagish "tribe" was small, numbering 70 or 80 individuals. Surveyor William Ogilvie (1897:20) suggested that the population appeared so small because a number of Tagish people may actually have moved down to the coast. In 1897, a North West Mounted Police inspector, newly arrived in the Yukon, wrote: "The village used to be a large and flourishing one, but only half a dozen houses are now left standing" (Wood 1899:41).

Skookum Jim and the Discovery of Gold

A singular glamour is associated with gold in any period of history, but its discovery in the Yukon in 1896 coincided with a world depression and gave hope to thousands of unemployed men and women. The Klondike was called a "poor man's gold rush," because individual prospectors could go to the Yukon with relatively little capital, egged on by dreams of fortunes waiting to be found in the creek beds and gravel bars. All that seemed to be required was a willingness to take the risks involved in travelling to the extreme northwest corner of North America. However, we know in hindsight that the Klondike gold rush was part of a much larger, less glamorous process: the expansion of the new Canadian state into what was seen as the margins. Very few gold seekers even found claims to stake by the time they had completed the strenuous trip over the coastal mountains and down the Yukon River. The most permanent effect of the gold rush was the establishment of a framework for administration of the territory from Ottawa, the new nation's capital. Institutions dating from this time continue to have far-reaching implications for everyone living in the Yukon.

This gold rush has produced an enormous literature, but in thousands of written pages we find very few references to indigenous peoples who watched the changes come and were profoundly affected by them. Between 1896 and 1900, tens of thousands of would-be prospectors and miners converged on one small area of the Klondike River. The vast majority came by one route, climbing the Chilkoot Pass and then travelling down the Yukon River to Dawson City. We are left to imagine the impact of this torrent of visitors on aboriginal people living along the route and at the site of Dawson City itself, because so few travellers even mentioned them in their journals.

One reference to Native people does turn up repeatedly in written accounts of the Klondike gold rush. The issue of how the initial "discovery" of gold was made has been controversial, partly because of the circumstances surrounding the claim. Names of individuals associated with the events appear repeatedly in written accounts of the gold rush: Skookum Jim, his sister Kate, Dawson Charlie — all Tagish people — and Kate's non-Native husband George Carmack (Ogilvie 1913:125-30; Berton 1958:42-43; Zaslow 1971:101-103; Wright 1976:287-90; Coates and Morrison 1988:79-81). The literature of the American West and the Canadian North is replete with popular stories that serve to locate and interpret social experience, and stories about Skookum Jim that appear in written accounts of the gold rush conform closely to this model. Such stories present him as a kind of frontier folk hero, the archetypal "self-made" man. His activities are often interpreted symbolically in such accounts, as evidence that even the most improbable individual can find riches and thereby transform his own life and the society around him.

Oral accounts from his own community, however, describe Skookum Jim from a very different perspective and give us a rare opportunity to compare the accounts in the gold rush literature with those passed on by individuals who knew the principal actors personally. A comparison of written and oral accounts shows the significance of cultural context in bringing the lens of interpretation to "facts."

Written Accounts

Skookum Jim's name appears early in historical records and popular accounts of the gold rush. In 1887, surveyor William Ogilvie employed him as a packer to carry supplies over the Chilkoot Pass and marvelled at the heavy loads he carried — 156 pounds of bacon on a single trip. He noted that this was the reason "Skookum" (meaning "strong" in Chinook jargon) had become part of his English name (Ogilvie 1913:133). In 1892, J.B. Moore wrote in his journal that Skookum Jim asked him to help retrieve two bear hides: Jim reported that he had killed one of them by ramming his gun down its muzzle and pelting it with rocks after he ran out of ammunition (Moore 1968:19).

The best known written account of Skookum Jim's adventures describes his association with the white prospector George Carmack, who was the husband of Jim's sister, Kate. In 1896, Jim, Kate, her husband Carmack, and Jim and Kate's sister's son, Charlie, travelled down the Yukon River allegedly prospecting for gold. Pierre Berton's popular book on the Klondike paints a rather one-dimensional picture of Skookum Jim, but one that makes him comprehensible — and attractive — to readers of gold rush folklore, a truly cross-cultural "man's man":

> [He was] a giant of a man, supremely handsome with his high cheekbones, his eagle's nose, and his fiery black eyes — straight as a gun barrel, powerfully built and known as the best hunter and trapper on the river....
> Just as Carmack wished to be an Indian, Jim longed to be a white man — in other words, a prospector. He differed from the others in his tribe in that he displayed the white man's kind of ambition. (Berton 1958:42, 43)

Near the Klondike River, they met another prospector, Robert Henderson, who told Carmack that he knew a good place to look for gold and was willing to share the information with Carmack, but not with his Indian friends. Incensed, Jim, Charlie, Carmack, and Kate went on their way, and when they accidentally found gold a few days later, very close to the place Henderson had identified, they neglected to go back to tell him. So rapid was the staking rush following their discovery that Henderson missed out and became the tragic figure in the drama, defeated by his own arrogance (Ogilvie 1913:127-29; Zaslow 1971:101-103; Wright 1976:287-89, 295; Carmack 1933).

Jim, Carmack, Kate, and Charlie went briefly to Seattle with their newfound wealth. By then, according to reports filed with the government, their gold production had exceeded $200,000. They set out to spend it, Klondike style. Seattle newspapers gleefully reported on their high-rolling life, including stories about Kate blazing her way up a stairway to her hotel room with a hatchet and of Kate and Jim and Carmack throwing nuggets from their hotel room window, gold rush stories which may easily have been invented because they are so typical of the genre (Berton 1958:400). Then life began to sour. Carmack married a white woman, Marguerite Saftig, and sent Kate back to Carcross. Dawson Charlie fell off a railway bridge and drowned in Carcross in 1908. Jim continued to prospect, making lengthy trips along the Teslin, Pelly, Macmillan, Stewart, and Upper Liard rivers, but he failed to make another major strike and his health began to deteriorate. He died in 1916.[1]

Oral Accounts

Many Yukon elders living in the southern Yukon knew Skookum Jim personally. During the 1980s Mrs. Angela Sidney, Mrs. Kitty Smith, and Mrs. Annie Ned each recorded her life story, and each made reference to Skookum Jim in her account.

Mrs. Sidney's father's mother and Skookum Jim's mother were sisters, making the two men brothers by the Tagish system of kinship reckoning. Consequently, Skookum Jim was Angela Sidney's uncle. She knew him from the time she was a child until his death in 1916 and helped to nurse him during his final illness. Mrs. Smith married Skookum Jim's sister's son, Billy Smith. After marriage, she also developed a close friendship with her husband's aunt, Kate Carmack, and heard her gold rush stories many times. Mrs. Ned said that her family and Skookum Jim's family began discussions about a possible marriage between the two of them. After some negotiations, her family decided that Skookum Jim's life had been changed too dramatically by the events of the gold rush and arranged for her to marry someone else. In the course of the discussions, however, she heard firsthand accounts about the events of the "discovery."

Skookum Jim's real name was Keish. His mother was a Tagish woman who had married a Tlingit man; the Tlingit name Keish belonged to her Dak̲l'aweidí clan but affirmed her husband's ancestry. At the time of Keish's birth, sometime after the mid-1800s, Tlingit economic influence in the interior was probably at its height (McClellan 1950). By now, trading partnerships reinforced by marriage alliances between coastal Tlingits and inland Tagish were common, and interior Tagish people were formally adopting Tlingit clans, clan names, personal names, traditions, and even the Tlingit language. Keish was born of such a union.

---

1   From the W.L. Phelps papers. W.L. Phelps, Skookum Jim's lawyer, kept detailed notes and copies of correspondence between himself, Jim, Jim's daughter Daisy, and Daisy's guardian, Percy R. Peele. Much of the correspondence deals with Jim's will; however, it also contains comments about the changes occurring in Jim's and Daisy's lives. Copies and an inventory of the papers are stored in the Yukon Archives manuscript collection.

When Mrs. Sidney talked about Skookum Jim, she drew attention not to his exceptional physical strength but rather to how well he understood the social obligations that were part of his world. She began by talking about how he came to have Frog as his spirit helper, and then described his encounter with another being, Tl'anaxéedákw or "Wealth Woman." She explained how Keish behaved as any Tagish man should, by taking responsibility for the safety of his sisters. She interpreted his behaviour from the perspective of events described in the following stories, rather than presenting him as having any desire to be a prospector.

As a young man, Keish once saved the life of a frog trapped in a deep hole. Later the same frog returned to him on two different occasions, once in its animal form when it healed a wound he had received, and again in the form of a woman, showing him a golden-tipped walking cane which would direct him toward his fortune downriver. People credit Keish's Frog helper with a significant role in his eventual discovery of gold. His encounter with Tl'anaxéedákw was equally significant. A complex figure in Tagish mythology, she richly rewards anyone who hears her, catches her, and follows a particular ritual that everyone who knows the story would remember. Both Jim and Charlie heard her, but run though they might, they were unable to overtake her, said Mrs. Sidney. Consequently, the money which came their way after the discovery of gold did not last.[1]

Anthropologist Catharine McClellan (1963) compared eight accounts of the Frog Helper story and numerous references to "Wealth Woman," showing how these narratives provided a conventional explanation for unprecedented events. She argued convincingly that such narratives cannot be pulled out of context and have to be understood in relation to the total bodies of oral literature in which they appear (McClellan 1970a). She also suggested that Tagish people were particularly careful to maintain intellectual consistency when they explained the dramatic contradictions accompanying the gold rush. Customary cognitive models helped make unfamiliar events seem comprehensible.

While superhuman beings may have helped Tagish people to explain the actual discovery of gold, Mrs. Sidney, Mrs. Smith, and Mrs. Ned also emphasized Keish's understanding of his social responsibilities when

---

1 For other versions of the story of Tl'anaxeedakw, see Swanton 1909:174 (Tale 94); De Laguna 1972, 2:821; Kamenskii 1985:67-70; and Cruikshank et al. 1990:56-65.

they talked about his life. Information provided by Mrs. Sidney when she was preparing her family history makes this clearer.

Keish's father, Ḵaachgaawáa, was a Tlingit man of the Deisheetaan clan who married a Tagish woman named Gus'dutéen, from the Daḵl'aweidí clan. Ḵaachgaawáa made his headquarters at the junction of Bennett and Nares Lakes at the site of the present village of Carcross. As local head of his clan, he claimed authority over all the land from there to the summit of the Chilkoot on the inland side of the pass. He and his wife had a large family, and eight of their children — two brothers and six sisters — survived to adulthood and were living in the 1890s (Figure 2).

By the late 1880s pressure from prospectors and traders was breaking down the Tlingit trade monopoly. However, marriages between coastal and interior people continued to be important, and Keish and his brother both married coastal Tlingit women during the time they worked as packers for prospectors entering the Yukon. But sometime early in the 1890s, the elder brother, Tlakwshaan, died in one of the influenza epidemics sweeping the coast.

Three of Keish's sisters also married coastal men, but in each case illness and death intervened. His eldest sister fell victim to influenza and died shortly after her marriage. Because marriages were contracts establishing important alliances between kin groups, rather than simply between individuals, her husband's clan requested that one of her sisters be sent to replace her, as was the custom. Another daughter, Aagé, travelled down to the coast to become the second wife. But even before this marriage could take place, the husband fell ill and died. Because the deceased man had no unmarried brother, custom dictated that his sister's son, who was of the same clan, should become Aagé's new husband. Aagé and her husband had a daughter, but a few years later and just before the birth of their second child, her husband was killed in a fight about which clan had the right to pack prospectors' goods over the pass. The young widow asked her husband's family to allow her to return to the interior, and they agreed, but only on the condition that she leave her eldest child with them to raise, a child Carcross elders remember by the English name Susie George. The marriages, the deaths, and the loss of her first child had taken a toll, and for a variety of reasons, Aagé asked her mother to look after her other child, Louise, while she left with a

JULIE CRUIKSHANK

prospector, "Mr. Wilson."[1] In this way, Aagé became the first of Skookum Jim's sisters to go downriver with a white prospector.

A third sister known as Kate or Shaaw Tláa also married a coastal Tlingit man, her mother's brother's son, in a conventional alliance. They had one baby daughter, but both father and child died of influenza. As in her sister's case, Kate's husband's Tlingit clan wanted her to remain on the coast so they could arrange an appropriate second marriage. But by now, her mother back in Carcross was so deeply distressed by the loss of her daughters that she insisted on Kate's return. The startling number of deaths was forcing people to improvise in cases of remarriage of widows. A fourth sister had recently married a white prospector/trader named George Carmack but she, too, died from the influenza that was ravaging interior communities by the early 1890s. Kate's mother insisted that it was more appropriate for Kate to return to the interior to marry her deceased sister's husband than to remain on the coast. Partnerships between brothers-in-law were very important, and with Carmack's second marriage into the family, he and Skookum Jim became strong allies. But shortly after this, Carmack and Kate followed her sister downriver, where rumours of gold were attracting prospectors.

Still another of Skookum Jim's sisters, Nadagaat' Tláa, died when she and her daughter were caught in an unexpected winter storm on a mountain pass as they returned from a potlatch. Only one sister, Kooyáy, remained with her parents, married in a customary alliance in the interior. She raised a large family, including the nephews who later accompanied Keish on his travels downriver. In a very few years, then, Keish lost one brother and three sisters. Of the surviving three sisters, two had gone "down the river" with white husbands, leaving only one still living safely at home. Local people insist that Skookum Jim was not prospecting with Carmack in 1896; instead, he was living on the southern lakes, preoccupied with the whereabouts of his two sisters. Angela Sidney began her account thus:[2]

---

1   This may be the same Wilson employed by John Healy, a long-time trader at Dyea, Alaska. Wilson ran one of Healy's posts near Haines, and J.B. Moore (1968:19), one of the founders of Skagway, Alaska, reported that Keish sold Wilson two bear skins in 1892.

2   Here I quote directly from the speakers, in their own words, making occasional changes to verb tenses for consistency with English usage.

In the first place, he wasn't looking for gold.

Skookum Jim went downriver to look for his two sisters, because they missed them.

They were gone two years already — no telegram, nothing!

He didn't know whether his two sisters were alive or not.

That's why he thought he'd go down the river too, to see if he could find his sisters, Aagé and Kate.

They were strict about that kind of thing, old people.

Mrs. Sidney went on to describe how a party was selected to go, who was chosen, who stayed behind, and why. Her own parents went part way, as far as Lake Laberge, but turned back when they considered how difficult it would be for their elderly relatives to survive the winter if they were delayed.

[Skookum Jim] took his wife and his two nephews — Dawson Charlie and Patsy Henderson.

My father was going too, but they turned back at Lake Laberge.

My father turned to my mother and he said, [looking back at the mountain behind Carcross]

"See that Chílíh Dzełe'?" And she started to cry.

"Why are you crying?"

"I'm just thinking about your poor crippled mother, and your sister and my mother.

Who is going to cut wood for them?

Who is going to help them get water?

They're sick and crippled and helpless."

And so my father and mother turned around and went back —

Otherwise, they might have found gold too.

Bad luck, eh?

But maybe it's just as well —

All those men who found gold split up with their wives.

Mrs. Smith's husband, Billy (Kenél'), was one of the young men who was left behind to look after his mother, Kooyáy. Mrs. Smith heard the story many times after her marriage, from the perspective of Kate who was living in Carcross by then:

Skookum Jim worries about his sister, you know.

"Oh my, [they're] going to get lost.
I don't want to get lost, my sister."
He talked about it all winter.
Dawson Charlie tells him,
"I guess we're going back to look for her.
We're going to bring her back," he tells his uncle.
Kate Carmack told me all that.
They just go look for her.
They're not looking for gold!

Her account attributed the overall success of the party to Kate's skills and to those of other women they met:

They lived one winter, Kate Carmack and him, her husband.
He's got a wife.
He's alright!
She does everything, that Indian woman, you know — hunts just like nothing, sets snares for rabbits.
That's what they eat.
I know her: that's my auntie, Kate Carmack, my old man's mother's sister.
One lady, Dawson people, gave them fish
She cut it up, Kate Carmack —
That's how they lived all winter.

In Mrs. Smith's version of the story, the actual discovery of the gold was secondary to Skookum Jim's journey down the river to find his missing sisters.[1] This pattern of a hero who uses all his powers to undertake a journey to find his wife or sisters is an important one in narratives from the southern Yukon, and occurs in many of the old stories.

---

1 A similar account came from Patsy Henderson, another of Skookum Jim's nephews and Dawson Charlie's younger brother. He was the youngest member of the party, though his name rarely appears in written accounts. His Tlingit name was Koolseen; his English name was given to him by George Carmack. Years later, in public lectures, he described the event as he remembered it (see Henderson 1950). When Catharine McClellan (personal communication, 1989) first heard the story from Patsy Henderson in the 1950s, his chief concern was to explain why, as a young man he had become frightened and "cried" at Wealth Woman, and hence had never become rich, like his uncle and brother. McClellan (n.d.) has recorded several other versions of the story.

One additional issue has continued to trouble Tagish people. K̲áa Goo̲x, Skookum Jim's sister's son, was with Jim when gold was discovered near the site named Dawson City, earning him the nickname Dawson Charlie. In written accounts he is invariably referred to as Tagish Charlie because whites identified him as coming from Tagish Lake. The misnomer causes confusion because a different Tagish man, Yeils'aagi, was known in the southern Yukon as Tagish Charlie. He was a prominent member of the Deisheetaan clan and was not involved in the discovery. To emphasize that these were two very different men, Mrs. Sidney and others pointed to their two graves in the Carcross cemetery, Tagish Charlie (Yéils'aagi) with his Deisheetaan beaver crest on his stone and Dawson Charlie (K̲áa Goo̲x) with his Dak̲l'aweidí wolf crest on his.

Stories of the aftermath of the gold rush focus on the close connection between wealth and tragedy. Carried away by their unexpected fortune, the men became involved in a lifestyle that cost each of them his family. Keish's wife left him and returned to her coastal Tlingit family. Her parents were disturbed by their daughter's violation of custom and they brought her back to her husband in Carcross, but Keish no longer seemed to care. She left again, taking their son while Keish kept their daughter Daisy. Dawson Charlie's wife, Sadusgé, left too. Alcohol played a part in his accidental death a few years later.

Kate returned to Carcross alone, abandoned by George Carmack who took their daughter, Graffie, south with him. Graffie's removal from the community was particularly devastating in a society which attaches such importance to matrilineal reckoning of kinship and where a child belongs to her mother's clan.[1] Kate died in 1920 at the age of 63, during the worldwide influenza epidemic. In the 75 years since her death, the story of the Klondike gold rush has been told in print many times. But Kate scarcely appears in written accounts of these events in which she was such a central player.

Skookum Jim's daughter, Daisy, studied acting briefly in California and made periodic trips back to Carcross, particularly when her father was ill. She was uncertain, however, about how she could fit into Car-

---

[1] In 1968, when I first heard these stories from women in Carcross, they were still deeply concerned about the whereabouts of Graffie, Kate and George Carmack's daughter. One of her relatives had a photograph, reportedly of Graffie in middle age in California.

JULIE CRUIKSHANK

cross life. She had grown up without any of the skills every Tagish woman would have learned. She once told Mrs. Sidney that she would like to marry and stay in Carcross, but it seemed that no man of the appropriate clan would have her: "She's too much white lady. Who wants to marry a white lady?" one prospective candidate told Mrs. Sidney. After her father's death in 1916, Daisy left, married, divorced, and remarried but her life was not a happy one. Her health deteriorated rapidly. According to papers filed with her father's lawyers, she died in 1938 at the age of 47.

Contrasting Views of Society

Part of the appeal of gold rush stories comes from the ideas they convey about social organization. They are rooted in general social concerns and dramatize areas of social life that seem problematic. Again, the question of which version is "correct" may not be as interesting or as useful as the question of what each version reveals about cultural values. A critical variable in the narratives is the way they construct the categories "individual" and "society," and especially the process by which the boundaries between those categories are established.

Between 1896 and 1898 tens of thousands of would-be prospectors and miners converged on one small area around the Klondike River. For many of them, the question of individual autonomy was crucial. Their commitment to achieving personal success and material wealth may have been reinforced by their direct experiences of unemployment during the 1896 depression. Many would have been familiar with the immensely popular stories written by Horatio Alger during the latter part of the century. In Alger's stories, individuals always succeed by their own efforts in spite of poverty and deprivation. Alger wrote over 120 books and those books sold over 20 million copies, making him one of the most successful writers of his day (Sharnhorst and Bales 1985). The Skookum Jim usually found in written accounts could easily have been a hero in one of Alger's books. White audiences learn about him simply as an idealized frontiersman, "an Indian who wanted to be a white man," and a lone prospector whose efforts are ultimately rewarded.

Prospectors brought their own myths about both Western and indigenous societies, myths which played a significant role in the ways they structured their accounts. Those myths were about social hierarchy as well as about the possibility of self-transformation. Unfamiliar "others" — the indigenous peoples — readily became symbols for representing these sometimes contradictory values (see Berkhofer 1978, Hegeman 1989). "Good Indians" gained attention by seeming to share some of the values of newcomers, and Skookum Jim's accidental discovery earned him such dubious compliments as "an exception to his race." Such an interpretation has less to do with any qualities Skookum Jim exhibited than with the newcomers' desire to confirm the advantages of an emerging social order in which individualism was a value widely shared, if problematic. Furthermore, the integration of Skookum Jim into prospector mythology acquired broader significance in Canadian society by casting an Indian as the original discoverer and exploiter of Yukon gold. It justified the exploitation of Native peoples that occurred in the Klondike by making the process seem natural. "Good Indians" were portrayed as exhibiting values just like those of prospectors, and indigenous people who resisted could then be dismissed as unwilling or unable to adapt to modern times.

Oral accounts from Skookum Jim's own community belong to a different tradition of narrative. In southern Yukon storytelling, many stories with a central male character dramatize a journey he makes with the assistance of an animal helper. In the course of his journey, the hero has new experiences which enable him to understand the world in a completely different way. If careful, he is able to bring insights back to his community in ways that benefit everyone (Cruikshank 1988:202–203). Oral traditions use familiar frameworks to explain Skookum Jim's actions, just as written records do, but the scaffolding comes from a distinctive understanding of how society functions.

By 1896, Native people in northwestern North America were dealing with unprecedented changes, as events occurring in Skookum Jim's own family confirm. Individual autonomy was not a troubling issue for Tagish men because every adult provider had been trained from childhood to perform, alone if necessary, a range of tasks associated with hunting. Ultimately their ability to act autonomously contributed directly to the survival of the group (McDonnell 1975:105–110). The major concern of Tagish people was to maintain the integrity of the group, already under enormous pressure from economic dislocation, illness, and death. Their accounts show a struggle to achieve consistency between old values and changing circumstances. Skookum Jim's personal success is attributed not to individualism but to his observance of long-standing values: his acquisition of an animal helper, his successful encounter with

Wealth Woman, his commitment to his obligations as a Daḵl'aweidí clan member, and his resolution to carry out responsibilities to his sisters and his maternal nephews. Many people suggest that while Skookum Jim followed the advice of his Frog helper carefully, his final days would have been happier had he also paid closer attention to Tl'anaxéedáḵw. People who knew Jim also describe him as a man strongly influenced by social and cultural customs important in his community. His concern about his sisters' whereabouts is entirely understandable to elders: his sisters and their children were members of his Daḵl'aweidí clan, not the clan of their husbands or fathers, so he was ultimately responsible for them. In his journey down the Yukon, he was carrying out his responsibilities as the senior surviving brother in his family.

We are faced again with the question of how the distinct contributions of differing kinds of narrative enhance our understanding of the past. In a related discussion, Terence Turner re-examines the conventional distinctions between Western notions of history and myth, suggesting that the important issue is not how they differ, for they do, but how they coexist and how both can be understood as representing particular kinds of historical consciousness. Turner defines myth as "the unself-conscious projection of structures of the existing social order as a framework of events that logically transcend the limits of that order" (1988:243). In this sense, Tagish narratives about the guiding framework provided by Skookum Jim's Frog helper, and prospector narratives about the possibility of individual self-transformation from poverty and deprivation to riches, both contribute to a mythic quality in all the accounts.

Turner (1988:244) goes on to define history as myth's polar opposite, "the awareness that social relations are not ... predetermined as the result of actions or events in an inaccessible past but are in significant respects shaped by individual or collective social action in the present" (1988:244). Again, this quality is present in both kinds of narrative. Skookum Jim's resolve to take responsibility for his sisters depicts him as a man committed to taking control of events. Likewise, some prospectors transformed their myth of individualism into programs for action. Most of those who achieved financial success did so not by finding gold but by initiating parallel business ventures, as traders, hoteliers, or providers of goods and services considered essential on the frontier. Mythic and historical consciousness interact, myth providing the framework for historical awareness and action.

This synthesis of myth and history returns us to ideas about narrative discourse. In his study of the relationship between narrative discourse and historical consciousness, Hayden White reiterates Hegel's suggestion that in human history there is an intimate relationship linking historical self-consciousness, law, and the narrative impulse. White (1987:14) proposes that *any* narrative representation of reality presenting itself to us as history invokes a social system. Outsiders' written and Tagish oral narratives about Skookum Jim both moralize: they construct, manipulate, and recast events. One set of narratives glorifies the social construction of the individual; the other idealizes the integrity of the group. Yet each perspective resonates with symbolic statements of culturally appropriate behaviour because they both invoke social process.

The lessons to be drawn from gold rush narratives for historical anthropology are certainly about the cultural relativity of texts, but they are also about power and domination. Written narratives use myths of individualism and the "good Indian" to rationalize the marginalization of Native society in the Yukon. From oral tradition, however, we hear stories of resilience and the assertion of cultural autonomy. Even though Keish's attempt to find his sisters and to maintain some continuity in Tagish society ended in personal tragedy, the narratives are structured to foreground resistance rather than defeat, community rather than individual circumstance, and ongoing attempts to maintain autonomy in the face of economic and cultural dislocation. Their regular retelling almost a century after the Klondike gold rush underscores the importance of storytelling in societies that have experienced rapid change and conflict.

Both written and oral accounts of the Klondike gold rush rely on conventional, culturally specific narrative genres that help members construct, maintain, and pass on an understanding of how the world works or should work. Some of the prospectors' stories became embedded in written accounts and were integrated into the literature of the dominant society; those of Tagish people were relegated to memory. A history that incorporates only a restricted repertoire of narratives does not adequately do justice to the complexities of events.

Oral tradition may teach us as much about differences in cultural values, attitudes, and interpretation as about past events. Ultimately, these contrasting narratives about the gold rush present two divergent models for society: one in which people are expected to succeed on individual merit and enterprise following Western values, and one in which ideas about success are more firmly embedded in family and community. Paying attention to the symbolic and structural nature of both written and oral accounts directs us away from a simple search for facts and closer to an investigation of the social processes in which all narratives are embedded.

References

Berkhofer, Robert K., Jr.

    1978   *The White Man's Indian: Images of the American Indian from Columbus to the Present Day.* New York: Knopf.

Berton, Pierre

    1958   *Klondike: The Life and Death of the Last Great Gold Rush.* Toronto: McClelland and Stewart.

Boyd, Robert T.

    1990   Demographic History, 1774-1784, in *Handbook of North American Indians*, vol. 7, *Northwest Coast.* Wayne Suttles, ed. Washington, DC: Smithsonian Institution Press. 412-21.

Carmack, George

    1933   *My Experiences in the Yukon.* Seattle, WA: privately printed.

Coates, Kenneth S., and William R. Morrison

    1988   *Land of the Midnight Sun: A History of the Yukon.* Edmonton, AB: Hurtig.

Cohen, David

    1989   *The Undefining of Oral Tradition*, in *Ethnohistory* 36(1):9-18.

Cruikshank, Julie

    1988   Myth and Tradition as Narrative Framework: Oral Histories from Northern Canada, in *International Journal of Oral History* 9(3):198-21455.

    1991   *Dan Dha Ts'edenintth'e/Reading Voices: Oral and Written Interpretations of the Yukon's Past.* Vancouver: Douglas and McIntyre.

Cruikshank, Julie, Angela Sidney, Kitty Smith, and Annie Ned

    1990   *Life Lived Like a Story: Life Stories of Three Yukon Elders.* Lincoln: University of Nebraska Press; Vancouver: University of British Columbia Press.

Darnton, Robert

    1984   *The Great Cat Massacre and Other Episodes in French Cultural History.* New York: Basic Books.

Davis, Natalie Z.

    1983   *The Return of Martin Guerre.* Cambridge, MA: Harvard University Press.

Dawson, George M.

1888 Notes on the Indian Tribes of the Yukon District and Adjacent
Northern Portion of British Columbia, 1887. *Annual Report of the
Geological Survey of Canada* n.s. 3(2):191b-213255B.

1898 *Report on an Exploration in the Yukon District, Northwest Territories and
Adjacent Northern Portion of British Columbia, 1887.* Ottawa:
Geological Survey of Canada.

De Laguna, Frederica

1972 Under Mount St. Elias: The History and Culture of the Yakutat
Tlingit. 3 vols. in *Smithsonian Contributions to Anthropology*, no. 7.
Washington, DC: Smithsonian Institution Press.

1990 Tlingit, in *Handbook of North American Indians*, vol. 7, *Northwest
Coast.* Wayne Suttles, ed. Washington, DC: Smithsonian Institution
Press. 203-228.

Dyen, Isadore, and David F. Aberle

1974 *Lexical Reconstruction: The Case of the Proto-Athapaskan Kinship System.*
Cambridge: Cambridge University Press.

Ginzberg, Carlo

1976 *The Cheese and the Worms: The Cosmos of a Sixteenth Century Miller.*
John and Anne Tedeschi, trans. Baltimore, MD: Johns Hopkins
University Press.

Hegeman, Susan

1989 History, Ethnography, Myth: Some Notes on the "Indian-centred"
Narrative, in *Social Text* 8(2):144-605.

Helm, June, ed.

1981 *Handbook of North American Indians*, vol. 6, *Subarctic.* Washington,
DC: Smithsonian Institution Press.

Henderson, Patsy

1950 Early Days at Caribou Crossing: the Discovery of Gold on the
Klondike. Recorded by Jennie May Moyer. Unpublished
manuscript. Pamphlet collection, Yukon Archives, Whitehorse.

Hill, Jonathan, ed.

1988 *Rethinking History and Myth: Indigenous Perspectives on the Past.*
Urbana: University of Illinois Press.

Kamenskii, Anatoli

1985 *Tlingit Indians of Alaska.* Sergei Kan, trans. and ed. Fairbanks:
University of Alaska Press.

Lévi-Strauss, Claude
  1966 *The Savage Mind*. Chicago: University of Chicago Press.
Lowie, Robert
  1917 Oral Tradition and History, in *Journal of American Folklore* 30:161-67.
McClellan, Catharine
  1950 Culture Change and Native Trade in the Southern Yukon Territory.
        Doctoral dissertation. Department of Anthropology, University of
        California, Berkeley.
  1961 Avoidance Between Siblings of the Same Sex in North America, in
        Southwestern Journal of Anthropology 17(2):103-123255.
  1963 Wealth Woman and Frogs among the Tagish Indians, in *Anthropos*
        58:121-28.
  1970a Indian Stories about the First Whites in Northwestern North
        America, in *Ethnohistory in Southwestern Alaska and Southern Yukon:
        Method and Content*. Margaret Lantis, ed. Lexington: University of
        Kentucky Press. 103-133.
  1970b The Girl Who Married the Bear, in *Publications in Ethnology*, no. 2.
        Ottawa: National Museums of Canada.
  1975 *My Old People Say: An Ethnographic Survey of Southern Yukon Territory*.
        2 vols. *Publications in Ethnology*, no. 6 (1 and 2). Ottawa: National
        Museums of Canada.
  1981 Tagish, in *Handbook of North American Indians*, vol. 6, *Subarctic*. June
        Helm, ed. Washington, DC: Smithsonian Institution Press. 481-92.
  n.d. My Old People's Stories. Unpublished manuscript.
McClellan, Catharine, Lucie Birckel, Robert Bringhurst, James A. Fall, Carol
  McCarthy, and Janice Sheppard
  1987 *Part of the Land, Part of the Water*. Vancouver: Douglas and McIntyre.
McDonnell, Roger
  1975 Kasini Society: Some Aspects of the Social Organization of an
        Athapaskan Culture Between 1900-1950. Doctoral dissertation,
        Department of Anthropology, University of British Columbia,
        Vancouver.
Malinowski, Bronislaw
  1926 *Myth in Primitive Psychology*. New York: Norton.
Moore, J. Bernard
  1968 *Skagway in Days Primeval*. New York: Vantage Press.

Ned, Annie

1984   *Old People in Those Days, They Told Their Story All the Time.*
Whitehorse: Yukon Native Language Project.

Netting, Robert M.

1987   Clashing Cultures, Clashing Symbols: Histories and Meanings of the
Latok War, in *Ethnohistory* 34(4):352-8055.

Obeyesekere, Gananath

1992   *The Apotheosis of Captain Cook: European Myth Making in the Pacific.*
Princeton, NJ: Princeton University Press.

Ogilvie, William

1897   *Information Respecting the Yukon Territory.* Ottawa: Department of the
Interior.

1913   *Early Days on the Yukon.* Ottawa: Thorburn and Abbott.

Phelps, W.L.

Notes and correspondence with Skookum Jim, Daisy (Saayna.aat),
and Percy R. Peele. Photocopies and inventory. Manuscript
collection, Yukon Archives, Whitehorse.

Price, Richard

1983   *First-Time: The Historical Vision of an Afro-American People.* Baltimore,
MD: Johns Hopkins University Press.

Radcliffe-Brown, A.R.

1952   *Structure and Function in Primitive Society.* Oxford: Oxford University
Press.

Rosaldo, Renato

1980   Doing Oral History, in *Social Analysis* 4:89-99.

Sahlins, Marshall

1985   *Islands of History.* Chicago: University of Chicago Press.

Scharnhorst, Gary, and Jack Bales

1985   *The Lost Life of Horatio Alger, Jr.* Bloomington: Indiana University
Press.

Schwatka, Frederick

1885   *Along Alaska's Great River.* Chicago: Henry Publishing.

Sidney, Angela

    1982 Tagish Tlaagu/Tagish Stories. Recorded by Julie Cruikshank. Whitehorse: Council for Yukon Indians and Government of Yukon.

    1983 Haa Shagoon/Our Family History. Julie Cruikshank, compiler. Whitehorse: Yukon Native Languages Project.

Sidney, Angela, Kitty Smith, and Rachel Dawson

    1977 My Stories Are My Wealth. Recorded by Julie Cruikshank. Whitehorse: Council for Yukon Indians.

Skookum Jim Friendship Centre

    1975 Interviews with Native men and women about Skookum Jim. Tape recordings. Manuscript collection, Yukon Archives, Whitehorse.

Slobodin, Richard

    1963 'The Dawson Boys' — Peel River Indians and the Dawson Gold Rush, in *Polar Record* 5:24-35.

Smith, Kitty

    1982 Nindal Kwadindur/I'm Going to Tell You a Story. Recorded by Julie Cruikshank. Whitehorse: Council for Yukon Indians and Government of Yukon.

Steinhart, Edward I.

    1989 Introduction, in *Ethnohistory* 36(1):1-8.

Swanton, John R.

    1909 *Tlingit Myths and Texts*. Bulletin no. 39, Washington, DC: Bureau of American Ethnology.

Turner, Terence

    1988 Ethno-Ethnohistory: Myth and History in Native South American Representations of Contact with Western Society, in *Rethinking History and Myth: Indigenous South American Perspectives on the Past*. Jonathan D. Hill, ed. Urbana: University of Illinois Press. 235-81.

Vansina, Jan

    1985 *Oral Tradition as History*. Madison: University of Wisconsin Press.

White, Hayden

    1987 *The Content of the Form: Narrative Discourse and Historical Representation*. Baltimore, MD: Johns Hopkins University Press.

Wood, Z.T.

    1899 Annual Report of Superintendent Z.T. Wood, Tagish, Upper
           Yukon, 1898, in *Annual Report of the Northwest Mounted Police,*
           Ottawa, 1899. 31-55.

Wright, Al

    1976 Prelude to Bonanza: The Discovery and Exploration of the Yukon.
           Sidney, BC: Gray's.

Zaslow, Morris

    1971 *The Opening of the Canadian North, 1890-1914*. Toronto: McClelland
           and Stewart.

Figure 1: The massive residential school in Edmonton must have been an imposing, perhaps terrifying first sight for its youthful inmates.

19

Reading Photographs, Reading Voices: Documenting the History of Native Residential Schools

J.R. Miller

THE TASKS OF uncovering and recounting the history of the residential schools for Inuit and status "Indian" children that existed in Canada until the late 1960s present many challenges. Three groups were involved in the creation and operation of these institutions, but the available records on these groups are not uniform in either quantity or quality. Aboriginal peoples, government, and Christian churches were all participants in the residential school story, but only the latter two entities created written records that, along with personal recollections, were systematically collected and preserved for the benefit of later generations. The constructive use of what materials exist often is further handicapped by an unacknowledged aversion to denominational records on the part of many twentieth-century investigators. Possibly unknowingly, scholars have often neglected or simplified the missionaries' role. In the increasingly secular atmosphere that has prevailed in Canada since the middle of this century, a tendency has developed to ignore religious figures, their actions, and their records.[1]

In the case of the Aboriginal peoples' involvement in schooling, the principal difficulty has been that most archival repositories have not collected much material generated in their societies. Ironically, a substantial portion of the written records that Native groups did create concerning their interaction with missions and schools is to be found in the denominational archives that researchers have largely ignored. Because much of the existing literature on residential schooling has failed to bring out Native roles in and contributions to residential schooling, the picture that is

---

1   L.H. Thomas noted the failure to take into account the Christian socialism of North America's first socialist government in "The CCF Victory in Saskatchewan, 1944," *Saskatchewan History* 34, no. 1 (1981):1-3; Ruth Compton Brouwer, "Transcending the 'unacknowledged quarantine': Putting Religion into English-Canadian Women's History," *Journal of Canadian Studies* 27, no. 3 (1992):47-61, points out how historians of women have neglected the sphere in which nineteenth-century Canadian women were probably most active outside the home.

available is at best a two-dimensional depiction, often presented in stark black and white without many of the colour tones that are usually present in any rendering of human affairs.

One peculiarity of the history of residential schooling is that Canadians, although they have never had a fully rounded treatment of the phenomenon made available to them, are inclined to think that they know the tale well because these institutions have been in the news a great deal during the past five years. A major event that created a false sense of knowing the residential school story occurred in 1990, when Phil Fontaine, head of the Assembly of Manitoba Chiefs, made public the fact that he, like many others, had been a victim of abuse at the Fort Alexander residential school that a Roman Catholic missionary order operated. Fontaine's revelations surfaced just as spectacular details of widespread mistreatment of orphans at Mount Cashel in Newfoundland and the Alfred institution for boys in Ontario were becoming known. They instantly sparked interest in Native residential schools as yet another setting in which abuse of defenceless children had taken place over many decades. Fontaine's initiative encouraged other victims to come forward and tell their stories, just as it stimulated major newspapers, magazines, and television news shows to prepare stories on the issue. Subsequently, the public hearings that the Royal Commission on Aboriginal Peoples conducted in various parts of Canada kept the subject of abuse in these schools alive in the popular media. Finally, in August 1994 the First Nations Health Commission of the Assembly of First Nations, the umbrella political organization for status Indians in Canada, issued a report that alleged that physical, sexual, and emotional abuse had been so widespread in residential schools that it was almost universal.[1] As a consequence of this barrage of publicity, many Canadians in the 1990s came to believe that they understood all too well what these custodial institutions had been about. The heavy documenting of one aspect of residential school life left the impression that it was the entire story.

However, among the many things that Canadians did not know about the subject was that residential schooling has a lengthy, if mixed, history in their country. In fact, the earliest boarding schools — or seminaries as they were known — were developed in seventeenth-century New France by Récollet and Jesuit priests, and Ursuline sisters. Because these early

---

1   Assembly of First Nations, First Nations Health Commission, "Breaking the Silence" (mimeo, August 1994).

French initiatives all failed, forays into residential schooling were abandoned in the late seventeenth century. An attempt by a British missionary body a century later to establish what it called an "Indian College" for young Native children in colonial New Brunswick similarly did not succeed in educating and training Micmac and Maliseet children.[1] Nonetheless, two other colonial efforts soon followed, one in Red River (Manitoba) under a Church of England missionary named John West in 1820, the other later in the same decade when the forerunner of what would become known as the Mohawk Institute was established near Brantford, Upper Canada (later Ontario).[2] Initially with Native cooperation, more institutions — then called "manual labour schools" — were set up in southern Ontario in the 1850s; finally, the Shingwauk Home was established near Sault Ste. Marie in the 1870s. This Anglican school, which still survives as part of Algoma University College, was the product of both missionary interest and Aboriginal initiative. The local Ojibwa chief, Shingwaukonce, had asked in the early 1830s for the creation of a mission, and later his son, Chief Augustin Shingwauk, called for the establishment of a "teaching wigwam" to prepare the youth of their people for a future with the European newcomers.[3]

The modern phase of residential schooling, the era whose results have been in the news so much, began in 1883 when three schools of a novel type were created in what were then the North-West Territories (now Saskatchewan and Alberta). The "industrial schools" that were established were usually located well away from reserves and were intended

---

1 Judith Fingard, "The New England Company and the New Brunswick Indians, 1786-1826: A Comment on the Colonial Perversion of British Benevolence," *Acadiensis* 1, no. 2 (1972):29-42; Grace Aiton, "The History of the Indian College and Early School Days in Sussex Vale," New Brunswick Historical Society, *Collections* 18 (1963):159-62.

2 Winona Stevenson, "The Red River Indian Mission School and John West's 'Little Charges,' 1820-1833," *Native Studies Review*, 4, nos. 1-2 (1988):129-65; Canada, *Sessional Papers 1929-30*, vol. 2, *Annual Report of the Department of Indian Affairs for the Year ended March 31, 1930*, 15-16; Jennifer Pettit, "From Longhouse to Schoolhouse: The Mohawk Institute, 1834-1970" (unpublished paper, Canadian Historical Association Annual Meeting, 1994).

3 Augustin Shingwauk, *Little Pine's Journal: The Appeal of a Christian Chippeway Chief on behalf of his People* (Toronto: Copp, Clark, 1872; facsimile edition Sault Ste. Marie: Shingwauk Reunion Committee 1991); Jean L. Manore, "A Vision of Trust: The Legal, Moral and Spiritual Foundations of Shingwauk Hall," *Native Studies Review* 9, no. 2 (1993-1994), 1-21.

by the federal government and Christian missionary bodies that ran them to do three things: to provide a basic academic training; to teach the children usable economic skills, including trades such as carpentry and blacksmithing; and to assimilate them culturally. The system that began with three industrial schools and a number of pre-existing boarding schools in 1883 expanded for the next half century, reaching at its height a total of eighty institutions. Although all of them were financed in part by the federal government, they were run by the churches. Roman Catholic missionary orders, both male and female, were in charge of about 60 per cent of the schools; Anglicans about one-third; and Methodists and Presbyterians the remainder. For most of the residential school system's existence only one-third to one-half of status Indian children were enrolled, and a much smaller fraction of all Native children came under their influence. Part of the reason for the incomplete coverage was Native resistance to the schools' harsh discipline and overwork of children, and their inadequate academic and vocational teaching. Increasingly in disfavour and subject to criticism after the Second World War, these schools were phased out in the 1960s as the Department of Indian Affairs moved toward a policy of integrated schooling. A little known fact is that in the 1990s, seven of them are still in operation, six under Native control and one operated by Indian Affairs.[1]

For the historian, the research challenge that Native residential schools present is to tell their long and complex story as systematically and comprehensively as possible. Although we have fragmentary accounts, there exists as yet no historical overview of the educational experiment as a whole. One reason for this lack is the sheer size of the task. It requires recovering the experiences and views of three distinct sets of actors – Native peoples, government, and missionaries. Compounding the problem of scale is the shortage of conventional records for Native peoples. The records of politicians and bureaucrats like Indian Affairs deputy minister Hayter Reed are conveniently arranged for researchers in archival repositories such as the National Archives of Canada in Ottawa.[2] Similarly, the various church denominations have seen to it

---

1 In Saskatchewan, Lebret, Gordon's, Duck Lake, Beauval, and Prince Albert still function; in Alberta, Blue Quills; and in British Columbia, Kamloops is now the site of several educational initiatives controlled by the Secwepemc Cultural Education Society.

2 National Archives of Canada [NA], MG 29 E 106 Hayter Reed Papers.

J.R. MILLER

that the records of many missionaries and teachers are collected and available in archives from Victoria (Sisters of St. Ann) to Toronto (General Synod Archives and United Church of Canada Archives), to Ottawa (Archives Deschâtelets of the Oblates), and to Montreal (Sisters of St. Ann and Daughters of the Heart of Mary). Records of some Aboriginal clergymen, such as the well-known Mississauga, Peter Jones, exist in government and church repositories.[1]

What are lacking, though, are records that tell the stories of the children who attended and of their families. What was it like for Inuit children to be taken far up the Mackenzie River to an Anglican school such as Hay River, which was located in alien forested territory where limited gardening was carried out using dogs to pull the plough? What was the reaction of Dene children from small settlements in northern Alberta when they got their first glimpse of the Methodists' enormous Edmonton Indian Residential School? More generally, what was it like to live and learn, work and play, be cared for or mistreated on a day-to-day basis in one of the eighty residential institutions run by missionaries on behalf of Ottawa between the 1880s and 1960s? The records of Native peoples, like those of many other groups that the dominant Euro-Canadian society has until recently regarded as marginal, for the most part remain uncollected. For the researcher who wants to sketch the history of Native residential schools, the challenge is to find the means to recover and recount the experiences – good, bad, and indifferent – of the Inuit and Indian children and of the families and communities they left behind, sometimes never to be seen again.

The appropriate way to respond to that challenge is to multiply the lines and techniques of inquiry. The papers of politicians, bureaucrats, and missionaries must be utilized, of course. In particular, a research approach known as ethnohistory can help us to extract the submerged experiences of Native peoples from the records of the dominant Euro-Canadians. Ethnohistory, which combines insights about Aboriginal societies derived from anthropology with the traditional sources and methods of history, may help to amplify the muffled voices of Native

---

1 For example, the Archives of Victoria University in the University of Toronto have rich Jones materials.

children and their families that are sometimes found in archival records.[1] For example, one can find letters, petitions, remonstrances, and protests from Aboriginal people, often mediated through missionary interpreters. Similarly, one can uncover in denominational archives fragments of children's writing, often in the form of school newsletters. All of these kinds of sources can and must be pressed into service.

Ultimately, however, written sources and collections cannot do the job as fully and effectively as one would like. Other forms of evidence and other techniques of inquiry are needed to recapture Native experiences of residential schooling as fully as possible. In particular, the contributions of visual and oral history are vital components in the multidisciplinary research strategy that is necessary to tell the story of residential schools.

Visual images are of great value in helping a researcher to grasp fully residential school experiences and to convey them vividly and forcefully to the reader. Many of the sensations that Native children experienced in the residential school environment were alien or frightening, and particular exercises of imaginative reconstruction are required to appreciate them properly. How intimidating it was coming to school for the first time, perhaps at night to the Methodists' school in Edmonton, can be understood better when the strangeness is perceived in pictorial form (see Figure 1). Another example is the powerful visual religious message that Roman Catholic residential school children were given. The famous (or infamous) teaching aid that Oblates and female religious used in many institutions, often known as Lacombe's Ladder, makes clear, in a way that mere words cannot, how frightening missionaries' depiction of the road to Hell might have been to impressionable children (see Figure 2). When one notes, too, that the lost souls on the path to perdition were mainly Aboriginal while those on the upward road to Paradise were Caucasian, one begins to appreciate how the evangelical message often served to reinforce the denigration and undermining of Native culture and belief that were central to the mandate of these schools.

Residential school experiences can be vividly reconstructed if visual images are juxtaposed to documents. Consider, for example, the "half-

1   See James Axtell, "Ethnohistory: An Historian's Viewpoint," *Ethnohistory* 26, no. 1 (1979):1-13; and "Some Thoughts on the Ethnohistory of Missions," *Ethnohistory* 29, no. 1 (Winter 1982): 35-41. Also useful are Bruce G. Trigger, *Natives and Newcomers: Canada's "Heroic Age" Reconsidered* (Montreal and Kingston: McGill-Queen's University Press, 1985), ch. 4, and "Ethnohistory: Problems and Prospects," *Ethnohistory* 29, no. 1 (1982):1-19.

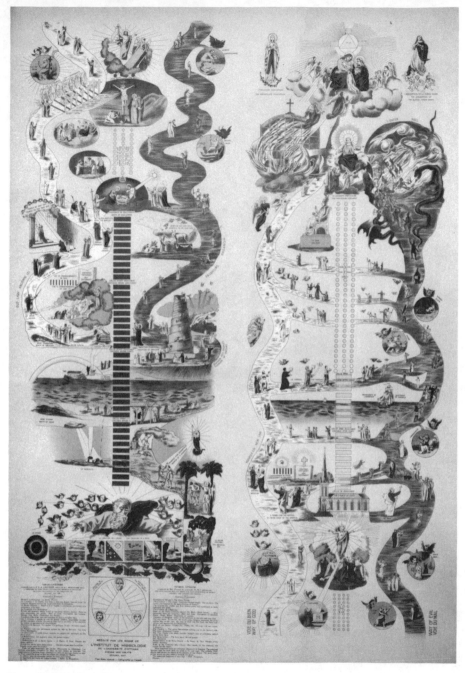

Figure 2: Catholic missionaries taught catechism by means of "Lacombe's Ladder," which made it clear that the road to heaven was smoother for converted Natives than it was for "pagans."

Figure 3: This image of boys sawing wood at the Sarcee school is compatible with the official version of the half-day system.

Figure 4: Woodpile at the ChooutlaSchool. The reality of the fuel requirements of a Yukon winter raised doubts about the underlying purpose of student labour in residential schools.

J.R. MILLER

day system," which in theory trained students in practical skills during the "half-day" that they spent working in barn or yard or about the school. (The other half-day, of course, was supposed to be spent learning academic subjects in the classroom.) The discrepancy between the theoretical justification of the half-day labour system and the onerous reality is perceived upon careful scrutiny of illustrations of children at work. If, for example, one sees a picture of a couple of boys cutting wood into stove lengths, it may mean little at first glance (see Figure 3). However, if we contemplate the reality of how much wood was required for the furnaces at Chooutla residential school near Carcross in the southern Yukon, it becomes clear that the volume of routine labour extracted from the Tutchone and Tlingit schoolboys at this Anglican school went far beyond anything justified by the theory that underlay the half-day system (see Figure 4). Naturally, the official records of government and the churches do not dwell on how hard-worked the children at Chooutla and other schools were. And complaints of former students about excessive labour may not register strongly or concretely in written form. The pictures make the scope and weight of the labour burden on students starkly clear.

Similar examples of how visual images can make students' experiences speak more forcefully to later generations may be drawn from the propaganda pictures that the Department of Indian Affairs used to illustrate what it was trying to accomplish in the residential schools (see Figure 5). In 1900, the department's annual report emphasized pictorial contrasts of dress and grooming between Quewich and his children in order to celebrate the success of the Lebret school in Saskatchewan. The photographs vividly evoked the cultural assimilation program that such schools were designed to carry out. The lengths to which bureaucratic propagandists were willing to go similarly come out in the before-and-after pictures of Thomas Moore, a student at the Regina Industrial School prior to the First World War. The obviously staged quality of Figures 6 and 7 testifies as eloquently to the federal government's reliance on propagandistic techniques as it does to Ottawa's hope of working a cultural transformation in residential school students.

Literary artifacts of the residential school experience also help to convey aspects of how students remember their experience — for both good and ill. Micmac poet Rita Joe makes clear the pain that she felt, and feels, as a result of attending the Shubenacadie school in Nova Scotia, in a poetic remembrance entitled "Hated Structure":

Figure 5: Quewich and his children supposedly illustrated the "civilizing" effect of residential school in the Department of Indian Affairs annual report for 1900.

I for one looked into the window
And there on the floor
Was a deluge of a misery
Of a building I held in awe
Since the day
I walked into the ornamented door.[1]

Equally revealing are students' recollections, written and oral, of a more positive nature. The youthful pleasure with which two middle-aged Regina women remembered and sang the school song for St. Paul's, the high school division of the Oblates' school at Lebret, Saskatchewan in the 1950s, is suggestive of some fond memories held by these former students.

St. Paul's forever.
Junior, Senior High.
Teach us to live and love,
laugh and never deny.

Pride of the Valley,
We'll keep your honour true.
Always the dearest and
the best of the love for you.[2]

One of these singers also wrote a letter to the editor of the Regina *Leader-Post* defending Lebret school from many of the charges of abuse that have been made in recent years. At least this residential school evokes some positive recollections.[3]

---

1   Rita Joe, "Hated Structure: Indian Residential School, Shubenacadie, N.S.," *Song of Eskasoni: More Poems of Rita Joe* (Charlottetown, PEI: Ragweed Press, 1988), 75. I am indebted to an editor and friend, Gerald Hallowell, who brought this poem to my attention.

2   Interview with Elizabeth Yuzicappi and Pat Lacerte, 6 February 1992, Regina, SK. The interview was conducted by Maynard Quewezance. "The Valley" was the Qu'Appelle Valley of southern Saskatchewan.

3   Pat Lacerte to Editor, Regina, SK *Leader-Post*, 31 January 1992. I am indebted to Maynard Quewezance, who kindly provided me with a copy of the clipping containing this letter.

Figure 6: Thomas Moore as he appeared when admitted to the Regina Indian Industrial School

J.R. MILLER

Figure 7: Thomas Moore after. Before and after portraits were crafted to emphasize the transforming influence of Regina Industrial School.

The singing of a school song remembered many years later by a pair of former students leads directly to consideration of the major contribution that can be made by oral history. Oral history evidence is invaluable for understanding and depicting all those nooks and crannies of everyday life in the residential school that are not found in the official record because they were not considered important enough to be reported by missionary or bureaucrat. These details are significant and revealing. Consider, for example, a tale of how the girls at St. Joseph's residential school in Spanish, Ontario managed to defy the rules and communicate with boys in the Jesuit-run institution across the road, something that was usually hard to do given the rigid segregation of the sexes in these institutions until the 1950s. The priest who came each morning to the sisters' establishment to say Mass did not know that for each visit a forbidden message written lovingly on a scrap of paper was craftily tucked into his hatband. Nor did he realize that the deferential girl who took his hat and coat would retrieve the message before placing his apparel in the cloakroom. After saying Mass, the good father was handed his hat by another apparently submissive girl, who had secreted a return message in the hatband. And so the Jesuit would make his way back to the boys' school, where another pair of hands would extract the hidden note and pass it on to its intended recipient. No official document in any archives could inform us about such subterfuges. Only an interview with someone who was there allowed the retrieval of that detail of subversive school life.

Interviews with former students and staff have brought out very clearly more serious areas of the residential school experience. For example, both former staff and students raised, explicitly or implicitly, the topic of gender distinctions in the schools. Time and again former students answered questions about activities and recreation in ways that show clearly how residential schools constructed and reinforced notions of gender. Boys did outdoor work, while girls spent their half-day of supposedly instructive labour in the kitchens and sewing room, or in cleaning the hallways and other spaces of the buildings. That is not to say that vocational instruction in the schools adhered absolutely to separate gender spheres. Recollections and pictures tell us that sometimes girls, such as those at the female-run school at Spanish, Ontario, worked in the barns as boys did, though never at the same time as boys. Likewise, boys sometimes learned to bake bread, or a favoured male student was sometimes chosen to wait on table in the staff dining room.

J.R. MILLER

The shortcomings of both instruction and supervision also emerge clearly from oral histories. Classroom instruction was often rudimentary and culturally inappropriate, as Euro-Canadian teachers with no training in cross-cultural education attempted in sterile settings to convey in a foreign tongue the contents of a curriculum that was little altered from that of non-Native schools. The differentiation between females and males continued to manifest itself in these settings, too. In the area of recreation, for example, boys recalled their active and intense involvement with sports as one of the too-infrequent bright spots in their stay at boarding school. From the earliest days, when efforts were made to inculcate cricket at Lebret, until the middle of the twentieth century when federal budgets began to supply equipment to hockey teams such as the "Blackhawks" at Brandon residential school in Manitoba or Latuque, Quebec's "Indiens du Québec," who participated in a tournament held in conjunction with the Quebec Winter Carnival in 1967, sports were vitally important.[1] (The contrast between the rudimentary equipment of the "Blackhawks" and the first-class gear of the "Indiens" also confirms that funding for residential schools was much better in the 1960s than it had been during the Depression.) However, it is also revealing that, while one learns of hockey teams known as the "Indiens du Québec" or the Brandon "Blackhawks," one never hears of a lacrosse team being started or encouraged at a residential school. That is an interesting omission, given the Aboriginal origins of that game in eastern and central North America.

Women who attended residential school recounted dramatically different memories about recreation. If the sports for boys were sometimes culturally inappropriate, as in the case of cricket, the males were at least provided with athletic activities. For females, there was essentially no physical recreation available. Although girls such as those at the United Church school at Portage la Prairie were often able to join organizations such as the Canadian Girls In Training (CGIT), and girls at Catholic schools were encouraged to join sodalities oriented toward devotional practices, there was little else for them to do. For most girls, recreation consisted of conversation and playing with dolls, although boys were able at some institutions to play table hockey or even pool when outdoor activities were not possible. In a few exceptional cases,

---

1 Western Canada Pictorial Index, University of Winnipeg, EWA026408432 (Brandon "Blackhawks," 1936); NA, PA 185843 (Latuque "Indiens").

girls could avail themselves of some activities that were at least interesting, such as the dance troupe at the Kamloops school, which also boasted an outdoor swimming pool.[1] Such diversions, however, were the exception rather than the rule.

In general, oral histories reveal a routine of school life that at best was monotonous and at worst destructive. For most it was an unaccustomedly structured life of rules, bells, and punishments for infringements. Sewing class was usually recalled as only slightly less tedious than the obligatory attendance at chapel. The routine sometimes was relieved by parental visits, easily in the case of the Anglicans' Alert Bay school in British Columbia or Shubenacadie in Nova Scotia, where the residential school was close to the village. But parents in the North whose children attended such schools as Chooutla or even Aklavik at the mouth of the Mackenzie River found it difficult to visit their offspring. Over time, visiting became more difficult at some schools. At Lebret in the Qu'Appelle Valley of Saskatchewan, for example, the hospitality that was shown to parents in the first decade after 1883 was replaced by discouragement. Indian Affairs officials had intervened vigorously to prevent frequent parental visits, arguing that they disrupted the work of the schools. This episode illustrated another generalization about residential school administration: missionary principals and staff, who worked closely with Native children and their families, were often more sympathetic than Indian Affairs bureaucrats, who were remote geographically or emotionally — or both — from the schools.

The memories collected through oral history inquiry also show that the absence of parental contact permitted neglect and mistreatment to develop and even to flourish.[2] Negative aspects of residential school life included poor clothing, about which both men and women have remarked ever since. Numerous former students also complained about inadequate medical care and negligence when it came to preventing illness. Teachers at residential schools oversaw not just inappropriate cur-

---

1   Celia Haig-Brown, *Resistance and Renewal: Surviving the Indian Residential School* (Vancouver: Tillacum Library, 1988), 71-72; Royal British Columbia Museum, PN 6660 (dancers); PN 6665 (swimming pool).

2   The importance of Sunday visits and how they shielded some children from physical abuse are recurrent themes in Isabelle Knockwood, *Out of the Depths: The Experiences of Mi'kmaw Children at the Indian Residential School at Shubenacadie, Nova Scotia* (Lockeport, NS: Rosewood Publishing, 1992), 27, 32-33, 44, 78-79, and 123-24.

riculum, but also a student body that often included some children who ought not to have been in class in their infectious state. Both governmental and church records contain evidence that this happened because hard-pressed principals often accepted unhealthy students to ensure maximum revenue from federal per capita grants. Photographs and interviews with former students and staff confirm that these dangerous conditions were allowed to exist. The existence of disease in classrooms, and its spread in overcrowded dormitories, inevitably resulted in serious illness and death. Oral history inquiries also corroborate other evidence of overwork, mistreatment, and both physical and sexual abuse.

The use of oral history evidence in this study inevitably carried with it a number of challenges and questions. Perhaps the first and most substantial was to try to ensure that informants were treated with sensitivity, consideration, and respect — especially respect for privacy. The key to meeting this challenge was the notion of "informed consent," on which all bodies that oversee research with human subjects insist and which all reputable investigators practise. Potential interview subjects, whether they were being questioned by the principal investigator or by an interviewer hired for the purpose, first heard a description of the research project on the history of residential schooling, the nature and purpose of the oral history portion of the investigation, and the rules and guidelines surrounding the collection and use of their memories. The interviewer told them that they should feel free to answer or decline to answer as they saw fit, as well as the fact they had the right to terminate the interview at any point. It was also explained that they could restrict the use of answers to particular questions. To protect their privacy if they wished to do so, they had the right to be identified either by name or by the institution and years they attended. Finally, potential informants were told that the tapes and notes of the interviews would be disposed of as they wished. These materials could be deposited in an archives that the researcher chose so as to be available to future investigators, placed in a repository that the interview subject chose, returned to the subject, or destroyed.

A variation on the interview was the questionnaire, which was administered by mail. In these cases, potential respondents received a written version of the explanations and options that an interview subject was provided orally, and they were asked to indicate on the completed questionnaire if they wished any of the information restricted and where they wanted the questionnaire deposited once the research project was completed. In a few cases respondents to a questionnaire provided their answers on audio tape, a format that often led them to answer specific questions more expansively than they might have otherwise. Both face-to-face interviews and questionnaires provided valuable information on everyday life in residential schools, and both types of inquiry yielded these data while protecting the privacy of individual respondents and their control over the knowledge they furnished.

Consideration of the safeguards that are called for in a program of oral history research leads fairly logically to another controversial aspect of this style of investigation. The debate over "voice" and "appropriation" that has been so strident, if not usually enlightening, during the past few years has not exempted the use of recollections of Aboriginal informants and other people of colour from its censorious consideration. According to some critics it is not appropriate for a non-Native investigator to attempt to tell the stories or speak in the voice of people of another cultural or racial group. It should be noted that there are, indeed, aspects of Aboriginal culture in which it is not appropriate for non-Natives to participate. Certain songs or dances in some Aboriginal cultures belong to particular individuals or families. It is as wrong for someone else to tell or perform these rites without permission as it would be in non-Native society for someone to break copyright by performing another's play. A somewhat analogous example is the oral tradition that the Gitksan and Wet'suwet'en peoples put before the courts of British Columbia in the late 1980s in order to demonstrate their relationship to and ownership of the lands they claimed. Their texts formed a complete and integral account, rather than isolated bits of evidence, and they needed to be told in their own right and in their own context. Extracting them from their cultural matrix as the court system demanded, and using them for purposes of another people, distorted their meaning and character.[1]

However, not all oral history material partakes of ritual or sacred tradition. Informed respondents often may willingly recount histories in which they have been involved. Those histories are not an "oral tradition" lifted whole from the Native environment, but rather recollections given freely by informed participants. Their answers, rather than resembling a Potlatch song that has meaning and validity only when sung by the person who possesses the right to sing it and in its own cul-

---

1 See the helpful comments of Julie Cruikshank, "Oral Tradition and Oral History: Reviewing Some Issues," *The Canadian Historical Review* 75, no. 3 (1994):403-418.

J.R. MILLER

turally defined context, are oral equivalents of the bureaucrat's recording of the events in a residential school from the governmental point of view. Their spoken words are the only way of recovering and preserving records of some activities and experiences that were considered too minor to be caught in the official paper net or too scandalous to be preserved by those whose negligence or wrongdoing they exposed.[1]

The historical investigation of residential schools involves – some might say implicates – both Aboriginal peoples and non-Native peoples, and both can contribute in vital ways to understanding the history of these institutions. The schools were the device by which an unsympathetic majority sought to assimilate and culturally eliminate a racial minority, but that very fact ensures that their story belongs to both racial communities. This biracial reality is necessarily reflected in any reputable research into residential schooling. Properly conducted oral history research will elicit information not only from former students, but also from former members of the schools' staffs. The importance of relying on both former staff and former students for oral history evidence about residential schools is exemplified by the story recounted earlier about the priest whose trips across the road to the girls' school at Spanish, Ontario to say Mass each day made him an unconscious conveyor of secret messages between romantically inclined boys and girls. The existence of that practice was uncovered solely because of an interview conducted with a female religious who had worked for many years at the Spanish girls' school.[2] It would appear that the Daughters of the Heart of Mary community at Spanish knew what was going on all the time. We would not have known about it without the use of interviews.

What documents should one use, then, to recover and recount the history of Native residential schools? The answer reflects the nature of the historical phenomenon. Because residential schools are a historical artifact of a process by which a numerically and politically dominant society tried to assimilate a racial minority, and because their creation and operation involved Native peoples, missionaries, and officials, we need an expanded definition of "documentation," one that allows the recovery

---

1 Note, for example, the heavy reliance on oral history evidence in "Breaking the Silence."

2 Interview with a Daughter of the Heart of Mary, 16 October 1990, Montreal.

of the recollections of all the participants. Researching the history of residential schools requires an integrative style of scholarship that combines the insights and revelations of many forms of memory.

While these recollections include not only the written records of both church and state, and the smaller amount of Native testimony preserved in the repositories of denominations and governments, they should encompass a wide range of other evidence as well. It is essential to consider why Alberta artist George Littlechild chose to depict the *Red Horse Boarding School* without any windows.[1] In comparison, the works of art that students of Alert Bay school produced for the Pacific National Exhibition in 1936 illustrate that not all principals and instructors denigrated or discouraged all expressions of Native culture.[2] It is necessary to examine cultural artifacts such as the Christian Passion Play that the Oblate missionaries staged at their school at Mission, BC. before audiences of thousands, and to contemplate the rich ironies of these enactments, which an uncharitable newspaper editorialist referred to as "Oblate Potlatches."[3] And, finally, it is essential to collect and listen empathetically to the oral histories of both former staff and former students to obtain a well-rounded picture of what residential school life was like, synthesizing all the available evidence responsibly and respectfully.

How should the researcher handle the documents so assembled? It is essential to view the sources in context in order to appreciate the ways in which their creators have mediated and presented their observations and recollections. Is a student's story of a hard-hearted adult who weeps at a cinematic portrayal of children's hardship, and then spurns children who ask for help outside the theatre, merely a formulaic story? Or might the apparently familiar tale be a residential school inmate's allegory of the cruelties and insensitivities of supervisors and teachers? If it is important to peruse any document to understand it properly in its context, it is also vital to peer into its gaps and listen for its silences. Just as it is worth not-

---

1   I am indebted to Donald B. Smith of the University of Calgary, who brought this oil painting to my attention.

2   Vancouver Public Library, 9359, Pacific National Exhibition (1936), Display of Indian Art and Artifacts by Students of Alert Bay School.

3   Royal British Columbia Museum, PN 8788. The reference to "'Oblate Potlatches'" is quoted in an article on Father J. Hugonnard by Jacqueline Gresko, which is forthcoming in the *Dictionary of Canadian Biography*; she generously provided a copy, for which my thanks.

ing that the pictures of boys playing games never reveal a lacrosse team (see p 475), so it is necessary to look carefully at the children's clothing for evidence about the quality of the care they were receiving. Similarly it is important in conducting and using interviews to listen for the things informants do not say, or express in opaque and oblique fashion. The researcher must try to interrogate the silences and scan the omissions.

The history of the residential school experience embraces the hopes, hurts, successes, and sufferings of many people. To document it, we must listen carefully and actively to as many voices as we can, and integrate the diversity of evidence that results into interpretive accounts that will speak directly of and to all groups.

Photo Credits:

Figure 1. Provincial Archives of Alberta A 13457.

Figure 2. Archives Deschâtelets, Ottawa.

Figure 3. Glenbow Archives, Calgary, NC-21-9.

Figure 4. Yukon Archives, Whitehorse, Anglican Diocese of Yukon Records, box G-142, Album 7, 1044.

Figure 5. National Archives of Canada, C 37113. The picture first appeared in the Annual Report of the Department of Indian Affairs for 1900, opposite 337.

Figure 6. Saskatchewan Archives Board R-A8223-1.

Figure 7. (From Canada: Sessional Papers, vol. XXI, no. 11, 1897) Saskatchewan Archives Board R-A8223-2.

Figure 1. Oronhyatekha, age 21 years, in ceremonial dress worn when he met the Prince of Wales as spokesman for Six Nations in 1860. Photograph 1862 by Hills & Saunders ("by Appointment to Her Majesty"), Oxford, England. The suit of clothing is now in the Natural History Museum of Los Angeles County.

TRUDY NICKS

20

Dr. Oronhyatekha's History Lessons: Reading Museum Collections as Texts[1]

Trudy Nicks

THE INSPIRATION FOR this paper is a large and eclectic assemblage of objects which was donated to the Royal Ontario Museum in Toronto in 1911. The collection is a particularly interesting subject for study because, unlike most museum collections, it was created by an aboriginal person. Oronhyatekha was a Mohawk born in 1841 on the Six Nations Reserve near Brantford, Ontario. By the time he assembled his artifacts and specimens at the turn of the century, Oronhyatekha had become a medical doctor, a successful international businessman, and an active participant in Iroquois politics.

Dr. Oronhyatekha's collection is an invaluable source for analyzing the social, cultural and political milieus in which many Indian people lived in nineteenth-century Canada. Like other ethnographic collections, it constitutes a material record of cross-cultural exchange and interaction and provides evidence for the innovations, associations, and motivations of the makers, users, and collectors of the objects it contains. It can also be read as an historical text which documents both its founder's deep involvement in Victorian society and his use of mainstream values to further specific Iroquoian interests. This reading, placing the collection within its several historical and cultural contexts, suggests that Dr. Oronhyatekha actively constructed his relationship with a dominant Victorian society which, for its part, was bent on the forced assimilation of aboriginal peoples.

Dr. Oronhyatekha's collection, viewed as text and in context, helps to provide a more balanced view of his life than that found in existing biographies which have either stereotyped him as a noble or not-so-noble savage, or criticized his activities without due consideration for the

1   I am grateful to Jeffrey Brown for assistance in the search for objects from the Oronhyatekha Historical collection in ROM departmental collections, and for assistance in archival research on Oronhyatekha. Tom Hill, Director of the Museum at the Woodland Cultural Centre in Brantford, Ontario, generously supplied information about Oronhyatekha from his files.

cross-cultural environment in which he lived and worked. It also adds perspective to contemporary Iroquoian reminiscences which place great emphasis on Oronhyatekha's connection with British royalty. Finally, the collection's later history provides a telling illustration of how traditional museum approaches to the organization and care of collections can submerge, or at least greatly bias, their value as coherent historical documents.

Oronhyatekha's Life and Career

Dr. Oronhyatekha became known mainly for his career as chief executive officer of the Independent Order of Foresters, a Toronto-based international insurance company organized along the principles of a fraternal society.[1] Viewed from the pinnacle of that career, his earlier life underwent some mythologizing by Oronhyatekha as well as his biographers. Oronhyatekha was not above misrepresenting his early educational accomplishments and did not correct the mistakes of others even when he had the opportunity (Comeau-Vasilopoulos 1994). Records do exist, however, which document his early years. Correspondence by and about him in the Bodleian Library in Oxford[2] and in Department of Indian Affairs files in the National Archives of Canada both provide information about his non-IOF activities. These sources document his involvement with both Iroquoian and Victorian society, and his problems as well as achievements in these sometimes contradictory contexts.

Oronhyatekha, or "Burning Cloud,"[3] was born at the Six Nations Reserve on 10 August 1841. His English baptismal name, which he used

---

1 "The Independent Order of Foresters is a fraternal benefit society, which offers a variety of benefits to our Members. We're a not-for-profit organization owned and operated for our Members for the mutual benefit of all of us. We have social activities, we work to better our communities, and we help others in times of need. We operate under a Court (lodge) system, and we have a representative form of government, meaning we elect and appoint our leaders. We are one of the largest fraternal benefit societies in the world with well over one million Members throughout Canada, the United States, and the United Kingdom" (Current IOF advertising pamphlet).

2 The items relevant to Oronhyatekha are in the papers of Sir Henry Wentworth Acland (MS Acland d.91 and d.101) and his daughter S.A. Acland (MS D on d.14).

3 This translation, provided in written records, is not accepted by some contemporary Mohawk people. A translation used at Tyendinaga is "Heavens on Fire."

rarely, was Peter Martin. He described his early education in an autobiographical sketch written in the 1860s:

> Attended a common school till about 10 years old during which time I learned enough to be able to write after a copy — to read in the 2nd Reader of the "Irish National Service" and to Cipher in simple addition. At the age of ten I went to the Mohawk Institution where the Indian children are taught the elementary branches of English and either the trade of a shoemaker, of a Blacksmith or of a waggon maker. At this school we were clothed, lodged and boarded.
>
> At this institution I remained about four years during which time I ran away three or four times, but either I was sent for the next day or my friends would take me back when I was always whipped for my misconduct and made to promise not to repeat it. About three years of my time was devoted exclusively to my studies and the last year I was half day at school and half day in the shoe-makers shop learning the trade. About the end of the fourth year I was informed that I had been instructed in all the trades which they teach and in consequence left for good. I was partially supplied with tools to work at my trade. (Acland MS d.91 f75)

He then worked for three months for a shoemaker on a piecework basis. It was not a good situation: "My associates were all bad and [I] soon learned to drink and the use of profane language and [so] that had not something occur[r]ed I would have made a good demonstration of the utter uselessness of educating the Indians."

Two fortuitous events preserved Oronhyatekha's prospects for continuing his education. First, the shoemaker failed to pay him for some work, which caused Oronhyatekha to quit the job and return home to the reserve. Second, while he was at home his family was visited by an American phrenologist, a practitioner of the then popular science of analyzing intellect and personality by studying the arrangement of bumps on a person's head (Stocking 1987:26,66). The phrenologist "proposed after examining my head that I should study" (Acland MS d.91 f75). After a second examination, Oronhyatekha accepted the phrenologist's advice and accompanied him on his return journey to the United States. Through this connection he entered the Wesleyan Academy at Wilbraham, Massachusetts, where he supported himself through various kinds of work, including shoemaking and mending.

Following one year at Wilbraham, he returned to Canada and found employment as a teacher, first with the Baptist Missionary Board and then with the New England Company, a Protestant missionary organization with head offices in London. At this time, according to his autobiographical sketch, Oronhyatekha decided to pursue training as a medical doctor and a missionary to "be the most service to my people." With the help of the New England Company agent and principal of the Mohawk Institute, Mr. Abram (Abraham) Nelles (Leighton 1982), he entered Kenyon College in Ohio. He completed nearly two years of study (1859-1860) before, short of funds and following an unspecified altercation between students and faculty, he returned to Canada and began teaching at the Iroquois reserve on the Bay of Quinte, at the east end of Lake Ontario (Acland MS d.91 f73). He was still teaching there when the Prince of Wales came to Canada to open the Victoria Bridge at Montreal in 1860 and to tour widely in Quebec, Ontario, and the United States. To Oronhyatekha fell the honour of representing the Six Nations reserve, reading a speech which he had prepared and which had been "adopted over two others written by the New England Company's agent" (Acland MS d.91 f73).

Later biographies of Oronhyatekha made much of his presentation to the Prince (Figure 1), suggesting that the royal listener was so impressed with the young Mohawk's performance that he sought him out and ultimately sponsored his studies at Oxford University. However, the primary sources do not support this story.[1] Rather, it was a chance meeting with Henry Wentworth Acland, the Oxford professor and physician travelling with the Prince's party, that provided Oronhyatekha with the contact that brought him to Oxford. Acland kept a sketchbook and diary of his travels with the Prince in 1860 (Burant 1991). At Niagara Falls he asked two Indians in ceremonial dress to pose for him. One of them was Oronhyatekha, who discussed with Acland both his interest in studying medicine and his concern that Iroquoian culture should be retained. Acland found little merit in the latter idea, but appears to have offered some encouragement to the idea of studying medicine in England. Still, he was surprised when Oronhyatekha arrived in Oxford in February, nearly penniless but determined to study medicine. With the

---

1   There are references to the possibility of applying to the Prince of Wales for a small grant on Oronhyatekha's behalf after he had returned to Canada following his short stay at Oxford. (Acland MS d.91 f36-39 and f40-42).

help of colleagues, Acland arranged funding for him through the British office of the New England Company.

Oronhyatekha's Oxford career was brief, lasting only about four months.[1] He arrived in February, 1862; was admitted to St. Edmund Hall on 6 May; and in June he was on his way back to Canada. He had deliberately avoided advising Mr. Nelles, the New England Company's agent at Six Nations, that he was leaving for England (Acland MS d.91 f86-87). Nelles must have had an unpleasant surprise when he learned not only that Oronhyatekha had gone without his knowledge, but that the head office of the company was expected to fund his studies. Nelles retaliated by writing to Oxford, or encouraging a Kenyon College professor to do so, suggesting that Oronhyatekha had been dismissed from Kenyon College in disgrace (Acland MS d.91 f86-87). This turned out to be false, but whether or not he could have stayed on at Oxford, Oronhyatekha chose to return to Canada to clear his name, a task that would take ten years to accomplish.[2]

Back in Canada he married Ellen Hill, a descendant of Joseph Brant and John Deseronto (Mohawk who moved to Canada in the 1780s following the American Revolution) [Montour 1960:137]. In 1866 Oronhyatekha completed his medical training at the University of Toronto, which entitled him to a provincial licence to practise "Physic Surgery and Midwifery" (Oronhyatekha letter to Acland, 5 May 1866, Acland d.101 f106). At that time he met Daniel Wilson, a distinguished profes-

---

1 His short stay at Oxford notwithstanding, Oronhyatekha is still celebrated by students attending his alma mater, St. Edmund Hall ("Teddy Hall"). Students decked out in face paint and feathered headbands and wielding toy tomahawks are pictured on a spree commemorating Oronhyatekha, "an honoured alumnus," in a recent *National Geographic* article on Oxford (Bryson, 1995:137). In addition, a guest room at St. Edmund Hall is named the Oronhyatekha Room; a ceremonial pipe-tomahawk attributed to Oronhyatekha hangs in the room. The Independent Order of Foresters presented a portrait of him, dressed in a representation of the suit of clothing which he wore for his 1860 meeting with the Prince of Wales, to St. Edmund Hall where it now hangs in the dining room. A label beneath the portrait reads: "Oronhyatekha Mohawk, Commoner of the Hall 1862, First Supreme Chief Ranger of the Independent Order of Foresters, Portrait presented by the Independent Order of Foresters 1968" (Letter, 17 July 1992 from Deborah Eaton, Librarian, St. Edmund Hall, to Trudy Nicks).

2 Oronhyatekha wrote to Acland from Stratford, Ontario on 8 July 1872 — on the letterhead of the Office of the Grand Worthy Chief Templar — enclosing a letter from the president of Kenyon College which certified that he had indeed been a student in good standing when he left the college in 1860 (Acland MS d.91 f91-92).

Figure 2. Painting of Dr. Oronhyatekha in uniform of Supreme Chief Ranger, Independent Order of Foresters. This portrait hangs in the Woodland Cultural Centre, Brantford, Ontario. Courtesy of the Woodland Cultural Centre.

sor later recognized as the founder of Canadian anthropology (Trigger 1966). Wilson described Oronhyatekha as a brilliant, hard-working student, and tried without success to help him gain an appointment as physician to the Six Nations Reserve (Daniel Wilson to Acland, 18 November 1866, Acland d.91 f106-l08).

After his graduation, Oronhyatekha worked as a medical doctor in three Ontario communities and served as physician to at least two reserve communities: the Mohawks of the Bay of Quinte, and the Oneidas of the Thames River near London, Ontario (Canada, RG10, Vol. 1879, file 1058 Part 0, Reel C-11105 and Vol. 2293, file 56,897, Part 0, Reel C-11194). He also undertook a brief, unsuccessful venture as a merchant, campaigned on behalf of the federal Tory party, and joined several fraternal organizations. By 1881 he had left medicine to become the chief executive officer or the "Supreme Chief Ranger" of one of these organizations, the Independent Order of Foresters (Figure 2). He remained in this office until his death on 3 March 1907. As Supreme Chief Ranger Oronhyatekha travelled the world, opening branches or "courts" of the IOF across North America, in England, Ireland, Scotland, Australia, New Zealand, Denmark, and Norway. Under his leadership a new headquarters building was opened in downtown Toronto in 1895. At eleven storeys in height, it was then the tallest building in the British Empire (Dendy 1993). His last projects were an orphanage for children of deceased IOF members (which did not endure), and a proposal for a home for retired company employees, both at Foresters Island in the Bay of Quinte near Deseronto.

In retrospect, an apparent flair for showmanship, more than for actuarial expertise, accounted for Oronhyatekha's success as head of the IOF. The policies he followed in setting its insurance rates, according to Dunn (1924), would ultimately have bankrupted the company. But his public relations skills were more impressive. Before corporate advertising was commonplace, Dr. Oronhyatekha heightened the visibility of the IOF through printed advertisements, annually placed an IOF booth at the Canadian National Exhibition in Toronto, and took advantage of the royal visit in 1905 to construct a street arch suitably embellished with a hugh royal crown and manned by members of the IOF in full dress uniforms.[1] One magazine called him "the Barnum of the insurance business" (cited in Potter and Oliver 1967:78). Under his regime, the IOF

---

1   A photograph of the arch is published in Potter and Oliver 1967:105.

Figure 3. Lawn party at Tyendinaga home of Dr. Oronhyatekha, c. 1904. The replica of the Westminster Abbey coronation chair, seen on the left-hand side of the picture, was commissioned for the IOF collection after Dr. Oronhyatekha attended the coronation of Edward VII in 1902. Courtesy of the Deseronto Public Library.

Figure 4. IOF commemorative medal, head of Dr. Oronhyatekha. Reverse side: Crest of Forestry order in centre with "The Supreme Court Independent Order of Foresters" around circumference, c. 1900 (ROM Canadiana collections 911.1.30).

　　　　　　　　　　　　　　　TRUDY NICKS

issued a steady stream of regalia and commemorative coins and medals (see, for example, Figure 4). As one obituary writer commented, "What the insurance companies bought with gold of the realm, he got in exchange for a few tawdry badges, a bit of gold lace and a brass band."[1]

Oronhyatekha remained involved with Indian communities and politics throughout his life. He maintained a farm at Deseronto, his wife's birthplace, as well as an imposing home known as the Castle on nearby Foresters Island. In 1872, as chairman of the Grand Indian Council (composed of delegates from the various tribes and bands in Ontario and Quebec), he petitioned Ottawa to amend the Indian Act of 1869 to allow Indians to own and register land "so that we can bargain among the whites," and to allow Indian women who married non-Indians to retain their status, arguing that the existing legislation merely promoted the evils of immorality or overly close intermarriage.[2]

However, he regularly provoked controversy in the Indian community. Although the Six Nations chose him as their spokesman in 1860, he was also charged by some with misappropriating funds set aside for the Prince of Wales's visit (Acland MS d.91 f75–76). His service as physician to the Mohawks of the Bay of Quinte, and later, the Oneidas of the Thames, was marred by complaints that he did not fulfil his medical obligations (Canada, RG10 Vol. 1897 File 1866 Part 0, Reel C-11107; Vol. 1942, File 4131 Part 0, Reel C-11117; Vol. 2283 File 56,897 Part 0, Reel C-11194). In all cases he was eventually exonerated, either by the Council or supervisors from the Indian Department. An ambitious and impatient man, Oronhyatekha was inclined to bypass local systems if they impeded his goals. He had more than one dispute with Mr. Nelles, the New England Company agent, of whom he wrote:

> Mr. Nelles has always been deeply impressed with the idea that no Mohawk could prosper without his approving smile [and] countenance, in consequence he acted as he pleased [and] when he pleased [and] unless one did nothing until he was commanded there was no hope of succeed-

---

1 *The Canadian Courier*, 1(15), 9 March 1907. A description of the "Honors and Emblems of the Independent Order of Foresters" appears in Potter and Oliver 1967:200–201.

2 Canada, RG10 Vol. 1934, file 3541, Part O, Reel C-11114. Oronhyatekha's interest in rights for women is further demonstrated by his campaign to have women admitted as members of the IOF. He succeeded in this endeavour in 1898.

Figure 5. Funeral procession of Dr. Oronhyatekha passing Independent Order of Foresters office building in downtown Toronto, 6 March 1907. The hearse was preceded by mounted police, marshals, members of the IOF on foot, two bands (48th Highlanders; Royal Foresters), and pallbearers in carriages, and followed by a Royal Foresters guard of honour, mourners, IOF Executive Council, honourary pallbearers, the mayor and aldermen, members of the Temple staff and citizens, all in carriages (The Canadian Courier 1(16), 16 March 1907:11).

TRUDY NICKS

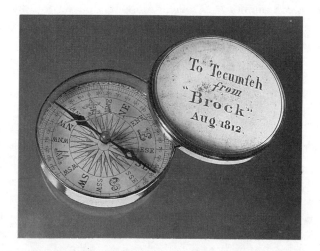

Figure 6. Brass compass attributed as a gift from General Brock to Tecumseh. Oshawana, Tecumseh's Ojibwa lieutenant, had the engraving added in Detroit after Tecumseh's death, according to the 1904 catalogue of Dr. Oronhyatekha's collection (ROM Ethnology collections HD6315).

ing with him.... He saw me prosperous [and] improving, he did not like it. For I worked for myself [and] improved without consulting him.[1]

Oronhyatekha's account was supported by Daniel Wilson, who stated in a letter to Acland:

From my own observations of Oronhyatekha, I am led to believe that he possesses an unusual amount of firmness and self-reliance for an Indian: and I am even led to suspect that this has something to do with his being held in disfavour both by Government Officials and Missionaries.... My own opinion is that the system of Indian Superintendence is carried to excess; so that they are kept in a state of pupilage like children; and if one

---

1   Acland MS d.91 f86-87. The document is not dated but it appears to have been written about the time Oronhyatekha left Oxford.

ventures to have a mind and will of his own, he forthwith is regarded as a troublesome fellow, and treated as a rebel against constituted authorities. (Acland MS d.91 fl06-l08)

These traits were probably factors in his troubles with some members of Iroquois communities in Ontario and with government officials who overlooked his qualifications in 1866. Yet he also developed tactical skills in dealing with superiors. In 1894 he enlisted the aid of the minister responsible for Indian Affairs in having himself and his family reinstated on the band list for Tyendinaga, his wife's home community. In a letter to W. Hayter Reed, Deputy Superintendent General of Indian Affairs, he wrote:

I trust the Minister may not have occasion to change his mind that in ordering my readmission to the Band he is acting in their best interest. I have no hesitation in assuring you that I and my friends will use our best endeavours to remove all causes of friction in the Band.

I may say to you that the primary and chief cause of all our troubles is the resident Minister and you will be doing great service to the Band if you can effect his removal. (Canada, RG10 Vol. 1956 File 4618, 10 August 1894)

Oronhyatekha had learned well the value of friends in high places, just as he never forgot the difficulties he had to overcome when local chiefs and agents had influence over his opportunities in life.

Dr. Oronhyatekha died on 3 March 1907 after a lengthy illness. His funeral included a stately procession, with bands and civic dignitaries, past the IOF Temple Building in Toronto, to a lying-in-state and memorial service at Massey Hall (Figure 5).[1] The next day his remains were taken by train to the family plot at Deseronto. At the funeral in Deseronto, "Indian choristers sang appropriate hymns and chants in the Mohawk language to an excellent organ accompaniment" (*The Forester* 1907:40).

Writings about Oronhyatekha at the time of his death and into the 1920s suggest white, mainstream society had some ambivalence toward an Indian who had achieved success in their world. Obituaries in *The Forester* (1907) and *The Canadian Courier* magazine (16 March 1907) trade heavily on stereotypes of Indians as savages both noble and fearful. *The Canadian Courier* described him as

A bronze Apollo, over six feet in height and massive in proportion; a well-chiselled face with every muscle in repose or control; a keen eye; a searching glance; a bold, almost audacious manner – these were some of the physical attributes which enabled him to dominate both men and women.

The same obituary also cited "the craftiness of his race [which] was his in the fullest degree," his "Indian's intuition," his natural skills as a "debater" and an "orator" and "the treachery of the Indian [which] does not seem to have come to this son of the Mohawk tribe." (A writer in 1896 had invoked similar stereotypes, finding his sense of humour remarkable because "it is generally thought [something] the Indian does not possess, or ... does not disclose" [cited in Potter and Oliver 1967:75].) He did not die or pass away; rather "his Spirit sought the Happy Hunting Grounds." At his death, an editorial in *The Forester* (cited in Potter and Oliver 1967:82) described him as "the great, honest, tender, true, noble Indian, Oronhyatekha." The IOF obituary cited "the immortal song of Longfellow's 'Hiawatha'" to explain his motivation in establishing an orphanage for children of IOF families (1907:42): we may hear him saying to a quarter million Foresters:

> In your watch and ward I leave them,
> See that never harm comes near them,
> See that never fear molest them,
> Never danger nor suspicion,
> Never want of food or shelter.

And even while acknowledging his many achievements in the world of Victorian society and business, F.J. Dunn felt obliged to point out that Dr. Oronhyatekha was an exception to the rule that Indians were inferior to Europeans:

The Doctor was imbued with great pride in his race.... He always stoutly maintained that the red race was the equal of the white race in every respect. This contention was pardonable as a matter of racial pride, but it was foolish when measured by the facts.... The Indian once possessed, owned and controlled the western hemisphere. The white man owns and controls it today. A superior civilization crowded out the inferior.... As individuals, there have been Indians who were, perhaps, in no respect inferior to the best the white race has ever produced. If so, then Doctor

Oronhyatekha was, no doubt, such an Indian. Still such comparisons must be confined to very narrow limits. You dare not carry them into the realms of painting, of sculpture, or architecture, or music, of invention, of literature, etc. In his belief the Doctor may have been sincere, but he was mistaken. Earnestness and sincerity are not necessarily evidence of the truth (1923:263-264).

The Oronhyatekha Historical Collection

A 1904 catalogue of the Oronhyatekha collection of artifacts, prepared by F. Barlow Cumberland of the Ontario Historical Society for the exhibition at IOF headquarters in downtown Toronto, listed over 800 objects including "mementos of the early history of Canada and of the United States bordering on the Great Lakes, and of the Royal annals of Great Britain" and "evidences of historic and prehistoric Indian days" (Cumberland 1904:9). Included also were replicas of architecture and statuary, IOF insignia and memorabilia, and "curios" and gifts which Dr. Oronhyatekha had acquired in the course of his international travels on behalf of the IOF. Another portion of the collection consisted primarily of over 1,000 specimens of marine shells, corals, and sponges, as well as a few bird specimens.

The ethnographic component of the collection included North American artifacts from the Northeast, the Great Lakes, the Plains, and the Arctic. Among the diverse non-North American ethnographic items, listed in the 1904 catalogue mainly as "Eastern Arts" or "Curios from Foreign Parts," were elephant goads, spears, scimitars, Indo-Persian battle axes, clubs from Fiji, a New Guinea lime spatula, Australian boomerangs, Japanese shoes or "geta," and drums from Burma. These and other "exotic souvenirs," including samples of flora and fauna, represented Dr. Oronhyatekha's

> travels around the world in planting the standard of Independent Forestry, and its beneficent advantages, [which] have taken him through many lands and so have brought together evidences of their history, taste, typical habits and natural beauties. (Cumberland 1904:9)

Dr. Oronhyatekha had a number of opportunities to observe collections which may have inspired him to create his own assemblage. During his brief career at Oxford, for instance, he visited the British Museum and the Ashmolean Museum.[1] Sir Henry Wentworth Acland, his

Oxford mentor, maintained a collection to which Oronhyatekha contributed "two or three skulls of an extinct nation of Indians — the Eries" after his return to Canada in 1863. Furthermore, his son, Acland Oronhyatekha, offered to donate an Indian costume to Sir Henry's collection in 1894.[2] In Toronto, Oronhyatekha would have witnessed the early development of the first provincial museum collection at the Toronto Normal School. And Daniel Wilson, whom he met at the University of Toronto in the 1860s, was a member of the Canadian Institute, one of the predecessors of the Royal Ontario Museum.

Collecting was a very Victorian habit. As historian Carl Berger (1983) has observed, collections of cultural objects and biological specimens represented the Victorians' passion for discovering the order of the natural world (which included indigenous peoples). Such activity fulfilled a need for recreation without sacrificing the virtue of industriousness. The habit of collecting was the sign of an educated and successful member of society. The introduction to the 1904 catalogue of Dr. Oronhyatekha's collection was explicit regarding the Victorian values behind its creation and display. Selected "by a cultivated and observant mind," the display was intended to encourage "a 'collecting mind' ... and a desire for further information." As Cumberland continued in his introduction,

Education, increased interest in history, nature, and art, and beyond all, thought and reading in the Home, the centre of every Forester's heart, may, it is hoped, be helped by a short study in this collection and so gladden the generous donor who has transferred his valued treasures to the general use. (1904:10)

Oronhyatekha, like other Victorians, did not build his collection from scratch; he also acquired existing collections or enlisted others to collect on his behalf.[1] The Woodlands and Great Lakes artifacts, many of

---

1 James Heywood of the New England Company wrote to Acland 25 February 1862, shortly after Oronhyatekha arrived in England, noting that he had taken "the young Mohawk" to see the British Museum (Acland MS d.91 f7-9). Oronhyatekha mentions speaking "before" the Ashmolean in a letter to Acland dated Shannonville, Bay of Quinte, 4 February 1963 (Acland MS d.91 f82-85).

2 Acland Oronhyatekha wrote from 24 Charing Cross, Whitehall on 31 December 1894 (Acland MS d.91 f97-98). He may have been offering Sir Henry the costume he wears in a photograph in the F. Barlow Cumberland files in the Archives of Ontario (MU3926/7).

which are attributed to known historical figures, were acquired by an employee of the IOF, George Mills McClurg. McClurg's success in acquiring these items appears to have been due to his association with Oronhyatekha, "in whose word ... Indians ... had implicit confidence."[2] McClurg was listed as the source of the sometimes lengthy entries for Iroquoian and Ojibwa artifacts in the 1904 catalogue. Most of the specific historical data which McClurg provided about the pieces have defied corroboration in other written sources. His records, evidently drawn from oral history, make a significant contribution to our understanding of Indian-white relations in the nineteenth century.

The collection also reflects a Victorian taste for objects connected with royalty. A replica of the British Coronation chair in Westminster Abbey, a quantity of commemorative coins and medals, including a gold Victoria Diamond Jubilee medal, as well as a collection of Maundy money[3] from three centuries, suggest the collector's interest in imperial matters. Contrary to oral tradition, the replica of the Westminster Abbey Coronation Chair was commissioned and purchased with IOF funds, and was not a personal gift to Oronhyatekha from Queen Victoria (*The Forester* 1904:35). The small marble sculptures in the collection were typical of pieces used as decorations in Victorian homes or for teaching in art schools. Besides six statues of Venus, there were various replicas of "Old Master" sculptures including a copy of "The Three Graces" apparently after a work by the early nineteenth-century Italian sculptor Antonio Canova.[4]

---

1   A large number of white metal and bronze commemorative Canadian medals manufactured by P.W. Ellis & Co. of Toronto had been assembled over a twenty-year period by Mr. William Tom while he was an employee of the Ellis company. Tom offered to provide information about them after they had come to the ROM, but the museum does not appear to have acted on his offer (letter from Tom to Mr Corsely [sic?] dated 28 July 1915, ROM Registration files).

2   Chief Johnson Paudash of Lindsay, Ontario to Sir Robert Falconer, president of the University of Toronto, 12 November 1929. ROM Registration Files. The ROM was part of the university at that time.

3   Maundy money refers to specially minted silver coins distributed by the British sovereign on Maundy Thursday (the Thursday before Easter).

4   The Toronto Normal School had a collection of similar Old Master sculptures. Oscar Wilde extolled the value of such copies for purposes of education when he lectured in Toronto in 1882 (Corey Keeble, personal communication).

The contents of the collection, the manner in which it was collected, and above all the manner in which it was displayed at the IOF, suggest that Oronhyatekha saw it primarily as a means to promote a good corporate image and, by extension, his own best interests. The 1904 catalogue lists contents for 34 exhibit cases in addition to free-standing pieces. There was no organizing storyline; rather, objects were loosely grouped according to similarity in form or relationship to places or events. The "exotic other," of such great interest to Victorian travellers, was very much a part of Dr. Oronhyatekha's historical collection and exhibition.

But the collection has another contradictory aspect that suggests a resistance to and denial of Victorian values: the ethnographic artifacts representing Great Lakes/Eastern Woodlands Indians. Many of these items relate to contexts in which their owners were arguably acting as members of sovereign nations. Several items were related to the War of 1812: military-style coats attributed to Ojibwa allies of the British;[1] silver gorgets and medals presented to Indian allies by grateful French and English sovereigns;[2] and a medal, compass, and pipe tomahawk which belonged to Tecumseh, Shawnee ally of General Brock (Figure 6).[3] The one wampum belt in the collection is claimed "to be an Indian record of what took place at the great Council in 1682, when the Indians ceded what is now Pennsylvania to William Penn" (Cumberland 1904:58–59).[4] It was ob-

---

1 Two "Indian Chiefs' Uniforms," that is, red coats with brass buttons and bullion braid, are listed in the 1904 catalogue as the property of Oshawana and of George King, "a Chippewa warrior of the Carodoc reservation." They were displayed as "Case 29" at the IOF headquarters. These coats are now in the ethnology collections of the Royal Ontario Museum.

2 The 1904 catalogue listed ten French and four English gorgets, or "waughasee," and attributed one of the English gorgets to Joseph Brant. The collection also contained five Indian chiefs' silver medals presented by George III. Most of these pieces came to the Royal Ontario Museum in 1911.

3 According to the history given by a Shawnee Indian woman named "Winnipe-goosquaw," cited in the 1904 catalogue, the compass was given to him by General Brock. Tecumseh thought the compass was a watch and lost interest in it when he discovered it always told the same time. Tecumseh gave the compass to one of his warriors, Chief Oshawana, who, according to the woman's story, had it engraved 'To Tecumseh from "Brock" Aug. 1812.' by a Detroit jeweller after Tecumseh's death. The compass, medal, and pipe tomahawk are in the ROM ethnology collections.

4 The belt is in the ethnology collections at the ROM.

tained from Chief Waubuno, or John B. Wampum, of the Delawares at Munceytown, Ontario, who took the belt with him on a visit to England in 1886 where he showed it to Queen Victoria (Cumberland 1904:59-61). There is also a suit of clothing[1] worn by Ojibwa Chief John Tecumseh Henry when he gave a speech on behalf of the Carodoc Indian Reserve to the Prince of Wales in 1860, as well as other items of clothing and personal belongings attributed to other Ojibwa leaders.[2] From the later nineteenth century there is a military medal awarded to Joseph Le Blanc of Kahnawake, one of the boatmen recruited by the British government for service on the Nile campaign of 1884-85.[3] All of these artifacts can be read as symbolic of nation-to-nation meetings, agreements, or alliances.

The issue of sovereignty was a significant one for the Iroquois throughout the nineteenth century as it is today. In Oronhyatekha's time the Canadian government no longer recognized the sovereign status of Indian peoples who had been important British allies against the French and Americans. For Oronhyatekha these artifacts surely served as a tangible reminder and evidence of the sovereign status which the Iroquois had enjoyed and still claimed. In his speech to the Prince of Wales in 1860, Oronhyatekha, then barely 20 years of age, spoke of keeping bright the chain of friendship that had existed between the Crown of England and the Six Nations Iroquois for more than 200 years (Acland d.91 f104-105). His collection, amassed over a quarter of a century later, seems to have served as another way of arguing the same point.

Oronhyatekha's connections to Oxford and the University of Toronto exposed him to the debates of the day concerning sociocultural evolution and doubtless reinforced his interest in affirming the standing of Iroquoian peoples. At Oxford he worked briefly with Friedrich Max

---

1 The suit consisted of coat, leggings, pouch, and headdress. These pieces are in the ROM collections. Chief John Tecumseh Henry appears in a photograph in Rogers (1978:767) wearing this or a very similar suit of ceremonial clothing.

2 About twenty individual Indian people from the Great Lakes area are identified in the 1904 catalogue, half of whom are known or probably Ojibwa.

3 Joseph Leblanc was listed as no. 40 of the Caughnawaga contingent recruited to take boats of soldiers over the cataracts of the Nile in the British attempt to relieve the siege of Khartoum (Stacey 1959:258). Leblanc stayed in Egypt for the first six-month contract only. The medal is in the ROM's Canadiana collections.

Muller, a professor of comparative philology whose work on language provoked dissent from "every one of the major classical evolutionary writers" (Stocking 1987:305). Oronhyatekha arrived at the University of Toronto just about the time Daniel Wilson published his best known work, *Prehistoric Man* in 1862, and he later provided Wilson with data on Iroquoian languages. Whatever his direct contact with evolutionism, Oronhyatekha remained convinced that Iroquoian cultures were the equal of European, a conviction demonstrated in his political actions, his writings, and his collection. Although willing to accommodate Victorian values of industry and education, he rejected theories and policies which relegated Indian people to a lowly position on a scale of savagery to civilization, and the accompanying doctrine that assimilation was the only salvation for Native people.

Bias in the Text: Problems of Museum Practice

Like any historical text, museum collections are inherently biased. They never include more than a limited range of the material culture existing at any given time or place; very large or perishable objects are seldom collected or preserved; and early collectors also appear to have been more interested in acquiring objects that were "unusual, historic, difficult to obtain and apparently bizarre," rather than commonplace (King 1982:9). Therefore, not even the largest museum collections provide fully adequate representations of most cultures (Feest 1994:90). Most of the objects in ethnology collections are also in some way influenced by European contact. These collections are therefore not very useful as evidence for "pristine" cultures; instead, they are informative mainly about interactions between Native peoples and Europeans over the centuries since contact.

The treatment of Dr. Oronhyatekha's collection upon its transfer to the Royal Ontario Museum in 1911 is a case study of how standard museum practices in organizing and caring for materials can introduce bias and obscure the textual value of a collection. In 1911, Dr. C.T. Currelly, Director of the Royal Ontario Museum, provided the following evaluation of the Oronhyatekha Historical Collection to the donor, the Independent Order of Foresters:

(1) A collection of Indian stone implements and pipes, which are of no particular value but which we should be very glad to have.

(2) A collection of personal historical things of Toronto, etc. for which we have no place in the constitution of the museum, with the exception of a piece or two, the value of which would compensate for the straining of the constitution of the Museum.

(3) The third section of objects picked up in travel, mainly in Egypt, are not only worthless but are objects which would have to be so labelled that they would bring discredit upon those from whom they came. There are two or three exceptions in this class that we would be glad to keep, and my private advice would be for the complete destruction of the remainder as they are not even copies of real things, but are fantastic creations that are very well known.

(4) The fourth class is a series of marble carvings from the modern Italian factories, and one of the objects of the Museum is to educate people away from things of that kind. (Currelly to Dr. Davidson of the IOF, 8 August 1911. ROM Registration files.)

Currelly's letter concludes, "Please do not consider that our gratitude is any the less than if the whole collection had been of first class importance."

It has not been possible to trace Dr. Oronhyatekha's natural history specimens in ROM collections. Perhaps they were not offered or not accepted. The artifacts that were kept, in accordance with standard procedures of the time, were dispersed according to their region of origin into departmental collections covering the Mediterranean World, the Far East, Africa, Oceania, Europe, and the Americas. Their dispersal effectively buried a significant source of information for the interpretation of Indian–European interactions in the Victorian and Edwardian eras in Canada and Great Britain.

Over the years a number of items in the Oronhyatekha Historical Collection also left the Royal Ontario Museum: three medals which had been loaned for the exhibit at IOF headquarters were returned to their Indian owners in the 1920s;[1] the replica marble statues were sent on long-term loan to Central Technical School in Toronto; a marble bust of Oronhyatekha was returned to the IOF in 1957;[2] and in the 1980s the

---

1   Receipt for three silver medals returned to Chief Johnson Paudash and Mrs. Isaac Johnson of Lindsay, Ontario, 18 February 1929. ROM Registration files.

3   Receipt for return of Oronhyatekha bust, 5 March 1957. ROM Registration files.

replica Coronation Chair was transferred to Casa Loma, a privately run tourist attraction in Toronto.[1] Other items were shunted from one department to another within the museum because they were not considered of first-class importance for various discipline-based collections. One artifact which emerged from a drawer during a search for Oronhyatekha items was a pen, pencil, and letter-opener set with handles carved from Pompeii lava, still in their original satin-lined presentation box. Since the piece had never been registered as part of the ROM collections, its source would not have been known except for an inscription across the inside of the lid in some ROM hand which proclaimed it to be a "Good Example of the Rubbish Bought in Italy by Tourists. Oron. Coll." While certainly not great art, the set is precisely the kind of artifact that demonstrates both Dr. Oronhyatekha's active involvement in mainstream Victorian culture and the interpretive power of his collection as an historical text.

Conclusion

This study of Dr. Oronhyatekha's collection, and of the contexts in which it was assembled and displayed, provides an example of the active responses which Indian people have made to the presence of non-Indian cultures in the postcontact period. To an extent, Oronhyatekha accepted some mainstream attitudes and values. But he also manipulated them to further Iroquoian interests during a period when the survival of Indian cultures was under threat from official policies which sought, by banning traditional languages, ceremonies, and political institutions, and through the use of Euro-Canadian schools, to force the aboriginal peoples of Canada to accept European values and cultural forms (see, for example, Pettipas 1994).

Other recent studies of ethnographic collections have focused on what these assemblages can reveal about the complex relationships between Indian and European cultures. Museum collections are becoming appreciated as archives which document the cultures of the collectors as well as the collected (Feest 1994:91,95; Krech 1989; 1994; Hail and Duncan 1989). Objects once thought unimportant for the interpretation

---

1 Casa Loma is a mock baronial mansion built just prior to the First World War by industrialist and monarchist Sir Henry Pellet. The replica Coronation Chair apparently was considered a fitting addition to a site with strong imperialist connections.

of Native cultures because they were made for cultural outsiders now help to reveal the dynamics of Indian-European interactions. Ruth Phillips's (1991) study of Huron moosehair embroidery work, for example, argues for the active contribution, reflected in materials, forms, and iconography, of both French nuns and Huron Indians to the development of the wide array of objects which the Hurons produced for sale to travellers to Quebec in the nineteenth century.

Reading collections as records of cultural exchange and interaction can lead us far beyond approaches which focus narrowly on using objects as clues for the construction of pristine, precontact cultures. An interactive model encompasses all materials, and does not require assumptions about cultural purity. It also privileges aboriginal perspectives when assessing the multiple significances of objects and collections. Phillips (1991) argues, for example, that the birchbark and moosehair souvenirs made by nineteenth-century Huron embroiderers provide a record of Huron world view and preferred self-images as well as representing economic responses to an emerging tourist market.

At a more general level, acknowledgement of the active manner in which aboriginal peoples have responded to the presence of Europeans serves to counter stereotypes, long perpetuated in museum exhibitions, of aboriginal cultures as unchanging and isolated from mainstream history and society. The restudying of old collections from new angles can help explain to museum visitors how aboriginal peoples have maintained vital and distinct cultures in spite of contact with dominant societies which have long expected them to vanish. They also open the door for effective collaboration with contemporary aboriginal people who have expressed concern, not just that some collections should be returned, but that they have a voice in how their histories and cultures are presented in mainstream museum exhibitions and programs.[1]

---

1   In North America aboriginal concerns regarding access to collections and objections to the static and isolated depictions of their cultures in museum exhibitions have resulted in legislation in the United States (United States Public Law 101-601, the Native American Grave Protection and Repatriation Act) and a national task force on Museums and First Peoples in Canada. The Canadian task force was jointly sponsored by the Assembly of First Nations and the Canadian Museums Association. A report which identified issues and recommendations for their resolution was published in 1992 under the title "Turning the Page: Forging New Partnerships Between Museums and First Peoples."

The case of Dr. Oronhyatekha and his historical collection illustrates the complexity surrounding the issue of aboriginal voice in museums. James Clifford (1988:248) recently wrote, "resourceful Native American groups may yet appropriate the Western museum." In gathering and displaying his historical collection with its embedded contrapuntal messages of Victorian values and Iroquoian sovereignty, it seems that Dr. Oronhyatekha anticipated Dr. Clifford and the mainstream museum world by a century.

References

Acland, Henry Wentworth.
    n.d. MS Acland d.91 and d.101. Bodleian Library, Oxford.

Acland, S.A.
    n.d. Portraits by S.A. Acland 1891-1900. MS D on d.14. Bodleian Library, Oxford.

Atlay, J.B.
    1903 *Sir Henry Wentworth Acland, Bart. K.C.B., F.R.S. Regius Professor of Medicine in the University of Oxford. A Memoir.* London: Smith, Elder.

Bayard, Mary Temple (Meg)
    1896 Dr. Oronhyatekha. *The Canadian Magazine* 7(2):135-142.

Berger, Carl
    1983 *Science, God, and Nature in Victorian Canada.* Toronto: University of Toronto Press.

Bryson, Bill
    1995 The Style and Substance of Oxford. *National Geographic* 188(5):114-137.

Burant, Jim
    1991 Sir Henry Wentworth Acland (1815-1900), in *A Place in History. Twenty Years of Acquiring Paintings, Drawings and Prints at the National Archives of Canada.* Ottawa: National Archives of Canada.

Canada
    Indian Affairs Records. National Archives of Canada, RG10 Red Series, 1872-1964.

The Canadian Courier
    1907 A Noble Red Man. 1(15):9. 9 March.

Clifford, James
    1988 *The Predicament of Culture. Twentieth Century Ethnography Literature and Art.* Cambridge: Harvard University Press.

Comeau-Vasilopoulos, Gayle M.

    1994 Oronhyatekha. *Dictionary of Canadian Biography*, vol. 13. 1901–1910. Toronto: University of Toronto Press. 791–95.

Cumberland, F. Barlow

    1904 *The Oronhyatekha Historical Collection*. Toronto: The Independent Order of Foresters.

    n.d. F. Barlow Cumberland Papers. Toronto: Archives of Ontario.

Dendy, William

    1993 The Temple Building, in *Lost Toronto. Images of the City's Past*. Toronto: McClelland and Stewart.

Dunn, F.J.

    1924 Dr. Oronhyatekha, in *Builders of Fraternalism in America*. Chicago: Fraternal Book Concern of Chicago.

Feest, Christian F.

    1994 Needs and opportunities for research in ethnographic museums. *Zeitschrift fur Ethnologie 118 (1903)*, 87–95.

The Forester

    1901 Oronhyatekha. 47–56.

    1904 A Coronation Chair in the Forester's Museum. 35.

    1907 Oronhyatekha Dead. 34–40.

    1907 Proclamation. 43.

Hail, Barbara A., and Kate C. Duncan

    1989 *Out of the North: The Subarctic Collection of the Haffenreffer Museum of Anthropology*. Bristol, RI: Brown University.

King, J.C.H.

    1982 *Thunderbird and Lightning. Indian Life in Northeastern North America 1600–1900*. London: British Museum Publications.

Krech, Shepard III

    1989 *A Victorian Earl in the Arctic: The Travels and Collections of the Fifth Earl of Lonsdale, 1888–89*. Seattle: University of Washington Press.

    1994 *Passionate Hobby. Rudolf Haffenreffer and the King Phillip Museum*. Bristol, RI: Haffenreffer Museum of Anthropology, Brown University.

Leighton, Douglas

    1982 Nelles, Abram (Abraham). *Dictionary of Canadian Biography*, vol. 11, 1881–1890. Toronto: University of Toronto Press. 639–40.

Macgillivray, Bro. Rev. A.

    1907 Oronhyatekha: A Historical Sketch. *The Forester* 40–43.

Mavor, James

    1923 Canada in 1892, in *My Windows on the Street of the World*, vol. 1. London: J.M. Dent & Sons.

Miller, J.R.

    1989 *Skyscrapers Hide the Heavens. A History of Indian-White Relations in Canada.* Toronto: University of Toronto Press.

Miller, Keith R.

    1971 Beyond Indian Leadership. *Tawow* 2(2):10-12.

Montour, Ethel Brant

    1960 *Canadian Portraits. Brant, Crowfoot, Oronhyatekha. Famous Indians.* Toronto: Clarke, Irwin.

Morgan, Henry James, ed.

1898   Oronhyatekha, M.D. *The Canadian Men and Women of the Times. A Hand-Book of Canadian Biography.* Toronto: William Briggs.

Pettipas, Katherine

    1994 *Severing the Ties That Bind: Government Repression of Indigenous Religious Ceremonies on the Prairies.* Winnipeg: University of Manitoba Press.

Phillips, Ruth B.

    1991 Glimpses of Eden: Iconographic Themes in Huron Pictorial Tourist Art. *European Review of Native American Studies* 5(2):19-28.

Potter, Warren, and Robert Oliver

    1967 *Fraternally Yours: A History of the Independent Order of Foresters.* London: Queen Anne Press.

Rogers, E.S.

    1978 Southern Ojibwa. *Handbook of North American Indians*, vol. 15, *The Northeast.* Washington, DC: Smithsonian Institution. 760-71.

Royal Ontario Museum.

    Registration files, Oronhyatekha collection.

Stacey, C.P.

    1959 *Records of the Nile Voyageurs 1884-85: The Canadian Voyageur Contingent*, vol. 37. Toronto: Champlain Society.

Stocking, George W., Jr., ed.

    1985 *Objects and Others: Essays on Museums and Material Culture.* Madison: The University of Wisconsin Press.

    1987 *Victorian Anthropology.* New York: Free Press.

Task Force on Museums and First Peoples

    1992   *Turning the Page: Forging New Partnerships Between Museums and First Peoples.* Ottawa: Assembly of First Nations and Canadian Museums Association.

Titley, Brian

    1986   *A Narrow Vision: Duncan Cameron Scott and the Administration of Indian Affairs in Canada.* Vancouver: University of British Columbia Press.

Trigger, Bruce G.

    1966   Sir Daniel Wilson: Canada's First Anthropologist. *Anthropologica* 7:3-37.

Vollick, Colin

    1987   Oronhyatekha, The Independent Order of Foresters, and the Forester Island Orphanage. *Lennox & Addington Historical Society Papers and Records* 17:55-75.

Contributors

Jennifer S.H. Brown, Dept. of History, University of Winnipeg, Manitoba.

Daniel Clayton, School of Geography and Geology, University of St. Andrews, Fife, United Kingdom.

Julie Cruikshank, Dept. of Anthropology and Sociology, University of British Columbia, Vancouver, British Columbia.

Jody F. Decker, Dept. of Geography, Wilfrid Laurier University, Waterloo, Ontario.

Olive P. Dickason, Dept. of History, University of Alberta, Edmonton, Alberta.

John Fierst, The John Tanner Project, Winnipeg, Manitoba.

Renée Fossett, Dept. of History, University of Manitoba, Winnipeg, Manitoba.

Frederic W. Gleach, Dept. of Anthropology, Cornell University, Ithaca, New York.

Alice Beck Kehoe, Dept. of Anthropology, Marquette University, Milwaukee, Wisconsin.

Frieda Esau Klippenstein, Parks Canada, Winnipeg, Manitoba.

Shepard Krech III, Dept. of Anthropology, Brown University, Providence, Rhode Island.

Maureen Matthews, CBC Radio, Winnipeg, Manitoba.

Bunny McBride, Dept. of Sociology and Anthropology, Kansas State University, Manhattan, Kansas.

J.R. Miller, Dept. of History, University of Saskatchewan, Saskatoon, Saskatchewan.

Trudy C. Nicks, Dept. of Ethnology, Royal Ontario Museum. Toronto, Ontario.

Laura Peers, SSHRC Postdoctoral Fellow, Dept. of History, University of Winnipeg, Manitoba.

David Pentland, Dept. of Linguistics, University of Manitoba, Winnipeg, Manitoba.

Roger Roulette, Association for Native Languages, Winnipeg, Manitoba.

Theresa Schenck, Dept. of Anthropology, Rutgers University, New Brunswick, New Jersey.

Erica Smith, Dept. of History, Carleton University, Ottawa, Ontario.

Winona Stevenson, Dept. of Native Studies, University of Saskatchewan, Saskatoon, Saskatchewan.

Elizabeth Vibert, Dept. of History, University of Victoria, British Columbia.

Germaine Warkentin, Dept. of English, Victoria College, University of Toronto, Ontario.

Index

A

acculturation myths, 386-387
Acland, Henry Wentworth: artifact collection of, 497; meeting with Oronhyatekha, 486-487
Acton, William: views on women, 368
Aiskabawis (Ojibwa shaman), 225-226
Amergoo (Inuit mapmaker), 89
Amerindians. SEE First Nations; and names of individual First Nations
Anderson, David, 367
Anderson, Thomas Gummersall, 269
Angus (Naamiwan's son), dream of: 348-350
anthropology: agenda in, 423; assumptions of, 384-385; methods of, 385
Archambaud, Jean (Spotted Elk's husband), 418-419
architecture: of 16th century First Nations, 16-18
Askenootow. SEE Pratt, Charles
Assiginack, Jean-Baptiste (Ottawa leader), 268-269, 271
Assiniboine (First Nation): medical practice of, 167
Atahuallpa (Inca): Belleforest's views on, 17
Atkinson, Geoffrey: views on Thevet, 13-14

B

Bakhtin, Mikhail: on language, 317-318
Barbue (Gwich'in leader), 184, 185, 187-188: last illness of, 204-207, 209-212; naming of, 192; as political leader, 197-198; relations of with HBC, 193; trading activities of, 193, 198
bawagaan. SEE "Our Grandfathers"
beads: as currency, 194-195
Beaglehole, J.C.: edition of Cook's travel narrative, 102-103

Beaver (First Nation): disease among, 203; medical practice of, 167, 169
beavers: disease epidemics among (1802-03), 225
Beechey, Captain Thomas, 75
Bell, John: Barbue's last illness and, 204-205; G. Simpson's views on, 185-186
Belleforest, François de, 6-7: cosmography of, 9-10; ethnographic methods of, 19-20; relations of with Thevet, 10-11, 14; views on First Nations, 15
Benedict, Ruth, 381
Berens, Chief William, xiii, 283, 330, 334, 335-336: bias of, 351-352
Berton, Pierre: representation of Skookum Jim (Keish), 441
bias, ix-xi, xvi-xvii, xviii: in accounts of Douglas-Kwah incident, 133-142; in historical accounts, 147-148; in language, xi-xiv, 351-352, 388; in missionary literature, 310-312; in museum collections, 501-503; in selection of evidence, xvii-xviii; in travel literature, 103-105, 114-119
biography: as historical method, 214, 419-422, 424; problems of, 405, 419-422; uses of, 422-423
Black, John: views on women, 368, 378-379
Black-Rogers, Mary: on discourse, xii
Blackfoot (First Nation): disease discourse of, 172; violence stories in, 387-388; Grease Melters band, 387; medical practice of, 169; sociocultural description of, 394-396
Boas, Franz: comparative methods of, 21; on Inuit maps, 75
Boehme, Johann: cosmography of, 5-6
boodade. SEE dream dance (Ojibwe)
Boucher, Nancy, 128, 135
boundaries, sociocultural, 48-49
Brightman, Robert: on Naamiwan's dream, 341
Brown, Jennifer S.H., xxii-xxiii

Brumble, H. David, xvi-xvii
Bry, Theodore de: travel accounts of, 4
burial practices, Gwich'in, 212

C

cannibalism: 15th century European
views on, 14-15
captivity narratives. SEE narratives, captivity
Carmack, George, 440, 441-442
Carmack, Kate, 440, 441-442, 445, 448
Carrier (First Nation), 124: accounts of
Douglas-Kwah incident, 139-142
Cartier, Jacques, 18
Cass, Lewis, 224
Cha-wa-cis (Saulteaux medicine man),
325-328
Chief All Over, Agnes, 384, 386, 387
Chipewyan (First Nation): disease
among, 203
Choné, Jean-Pierre, 272
Christinos, 65, 66: at Feast of the Dead,
63-64. SEE ALSO Cree
cities and towns, North American: in
16th century, 16-17, 18
clans. SEE totems
Clark, William, 224
Clayton, Daniel, xiv, xxv, 72-73
Clifton, James: on biography, 424
Coldwell, William, 364-365
collecting and collections, 483-484,
496-499, 501-502
Connolly, Amelia. SEE Douglas,
Amelia Connolly
Connolly, Henry: account of Douglas-
Kwah incident, 132-133, 135
Connolly, Julia, 133
Connolly, William, Jr, 129, 132
Connolly, William, Sr, 126, 131, 135-
136
Cook, Captain James, xiv, xxv, 95-97:
aboriginal accounts of, 107-111;
bias in travel narrative, 114-119;
contemporary views on, 95; officers' accounts of voyage, 112-113,
117; travel narrative of, 99-103
Corbett, Abigail, 365, 369-370
Corbett, Griffith Owen, 364

corn (maize): symbolic meaning of to
Powhatan, 35
Cornut, Jacques-Philippe: dictionary of
Canadian plants, 12
cosmography: European, 5-10, 97-98
Cree: disease discourse of, 169, 172.
SEE ALSO Christinos
Cronon, William, xviii
Cruikshank, Julie, xxvii, 430: on construction of knowledge, xviii-xix;
on oral testimony, 324
cultural change: conditions for, 286
cultural practice: disease and, 158, 159-
162

D

Davis, Matilda, 377-378
Dawson Charlie, 440, 441
De Smet, Pierre-Jean, 286
Dease, Charles, 186
Dease, Peter Warren: Barbue's last illness and, 205; G. Simpson's views
on, 186-187; on Gwich'in disease
theory, 207-208
Decker, Jody, xxv-xxvi, 154
Delgamuukw decision (B.C. Supreme
Court), xiii, 120
Dickason, Olive Patricia, xxv, 2
discourse: on aboriginal people, 14-16;
on abuse, 462; medical, 156, 163-
164; missionary, 310-311, 317; sexual, 366-369, 374-375; on women,
365, 373-377, 404
discourse analysis: as historical method,
xi-xii
disease: changing pathology of, 164-
165; cultural practices and, 158,
159-162; defined, 163; discourse
on, 156, 163-164, 172; environment and, 157-158; in First Nations, 203-206; population size/density and, 158-161; theories of origin
and nature of, 165-166, 168-169,
171-173, 209; transmission of, 156,
171. SEE ALSO illness (morbidity)
documents, historical: editing of, 235-
236
Donnacona (Iroquoian leader), 18
Dorris, Michael: on bias, ix-x

Douglas, Amelia Connolly, 128, 135
Douglas, James, xvii, xxv, 125
Douglas, John: edition of Cook's travel narrative, 99-102, 105-106, 112
Douglas, Thomas. SEE Selkirk, 5th Earl of
dream dance (Ojibwe), 331, 335-337: pavilion for, 334-335
dreams and dreaming: in Insima's testimony, 392; in Ojibwa worldview, 228-229; in Spotted Elk's diary, 408-409; in Tanner's *Narrative*, 228, 231-232. SEE ALSO Naamiwan's dream
dress: prostitution and, 367-368
drum(s), dream dance, 331, 348, 352-353

E

education: of women in Red River, 377-379
Eggan, Fred, 21
English, Mary Warren, 243
environment, physical: disease and, 157-158
ethnohistory, xxii-xxiii
Evans, James: and Rice Lake letter, 270
evidence, historical: bias and reliability of, x, xi, xvi-xvii, xviii, 134-139, 351-352, 433-434; material culture as, 483, 501-503; oral histories as, 385; oral sources as, 385-388; oral testimony as, 124, 245, 254-255, 307-308, 324, 334, 474; relative value accorded to, 120, 124-125, 147, 148, 433, 434; second-hand, 130-131; selection of, xvii-xviii, 184-185, 414, 421-422, 503; visual images as, 466, 480-481; written sources of, 470-471
exploration literature. SEE literature, travel

F

Fabian, Johannes: on texts and contexts, xx-xxi
Fair Wind. SEE Naamiwan

Feast of the Dead, 56-57, 65, 66: Radisson's account of, 52, 58-64
Fierst, John, xxvi, 218
First Nations: self-representations of, 317-319, 321, 480-481, 499-501, 503; 16th century architecture of, 16-18; 15th century European views on, 14-16
Fort George: 1823 murders at, 125-126
Fort Good Hope, 190, 194: relocation of, 201-202
Fort St. James National Historic Site, 124
Fossett, Renée, xxv, 72
Fracastoro, Girolamo: on disease contagion, 171
Frog helper: role of in Keish's life, 443

G

George Simpson Centennial Celebration (1928), 142-147
gifts: cultural meaning of, 59-60, 63-64; of "Our Grandfathers", 347
Gitksan: and Delgamuukw decision, xiii; oral histories of, 478
Gleach, Frederic, xxv, 2-3
Gold Rush, Klondike, 439-440
Gorham, Deborah: on Victorian sexual discourse, 376
guardian spirits: in Plateau peoples' worldview, 291, 293
Gwich'in (First Nation), 188-191: burial practices of, 212; commercial activities of, 193-196; conflict with Inuvialuit, 198-200, 203; and European fur trade, 190-191; leadership in, 198; medical practices of, 188, 206-211; mourning practices of, 212; naming practices of, 192; theories of disease origin, 204-205; warfare and, 195, 196-197, 198, 203

H

Hall, Charles Francis, 86
Hall, Lizette: account of Douglas-Kwah incident, 140, 141, 142

Hallowell, A. Irving, xiii, 283, 300: account of Naamiwan's dream, 337-341; cultural bias in ethnography of, 353; description of dream dance, 333, 335-337; on Ojibwe empiricism, 341

Hanipaux, Joseph, 272

Hare (First Nation): disease among, 203, 204

Harmon, Daniel, 140-141: meeting with Kwah, 125

Hatfield, Harley, xxiv

Henderson, Patsy: account of Klondike gold discovery, 447

Henderson, Robert, 441

Hickerson, Harold: views on Radisson's narrative, 57-58

history, official public interpretations of, 142-147

Hochelaga (Iroquoian town), 18

Holy Cross Mission (Manitoulin Island), 272

Hudson's Bay Company: northern departments of, 191-192; official version of Douglas-Kwah incident, 138-139; relations with Gwich'in, 196

I

Igjugarjuk (Inuit mapmaker), 84-85

Iillak (Inuit hunter), 89

Iligliuk (Inuit mapmaker), 76-78, 79, 82: concern with personal names, 87; mapping of, 82, 84

illness (morbidity): defined, 163; human responses to, 174-175. SEE ALSO disease

Independent Order of Foresters: Oronhyatekha's management of, 489-491

Insima (Blackfoot woman), 382: family of, 384, 393; oral testimony of, 386, 387, 389-397

Inuvialuit (First Nation): conflict with Gwich'in, 195-196, 198-200, 203; perceived as warlike, 201

Itoyatin (Powhatan district chief), 32, 38

J

James, Edwin, xi, 223, 229-231: edits Tanner's *Narrative*, 227

Jennings, David: on disease, 163

Jesuits: conversion strategies of, 288-291; ideas of womanhood, 288, 290-291; perceptions of Virgin Mary, 288-291

John Tanner Project, 221

Jones, Peter: describes Manitoulin Island, 272-273

K

Kash-kau-ko (Ojibwa warrior), 221

Kateri Tekakwitha, 408

Kehoe, Alice B., xxvi

Keish (Skookum Jim; Tagish man), 442-443: family of, 444-445; representations of in oral histories, 442-449; representations of in written histories, 440-442; spirit helpers of, 443

Kekataugh (Powhatan district chief), 32, 35, 38

kidnapping, intercultural: reasons for, 221-222. SEE ALSO narratives, captivity; Tanner's *Narrative*

Klippenstein, Frieda Esau, xvii-xviii, xxv, 73

Klutschak, Heinrich: on Inuit mapping, 82

knowledge, cultural construction of, x-xi, xviii-xix, xx-xxi, 39, 111, 324, 366, 435-436, 449-451

Kohl, Johann Georg: on Ojibwa totems, 248

Krech, Shepard, xxvi, 154-155

Krupat, Arnold: on aboriginal literature, 317, 318

Kwah (Carrier chief), xvii-xviii, xxv, 124-125

L

Labrador: architecture (16th century), 17-18

language: bias in, xi-xiv, 351-352, 388; Christian elements in Ojibwe, 354-355; cultural meaning in, xii-xiv, 317-318

leadership, First Nations, 15: Gwich'in, 198

Lemay, J.A. Leo: on Pocahontas-Smith story, 23

Lery, Jean de: views on Thevet, 13

literature, aboriginal, 317-319: as sources of historical evidence, 470-471; themes in, 319, 321

literature, missionary: bias in, 310-312

literature, travel: bias in, 103-105, 114; 14th century, 6; 16th century, 11-12; 18th century, 101-102

literature, women's: themes in, 414-415

Little Plume, Jim, 382

Loucheux (First Nation): disease among, 204. SEE ALSO Gwich'in (First Nation)

Lyon, Commander George, 79

M

Mackenzie, Alexander, 190

MacLaren, Ian S.: on travel literature, 103

Mal de Gorge (Carrier hunter), 133

Mandeville, John, 12: travel accounts of, 6

Manito-o-geezhik (Ojibwa warrior), 221, 223

Manitoulin Island: community at, 271; missions at, 271-272; subsistence activities at, 272-273

Manitouwaning reserve. SEE Manitoulin Island

Maniwaki Indian Reserve, 274-275

maple syrup in America: described by Thevet, 12

maps and mapping, European: orality of, 91: purpose of, 76, 79, 83, 91

maps and mapping, Inuit: cooperative nature of, 88; legend and symbol in, 85-86; orality of, 74, 75, 79-82, 85, 86, 91-92; orientation in, 82; place-names in, 86-87; purpose of, 75, 79-82, 83; resource sites in, 82; scale and distance in, 83; time dimension in, 83-85; women as mapmakers, 88-91

maps and mapping, Shoshoni, 75

Mary (The Virgin): Jesuits' perceptions of, 288-291; Plateau peoples' devotion to, 288-289, 299-300; Salish perceptions of, xv, 293-294, 296-299

Matthews, Maureen, xiii, xxvi, 283

McBride, Bunny, xvii, xxvi-xxvii

McClellan, Catharine: on spirit helper stories, 443

McClintock, Captain Leopold, 75: and Inuit mapmaker, 89

McEachern, Chief Justice Allan, 120: and Delgamuukw decision, xiii

McLean, John: account of Douglas-Kwah incident, 125, 126-129, 130-131; on trading post medical practice, 167-168

medical discourse. SEE UNDER discourse

medical practice (19th century): First Nations, 167, 169-170, 188, 206-211; at HBC posts, 166-168, 205-206

medicine, First Nations, 208-209: Monardes' compilation of, 11-12

Mednick, Mel, 21-22

Mengarini, Gregory, 286-287

methodology, anthropological: discourse analysis, 397; oral sources, 385, 398, 413-414

methodology, historical, 465-466: biography, 214, 419-422, 424; comparative, 21, 245, 334; discourse analysis, xi-xii; ethnohistory, xxii-xxiii; multidisciplinarity in, 182; oral sources, 477-479; speculation, 21-22, 24-27; theoretical approach, 306

Mexico: architecture of (16th century), 16-17

Meyerhoff, Barbara: on ethnographic representations, 421

Midewiwin, 251: ceremonial pavilion for, 335

Miller, J.R., xv, xxvii, 431

Mills, Harriet, 377

Monardes, Nicolas, 11-12

Moore, Jean Archambaud (Spotted Elk's daughter), 407–408, 422
More, Hannah: on women's education, 378
Moresby, Fairfax: account of Douglas-Kwah incident, 128–129
mourning practices, Gwich'in, 212
Munster, Sebastian: cosmography of, 5
Murray, David: on aboriginal literature, 318–319, 321
museum collections: bias in organization of artifacts, 502

N

Naamiwan (Fair Wind), xiii, 283, 330–331: power of over death, 341; restores grandson to life, 341–342; syncretic religious beliefs of, 348, 350–352. SEE ALSO Naamiwan's dream
Naamiwan's dream, 334: Hallowell's account of, 337–341; Owen's account of, 342–347; R. Brightman on, 341; source of, 355–359
names and naming practices: Gwich'in, 192; Inuit, 86–87; Ojibwa, 251. SEE ALSO place names
narrative(s): captivity, 222; cultural construction of, xviii–xix, 435–436, 449–451, 452–453
Ned, Annie, 435, 442
Nelson, Horace, 404
Nelson, Molly. SEE Spotted Elk, Molly
Nelson-Bauman, Eunice, 407, 422
Netnokwa (Ottawa woman), 223
Nicks, Trudy, xxvii, 431–432
Nootka Sound: naming of, 98–99; Spanish visits to, 106–107
Nootka Sound people: histories of Cook's visit, 107–111, 114
The Nor'Wester: coverage of Corbett trial, 365, 372–373; on women's roles, 378
North West Company, 124: in Mackenzie River district, 190
nudity: 15th century European views on, 14–15
Nute, Grace Lee, 45

Nuu-chah-nulth (Nootka Sound aboriginal people). SEE Nootka Sound people

O

objectivity. SEE knowledge, construction of
Ohudlerk (Inuit man), 90
Ohudlerk's wife (Inuit): as navigator, 90
Ojibwa (First Nation): dreams in worldview of, 228–229; naming practice of, 251; reasons of for war, 249, 251–252; relations with Dakota, 251; relations with Dakota and Fox, 249–250; rhetorical style of, 271, 276; totemic traditions of, 246–249; westward expansion of, 224, 246, 248, 249–250, 251; worldview of, 225–226
Ojibwa-Ojibwe: alternate spellings of, 283
Oka, community at, 273–275
O'Meara, Frederick A., 271
Oonalee (Inuit mapmaker), 75
Opechancanough (Powhatan war chief), 27–28, 29, 38
oral history. SEE UNDER evidence, historical
oral sources: sex-gender differences in, 386–388
oral testimony. SEE UNDER evidence, historical
Oronhyatekha (Mohawk man), 483, 484–494: artifact collection of, 483–484, 496, 498–499; collecting as protest, 499–501, 503; education of, 485, 487; IOF career of, 489–491; medical career of, 489; obituaries of, 494–496; relations of with Indian communities, 491–494
Ottawa (First Nation), 223–224: dreams in worldview of, 228–229; letter to Algonquin chiefs. SEE ALSO Ottawa letter to Algonquin
Ottawa letter to Algonquin, 262–265: compared to Rice Lake letter, 270–271; purpose of, 269; rhetoric of, 266, 271, 276; text of, 264–265

S

Sacsahuaman (Inca city), 17

Salish (First Nation): perceptions of Virgin Mary, 284-285, 293-294; religious conversion of, 286-287; women's roles among, 292-293

Schenck, Theresa M., xxvi, 218-219

Schoolcraft, Henry Rowe: on J. Tanner, 232-234, 236; on Ojibwa totems, 249

Schoolcraft, James L.: murder of, 236

schools, native residential, xv, 461-464: discourse on abuse at, 462; gender bias in activities at, 475-476; histories of neglected, 462, 464-465; industrial, 463-464; sources of historical evidence on, 461, 464-465, 466-469, 474-478

Selkirk, 5th Earl of (Thomas Douglas), 224-225

Shawnee Prophet movement, 226

Sidney, Angela, 435: account of Klondike gold discovery, 445-447; history of Keish (Tagish man), 442-443

Simpson, George: Gwich'in trade and, 195; official account of Ft George murders, 137-138

Skookum Jim. SEE Keish (Tagish man)

smallpox (1779-83), 161-162, 170

Smith, Erica, xxvi

Smith, Captain John, xi, xxv, 22-24, 27: captivity narrative of, 28-33, 35-39

Smith, Kitty, 435, 442: account of Klondike gold discovery, 447

Smithurst, John: on native missionaries, 312-313

smoke in dream dance, 337

snowshoes described by Thevet, 12

sodalities, as aids to conversion, 289-290

Sommers, Sue, 381: ethnographic methods of, 387-88

sovereignty claims: by right of 'discovery', 18-19, 97; by right of invitation, 119

speculation. SEE UNDER methodology, historical

spirits, divine. SEE "Our Grandfathers"

Spotted Elk, Molly, xvii, 403: biculturalism of, 415; career of, 417-418; coping with racism, 417; diaries of, 410-413; education of, 415, 417; purpose of life, 423; search for self-definition, 404-405, 414

Stadacona (Iroquoian town), 18

Stafford, Barbara Maria: on European explorers, 101-102

status displays, 65-66

Stevenson, Winona, xvi, xxvi, 282-283

Stuart Lake. SEE Fort St. James

Swift, Graham, xviii

syphilis, 164

T

Tagish (First Nation): disease history of, 438; relations with Tlingit, 437-439; social organization of, 436-437; Tail Feather Woman (Sioux woman), 331

Tanner, John, xi, xxvi: kidnapping of, 221, 222-223; return to U.S. society, 226-227 SEE ALSO Tanner's *Narrative*

Tanner's *Narrative*, 227-228: 1994 edition of, 234; editing of, 235-236; as historical evidence, 235, 237; Ojibwa worldview in, 228-229

Tawgaweninne (Ojibwa man), 223-224

Tekakwitha. SEE Kateri Tekakwitha

Tenochtitlan (Mexican city), 16-17

Tenskwatawa, The Prophet (Shawnee), 226

Themistitan. SEE Tenochtitlan

Thevet, André, 12-13: cosmography of, 6-9; ethnographic methods of, 19-20; relations of with Belleforest, 10-11; reputation of, 13-14; views on Amerindians, 15-16

Thomas, Maria, 364, 368, 379-380: Ross's characterization of, 365, 367, 372, 375

Thou, Jacques-Auguste de: views on Thevet, 13

Thunderbird: as source of Naamiwan's dreams, 355-359

time element in Inuit mapping, 84

Tiriksiu (Inuit mapmaker), 85

Tlingit (First Nation), 437–439
tobacco: in dream dance, 337
Tod, John: account of Douglas-Kwah incident, 126, 129–131, 134–135
Toolemak (Inuit mapmaker), 86
Toolookah (Inuit mapmaker), 86
totems: Ojibwa, 246–249; Penobscot, 403
towns. SEE cities and towns
translation of texts: difficulties of, 53–54
travel literature. SEE literature, travel
Trimble, Michael: on disease transmission, 161–162, 174
Turner, Terence: on history and myth, 451
Tweroong (Inuit mapmaker), 89
Tzoelhnolle, 139

U

unicorns, 13–14

V

Vennum, Thomas: on dream drums and Christianity, 352
Vespucci, Amerigo: travel accounts of, 6
Vibert, Elizabeth, xxiii–xxiv

W

Warkentin, Germaine, xiv–xv, xxv, 3
Warren, William W., xxvi, 243–245. SEE ALSO Warren's *History*
Warren's *History*: errors in 252–254; point of view in, 245–246; reliabil-

ity of, 250–251, 254–255; reputation of, 242–243
Wealth Woman, 447, 450–451: role of in Keish's life, 443
Wet'suwet'en: and Delgamuukw decision, xiii; oral histories of, 478
White, Hayden: on historical texts, 316–317; on narrative, 452
White, Richard: on sociocultural boundaries, 48
Wilson, Daniel, 497: on race and miscegenation, 373; views on Oronhyatekha, 487–489, 493–494
windigo, 168
Wissler, Clark: on Blackfoot women, 394
women: Blackfoot, 394; 392–393; discourse on, 365, 373–377, 404; divinities: female deities in Salish worldview, 291–292, Virgin Mary, 288–291, 293–294, 296–300, Wealth Woman, 447, 450–451; education of, 377–379, 475–476; Inuit navigators and mapmakers, 88–91; Jesuit views on, 288, 290–291; in Plateau societies, 292–293; status of in Red River, 375–377; themes in writings of, 414–415; Victorian views on, 365, 368–369, 371–372, 373–377; Victorian views on prostitution, 366–367

Y

Yale, James, 126, 136–137
Yellow Kidney (Blackfoot man), 382–383, 384–385, 396: oral histories told by, 385
Yellow Wolf (Blackfoot man), 393–394